Nuclear Non-Proliferation in International Law

Volume II

Jonathan L. Black-Branch · Dieter Fleck
Editors

Nuclear Non-Proliferation in International Law

Volume II
Verification and Compliance

ASSER PRESS

Springer

Editors
Jonathan L. Black-Branch
School of Management—Law
Royal Holloway, University of London
Egham, Surrey
UK

Dieter Fleck
Cologne
Germany

ISBN 978-94-6265-074-9 ISBN 978-94-6265-075-6 (eBook)
DOI 10.1007/978-94-6265-075-6

Library of Congress Control Number: 2015945599

Published by T.M.C. ASSER PRESS, The Hague, The Netherlands www.asserpress.nl
Produced and distributed for T.M.C. ASSER PRESS by Springer-Verlag Berlin Heidelberg

Printed on acid-free paper

Springer Science+Business Media B.V. Dordrecht is part of Springer Science+Business Media
(www.springer.com)

Preface

Nuclear non-proliferation continues to dominate political, diplomatic and legal discussions worldwide. Legal issues regarding the non-proliferation of nuclear weapons, the use of nuclear energy for peaceful purposes and nuclear disarmament must be viewed within their relevant context, which is what this book series endeavours to achieve. Volume I[1] was widely received with encouraging praise by academics and practitioners alike. This warm reception demonstrates the need for continued efforts to explore such issues further, from an abstract analytical perspective but also from a practical stance.

The present volume focuses on verification and compliance. The main body of contributions presented are the results of a research conference on *Verification of Nuclear Non-Proliferation Obligations* held in Cologne from 13–14 November 2014 in cooperation with the Cologne Institute of International Peace and Security Law. This follows in the tradition of gathering relevant experts to discuss areas pertinent to nuclear weapons, non-proliferation and contemporary international law through a series of Round Table Discussions, which have already led to a comprehensive report on *Legal Aspects of Nuclear Disarmament*, presented at the most recent conference of the International Law Association (Washington 2014).[2] The Cologne event was of major significance for clarifying issues regarding verification problems. It created a better understanding for verification tasks of the IAEA, the CTBTO and EURATOM, providing an instructive interdisciplinary approach to technical possibilities of verification and gaps in current legal regulation which may help to explore implications for treaty design and the implementation of the best practice rules. Moreover, it contributed to greater consensus related to existing legal controversies regarding countermeasures, remedies for wrongful acts and peaceful settlement of disputes.

We would like to express our sincere gratitude to Prof. Claus Kreß, Director of the Cologne Institute of International Peace and Security Law and his assistants,

---

[1]J.L. Black-Branch and D. Fleck (eds.) Nuclear Non-Proliferation in International Law, Vol. I, with a foreword by Mohamed ElBaradei. T.M.C. Asser Press 2014.

[2]See http://www.ila-hq.org/en/committees/index.cfm/cid/1025.

for co-organizing this event in conjunction with the ILA Committee on Nuclear Weapons, Non-Proliferation and Contemporary International Law and the Nuclear Round Table Forum. We are particularly indebted to the Fritz Thyssen Foundation for kindly supporting the event, and in particular to Dr. Thomas Suermann and his team for hosting our conference, providing an intimate and professional environment in which to advance these important discussions.

Special acknowledgement must be expressed to our peer reviewers, who have offered their critical advice, encouragement and invaluable suggestions. The various authors appreciate the double anonymous review process and we wish to express our sincere gratitude on both our behalf as well as the contributing authors who benefited from their efforts.

A third volume is under preparation. It will be devoted to legal aspects of the use of nuclear energy for peaceful purposes.

Oxford, Cologne, April 2015

Jonathan L. Black-Branch
Dieter Fleck

Contents

Abbreviations

ABACC	Brazilian–Argentine Agency for Accounting and Control of Nuclear Materials
AP	Additional Protocol
ARSIWA	Articles on Responsibility of States for Internationally Wrongful Acts (2001)
CPPNM	Convention on the Physical Protection of Nuclear Material (30 March 1980)
CSA	Comprehensive Safeguards Agreement
CTBT	Comprehensive Nuclear Test-Ban Treaty (24 September 1996)
CTBTO	Preparatory Commission for the Comprehensive Nuclear Test-Ban Organization
CWC	Convention on the Prohibition of the Development, Production, Stockpiling and Use of Chemical Weapons and on Their Destruction (13 January 1993)
DARIO	Draft Articles on Responsibility of International Organizations (2011)
DPRK	Democratic People's Republic of Korea
EAEC	European Atomic Energy Community
ECSC	European Coal and Steel Community
ESA	EURATOM Supply Agency
EU	European Union
EURATO	European Atomic Energy Community
GICNT	Global Initiative to Combat Nuclear Terrorism
GTRI	Global Threat Reduction Initiative
IAEA	International Atomic Energy Agency
IHL	International Humanitarian Law
ICJ	International Court of Justice
ILA	International Law Association
ILC	International Law Commission
INFCIRC	Information Circulars, IAEA

INS	Intense Neutron Sources
LOFs	Locations Outside Facilities
LWR	Light Water Moderated Fission Reactor
MOX	Mixed Oxide Fuel
NAM	Non-Aligned Movement
NNWS	Non-Nuclear-Weapon States
NPT	Treaty on the Non-Proliferation of Nuclear Weapons (1 July 1968)
NSG	Nuclear Suppliers Group
NWFZ	Nuclear-Weapon-Free Zone
NWS	Nuclear-Weapon States
PrepCom	Preparatory Committee
PSI	Proliferation Security Initiative
SC	Security Council
SIP	Statement of Interdiction Principles
SIR	Safeguards Implementation Report
SLC	State-Level Concept
SNS	Spallation Neutron Source
TEU	Treaty on European Union (2012)
TFEU	Treaty on the Functioning of the European Union (2012)
UN	United Nations
UNMOVIC	United Nations Monitoring, Verification and Inspection Commission
UNSCOM	United Nations Special Commission
UNTS	United Nations Treaty Series
WMD	Weapons of Mass Destruction

Chapter 1
Verification of and Compliance with Nuclear Non-Proliferation Obligations: A Comprehensive Synopsis of Outstanding Issues

Jonathan L. Black-Branch and Dieter Fleck

Abstract Nuclear non-proliferation practice is characterized by a wide range of government practice and activities of specialist institutions, seeking to monitor, implement and enforce a legal framework that is often met with non-compliance. Pertinent legal obligations are deriving from various fields of international law, not always regulated in similar forms. This chapter provides a synopsis of relevant work in this area. It reviews current developments regarding the verification of, and compliance with, international standards in the wider field of nuclear security, non-proliferation and disarmament, highlighting the unique nature of this evolving area of international law, addressing the need for specialist legal interpretation, and trying to offer some conclusions which need to be further developed within this rather distinctive domain of international cooperation.

Keywords Compliance · International Atomic Energy Agency (IAEA) · Nuclear disarmament · Peaceful uses of nuclear energy · Treaty on Non-Proliferation of Nuclear Weapons (NPT) · Verification

---

Jonathan L. Black-Branch—Professor of International Law, Royal Holloway University of London; a member of Wolfson College, Oxford; Chairman of the International Law Association (ILA) Committee on Nuclear Weapons, Non-Proliferation and Contemporary International Law.

Dieter Fleck—Former Director International Agreements and Policy, Federal Ministry of Defence, Germany; Member of the Advisory Board of the Amsterdam Center for International Law (ACIL); Honorary President, International Society for Military Law and the Law of War; Rapporteur of the ILA Committee on Nuclear Weapons, Non-Proliferation and Contemporary International Law.

J.L. Black-Branch (✉)
Perseverance Cottage, 74 Old High Street, Old Headington, Oxford OX3 9HW, UK
e-mail: blackbranch@binternet.com

D. Fleck (✉)
Richard-Wagner-Str 30, 50999 Cologne, Germany
e-mail: DieterFleck@t-online.de

J.L. Black-Branch and D. Fleck (eds.), *Nuclear Non-Proliferation in International Law - Volume II*, DOI 10.1007/978-94-6265-075-6_1

Contents

1.1 Introduction

Activities regarding the verification of, and compliance with, international nuclear obligations remain ambiguous, often uncertain in their effects, and sometimes controversial. This explains the need for continued discussion in an area of law requiring legal certainty.

This chapter presents an overview of current work in this field, which still requires much further development. Underlining the need for this series, the chapter highlights the unique nature of pertinent obligations and the need for specialist legal interpretation in this area, introducing the present volume as part of a larger legal study. Section 1.2 focuses on the main legal framework and the institutions currently involved in issues of verification and compliance regarding nuclear non-proliferation obligations. Section 1.3 provides a précis of the main contributions to this volume highlighting the authors' main arguments and conclusions. Section 1.4 offers some conclusions, addressing the relevance of clarifying ambiguities and advancing understandings in this important area. It also highlights current developments and the unique nature of the nuclear non-proliferation domain.

The primary objective of this series remains to identify and critically assess legal rules regarding nuclear armament and the development and use of nuclear energy for peaceful purposes. This includes identifying gaps in legal regulation and examining emerging trends in this often complicated area of law and diplomacy. In presenting this analysis we seek to address an absence in the literature of legal scholarship on nuclear non-proliferation issues, an area that is largely dominated by political debate and a clear interest of States to keep important information classified. As editors, we believe that discussion and transparency is required in order to ensure that existing problems can be addressed and approached in a professional and effective manner. Debate, discussion and dialogue should be paramount to secrecy, confusion and confrontation. Legal analysis and independent expertise is of particular relevance for such debate in an environment that often compounds veritable information with political rhetoric. The principles and rules on the law of nuclear non-proliferation are forming a new, and indeed developing, discrete branch of international law today where nuclear weapons and non-proliferation law should constitute a subject discipline in its own right, interrelated to, yet distinct from other fields of international law, and to be distinguished from the law of control of conventional weapons and international humanitarian law.

Indeed, '[t]here is the need for a paradigm-shift in how we approach, interpret, and apply this area of law, separate from other forms of law',[1] making interpretive contributions and comparative assessments indispensable. This volume seeks to contribute to the exploration of this emerging field of international law by presenting impartial analysis, apprehensive of State practice, yet independent of political considerations.

The practical-oriented nature of such contributions becomes most apparent in the International Law Association's current Committee on Nuclear Weapons, Non-Proliferation and Contemporary International Law,[2] which aims to prepare a *Declaration on Legal Issues of Nuclear Weapons, Non-Proliferation and Peaceful Uses of Nuclear Energy* with a commentary to describe the contents and nature of pertinent principles and rules, and to explain options for future development in this field. To fully comply with the Committee mandate it will not suffice to note the different, and at times contentious, opinions developed on various relevant issues; rather it is unavoidable to weigh arguments and counter-arguments and eventually take a position and try to enlarge acceptance in the international community. The ILA Committee is, indeed, an appropriate forum to air such differences with the view to finding common ground as well as to work towards exploring approaches to settle contentious issues and to develop frameworks for dealing with dissentient views. Likewise, it provides a framework for evaluating open issues, identifying gaps in legal regulation, and helping to avoid situations of *non liquet.*

The ILA Committee has taken first steps on this route with its Report on *Legal Aspects of Nuclear Disarmament*, submitted at the last ILA Conference (Washington, D.C., 2014). It will continue its efforts by reporting to the forthcoming Conference (Johannesburg, 2016) on *Legal Aspects of Verification of Nuclear Non-Proliferation Commitments*. The present book series is meant to enhance these activities by enlarging expertise on the wide-ranging issues involved, widening networks, facilitating information exchange and increasing transparency in cooperation at a global level. Taking up earlier activities in this field,[3] it aims at developing new ideas that are required to achieve a better understanding of existing law and to develop proposals *de lege ferenda*.

The significance of this series may be seen from three different perspectives: providing a clear focus on legal rather than political science issues; taking a fresh look at nuclear non-proliferation, safety of nuclear energy and nuclear disarmament within a contemporary context; and giving full consideration to issues of implementation, compliance control and dispute settlement:

---

[1] Black-Branch and Fleck 2014, p. 2; as quoted from J. Black-Branch, Opening Remarks to the Third Round Table (London) on Nuclear Weapons, Nuclear Energy and Non-Proliferation under International Law: Current Challenges and Evolving Norms (14–15 February 2013 Oxford and Cambridge Club)', http://www.ila-hq.org/en/committees/index.cfm/cid/1025.

[2] http://www.ila-hq.org/en/committees/index.cfm/cid/1025.

[3] See e.g. Dahlitz 1991, 1994, 1996, 1999.

- Legal requirements are often missed in discussions on nuclear issues. Many important decisions are taken without objective or full consultation with legal experts. Even when objective discussion is requested, this is often done by physicists or political scientists rather than in cooperation with legal advisors and those involved in legal research. While a considerable amount of legal principles and rules is available in this field, its relevance for decision-making needs to be made more visible.
- All three pillars of the 1968 Nuclear Non-Proliferation Treaty (NPT)[4]—i.e. non-proliferation of nuclear weapons and their means of delivery; the right to develop research, production and use of nuclear energy for peaceful purposes and its resulting obligations; and cessation of the nuclear arms race, nuclear disarmament, and general and complete disarmament—must be pursued within their context; they cannot be fully understood nor effectively implemented in isolation; and they must be considered in their entirety.
- Effective implementation requires continuous efforts to ensure compliance and dispute settlement. To be successful, such efforts may not rely solely on existing institutions and procedures, but must include innovative and balanced approaches, and must be developed in cooperation.

In meeting these aspirations, it is required not only to contribute to interpreting and implementing existing treaty law in this field, but also to identify evolving new principles and rules of customary international law and to support their further development in *opinio juris* and best-practice. Given the wide range of treaty regulation in place,[5] specialist analysis is required by a range of legal experts. It is in this spirit that the contributions presented in this volume are focussing on verification of, and compliance with, nuclear non-proliferation obligations.

1.2 Legal and Institutional Frameworks for Verification and Compliance

The legal obligations regarding non-proliferation of nuclear weapons and other nuclear devices are established in the NPT as part of a package including the obligations on nuclear disarmament and an assured use of nuclear energy for peaceful purposes. While the NPT enjoys wide acceptance and has been extended indefinitely in 1995, some issues cause a continuing concern in relation to the interrelationship of its fundamental three pillars highlighted above. Important military Powers continue to abstain from becoming Parties to the NPT, and other forms

[4]Treaty on the Non-Proliferation of Nuclear Weapons (1 July 1968) 729 UNTS 161.

[5]See Nuclear Weapons, Non-Proliferation & Contemporary International Law: Relevant Treaties, Other International Instruments and Case Law, http://www.ila-hq.org/en/committees/index.cfm/cid/1025.

of cooperation are still unexplored. There is little transparency in this respect. Furthermore, there is no consensus on questions of whether, and to what extent, certain treaty obligations are developing into custom. As a result, many issues of compliance and enforcement remained controversial. Safety and security of peaceful uses of nuclear energy have often been unsatisfactory and underexplored. Furthermore, the interrelationship between the NPT's three pillars is in itself characterized by different views as to the interpretation and implementation of relevant rules.

States and international organizations, including the International Atomic Energy Agency (IAEA), the Preparatory Commission for the Comprehensive Nuclear-Test-Ban Treaty Organization (CTBTO), and the European Atomic Energy Community (EURATOM) have revealed severe gaps in compliance with nuclear non-proliferation obligations through intrusive verification measures and the use of national technical means. The revolution in information technology has effectively supported control activities and made results publicly accessible. This has contributed to worldwide monitoring activities and an open discussion of contentious developments. Activities, which in former times might have been obscured more easily, are now more obvious and difficult to camouflage. It is less likely today than decades ago that agreed limitations in armament could be circumvented in secrecy. Yet cooperative action, which is necessary to ensure relevant safeguards, remains often less than effective. States would not accept verification measures that are not clearly agreed to and confirmed in practice. Enforcement measures, even if taken by the Security Council acting under Chapter VII of the UN Charter, have often proven unsuccessful. Nuclear-weapon States, non-nuclear-weapon States and international organizations share responsibilities in this context.

While countermeasures and enforcement have become part of daily reality in the practice of States and international organizations, procedures and objectives of verification (including on abilities or quantities; numbers of warheads or general ceilings; transparency of information assessment), as well as technical issues of data exchange and data publication must still to be assessed more thoroughly, to ensure effectiveness of follow-up measures. Although hidden stockpiles may have a rather limited role for deterrence purposes, they continue to exist and the assumption of their existence may have negative effects on confidence building. Nuclear capacities could be detrimental if used for aggressive purposes, irrespective of whether such purposes are intended or perceived. Hence cooperative action will be essential on the route to nuclear balance at lower levels. More transparency is needed on issues of security and safety of the use of nuclear energy for peaceful purposes. Hence verification is essential for all three pillars of the NPT and it needs to become even more transparent. Furthermore, disputes must be settled at an early stage and in a cooperative manner. To the extent that countermeasures and sanctions in case of non-compliance have to be applied, their legal conditions, effectiveness and consequences for future cooperation must be considered.

The role of non-governmental organizations, a well-informed public opinion, and in-depth academic research on these issues cannot be underestimated. It may help to objectively assess existing problems, fully understand their implications and facilitate possible solutions. To achieve effective results, comprehensive approaches and a distinct openness for different lines of thought will be necessary, rather than insisting on specialized yet controversial ideas. This circumscribes the challenges involved with implementing the agreed Work Plan of the ILA Committee,[6] challenges which those engaged in its implementation do perceive as chances for making progress. Fully considering the variety of pertinent issues,[7] it may be appropriate to present the law of nuclear non-proliferation as a special legal regime that may become a useful analytical tool to employ in the future work,[8] but it remains important to assess relevant norms in their context and compare, whether and to what extent they differ from the general rules of public international law or the rules of other special regimes.

1.3 A Précis of Verification and Compliance Contributions

International verification activities are examined in this book both in their complexity and incompleteness of legal regulation. Experts from different backgrounds and expertise are exploring the means and methods of current verification activities; existing technical possibilities and gaps; and remedies for wrongful acts including means and methods of dispute settlement. All contributions are practice-oriented. They are reviewing existing obligations as based on treaty law, unilateral commitments and developing custom. Legal loopholes and consequences of non-compliance are also considered in-depth.

Tariq Rauf portrays the work of the International Atomic Energy Agency (IAEA). He insists that the Agency is the competent authority responsible for verifying and assuring compliance with its safeguards agreements, explaining that in order to carry out its safeguards obligations and to maintain its credibility, it must consider, investigate, draw conclusions and decide on necessary actions in accordance with its mandate and use its capabilities to assess the provenance and authenticity of third-party (intelligence) information. A critical evaluation of existing safeguards agreements is presented by *Pierre-Emmanuel Dupont*. He argues that existing rules of interpretation, including an enquiry into subsequent agreement and practice, do not lend unconditional support to the interpretation that the IAEA is entitled to verify completeness of national reports, unless an Additional Protocol to the Comprehensive Safeguards Agreement is brought into force between the Agency and the respective State. This position is not shared by other contributors. *Laura Rockwood* and *Larry Johnson*, evaluating treaty obligations and assessing multiple decisions of the IAEA policy-making organs, confirm the

[6]See http://www.ila-hq.org/en/committees/index.cfm/cid/1025.

[7]See Pant 2012.

[8]See Joyner and Roscini 2012, p. 277.

right and obligation of the Agency to verify both the correctness and completeness of these reports and its authority to do so efficiently. They also explain that the Model Additional Protocol was not developed to broaden the IAEA's right to verify both correctness and completeness, but to provide the Agency with additional tools with which to fulfil that obligation more effectively. *Masahiko Asada* undertakes a comprehensive assessment of the Model Additional Protocol and its importance for the IAEA in performing its mandate under the NPT. He explains that the IAEA, wishing to further develop its cooperative verification efforts, never stated that States were obliged to conclude an AP (this would, indeed, be counterproductive for the cooperative approach taken with the AP). On the other hand the Agency is mandated and authorized to use information also from other sources, in addition to national reports of the State under review. The question is thus not confined to issues of interpretation of safeguard agreements (although full cooperation under INFCIRC/153 and INFCIRC/540 would be preferable), but it extends to the issue of what belongs to the obligations of States under Articles I, II and III NPT on the one hand and how far is the reach of the IAEA's mandate on the other.

The experience gathered so far by the Preparatory Commission for the Comprehensive Nuclear-Test-Ban Treaty Organization (CTBTO) is discussed by *Sabine Bauer and Cormac O'Reilly,* who demonstrate that compliance with the comprehensive nuclear test ban can be effectively verified even before the CTBT[9] enters into force. *Wolfgang Kilb* discusses the long-standing safeguards practice of the European Atomic Energy Community (EURATOM) as a regional cornerstone of the verification of nuclear non-proliferation obligations in the European Union.

Technical possibilities, informal ways of cooperation and gaps in current regulation are presented in interdisciplinary approaches. *Gerald Kirchner* and *Stefan Oeter* carry the interdisciplinary approach further to verification capabilities by evaluating to what extent existing technological perspectives would affect the current treaty design. Underlining that the NPT regime is based on a fundamental *do ut des*, with a basic feature of reciprocity between rights and duties of the different groups of contracting States, they conclude that more intrusive safeguards and additional means of monitoring and verification of suspected violations of non-proliferation obligations will only be possible if the nuclear powers show a serious commitment to make significant progress in nuclear disarmament. *Matthias Englert and Anne I. Harrington,* endorsing this approach from a different perspective, explain that next generation nuclear technologies including intense neutron sources and facilities that are not originally designed for fissile material production, but could well be used for that purpose, are not directly covered by existing IAEA safeguards. *Gabriella Venturini* presents a review of legal issues relating to the Proliferation Security Initiative (PSI), stressing that its activities would benefit from a greater involvement of law enforcement authorities for the interdiction of dual-use goods, as well as from a geographical expansion of its scope.

---

[9]Comprehensive Nuclear-Test-Ban Treaty (CTBT) of 24 September 1996, http://www.ctbto.org/fileadmin/content/treaty/treaty_text.pdf.

Countermeasures, remedies for wrongful acts, and peaceful settlement of disputes conclude this book. *Barry Kellman* undertakes to develop objective criteria by which the NPT verification system may be judged and put into practice. Asserting that the core imperative of verification must be to enable detection of violations of non-proliferation obligations, and frames the International Atomic Energy Agency's (IAEA) role in verifying compliance with States' mutual commitment to nuclear non-proliferation, he addresses two controversies associated with nuclear non-proliferation verification, respectively: the scope of States' legal obligation to allow the IAEA to resolve doubts about compliance, and the Security Council's authority to impose sanctions for non-compliance with nuclear non-proliferation obligations pursuant to recent international law decisions. He concludes that the IAEA is fully mandated to verify not only the correctness but also the completeness of a State's reports, and the Security Council has unreviewable authority to enforce international obligations in the maintenance of peace and security. *Ilaria Anna Colussi* and *Maurizio Martellini*, again taking an interdisciplinary effort, discuss best-practice guidelines for enhancing cooperative compliance with nuclear non-proliferation obligations, in particular through monitoring, reinforcing the structure and action of the IAEA, involving other UN bodies, States and civil society, and promoting the rule of law, impartiality and non-discrimination transparency. *Eva Kassoti* offers an assessment of unilateral security assurances by nuclear-weapon States, explaining their legal status and relevance, and asserting that these security assurances, despite their shortcomings in terms of scope and content, may be validly considered as binding undertakings to the extent that they manifest the intention of their authors to be bound. *Gabriella Venturini,* evaluating the legal consequences of unilateral moratoria and reductions of stockpiles in her second contribution, addresses several questions regarding the effective implementation and expediency of unilateral initiatives in nuclear non-proliferation, especially the absence of obligatory verification measures and the need to secure transparency as a voluntary confidence-building measure based on disclosure, accessibility and reliability of information. *Francis Grimal* provides an assessment of legal theory with reference to practical examples on the threat or use of nuclear weapons under the right of self-defence, addressing the exact point at which a State can lawfully respond with recourse to nuclear weapons and stressing that only under exceptional circumstances would a State meet the cardinal requirements of 'necessity' and 'proportionality'. *Jonathan Black-Branch*, explaining the requirement that countermeasures in cases of non-compliance with verification obligations must be in line with the principles and rules on international responsibility of States and international organizations, comments on existing legal limitations for action in this field. He concludes that not only are countermeasures permissible under the 2001 Articles on Responsibility of States for Internationally Wrongful Acts and the 2011 Draft Articles on Responsibility of International Organizations, but they may be necessary to ensure compliance with *erga omnes* obligations and may prove to be an effective and indeed favourable device for enforcing the Nuclear Non-Proliferation Treaty and other relevant obligations. *Dieter Fleck*, evaluating means and methods for the settlement of disputes on nuclear non-proliferation obligations, reviews cases of non-compliance with the NPT in light of the fact that none of the cases reported to the Security Council have been successfully resolved by measures under Chapter VII of the UN Charter. He concludes that new rules on nuclear non-proliferation may not be necessary, but the principles and rules on pacific dispute settlement, as set out in Article 2(3) and Chapter VI, need to be better implemented and further developed in multilateral cooperation.

Taken together, this complex picture of different commitments, gaps in legal regulation and difficulties in compliance control should help to better understand existing challenges for a comprehensive legal assessment, and also contribute to making pertinent general principles and rules more apparent.

1.4 Conclusions and Outlook

The research presented in this book will invariably be of great support to those involved in the implementation and application of nuclear obligations. It will assist in preparing the forthcoming ILA Declaration on legal issues of nuclear weapons, non-proliferation and peaceful uses of nuclear energy and its commentary. The Declaration will examine the interrelationship between nuclear non-proliferation, nuclear disarmament and nuclear safety and security as a whole, including the future goals regarding an in-depth evaluation of relevant legal aspects of ensuring the safety and security of peaceful uses of nuclear energy. A research project on this latter topic is already under preparation and its results will be published in Volume III of this book series.

New developments within the wider field of nuclear non-proliferation law convincingly show that the process of discussion and exchange, which we have started with this book series, must continue. The recent Vienna Conference on the Humanitarian Impact of Nuclear Weapons (8–9 December 2014) has marked a new willingness for open dialogue, including representatives from two nuclear-weapon States Parties to the NPT, on ways and means for pursuing the goal of achieving a world free from nuclear weapons. New perspectives for the continuation of that dialogue are being developed.[10] The case brought by the Marshall Islands against all nine nuclear-weapon States to the ICJ regarding their obligations on cessation of the nuclear arms race and to nuclear disarmament has opened a new path for jurisprudence. In respect of India, Pakistan and the United Kingdom the Applicant has invoked, as basis for the Court's jurisdiction, the acceptance of compulsory jurisdiction of the Court under Article 36(2) of the ICJ Statute; with respect to the six other States (China, the Democratic People's Republic of Korea, France, Israel, the Russian Federation and the United States of America), the Marshall Islands seeks to establish the Court's jurisdiction, pursuant to Article 38(5) of the Rules of

[10]See http://www.bmeia.gv.at/en/european-foreign-policy/disarmament/weapons-of-mass-destruction/nuclear-weapons-and-nuclear-terrorism/vienna-conference-on-the-humanitarian-impact-of-nuclear-weapons/.

Court, on the consent of those States. The Applicant's claims are based not only on Article VI NPT of which six of the nine Defendants are Parties, but also on customary international law.[11] The 2015 NPT Review conference, although unable to adopt a Final Document, provided an opportunity to take stock of what has been accomplished so far and to diagnose the obstacles that continue to inhibit progress on the Action Plan, which was agreed in 2010.[12] The 60th anniversary of the use of nuclear weapons in Hiroshima and Nagasaki on 6 and 8 August 2015 will challenge non-nuclear-weapon States and nuclear-weapon States alike to play a more active role in activities to reach a world free from nuclear armament.[13]

Whilst important issues of verification of, and compliance with, international nuclear obligations will remain open to various interpretations leaving ambiguity in a field requiring certainty, this volume attempts to clarify various ambiguities or at least to present varying differences in a clear and concise manner with the hope of advancing understandings of these important issues regarding verification of and compliance with nuclear non-proliferation obligations in the international community. Moreover, the discussion highlights the unique nature of this evolving area of international law on nuclear non-proliferation and the continuing need for specialist legal interpretation in this distinctive domain. Special approaches by theorists, practitioners and governments alike, and openness for the interrelationship of the various issues involved remain as necessary as public participation in relevant debates on these issues.

References

Black-Branch J, Fleck D (2014) Nuclear weapons, non-proliferation and disarmament: a comprehensive audit of relevant legal issues and international concerns. In: Black-Branch J, Fleck D (eds) Nuclear non-proliferation and international law, vol I. TMC Asser Press, The Hague, pp 1–21

Dahlitz J (ed) (1991) Arms control and disarmament law, vol I. The international law of arms control and disarmament. United Nations, Geneva

Dahlitz J (ed) (1994) Arms control and disarmament law, vol II. Avoidance and settlement of arms control disputes. United Nations, Geneva

Dahlitz J (ed) (1996) Arms control and disarmament law, vol III. Future legal restraints on arms proliferation. United Nations, Geneva

Dahlitz J (ed) (1999) Peaceful resolution of major international disputes. United Nations, Geneva

Joyner DH, Roscini M (2012) Conclusions. In: Joyner DH, Roscini M (eds) Non-proliferation law as a special regime. A contribution to fragmentation theory in international law. Cambridge University Press, pp 270–277

Pant HV (ed) (2012) Handbook of nuclear proliferation. Routledge, London

[11]See http://www.icj-cij.org/presscom/files/0/18300.pdf; see also http://www.icj-cij.org/docket/files/160/18332.pdf.

[12]See http://www.un.org/disarmament/WMD/Nuclear/NPT_Review_Conferences.shtml.

[13]See http://www.japantimes.co.jp/news/2015/01/04/national/politics-diplomacy/experts-urge-japan-play-greater-role-nuclear-disarmament-process/.VLD9R1rgq8o.

Chapter 2
The General Framework of IAEA Safeguards

Tariq Rauf

A prudent ruler cannot keep his word, nor should he, where such fidelity would damage him, and when the reasons that made him promise are no longer relevant.
Niccolò Machiavelli 1513, pp. 61–62

The very meaning of a line in the law is that you intentionally may come as close to it as you can if you do not pass it.
Justice Oliver Wendell Holmes 1920, p. 395

Almost all nations observe almost all principles of international law and almost all of their obligations almost all of the time.
Louis Henkin 1979, p. 47

In my experience [States] will keep their bargains as long as it is in their interest.
Hans J. Morgenthau 1948, p. 560

Abstract Starting with a consideration of some main reasons for States to comply with international treaty obligations, this chapter portrays the general framework of IAEA Safeguards as the process, to assess whether others are complying with their obligations. To be credible, this process should rely on five key elements: treaty language, monitoring, analysis, evaluation and findings. It should detect evidence of violations, deter violations and help to build confidence among States. The IAEA Safeguards System is discussed and its implementation in the interplay between the Director General and the Board of Governors characterized as an effort to ensure zero-tolerance in case of non-compliance. The chapter concludes

Director, Disarmament, Arms Control and Non-Proliferation Programme, Stockholm International Peace Research Institute; Senior Advisor to the Chairman of the 2014 NPT PrepCom; formerly Head, Verification and Security Policy Coordination, International Atomic Energy Agency (2002–2011).

T. Rauf (✉)
Stockholm International Peace Research Institute, Signalistgatan 9, 16970 Solna, Sweden
e-mail: rauf@sipri.org

J.L. Black-Branch and D. Fleck (eds.), *Nuclear Non-Proliferation in International Law - Volume II*, DOI 10.1007/978-94-6265-075-6_2

that in order to carry out its safeguards obligations and to maintain its credibility the IAEA must consider, investigate, draw conclusions and decide on necessary actions in accordance with its mandate and use its capabilities to assess the provenance and authenticity of third-party (intelligence) information.

Keywords Compliance · Comprehensive Safeguards Agreements (CSAs) · International Atomic Energy Agency (IAEA) · IAEA safeguards · Model additional protocol · Verification

Contents

2.1 Introduction

It is a safe assumption that the general propensity of States is to comply with their international obligations undertaken through negotiated treaties and other related international legal instruments. One might well ask, why? A number of considerations lend support to this proposition. These are: efficiency, interests and norms.[1]

Efficiency: Policy decisions do not take place in a vacuum nor are they a free good. Decision-making theory holds that individuals and entities (organizations) seek to conserve resources for the most critical and urgent matters.[2] Efficiency leads to considerable policy continuity, thus in the areas of treaty obligations, the alternative to recalculation is to follow the established rule. In other words, instead of the continuously recalculating, maximizing rational actor, a 'satisficing' model of bounded rationality reacts to problems as they arise and devises solutions within a familiar and accustomed repertoire.[3] Bureaucratic organizations generally function according to routines and standard operating procedures, mainly governed by authoritative rules and regulations. The adoption of a treaty, much as the enactment of any other law, establishes an authoritative rule system, which leads to compliance as the normal organizational behaviour. Bureaucracy, however, is not monolithic, and may well include opponents to a treaty regime. Controversies over rule implementation or interpretation are generally resolved in accordance

[1]For a useful and stimulating work on thinking broadly about compliance matters see Chayes and Chayes 1995.

[2]See Lindblom 1968, p. 14.

[3]See Allison 1971, Chaps. 3–4.

with normal bureaucratic practices in which the presumption is in favour of following the rule, as an outright violation would be a much heavier case to make, except in circumstances where the State might perceive that international norms are not being applied in a fair and consistent manner.

Interests: It is a basic principle of international law that States cannot be legally bound except with their own consent, as such most arms control treaties include provisions permitting a State party to withdraw from the treaty in extenuating circumstances which have jeopardized its supreme national interests. Hence, a State need not enter into a treaty that it does not regard as being in its own interest. Treaties, as other legal instruments, are artefacts of political choice and the process by which they are formulated, negotiated and concluded is designed to ensure that the interests of all negotiating parties are accommodated to a greater or lesser extent. Treaty formulation and negotiation, at its best, is a creative exercise through which the parties not only assess the benefits and burdens of obligations but redefine and sometimes even discover their interests. It can be a learning process in which national positions and concepts of national interests evolve. Furthermore, negotiators often have to take a long-range view, as they may end up with operational responsibility for the treaty after its conclusion. They are likely to attach considerable importance to developing governance norms and practices that will operate predictably over time. These elements tend to influence broad-based conceptions of national interest that contribute to induce compliance. A good treaty is one that reflects bargains and is perceived to be in the interest of all negotiating parties. If issues of non-compliance and enforcement become endemic, then the root cause likely is that either the original bargain did not adequately reflect the interests of all parties rather than mere disobedience or that concerns about fairness and impartiality regarding the treaty regime have risen to the fore. While States may know that they can violate treaty commitments in crunch situations, they do not negotiate agreements with the notion that they can violate the treaty as a matter of routine. The international situation that led to a treaty does not remain static. Lasting treaty regimes must be able to adapt to changes in the international setting, not only through formal amendments but also through interpretations agreed by contracting parties, which in turn are supportive of the default mode of compliance.

Norms: The fundamental norm of international law is *pacta sunt servanda* (treaties are to be obeyed). In many States, treaties are enshrined in domestic legislation. Thus, treaties are legally binding on the States that have ratified them and this in turn entails a legal obligation to obey the provisions. The effort put in by States to negotiate a treaty, or to accede to it, is reflective of the understanding that entering into a treaty commitment will constrain the State's own sovereignty and freedom of action. This effort also reflects the State's interest that in constraining its own sovereignty it is also similarly constraining the sovereignty of other States parties and thus contributing to the well-being of all parties. This highlights the general rule that States acknowledge an obligation to comply with the agreements they have signed.

2.2 Verification of Compliance

The above discussion reflects the view that ordinarily States will comply with the treaties that they are a party to, and that non-compliance is a deviant rather than an expected behaviour. Arms control treaties concern core national security interests and the authority and value of such legal agreements is enhanced when compliance can be assured, especially through a credible and impartial verification regime. International security treaties require the active participation and compliance of the States' parties and verification of such compliance by international mechanisms, as such treaties can be sustained only through cooperative verification measures between the States' parties and the international verification organization. The long-term sustainability of international arms control arrangements is not possible without credible verification of compliance. Assessment of compliance of international arms control agreements is vested in international verification organizations, such as the International Atomic Energy Agency (for the Non-Proliferation Treaty), the Comprehensive Nuclear-Test Ban Treaty Organization (for the CTBT) and the Organization for the Prohibition of Chemical Weapons (for the CWC).

Verification can be described as the processes that States use, to assess whether other States are complying with their arms control agreement obligations. To verify compliance, a State party must be assured that the forces or activities of another State are within the constraints established by the limits and obligations in the agreement. A verifiable treaty contains an interlocking web of constraints and provisions designed to deter non-compliance, to make non-compliance more complicated and more expensive, and to make its detection more timely.[4] A credible verification regime relies on five key elements: treaty language, monitoring, analysis, evaluation and findings (conclusions). The verification system for an arms control treaty cannot remove all doubts about the existence of possible non-compliance. But it can provide States' parties with confidence in compliance with the treaty if it meets three objectives. First, the verification should detect evidence of any violations in a timely manner. The data collected by the monitoring systems, when combined with the restrictions in the treaty, should enable identification of violations in a timely manner. Second, the verification system should deter violations of the treaty through early detection. Third, the verification system should help build confidence in the viability of the treaty through conclusions that the States' parties are complying with limits and obligations in the treaty.

2.2.1 The Role of IAEA Safeguards

The IAEA safeguards system fulfils all three criteria. The principal role of IAEA safeguards is to verify compliance by States' parties with their undertakings

[4]See A.F. Woolf, Monitoring and Verification in Arms Control, Congressional Research Service, 23 December 2011.

under the nuclear-weapon-free zone (NWFZ) treaties and compliance with Non-Proliferation Treaty (NPT) comprehensive safeguards agreements.

NWFZ treaties and the NPT require NNWS parties to use nuclear energy exclusively for peaceful purposes. Verification of this obligation is fulfilled by bringing into force a comprehensive safeguards agreement with the Agency. The basic undertaking of the State is to accept safeguards on all source or special fissionable material in all peaceful nuclear activities within its territory, under its jurisdiction or carried out under its control anywhere, for the exclusive purpose of verifying that such material is not diverted to nuclear weapons or other nuclear explosive devices.[5] For its part, the IAEA has the corresponding right and obligation to ensure that safeguards are applied in accordance with the Agency's safeguards system.[6]

In February 1992, the IAEA Board of Governors affirmed that the scope of comprehensive safeguards agreements was not limited to nuclear material actually declared by a State, but included all material that is required to be declared. In other words, the Board confirmed that the organization has the right and obligation, under such agreements, to verify not only that State declarations of nuclear material subject to safeguards are 'correct' (i.e. they accurately describe the types and quantities of the State's declared nuclear material holdings), but that they are also 'complete' (i.e. that they include all material that should have been declared).

The objective of IAEA safeguards is the timely detection of diversion of significant quantities of nuclear material from peaceful nuclear activities to the manufacture of nuclear weapons or of other nuclear explosive devices or for purposes unknown, and deterrence of such diversion by the risk of early detection. The 'timely detection' of the diversion of 'significant quantities' is based on the premise that, in case a certain quantity of nuclear material cannot be accounted for, the possibility of the State manufacturing a nuclear explosive device cannot be excluded. Furthermore, a certain amount of time is required for the State to convert nuclear material into a weapon-usable form. Goal quantities and timeliness requirements are established for detecting diversion of different categories and forms of nuclear material (e.g. low-enriched uranium and high-enriched uranium; bulk form or fresh reactor fuel assemblies).

Achievement of the second objective, that is, the detection of undeclared nuclear material and activities in a State, requires different tools from those needed for the timely detection of the diversion of declared nuclear material. These are a broader range of information, more emphasis on the evaluation of information, more access for inspectors to locations and a more analytical approach in implementing safeguards. It also requires the evaluation of the State's entire nuclear fuel cycle capabilities (i.e. the State 'as a whole') in addition to individual facilities.

[5](International Atomic Energy Agency Information Circular), INFCIRC/153 (Corr.), para 1.

[6]IAEA: Guidance for States Implementing Comprehensive Safeguards Agreements and Additional Protocols, (IAEA Services Series 21), pp. 1–2.

The IAEA has defined three safeguards objectives[7] that are common to all States with CSAs, as follows:

- to detect undeclared nuclear material and activities anywhere in the State;
- to detect undeclared production or processing of nuclear material at facilities and Locations Outside Facilities (LOFs) where nuclear material is customarily used; and
- to detect diversion of declared nuclear material at facilities and LOFs.

In order to meet the overall objective the Agency determines an optimized combination of safeguards measures needed to achieve State-specific technical objectives, based on the evaluation of all available information on the State. The concept of considering the State as a whole provides the opportunity to focus verification efforts and resources, where needed, to meet the State-specific objectives. The methodology and approach are based on a comprehensive State evaluation that takes State-specific factors into consideration in all stages of safeguards implementation.

In determining how generic safeguards objectives are to be addressed for a particular State, the Agency conducts an analysis of all technically plausible paths by which that State could pursue the acquisition of nuclear material for the development of a nuclear weapon or other nuclear explosive device. Such an acquisition path could involve the diversion of declared nuclear material, unreported imports of nuclear material, unreported production or processing of nuclear material at declared nuclear facilities or LOFs, undeclared nuclear material and activities or any combination of these. The Agency then establishes technical objectives for each path.

Thus, the generic and technical objectives and applicable safeguards measures to address them form the basis of a State-level safeguards approach for a State.

The IAEA may carry out three kinds of inspections: ad hoc, routine and special inspections, as well as complementary accesses. States must ensure the inspectors are able to carry out their activities, by providing access to locations and to information necessary to meet independently the objectives of the inspection. States, and NWFZ regional control mechanisms, have the right to have IAEA personnel accompanied during inspections, provided that in doing so, inspectors are not delayed or otherwise impeded in carrying out their functions. States have the right to reject the designation of any inspector at any time without assigning reasons, and also to refuse visas to designated inspectors.

Ad hoc inspections are normally conducted to verify the information contained in the initial report by a State to the IAEA, before Subsidiary Arrangements have been concluded and Facility Attachments have been prepared, or to verify nuclear material before it is exported or upon receipt in the importing State.

Routine inspections[8] are conducted after the Subsidiary Arrangements and Facility Attachments have been concluded and specific information has been incorporated in the Attachments, including information on 'strategic points' in

[7]See, 'The Safeguards System of the International Atomic Energy Agency'. http://www.iaea.org/safeguards/documents/safeg_system.pdf.

[8]The purposes of routine inspections are listed in para 72 of INFCIRC/153.

each facility. Once the broader conclusions are drawn in a State with an AP in force, the IAEA has the right under certain conditions to conduct inspections on a random basis, with a minimum advance notification to the State and operator or to select part of the routine inspection activities randomly.

The IAEA may require special inspections which may be either additional to the routine inspection effort, or involve access to information or locations which are additional to those involved in routine and ad hoc inspections, or both. Special inspections can be triggered by the IAEA in situations where there are indications of undeclared nuclear activities, and/or if the IAEA considers that information made available by the State is not adequate for the Agency to fulfil its responsibilities in the implementation of safeguards. Furthermore, under the Additional Protocol (INFCIRC/540 Corr.), the IAEA can request 'complementary access' to resolve questions or inconsistencies, or to seek additional information, in the course of the implementation of safeguards. It is worth noting that the procedure to initiate a special inspection is far more complex that the one established for a complementary access under the Additional Protocol.[9] While special inspections have rarely been carried out, they are an important element of the Agency's legal authority to implement safeguards, and may be necessary for the IAEA to achieve the objectives of NWFZ treaty and NPT safeguards.

Complementary access refers to access provided to IAEA inspectors by a State under an Additional Protocol, to enable the inspectors to carry out specific verification and assessment activities to meet the Agency's safeguards objectives. The Agency may request complementary access to a variety of locations in a State with an Additional Protocol in force.[10] Each type of access requested has specific advance notice requirements; in some cases this may be less than 2 h. In addition to locations associated with State declarations under an AP, the IAEA may also request complementary access to any location in the State.[11]

Managed access refers to steps taken by the State to prevent the dissemination of proliferation-sensitive information,[12] to meet safety or physical security requirements, or to protect proprietary or commercially sensitive information, in such a manner as to not impede the IAEA's activities to fulfil the purpose of the access. Arrangements for managed access shall not preclude the Agency from conducting activities necessary to provide credible assurance of the absence of undeclared nuclear material and activities at the location in question. Ultimately, the State must provide sufficient access to information and locations during managed access to allow the IAEA inspectors to fulfil the purpose of the access.

The discovery in 1991 of Iraq's clandestine nuclear weapons programme highlighted the shortcomings of safeguards implementation focusing essentially on

---

[9]In some cases the IAEA may seek a complementary access with advance notice of 2 h, or even less than 2 h.

[10]INFCIRC/540, Article 5.

[11]INFCIRC/540, Article 4.

[12]Such as uranium enrichment or plutonium separation.

declared nuclear material and safeguards conclusions drawn at the facility level. This set the stage and provided the catalyst for far-reaching efforts to strengthen the safeguards system, in particular the Agency's ability to detect undeclared nuclear material and activities in States with comprehensive safeguards agreements. The objective, as endorsed by the Board of Governors, was to develop a safeguards system that could verify not only the correctness of States' declarations of nuclear material, but also the completeness thereof. The result was the Model Additional Protocol, which was approved by the Board on 15 May 1997, and subsequently published as INFCIRC/540 (Corr.). Additional protocols for States with comprehensive safeguards agreements in force must include all of the measures contained in the Model Additional Protocol. Enhanced evaluation of all information available to the Agency about a State's nuclear material, activities and plans, including information in States' declarations and voluntary reports, the results of the Agency's verification activities and information from open and other sources, is key to the strengthened safeguards system. No verification system in the world anywhere can provide an absolute guarantee of detecting violations if a state is taking active concealment measures, on the other hand, the suite of safeguards technologies and methodologies being implemented by the IAEA currently make it very difficult for a state to have the assurance of the non-detection of clandestine nuclear activities by the Agency.

2.2.2 Non-Compliance with IAEA Safeguards

The basic undertaking by NNWS in the comprehensive safeguards agreement, in accordance with Article III.1 of the NPT, is to accept safeguards on all source or special fissionable material in all peaceful nuclear activities within its territory, under its jurisdiction or carried out under its control anywhere, for the exclusive purpose of verifying that such material is not diverted to nuclear weapons or other nuclear explosive devices.[13]

The IAEA Board of Governors, upon report of the Director General, may decide that an action by the State is *essential and urgent* in order to ensure verification that nuclear material subject to safeguards is not diverted from peaceful uses to nuclear weapons or purposes unknown and is being used in accordance with the State's declaration in peaceful applications. In the event, the Board may call upon the State to take the required action without delay, irrespective of whether procedures for the settlement of a dispute have been invoked.[14]

The Board, upon examination of relevant information reported to it by the Director General, may find that the Agency is not able to verify that there has been no diversion of nuclear material required to be safeguarded, and may make the

---

[13]INFCIRC/153 (Corr.), para 1.

[14]Ibid., para 18.

reports provided for in para C of Article XII of the Statute and also may take, where applicable, the other measures provided for in that paragraph. In taking such action the Board shall take account of the degree of assurance provided by the safeguards measures that have been applied and shall afford the State every reasonable opportunity to furnish the Board with any necessary reassurance.[15]

In describing the IAEA's functions the Statute provides that the Agency submit reports, when appropriate, to the Security Council. If in connection with the activities of the Agency there should arise questions that are within the competence of the Security Council, the Agency shall notify the Security Council, as the organ bearing the main responsibility for the maintenance of international peace and security, and may also take the measures open to it under the Statute, including those provided in para C of Article XII.[16]

The IAEA Statute also provides that Agency inspectors shall report any non-compliance to the Director General who shall thereupon transmit the report to the Board of Governors. The Board shall call upon the State or States to remedy forthwith any non-compliance which it finds to have occurred. The Board shall report the non-compliance to all members and to the Security Council and the General Assembly of the United Nations.[17]

The Statute is not self-implementing; it requires a safeguards agreement as a vehicle for bringing reports by the Director General to the Board of Governors for its consideration. In practice, over the years, determination of findings of non-compliance has been within the remit of the Board and not the Director General. The Board has made findings on non-compliance by Iraq, the Democratic People's Republic of Korea (DPRK), Romania, Iran, Syria and Libya. In the cases of Iraq, the DPRK, Iran and Syria, the Board decided to report the non-compliance to the Security Council along with Board resolutions requesting the States concerned to remedy the non-compliance and to cooperate with the IAEA in that regard. In the case of Romania and Libya, the Board reported the non-compliance to the Security Council 'for information only'. And, in the cases of undeclared nuclear activities carried out by Egypt and South Korea, the Board chose not to make any findings of non-compliance. This record of the Board is indicative of political considerations introduced by Board members in considering reports of the Director General. And, similarly, the actions of the Security Council in this context have also been politically driven.

The correct approach should be the one as stated by Director General Mohamed ElBaradei in November 2002:

> I believe that while differing circumstances may necessitate asymmetric responses, in the case of non-compliance with non-proliferation obligations, for the credibility of the regime, the approach in all cases should be one and the same: zero tolerance.[18]

---

[15]Ibid., para 19.

[16]IAEA Statute, Article III.B.4.

[17]Ibid., Article XII.C.

[18]IAEA, 'Reinforcing the World's Regime Against Nuclear Weapons', 14 November 2002, www.iaea.org/NewsCenter/News/2002/11-13-903199.shtml.

Consistency and predictability are essential if the decisions of the Board are to be seen as credible and to maintain confidence in the integrity of the Agency's safeguards system.

2.3 Conclusion

To wrap up, I have stated that in general States have the propensity to honour their international treaty obligations. In the nuclear non-proliferation field this proposition is borne out by the fact that the IAEA is implementing safeguards in more than 180 States and there has not been any finding of non-compliance since June 2011 (Syria). In total, in the 57-year history of the Agency, and the 44-year history of the NPT, there have been only six cases of determinations of non-compliance.

The IAEA safeguards system has been working well. Measures to strengthen the safeguards system were put in place between 1991 and 1997 and have been updated since then. The challenges emanate from the political machinations of States and their rivalries and conflicts that spill into the realm of nuclear verification. Nuclear materials in use around the world are increasing continuously, but the financial resources provided by States for IAEA nuclear verification remain paltry.

NPT States have affirmed that the IAEA is the competent authority responsible for verifying and assuring, in accordance with the Statute of IAEA and the IAEA safeguards system, compliance with its safeguards agreements with States parties undertaken in fulfilment of their obligations, with a view to preventing diversion of nuclear energy from peaceful uses to nuclear weapons or other nuclear explosive devices. Nothing should be done to undermine the authority of IAEA in this regard. States' parties that have concerns regarding non-compliance with the safeguards agreements by other States' parties should direct such concerns, along with supporting evidence and information, to the IAEA to consider, investigate, draw conclusions and decide on necessary actions in accordance with its mandate. In this regard it is essential that the IAEA has the capabilities to authenticate the provenance and authenticity of third-party (intelligence) information in order to carry out its safeguards obligations and to maintain its credibility. The international legal community can assist by ensuring that treaty undertakings are interpreted fairly and without political overtones.

References

Allison GT (1971) The essence of decision: explaining the Cuban missile crisis. Scott Foresman, Glenview

Chayes A, Chayes AH (1995) The new sovereignty: compliance with international regulatory agreements. Harvard University Press, Cambridge

Henkin L (1979) How nations behave, 2nd edn. Columbia University Press, New York

Lindblom CE (1968) The policy making process. Prentice-Hall, Englewood Cliffs
Machiavelli N (1513) The prince (trans: Skinner Q, Price R, Machiavelli, The Prince), Cambridge University Press
Morgenthau HJ (1948) 1978) Politics among nations: the struggle for power and peace, 5th edn. Alfred A. Knopf, New York
Wendell Holmes Justice O (1920), Superior Oil Co. v. Mississippi, 280 U.S. 390

Chapter 3
Interpretation of Nuclear Safeguards Commitments: The Role of Subsequent Agreements and Practice

Pierre-Emmanuel Dupont

Abstract This chapter addresses an interpretative issue concerning the scope of safeguards applied by the IAEA under comprehensive safeguards agreements (CSAs) concluded by non-nuclear-weapon States pursuant to the obligation set out in Article III of the NPT. It aims at assessing the way rules for treaty interpretation ought to be applied, and have *de facto* been applied, in the context of a controversy surrounding the interpretation of para 2 of IAEA document INFCIRC/153 (Corr.), which provides the basis for CSAs, concerning the scope of safeguards under such agreements. The controversial issue is whether this provision is to be read as implying that the IAEA is authorized to verify the absence of 'undeclared' nuclear activities in the State subject to safeguards under CSAs, i.e. the 'completeness' of the declarations made by the State on the extent of its nuclear activities. I argue that existing rules of interpretation, including an enquiry into subsequent agreement and practice, do not lend unconditional support to the interpretation according to which such provision is to be read as implying that the IAEA under CSAs is entitled to verify the 'completeness' of declarations made by States. It appears that a textual approach, together with examination of the context and the object and purpose of CSAs and recourse to the *travaux préparatoires* gives some weight to the 'completeness' argument; and it may be assumed that this embodies a correct interpretation of the disputed provision. But this position is in turn weakened by the consideration of other relevant elements. Indeed, various sources point to the fact that, at the time of entry into force of the NPT and of negotiation of the INFCIRC/153 safeguards system—and at least until the 1990s—there was no shared understanding on the disputed interpretation of para 2 of INFCIRC/153. The various decisions of the IAEA Board of Governors in 1992–1995 often invoked as supporting the 'completeness'

Head of Public International Law and Dispute Settlement, London Centre of International Law Practice; Member of the ILA Committee on Nuclear Weapons, Non-Proliferation and Contemporary International Law.

P.-E. Dupont (✉)
Centre of International Law Practice, Second Floor, Gray's Inn Chambers,
19–21 High Holborn, London WC1R 5JA, UK
e-mail: p.dupont@lcilp.org

J.L. Black-Branch and D. Fleck (eds.), *Nuclear Non-Proliferation in International Law - Volume II*, DOI 10.1007/978-94-6265-075-6_3

argument do not in fact embody a common unequivocal endorsement by the Board. As a matter of fact, such disagreements on interpretation have persisted to date, with a few States expressing reservations on the 'completeness' argument. The present author has been unable to identify relevant subsequent agreement or subsequent practice that would confirm the 'completeness' argument. Therefore, he expresses the view that the confirmation by the IAEA of the 'completeness' of declarations of States can only derive, practically if not even legally, from the application of an Additional Protocol.

Keywords Completeness · Comprehensive Safeguards Agreements (CSAs) · Correctness; International Atomic Energy Agency (IAEA) · IAEA safeguards · Nuclear safeguards commitments · Subsequent practice · Verification

Contents

3.1 Introduction

Treaty interpretation is of critical importance to the effectiveness of arms control, disarmament and non-proliferation treaties, since compliance by States' Parties with substantive obligations set out by such treaties rests to a large extent upon the correct interpretation of the relevant treaty provisions. An assessment of State practice as well as of the practice of relevant international organizations shows that divergences of views on the authentic meaning of arms control, disarmament and non-proliferation commitments, which may in turn give rise to legal disputes, are indeed a common feature in contemporary international law. The various international agreements comprising the so-called 'non-proliferation regime' make no exception in that respect.[1]

The present paper focuses on one major interpretative issue concerning safeguards agreements concluded pursuant to the obligation set out in the main multilateral agreement on nuclear non-proliferation, i.e. the 1968 Non-Proliferation

[1]On the non-proliferation regime in the legal literature, see Goldblat 1995, 2002; Joyner 2009, at pp. 3 et seq., 2011; Blix 1989, 1983; Priest 1995; Njølstad 2011; Joyner and Roscini 2012; Black-Branch and Fleck 2014.

Treaty (NPT).[2] It aims at assessing the way rules for treaty interpretation ought to be applied, and have *de facto* been applied, in the context of a controversy surrounding the interpretation of the authority of the IAEA (and the corresponding obligations of States) in the field of nuclear safeguards to be applied by the IAEA in non-nuclear-weapon States (NNWSs) pursuant to the obligation set out in Article III of the NPT.[3]

This interpretation issue, which has long been outstanding and remains to date unsettled, concerns interpretation of a clause found in INFCIRC/153,[4] which is restated in each CSA entered into by the IAEA on the one hand, and individual NNWSs on the other hand. The clause in question concerns the scope of safeguards to be applied by the IAEA under CSAs. The conflicting positions can be summarized as follows: most Member States of the IAEA, as well as the IAEA secretariat, consider that under CSAs, the IAEA is entitled to verify that State declarations of nuclear material subject to safeguards are not only 'correct', but are also 'complete'. On the contrary, a few States hold that under a CSA, the IAEA does not have the legal authority to verify both the 'correctness' and 'completeness' of declarations of States, and that such authority can only stem from an Additional Protocol (AP),[5] or in other words that, for the IAEA to be in a position to effect such verification, the

[2]Treaty on the Non-Proliferation of Nuclear Weapons (1 July 1968) 729 UNTS 161. The NPT entered into force in 1970.

[3]For a strictly legal (rather than technical) treatment of issues related to nuclear safeguards, see e.g. Szasz 1970; Rainer and Szasz 1993; Edwards 1984; Szasz 1985; Sur 1998; Rockwood 2010; Gruemm 1983; Kofstadmoen and Reistad 2010; Myjer and Herbach 2012; Rockwood 2013. The basic legal materials are found in the two-volume work edited by ElBaradei et al. 1993.

[4]CSAs are agreements (bilateral for most of them) entered into between the IAEA and non-nuclear-weapon States party to the NPT, pursuant to the obligation set out by Article III of the NPT. They are based on a document developed in 1970–1972 by a Safeguards Committee set up by the IAEA Board of Governors on the structure and content of such agreements (INFCIRC/153 (Corr.). A model agreement based on INFCIRC/153 (Corr.) was eventually developed and published in 1974 as GOV/INF/276, Annex A. Accordingly, CSAs are also frequently referred to as INFCIRC/153 agreements, see IAEA 1972. For an overview of the safeguards system, see IAEA (undated), The Safeguards System of the International Atomic Energy Agency, http://www.iaea.org/OurWork/SG/documents/safeg_system.pdf.

[5]APs are individual protocols between the IAEA and States with a safeguards agreement in force, which provide for 'those measures for strengthening the effectiveness and improving the efficiency of IAEA safeguards which could not be implemented under the legal authority of safeguards agreements', IAEA 2002, para 1.15. States having a CSA and an AP in force are required to provide additional information and grant complementary access to IAEA inspectors, going beyond the requirements of CSAs. The individual APs to CSAs are based on the IAEA Model Additional Protocol 1997, reproduced in IAEA document INFCIRC/540 (Corr.). The measures provided for in CSA APs include inter alia the provision of information about, and inspector access to, all aspects of a State's nuclear fuel cycle, from uranium mines to nuclear waste and any other location where nuclear material intended for non-nuclear uses is present; information about, and short notice inspector access to, all buildings on a nuclear site, as well as to fuel cycle related research and development activities; collection of environmental samples beyond declared locations when deemed necessary by the IAEA. See e.g. Rockwood 2013, p. 13.

State concerned shall have signed and brought into force an AP with the Agency. The controversy has at times had very practical consequences, as confirmed by the case of the IAEA verification activities regarding the Iranian nuclear programme.[6]

In order to assess the correctness of these two contrary interpretations, recourse will be made in this chapter to the general rule of treaty interpretation, as set out in the 1969 and 1986 Vienna Conventions,[7] with a specific focus on the role of subsequent agreement and subsequent practice of parties to a treaty in interpretation of the latter, as referred to in Article 31(3)(a) and (b) of the Vienna Conventions. As will be recalled, these two means of interpretation, adequately described as features 'designed to ensure that evolving circumstances are taken into account in a way which is compatible with the agreement of the parties',[8] raise complex issues (notably as to their application to concrete cases), for most of them unsettled so far, and the matter is part of the programme of work of the UN International Law Commission (ILC) since 2008.[9] As of the time of writing, two reports have been issued by the Special Rapporteur, Professor G. Nolte,[10] but significant matters forming part of the topic remain to be addressed by the Commission.[11]

[6]See Sect. 3.2 below.

[7]Vienna Convention on the Law of Treaties, 23 May 1969, entered into force on 27 January 1980, 1155 UNTS 331 (hereinafter the '1969 Vienna Convention'); Vienna Convention on the Law of Treaties between States and International Organizations or between International Organizations, 21 March 1986, not yet in force (hereinafter the '1986 Vienna Convention'). In the present chapter, the term 'Vienna Conventions' refers to both conventions envisaged together. See Sorel and Boré Eveno 2011, pp. 804–837 (for the 1969 Convention) and pp. 838–840 (for the 1986 Convention). It is to be noted that as regards interpretation issues concerning provisions of IAEA safeguards agreements, which are international agreements concluded between a State and the IAEA, the relevant instrument as regards interpretation is the 1986 Vienna Convention (see its Article 1, 'Scope of the present Convention'), despite the fact that the 1986 Convention has not yet entered into force (and despite the non-retroactivity clause found in Article 4 of the Convention), provided that the relevant provisions be considered as reflective of customary international law.

[8]ILC, Report on the work of its sixtieth session (2008), *General Assembly Official Records, Sixty-third Session*, Supplement No. 10 (A/63/10), para 11.

[9]The International Law Commission decided in 2008 to include the topic 'Treaties over time' in its programme of work (see ILC Report 2008, *Official Records of the General Assembly, Sixty-third Session, Supplement No. 10* (A/63/10), para 353). In 2009, the ILC established a Study Group on that topic, chaired by professor Georg Nolte. See e.g. Nolte (2010). The format of work on the topic within the ILC was subsequently amended and its title has become 'Subsequent agreements and subsequent practice in relation to interpretation of treaties' (see ILC's 3136th meeting, 31 May 2012).

[10]See First report on subsequent agreements and subsequent practice in relation to treaty interpretation by Georg Nolte, Special Rapporteur (A/CN.4/660), 19 March 2013; Second report on subsequent agreements and subsequent practice in relation to the interpretation of treaties by Georg Nolte, Special Rapporteur (A/CN.4/671), 26 March 2014.

[11]See Second report on subsequent agreements and subsequent practice in relation to the interpretation of treaties by Georg Nolte, Special Rapporteur (A/CN.4/671), 26 March 2014, para 167.

Insofar as the solution of the interpretation exercise in the case considered rests to a large extent on the accuracy of claims that either a 'subsequent agreement' has been reached regarding the interpretation of the disputed treaty provision, or that a 'subsequent practice' in its application can be established, this paper will analyse the operation of both means of interpretation in general, and then evaluate whether and to what extent, in the case of the interpretation issue at hand, subsequent agreement and/or subsequent practice may come into play to support the disputed interpretation.[12]

3.2 The Issue of the Scope of Comprehensive Safeguards Agreements: The 'Correctness' and 'Completeness' Debate

The scope of application of safeguards to be applied by the IAEA under comprehensive safeguards agreements, based on the INFCIRC/153 document, is set out in para 2 of INFCIRC/153, under the heading 'Application of Safeguards', as follows:

> The Agreement should provide for the Agency's right and obligation to ensure that safeguards will be applied, in accordance with the terms of the Agreement, on all source or special fissionable material in all peaceful nuclear activities within the territory of the State, under its jurisdiction or carried out under its control anywhere, for the exclusive purpose of verifying that such material is not diverted to nuclear weapons or other nuclear explosive devices.

The issue in dispute is the following: whether the IAEA, by virtue of this and other provisions in INFCIRC/153, is empowered to verify 'both the non-diversion of nuclear material from declared activities (i.e. correctness) and the absence of undeclared nuclear activities in the State (i.e. completeness)'.[13] In other words, the question is whether para 2 of INFCIRC/153 is to be read (possibly in conjunction with other relevant provisions) as implying that the IAEA is authorized to verify the absence of 'undeclared' nuclear activities in the State subject to safeguards, i.e. the 'completeness' of the declaration made by the State on the extent of its nuclear activities. A typical statement of an affirmative answer to this question may be found in a report of the IAEA Director-General issued in 1997:

---

[12]It is to be mentioned that the ongoing work of the ILC on subsequent agreement and practice has revived interest for the topic in legal literature: see e.g. Nolte 2013.

[13]See e.g. GOV/2012/55, para 53, footnote 56.

> Beginning in 1992, a number of decisions by the Board of Governors reaffirmed the requirements that Agency safeguards provide assurance regarding both the correctness and the completeness of nuclear material declarations by States with comprehensive safeguards agreements.[14]

The dispute has materialized notably in the context of the controversy surrounding the Iranian nuclear programme.[15] The recent IAEA Director-General's reports on the application of safeguards in Iran routinely include the affirmation that

> [w]hile the Agency continues to verify the non-diversion of declared nuclear material at the nuclear facilities and LOFs declared by Iran under its Safeguards Agreement, as Iran is not providing the necessary cooperation, including by not implementing its Additional Protocol, the Agency is unable to provide credible assurance about the absence of undeclared nuclear material and activities in Iran, and therefore to conclude that all nuclear material in Iran is in peaceful activities.[16]

In its successive reports on safeguards in Iran, the IAEA refers (in a footnote related to the previous statement), in support of its assertion on the scope of safeguards to be applied in Iran, to the following consideration:

> The Board [of Governors of the IAEA] has confirmed on numerous occasions, since as early as 1992, that para 2 of INFCIRC/153 (Corr.), which corresponds to Article 2 of Iran's Safeguards Agreement, authorizes and requires the Agency to seek to verify both the non-diversion of nuclear material from declared activities (i.e. correctness) and the absence of undeclared nuclear activities in the State (i.e. completeness) (see, for example, GOV/OR.864, para 49 and GOV/OR.865, paras 53–54).[17]

---

[14] 'Strengthening the Effectiveness and Improving the Efficiency of the Safeguards System', Report by the Director General to the General Conference, GC(41)/22, 17 September 1997, para 2.

[15] For general background information on the controversy, see e.g. Kile 2005, 2008, pp. 338–349, 2009, 2011; Ronen 2010; Dupont 2012, 2014; Jansen Calamita 2009; Rockwood 2014; Rauf and Kelley 2014.

[16] 'Implementation of the NPT Safeguards Agreement and relevant provisions of Security Council resolutions in the Islamic Republic of Iran', 20 February 2014 (GOV/2014/10), para 74.

[17] GOV/2014/10, para 74, footnote 50. This assertion appears also, for instance, in the Background paper prepared by the IAEA Secretariat for the 2010 NPT Review Conference: see Activities of the International Atomic Energy Agency relevant to Article III of the Treaty on the Non-Proliferation of Nuclear Weapons: Background paper prepared by the Secretariat of the International Atomic Energy Agency (NPT/CONF.2010/25), also reprinted in the Final Document of the 2010 Review Conference of the Parties to the Treaty of the Non-Proliferation of Nuclear Weapons (NPT/CONF.2010/50 (Vol. II)), at p. 213: 'Under comprehensive safeguards agreements (CSAs) in NNWS, IAEA verifies that State declarations of nuclear material subject to safeguards are not only "correct" (i.e. accurately describe the type(s) and quantity(ies) of a State's declared nuclear material holdings), but also are "complete" (i.e. that they include everything that is required to be declared)'. See also Rockwood 2013, at p. 19: 'In February 1992, the Board of Governors affirmed that the scope of comprehensive safeguards agreements was not limited to verification of the non-diversion of nuclear material actually declared by a State, but included verifying the absence of undeclared nuclear material and activities in the State. Expressed differently, the Board confirmed that, in accordance with para 2 of INFCIRC/153 (Corr.), the IAEA has the right and obligation under such agreements to verify not only that State declarations of nuclear material subject to safeguards are "correct", but that they are also "complete".'

This interpretation is also found in a recent report (2013) of the IAEA Director General on the new concept of State Level Safeguards (SLC)[18] which, as a reminder, recalls that:

> [u]nder comprehensive safeguards agreements (CSAs), the Agency has both the right and the obligation to verify the correctness and completeness of States' declarations so that there is credible assurance of the non-diversion of nuclear material from declared activities and of the absence of undeclared nuclear activities.[19]

It is noteworthy that this statement refers (in a footnote) to various decisions of the Board of Governors, i.e. 'GOV/DECISIONS 1991–92, 91–92/21; GOV/OR.776, paras 48, 83 and 84; GOV/DECISIONS 1994–95, 94–95/28; GOV/OR.864, para 49; GOV/OR.865, paras 53–54'.[20]

The same report emphasizes that

> [b]etween 1991 and 1993, the Board of Governors took decisions in which it, inter alia, requested the Director General to verify the correctness and completeness of States' declarations under CSAs [reference to: GOV/DECISIONS 1990–91, 90–91/71; GOV/2547/Rev.1 (11 September 1991); GOV/DECISIONS 1992–93, 92–93/19; GOV/2636 (26 February 1993)] and reaffirmed the Agency's right under CSAs to ensure that all nuclear material in peaceful nuclear activities was under safeguards [reference to: GOV/DECISIONS 1991–92, 91–92/21; GOV/OR.776, paras 48, 83 and 84].[21]

I will revert to these various IAEA Board decisions later in this chapter.

---

[18]The 'State-level concept' (SLC) has been described as 'a comprehensive approach to implementing safeguards that emphasizes using all available and relevant information about a State's nuclear programme to guide the Agency's safeguards activities in that State, instead of focusing on specific facilities' (see James Martin Center for Nonproliferation Studies and Vienna Center for Disarmament and Nonproliferation, Factsheet No. 3, September 2014, at http://www.nonproliferation.org/wp-content/uploads/2014/09/2014_IAEA_GC_QA_Safeguards.pdf). 'A safeguards implementation plan for a specific State that uses this concept is called a State-level approach. According to the IAEA, applying State-level approaches allows it to more efficiently use its limited resources and focus more on detection of possible undeclared activities. The IAEA began implementing State-level approaches taking into account State-specific factors for several States in 2001. The secretariat first introduced the term "State-level concept" in the Safeguards Implementation Report in 2005' (ibid.). The SLC has attracted various criticisms from a number of States, some of which point to the risk of politicization of the safeguards system, as well as to the risk of undue interference into the affairs of States unrelated to the nuclear sphere, and refer to instances of '[f]alse allegations [of nuclear proliferation] generated by interested parties in order to exercise political pressure on a State' (see e.g. 'Statement by the Head of the Delegation of the Russian Federation at the Symposium on International Safeguards', Vienna, 20–24 October 2014).

[19]'The Conceptualization and Development of Safeguards Implementation at the State Level', Report by the Director General (GOV/2013/38), para 3.

[20]'Idem., para 3, footnote 2.

[21]Idem., para 5 (with footnotes 5 and 6 integrated into our quote).

Most of the Member States of the IAEA have held for many years the same position asserting the right of the IAEA to verify the 'completeness' of declarations of States, as evidenced for example by their statements during IAEA General Conferences or before the IAEA Board of Governors.[22]

Thus, it appears that, for the IAEA as well as for most of its Member States, para 2 of INFCIRC/153 is to be interpreted as granting the IAEA the authority to verify both the non-diversion of nuclear material from declared activities (i.e. the correctness of declarations made by States) *and* the absence of undeclared nuclear activities (i.e. the completeness of declarations made by States). There is however, at least at first sight, some inconsistency in the identification of the legal basis for such interpretation.

Some argue that the interpretation according to which the IAEA is entitled under CSAs to verify both 'correctness' and 'completeness' of declarations of States stems from a plain reading of Article 2 INFCIRC/153 as it is worded, and in light of its object and purpose. For example, at the 57th IAEA General Conference (2013), the legal officer for the Committee of the Whole stated that,

> [t]he fundamental right and obligation of the Agency to verify the correctness and completeness of a State's declarations under a comprehensive safeguards agreement unequivocally derive[s] from para 2 of document INFCIRC/153.[23]

Similarly, the representative of Spain stated that

> it was not necessary to consider the legal status of the Board decision taken in 1995 because, as had been explained by the Secretariat, the legal basis for the Agency's verifying the correctness and completeness of a State's declarations was Article 2 of the comprehensive safeguards agreement with that State and did not derive from any type of Board decision taken in 1995.[24]

On the other hand, reference is often made to the decisions of the IAEA Board of Governors referred to above as supporting the disputed interpretation. For example, the above-mentioned statement by the IAEA Director-General regarding Iran, as well as the 2013 Report of the Director-General on SLS, obviously purport to ground such interpretation in the authority of the Board of Governors. In other words, the legal reasoning of the IAEA as implied in these documents is that the above interpretation of para 2 of INFCIRC/153 would be the correct and authoritative interpretation because it has been 'confirmed on numerous occasions, since as early as 1992' by the Board. The underlying assumption is that there would have

---

[22]See e.g. for the US position, IAEA Board of Governors, *Record of the 861st meeting,* para 17, excerpt appended as Annex 3 to 'Strengthening the Effectiveness and Improving the Efficiency of the Safeguards System', Report by the Director General to the General Conference (GC(39)/17), 22 August 1995.

[23]IAEA 57th General Conference, Committee of the Whole, *Record of the Seventh Meeting*, 19 September 2013 (GC(57)/COM.5/OR.7), para 48.

[24]Idem., para 52. The reference to the 'Board decision taken in 1995' is obviously a reference to the discussions within the Board in March 1995 in GOV/OR.864 and GOV/OR.865, to which I will revert later in this chapter.

been either a 'subsequent agreement' regarding the interpretation of para 2 of INFCIRC/153, or a 'subsequent practice' in its application, which would support the reading of this provision as including a mandate granted to the IAEA to verify both the 'correctness' and 'completeness' of declarations made by States. For the sake of completeness, however, it shall be mentioned that the assertion that the 'completeness' argument stems from the plain wording of para 2 INFCIRC/153, does not necessarily exclude a reference to subsequent agreement and practice as confirming the 'completeness' argument, since the main function of subsequent agreement and practice in the interpretative process is precisely to *confirm* the meaning of a treaty provision arrived at through the operation of the general rule of interpretation.[25]

3.3 The Process of Interpretation

3.3.1 General Framework

Before the analysis turns to the notions of subsequent agreement and subsequent practice and to their application to the treaty provisions considered, the present section will attempt at identifying the correct interpretation of Article 2 of CSAs under the general rule of interpretation found in the 1986 Vienna Convention.[26] It is a truism to mention in that respect that it is now undisputed that the rules of treaty interpretation set out in the VCLT constitute a 'general expression of the principles of customary law',[27] as such relevant to the interpretation of the provisions at hand.

It is important at the outset to take into account the specific characteristics of the object of the interpretative exercise. CSAs have been rightly described as a type of bilateral agreement of a unique legal character, in that

> [t]he rights and obligations of the two parties to these agreements are derived from a specific, qualified obligation set forth by a multilateral treaty, [the NPT].
>
> It is an unusual trilateral legal construct in that a multilateral treaty—the NPT—contains a binding obligation for some of its parties, the non-nuclear-weapon states (NNWS) to conclude a bilateral agreement (safeguards) with an intergovernmental organization (IAEA) for the purpose of allowing verification of fulfilment of their individual obligations under the NPT.[28]

---

[25]See e.g. Sorel and Boré Eveno 2011, at p. 826.

[26]See above n. 7 on the relevance of the 1986 Vienna Convention in interpretation of CSAs.

[27]See e.g. Sinclair 1984, p. 153; *Case Concerning the Territorial Dispute (Libya v. Chad)* [1994] ICJ Rep. 3, para 41; *Case Concerning Maritime Delimitation and Territorial Questions (Qatar v. Bahrain)* (Jurisdiction and Admissibility) [1995] ICJ Rep. 6, para 33; *Case Concerning Legality of Use of Force (Serbia and Montenegro v. Belgium)* [2004] ICJ Rep. 279, para 100.

[28]Jankowitsch-Prevor 2010, at pp. 20–21.

CSAs may also be seen, from another perspective, as 'unusual' agreements since all CSAs are based on, and follow closely, the same the structure and substance of INFCIRC/153. This raises the issue of the link between INFCIRC/153 and actual CSAs under the VCLT rules on interpretation. It may be thought that INFCIRC/153 qualifies as 'preparatory work' (in the meaning of Article 32 VCLT) of actual CSAs, which means that, should the meaning of the text appear ambiguous or obscure, recourse may be had to INFCIRC/153 to interpret a provision of an actual CSA. It may be noted in that respect that in the field of investment treaties, it has been suggested that 'model' bilateral investment treaties (BITs) drafted by capital-exporting countries to conduct the negotiations of actual BITs may be relevant, as *travaux préparatoires* within the meaning of Article 32 VCLT, to the interpretation of provisions of the latter, when it is known that the relevant BIT was based on the model BIT.[29] Applied to the case at hand, such reasoning would imply that the work of the Safeguards Committee in drafting INFCIRC/153 in 1970–1972 shall be taken into account in the interpretation of actual CSAs, under the conditions set out in Article 32 VCLT. The issue of the light that the *travaux préparatoires* of INFCIRC/153 may shed on the correct interpretation of Article 2 of CSAs will be examined below. However, at this stage it may be noted that, while as a matter of principle the *preparatory* work of INFCIRC/153 may be relevant to the interpretation of actual CSAs, it cannot be admitted that *subsequent* work of interpretation of, let alone of amendment of, INFCIRC/153 within the framework of the IAEA be relevant to such interpretation.

An analogous issue, that of interpretation of bilateral tax treaties based to some extent on the OECD Model Tax Convention and its Commentaries, has been explored comprehensively by the legal literature.[30] It has been rightly stressed in that respect that, while the OECD Model Convention (and the related OECD Commentary) is clearly relevant to interpretation of provisions of double taxation conventions following the 'model' wording, since it is 'reasonable to assume that the contracting States intended such a provision to have the meaning it has in the OECD Model, as outlined in the OECD Commentary', later amendments to the OECD Commentary 'cannot serve to establish the parties' intentions upon conclusion of a double taxation convention'.[31] Applying the same reasoning to the case examined here, it may be reasonably assumed that the negotiators of a given CSA had the structure and contents of INFCIRC/153 in mind when they negotiated this CSA. Where the CSA conforms to INFCIRC/153 (which is, to our knowledge, almost always the case), it is possible to conclude that CSA negotiators intended to create provisions having the same meaning as in INFIRC/153. Therefore, INFCIRC/153 can be deemed part of the material to be taken into account when interpreting the provision of the CSA,[32] where the conditions set out in Article 32

[29]See Salacuse 2009, pp. 154–155, who notes however that there is no jurisprudence of arbitral tribunals on this issue.

[30]See e.g. Engelen 2004.

[31]Lang and Brugger 2008, at p. 107.

[32]For similar assumptions applied to the interpretation of tax treaties based on the OECD Model, see e.g. Engelen 2004, p. 447.

VCLT are met. On the contrary, if one considers the regime of subsequent 'interpretative agreements' on certain provisions of INFCIRC/153 adopted in the framework of the IAEA Board or GCs *after* the conclusion of a given CSA to be interpreted, it can be thought that these agreements qualify neither as part of the general rule of interpretation of Article 31 VCLT, nor as supplementary means of interpretation to which recourse may be had under Article 32 VCLT.

3.3.2 Application of the General Rule of Interpretation

3.3.2.1 Text and Context

According to Article 31(1) VCLT, a treaty 'shall be interpreted in good faith in accordance with the ordinary meaning to be given to the terms of the treaty in their context and in the light of its object and purpose'. The wording of the disputed provision is thus to be examined first. This focus on the text as a point of departure in interpretation is often referred to as the principle of actuality (or textuality),[33] which was stated by Fitzmaurice as follows: 'Treaties are to be interpreted primarily as they stand, and on the basis of their actual texts',[34] that is to say 'prima facie, without reference to extraneous factors'.[35]

However, on its face, it appears that the provision of para 2 INFIRC/153 is unclear as to whether it implies that the IAEA is entitled to verify both the non-diversion of nuclear material (correctness of declarations) and the absence of undeclared nuclear activities (completeness of declarations). There are obviously some serious textual and logical arguments supporting the view that such interpretation is correct. A report on the negotiating history of INFIRC/153 prepared for the US Government by a private consultancy firm (with the participation of one of the principal negotiators) in 1984 asserts that there is 'an unmistakeable record as to the obligation to accept safeguards on all nuclear material in all peaceful uses, *regardless of whether reported by the State*'.[36] This report points to various provisions in INFCIRC/153 supporting this argument, and asserts that:

> INFCIRC/153 and its negotiating history provide incontrovertible grounds for the conclusion that 'all nuclear material in all peaceful nuclear activities' is to be safeguarded and that the Agency is under an obligation to apply its safeguards to all such material. These obligations are not only explicit in Paras 1 and 2, which are understood to specify the fundamental undertakings of safeguards agreements, but are supported by an extensive number of references to 'all' material, and *each* facility in a number of other paragraphs.

[33] Thirlway 2013, at p. 273.

[34] Fitzmaurice 1957, at p. 211.

[35] Fitzmaurice 1957, at p. 212.

[36] See International Energy Associates Limited (1984), at p. 35 (emphasis in original).

> On the basis of these provisions, there can be no doubt that a State is under an obligation to record and 'declare' all material, and that it is in violation of the agreement if it fails to do so; and that there is a corresponding right *and obligation* of the Agency to apply its safeguards to all materials.[37]

The report goes on to argue that:

> [t]he very absence from INFCIRC/153 of references to declared or undeclared materials strengthens the conclusion that no distinction was intended, or could have been intended, with respect to the right and obligation of the Agency to apply safeguards to all nuclear material.[38]

These are no doubt very convincing arguments. However, it remains that the mere fact that the IAEA Director General sought in 1995 to obtain confirmation from the BoG that 'the purpose of comprehensive safeguards agreements is the continuing verification of the correctness and completeness of States' declarations of nuclear material'[39]—a fact that will be analysed later in this chapter—is in itself evidence that such interpretation of Article 2 INFCIRC/153 was not self-evident. Moreover, it is to be stressed that the very purpose of APs is precisely to enable the IAEA to reach conclusions on correctness and completeness of States declarations. In other words, it is precisely the restricted scope of safeguards under INFCIRC/153 that prompted initiatives within the IAEA, starting in the early 1990s, which led to the adoption of the model AP, which undeniably is designed to allow the IAEA to verify both the correctness and the completeness of declarations made by States.[40] As it has been noted,

> [u]sing the additional information and access provided under the AP, the Agency is no longer limited to reaching a conclusion on the non-diversion of declared nuclear material, but is able to reach a conclusion on the absence of undeclared nuclear material and activity in the state as a whole.[41]

Former IAEA Director General H. Blix acknowledged along the same lines that under INFCIRC/153-type CSAs,

---

[37]Idem., at p. 40 (emphasis in original). It is noteworthy that the report notes that '[a]s a practical matter, however, [under INFCIRC/153-type CSAs] the Agency lacks the capability to search out activities or facilities which have not been reported to it' (at p. 43).

[38]Idem., at p. 41.

[39]'Strengthening the Effectiveness and Improving the Efficiency of the Safeguards System', Report by the Director General to the Board of Governors (GOV/2784), 21 February 1995, para 110(A).

[40]Goldblat 1995, at p. 33, States that the INFCIRC/153-type CSA 'is becoming obsolete. Its implementation has been improved by agreed broad interpretation of its provisions, but new verification measures will require complementary legal authority'. That is, according to Goldblat, the *raison d'être* of the '93 + 2' process.

[41]Carlson and Leslie, Special Inspections Revisited. Paper presented at INMM 2005 symposium (Phoenix, USA), https://www.dfat.gov.au/asno/publications/inmm2005_special_inspections.pdf, at p. 6.

> Agency inspection was in principle confined to declared nuclear material in declared installations. The correctness and consistency of declarations could and should be verified by the Agency—but not their completeness.[42]

Apart from the wording itself of the disputed provision, the question arises of whether an examination of the 'context' of the disputed provision, in the meaning of Article 31(1) VCLT, is able to shed some light on its correct interpretation. It is admitted in general that the consideration of the 'context' of a disputed treaty provision for the establishment of its correct meaning is justified by the fact that treaty provisions are not drafted in 'isolation', so that the interpreter has to read the provision in the context of the text of the entire treaty. The 'context' in the meaning of Article 31 is thus understood to include 'remaining terms of the sentence and of the paragraph; the entire article at issue; and the remainder of the treaty, i.e. its text, including its preamble'.[43] Thus recourse to the context aims at avoiding 'inconsistencies between the individual term and its textual surroundings'.[44]

Regarding the 'context' of Article 2 of INFCIRC/153-type CSAs, it appears that the whole safeguards system embodied in INFCIRC/153, especially in Part II of the latter aimed at specifying 'the procedures to be applied for the implementation of the safeguards provisions',[45] provides no decisive evidence in support of the assertion that safeguards would extend to the verification by the IAEA of the completeness of States' declarations. Basically, the safeguards system embodied in INFCIRC/153 (especially in Part II thereof), as summarized by H. Blix,

> has three basic features: *material accounting*, involving a system of records of nuclear materials kept by persons who possess such material and of reports to the Agency based on those records; *containment and surveillance measures*, which take advantage of physical barriers (e.g. walls, containers) and such things as seals and cameras to restrict or control the movement of or access to nuclear materials; and *on-site inspection* designed to verify the information provided to the Agency.[46]

This is to say that the role of IAEA in this system is primarily limited to verifying the correctness and consistency of declarations made by States.[47] The only provisions of INFCIRC/153 which were designed to allow the IAEA to go beyond States' declarations were those on 'special inspections', found in para 73 of INFCIRC/153, under which the IAEA is entitled to make special inspections if it

---

[42] Blix 2011, at p. 5.

[43] Villiger 2011, pp. 109–110.

[44] Villiger 2011, p. 110.

[45] See INFCIRC/153, para 27.

[46] Blix 1989, p. 236.

[47] Blix 2011, p. 5.

'considers that information made available by the State [...] is not adequate for the Agency to fulfil its responsibilities to ensure safeguards are applied to all nuclear material in peaceful nuclear activities in the State'.[48]

Therefore, it appears that a holistic approach to interpretation of INFCIRC/153 (and actual CSAs) does not lend unconditional support to the argument that safeguards under CSAs would extend to the verification of the 'completeness' of declarations of States.

However, an argument is frequently made, based on a distinction between, on the one hand, the 'rights' or 'authority' of the IAEA under the NPT and CSAs, and the 'tools' at its disposal to fulfil its role, on the other hand. According to this widely used argument, while '[t]he scope of INFCIRC/153 was not limited to the nuclear material actually declared by the State', but rather also included 'that which should be declared', as a matter of fact 'the [safeguards] system such as it had developed up to the Iraqi case, had limited capability to deal with completeness. *This was the result of practical, rather than legal, considerations*'.[49]

The same argument may be found, for example, in a paper prepared in 2010 by the IAEA Secretariat,[50] which refers to the 1992 debate within the IAEA Board of Governors on the question of the scope of safeguards under INFCIRC/153 CSAs. It argues that the Board 'affirmed' at that time that 'the scope of CSAs was not limited to nuclear material actually declared by a State but included any material that is required to be declared', and that this affirmation 'was a major *catalyst for efforts* to equip the safeguards system with important additional tools, to better verify the correctness and completeness of States' declarations under CSAs'.[51]

However, it is *prima facie* difficult to accept that INFCIRC/153 would have granted 'rights' to the IAEA under the NPT and CSAs, without at the same time providing it with the procedural and technical 'tools' necessary to fulfil this role.[52] It could be deemed more realistic to assume that the negotiators of INFCIRC/153 intended to correlate (i) the rights of the IAEA and (ii) the technical procedures of verification that it could use to fulfil its mission. The IAEA has admitted that this was the implicit understanding of States on the scope of safeguards under INFCIRC/153 at the time of its drafting and during the following decades:

---

[48]INFCIRC/153, para 73(b). When such circumstances arise, INFCIRC/153 provides for consultations between the State concerned and the IAEA. It may be observed that the IAEA Board of Governors discussed the issue of use of special inspections in December 1991, and in February 1992 concluded that special inspections should occur 'only on rare occasions'. See GOV/OR.776, para 48. See also Carlson and Leslie, above n. 41, at p. 6.

[49]'Strengthening the Effectiveness and Improving the Efficiency of the Safeguards System', Report by the Director General to the Board of Governors (GOV/2784), 21 February 1995, para 5 (emphasis added).

[50]Background paper prepared by the Secretariat of the International Atomic Energy Agency (NPT/CONF.2010/25), also reprinted in the Final Document of the 2010 Review Conference of the Parties to the Treaty of the Non-Proliferation of Nuclear Weapons (NPT/CONF.2010/50 (Vol. II)), at p. 213.

[51]Idem., at p. 213 (emphasis added).

[52]This point has been also highlighted by Joyner 2014.

> Since most governments were unwilling to give the IAEA a free hand to scout for undeclared plants or stocks, the 1970–1971 safeguards focused almost exclusively on verifying that there was no diversion of nuclear material that the governments concerned *had declared and placed under safeguards*. The possibility that undeclared plants might exist was, of course, recognized by the architects of the 1970–1971 system, but it was tacitly assumed that if such plants were built they would be detected by means other than IAEA safeguards. In practice, accounting for nuclear material in declared nuclear operations thus became the main task of IAEA safeguards. [53]

In this context, it may also be relevant to mention that during the negotiating process of the AP, a consensus emerged on the need for additional legal authority (additional to the legal authority provided for in INFCIRC/153) for some of the contemplated measures of strengthening of safeguards. As was reported in a report issued in the US in 2010:

> Although the issue of whether additional legal authority was needed for many of the proposed measures for strengthening safeguards was fundamental to many of the decisions of the Board and Committee 24, it received relatively little debate in either forum. Both the Secretariat and the member states either wanted new explicit authority or seemed prepared to proceed on the basis of an assumption of the need for additional legal authority. This would, thereby, avoid a lengthy and possibly contentious and inconclusive debate as to which measures did and which did not require additional legal authority. Although suggestions arose that would have permitted States to use different mechanisms for providing the IAEA with the necessary authorities, a consensus emerged, and is reflected in the Model Additional Protocol, that a single instrument was best. This would achieve uniformity and avoid any risk of different interpretations arising.
>
> Although some Board actions during the period from 1991–1997 suggest that the Agency might have the legal authority to apply protocol measures in States with comprehensive safeguards agreements that have not concluded a protocol, the fact of the Additional Protocol, itself, suggests otherwise politically, if not also legally. As a result, obtaining universal adherence to Additional Protocols is the best, perhaps, the only way, to provide the Agency everywhere with the authorities contained in the Model Additional Protocol.[54]

Should it reflect accurately the reality of the negotiating process of the AP, such statement appears difficult to reconcile with the assumption of a dichotomy between the 'rights' or 'authority' of the IAEA under the NPT and CSAs, and the 'tools' at its disposal to fulfil its role under the same.

3.3.2.2 Object and Purpose

As a matter of principle, a treaty's *object and purpose* may be used as one of the primary means to determine the ordinary meaning of a term, as provided for in Article

[53] IAEA, *The Evolution of IAEA Safeguards* (Vienna: International Atomic Energy Agency 1998), p. 14.

[54] M.D. Rosenthal et al., Review of the Negotiation of the Model Protocol Additional to the Agreement(s) between State(s) and the International Atomic Energy Agency for the Application of Safeguards, INFCIRC/540 (Corr.), Vol. II (Brookhaven National Laboratory 2010), http://www.bnl.gov/isd/documents/71014.pdf, at p. 11.

31(1) VCLT. Usually the object and purpose of a treaty is to be sought in the preamble, or in a general clause at the beginning of the treaty.[55] Applied to an INFCIRC/153-based CSA, the object and purpose may be identified in Article 1 ('Basic undertaking'), which provides that the 'exclusive purpose' of safeguards' is 'of verifying that [nuclear] material is not diverted to nuclear weapons or other nuclear explosive devices'.[56] This is *prima facie* inconclusive as to the correctness of the disputed interpretation of Article 2 of CSAs. On a more general level, it is to be recalled that, while the consideration of a treaty's object and purpose aims at ensuring the effectiveness of its terms (*ut res magis valeat quam pereat*, the *effet utile*), it remains that 'interpretation in the light of a treaty's object and purpose finds its limits in the treaty text itself'.[57] That is to say that consideration of the object and purpose of a treaty cannot be used as to allow for *de facto* 'legislation', or in other words to revision of the treaty.[58] It is commonly admitted that the correct understanding of the principle *ut res magis valeat quam pereat* is that (i) no treaty provision shall be deprived of its effect, but at the same time (ii) it cannot allow to give to a treaty provision an effect that it does not have per se, even if such effect would be useful (*effet utile*).[59] In other words, the principle cannot be invoked in favour of an extensive interpretation of a treaty provision, aiming at a 'maximum effect' of the treaty.[60]

Against this background, it may be opportune to consider the argument of 'evolutive interpretation' that some have purported to apply to CSAs. The allegation that the IAEA is entitled under Article 2 of CSAs to verify both the correctness and the completeness of States' declarations may indeed be related to an argument of 'effectiveness' of safeguards agreements, i.e. a claim that, since the IAEA safeguards system evolves over time, States shall be deemed to have given in advance their consent to the application of new verification activities by the IAEA, which the latter would develop over time (and that the competent organs of the IAEA would approve). By virtue of this argument, an evolutive interpretation shall be applied to Article 2 of CSAs.

It shall be mentioned that, on a theoretical level, this argument is controversial and raises important difficulties. As noted by Charles de Visscher, '[t]he purpose of interpretation is not to perfect an instrument, to adapt it more or less to achieve what may be deemed to be the logically postulated objective, but to shed light on the real intention of the parties'.[61] Sir Gerald Fitzmaurice expressed the same idea, stressing that:

---

[55]Villiger 2011, at p. 110.

[56]INFCIRC/153, para 1.

[57]Villiger 2011, at p. 110.

[58]See ILC Rep. 1966, ibid., Vol. II, at p. 219, paras 6 and 220, para 11; ICJ, *Interpretation of Peace Treaties with Bulgaria, Hungary and Romania*, Advisory Opinion of 30 March 1950, ICJ Rep. (1950) at 229; also the statement in Vienna by J. de Aréchaga of the Uruguyan delegation, *Official Records*, Vol. I, at p. 170, para 67; Yasseen 1976, para 4; Villiger 2011, p. 110.

[59]Yasseen 1976, p. 74.

[60]Yasseen 1976, p. 72.

[61]De Visscher 1963, the English translation of which is found in Ost 1992, p. 288.

> [t]he objectives of a treaty do not exist in the abstract; they derive from the intention of the parties and expressed in the terms of the treaty or as evidenced by them and are closely in relation to them as they are their only source [...]. They (the intentions of the parties) cannot be introduced afterwards in the guise of objectives which were not contemplated at the time.[62, 63]

A parallel may be established between this argument and the argument according to which, since Article III, para 1, of the NPT provides for the conclusion of an agreement in accordance with 'the [IAEA's] safeguards system', the obligation under this provision may evolve as the IAEA's 'safeguards system' evolves, implying that the AP is an evolved form of IAEA's 'safeguards system'. However, as rightly noted by Professor Asada, the power to give authentic interpretation of treaty provisions lies with its States' Parties (to the NPT, in the case considered), subject to possible rulings of the competent courts and tribunals. Therefore, such argument is to be rejected. Otherwise, as Asada observes, 'it would follow that NPT parties could, in effect, continue to be bound automatically by documents that are produced by a body whose membership is not identical with them, which seems to be something the NPT parties did not accept in signing and ratifying the Treaty'.[64] The contrary solution could only be true if the NPT explicitly mandated the IAEA to update as necessary its 'safeguards system' in the meaning of NPT Article III—which as a matter of fact it does not.

The same considerations apply *mutatis mutandis* to the case of CSAs. When a State enters into a CSA with the IAEA, it gives its consent to the application of certain measures, under precise conditions (especially in terms of scope, etc.) and under technical modalities set out in the agreement (as well as in subsidiary arrangements). But it is not to be presumed that the State in doing so has given in advance its consent to an indefinite evolution of such measures and modalities, so that its obligations under CSAs would evolve over time as new technological developments occur and are endorsed by the IAEA. It may be noted that Brazil stated in 1995 before the Board of Governors in that respect that

> technological developments in the safeguards field should not be confused with the evolution of the safeguards system itself. The system had evolved from one based on safeguards agreements deriving from the Statute to one based on comprehensive safeguards agreements deriving from document INFCIRC/153, but a safeguards agreement was a legal instrument not subject to evolution; if additional undertakings were to be entered into, that called for a protocol or some other form of additional legal instrument acceptable to the parties.[65]

---

[62] Cited by Ost 1992.

[63] See also Dupuy 2011, at p. 127.

[64] Asada 2011, at pp. 8–9. See also Chap. 5 by Asada in this volume.

[65] See IAEA Board of Governors, *Record of the 860th meeting,* para 109, excerpt appended as Annex 3 to 'Strengthening the Effectiveness and Improving the Efficiency of the Safeguards System', Report by the Director General to the General Conference (GC(39)/17), 22 August 1995.

3.3.3 Drafting History

An examination of the drafting history of an international agreement may also prove necessary, according to Article 32 VCLT, either in order to *confirm* the meaning of a provision resulting from the application of Article 31 VCLT, or if the application of the standard rule of Article 31(1) VCLT does not yield sensible results, i.e. in a situation when the interpretation according to Article 31 VCLT 'leaves the meaning ambiguous or obscure' or 'leads to a result which is manifestly absurd or unreasonable'. In the case of Article 2 of CSAs, it may be deemed that interpretation under Article 31 has indeed left the meaning ambiguous, at least as regards the question of whether it provides for the IAEA's right to verify the 'completeness' of declarations of States. Therefore, recourse to preparatory work would be appropriate.

As is well known, Article 32 VCLT is lacunar about the concept of preparatory works, as well as about the operation of this means of interpretation and its relationship with interpretation under Article 31. What is uncontroversial is that preparatory works may be used to 'reconstruct the real and actual intent of the contracting parties at the time of the conclusion of the treaty'.[66] In other words, as emphasized by Waldock, the role of preparatory works should be to 'furnish proof of the common understanding of the parties as to the meaning attached to the terms of the treaty'.[67]

While it is known that in the course of the preparation of INFCIRC/153, extensive discussions took place on the proper function of Agency safeguards,[68] to our knowledge the relevant materials have never been made public. The 1984 report on the negotiating history of INFCIRC/153 commissioned by the US government, already mentioned, sheds some light on discussions surrounding Article 2, and asserts that the issue of undeclared material and activities was dealt with explicitly during these discussions. It mentions that South Africa had recommended that 'safeguarding and inspection [...] shall be concerned solely with the material reported upon by the State concerned [...]', but that such proposal was 'explicitly objected to by Hungary, received no support, and was omitted from Paras 1 and 2 of INFCIRC/153'.[69]

Be that as it may, it remains that, as far as I am aware, there was no explicit and unequivocal understanding among the drafters of INFCIRC/153 on the disputed interpretation of Article 2. Again, this lack of agreed understanding is confirmed above all by the fact that in 1995 the IAEA DG sought to obtain confirmation from the BoG that 'the purpose of [CSAs] is the continuing verification of the

---

[66]Scolbi 2011, at p. 151; see generally Lauterpacht 1934.

[67]Waldock 1964, at p. 58, para 21.

[68]Rainer and Szasz 1993, at p. 271. Supporting footnote 9 refers to: GOV/COM.22/166; GOV/COM.22/OR, paras 1–82.

[69]See above n. 36, at p. 35.

correctness and completeness of States' declarations of nuclear material'.[70] This is in itself sufficient proof that there was at that time no common and authoritative understanding of the correct meaning of Article 2 of INFCIRC/153. The *travaux préparatoires* of INFCIRC/153 being unavailable to the public, it remains possible to refer to individual opinions on the scope of IAEA safeguards under the NPT. P.C. Szasz in an official IAEA publication asserted the following:

> Even more broadly than the Tlatelolco Treaty, the safeguards Under the Non-Proliferation Treaty are to relate to all peaceful nuclear activities within the territory of each non-nuclear-weapon State, or otherwise 'under its jurisdiction, or carried out under its control anywhere'. Again *the Agency under its present system will only be able to control those activities that are reported to it—and thus both unregistered items and those officially declared to be used for a non-weapon military purpose will escape its scrutiny* (65); unlike the Latin American instrument, the Non-Proliferation Treaty does not provide for special inspections to be carried out on the basis of accusations.[71]

The same authors highlighted the fact that 'this was confirmed by the testimony of William Foster, the principal US negotiator of the Treaty, in his testimony on its ratification'.[72] As a matter of fact, W. Foster testified in 1968 before the US Senate as follows:

> EXTENT OF IAEA INSPECTION
>
> Another question: Will the [IAEA] inspection be restricted only to the declared peaceful nuclear facilities or will they also apply to the undeclared or clandestine facilities? How will they be sought out?
>
> Secretary RUSK. The undeclared and clandestine?
> Mr. FOSTER. The IAEA inspection would only be as to declared. If there were undeclared, if they were found, this would be a breach of the treaty.
> Senator PELL. But under the treaty there is no provision for searching out the clandestine?
> Mr. FOSTER. No, sir.
> Senator PELL. Just as there is no sanction?
> Mr. FOSTER. But there would be great alertness on the part of many, including ourselves, on that latter point, Senator (at p. 52).[73]

These sources seem to confirm that at the time of entry into force of the NPT and at the time of negotiation of the INFCIRC/153 safeguards system, there was no shared understanding on the disputed interpretation of para 2 of INFCIRC/153. As we have seen, recourse to the general rule of interpretation of the 1986 Vienna Convention on the Law of Treaties between States and International Organizations

---

[70]'Strengthening the Effectiveness and Improving the Efficiency of the Safeguards System', Report by the Director General to the Board of Governors (GOV/2784), 21 February 1995, para 110(A).

[71]Szasz 1970, p. 549 (emphasis added).

[72]Szasz 1970, footnote 65 supporting the assertion at p. 549 quoted above.

[73]Hearings on Nonproliferation Treaty before the Committee on Foreign Relations of the Senate, 90th Cong., 2nd Sess., p. 52 (1968). See also S. Exec. Rep. No. 9, 90th Cong., 2nd Sess., p. 5 (1968).

or between International Organizations does not clarify absolutely the question, and leaves the meaning of the disputed provision to some extent 'ambiguous or obscure'. In my view, in order to prove that the correct interpretation of para 2 of INFCIRC/153 is the interpretation according to which the IAEA is entitled to verify the 'completeness' of declarations of States, it would thus be necessary to establish that either a 'subsequent agreement' has been reached regarding the interpretation of the disputed provision, or that a 'subsequent practice' in its application—supporting the disputed interpretation—can be established.

3.3.4 Subsequent Agreement and Subsequent Practice

It may be useful here to give a brief overview of the rules governing recourse to 'subsequent agreement' and 'subsequent practice' in the process of interpretation of a treaty provision, found in both the 1969 and 1986 Vienna Conventions.[74] Article 31(3) of each of the Vienna Conventions provides in relevant part in similar terms as follows:

> There shall be taken into account, together with the context:
> (a) any subsequent agreement between the parties regarding the interpretation of the treaty or the application of its provisions;
> (b) any subsequent practice in the application of the treaty which establishes the agreement of the parties regarding its interpretation.

The recognition by the Vienna Conventions of the role that subsequent agreement and subsequent practice play in the interpretation of treaties, obviously a significant development in the law of treaties, left open many issues related to application *in concreto* of these means of interpretation. As rightly noted by Professor Nolte,

> [d]espite their great practical importance the means of interpretation contained in Article 31(3)(a) and (b) VCLT have hardly been analysed by international tribunals beyond what the cases at hand required. In addition, these means of interpretation have rarely been the subject of extensive empirical, comparative or theoretical research. In fact, relevant subsequent agreement and subsequent practice of States is not always well-documented and often only comes to light in legal proceedings.[75]

3.3.4.1 Subsequent Agreement

Subsequent agreements have basically the function of clarifying the meaning of provisions of treaties.[76] The ILC in the course of its work on the law of treaties made clear that

---

[74]See above n. 3.

[75]G. Nolte, Treaties over time, in particular: Subsequent Agreement and Practice, Annex A to the ILC Report 2008, Official Records of the General Assembly, Sixty-third Session, Supplement No. 10 (A/63/10), para 13.

[76]Gardiner 2008, p. 208.

> an agreement as to the interpretation of a provision reached after the conclusion of the treaty represents an authentic interpretation by the parties which must be read into the treaty for the purposes of its interpretation.[77]

As regards their function in interpretation, it has been observed that subsequent interpretative agreements and subsequent practice 'seem more in the order of confirmation rather than assertion'.[78] Indeed, if subsequent agreement and subsequent practice are not characterized as 'supplementary', in that they are considered 'at the same time as the context', they are 'nevertheless inscribed into a logical order of consideration in the absence of a clear solution based on the means of interpretation enunciated in [Article 31, paras 1 and 2]'.[79]

It is generally admitted that such agreements 'may be recorded in a formal instrument of the same legal standing as the original treaty or in a less formal record of agreement or understanding on interpretation'.[80] In other words, '[p]rovided the purpose is clear, the agreement can take various forms, including a decision adopted by a meeting of the parties'.[81]

That being recalled, it shall be borne in mind that the provision the interpretation of which is disputed is found in CSAs, which are treaties between the IAEA and individual States. Should a subsequent agreement occur in this case, it would thus necessarily consist in an agreement between the IAEA and an individual State (or several States). It may be recalled in this respect that INFCIRC/153 provides for a dispute settlement mechanism under which 'any dispute arising out of the interpretation or application [of a CSA] [...] which is not settled by negotiation or another procedure agreed to by the parties should, on the request of either party, be submitted to an arbitral tribunal'.[82]

This implies that, should it exist, an agreement reached within the Board of Governors of the IAEA, or within the IAEA General Conference, would not be legally dispositive of the interpretation of actual CSAs. A consideration of decisions of 'review conferences' of the NPT would of course be relevant to the interpretation of provisions of the NPT.[83] As a matter of fact most review conferences

---

[77]ILC Yearbook 1966, Vol. II, 221, para 14.

[78]Sorel and Boré Eveno 2011, pp. 804–837 (for the 1969 Convention) and pp. 838–840 (for the 1986 Convention), at p. 826.

[79]Sorel and Boré Eveno 2011, pp. 825–826.

[80]Gardiner 2008, p. 208.

[81]Aust 2007, p. 191.

[82]INFCIRC/153, para 22. The same provision excludes from the scope of arbitration any 'dispute with regard to a finding by the Board under para 19 [i.e. a finding that the Agency is not able to verify that there has been no diversion of nuclear material] or an action taken by the Board pursuant to such a finding'.

[83]See generally Carnahan 1987. The 1959 Antarctic Treaty was an early example of a treaty providing for a review conference mechanism. The NPT contains a similar feature, as well as, for instance, the 1972 Convention on Biological and Toxin Weapons and the Rome Statute of the International Criminal Court.

adopt final declarations that State, article by article, the conference's conclusions on the operation of the agreement under review.[84] Such declarations, as was rightly noted, are not legally binding in and of themselves, but they may have juridical significance, especially as a source of authoritative interpretations of the treaty'.[85] The final declaration of a review conference, especially if adopted by consensus, would probably fit within either or both of (i) 'subsequent agreement between the parties regarding the interpretation of the treaty or the application of its provisions' in the meaning of Article 31(3)(a) of the Vienna Convention, and (ii) 'subsequent practice in the application of the treaty which establishes the agreement of the parties regarding its interpretation' in the meaning of Article 31(3)(b) of the Vienna Convention.[86] But again, in the case of interpretation of a (bilateral) CSA, the decisions of the organs or bodies of the IAEA cannot be deemed dispositive.

Now let us suppose, however, for the sake of argument, that such decisions would nonetheless be to some extent relevant to interpretation of Article 2 of CSAs. In that case, it would be necessary to examine whether the various decisions of the Board of Governors referred to by the IAEA in the statements quoted above lend in fact support to the assertion that the Agency's mandate extends to verify 'both the non-diversion of nuclear material from declared activities (i.e. correctness) and the absence of undeclared nuclear activities in the State (i.e. completeness)'.[87]

A closer look at the so-called '93 + 2' process (i.e. the process within the IAEA which led during the 1990s to the drafting of the AP), as it has been analysed and reported by the IAEA itself, is necessary in that respect. The context of this process was marked by the proliferation cases of the 1990s in Iraq and North Korea, together with the Agency's 'positive experience in verifying the declared nuclear inventory in South Africa'.[88] It has often been stressed that this context 'changed the circumstances and requirements of the safeguards system'.[89] This situation led indeed the IAEA secretariat to consider it imperative to update the safeguards system 'by integrating into it measures that will give the Agency an improved capability of detecting clandestine nuclear activities if such exist'.[90] The IAEA Director General stressed in 1995 that

---

[84]Carnahan 1987, p. 229.

[85]Carnahan 1987, p. 229.

[86]Carnahan 1987, pp. 229–230.

[87]See Joyner, The IAEA Applies Incorrect Standards, Exceeding its Legal Mandate and Acting Ultra Vires Regarding Iran, http://armscontrollaw.com/2012/09/13/the-iaea-applies-incorrect-standards-exceeding-its-legal-mandate-and-acting-ultra-vires-regarding-iran/.

[88]'Strengthening the Effectiveness and Improving the Efficiency of the Safeguards System', Report by the Director General to the General Conference (GC(39)/17), 22 August 1995, para 1.

[89]Rockwood 2013, p. 19.

[90]'Strengthening the Effectiveness and Improving the Efficiency of the Safeguards System', Report by the Director General to the General Conference (GC(39)/17), 22 August 1995, para 1.

> [r]ecent events have demonstrated the need for the IAEA safeguards system to provide credible assurances *not only regarding declared nuclear activities but also regarding the absence of undeclared nuclear activities*.[91]

To that effect, the IAEA Director General exposed the measures envisioned under the '93 + 2' programme for 'updating' and 'strengthening' the safeguards system, and invited the Board of Governors to confirm, *inter alia*, that:

> A. The purpose of comprehensive safeguards agreements is the continuing verification of the correctness and completeness of States' declarations of nuclear material in order to provide maximum assurance of the non-diversion of nuclear material from declared activities and of the absence of undeclared nuclear activities.
> B. The safeguards system of the IAEA should be so designed as to give effect to that purpose. The IAEA should be enabled to fulfil its mandate under such agreements, either on the basis of existing authority provided for in such agreements or on the basis of complementary authority to be conferred.[92]

At the March 1995 session of the IAEA Board of Governors, such 'invitation' was largely debated. The United States,[93] Australia,[94] Romania[95] and Japan,[96] *inter alia*, endorsed the specific proposal contained in para 110 of GOV/2784. But the proposal also met with significant opposition from several members of the Board. For instance, the governor from Cuba, stated that

> [t]he aim of comprehensive safeguards agreements was to detect swiftly any diversion to non-peaceful uses of significant quantities of nuclear material, and the means of doing so was by verifying the nuclear material declarations of States. Therefore, the Board could not confirm what was recommended in para 110 A of the document within the current legal framework.[97]

---

[91]Idem., para 1 (emphasis added).

[92]Idem., para 110.

[93]See IAEA Board of Governors, *Record of the 861st meeting,* para 17, excerpt appended as Annex 3 to 'Strengthening the Effectiveness and Improving the Efficiency of the Safeguards System', Report by the Director General to the General Conference (GC(39)/17), 22 August 1995.

[94]Idem., paras 89–92. 'As to para 110.A, it seemed self-evident that if safeguards were to verify "all source or special fissionable material in all peaceful nuclear activities within the territory of the State, under its jurisdiction or carried out under its control anywhere", as required under para 2 of INFCIRC/153, then they must verify the correctness and completeness of declared inventories, and thereby necessarily also the absence of undeclared activities' (para 91).

[95]Idem., paras 130–134. 'His authorities also concurred with the view expressed in the report that the purpose of comprehensive safeguards agreements was the continuing verification of the correctness and completeness of a State's declaration of nuclear material in order to provide maximum assurance of the non-diversion of nuclear material from declared activities. His delegation considered that the Agency's safeguards system should be designed to give effect to that aim, and also that the Agency should be able to fulfil its mandate on the basis of the authority it had under the terms of existing safeguards agreements' (para 133).

[96]Idem., para 59.

[97]Idem., para 3.

Reservations vis-à-vis the Director-General's request were formulated among others by Mexico,[98] India,[99] Pakistan,[100] China,[101] Algeria,[102] Turkey[103] and the Russian Federation.[104] The most elaborated criticism of the Director-General's invitation came from the governor from Brazil, Ms. Machado Quintella, whose statement is worth being quoted extensively:

> regretfully her delegation had some difficulty in accepting the present wording of paragraph 110, although it believed that there would be scope for consensus after some adjustments, as no one was likely to deny the desirability of increasing the level of assurance provided by the safeguards system. All were committed to strengthening the system; the question on which views differed was how to achieve that common goal.
>
> 100. What the Board was being asked to approve in subparagraph 110.A was not a confirmatory interpretation of document INFCIRC/153, but rather a new concept regarding the purpose of comprehensive safeguards agreements—one that would require the modification of existing agreements or their amplification by additional legal instruments.
>
> 101. As things stood at present, the purpose of existing comprehensive safeguards agreements was to verify that there was no diversion of nuclear material to the manufacture of nuclear weapons or of any other explosive device. Confirming what was stated in subparagraph 110. A, that the purpose of such agreements was the continuing verification of the correctness and completeness of States' declarations of nuclear material, would thus represent a substantial departure, with no legal basis, from the original purpose as defined in para 2 of document INFCIRC/153 and in Article III(l) of the NPT.
>
> 102. The assertion made in para 5 of document GOV/2784 regarding the intentions of the drafters of document INFCIRC/153 was entirely uncorroborated by the records of the Board's Safeguards Committee (1970), which she had studied at length. In approving the concept put forward in document GOV/2784 regarding the purpose of comprehensive safeguards agreements, the Board would therefore not be confirming previous understandings, but introducing new ideas which would require amendments or protocols to existing agreements in order that the envisaged new safeguards measures might be applied. Such measures could, of course, be introduced on the basis of bilateral arrangements between the Agency and each Member State concerned, but there was as yet no proper legal basis for changing the Agency's safeguards system from one aimed at the verification of non-diversion to one aimed at verification of the non-existence of undeclared activities.
>
> 103. Verification of the absence of undeclared nuclear materials or activities required actions that had not been considered by the drafters of document INFCIRC/153 [...]
>
> 109. With regard to paragraphs 2, 3 and 4, where there were references to the continuous development of safeguards, she believed that technological developments in the safeguards field should not be confused with the evolution of the safeguards system itself. The system had evolved from one based on safeguards agreements deriving from the Statute to one based on comprehensive safeguards agreements deriving from document

[98]Idem., paras 11, 13.

[99]Idem., para 15.

[100]Idem., paras 36, 38.

[101]Idem., paras 53, 55–56.

[102]Idem., paras 62 et seq.

[103]Idem., para 72.

[104]Idem., paras 75–80.

INFCIRC/153, but a safeguards agreement was a legal instrument not subject to evolution; if additional undertakings were to be entered into, that called for a protocol or some other form of additional legal instrument acceptable to the parties.

110. The statement in paragraph 6 that in February 1992 the Board had reaffirmed the requirement that the Agency provide assurance regarding the correctness and completeness of nuclear material declarations by States was misleading: that requirement had been affirmed not as a general principle, but in respect of the initial inventories of two specific countries—and on both occasions Brazil had expressed reservations.[105]

This review of the March 1995 Board discussions shows that it can hardly be contended that a subsequent agreement was reached at that time regarding the interpretation or application of INFCIRC/153-type CSAs between States' parties to the IAEA Statute and/or parties to the NPT. But again, the fundamental point is that such decisions of the Board are irrelevant to authoritative interpretation of earlier CSAs, since the latter are bilateral treaties between the IAEA and individual States, the interpretation of which lies with the contracting parties.

Now we may turn to the various Board decisions already referred to, invoked as supporting the 'completeness' argument.

The first decision, GOV/2547/Rev.1 was a resolution adopted by the IAEA Board (11 September 1991) by which the Board requested the IAEA DG to verify the 'correctness and completeness of the inventory of South Africa's nuclear installations and material' under its newly approved comprehensive safeguards agreement.[106]

The second, GOV/OR.776 (paras 48, 83 and 84) took place during discussions within the Board on special inspections in accordance with CSAs. During its 25 February 1992 meeting, the Board reached the following decision on the issue of special inspections:

> The Board urged the full exercise of all Agency rights and obligations as provided under the Statute and in all comprehensive safeguards agreements (i.e. those which are based on the guidelines set forth in INFCIRC/153 (Corrected), as well as others which provide for the application of Agency safeguards to all nuclear materials in all peaceful nuclear activities within a State). The Board reaffirmed the Agency's right to undertake special inspections, when necessary and appropriate as described in the above-mentioned agreements and to ensure that all nuclear materials in peaceful nuclear activities are under safeguards. The Board anticipates that these special inspections should only occur on rare occasions. The Board further reaffirmed the Agency's rights to obtain and to have access to additional information and locations in accordance with the Agency's Statute and all comprehensive safeguards agreements.[107]

The third, GOV/2636 (26 February 1993) was a Board resolution on the implementation of safeguards in North Korea. In this resolution, the Board, '[t]aking account of the rights and obligations under the Safeguards Agreement between the

[105]Idem., paras 99–110.

[106]See 'Safeguards: Draft Resolution Submitted by Egypt, Morocco, Nigeria and Tunisia on Behalf of the Africa Group' (GOV/2547/Rev.1) 11 September 1991.

[107]GOV/OR.776, para 48.

[DPRK] and the [IAEA]', stressed 'that it is essential to verify the correctness and assess the completeness of the [DPRK]'s Initial Report'.[108]

Finally, the fourth and last reference invoked in favour of the 'completeness' argument is GOV/OR.864 (para 49), which refers to a 'summing-up' of the Board's discussions in March 1995, drafted by the Chairman and proposed for adoption at the Board's 864th meeting. In this draft, the Board was requested to 'reiterate' that 'the purpose of comprehensive safeguards agreements, where safeguards are applied to all nuclear material in all nuclear activities within the territory of a State party to such an agreement, under its jurisdiction or carried out under its control anywhere, is to verify that such material is not diverted to nuclear weapons or other nuclear explosive devices. To this end, the safeguards system for implementing comprehensive safeguards agreements should be designed to provide for verification by the Agency of the correctness and completeness of States' declarations, so that there is credible assurance of the non-diversion of nuclear material from declared activities and of the absence of undeclared nuclear activities'.[109] This proposal met with significant opposition, as previously mentioned. GOV/OR.865 (paras 53–54) refers to the part of the official records of the Board's 865th meeting, where the Chairman mentioned that 'a basis for agreement' on the summing-up 'appeared to have been found during informal consultations'. The Chairman's summing-up was indeed 'accepted' by the Board.[110] By this decision, the Board,

> [w]hile not taking a decision at those meetings on the specific measures proposed in GOV/2784 or on their legal basis, [...] endorsed the general direction of 'Programme 93 + 2' for a strengthened and cost-effective safeguards system.[111]

---

[108]'Report on the Implementation of the Agreement between the Agency and the Democratic People's Republic of Korea for the Application of Safeguards in Connection with the Treaty on the Non-Proliferation of Nuclear Weapons', Resolution adopted by the Board on 25 February 1993 (GOV/2636): [*Preamble*] '(a) Having considered the Report of the Director General and the statements by the Representative of the [DPRK] on the Implementation of the Safeguards Agreement between the [DPRK] and the [IAEA]; (b) Taking account of the rights and obligations under the Safeguards Agreement between the between the [DPRK] and the [IAEA] (INFCIRC/403) [...]' [*Operative paragraphs*] '1. Calls for full and prompt implementation of the Safeguards Agreement between the [DPRK] and the [IAEA]; 2. Stresses that it is essential to verify the correctness and assess the completeness of the [DPRK]'s Initial Report.'

[109]See IAEA Board of Governors, *Record of the 864th meeting,* para 49, excerpt appended as Annex 3 to 'Strengthening the Effectiveness and Improving the Efficiency of the Safeguards System', Report by the Director General to the General Conference (GC(39)/17), 22 August 1995.

[110]See IAEA Board of Governors, *Record of the 865th meeting,* paras 53–54, excerpt appended as Annex 3 to 'Strengthening the Effectiveness and Improving the Efficiency of the Safeguards System', Report by the Director General to the General Conference (GC(39)/17), 22 August 1995: '53. The CHAIRMAN said that a basis for agreement appeared to have been found during informal consultations. Accordingly, he took it that the Board wished to accept his summing-up with the two amendments suggested by him at the start of the meeting. 54. It was so decided.'

[111]See GOV/2807, 12 May 1995, para 2.

To summarize, the first and third decisions (i.e. GOV/2547/Rev.1 and GOV/2636) were adopted with respect to specific cases (South Africa and the DPRK respectively), and it is difficult to draw general conclusions from these on the scope of safeguards under CSAs. The third decision (GOV/OR.776) was concerned with the issue of special inspections under CSAs. And the fourth decision (GOV/OR.864 and 865) can hardly be deemed more than a mere 'endorsement' of the 'general direction' of the 93 + 2 Programme.

My conclusion is thus that none of these four decisions appears to embody a common understanding within the Board that the IAEA would be entitled under CSAs to verify both the correctness and the completeness of States' declarations.

As a matter of fact, such disagreements on the interpretation of Article 2 of CSAs have persisted to date. At the 57th IAEA General Conference (2013), during the debate in the Committee of the Whole on the draft resolution on 'Strengthening the effectiveness and improving the efficiency of the safeguards system and application of the Model Additional Protocol',[112] Russia expressed its opposition to preambular paragraph (g) of the draft resolution, worded as follows:

> (g) Noting that the implementation of comprehensive safeguards agreements should be designed to provide for verification by the Agency of the correctness and completeness of a State's declarations.

It is also to be noted that the representative of Saudi Arabia stated that, if the Agency had the right and obligation to verify the correctness and completeness of a State's declarations under the [CSA] with that State, he did not see what purpose was served by the Model Additional Protocol.[113] At the same meeting, the Russian Federation expressed the view that the March 1995 decision of the Board examined above did not entail acceptance of the 'completeness' argument, stressing that 'ultimate acceptance of the Chairman's summing-up on that occasion could certainly not be regarded as a formal decision of the Board'.[114] Referring to these statements, L. Rockwood has deplored that on this occasion

> [s]ome [IAEA] member states have used this opportunity [i.e. the discussions on the State-level concept at the IAEA GC] to call into question important measures to strengthen safeguards that have been in place since the early 1990s. Most disconcerting have been challenges to IAEA authority under comprehensive safeguards agreements to verify the nondiversion of declared nuclear material and the absence of undeclared nuclear material and activities in a state with such an agreement.[115]

But again, the mere fact of these disagreements is evidence of the lack of a common understanding of para 2 of INFCIRC/153.

---

[112]GC(57)/COM.5/L.9/Rev.1.

[113]IAEA 57th General Conference, Committee of the Whole, *Record of the Seventh Meeting*, 19 September 2013 (GC(57)/COM.5/OR.7), para 47.

[114]Idem., paras 49, 54–55.

[115]Rockwood 2014. D.H. Joyner has made critical comments on this article in A Response to Laura Rockwood, Arms Control Law blog, 14 September 2014, http://armscontrollaw.com/.

3.3.4.2 Subsequent Practice

As emphasized by the ILC,

> The importance of such subsequent practice in the application of the treaty, as an element of interpretation, is obvious; for it constitutes objective evidence of the understanding of the parties as to the meaning of the treaty. Recourse to it as a means of interpretation is well-established in the jurisprudence of international tribunals.[116]

It is necessary to examine first the main characteristics that subsequent practice is supposed to display in order to be taken into account in the meaning of Article 31(3)(b), it is undisputed that the latter provision requires at least active practice of some parties to the treaty, and that the active practice 'should be consistent rather than haphazard and it should have occurred with a certain frequency'.[117] Moreover, the subsequent practice must establish the agreement of the parties regarding its interpretation. 'Thus, it will have been acquiesced in by the other parties; and no other party will have raised an objection'.[118] Practice has to be concordant and common to all parties.[119] This requirement has been affirmed, for example, by the WTO Appellate Body in *Japan–Alcoholic Beverages*:

Generally, in international law, the essence of subsequent practice in interpreting a treaty has been recognized as a 'concordant, common and consistent' sequence of acts or pronouncements which is sufficient to establish a discernible pattern implying the agreement of the parties regarding its interpretation. An isolated act is generally not sufficient to establish subsequent practice; it is a sequence of acts establishing the agreement of the parties that is relevant.[120] If these conditions are not met, such practice may still serve as a supplementary means of interpretation according to Article 32 of the Vienna Conventions.[121, 122]

---

[116]ILC Yearbook 1966, Vol. II, 221, para 15. This statement has been endorsed by the ICJ in the *Kasikili/Sedudu Island (Botswana/Namibia) case*, ICJ Rep. 1999, p. 1045 at p. 1076.

[117]See the statement during the Vienna Conference by the delegation of Argentina, OR 1968 CoW 180, para 23; Waldock Report III, YBILC 1964 II 59, para 24; the *avis de droit* of the Swiss Federal Department for Foreign Affairs, SJIR 38 (1982) 86, according to which two règlements of the WHO were insufficient in this respect.

[118]Villiger 2009, p. 431. This requirement is affirmed by Waldock 1966, paras 15 and 18. See also the observation by the US Government, ibid., 359; See the 1977 Beagle Channel Arbitration, ILR 52 (1979) 224, paras 172, and 169; the 1980 Young Loan Arbitration, ibid., 59 (1980) 541, para 31 ('tacit subsequent understanding'); the 1963 Air Transport Arbitration (France/US), ibid., 38 (1969) 249 et seq. This qualified passive conduct approximates to customary law, Müller 1971, p. 132.

[119]Sorel and Boré Eveno 2011, pp. 804–837 (for the 1969 Convention) and pp. 838–840 (for the 1986 Convention), at p. 826. See also Gardiner 2008, pp. 227–228.

[120]*Japan–Taxes on Alcoholic Beverages*, AB-1996-2, Report of 4 October 1996, WT/DS8/AB/R, WT/DS10/AB/R, WT/DS11/AB/R, at pp. 12–13.

[121]Villiger 2009, p. 432.

[122]Torres Bernadez 1998, p. 726 et seq.

Regarding the effect of subsequent practice of the parties to a treaty, it is admitted that it may *confirm* an interpretation of a treaty provision.[123] This concept of subsequent practice as a means of *confirmation* of a given treaty interpretation is expressed in the case law of the ICJ, for instance in the 1984 judgment in *Military and Paramilitary Activities*, where the Court observed that its vision of the interpretation of Article 36(5) of its Statute was 'confirmed by the subsequent conduct of the Parties to the treaty in question, the Statute of the Court'.[124] The same approach was followed by the ICJ in the *Gabčíkovo-Nagymaros Project* case,[125, 126] where the Court made clear that subsequent practice cannot be deemed to have caused an *amendment* or a termination of a treaty by lapse. The function of subsequent practice in interpretation is therefore primarily to *confirm* the meaning of a treaty provision.

Regarding the role of subsequent practice in the context of interpretation of CSAs, three main elements need to be taken into account.

First, the subsequent practice of the IAEA or its organs in the interpretation of INFCIRC/153 is *stricto sensu* irrelevant to interpretation of an actual CSA, as such practice is not the practice *of the parties* to the treaty concerned. It is undisputed that to be taken into account as a means of interpretation according to Article 31(3)(b) of the Vienna Convention, subsequent practice in the application of the treaty is supposed to be a treaty practice which 'establishes the agreement of the parties regarding its interpretation or application.[127] The practice of the IAEA alone (or its organs) cannot therefore in my view be taken into account under Article 31(3)(b) for the purposes of interpretation of a CSA, even though it may reasonably be argued that the role of the IAEA is incorporated by reference in the NPT and in INFCIRC/153.

Second, it is important to observe that for each State with a CSA in force but no AP in force, the IAEA refrains from reaching a conclusion as to the absence of 'undeclared' nuclear activities. As noted by L. Rockwood, the conclusion which the IAEA draws for any State with a CSA (but no AP) in force 'relates only to the non-diversion of declared nuclear material, i.e. that all declared nuclear material remained in peaceful activities'.[128] It is plausible to argue that this reflects a policy decision from the part of the IAEA, not a legal position. But it may also be argued that the very measures provided for in an AP allow the Agency to reach a conclusion on the absence of undeclared nuclear material in a given State.[129]

---

[123]Sorel and Boré Eveno 2011, pp. 804–837 (for the 1969 Convention) and pp. 838–840 (for the 1986 Convention), at pp. 825–826.

[124]*Military and Paramilitary Activities in and against Nicaragua (Jurisdiction and Admissibility)*, Judgment of 24 November 1984, ICJ Rep. 1984, 411, para 42.

[125]Judgment of 25 September 1997, ICJ Rep. 1997, 66–69, paras 100 and 114.

[126]Sorel and Boré Eveno, at 828.

[127]See First report on subsequent agreements and subsequent practice in relation to treaty interpretation by Georg Nolte, Special Rapporteur (A/CN.4/660), 19 March 2013, para 118.

[128]Rockwood 2013, at p. 29.

[129]Carlson and Leslie, above n. 41, at p. 6.

Third, an examination of the practice of the IAEA in the implementation of safeguards in various countries found in non-compliance with their CSA undertakings is also relevant in this context. The case of Egypt is of particular interest. Following IAEA enquiries, Egypt, between 2004 and 2005, disclosed past-undeclared nuclear activities and material to the Agency.[130] Egypt had failed to report information on several nuclear facilities and materials.[131] Following a process of verification during which Egypt provided nuclear material accounting reports and clarifications on its past undeclared nuclear activities, the IAEA 'found no indication of the diversion of declared nuclear material in Egypt' and was therefore in a position to conclude for Egypt that all declared nuclear material remained in peaceful activities'.[132] It is clear that the IAEA's verification process in this case did not include verification of the absence of *undeclared* nuclear activities in Egypt (i.e. the completeness of Egypt's reported nuclear materials).

The same conclusion may be drawn from the case of South Korea. Following Agency enquiries, in 2004 the Republic of Korea (ROK) disclosed to the Agency past undeclared activities.[133] At that time, the POK had just signed an Additional Protocol. In August 2004, in its initial declaration pursuant to its Additional Protocol, the ROK declared that experiments on uranium enrichment had been previously carried out without having been reported to the Agency. Also, the ROK acknowledged past undeclared experiments which involved *inter alia* uranium conversion and chemical enrichment of uranium. These activities should have been reported to the Agency in accordance with the ROK's obligations under its safeguards agreement.[134] Following the disclosure of these activities, and since there in the meantime the ROK had signed an AP and the latter had come into force, the IAEA implemented an action plan for the verification of the *correctness* and *completeness* of the ROK's declarations, including clarification of the extent of past undeclared activities, leading to the clarification of all issues relating to past undeclared activities.[135] The verification process came to an end in 2007, when the Agency found no indication of the diversion of *declared* nuclear material, and no indication of *undeclared* nuclear material and activities in the ROK.[136] This is precisely because an Additional Protocol was in force that the IAEA's assessment also extended to potential *undeclared* nuclear material and activities.

---

[130]Safeguards Statement for 2008, para 43.

[131]Idem., para 44.

[132]Idem., para 48.

[133]Idem., para 31.

[134]Idem., para 32.

[135]Idem., para 33.

[136]Idem., para 35.

3.4 Concluding Remarks

Application of the rule of interpretation of the 1986 Vienna Convention to para 2 of INFCIRC/153 (and Article 2 of individual CSAs), including an enquiry into subsequent agreement and practice, does not lend unconditional support to the interpretation according to which such provision is to be read as implying that the IAEA under CSAs is entitled to verify both the 'correctness' and 'completeness' of declarations made by States. It appears that a textual approach, together with examination of the context and the object and purpose of CSAs and recourse to the *travaux préparatoires* (or more exactly to what is publicly known of the *travaux*) gives some weight to the 'completeness' argument; and it may be assumed that this embodies a correct interpretation of the disputed provision. But this position is in turn weakened by the consideration of other relevant elements. Indeed, one cannot fail to notice that various sources point to the fact that, at the time of negotiation of the INFCIRC/153 safeguards system—and at least until the 1990s—there was no shared understanding on the disputed interpretation of para 2 of INFCIRC/153. The various decisions of the IAEA Board in 1992–1995 invoked as supporting the 'completeness' argument do not in fact embody a common unequivocal understanding within the Board that the IAEA would be entitled under CSAs to verify both the correctness and the completeness of States' declarations. It is also noteworthy that as a matter of fact, such disagreements on the interpretation of Article 2 of CSAs have persisted to date by a few Member States of the IAEA, who have expressed reservations or dissenting opinions on this interpretation. Most of all, I have been unable to identify relevant subsequent agreement or subsequent practice that would confirm the 'correctness' argument. Therefore, taking into account the remaining uncertainty surrounding the correct interpretation of para 2 of INFCIRC/153 (and Article 2 of individual CSAs), I cannot but express the view that the confirmation by the IAEA of the 'completeness' of declarations of States can only derive, practically if not even legally, from the application of an AP. In expressing this view, I share the opinion, already referred to, that 'obtaining universal adherence to Additional Protocols is the best, perhaps, the only way, to provide the Agency everywhere with the authorities contained in the Model Additional Protocol'.[137]

On a more general level, I observe that claims are often made that nuclear non-proliferation instruments, particularly those setting out obligations regarding safeguards to be applied to nuclear materials, shall be subject, in one way or another, to 'evolutive' interpretation. In support of such proposition, it is often stated that the technical character of the matter, and the evolutions witnessed both in nuclear technologies and in non-proliferation verification techniques,[138] are such as to require that relevant provisions of safeguards instruments be recognized as displaying an 'evolutive' character. Should such reasoning be accepted, from the

[137]M.D. Rosenthal et al. Review of the Negotiation of the Model Protocol Additional to the Agreement(s) between State(s) and the International Atomic Energy Agency for the Application of Safeguards, INFCIRC/540 (Corrected), Vol. II (Brookhaven National Laboratory, 2010), http://www.bnl.gov/isd/documents/71014.pdf, at p. 11.

[138]IAEA 1998, p. 24.

point of view of the law of treaties it would prove difficult to distinguish between 'evolutive interpretation' of treaty provisions, and amendments to a treaty.[139] Moreover, in my view such trends are of such a nature as to reinforce the concerns often expressed by some non-nuclear weapon States, and as such could even impair the future and strengthening of the non-proliferation regime.

References

Asada M (2011) The treaty on the non-proliferation of nuclear weapons and the universalization of the additional protocol. J Conflict Secur Law 16:3–34

Aust A (2007) Modern treaty law and practice. Cambridge University Press, Cambridge

Black-Branch JL, Fleck D (eds) (2014) Nuclear non-proliferation in international law, vol 1. TMC Asser Press, The Hague

Blix H (1983) Aspects juridiques des garanties de l'Agence Internationale de l'Energie Atomique. Annuaire Français de Droit International 29:37–58

Blix H (1989) The role of the IAEA in the development of international law. Nordic J Int Law 58:231–242

Blix H (2011) Introduction. The present nuclear order, how it came about, why it may not last. In: Njølstad O (ed), Nuclear proliferation and international order. Challenges to the non-proliferation treaty. Routledge, Abingdon, pp 5 et seq

Carnahan BM (1987) Treaty review conferences. AJIL 81:226–230

De Visscher C (1963) Problèmes d'interprétation judiciaire en droit international public. Pédone, Paris

Dupont PE (2012) The EU-Iran dialogue in the context of the nuclear crisis. Central Eur J Int Secur Stud 3:97–112

Dupont PE (2014) Compliance with treaties in the context of nuclear non-proliferation: assessing claims in the case of Iran. J Conflict Secur Law 19:161–210

Dupuy PM (2011) Evolutionary interpretation of treaties: between memory and prophecy. In: Cannizzaro E (ed) The law of treaties beyond the Vienna Convention. Oxford University Press, Oxford, pp 123–137

Edwards DM (1984) International legal aspects of safeguards and the non-proliferation of nuclear weapons. ICLQ 33:1–21

ElBaradei M et al (1993) The international law of nuclear energy: basic documents. Martinus Nijhoff Publishers, Dordrecht

ElBaradei M et al (1995) International law and nuclear energy: overview of the legal framework. IAEA Bulletin 37:16–25

Engelen FA (2004) Interpretation of tax treaties under international law. IBFD, Amsterdam

Fitzmaurice G (1957) The foundations of the authority of international law and the ICJ 1951–54: treaty interpretation and other treaty points. BYBIL 33:203

Gardiner RK (2008) Treaty interpretation. Oxford University Press, Oxford

Goldblat J (1995) The nuclear non-proliferation régime: assessment and prospects. Recueil des Cours 256:9–192

Goldblat J (2002) Arms control: the new guide to negotiations and agreements. PRIO/SIPRI, Oslo

Gruemm H (1983) Safeguards verification: its credibility and the diversion hypothesis. IAEA Bulletin 25:27–29

[139]See e.g. Nolte 2010, paras 344–354.

IAEA (1972) 'The Structure and Content of Agreements Between the Agency and States Required in Connection With the Treaty on the Non-Proliferation of Nuclear Weapons' as an IAEA information circular (INFCIRC/153 (Corr.). www.iaea.org/Publications/Documents/Infcircs/Others/infcirc153.pdf
IAEA (1997) Model Protocol Additional to the Agreement(s) between State(s) and the IAEA for the Application of Safeguards (INFCIRC/540 (Corr.)), approved by the IAEA Board of Governors in 1997, referred to as the Model Additional Protocol
IAEA (1998) The evolution of IAEA safeguards. IAEA, Vienna
IAEA (2002) IAEA safeguards glossary, 2001 edn. IAEA, Vienna
International Energy Associates Limited (1984) Review of the Negotiating History of the IAEA Safeguards Document INFCIRC/153. Prepared for the US Arms Control and Disarmament Agency, Vol. I, http://cgs.pnnl.gov/fois/doclib/INFCIRC153Ch1-3.pdf
Jankowitsch-Prevor O (2010) The normative role of the International Atomic Energy Agency (IAEA): legal basis and legal sources. In: OECD Nuclear Energy Agency, international nuclear law: history, evolution and outlook, pp 13–30. http://www.oecd-nea.org/law/isnl/10th/isnl-10th-anniversary.pdf
Jansen Calamita N (2009) Sanctions, countermeasures, and the Iranian nuclear issue. Vanderbildt J Transnational Law 42:1393–1442
Joyner DH (2009) International law and the proliferation of weapons of mass destruction. Oxford University Press, Oxford
Joyner DH (2011) Interpreting the nuclear non-proliferation treaty. Oxford University Press, Oxford
Joyner DH, Roscini M (eds) (2012) Nonproliferation law as a special regime. Cambridge University Press, Cambridge
Joyner (2014) A Response to Laura Rockwood, Arms Control Law blog, 14 September 2014, http://armscontrollaw.com/
Kile SN (ed) (2005) Europe and Iran. Perspectives on nonproliferation. Oxford University Press/SIPRI, Oxford
Kile SN (2008) Nuclear arms control and non-proliferation. In: SIPRI yearbook 2008. Armaments, Disarmament and International Security, pp 337 et seq.
Kile SN (2009) Nuclear arms control and non-proliferation. In: SIPRI yearbook 2009. Armaments, Disarmament and International Security, pp 387 et seq.
Kile SN (2011) Nuclear arms control and non-proliferation. In: SIPRI yearbook 2011. Armaments, Disarmament and International Security, pp 363 et seq.
Kofstadmoen H, Reistad O (2010) The role of IAEA in multilateral nuclear disarmament verification. Paper presented at the 2010 IAEA safeguards symposium (Doc. IAEA-CN-184/280)
Lang M, Brugger F (2008) The role of the OECD commentary in tax treaty interpretation. Australian Tax Forum 23:95–108
Lauterpacht H (1934) Les travaux préparatoires et l'interprétation des traités. Recueil des Cours 48-II
Müller JP (1971) Vertrauensschutz im Völkerrecht. Köln, Heymanns
Myjer E, Herbach J (2012) Violation of non-proliferation treaties and related verification treaties. In: Joyner DH, Roscini M (eds) Nonproliferation law as a special regime. Cambridge University Press, Cambridge, pp 119–150
Njølstad O (ed) (2011) Nuclear proliferation and international order. Challenges to the non-proliferation treaty. Routledge, Abingdon
Nolte G (2010) Introductory Report for the Study Group on Treaties over Time. Jurisprudence of the International Court of Justice and arbitral tribunals of ad hoc jurisdiction relating to subsequent agreements and subsequent practice', in ILC Report 2010, *Official Records of the General Assembly, Sixty-fifth Session*, Supplement No. 10, (A/65/10), Chap. X, 334–335, paras 344–354
Nolte G (2013) (ed) Treaties and subsequent practice. Oxford University Press, Oxford

Ost F (1992) The original canons of interpretation of the European Court of Human Rights. In: Delmas-Marty M (ed) The European convention for the protection of human rights: international protection versus national restrictions. Martinus Nijhoff Publishers, Dordrecht
Priest J (1995) IAEA safeguards and the NPT: examining interconnections. IAEA Bull 37:2–13
Rainer RH, Szasz PC (1993) Supplement 1 to the 1970 edition of Legal Series No. 7, IAEA
Rauf T, Kelley R (2014) Nuclear verification in Iran. Arms Control Today 44:8–17
Rockwood L (2010) The IAEA safeguards system. OECD nuclear energy agency, international nuclear law: history, evolution and outlook. OECD, Paris, pp 243–269
Rockwood L (2013) Legal framework for IAEA safeguards. IAEA, Vienna
Rockwood L (2014) The IAEA's state-level concept and the law of unintended consequences. Arms Control Today. http://www.armscontrol.org/act/2014_09/Features/The-IAEAs-State-Level-Concept-and-the-Law-of-Unintended-Consequences
Ronen Y (2010) The Iran nuclear issue. Hart Publishing, Oxford
Salacuse JW (2009) The law of investment treaties. Oxford University Press, Oxford
Scolbi L (2011) Supplementary means of interpretation. In: Cannizzaro E (ed) The law of treaties beyond the Vienna Convention. Oxford University Press, Oxford, pp 145–163
Sinclair I (1984) The Vienna convention on the law of treaties, 2nd edn. Manchester University Press, Manchester
Sorel JM, Boré Eveno V (2011) Article 31. In: Corten O, Klein P (eds), The Vienna Conventions on the law of treaties. Oxford University Press, Oxford, pp 804–837
Sur S (1998) Vérification en matière de désarmement. Recueil des Cours 273:9–102
Szasz PC (1970) The law and practices of the International Atomic Energy Agency. IAEA, Vienna
Szasz PC (1985) IAEA safeguards: sanctions. In: Goldblat J (ed) Safeguarding the atom: a critical appraisal. SIPRI/Taylor and Francis, London, pp 135–152
Thirlway H (2013) The law and practice of the International Court of Justice, vol I. Oxford University Press, Oxford
Torres Bernardez S (1998) Interpretation of treaties by the International Court of Justice following the adoption of the 1969 Vienna Convention on the law of treaties. In: Hafner G et al (eds) Liber amicorum professor Ignaz Seidl-Hohenveldern. Kluwer Law International, The Hague, pp 721–748
Villiger ME (2009) Commentary on the 1969 Vienna Convention on the law of treaties. Martinus Nijhoff Publishers, The Hague
Villiger ME (2011) The rules on interpretation: misgivings, misunderstandings, miscarriage? The 'crucible' intended by the International Law Commission. In: Cannizzaro E (ed) The law of treaties beyond the Vienna Convention. Oxford University Press, Oxford, pp 105–122
Waldock H (1964) Third Report on the Law of Treaties, YILC 1964 II. pp 5–65
Waldock H (1966) Sixth Report on the Law of Treaties, YILC 1966 II. pp 51–103
Yasseen MK (1976) L'interprétation des traités d'après la Convention de Vienne sur le droit des traités. Collected Courses 151:1–114

Chapter 4
Verification of Correctness and Completeness in the Implementation of IAEA Safeguards: The Law and Practice

Laura Rockwood and Larry Johnson

Abstract Pursuant to Article III.1 of the Treaty on the Non-Proliferation of Nuclear Weapons (the NPT) each non-nuclear-weapon State (NNWS) Party to the Treaty undertakes to conclude with the International Atomic Energy Agency (IAEA) an agreement for the application of safeguards on all source or special fissionable material in all peaceful nuclear activities within the territory of such State, under its jurisdiction, or carried out under its control anywhere. As provided for in Article III.1 of the NPT, the purpose of these agreements, referred to as comprehensive safeguards agreements (CSAs), is the 'verification of the fulfilment of [the NNWS's] obligations assumed under this Treaty with a view to

Laura Rockwood retired in 2013 from the International Atomic Energy Agency as the Section Head for Non-Proliferation and Policy Making in the Office of Legal Affairs, where she had served since 1985. During her employment with the IAEA, she was involved in all aspects of the negotiation, interpretation and implementation of IAEA safeguards, and was the principal author of the document that became the Model Additional Protocol. She is currently a Senior Research Fellow at the Harvard University's Kennedy School Belfer Center, Project on Managing the Atom. In June 2015, she took up the position of Executive Director of the Vienna Center for Disarmament and Non-Proliferation in Vienna, Austria. Prior to working for the IAEA, she was employed by the US Department of Energy as a trial attorney in radiation injury cases, and as counsel in general legal matters.

Larry Johnson served as Assistant Secretary-General for Legal Affairs in the United Nations from 2006 to 2008, having served in the UN Office of Legal Affairs for over 25 years, including 15 years in the Secretariat of the International Law Commission and 10 years in the Office of the Legal Counsel, providing legal advice on a variety of international law issues including on law of treaties matters. He was also Legal Adviser of the International Atomic Energy Agency from 1997 to 2001 and Chef de Cabinet in the Office of the President of the International Criminal Tribunal for the former Yugoslavia from 2003 to 2005. He is currently Adjunct Professor of Law at Columbia Law School and Professorial Lecturer at the Vienna Diplomatic Academy.

L. Rockwood (✉)
Schwarzenbergstrasse 8/17, A-1010, Vienna, Austria
e-mail: Laura_Rockwood@hks.harvard.edu

L. Johnson (✉)
141 East 88th St., Apt. 3H, New York, NY 10128, USA
e-mail: ldjohnson7@earthlink.net

J.L. Black-Branch and D. Fleck (eds.), *Nuclear Non-Proliferation in International Law - Volume II*, DOI 10.1007/978-94-6265-075-6_4

preventing diversion of nuclear energy from peaceful uses to nuclear weapons or other nuclear explosive devices'. These safeguards agreements are highly standardized and are based on a document negotiated by a committee of the IAEA's Board of Governors and approved by the Board in 1971, INFCIRC/153 (Corr.). Paragraph 2 of INFCIRC/153, which is reproduced mutatis mutandis, in every CSA concluded by the IAEA, provides that the IAEA shall have the 'right and obligation to ensure that safeguards will be applied … on all source or special fissionable material …'. Between 1971 and the early 1990s, the implementation of safeguards under these agreements was primarily, although not exclusively, focused on the verification of nuclear material and facilities declared by the State concerned. The discovery in 1993 of Iraq's clandestine nuclear programme made it clear that more should, and could, be done by the IAEA, as authorized and required by para 2 of INFCIRC/153, and the corresponding articles of CSAs, with a view to providing assurances not just of the non-diversion of declared nuclear material, but of the absence of undeclared nuclear material and activities in such States. This right and obligation has been confirmed consistently by the policy-making organs of the IAEA since the early 1990s. In 1997, the Board approved a Model Additional Protocol, designed as a model for protocols to be concluded with States party to CSAs, with a view to providing the IAEA with complementary authority to request access, on a more routine basis, to additional information and locations related to a State's nuclear fuel cycle, with a view to strengthening the IAEA's ability to fulfil its obligations under such agreements. In recent years, Iran, supported by a very few other Member States of the IAEA and a small number of academics, has challenged the IAEA's efforts to verify the completeness of Iran's declarations under its CSA, arguing that, without an additional protocol to that agreement, the IAEA has no authority to do so. In accordance with the general rules of interpretation codified in both the Vienna Convention on the Law of Treaties between States and the Vienna Convention on the Law of Treaties between States and International Organizations or between International Organizations, these safeguards agreements must be interpreted in good faith in accordance with the ordinary meaning to be given to the terms of the agreements in their context and in the light of their object and purpose. Account is also to be taken of any subsequent agreement between the parties regarding the interpretation of the agreements or the application of its provisions and any subsequent practice in the application of the treaty which establishes the agreement of the parties regarding its interpretation. Recourse to supplementary means of interpretation, such as the preparatory work of the treaty and the circumstances of its conclusion, may be had in order to confirm the meaning resulting from the application that general rule, or to determine the meaning when the interpretation in accordance with that rule leaves the meaning ambiguous or obscure or leads to a result which is manifestly absurd or unreasonable. As discussed in this chapter, a plain reading of INFCIRC/153 clearly demonstrates the IAEA's right and obligation to verify the non-diversion of the declared nuclear material and the absence of undeclared nuclear material and activities—that is to say, to provide assurances of the correctness and completeness of States' declarations under such agreements. The text of INFCIRC/153 is clear on its face. This is clearly supported by the context of these agreements, and in the light of their object and purpose. This unambiguous meaning is confirmed by the subsequent agreement and practice of the parties to those agreements, as reflected in the documents adopted by the States Parties to the NPT in their quinquennial review conferences, the decisions of the IAEA policy-making organs and the consistent practice of the IAEA since the early 1990s—long before the Model Additional Protocol was approved by the Board of Governors. The travaux prėparatoires reflected in the negotiation history of INFCIRC/153 further confirms that interpretation. With the approval of the Model Additional Protocol in 1997, and the conclusion of additional protocols based on the model, the IAEA has been able to more effectively and efficiently implement its right and fulfil its obligation under CSAs to provide the necessary assurances. To interpret INFCIRC/153, and the agreements concluded on the basis of that document, in such a way as to preclude IAEA verification of the correctness and completeness of States' declarations under such agreements would defeat the very object and purpose of such agreements, and the very foundations of such agreements, the NPT, which is to ensure the timely detection of the diversion of nuclear material to nuclear weapons and other nuclear explosive devices and the deterrence of such diversion through the risk of timely detection.

Keywords Completeness · Correctness · Inspections · International Atomic Energy Agency (IAEA) · IAEA Safeguards · Nuclear non-proliferation · Programme 93 + 2 · Safeguards Implementation Report (SIR) · State-level concept · Verification

Contents

4.1 Background

Pursuant to Article III.1. of the Treaty on the Non-Proliferation of Nuclear Weapons (the NPT)[1] each non-nuclear-weapon State (NNWS) Party to the Treaty undertakes:

[1]Treaty on the Non-Proliferation of Nuclear Weapons (1 July 1968), 729 UNTS 161.

> … to accept safeguards, as set forth in an agreement to be negotiated and concluded with the International Atomic Energy Agency in accordance with the Statute of the International Atomic Energy Agency and the Agency's safeguards system, for the exclusive purpose of verification of the fulfilment of its obligations assumed under this Treaty with a view to preventing diversion of nuclear energy from peaceful uses to nuclear weapons or other nuclear explosive devices. Procedures for the safeguards required by this Article shall be followed with respect to source or special fissionable material whether it is being produced, processed or used in any principal nuclear facility or is outside any such facility. The safeguards required by this Article shall be applied on all source or special fissionable material in all peaceful nuclear activities within the territory of such State, under its jurisdiction, or carried out under its control anywhere.

Following the entry into force of the NPT on 5 March 1970, the Board of Governors of the International Atomic Energy Agency (the IAEA) adopted a resolution in April 1970 establishing a committee (Committee 22 or the Safeguards Committee), with participation open to all Member States of the IAEA, to consider the form and content of the necessary safeguards agreements.[2] A year later, the Board of Governors approved the text of a document tabled by the Committee entitled 'The Structure and Content of Agreements between the Agency and States required in Connection with the Treaty on the Non-Proliferation of Nuclear Weapons' (INFCIRC/153 (Corr.)),[3] (frequently simply referred to as 'INFCIRC/153'). In approving the text, the Board requested the Director General to use the material reproduced in that document as the basis for negotiating safeguards agreements between the IAEA and NNWS's party to the NPT. Given that the scope of such agreements was to cover all nuclear material in a State, they were referred to as 'full scope safeguards agreements', or, as they are more currently referred to, 'comprehensive safeguards agreements' or 'CSAs'.

All comprehensive safeguards agreements concluded by the IAEA are based on INFCIRC/153,[4] and the model agreement derived from it reproduced in GOV/INF/276.[5] Each of these agreements contains articles which correspond to

---

[2]The text of that resolution is reproduced in IAEA Doc. GOV/INF/222, 6 April 1970. The website of the US Department of State Office of the Historian contains an extract from a talking paper prepared by the Chairman of the US Atomic Energy Commission, Glenn Seaborg, in anticipation of a meeting with the Ambassador of the Soviet Union to the United States on the subject of the draft resolution. See Journal Entry by the Chairman of the Atomic Energy Commission (Seaborg), Washington, March 18, 1970 at: https://history.state.gov/historicaldocuments/frus1969-76ve02/d47. Forty-eight of the then 98 Member States of the IAEA, roughly half, participated in the Committee's deliberations. The Committee held 82 meetings between June 1970 and mid-March 1971. Sanders 1975, p. 7.

[3]IAEA, The Structure and Content of Agreements Between the Agency and States Required in Connection with the Treaty on the Non-Proliferation of Nuclear Weapons, (International Atomic Energy Agency Information Circular) INFCIRC/153 (Corr.), June 1972.

[4]CSAs can also be concluded by more than one State, and by non-State organizations, such as those concluded by the IAEA with EURATOM and the Member States of the European Community (e.g. INFCIRC/193) and that concluded with Argentina, Brazil and the Brazilian–Argentine Agency of Accounting and Control (ABACC) (INFCIRC/435).

[5]IAEA Doc. GOV/INF/276, Annex A, 'The Standard Text of Safeguards Agreements in Connection with the Treaty on the Non-Proliferation of Nuclear Weapons', 22 August 1974.

paras 1 and 2 of INFCIRC/153 relating, respectively, to the basic undertaking of the State to accept safeguards (para 1) and the IAEA's right and obligation to apply safeguards (para 2).

Paragraph 1 of INFCIRC/153 reads as follows:

> The Agreement contain, in accordance with Article III.2 of the [NPT], an undertaking by the State to accept safeguards, … on *all* source or special fissionable material in all peaceful nuclear activities within its territory, under its jurisdiction or carried out under its control anywhere, for the exclusive purpose of verifying that such material is not diverted to nuclear weapons or other nuclear explosive devices. (Emphasis added.)

Paragraph 2 of INFCIRC/153 reads as follows:

> The Agreement should provide for the Agency's *right and obligation* to *ensure that safeguards will be applied, … on all source or special fissionable material* in all peaceful nuclear activities within the territory of the State, under its jurisdiction or carried out under its control anywhere, for the exclusive purpose of verifying that such material is not diverted to nuclear weapons or other nuclear explosive devices. (Emphasis added.)

Paragraph 1 makes clear the obligation of the State to place under safeguards *all* source or special fissionable material (hereafter referred to collectively as 'nuclear material'[6]); Paragraph 2 provides for the corresponding right and responsibility of the IAEA to ensure, through appropriate verification, that *all* nuclear material is in fact declared by the State and placed under safeguards, to ensure that no such material is misused for prohibited purposes. In other words, the objective of IAEA safeguards under such agreements is verification of not just the non-diversion of declared nuclear material (the correctness of State declarations), but also the absence of undeclared nuclear material and activities in the State (the completeness of State declarations).

Between 1971 and 1990, the IAEA's verification activities under comprehensive safeguards agreements were primarily focused on nuclear material and facilities declared by the State. However, as described below, that was neither exclusively so, nor was it done because of a lack of authority, but rather for practical reasons.

Between 1991 and 1993, following the discovery in 1991 of a clandestine nuclear weapons programme in Iraq (a party to the NPT with a CSA in force), the IAEA Board and General Conference took a number of decisions reaffirming the IAEA's existing right and obligation under comprehensive safeguards agreements to ensure that no nuclear material, whether declared or undeclared, is diverted to nuclear weapons or other nuclear explosive devices, that is to say, to verify the correctness and completeness of States' declarations under such agreements.

---

[6]The terms 'source material' and 'special fissionable material' are defined in Article XX of the IAEA Statute. In para 112 of INFCIRC/153 (Corr.), 'nuclear material' is defined as 'any source or any special fissionable material as defined in Article XX of the Statute', while excluding from the definition of source material ore or ore residue. It is interesting to note that para 112 does not simply define that term as 'source or special fissionable material as defined in Article XX', but emphasizes that it means '*any* source or *any* special fissionable material as defined in Article XX'.

At the end of 1993, the IAEA Secretariat, at the request of the Board, embarked on a programme, known as Programme 93 + 2, to develop a comprehensive set of measures for strengthening safeguards. These efforts resulted in the approval by the Board of Governors in May 1997 of the 'Model Protocol Additional to the Agreement(s) between State(s) and the International Atomic Energy Agency for the Application of Safeguards' (the Model Additional Protocol),[7] a document designed for States with a safeguards agreement with the IAEA, 'in order to strengthen the effectiveness and improve the efficiency of the safeguards system as a contribution to global nuclear non-proliferation objectives'.[8] In approving the Model Additional Protocol, the Board of Governors requested the Director General to use the model as 'the standard for additional protocols that are to be concluded by States and other parties to comprehensive safeguards agreements with the Agency', and decided that such protocols must include all of the measures in the model.[9]

The IAEA's right and obligation to verify the correctness and completeness of States' declarations under CSAs derives from the ordinary meaning of the terms of such agreements, in particular with reference to para 2 of INFCIRC/153. That authority has been recognized, confirmed and reaffirmed on multiple occasions by both policy-making organs of the IAEA (the Board of Governors and the General Conference) since 1991. It has been the practice of the IAEA since the early 1990s to attempt to verify the correctness and completeness of States' declarations under CSAs on a routine basis. The fulfilment of the IAEA's obligation was facilitated with the Board's approval of the Model Additional Protocol in 1997 and the implementation of the additional measures provided for in the protocols concluded on the basis of that model.[10] However, the IAEA routinely looks for indications of the diversion of declared nuclear material and for any indications of undeclared nuclear material and activities under CSAs, regardless of whether the State in question has concluded an additional protocol, and reports to the Board of Governors in the event that it finds such indications.

In early 2003, the IAEA discovered in Iran nuclear material, facilities and activities which were required to have been also declared under Iran's NPT CSA but had not been. Iran signed an additional protocol in late 2003, and implemented it voluntarily until early 2006. However, the additional protocol is not yet in force. While the IAEA has been able to verify the non-diversion of nuclear material which has actually been declared by Iran under its safeguards agreement, the IAEA is 'not in a position to provide credible assurance about the absence of

---

[7]IAEA, Model Protocol Additional to the Agreement(s) Between State(s) and the International Atomic Energy Agency for the Application of Safeguards, INFCIRC/540 (Corr.), September 1997.

[8]Ibid., Foreword.

[9]Ibid.

[10]L. Rockwood, The IAEA's State-level concept and the law of unintended consequences. Arms Control Today (September 2014), https://www.armscontrol.org/act/2014_09/Features/The-IAEAs-State-Level-Concept-and-the-Law-of-Unintended-Consequences).

undeclared nuclear material and activities in Iran, and therefore to conclude that all nuclear material in Iran is in peaceful activities'.[11]

Iran has challenged the IAEA's efforts to verify the completeness of Iran's declarations under its CSA, arguing that, without an additional protocol to that agreement, the IAEA has no authority to do so. That view has been echoed by a very few other Member States of the IAEA (among whom number Brazil, Cuba and Venezuela) and supported by a small number of academics.

This chapter is offered in the hope of providing a better understanding of the legal authority of the IAEA under CSAs, and, in doing so, putting to rest this challenge.

4.2 Historical Overview

4.2.1 INFCIRC/153 and Comprehensive Safeguards

Paragraph 2 of INFCIRC/153 describes the Agency's role under a CSA. It provides that '... the Agency has the right and the obligation to ensure that safeguards will be applied ... on *all* source or special fissionable material ...' (emphasis added), a formulation agreed upon by the drafters of INFCIRC/153 after due consideration—and explicit rejection—of a proposal by one Member State that 'safeguarding and inspection ... shall be concerned solely with the material reported upon by the State concerned'.[12]

In anticipation of the possibility that a State might try to circumvent its obligations under a CSA by not declaring nuclear material to the Agency, the drafters of INFCIRC/153 included specific measures for the IAEA to use to ensure that all nuclear material is *in fact* placed under safeguards, in particular the provisions related to ad hoc and special inspections. By way of explanation, INFCIRC/153 requires that, upon entry into force of a CSA, the State is to submit to the IAEA an initial report of all nuclear material which is to be subject to safeguards and information with respect to all existing nuclear facilities (design information).[13] It authorizes the IAEA to request access to the State to verify such information. Such access is available to the IAEA, inter alia, through three types of inspections: ad hoc, routine and special inspections.[14] The purposes for which these inspections

[11]IAEA Doc. GOV/2015/15, Implementation of the NPT Safeguards Agreement and relevant provisions of Security Council resolutions in the Islamic Republic of Iran, 19 February 2015, para 71.

[12]GOV/COM 22/OR.6, para 22; M. Kratzer, International Energy Associates Limited, 1984, Review of the Negotiating History of the IAEA Safeguards Document INFCIRC/153. Prepared for the US Arms Control and Disarmament Agency, Vol. I, http://cgs.pnnl.gov/fois/doclib/INFCIRC153Ch1-3.pdf, at pp. 33–44.

[13]IAEA Doc. INFCIRC/153, paras 62 and 42 respectively.

[14]The IAEA also has an additional right of access under CSAs: the right to carry out design information verification (DIV) at nuclear facilities. DIVs, the relevant provisions for which are set out in paras 42–48 of INFCIRC/153, are separate and distinct from inspections, which are addressed in detail in paras 70–89 of INFCIRC/153.

may be carried out are described in paras 71, 72 and 73 INFCIRC/153, respectively. The places to which the IAEA has a right of access to carry out inspections are defined in paras 76 and 77 of INFCIRC/153, as described below.

Ad hoc inspections are utilized, inter alia, for verifying the information contained in a State's initial report on nuclear material subject to safeguards under its CSA, and changes in the situation which occur after the date of the initial report (para 71(a) and (b)).[15] Paragraph 76(a) provides that ad hoc inspections for such purposes may be carried out at 'any location where the initial report or *any inspections carried out in connection with [the initial report] indicate that nuclear material is present*' (emphasis added), thereby permitting the IAEA to request access not only to locations declared by the State in its initial report, but to other locations not declared by the State.

Routine inspections are those inspections carried out at facilities, and at locations outside facilities where nuclear material is customarily used (LOFs), at strategic points agreed upon between the Agency and the State in the Subsidiary Arrangements to the CSA.[16] As provided for in para 72(c), the purpose of such inspections is to verify consistency of the State's reports with its records, to verify 'the location, identify, quantity and composition of *all* nuclear material subject to safeguards under the Agreement' (emphasis added) and to verify possible causes of material unaccounted for, shipper/receiver differences and uncertainties in the book inventory. Paragraph 76 limits the Agency's access under routine inspections to the agreed strategic points and to the records maintained pursuant to the CSA.[17]

Paragraph 73 of INFCIRC/153 authorizes the Agency to carry out special inspections, inter alia, if it 'considers that information made available by the State, including explanations from the State and information obtained from routine inspections, is not adequate for the Agency to fulfil its responsibilities under the Agreement'

---

[15]Ad hoc inspections are also used to verify material before its transport out of or upon its transfer into a State, pursuant to para 71(c). This type of ad hoc inspection is not addressed further in this chapter.

[16]The highly standardized subsidiary arrangements under a CSA consist of two parts: the 'general part' containing provisions applicable to the State in general (such as Code 3.1, which details the timing of the State's submission of design information for nuclear facilities); and 'attachments' thereto for each facility or other locations where nuclear material is customarily used (LOFs) ('facility attachments' and 'LOF attachments'). It is in the latter part of the subsidiary arrangements (i.e. facility and LOF attachments) where the strategic points agreed upon between the State and the IAEA are identified. A 'strategic point' is defined in para 116 of INFCIRC/153 as 'a location selected during the examination of design information where, under normal conditions and when combined with the information from all "strategic points" taken together, the information necessary and sufficient for the implementation of safeguards measures is obtained and verified; a 'strategic point' may include any location where key measurements related to material balance accountancy are made and where containment and surveillance measures are executed.' A strategic point need not be a place where nuclear material is present or declared to be present.

[17]The records required to be maintained under a CSA are described in paras 51–58 of INFCIRC/153.

(INFCIRC/153, para 73(b)).[18] As reflected in para 2 of INFCIRC/153, those responsibilities include ensuring that safeguards are applied on *all* source and special fissionable material required to be declared by the State. Paragraph 73 explicitly provides that

> an inspection shall be deemed to be special when it is either additional to the routine inspection effort provided for in paragraphs 78–82 [of INFCIRC/153], or *involves access to information or locations in addition to the access specified in paragraph 76 for ad hoc and routine inspections, or both* (emphasis added).[19]

Paragraph 19 of INFCIRC/153 provides that, if the Board, upon examination of relevant information reported to it by the Director General, finds that the IAEA is 'not able to verify that there has been no diversion of nuclear material *required to be safeguarded* under the Agreement to nuclear weapons or other nuclear explosive devices' (emphasis added), the Board 'may make the reports provided for in para C of Article XII of the Statute and may also take, where applicable, the other measures provided for in that paragraph'.[20] The formulation of para 19 reaffirms the Agency's right to ensure not just that no declared nuclear material is diverted to proscribed purposes, but that *no* nuclear material is diverted, whether declared or undeclared.[21]

---

[18]Paragraph 73(a) of INFCIRC/153 provides that the IAEA may also make special inspections in order to verify information contained in a special report make by a State under its CSA. Special reports are to be provided to the IAEA if any unusual incident or circumstances lead the State to believe that there is or may have been loss of nuclear material in excess of the limits specified in the Subsidiary Arrangements or if the containment has unexpectedly changed from that specified in the Subsidiary Arrangements to the extent that unauthorized removal of nuclear material has become possible. The IAEA carried out just such a special inspection in Romania in 1991 (see text above).

[19]Paragraph 77 requires that, in circumstances which may lead to special inspections, the State and the IAEA are to consult 'forthwith'. It provides further that, as a result of such consultations, the IAEA 'may obtain access in agreement with the State to information or locations in addition to the access specified in para 76 above for ad hoc and routine inspections'. Any disagreement concerning the need for additional access is to be resolved in accordance with paras 21 and 22 of INFCIRC/153 (i.e. the provisions related to settlement of disputes), unless action by the State is 'essential and urgent', in which case para 18 applies. If the Board decides that that an action is 'essential and urgent', as provided for in para 18, the State is required to take that action 'without delay, irrespective of whether procedures for the settlement of a dispute have been invoked'.

[20]Article XII.C of the IAEA Statute requires the Director General to transmit to the Board of Governors reports of non-compliance. It provides further that the Board 'shall call upon the recipient State or States to remedy forthwith any non-compliance which it finds to have occurred. The Board shall report the non-compliance to all members of the Security Council and General Assembly of the United Nations … .'

[21]Indeed, there are numerous other provisions in INFCIRC/153 which demonstrate the drafters' clear intention that the Agency's right and obligation extends to nuclear material and activities that the State is *required* to declare, and not just to those which the State actually does declare. Paragraphs 7, 8, 11, 12, 13 and 18 all refer to 'nuclear material subject to safeguards', which was understood by the Committee to mean not simply that material which was being safeguarded but that which is required to be safeguarded. Myron Kratzer, the lead US negotiator participating in that Committee, notes in his negotiating history of INFCIRC/153, that the use of 'the more explicit and emphatic term "nuclear material required to be safeguarded" [including in para 19] was employed, with a recognition … that the meaning was perhaps clearer, but not different from that of "nuclear materials subject to safeguards"'. M. Kratzer, International Energy Associates Limited, 1984, Review of the Negotiating History of the IAEA Safeguards Document INFCIRC/153. Prepared for the US Arms Control and Disarmament Agency, Vol. I, http://cgs.pnnl.gov/fois/doclib/INFCIRC153Ch1-3.pdf, at p. 35.

As described in para 28 of INFCIRC/153, the objective of safeguards under such agreements is two-fold:

> The Agreement should provide that the objective of safeguards is the *timely detection of diversion* of significant quantities of nuclear material from peaceful nuclear activities to the manufacture of nuclear weapons or other nuclear explosive devices or for purposes unknown, and *deterrence of such diversion by the risk of early detection*. (Emphasis added.)

In the early days of the implementation of CSAs, this dual-pronged objective was pursued through the implementation of safeguards focused on the drawing of safeguards conclusions at the level of individual nuclear facilities, rather than looking at the State as a whole. Prescriptive quantitative criteria for achieving that objective at each type of nuclear facility were developed by the Secretariat with the aim of standardizing safeguards implementation and avoiding discrimination. While there were limited criteria related to the detection of undeclared production of nuclear material at declared facilities, there were no specific criteria developed for verifying that there was no undeclared nuclear material, or undeclared facilities or activities, elsewhere in a CSA State. The assumption was that indications of undeclared material, facilities or activities would likely be infrequent and would have to be handled on a case by case basis, most likely involving invocation of the provisions related to special inspections. Thus it was that the IAEA's routine verification activities were, as a practical matter—not a legal matter, primarily, not exclusively, focused on verifying declared nuclear material at declared nuclear facilities and other declared locations.[22]

With the discovery of Iraq's undeclared nuclear programme in 1991, it became clear that this facility level approach did not provide the necessary assurances about the non-diversion of nuclear material, whether declared or undeclared. What was needed was a new approach to the implementation of safeguards under CSAs that would permit the IAEA, pursuant to its obligation under para 2 of INFCIRC/153, 'to ensure that safeguards will be applied … on *all* source and special fissionable material', not just that which is declared. As later noted by Director General Blix in a report to the General Conference, the IAEA's safeguards system had, since its inception in 1970,

> evolved and been strengthened by the regular introduction of new methods and techniques, improving both its effectiveness and efficiency for detecting diversion of nuclear material placed under safeguards. The increasing importance of assurance regarding the absence of any nuclear activities and installations in States with comprehensive safeguards agreements [had] made it imperative to update the safeguards system by integrating into it measures that [would] give the Agency an improved capability of detecting clandestine nuclear activities if such exist.[23]

---

[22] In addition to nuclear material at facilities, the Agency also verifies nuclear material at locations outside facilities where such material is customarily used in amounts of one effective kilogramme or less (INFCIRC/153, paras 49–50), commonly referred to as 'LOFs', and defined as such in INFCIRC/540 (Corr.). What constitutes an 'effective kilogramme' depends on the type of nuclear material involved, and is calculated in accordance with INFCIRC/153, para 104.

[23] IAEA, 'Strengthening the Effectiveness and Improving the Efficiency of Agency Safeguards: Report by the Director General to the General Conference', GC(40)/17, 23 August 1996, para 1.

4.2.2 Programme 93 + 2 and the Model Additional Protocol

In December 1993, the IAEA Secretariat, at the request of the Board of Governors, embarked on an ambitious programme, known as Programme 93 + 2, to develop a comprehensive set of measures for strengthening safeguards.[24] The goal was to complete that task and report back to the Board before the 1995 NPT Review and Extension Conference to be convened in April 1995.

The Director General submitted his report to the Board in February 1995.[25] Following its consideration of the Director General's report at its March 1995 meeting, the Board, through an agreed chairman's summary of the Board's deliberations, endorsed the general direction of Programme 93 + 2 for a strengthened and cost-effective safeguards system and requested the Director General to submit a follow-up report in time for its June meeting. The Board also reiterated that:

> … the purpose of comprehensive safeguards agreements, where safeguards are applied to all nuclear material in all nuclear activities within the territory of a State party to such an agreement, under its jurisdiction or carried out under its control anywhere, is to verify that such material is not diverted to nuclear weapons or other nuclear explosive devices. To this end, the safeguards system for implementing comprehensive safeguards agreements *should be designed to provide for verification by the Agency of the correctness and completeness of States' declarations, so that there is credible assurance of the non-diversion of nuclear material from declared activities and of the absence of undeclared nuclear activities.*[26]

In May 1995, the Director General submitted the requested follow-up report.[27] The report described in greater detail the comprehensive set of measures, and distinguished those which could, in the Secretariat's view, be implemented under the IAEA's existing legal authority (the 'Part 1' measures[28]) from those which it

[24]IAEA, 'Strengthening the Effectiveness and Improving the Efficiency of Agency Safeguards: Report by the Director General to the General Conference', GC(39)/17, 22 August 1995, Annexes 1 and 4.

[25]GOV/2784, 21 February 1995, reproduced as Annex 1 to GC(39)17, 22 August 1995.

[26]GOV/OR.864, para 49 and GOV/OR.865, paras 1–54, reproduced in Annex 3 to GC(39)17, 22 August 1995. Assertions to the contrary notwithstanding, including those of the Russian Federation at the 2013 General Conference (GC(57)/COM.5/OR.7, para 55), the decision to accept the Chairman's summary was in fact taken by consensus of the entire Board—including the representative of the Philippines, who had simply asked that the record reflect that he would like to see all Agency safeguards strengthened, not just safeguards under CSAs. For a fuller description of the Board's discussion, see D. Albright, O. Heinonen and O. Kittrie, Understanding the IAEA's Mandate in Iran: Avoiding Misinterpretations. http://www.isis-online.org/uploads/isis-reports/documents/Misinterpreting_the_IAEA_27Nov2012.pdf.

[27]GOV/2807, 12 May 1995, reproduced as Annex 4 to GC(39)/17, 22 August 1995.

[28]Ibid., at Table 1. The Part 1 measures included, for example: the taking of environmental samples at any location to which the IAEA has access; improved analysis of information available to the IAEA about the State; the early provision of nuclear facility design information by the State to the IAEA; and the introduction of advanced safeguards technologies, such as the remote monitoring and transmission of safeguards equipment and data.

believed would be useful to implement under complementary legal authority (the 'Part 2' measures,[29] which subsequently served as the basis for the Model Additional Protocol.[30]

One the most significant Part 1 measures was a change in the way the IAEA would evaluate information available to it about a State. Instead of assessing the results of its verification activities separately for each individual facility in a State, the IAEA would visualize the State's nuclear programme in a coherent and connected way by looking at the State as a whole with a view to drawing conclusions regarding the non-diversion of declared nuclear material and the absence of undeclared nuclear material and activities.

At its meeting in June 1995, again through a chairman's summary, the Board took note of the Director General's plan to implement at an early date the measures described in Part 1, and urged States party to CSAs to cooperate with the Secretariat to facilitate such implementation.[31]

In September of that year, the General Conference adopted a resolution in which it requested the Director General: to continue to develop the measures proposed under Programme 93 + 2 'in order to bring about a more effective and efficient system covering all nuclear material in all peaceful nuclear activities within the territory of a State which has concluded a comprehensive safeguards agreement'; to make arrangements to implement the Part 1 measures at an early date; and to provide the Board of Governors as soon as possible with clear proposals for the measures proposed in Part 2.[32]

In May 1996, the Director General submitted a formal report to the Board for consideration at its meeting in June 1996.[33] Annex 3 of that report was a draft model protocol proposed by the Secretariat as the mechanism through which States with CSAs could grant the IAEA the additional authority to implement the Part 2 measures. The Board established an open-ended committee, Committee 24, tasked with drafting a model protocol based on that annex. The Committee completed its deliberations by April 1996 and submitted a draft text to the Board of Governors for its approval. In a special session convened in May 1997, the Board, through a chairman's summary, approved the text of the Model Additional Protocol and requested the Director General to use it as the standard for all additional protocols to comprehensive safeguards agreements.

The first additional protocol was brought into force by Australia in December 1997. As of June 2014, there were additional protocols in force for 118 States with comprehensive safeguards agreements.

---

[29]Ibid.

[30]IAEA, Model Protocol Additional to the Agreement(s) Between State(s) and the International Atomic Energy Agency for the Application of Safeguards, INFCIRC/540 (Corr.), September 1997.

[31]GOV/OR.872, paras 7–10.

[32]IAEA Doc. GC(39)/RES/17.

[33]IAEA Doc. GOV/2863, 'Proposals for Implementation under Complementary Legal Authority', 6 May 1996, reproduced as Annex 1 to GC(40)/17, 23 August 1996.

4.2.3 Drawing Safeguards Conclusions

In the first half of each year, the Secretariat prepares a Safeguards Implementation Report (SIR) on the implementation of safeguards during previous calendar year. The report is then submitted to the Board of Governors for consideration at its June meeting. In what is now referred to as the 'Safeguards Statement' of the SIR, the Director General summarizes the safeguards findings and the conclusions that the IAEA has been able to draw, by type of agreement, for States with a safeguards agreement in force.[34] The findings and conclusions are based upon an evaluation of all information available to the IAEA in exercising is safeguards obligations for that year.

In the case of States with CSAs, the IAEA presents its conclusions as follows:

- For States which have both a CSA and an AP in force:
  - For those in which the Secretariat found no indication of the diversion of declared nuclear material from peaceful nuclear activities and no indication of undeclared nuclear material or activities, the Secretariat concludes that "all nuclear material remained in peaceful activities". This is commonly referred to as the "broader conclusion".
  - For those in which the Secretariat found no indication of the diversion of declared nuclear material from peaceful nuclear activities, but for which evaluations regarding the absence of undeclared nuclear material and activities remain ongoing, the Secretariat's conclusion is limited to confirming that the declared nuclear material remained in peaceful activities.
- For States which have a CSA in force, but no AP:
  - If the Secretariat has found no indication of the diversion of declared nuclear material from peaceful nuclear activities, the Secretariat's conclusion is likewise limited to confirming that the declared nuclear material remained in peaceful activities.

The Board routinely releases to the public the Safeguards Statement and the section immediately following the Safeguards Statement, which provides background information in connection with the Safeguards Statement.[35]

As described in the background to the Safeguards Statement, although the Agency has the authority under a CSA to verify the peaceful use of all nuclear material in a State (i.e. the correctness and completeness of the State's declarations), the tools available to the Agency under such an agreement are limited. As

[34]Conclusions are provided for States with CSAs, for States with voluntary offer agreements (the five nuclear-weapon States party to the NPT) and for States with item-specific safeguards agreements (India, Israel and Pakistan).

[35]The executive summaries containing the 'Safeguards Statement', and the background to them, are released to the public, although the detailed remainder of the SIRS are not. See, for example, the Safeguards Statement for 2013, available at http://www.iaea.org/safeguards/documents/Statement_for_SIR_2013_GOV_2014_27.pdf.

further explained in that section, the Model Additional Protocol equips the Agency with important supplementary tools that provide broader access to information and locations. The measures provided for under an additional protocol thus significantly increase the Agency's ability to verify the peaceful use of all nuclear material in a State with a CSA.

As further noted in the background, in the course of its evaluation for States with a CSA and no AP, the IAEA also seeks to determine whether there is any indication of undeclared nuclear material or activities in the State which would need to be reflected in the Safeguards Statement. However, without the measures provided for in the Model Additional Protocol being implemented, the Agency is not able to provide credible assurance of the absence of undeclared nuclear material and activities for the State as a whole.

Thus, although the IAEA does in fact review all of the information available to it for indications of undeclared nuclear material and activities in all CSA States, it will not extend on behalf of the State any assurance about the absence of such material and activities unless the State also has an additional protocol in force, or is implementing it provisionally.

4.3 Treaty Interpretation

The conventions applicable to a discussion of treaty interpretation in this context are the Vienna Convention on the Law of Treaties between States[36] and the Vienna Convention on the Law of Treaties between States and International Organizations or between International Organizations.[37] These treaties are generally recognized as codifying the customary international law governing the law of treaties as it applies to treaties to between States and to treaties to which both States and international organizations are party. It bears noting that, while the 1986 treaty is not in force, the IAEA gave its consent to be bound by its provisions by depositing an instrument of accession in 2001 and will thus be a party to the Convention once it enters into force.[38] Insofar as the relevant provisions of both Conventions are substantively identical, for ease of reference, they will collectively be referred to in this chapter as 'the VCLTs'.

Article 31 of the VCLTs provides the key 'General rule of interpretation':

1. A treaty shall be interpreted in good faith in accordance with the ordinary meaning to be given to the terms of the treaty in their context and in the light of its object and purpose.

---

[36]Vienna Convention on the Law of Treaties (23 May 1969), 1155 UNTS 331.

[37]Vienna Convention on the Law of Treaties between States and International Organizations or between International Organizations (21 March 1986), Doc. A/CONF.129/15.

[38]The 1986 Convention requires 35 States to express consent to be bound in order for its entry into force; as of this writing, four more accessions/ratifications by States are necessary in order to reach that number.

2. The context for the purpose of the interpretation of a treaty shall comprise, in addition to the text, including its preamble and annexes:
   (a) Any agreement relating to the treaty which was made between all the parties in [connection] with the conclusion of the treaty;
   (b) Any instrument which was made by one or more parties in [connection] with the conclusion of the treaty and accepted by the other parties as an instrument related to the treaty.
3. There shall be taken into account, together with the context:
   (a) Any subsequent agreement between the parties regarding the interpretation of the treaty or the application of its provisions;
   (b) Any subsequent practice in the application of the treaty which establishes the agreement of the parties regarding its interpretation;
   (c) Any relevant rules of international law applicable in the relations between the parties.
4. A special meaning shall be given to a term if it is established that the parties so intended.

Article 32 of the VCLTs provides for 'supplementary means of interpretation' as follows:

> Recourse may be had to supplementary means of interpretation, including the preparatory work of the treaty and the circumstances of its conclusion, in order to confirm the meaning resulting from the application of Article 31, or to determine the meaning when the interpretation according to Article 31: (a) leaves the meaning ambiguous or obscure; (b) leads to a result which is manifestly absurd or unreasonable.

4.3.1 The NPT

Comprehensive safeguards agreements are implementing, supplementary agreements of the NPT. All NPT NNWS safeguards obligations flow from the basic obligations contained in the NPT. The basic obligations of NNWSs under the NPT are as follows:

> Article II. Each non-nuclear-weapon State Party to the Treaty undertakes not to receive the transfer from any transferor whatsoever of nuclear weapons or other nuclear explosive devices or of control over such weapons or explosive devices directly, or indirectly; not to manufacture or otherwise acquire nuclear weapons or other nuclear explosive devices; and not to seek or receive any assistance in the manufacture of nuclear weapons or other nuclear explosive devices.

> Article III.1. Each non-nuclear-weapon State Party to the Treaty undertakes to accept safeguards, as set forth in an agreement to be negotiated and concluded with the International Atomic Energy Agency in accordance with the Statute of the International Atomic Energy Agency and the Agency's safeguards system, for the exclusive purpose of verification of the fulfilment of its obligations assumed under this Treaty with a view to preventing diversion

of nuclear energy from peaceful uses to nuclear weapons or other nuclear explosive devices. Procedures for the safeguards required by this Article shall be followed with respect to source or special fissionable material whether it is being produced, processed or used in any principal nuclear facility or is outside any such facility. The safeguards required by this Article shall be applied on all source or special fissionable material in all peaceful nuclear activities within the territory of such State, under its jurisdiction, or carried out under its control anywhere.

As is clear from the above, in Article III.1, NNWSs agree to accept safeguards to verify the fulfilment of the obligations they have assumed under Article II. Those safeguards are to be set forth in an agreement concluded with the IAEA in accordance with its Statute. What are those obligations? They are:

(a) Not to receive the transfer from any transferor whatsoever of nuclear weapons or other nuclear explosive devices or of control over such weapons or explosive devices directly, or indirectly;
(b) Not to manufacture or otherwise acquire nuclear weapons or other nuclear explosive devices; and
(c) Not to seek or receive any assistance in the manufacture of nuclear weapons or other explosive devices.

Article III.1 also requires that each NNWS accept safeguards, as set forth in an agreement with the IAEA in accordance with the latter's Statute and its safeguards system. It specifies that the exclusive purpose of such agreements is the verification of the fulfilment of the obligations assumed under the NPT 'with a view to preventing the diversion of nuclear energy from peaceful uses to nuclear weapons or other nuclear explosive devices'. The NPT further specifies that the procedures for the required safeguards be followed with respect to 'source or fissionable material whether it is being produced, processed or used in *any* principal nuclear facility *or* outside any such facility' (emphasis added). It is thus clear that safeguards are to be applied to such material produced, processed or used anywhere in the State.

This conclusion is spelled out in the final sentence of para 1 of Article III, which provides that the required safeguards 'shall be applied on *all* source or fissionable material in *all* peaceful nuclear activities within the territory of such State, under its jurisdiction, or carried out under its control anywhere' (emphasis added).

The question has been raised as to whether the core NPT obligation of NNWSs to use nuclear material only for peaceful purposes (i.e. not for nuclear weapons or other nuclear explosive devices) necessarily means that the safeguards system and the agreements established to implement Article III of the NPT may—or perhaps must—include the means to verify—to the extent one can verify a negative—that there are no clandestine activities in violation of the core obligation.[39] The answer

[39]The testimony of William Foster, the Director of the US Arms Control and Disarmament Agency, before the Senate Foreign Relations Committee in July 1968 has been cited as evidence to the contrary. In response to a question as to whether IAEA inspection would be restricted only to declared peaceful nuclear facilities or whether it would also apply to undeclared or clandestine facilities, Foster is quoted as saying "The IAEA inspection would only be as to declared". In response to a further question by a Senator as to whether there would be provision for "searching out the clandestine" under the treaty, he replied in the negative. Hearings on Non-Proliferation Treaty before the Committee on Foreign Relations of the Senate, 90th Congress, 2nd Sess., p. 52

to that question—as to how the IAEA was to ensure that its safeguards system would be able to accomplish the task assigned to it by the NPT Parties, and what was to be included in the safeguards agreement between the IAEA and each NNWS—was left to the IAEA and its governing bodies to determine.

A specious argument could be made that, since any clandestine activities would most likely not be 'peaceful nuclear activities', those need not be safeguarded. But that would be manifestly absurd and unreasonable in light of the object and purpose of the NPT itself. By becoming a party to the NPT, a NNWS has promised not to receive, manufacture, develop or otherwise acquire a nuclear weapon and, to that end, to place under IAEA safeguards all nuclear material in activities carried out on its territory (or under its jurisdiction or control) so that the IAEA is able to verify that it is only being used for peaceful purposes and has not been diverted to a nuclear weapon or other nuclear explosive purpose.

As indicated above, Article 32 of both VCLTs on 'supplementary means of interpretation' only comes into play if there is a need to need to confirm the meaning resulting from the application of Article 31, or to determine the meaning when the interpretation according to that article leaves the meaning ambiguous or obscure or leads to a result which is manifestly absurd or unreasonable. It is submitted that there is no need for supplementary means to interpret the meaning of the NPT. It is clear from the ordinary meaning to be given to the terms of the NPT in their context and in the light of its object and purpose that all source or special fissionable material within the territory of a NNWS[40] is required to be made subject to IAEA safeguards. It is difficult to imagine an argument that the word 'all' does not mean 'all'—whether publicized, proclaimed, admitted, hidden or secret (or, in later parlance, whether 'declared' or 'undeclared'). And there is no indication that the drafters of the NPT intended to give a special meaning to the word 'all'.

This unambiguous meaning is also confirmed when applying para 3 of Article 31: taking into account (a) subsequent agreements between the parties regarding the interpretation of the NPT or the application of its provisions and (b) subsequent practice in the application of the treaty which establishes the agreement of the parties regarding its interpretation. How are such subsequent agreements, or subsequent practice establishing the agreement, of the States Party to the NPT determined? The answer is found in the documents emanating from the 5-year review conferences of the NPT States Parties convened under Article VIII(3) of the NPT, inter alia, to review the operation of the treaty with a view to assuring that the purposes of the Preamble and the provisions of the Treaty are being realized.

Footnote 39 (continued)

(1968). However, his testimony predated the IAEA's development of INFCIRC/153 and the comprehensive safeguards system and was based on his assessment of safeguards as they were implemented in 1968—on declared nuclear material and facilities. Moreover, Foster confirmed that, if there were undeclared facilities, this would be a breach of the NPT.

[40]Or in peaceful nuclear activities carried out under its jurisdiction and control anywhere. NPT, Article III.1.

4.3.1.1 Subsequent Agreement and Subsequent Practice: NPT Review Conferences

Since the entry into force of the NPT, there have been eight Review Conferences as of the time of this writing, with the ninth to be held in New York in April/May 2015. The States Parties have adopted final documents and/or decisions at the first, third, fifth, sixth and eighth conferences, as described below.

At the conclusion of the first Review Conference in 1975, the States Parties adopted a Final Declaration by consensus (e.g., with the agreement of all States Parties).[41] In the preamble to that Final Declaration, the States recognized 'that the accelerated spread and development of peaceful applications of nuclear energy will, in the absence of effective safeguards, contribute to further proliferation of nuclear explosive capability' and 'the continuing necessity of full cooperation in the application and *improvement* of [IAEA] safeguards on peaceful nuclear activities' (emphasis added). The States Parties declared with respect to their review of Article III that '[t]he Conference recommends that more attention and fuller support be given to the *improvement of safeguards techniques, instrumentation, data-handling and implementation* in order, among other things to ensure optimum cost-effectiveness' (emphasis added).

It is thus clear that the States Parties saw safeguards not as a static, rigid system, but rather one constantly subject to improvement, particularly in technical areas. Therefore, it would be only logical that the agreements concluded for the application of such safeguards should allow for improvements in technology and implementation. And they do, as described below.

At the third Review Conference in 1985, the States Parties adopted, again by consensus, a Final Declaration that included a review of Article III and preambular paras 4 and 5 of the NPT.[42] In that review, the Conference expressed 'the conviction that IAEA safeguards provide assurance that States are complying with their undertakings and assist States in demonstrating this compliance'. It furthermore stated that '*[u]nsafeguarded nuclear activities* in non-nuclear-weapon States pose serious proliferation dangers' (emphasis added). The Conference noted with satisfaction that the IAEA, in carrying out its safeguards activities had not detected 'any diversion of a significant amount of safeguarded material to the production of nuclear weapons, other nuclear explosive devices or to purposes unknown'. No mention is made of 'declared'; rather the emphasis is on all material being safeguarded and none being diverted. There is a clear assumption that 'unsafeguarded nuclear activities' were appropriately within the purview of the Parties' attention.

---

[41]NPT/CONF/35/I, Review Conference of the Parties to the Treaty: Final Document, https://unoda-web.s3.amazonaws.com/wp-content/uploads/assets/WMD/Nuclear/pdf/finaldocs/1975%20-%20Geneva%20-%20NPT%20Review%20Conference%20-%20Final%20Document%20Part%20I.pdf.

[42]NPT/CONF.III/64/I, Review Conference of the Parties to the Treaty on the non-proliferation of nuclear weapons, https://unoda-web.s3.amazonaws.com/wp-content/uploads/assets/WMD/Nuclear/pdf/finaldocs/1985%20-%20Geneva%20-%20NPT%20Review%20Conference%20-%20Final%20Document%20Part%20I.pdf.

In addition, the third Review Conference in its review of Article III noted with satisfaction the improvement of IAEA safeguards and emphasized the importance of

> continued improvements in the effectiveness and efficiency of IAEA safeguards, for example, but not limited to: ... (b) The expeditious implementation of new instruments and techniques; (c) The further development of methods for evaluation of safeguards effectiveness in combination with safeguards information; [and] (d) Continued increases in the efficiency of the use of human and financial resources and of equipment. (emphasis added).

Again, the States Parties demonstrated a clear agreement that technological advances should be incorporated in the safeguards system and that safeguards should not be static and implemented rigidly, but rather constantly improved.

The fifth NPT Review Conference in 1995 was convened within just 1 month after the Board of Governors had met to discuss strengthening the effectiveness and improving the efficiency of safeguards in March. While the Conference was unable to adopt a final declaration on the review of the operation of the Treaty, it did adopt, without a vote (no State party requested a vote, implying non-objection to the texts), one resolution[43] and three decisions, Decision 2 of which on 'Principles and objectives for nuclear non-proliferation and disarmament' is highly relevant to the issue at hand.[44] By that Decision, the Conference of States Parties to the NPT affirmed 'the need to continue to move with determination towards the full realization and effective implementation of the provisions of the Treaty', and accordingly adopted principles and objectives regarding, inter alia, safeguards, which included the following:

> 9. The International Atomic Energy is the competent authority responsible to verify and assure, in accordance with the Statute of the Agency and the Agency's safeguards system, compliance with its safeguards agreements with States parties undertaken in fulfillment of their obligations under Article III, paragraph 1, of the Treaty, with a view to preventing diversion of nuclear energy from peaceful uses to nuclear weapons or other nuclear explosive devices. ... States parties that have *concerns regarding non-compliance* with the safeguards agreements of the Treaty by States parties should direct such concerns, along with supporting evidence and information, to the Agency to consider, investigate, draw conclusions and decide on necessary actions in accordance with its mandate....
>
> 11. International Atomic Energy Agency safeguards should be regularly assessed and evaluated. Decisions adopted by the Board of Governors aimed at further strengthening the effectiveness of Agency safeguards should be supported and implemented and the Agency's *capability to detect undeclared nuclear activities should be increased. ...* (emphasis added).

For the first time in a decision concerning safeguards, the Conference of States Parties used the term 'undeclared nuclear activities', but not in any sense that it was a new objective or concept. Quite the contrary: it stated that the IAEA's capability to detect such undeclared activities 'should be increased'; not created, established,

---

[43]Resolution on the Middle East, http://www.un.org/disarmament/WMD/Nuclear/1995-NPT/pdf/Resolution_MiddleEast.pdf.

[44]Reproduced at http://www.un.org/disarmament/WMD/uclear/1995-NPT/pdf/1995-NY-NPTReviewConference-FinalDocumentDecision_2.pdf.

studied or considered, but rather *increased* from what it was then. There can be no doubt from the plain and ordinary meaning of the terms that the States Parties were of the view that the objective of IAEA safeguards included detection of undeclared nuclear activities; what was needed, the Parties agreed, was an increased capability to detect such prohibited activities. Having adopted that view without a vote, it can confidently be concluded that the parties to the NPT have, pursuant to Article 31 of the Vienna Convention, subsequently agreed that the application of the provisions of the Treaty regarding safeguards includes coverage of undeclared nuclear activities. That subsequent agreement can be seen as a confirmation of their understanding of the plain and ordinary meaning of the terms of Article III.1 as well.

This position of the States Parties was reinforced at the next, sixth Review Conference in 2000 which adopted, by consensus, a Final Document which included the following of relevance.[45] In Part I, entitled 'Review of the operation of the Treaty, taking into account the decisions and the resolution adopted by the 1995 Review and Extension Conference', in the section concerning Article III, the Conference reiterated some of the language from previously agreed documents, but included the following new statements of relevance:

> 14. The Conference notes with concern that IAEA continues to be unable to verify the *correctness and completeness* of the initial declaration of nuclear material made by the Democratic People's Republic of Korea, and is therefore unable to conclude that there has been no diversion of nuclear material in that country ….
>
> 17. The Conference reaffirms that the implementation of comprehensive safeguards agreements pursuant to Article III, paragraph 1, of the Treaty should be designed to provide for verification by IAEA of the correctness and completeness of a State's declaration so that there is a credible assurance of the non-diversion of nuclear material from declared activities and of the *absence of undeclared nuclear material and activities*.
>
> 18. The Conference notes the measures endorsed by the IAEA Board of Governors in June 1995 for strengthening and making more efficient the safeguards system, and notes also that *these measures are being implemented pursuant to existing legal authority conferred upon IAEA by comprehensive safeguards agreements* ….
>
> 20. The Conference recognizes that comprehensive safeguards agreements based on document INFCIRC/153 have been successful in their main focus of providing assurance regarding declared nuclear material and have also provided *a limited level of assurance regarding the absence of undeclared nuclear material and activities*." (emphasis added)

Thus, the States Parties confirmed that the safeguards system envisaged in Article III.1 of the NPT, and the IAEA's comprehensive safeguards agreements based on that Treaty, were to cover undeclared nuclear material and activities, but recognized that such agreements had only provided a limited level of assurance regarding the absence of such material and activities. Legally, the authority was there; it was simply a question of how to exercise that authority and implement the intent of the Parties. Again, the Parties not only established their subsequent agreement regarding their interpretation of the Treaty and the application of its

[45]NPT/CONF.2000/28 (Parts I and II), http://daccess-dds-ny.un.org/doc/UNDOC/GEN/N00/453/64/PDF/N0045364.pdf?OpenElement.

provisions, but also confirmed their practice in the application of the Treaty which established their agreement regarding its interpretation.

The eighth Review Conference in 2010 did not adopt a section on its review of the operation of the Treaty. Instead, it rather took note of a document on that topic which the President of the Conference had drafted reflecting, to the best of his knowledge, what had transpired at the Conference with regard to matters under review. In that review, it was noted that:

> 17. The Conference recognizes that comprehensive safeguards agreements based on IAEA document INFCIRC/153 (Corrected) have been successful in their *main focus* of providing assurance regarding declared nuclear material and *have also provided a limited level of assurance regarding the absence of undeclared nuclear material and activities*. The Conference notes that the implementation of measures specified in the model additional protocol provides, in an effective and efficient manner, *increased* confidence about the absence of undeclared nuclear material and activities in a State as a whole. The Conference notes that numerous States were of the view that those measures have been introduced as an integral part of the IAEA safeguards system. The Conference also notes that it is the sovereign decision of any State to conclude an additional protocol, but once in force, the additional protocol is a legal obligation.[46]

The Conference also adopted 'Conclusions and recommendations for follow-on actions' by which it recalled and reaffirmed Decision 2 of the 1995 Review Conference, noting the elements relevant to Article III of the Treaty, in particular paras 9–13 of Decision 2. Paragraphs 9 and 11 are directly relevant and are quoted above. It should be recalled that para 11 of the 1995 document includes the statement that '... the Agency's capability to detect undeclared nuclear activities should be increased', which was recalled and reaffirmed in 2010.

The declarations, decisions and documents adopted over the years by the States Parties to the NPT make clear their interpretation as to the meaning of Article III.1, and their understanding of what IAEA safeguards should cover: verification of the non-diversion of declared nuclear material and the detection of undeclared nuclear material and activities. This is clear not only from the ordinary meaning of the text of the Treaty but also from the decisions of the Parties to the Treaty that establish their agreement as to how the Treaty is to be applied and interpreted in law and practice.

If Parties have changed their positions and no longer agree with prior understandings, they are of course always free to make proposals at the next Review Conference to try to get the Parties to change their positions as well.

4.3.2 INFCIRC/153 and Comprehensive Safeguards Agreements

Just as for the NPT, the ordinary meaning of the terms of INFCIRC/153 and the CSAs concluded by the IAEA on the basis of that document must be interpreted in their context and in the light of the object and purpose of those instruments.

[46]2010 Review Conference of the Parties to the Treaty on the Non-Proliferation of Nuclear Weapons, Final Document, reproduced at http://www.un.org/ga/search/view_doc.asp?symbol=NPT/CONF.2010/50%20(VOL.I).

As indicated above, it was the clear intent of the States Parties to the NPT that the safeguards agreements required to be concluded with the IAEA would be the implementing technical agreements for Article III.1 of the NPT and the means by which the fulfilment of the NNWSs' obligations assumed under the NPT would be verified, leaving it for the IAEA to determine what needed to be included in such agreements.

That CSAs are intended as the implementing instruments for the NPT is reflected in the title of INFCIRC/153. In addition, paras 1 and 2 of INFCIRC/153, which relate to the basic undertaking of the State and the IAEA's right and obligation in the implementation of safeguards, respectively, use language directly derived from Article III.1 of the NPT, i.e. that safeguards 'shall be applied on all source or special fissionable material in all peaceful nuclear activities within the territory of such State, under its jurisdiction, or carried out under its control anywhere'. For the reasons cited above, the language of that article must be understood as entrusting the IAEA with verifying that no nuclear material of the State—whether declared or undeclared—is use for prohibited purposes.

It follows, therefore, that the ordinary meaning of the terms of INFCIRC/153, and the CSAs concluded by the IAEA on the basis of that document, in their context and in the light of their object and purpose, must likewise be interpreted as meaning that IAEA safeguards under those agreements were intended to provide for verification of the non–misuse of any nuclear material of a State, whether declared or undeclared. If anything, the text of INFCIRC/153 makes even clearer that agreements based on that document provide for IAEA verification of the correctness and completeness of States' declarations.

Why then the need for the Model Additional Protocol and additional protocols to comprehensive safeguards agreements? As foreseen in the various reports on Programme 93 + 2, the measures of the Model Additional Protocol were never intended to be simply superimposed as a new layer of activity on top of safeguards as implemented under INFCIRC/153 and the earlier strengthening measures.[47] The expectation was that the measures proposed under Programme 93 + 2 (Parts 1 and 2), taken together, would provide the Agency with a new kind of 'observational vantage point'—a more complete picture of the State's nuclear programme—which would enhance the ability of the Agency to draw the necessary safeguards conclusions regarding the correctness and completeness of States' declarations.

The issue was raised by the Representative of Saudi Arabia during the 2014 meeting of the General Conference. He noted that, if the IAEA had the right to verify the correctness and completeness of a State's declarations under the comprehensive safeguards agreement, he did not see what purpose was served by the Model Additional Protocol. In response thereto, the Legal Officer for the Committee of the Whole stated that:

---

[47]Part II, Section D of GOV/2807, 12 May 1995, reproduced as Annex 4 to GC(39)/17, 22 August 1995.

> [P]ursuant to paragraph 2 of the document INFCIRC/153, Member States had invested in the Agency the right and obligation to ensure that all source and special fissionable material was placed under safeguards under a comprehensive safeguards agreement. The purpose of additional protocols based on the Model Additional Protocol … was to provide the Agency with additional tools for doing that more efficiently and effectively on a more routine basis. The fundament right and obligation of the Agency to verify the correctness and completeness of a State's declarations under a comprehensive safeguards agreement unequivocally derived from paragraph 2 of document INFCIRC/153.[48]

As further noted by the Representative of Spain, 'it was not necessary to consider the legal status of the Board's decision taken in 1995 because … the legal basis for the Agency's verifying correctness and completeness of a State's declarations was Article 2 of the Comprehensive safeguards agreement with that State and did not derive from any type of Board decision taken in 1995. An additional protocol "simply made it easier for the Agency to achieve its verification objective'.[49]

The IAEA has never asserted that its right—and obligation—to verify the correctness and completeness of States' declarations under CSAs derive from the decisions taken by its policy-making organs post-1990. Those decisions have only been cited as affirmations of that right and obligation. Notwithstanding, there is adequate evidence from which to conclude that those decisions, and the consistent practice of the IAEA in implementing CSAs on that basis since the early 1990s, could be interpreted as reflecting 'subsequent agreement between the parties regarding the interpretation of the treaty or the application of its provisions' and 'subsequent practice in the application of the treaty which establishes the agreement of the parties regarding its interpretation', as contemplated in Article 31 of the VCLTs.

4.3.2.1 Subsequent Agreement

Well before Programme 93 + 2 was initiated or the Model Additional Protocol even contemplated, the Board of Governors and the General Conference took a number of decisions confirming that the IAEA had not just the right but the obligation to verify that all nuclear material required to be safeguarded under a comprehensive safeguards agreement was in fact under safeguards. These decisions addressed a range of countries and issues.

- *Iraq*: In July 1991, the 35-member Board of Governors adopted a resolution in which it found that Iraq's failure to declare nuclear material and facilities constituted non-compliance with its CSA, and requested the Director General to report the matter to the IAEA Member States, and to the United Nations

[48]GC(57)/COM.5/OR.7, at paras 47 and 48.

[49]Ibid., at para 52.

Security Council and General Assembly.[50] In September 1991, the Board, through the mechanism of a chairman's summary of the Board's deliberations, took note of Iraq's further non-compliance and requested the Director General to report again to the Security Council.[51] Immediately following that Board meeting, the General Conference of the entire membership of the IAEA also adopted a resolution in which it, *inter alia*, supported the actions taken by the Board of Governors and strongly condemned Iraq's non-compliance with its nuclear non-proliferation obligations, including its safeguards agreement with the IAEA.[52]

- *South Africa*: In September 1991, IAEA Member States, in resolutions adopted by the Board[53] and the General Conference,[54] requested the Director General to verify the correctness and completeness of the inventory of South Africa's nuclear installations and material' under its newly approved comprehensive safeguards agreement. In her introduction of the resolution to the Board of Governors, the representative of Egypt, speaking on behalf of the African Group stated that:

> ... pleased as they were that South Africa had acceded to the NPT, the African delegations on the Board had *grounds for concern* .... In order not to make a mockery of the safeguards system in the future, especially as the situation at issue was unique and *there was some doubt about South Africa's military nuclear capability*, the sponsors of the draft resolution before the Board wanted the DG, the Agency and all Member States, including South Africa, to help ensure that the inventory established for South Africa was complete. (Emphasis added.)

- *Special inspections*: In February 1992, the Board, acting through a chairman's summary, reaffirmed the IAEA's right under comprehensive safeguards

---

[50]IAEA Doc. GOV/2532, 18 July 1991; the draft resolution was submitted by China, France, the USSR, the United Kingdom and the United States, and co-sponsored by 12 other States. A decision was taken by a vote, with 29 in favour, one against (Iraq) and three abstentions (Cuba, Nigeria, and Tunisia). As noted in the Director General's opening remarks to the Board at that meeting, '[t]he rationale of the safeguards system was to create confidence about the peaceful purpose of nuclear activities by ensuring that they were openly declared to the IAEA and inspected by the Agency. The large enrichment programme in Iraq had been clandestine, it had not been placed under safeguards, and there could be no confidence that it had peaceful purposes'. (GOV/OR.758, para 12, reproduced in GC(XXXV)/978, 16 September 1991, Attachment 8).

[51]GOV/OR.763, paras 47–53, reproduced in GC(XXXV)/978/Add.1,16 September 1991.

[52]GC(XXXV)/RES/568 (20 September 1991); GC(XXXV)/OR.341, paras 77–79. The vote on the draft resolution, which was submitted by 14 States (including the UK, the US and the USSR) and co-sponsored by 21 States, was 71 in favour, 1 against (Iraq), and 7 abstentions (Algeria, Cuba, Jordan, Libya, Morocco, Namibia and Sudan).

[53]IAEA, 'Safeguards: Draft Resolution Submitted by Egypt, Morocco, Nigeria and Tunisia on Behalf of the Africa Group', GOV/2547/Rev.1, 11 September 1991.

[54]IAEA, 'South Africa's Nuclear Capabilities', GC(XXXV)/RES/567, September 1991. The draft resolution, submitted by Zaire on behalf of the African Group, was adopted by consensus (i.e. without a vote).

agreements to ensure that all nuclear material in all peaceful nuclear activities is under safeguards.[55] The discussion was centred on a paper submitted to the Board of Governors by the Secretariat on the use of special inspections. In the agreed summary, the Board urged the full exercise of all of the IAEA's rights and obligations under the Statute and comprehensive safeguards agreements, reaffirmed the IAEA's right to undertake special inspections to "ensure that all nuclear materials in all peaceful nuclear activities are under safeguards", and reaffirmed the IAEA's rights to obtain and have access to additional information and locations in accordance with the Statutes and comprehensive safeguards agreements.[56]

- *Romania*: In June 1992, the Board, again acting through a chairman's summary, took note of Director General Hans Blix's report on non-compliance by the former regime in Romania with certain provisions of its comprehensive safeguards agreement which had been brought to the IAEA's attention by the successor Romanian Government, and requested that the Director General report the non-compliance to the UN Security Council 'for information purposes'.[57]
- *Strengthening safeguards*: In September 1992, the General Conference adopted a resolution in which it noted the 'decisions taken by the Board over the preceding 12 months to strengthen the safeguards system' and called upon Member States to cooperate with the IAEA in implementing those decisions.[58]
- *DPRK*: In February 1993, Director General Blix submitted a report to the Board informing it of an anomaly the Secretariat had discovered in the Democratic People's Republic of Korea (the DPRK), and that the anomaly had given rise to doubts about the completeness of the country's initial report of nuclear material under its comprehensive safeguards agreement.[59] Based on the Director General's report and a detailed Secretariat briefing, the Board adopted a resolution in which it stressed that it was 'essential to verify the correctness and assess the completeness' of North Korea's initial report. The Board also decided that the access to additional information and locations requested by the Director General pursuant to the provisions related to special inspections was 'essential

[55]IAEA, 'Record of GOV/OR Meeting 776', GOV/OR.776, February 25, 1992, paras 48, 83, and 84. As reported by the Chairman, consensus had been reached on the text of the conclusion agreed upon in informal discussions, GOV/OR.776, paras 48, 83 and 84 (25 February 1992).

[56]IAEA, Record of GOV/OR Meeting 776, February 1992, paras 48, 83–84; GOV/2554, 12 November 1991.

[57]IAEA, Record of GOV/OR Meeting 783, GOV/OR.783, June 17, 1992, paras 90–93.

[58]IAEA, 'Strengthening of the Safeguards System', GC(XXXVI)/RES/586, October 1992.

[59]The DPRK's CSA, reproduced in IAEA document INFCIRC/403, May 1992, was approved by the Board of Governors on 12 September 1991, signed on 30 January 1992 and came into force on 10 April 1992.

and urgent in order to resolve differences and to ensure verification of compliance' by North Korea with its comprehensive safeguards agreement.[60] In April 1993, the Board adopted a further resolution in which it found the DPRK to be in non-compliance for having failed to grant the required access; it also found that the IAEA was unable to verify the non-diversion of nuclear material, and decided to report both findings to the United Nations Security Council.[61] Following the Board's adoption of yet another resolution on the DPRK in September 1993, the General Conference at its meeting the following week, adopted a resolution, co-sponsored by 48 Member States, in which it strongly endorsed the actions taken in this regard by the Board.[62]

Again, each of these decisions was taken long before the idea of additional legal authority was contemplated.

The policy-making organs have taken other decisions over the years since then which further confirm the collective interpretation of INFCIRC/153 and the CSAs concluded, on the basis of that document.

In connection with Programme 93 + 2, the Board of Governors approved, by consensus, the Chairman's summary in March 1995 in which he stated the following

> The Board reiterates that the purpose of comprehensive safeguards agreements, where safeguards are applied to all nuclear material in all nuclear activities within the territory of a State party to such an agreement, under its jurisdiction or carried out under its control anywhere, is to verify that such material is not diverted to nuclear weapons or other nuclear explosive devices. To this end, the safeguards system for implementing comprehensive safeguards agreements should be designed to provide for verification by the Agency of the correctness and completeness of States' declarations, so that there is credible assurance of the non-diversion of nuclear material from declared activities and of the absence of undeclared nuclear activities.[63]

[60]IAEA Board of Governors, Report on the Implementation of the Agreement Between the Agency and the Democratic People's Republic of Korea for the Application of Safeguards in Connection With the Treaty on the Non-Proliferation of Nuclear Weapons, GOV/2636, February 26, 1993. The draft resolution, co-sponsored by 28 members of the 35-member Board of Governors, was adopted without a vote. The Director General's report and the official records of the Board's discussion, which was held in closed session, have not been publicly released by the IAEA.

[61]GOV/2645, 1 April 1993; the draft resolution (GOV/2644) was submitted by 21 States (including the Russian Federation, the UK and the US), and was adopted by a vote of 28 in favour, 2 against (China, Libya) and 4 abstentions (India, Pakistan, Syria and Vietnam).

[62]GC(XXXVII)/RES/624, 1 October 1993; GC(XXXVII)/OR. 361, paras 49–159. The draft resolution was co-sponsored by 48 Member States and adopted by a vote of 72 in favour, 2 against (DPRK and Libya) and 11 abstentions (Bangladesh, China, Cuba, India, Iran, Namibia, Pakistan, Syria, Tanzania, Vietnam and Zimbabwe).

[63]GOV/OR.864, para 49, and GOV/OR.865, paras 2, 63 and 71, and reproduced in GC(39)/17, Annex 3, at pp. 55, 63 and 71.

The Chairman's summary also noted that 'the Board endorses the general direction of Programme 93 + 2 for a strengthened and cost-effective safeguards system'.

Much has been made by some academics of the Director General's recommendation in para 110.A and B of GOV/2784, the 21 February 1995 report to the Board on strengthening safeguards, that the Board confirm that the purpose of comprehensive safeguards agreements was the continuing verification of the correctness and completeness of States' declarations, and that the safeguards system of the IAEA should be so designed as to give effect to that purpose, suggesting that had the authority been clear, there would have been no need to seek such confirmation.

The proponents of that question might refer to the Director General's response to comments made during the Board's deliberations in March 1995, in which he stated that:

> 51. Given the experience of recent years, in which the Board had been closely involved, it should not be surprising that a major aim of Programme 93 + 2 was to *strengthen the ability of Agency safeguards to verify the completeness and correctness of declarations of countries' nuclear inventories*. After the events in Iraq there could be no excuse for not realizing how necessary that was, and he hoped the Board would convey that message to the NPT Review and Extension Conference.
>
> 52. Document *INFCIRC/153 fully justified efforts to verify that no nuclear material had been diverted from non-declared installations, for it stated that all nuclear material was subject to safeguards, whether it had been declared or not*, and the Agency could carry out such verification only if it could confirm that countries' declarations were correct and complete—that nothing had been forgotten or hidden.[64] (Emphasis added.)

Much has also been made of the reservations that were expressed by some Member States in the course of the Board's deliberations on GOV/2784, with special attention given to an intervention by the Representative of Brazil[65] who asserted, in relevant summary, the following:

- What the Board was asked to approve in para 110.A was not a confirmatory interpretation of INFCIRC/153, but rather a new concept that would require the modification of existing agreements or their amplification with additional legal instruments. There was no legal basis, from the original purpose as defined in para 2 of document INFCIRC/153 and Article III.1 of the NPT, for confirming that the purpose of such agreements was the continuing verification of correctness and completeness. The Secretariat's assertion in para 5 of GOV/2784[66] that

[64] GOV/OR.862, paras 51 and 52, reproduced in GC(39)/17, Annex 3, at p. 55.

[65] GOV/OR.860, paras 99–110, reproduced in GC(39)/17, Annex 3, at pp. 5–8.

[66] Paragraph 5 of GOV/2784 reads as follows: 'The problem of undeclared activities was highlighted in Iraq, but was not unknown. Indeed, the need for the safeguards system to provide assurances regarding both the correctness and the completeness of a State's nuclear material declarations was considered by the drafters of the INFCIRC/153 (Corr.), the basis for comprehensive safeguards agreements. The scope of INFCIRC/153 was not limited to the nuclear material actually GOV/2784 declared by the State; it also includes that which should be declared. However, the system such as it had developed up to the Iraqi case, had limited capability to deal with completeness. This was the result of practical, rather than legal, considerations.'

the drafters of INFCIRC/153 had considered the need for the safeguards system to provide assurances regarding both the correctness and the completeness of a State's nuclear material declarations was 'entirely uncorroborated by the records of the Board's Safeguards Committee', and that verification of the absence of undeclared nuclear materials or activities required actions that had not been considered by the drafters of INFCIRC/153; and
- The statement in para 6 of GOV/2784 to the effect that, in February 1992, the Board had reaffirmed the requirement that the IAEA provide assurances regarding correctness and completeness was misleading since 'that requirement had been affirmed not as a general principle, but in respect of initial inventories of two specific countries and on both occasions Brazil had expressed reservations.

With respect to the first point, it is difficult to understand how, in light of the Official Records of the Safeguards Committee, the Brazilian Representative could assert that the Secretariat's statement to the effect that the drafters of INFCIRC/153 had considered the need for the safeguards system to provide assurances of the correctness and completeness of States' declarations was 'entirely uncorroborated'. While the drafters did not use the phrase 'correctness and completeness', the official records of the Committee's meetings demonstrate unequivocally that the Committee considered—and explicitly rejected—a proposal to limit the safeguards system to verifying only the nuclear material declared by a State (see discussion below).

The second point by Brazil relates to a reference in GOV/2784 to the decision taken by the Board of Governors in February 1992 in connection with the Board's consideration of special inspections, in which it had reaffirmed the IAEA's right to undertake special inspections to 'ensure that all nuclear materials in all peaceful nuclear activities are under safeguards'—i.e. to ensure that a State's declarations are not just correct but complete. The Board's discussions on that paper was not 'in respect of initial inventories' of any individual countries, but rather in the overall context of initial discussions on strengthening safeguards under comprehensive safeguards in general.[67] More significantly, however, it is manifestly absurd to argue that the reaffirmation of the right of special inspections by the Board in that instance was distinguishable because the decision was taken in the context of

[67]Paragraph 6 of GOV/2784 on which the Her remarks were made reads in relevant part as follows: 'The discoveries in Iraq, the problems which have arisen in the Agency's efforts to verify the declared nuclear inventory in the DPRK, the Agency's positive experience in verifying the declared nuclear inventory in South Africa and the increasing importance of assurance regarding the absence of any undeclared nuclear activities and installations in States committed by treaty to non-proliferation have made it imperative to update the safeguards system by adding to it measures that will give the Agency an improved capability of detecting clandestine nuclear activities. In February 1992 the Board of Governors reaffirmed the requirement that the Agency provide assurance regarding the correctness and completeness of nuclear material declarations by States with comprehensive safeguards agreements. …' It is not entirely clear to which two States the Brazilian Representative was referring in here statement of March 1995, i.e. Iraq, South Africa or the DPRK, but it is not necessary to determine that as all three agreements are substantively identical to INFCIRC/153, including with respect to the provisions related to special inspections.

specific States, even had that been the case—and it was not—the underlying legal instruments to which she was referring are, *mutatis mutandis*, identical, and are based on the same document as all other comprehensive safeguards agreements concluded by the IAEA, INFCIRC/153 (Corr.).[68]

It was clearly Brazil's view that the IAEA did not have the authority under INFCIRC/153 to verify the correctness and completeness of States' declarations under comprehensive safeguards agreements. However, while the view of Brazil, and the reservations expressed by some other States were duly noted, none of these States blocked consensus on the Board's decision to approve the Chairman's summary. Moreover, as evidenced by the Board's decision in March 1995, and in numerous other decisions taken by both policy-making organs over the next 20 years, Brazil's views differed from the IAEA's interpretation, as expressed not only by the organ with responsibility for the implementation of safeguards—the Board of Governors—but the policy-making organ of all Member States the General Conference.[69]

In September 1995, the General Conference adopted a resolution on strengthening the effectiveness and improving the efficiency of safeguards in which it, inter alia, noted in preambular para (d) that 'decisions of the Board aimed at further strengthening the effectiveness of IAEA safeguards should be supported and implemented and that that *IAEA's capability to detect undeclared nuclear activities should be increased*' (emphasis added), and in operative para 2 affirmed that '*increasing* the Agency's capability to detect undeclared nuclear activities in contravention of safeguards agreements will contribute to strengthening the effectiveness of safeguards' (emphasis added).[70] It warrants notice that, yet again, the

---

[68]During the General Conference's deliberations on the safeguards resolution in 2013, the Russian Federation seemed to echo the Brazilian objection. In the seventh meeting of the Committee of the Whole (CoW), the delegate of Saudi Arabia questioned the genesis of a preambular paragraph which read 'Noting that the implementation of comprehensive safeguards agreements should be designed to provide for verification by the Agency of the correctness and completeness of a State's declarations.' In her reply to that question, the Director of the Department of Safeguards' Division of Concepts and Planning replied that it had derived from a decision taken by the Board of Governors in 1995. In response to that intervention, the representative of the Russian Federation asked the Secretariat 'to indicate the specific decisions to which it had referred, and whether they had related to decisions regarding specific countries' dossiers'. The resolution ultimately adopted by the General Conference retained the preambular paragraph from the draft resolution, which, as pointed out by the Chairman of the CoW, was identical to that used in previous resolutions adopted by the General Conference. See GC(57)/COM.5.OR.7, at paras 31–40.

[69]The same language does in fact occur in the GC resolutions adopted in 2010, (there was no SG resolution in 2011) 2012, 2013 and 2014—even during the most contentious discussions on the safeguards resolution and the State-level concept. The relevant preambular paragraph in each of those resolutions reads as follows: 'Noting that the implementation of comprehensive safeguards agreements should be designed to provide for verification by the Agency of the correctness and completeness of a State's declarations.'

[70]GC(39)/RES/17, 'Strengthening the Effectiveness and Improving the Efficiency of the Safeguards System', 22 September 1995.

General Conference referred to 'increasing' the Agency's ability to detect undeclared nuclear activities, not 'establishing', 'creating' or 'conveying'.[71]

The 2005 resolution of the General Conference contains a paragraph corresponding to preambular para 5 of the 1995 resolution, and includes as well:

- An additional preambular para (k) 'Noting that additional protocols constitute one of the important instruments in enhancing the Agency's ability to derive safeguards conclusions regarding the absence of undeclared nuclear material and activities'
- And an operative para 14, in which, referring to para 13 requesting all concerned States and other parties to safeguards agreements, including nuclear-weapon States, to sign and bring into force additional protocols as soon as possible, it '[noted] in this regard that, for States with both a comprehensive safeguards agreement and an additional protocol in force, or being otherwise applied, Agency safeguards can provide increased assurances regarding both the non-diversion of nuclear material placed under safeguards and the absence of undeclared nuclear material and activities for a State as a whole'. Implicit in this language is that, while the IAEA may be able to provide some assurance of the absence of undeclared nuclear material and activities without an AP, clearly it can provide better assurances with an AP in place.
- Both preambular para (k) and operative para 14 are reiterated in every successive GC resolution through and including the resolution adopted in September 2014

Many years later, the Russian Federation challenged the Secretariat's reference to the March 1995 decision, asserting that, in his view, this was not a 'decision' by the Board of Governors since it did not involve a 'formal decision' of the Board but simply broad acceptance of the Chairman's summing-up. That view is not consistent with the long-standing practice of the Board of Governors. As noted by the Legal Officer of the CoW, the Board had taken decisions for many years through the mechanism of accepting summing-ups read out by its Chairman.[72]

The Statute of the IAEA provides that non-budgetary questions are to be decided by the Board of Governors by a majority of those present and voting (Article VI.E). Just as in the case of the General Assembly of the United Nations, the practice has developed among the Member States of the IAEA to seek to have decisions taken by consensus, by general agreement or without a vote. The search for common agreement is for policy reasons, but is not legally required. From the

[71]Similar paragraphs have been included in every General Conference resolution on safeguards adopted thereafter.

[72]GC(57)/COM.5.OR.7, at paras 49–52. The Russian Representative also challenged the status of the Board's decision, asserting that, during the March 1995, the proposed summary of the Chairman had been contested by 'some Board members over several hours'. He specifically referred to the objection expressed by the Philippines. However, that objection related to the process, not the substance of the Chairman's summary, and the Philippines, just as every other member of the Board of Governors, eventually joined in the consensus to accept the Chairman's summary.

legal point of view, every Member of the organization has the right to insist on a vote; consensus cannot be required. Nor does consensus change the legal validity or weight of the decision taken—a resolution or decision adopted by the Board is valid whether adopted by consensus or by a bare majority. Unanimity is not required, and if members of the Board of Governors wish to contest a given proposition, each is free to oppose it, amend it or otherwise seek its rejection or withdrawal following the applicable rules of procedure.

What is clear is that if a State party to a comprehensive safeguards agreement disagrees with the interpretation given by the IAEA, it is not free to unilaterally adjust that agreement, ignore the interpretation or withdraw from the agreement (as long as it remains party to the NPT[73]).

4.3.2.2 Subsequent Practice

As indicated above, the assertion of the IAEA's right and obligation to verify the correctness and completeness of States' obligations under INFCIRC/153 does not derive from subsequent agreement or subsequent practice. Having said that, there is sufficient evidence to demonstrate that the practice of the IAEA since the early 1990s in implementing that right and obligation, and the active concurrence of the policy-making organs clearly confirms that interpretation.

Prior to 1990, the primary focus of IAEA safeguards under comprehensive safeguards agreements was on verifying the non-diversion of declared nuclear material from declared facilities and other declared locations. However, as noted above, it was not the sole focus. The IAEA also established procedures for ensuring that there was no undeclared nuclear material at such facilities, in particular the undeclared production or processing of nuclear material. The resolution of issues associated with indications of undeclared nuclear material and activities were left to ad hoc solutions, rather than through a routine practice. The issue of the IAEA's authority to verify the absence of undeclared nuclear material and activities elsewhere in the State was never debated in the policy-making organs, and no decision was ever taken with respect to that right, whether in the affirmative or the negative. The IAEA primarily focused on declared nuclear material and activities—and the word 'primarily' needs to be emphasized—simply as a practical matter, not because it did not have the right.

If, as it is said that, in order to establish a 'subsequent practice in the application of the treaty which establishes the agreement of the parties regarding its interpretation', it is necessary that the practice be at least the active practice of some parties to the treaty and that the active practice should be consistent rather than haphazard and should have occurred with a certain frequency, the IAEA's approach to verification under INFCIRC/153 can hardly be said to satisfy those requirements. There simply was no practice, The fact that the IAEA did not

---

[73]IAEA Doc. INFCIRC/153, para 26, provides that the agreement is to remain in force as long as the State is party to the NPT.

implement all of its authority under comprehensive safeguards agreements does not lead to the conclusion either that it relinquished that authority or that the first 20 years reflect 'subsequent practice' of the parties confirming an interpretation' that it did not have such authority.

The same is not true of the IAEA's practice since the 1990s, which has been concordant, common and consistent. The Board of Governors and the General Conference of the IAEA have consistently supported the exercise of that authority by the Secretariat. It began routinely to evaluate all information available to it about a State with a view to identifying possible indications of undeclared nuclear material and activities in a State, as well as indications of diversion of declared nuclear material, as early as 1995 (even before the drafting of the Model Additional Protocol), and has been routinely reporting the results of those efforts to the Board of Governors.

It was precisely this verification practice which led to the discovery of undeclared nuclear material and activities in Iran, and of over 10 years of resolutions by the Board of Governors and the United Nations Security Council supporting the efforts of the IAEA to verify the correctness and completeness of Iran's declarations under its comprehensive safeguards agreements. It is this practice which led to the successful verification of Libya's dismantlement of its nuclear weapons programme and the drawing of a broader conclusion for Libya. It was this practice that also led to the IAEA's discovery of undeclared nuclear material and activities in the Republic of Korea and Egypt.

It has been suggested that the case of Egypt supports an interpretation that the IAEA has no authority to verify the absence of undeclared nuclear material and activities in a State which does not have an additional protocol in force. In asserting that argument, the proponents assert that, because the IAEA "found no indication of the diversion of declared nuclear material in Egypt", its verification process did not include verification of the absence of undeclared nuclear activities in Egypt. That could not be further from the truth. As noted above, the IAEA looks for indications of possible undeclared nuclear material and activities in any State with a comprehensive safeguards agreement in force, regardless of whether the State also has an additional protocol in place, and will report any findings of indications of proliferation concern to the Board of Governors. That the IAEA was able to draw a conclusion regarding the non-diversion of material declared by Egypt does not imply any conclusion at all regarding the absence of undeclared nuclear material or activities in the State concerned—whether positive or negative. The IAEA simply will not extend on behalf a State any assurances about the absence of nuclear material and activities unless it has the increased confidence which it derives from the routine expanded access to information and locations provided for under an additional protocol.

Sceptics contend that, while that the IAEA's practice since the 1990s may confirm the interpretation of comprehensive safeguards agreements by one party—that of the IAEA—such practice cannot establish the agreement of the other parties regarding the its interpretation or application.

If a party to a comprehensive safeguards agreement disagrees with an interpretation or application of its provisions by the IAEA, it is perfectly free to invoke the provisions related to 'Interpretation and Application of the Agreement and Settlement of Disputes' contained in that agreement, which provide various avenues for resolving any such questions, such as consultation, consideration by the Board or submission to an arbitral tribunal.[74] However, none have done so—regardless of whether the State has concluded a comprehensive safeguards agreement before *or* after that interpretation was established.

A case in point is Brazil. The week following the Board's approval in September 1991 of South Africa's new CSA, the General Conference adopted its resolution requesting the Director General to verify the correctness and completeness of South Africa's declarations under its CSA. The resolution was adopted without a vote. Following the adoption of the resolution, the Brazilian Representative intervened to assert that, although Brazil had joined the consensus, the request contained 'did not fall within the mandate of the Director General' and thus 'should not be held to constitute a precedent or a new guideline for the application of safeguards by the Agency'.[75] Notwithstanding, 3 months later, Brazil, joined by Argentina and the Brazilian–Argentine Agency for the Accounting and Control of Nuclear Material (ABACC), sought Board approval of their new quadripartite CSA with the IAEA—an agreement containing the same language, mutatis mutandis, as that contained in para 2 of INFCIRC/153. Brazil might have chosen to negotiate different language but did not. Nor has it ever invoked the disputes resolutions provided for in that agreement to challenge the interpretation of the IAEA with respect to that provision.

To conclude otherwise would lead to 'a result which is manifestly absurd or unreasonable', given the context, object and purpose of the NPT and INFCIRC/153. That is, it would lead to a conclusion that, while the IAEA was tasked with 'verifying fulfillment of the [NNWSs'] fulfillment of t[heir] obligations assumed under [the NPT] with a view to preventing diversion of nuclear energy' to prohibited purposes, it has no right to ensure that nuclear material is not intentionally withheld from safeguards for its use in clandestine activities dedicated to such prohibited purposes.

---

[74]IAEA Doc. INFCIRC/153, paras 20–22. Paragraph 20 provides that the parties to the agreement 'shall, at the request of either, consult about any question arising out of the interpretation or application thereof'. Paragraph 21 provides further that 'the State shall have the right to request that any question arising out of the interpretation or application thereof be considered by the Board … and that the State shall be invited by the Board to participate in the discussion of any such question by the Board'. Paragraph 22 provides that 'any dispute arising out of the interpretation or application thereof except a dispute with regard to a finding by the Board under para 19 above or an action taken by the Board pursuant to such a finding which is not settled by negotiation or another procedure agreed to by the parties should, on the request of either party, be submitted to an arbitral tribunal…'.

[75]GC(XXXV)/OR.341 51. The Brazilian Representative stated that 'her delegation had joined the consensus and understood and shared the concerns and apprehensions of the sponsors, but wanted to place on record its view that the request contained in operative para 2 of the resolution did not fall within the mandate of the Director General. For that reason, that paragraph should not be held to constitute a precedent or a new guideline for the application of safeguards by the Agency'.

In the face of such a 'manifestly absurd' and 'unreasonable' conclusion, the VCLTs allow for recourse to 'supplementary means of interpretation, including the preparatory work of the treaty and the circumstances of its conclusion' (VCLT, Article 32). That would include reference to the *travaux préparatoires* of INFCIRC/153.

4.3.2.3 Travaux Préparatoires

There is extensive evidence in the official records of Committee 22, the Committee tasked with the negotiation of the document that became INFCIRC/153, that the drafters intended that all nuclear material in the State be placed under IAEA safeguards to ensure that none of it was used for prohibited purposes, and that, to ensure that such was the case, the IAEA had the authority to verify not only that the material declared by the State was not diverted to such purposes, but that no material—whether declared or undeclared—was used for such purposes.

The most compelling evidence in support of that proposition is that the Committee had before it a proposal to limit the IAEA's authority to the verification of material declared by a State, that it was explicitly objected to and that it was not accepted. It is difficult to understand how such evidence can be construed otherwise. That is especially so given other aspects of INFCIRC/153 that were included by the Member States, most significantly, the provisions related to ad hoc and special inspections (see discussion above), which were intentionally designed to secure access by the IAEA to information and/or locations beyond those declared by a State, and the formulation of para 19, which refers to the consequences of the IAEA's inability to verify that there has been 'no diversion of nuclear material required to be safeguarded under the Agreement', as discussed above.[76]

Mention has at times been made of the role of the IAEA's Board of Governors in developing the safeguards system. This is only as it should be considering Article XII.C of the Statute, the IAEA's constituent instrument. It is the Board which receives reports of non-compliance from the Director General and it is the Board which reports any non-compliance to IAEA Member States and to the United Nations Security Council and General Assembly. More generally, Article VI.F of the Statute provides that it is the Board of Governors which has the authority to carry out the functions of the Agency in accordance with its Statute, subject to its responsibilities to the General Conference as provided in the Statute. As indicated in a 1983 Board document entitled 'Compatibility of safeguards agreements and the Agency's Statute',

> The application of the Statute in matters relating to the safeguards has been the province of the Board throughout the Agency's history. The authority of the Board derives from

[76]While the records of Committee 22 may not have been made available to the general public in their entirety, they have always been available to all Members States of the IAEA, who accordingly must be considered to be at least on constructive notice of the contents of such records.

Article VI.F of the Statute. Various statements made at the Conference on the Statute confirm the Board's role and authority in determining the form and extent of particular safeguards.[77]

A legitimate question might be, given the clear intent of the States Party to the NPT, as reflected in its decisions noted above, why the IAEA, in the beginning, did not devote greater effort to devising techniques to be able to provide assurances regarding the absence of undeclared material and activities. Clearly, if a NNWS Party to the NPT were able to conduct clandestine nuclear activities contrary to its NPT obligations and the IAEA had no authority to implement safeguards designed to detect such non-compliance, then the system would not be functioning as intended. Such was the case with the discovery of Iraq's programme.

The answer to the question is a mix of political will and technological possibilities. In 1970, there were few techniques that could be easily utilized to achieve such detection, such as environmental sampling, a technique developed by the IAEA in its early investigations into Iraq's nuclear programme and utilized to excellent effect in the case of the DPRK. Thus, the option would be searching through the territory of a State attempting to 'prove a negative' without any specific indication of a need for such intrusive inspections; it was believed that States would not accept such a regime. As highlighted in the IAEA publication 'The Evolution of IAEA Safeguards' (1998), the former Director General of the IAEA Hans Blix had indicated 'that the IAEA could not scour the territories of upwards of 150 NPT non-nuclear-weapon States "in a blind search" for clandestine nuclear activities'. It was therefore important to rely not only on special inspections, but also 'national technical means' of verification obtained by States and submitted to the IAEA. Obviously, after Iraq, it became clear that the foregoing was insufficient to meet the object and purpose of the NPT and the understandings of what was required by the Parties to the NPT. More needed to be done, whether through more effective use of the measures already provided for in INFCIRC/153 or the implementation of additional measures, such as those which were incorporated into the Model Additional Protocol.

4.4 Concluding Remarks

Article III.1 of the NPT is clear on its face that the purpose of IAEA safeguards is to ensure that no nuclear material—whether declared or undeclared—is diverted from peaceful nuclear activities to nuclear weapons or other nuclear explosive

[77]IAEA document GOV/INF/433, 21 January 1983, at para 8. The document was prepared by the IAEA Secretariat in response to a request by the Board of Governors in 1982 for 'a study to determine the degree of compatibility between the provisions of the safeguards agreements in force and the Statute as regards the statutory legitimacy of non-explosive military applications and nuclear material subject to the Agency's safeguards system'.

devices, and that, to that end, safeguards are to be applied on all nuclear material, regardless of its location. A review of the NPT conference results confirms that understanding of the States Parties to the NPT. The comprehensive safeguards agreements concluded by the NPT NNWSs are intended as the implementing agreements of that primary obligation, and as such, cannot deviate or be interpreted contrary to the clear and express collective intent of the Parties to the NPT, not the intention of individual parties or individual parties to the bilateral safeguards agreements.

INFCIRC/153, and the comprehensive safeguards agreements concluded with the NPT NNWSs on the basis of that document, are consistent with that intention. A plain reading of INFCIRC/153 clearly demonstrates the IAEA's right and obligation to verify the non-diversion of the declared nuclear material and the absence of undeclared nuclear material and activities—that is to say, to provide assurances of the correctness and completeness of States' declarations under such agreements. The text of INFCIRC/153 is clear on its face that the purpose of IAEA verification under comprehensive safeguards agreements is to provide assurances that no nuclear material in a CSA State is diverted to nuclear weapons or nuclear explosive devices—whether declared or undeclared. That is clear from the framing of the basic undertakings, but is further evidenced in other provisions of INFCIRC/153. The negotiation history of INFCIRC/153 supports that conclusion—the drafters considered and rejected a proposal to limit IAEA verification to nuclear material declared by a State. The early practice of focusing routine verification primarily on declared nuclear material and facilities developed as a practical matter, and not a legal matter. And it is important to note the IAEA did in fact implement measures designed to detect undeclared nuclear material at declared nuclear facilities. Just because the IAEA did not routinely exercise its right to verify the absence of undeclared nuclear material elsewhere in the State does not mean that the IAEA did not have such authority.

The Agency's practice has been, since the early to mid-1990s, even before the Board's approval of the Model Additional Protocol, to attempt to verify the correctness and completeness of States' declarations under CSAs. There have been multiple decisions of the policy-making organs since then encouraging the IAEA to continue to do just that. The Model Additional Protocol was not developed to expand the Agency's authority to permit verification of the completeness of States' declarations under CSAs; the technical measures available to the IAEA under additional protocols, such as broader access to information and locations, simply provide the IAEA with additional tools with which to fulfil that obligation more effectively. The Agency's practice of not drawing a broader conclusion that all nuclear material has remained in peaceful activities for States which do not have an additional protocol in force is a function of a policy decision, not a legal decision. Although the IAEA does in fact review all of the information available to it for indications of undeclared nuclear material and activities in all CSA States, regardless of whether the State concerned has concluded an additional protocol or not, the IAEA will not extend on behalf of such a State any about the absence of nuclear material and activities unless the State also has an additional protocol in force, or is implementing it provisionally. This practice, about which the Board of Governors and the General Conference are reminded each year, has been implemented by the Secretariat since the late 1990s, and has not been challenged by either of the policy-making organs of the IAEA. Nor has any individual State exercised its right to resort to the mechanisms provided for in all comprehensive safeguards agreements for the resolution of questions arising from the interpretation or application of such agreements.

The IAEA has never asserted that its right to verify correctness and completeness derives from decisions by the Board of Governors reaffirming the Agency's right and obligation to verify correctness and completeness. These decisions simply reflected confirmation by the relevant policy-making organ of the IAEA of that right and obligation. However, such decisions could be considered as confirming the interpretation. And the consistent practice of the IAEA in implementing safeguards on that basis since the mid-1990s can be seen to constitute subsequent practice, a practice of which the Board of Governors was fully informed, and which it and the General Conference of the entire membership of the IAEA consistently supported in the decisions taken by those bodies. The Board's actions in requesting the IAEA to verify the completeness of the declarations of States with comprehensive safeguards agreements—long before the Model Additional Protocol was even considered—clearly demonstrates its concurrence in the conclusion that the right derived from the CSA itself, and not a later instrument. And it is absurd to contend that, simply because the decisions were taken in the context of specific States—the underlying legal instruments were, mutatis mutandis, identical, and are based on the same document as all other comprehensive safeguards agreements concluded by the IAEA, INFCIRC/153 (Corr.).

Whether those decisions are taken in the Board of Governors or the General Conference by consensus or by a simple majority of the States is irrelevant. Had any of the States that have expressed reservations to the interpretations of their respective comprehensive safeguards agreement, they could have done so, either in the initial conclusion of their agreements, or subsequently, in accordance with the provisions in the agreement for the interpretation and application of the agreement and settlement of disputes. None have done so. Even Iran, which is clearly motivated to challenge such authority, has not formally invoked those procedures.

The fact that a small number of States take issue with that right is not based on law; indeed, some are based on a misunderstanding of the facts, and, in my view, incorrect legal interpretations (e.g. that the policy-making organs cannot take decisions through the mechanism of agreement on a chairman's summary). Moreover, those States which actively participated in the relevant decisions taken by the Board and General Conference concerning the Agency's right to verify correctness and completeness should be estopped from arguing otherwise.

To interpret INFCIRC/153, and the agreements concluded on the basis of that document, in such a way as to preclude IAEA verification of the correctness and completeness of States' declarations under such agreements would defeat the very object and purpose of such agreements, and the very foundations of such agreements, the Treaty on the Non-Proliferation of Nuclear Weapons, which is to ensure the timely detection of the diversion of nuclear material to nuclear weapons and other nuclear explosive devices and the deterrence of such diversion through the risk of timely detection.

References

IAEA (1972) The structure and content of agreements between the agency and states required in connection with the Treaty on the Non-Proliferation of Nuclear Weapons, INFCIRC/153 (Corr.). www.iaea.org/Publications/Documents/Infcircs/Others/infcirc153.pdf

IAEA (1995) Strengthening the effectiveness and improving the efficiency of agency safeguards: report by the director general to the general conference, GC(39)/17

IAEA (1996) Strengthening the effectiveness and improving the efficiency of agency safeguards: report by the director general to the general conference, GC(40)/17

IAEA (1997) Model protocol additional to the agreement(s) between state(s) and the IAEA for the application of safeguards (INFCIRC/540 (Corr.)

Kratzer M, Hooper R, Wulf N (2005) A retrospective of INFCIRCs 153 and 540. http://cgs.pnnl.gov/fois/doclib/Retroworkingfinal.pdf

Rockwood L (2013) Legal framework for IAEA safeguards. IAEA, Vienna

Chapter 5
The NPT and the IAEA Additional Protocol

Masahiko Asada

Abstract The importance of having in place an effective verification system that goes beyond declaration-based verification under the Comprehensive Safeguards Agreement, and thus the importance of the Additional Protocol and of its universalization, has long been recognized and expressed within the framework of both the IAEA and the NPT. However, despite the recent increase in the number of States that have brought an Additional Protocol into force, its universalization still is a distant goal. This chapter first considers whether one can argue that the conclusion and bringing into force of an Additional Protocol is an obligation under the NPT. It then discusses the ways and means to make the Additional Protocol universal. Such ways and means may take the form of a direct call for the conclusion of an Additional Protocol. Its universalization may also be pursued indirectly by requiring a State to conclude an Additional Protocol as a condition for benefiting in nuclear cooperation. Possibilities and limitations are explored for both of these (direct and indirect) approaches.

Keywords Additional protocol · Comprehensive Safeguards Agreement (CSA) · International Atomic Energy Agency (IAEA) · Nuclear Suppliers Group (NSG) · Treaty on Non-Proliferation of Nuclear Weapons (NPT) · Verification

---

Professor of International Law, School of Government, Kyoto University; Member of the ILA Committee on Nuclear Weapons, Non-Proliferation and Contemporary International Law.
This is a revised and updated version of the author's Article entitled, 'The Treaty on the Non-Proliferation of Nuclear Weapons and the Universalization of the Additional Protocol', *Journal of Conflict and Security Law*, Vol. 16, No. 1 (Spring 2011), pp. 3–34.

M. Asada (✉)
School of Government, Kyoto University, Sayo-Ku, Kyoto 606-8501, Japan
e-mail: asada@law.kyoto-u.ac.jp

J.L. Black-Branch and D. Fleck (eds.), *Nuclear Non-Proliferation in International Law - Volume II*, DOI 10.1007/978-94-6265-075-6_5

Contents

5.1 Introduction

There is no question that the Treaty on the Non-Proliferation of Nuclear Weapons (NPT) is the cornerstone of the global non-proliferation architecture. At the same time, it is no denial that the NPT has been under serious strain for more than two decades. It seems that such strain started with the UN mandated inspection team's 'discovery' after the 1991 Gulf War of the fact that Iraq had been clandestinely working on the development of nuclear weapons in undeclared facilities. They were located adjacent to the facilities that had been declared to the International Atomic Energy Agency (IAEA) under the Comprehensive Safeguards Agreement[1] (CSA). This fact prompted the IAEA Board of Governors to adopt in May 1997 the Model Additional Protocol[2]

[1]IAEA, The Structure and Content of Agreements between the Agency and States Required in Connection with the Treaty on the Non-Proliferation of Nuclear Weapons, (International Atomic Energy Agency Information Circular) INFCIRC/153 (Corr.), June 1972. Under the CSA, each non-nuclear-weapon State Party to the NPT is obliged to accept safeguards on all source or special fissionable material in all peaceful nuclear activities within its territory, under its jurisdiction, or carried out under its control anywhere. The pre-NPT safeguards regime under INFCIRC/66 is focused on the particular facilities and material in order to verify that they are not used for military purposes, rather than applying to all nuclear material in peaceful activities of the State.

[2]IAEA, Model Protocol Additional to the Agreement(s) between State(s) and the International Atomic Energy Agency for the Application of Safeguards, INFCIRC/540 (Corr.), September 1997. The Model Additional Protocol was designed not only for non-nuclear-weapon States Parties to the NPT but also for nuclear-weapon States and non-NPT parties. See 'Foreword', INFCIRC/540 (Corr.). However, we confine our discussions to the conclusion of an Additional Protocol by non-nuclear-weapon States Parties to the NPT, as we discuss non-proliferation efforts under the NPT here.

(INFCIRC/540) to the IAEA safeguards agreements. The Additional Protocol would give the IAEA a much broader power than the CSA in terms of both rights of access to information and sites (called the 'expanded declaration' and the 'complementary access', respectively).[3] The Protocol would require its parties to provide information about, and IAEA inspector access to, all parts of their nuclear fuel cycle, as well as to any other location where nuclear material is or may be present. Under the Protocol's 'complementary access' system, the IAEA would have the right to collect environmental samples at locations beyond declaration if it deems necessary to do so. As a result, the Additional Protocol would equip the IAEA with new tools to provide 'credible assurance of the absence of undeclared nuclear material and activities'.[4]

The importance of having in place an effective verification system that goes beyond declaration-based verification under the CSA, and thus the importance of the Additional Protocol, was most dramatically shown by the following episode. In August 2004, the Republic of Korea (South Korea) declared that it had conducted uranium enrichment activities in 2000 without reporting them to the IAEA as required under its CSA. South Korea declared this after receiving a report from the Korea Atomic Energy Research Institute (KAERI) in June 2004 that it had conducted the experiments in question. It has been said that the KAERI reported its experiments because it thought that the fact would in any case be revealed when the IAEA conducted environmental sampling in the country as part of the complementary access that would take place in accordance with the Additional Protocol that had entered into force for South Korea in February of that year.[5]

Indeed, the importance of the Additional Protocol and of its universalization has long been recognized and expressed within the framework of both the IAEA and the NPT. However, despite the recent increase in number of States that have brought an Additional Protocol into force, its universalization still is a distant goal. Of the 185 non-nuclear-weapon States Parties to the NPT,[6] 124 have Additional Protocols in force (as of 31 December 2014).[7]

---

[3]Articles 2 and 5 of the Model Additional Protocol. For the significance of the Additional Protocol, see, e.g. Hirsch 2004, pp. 143–144.

[4]IAEA, 'The Safeguards System of the International Atomic Energy Agency' (date and year not given), p. 2, para 7. http://www.iaea.org/OurWork/SV/Safeguards/safeg_system.pdf. Accessed 10 September 2008.

[5]See J. Kang et al., South Korea's Nuclear Mis-Adventures, Special Report, Nautilus Institute, 10 September 2004.

[6]The number, which includes North Korea as a State Party to the NPT, is according to the web site of the UN Office for Disarmament Affairs (ODA). http://disarmament.un.org/treaties/t/npt. Accessed 31 January 2015. The author holds a different view concerning the North Korean status under the NPT. See Asada 2004, pp. 331–355.

[7]In addition, the IAEA also applies safeguards, including the measures foreseen in the Model Additional Protocol, in Taiwan. States not having an Additional Protocol in force include Argentina, Brazil, Egypt, Iran, Israel, Malaysia, Myanmar, North Korea, Pakistan, Syria and Venezuela. http://www.iaea.org/safeguards/documents/AP_status_list.pdf. Accessed 31 January 2015.

This article will first consider whether one can argue that the conclusion and bringing into force of an Additional Protocol is an obligation under the NPT. It will then discuss the ways and means to make the Additional Protocol universal. Such ways and means may take the form of a direct call for the conclusion of an Additional Protocol. Its universalization may also be pursued indirectly by requiring a State to conclude an Additional Protocol as a condition for benefiting in nuclear cooperation. Possibilities and limitations will be explored for both of these (direct and indirect) approaches. In doing so, an analysis of the discussions at the latest NPT Review Conference held in May 2010 in New York will also be provided.

5.2 Safeguards Obligations Under the NPT and the Conclusion of Additional Protocol

If the conclusion of an Additional Protocol is a legal obligation under the NPT, there will be no problem to be further addressed from a legal point of view. No Additional Protocol put in place in that case would simply mean non-compliance with that obligation and the whole problem would become political rather than legal. Thus, the first question to be asked for the universalization of the Additional Protocol is whether non-nuclear-weapon States Parties to the NPT are legally required to conclude an Additional Protocol.[8]

The relevant NPT provisions are contained in its Article III.1, which provides that:

> Each non-nuclear-weapon State Party to the Treaty undertakes to accept *safeguards*, as set forth in an agreement to be negotiated and concluded with the International Atomic Energy Agency in accordance with the Statute of the International Atomic Energy Agency and the Agency's safeguards system, for the exclusive purpose of verification of the fulfilment of its obligations assumed under this Treaty with a view to preventing diversion of nuclear energy from peaceful uses to nuclear weapons or other nuclear explosive devices. … The *safeguards* required by this Article shall be applied on *all source or special fissionable material in all peaceful nuclear activities* within the territory of such State, under its jurisdiction, or carried out under its control anywhere. (emphasis added)

[8]During the drafting of the Model Additional Protocol, the question of whether adherence to the Additional Protocol is obligatory was left open. On 31 January 1997, during the debate in the Committee on Strengthening the Effectiveness and Improving the Efficiency of the Safeguards System (Committee 24), which drafted the Model Protocol, Mohamed ElBaradei, then Assistant Director General, Division of External Relations, provided the Secretariat interpretation of Article 1 of the draft Model Additional Protocol that the Article 'did not seek to determine the question of the existence or non-existence of a legal obligation to adhere to the Protocol'. GOV/COM.24/OR.48 (31 January 1997), para 3. He also made clear concerning an abortive draft provision (the Protocol shall be considered as an integral part of the Safeguards Agreement) that: 'stating in the Protocol that it was "an integral part of the Safeguards Agreement" would not create a legal obligation to conclude the Protocol'. GOV/COM.24/OR.47 (30 January 1997), para 52.

There is no reference there[9] to *specific types* of 'safeguards',[10] such as those in a CSA or its model ('Structure and Content') as contained in INFCIRC/153. The provision only prescribes that the safeguards must cover 'all source or special fissionable material [hereinafter collectively referred to as "nuclear material"] in all peaceful nuclear activities' of the State Party concerned. Safeguards covering all nuclear material in all peaceful nuclear activities of a State are commonly called 'comprehensive safeguards' or 'full-scope safeguards'. However, measures contained in an Additional Protocol based on the Model Additional Protocol also cover all nuclear material in all peaceful nuclear activities of a State. Thus, the above NPT provision does not necessarily point only to the CSA.

In considering the implications of Article III, recall that States such as Australia and Canada proposed in a Preparatory Committee for the 2005 NPT Review Conference that the NPT Review Conference take a decision to the effect that 'the AP [i.e. Additional Protocol] is mandatory under Article III of the Treaty'.[11] In order to justify this proposal, they argued that 'safeguards requirements have evolved over time and must continue to evolve to meet present and future challenges', and that '[t]he international community must remain vigilant, remembering that no non-proliferation tool is perfect'.[12] They also contended that 'safeguards' referred to in Article III of the NPT is not a static concept,[13] but a concept that could evolve as the objective security environment changes. For example, a Model Additional Protocol was adopted by the IAEA Board of Governors in May 1997 to respond to the newly revealed proliferation risks. Thus, they argued, it is natural for the NPT States Parties to conclude an Additional Protocol based on that Model Protocol. This is a convincing argument from a nuclear non-proliferation viewpoint. But is it tenable to say that Additional Protocol is 'mandatory' under the NPT?

In the Chairman's Working Papers of Preparatory Committees for the 2010 NPT Review Conference in which the need to universalize the Additional Protocol was reaffirmed and the strengthened safeguards system—a CSA coupled with an

[9]There are certain treaties establishing a nuclear-weapon-free zone, which refer to a specific type of safeguards that the parties thereto are obliged to accept. The 1985 Treaty of Rarotonga for a South Pacific Nuclear Free Zone in its Annex 2 specifies INFCIRC/153 as the basis on which the parties are required to conclude an agreement with the IAEA, while the 2006 Treaty of Semipalatinsk on a Nuclear-Weapon-Free Zone in Central Asia in Article 8 refers to an Additional Protocol among the agreements its parties undertake to conclude with the IAEA.

[10]It is natural that no reference was made in the NPT to a specific document containing safeguards system for non-nuclear-weapon States Parties to the NPT, because such a document was to be drawn up after the Treaty was signed or entered into force.

[11]Third Preparatory Committee for the 2005 NPT Review Conference, Cluster II Issues, Statement by Mr. David Mason, Deputy Head of Mission, Australian Permanent Mission to the UN, Vienna, 29 April 2004 (statements at the NPT Review Conferences and their Preparatory Committees are hereinafter cited in the following manner: 'Statement by Australia, Cluster II, 29 April 2004'), p. 1; Statement by Canada, Cluster II, 29 April 2004, p. 2.

[12]Ibid.

[13]Ibid.

Additional Protocol—was referred to as the NPT's verification standard, views were also recorded that concluding an Additional Protocol should remain 'a voluntary confidence-building measure'.[14] This largely reflected the non-aligned movement (NAM) countries' desire to stress that 'it is fundamental to make the distinction between legal obligations and voluntary confidence-building measures, in order to ensure that such voluntary undertakings are not turned into legal safeguards obligations'.[15]

For the non-proliferation promoters to counter such arguments, it is necessary to forge strong and persuasive arguments in favour of the universalization of the Additional Protocol as a mandatory measure under the NPT. Legally, however, it is not easy to do so. Against the Australia–Canadian proposition, several counter-arguments could be made.

5.2.1 Article III Obligation Is Fulfilled by Concluding a CSA

First, it is true that Article III.1 of the NPT does not refer to the CSA or INFCIRC/153 specifically, and leaves some leeway for an evolutive interpretation of the provisions. However, those States Parties to the NPT that had concluded a CSA before the adoption of the Model Additional Protocol in 1997 must consider that they have already fulfilled their obligations under Article III.1 of the Treaty by concluding the former agreement. In fact, the Final Declaration of the Third Review Conference of the NPT held in 1985, for instance, stated that '[t]he Conference notes with satisfaction that the commitments in Articles I-III have been met and have greatly helped prevent the spread of nuclear explosives'.[16]

In addition, the first paragraph of the model ('Structure and Content') for a CSA (INFCIRC/153) provides that: 'The Agreement should contain, *in accordance with Article III. 1 of the Treaty on the Non-Proliferation of Nuclear Weapons*, an undertaking by the State to accept safeguards, in accordance with the terms of the Agreement, on all source or special fissionable material …'[17] (emphasis added). This sentence implies that by concluding a CSA the obligation under Article III.1 of the NPT is met. Although one may say that this represents no more than a recommendation on the part of the IAEA, because INFCIRC/153 is a 'model' produced by the IAEA, non-nuclear-weapon States Parties to the NPT

[14]NPT/CONF.2010/PC.II/WP.43, 9 May 2008, para 38; NPT/CONF.2010/PC.I/WP.78, 11 May 2007, para 30.

[15]Statement by NAM, Cluster II (date not given) 2008, p. 1; Statement by NAM, Cluster II, 9 May 2007, p. 2.

[16]NPT/CONF.III/64/I, Geneva, 1985, Annex I, p. 3, para 3.

[17]INFCIRC/153 (Corr.), above n. 1, para 1.

have nevertheless demonstrated that they hold the same view by repeating essentially the same sentence in their respective CSAs with the IAEA.[18]

Moreover, although not a globally applicable treaty, there is a nuclear-weapon-free zone treaty containing a provision which suggests that the CSA and the Additional Protocol have a different legal status under the NPT. The Treaty of Semipalatinsk on a Nuclear-Weapon-Free Zone in Central Asia, signed in September 2006 and brought into force in March 2009 with the ratification by all five signatories, in Article 8 provides that each Party undertakes to conclude with the IAEA and bring into force, if it has not already done so, 'an agreement for the application of safeguards *in accordance with the NPT* (INFCIRC/153 (Corr.)), and an Additional Protocol (INFCIRC/540 (Corr.))' (emphasis added) not later than 18 months after the entry into force of the Treaty. This provision clearly distinguishes between the CSA (INFCIRC/153 (Corr.)) which is to be concluded 'in accordance with the NPT' and the Additional Protocol which is not necessarily so. A similar sentence can be found in the Final Document of the 2010 NPT Review Conference, as we will see in Sect. 5.3.3.

Furthermore, if the conclusion of an Additional Protocol was an obligation under Article III.1, it would follow that quite a number of NPT States Parties are in 'violation' of that paragraph, given that only 124 out of 185 non-nuclear-weapon States Parties to the NPT have concluded an Additional Protocol. However, there is little hint of States Parties viewing the situation that way. In arguing against the idea of mandatory Additional Protocol, one delegation in the 2010 NPT Review Conference insisted that, having arrived to the Review Conference in compliance with the Treaty, it 'would not leave in non-compliance'.[19] Even Australia and Canada, which were advocating the idea, were merely *proposing* that the States Parties should agree that the conclusion of an Additional Protocol is mandatory under the NPT.

5.2.2 Additional Protocol as a Product of the IAEA

A second possible counter-argument against the proposition in favour of the mandatory conclusion of an Additional Protocol is related to the fact that the Model Additional Protocol was adopted by the IAEA's Board of Governors. Of course, there is a close link between the NPT and the IAEA as exemplified by the very provisions of Article III.1. The IAEA was also described in a decision of the 1995 NPT Review and Extension Conference as '*the* competent authority' (emphasis

[18]See, e.g. Agreement between the Government of Japan and the International Atomic Energy Agency in Implementation of Article III.1 and 4 of the Treaty on the Non-Proliferation of Nuclear Weapons, INFCIRC/255, March 1978, p. 2, Article 1.

[19]W. Potter et al., The 2010 NPT Review Conference: Deconstructing Consensus, CNS (James Martin Center for Nonproliferation Studies) Special Report, 17 June 2010, p. 14.

added) responsible for verifying compliance with its safeguards agreements with NPT States Parties under the said article.[20]

However, strictly speaking, the IAEA is not the implementing organization of the NPT so much as the Organisation for the Prohibition of Chemical Weapons (OPCW) is the implementing organization of the Chemical Weapons Convention (CWC). In fact, the membership of the IAEA is different from that of the NPT: India, Israel and Pakistan, which are outside the NPT, are members of the IAEA and two of them (India and Pakistan) are usually Board members, whereas a number of NPT parties are not members of the IAEA at all.[21] Therefore, those States Parties to the NPT that are not members of the IAEA may contend that they cannot accept something produced by a body that they have nothing to do with as non-members.

Admittedly, INFCIRC/153 is also a product of the IAEA, and non-nuclear-weapon States Parties to the NPT are nevertheless bound to conclude a safeguards agreement based on that document, even if they are not members of the IAEA. This is, however, because Article III.1 provides to that effect, albeit rather vaguely for necessary reasons.[22]

It could be argued that since Article III.1 of the NPT provides for the conclusion of an agreement in accordance with 'the [IAEA's] safeguards system', the obligation under this paragraph may evolve as the IAEA's 'safeguards system' evolves, implying that the Additional Protocol is an evolved form of IAEA's 'safeguards system'. However, the power to give authentic interpretation of treaty provisions lies with its States Parties, subject to possible rulings of the competent courts and tribunals.[23] Unless the NPT (States Parties) explicitly mandates the IAEA to update as necessary its 'safeguards system' in the meaning of Article III.1 such an argument would not easily be accepted by the holders of the authority. And indeed, despite the Australian claim otherwise,[24] an overwhelming majority of the NPT States Parties (including 116 States Parties to the Non-Aligned Movement—NAM—) hold the view that they are not legally obliged to conclude

[20]NPT/CONF.1995/32 (Part I), New York, 1995, Annex, Decision 2, para 9.

[21]The members of the IAEA number 162 as of 31 December 2014, while the NPT has 190 States Parties as of the same day.

[22]See above n. 10.

[23]In an Advisory Opinion delivered on the 'Question of Jaworzina', the Permanent Court of International Justice (PCIJ) stated that: 'it is an established principle that the right of giving an authoritative interpretation [le droit d'interpréter authentiquement] of a legal rule belongs solely to the person or body who has power to modify or suppress it'. P.C.I.J., Ser. B, No. 8 (6 December 1923), p. 37. See also Jennings and Watts 1992, pp. 1268–1269; Brownlie 2008, p. 630.

[24]Australia claimed that 'Australia and many others are of the firm view that the "Agency's safeguards system" which non-nuclear weapon state NPT Parties are obliged to accept comprises the Additional Protocol together with a comprehensive safeguards agreement'. Statement by Australia, Cluster II, 29 April 2004, p. 1.

an Additional Protocol.[25] In other words, concluding an Additional Protocol is considered to be optional. Otherwise, it would follow that NPT parties could, in effect, continue to be bound automatically by documents that are produced by a body whose membership is not identical with them, which seems to be something the NPT parties did not accept in signing and ratifying the Treaty.

5.2.3 Procedural Requirement Under Article III

A third possible counter-argument against the above-stated proposition would be that if the obligation under Article III.1, included the conclusion of an Additional Protocol, then Article III.4 would lose nearly all its meaning. This paragraph provides for the deadlines for the conclusion of an agreement with the IAEA 'to meet the requirements of this Article'. According to it, States Parties to the NPT must commence negotiation of such agreements within 180 days from the original entry into force of the Treaty (5 March 1970), except that those adhering to the NPT after the 180-day period must commence the negotiation not later than the date of adherence. In either case, the agreement must enter into force not later than 18 months after the initiation of negotiations.

These provisions are almost irrelevant to the conclusion of an Additional Protocol. This is because it was impossible for those many States Parties to the NPT that adhered to the Treaty years before the adoption of the Model Additional Protocol in May 1997 to commence the negotiation on an Additional Protocol not later than the date of' adherence. Article III.4, could be relevant to the Additional Protocol only in relation to those very few States Parties that adhered to the Treaty in May 1997 or later. It is reasonable to assume that NPT negotiators must have thought that 'safeguards' as referred to in Article III.1, were those that were to be contained in the eventual INFCIRC/153, and that they did not envision that any new safeguards documents would be developed afterwards in the context of the said Article.

It is true that INFCIRC/153 on which all CSAs are based was approved by the IAEA Board of Governors in March 1971, *more than* 180 days after the original entry into force of the NPT.[26] Thus, technically, the commencement of negotiation on safeguards agreements by a number of NPT parties was also not in strict compliance with the time frame set by Article III.4. However, it must be understood that Article III required NPT States Parties to conclude an agreement with a third party (IAEA) over whose work they had no absolute control. It should be permissible, therefore, that the conclusion of CSAs was somewhat delayed, because there was no assured way to meet the prescribed time limit without fail.

---

[25] See below n. 51 and accompanying text.

[26] Fischer 1997, p. 257.

5.2.4 Possible Rebuttal Based on 'Fundamental Change of Circumstances'

There may be a rebuttal to these counter-arguments, employing a rule concerning the fundamental change of circumstances. Although those States Parties to the NPT that have concluded a CSA may have been regarded as having already fulfilled the obligation under Article III.1, the circumstances may have fundamentally changed after the revelation of (attempted) nuclear weapons development by Iraq and North Korea as well as the suspected development by Iran with a CSA in place, leading to a change of the content of the obligation under the said provision of the NPT now to include the conclusion of an Additional Protocol. Is such an argument justifiable?

'Fundamental change of circumstances' has long been recognized as a rule having a theoretically sound basis,[27] while at the same time the possibility of its abuse in actual application has also been cautioned. Under the Vienna Convention on the Law of Treaties of 1969, the relevant article includes extremely strict conditions for the invocation of this concept, which is defined as 'fundamental change of circumstances which has occurred with regard to those existing at the time of the conclusion of a treaty, and which was not foreseen by the parties'. Article 62, para 1, enumerates the conditions for its invocation as follows:

(a) the existence of those circumstances constituted an essential basis of the consent of the parties to be bound by the treaty; and
(b) the effect of the change is radically to transform the extent of obligations still to be performed under the treaty.

It does not seem easy to meet these two cumulative conditions satisfactorily, though it is true that the current international situation offers a new, grave challenge to the nuclear non-proliferation regime.

More critical, even supposing it is proved that the current situation meets the above two conditions, one could still not say that the conclusion of an Additional Protocol is now an obligation under the NPT, because as far as the provisions of the Vienna Convention are concerned, the rule of 'fundamental change of circumstances' is for the termination or suspension of the operation of a treaty or withdrawal from a treaty, and not one for changing its interpretation.

---

[27]The rule on 'fundamental change of circumstances' has been recognized as constituting part of customary international law. In the cases of the Fisheries Jurisdiction and the Gabcikovo-Nagymaros Project, the International Court of Justice (ICJ) declared that Article 62 of the Vienna Convention on the Law of Treaties 'may in many respects be considered as a codification of existing customary law'. *Fisheries Jurisdiction* case (*United Kingdom v. Iceland*), Jurisdiction, Judgment, ICJ Rep. 1973, p. 18, para 36; *Fisheries Jurisdiction* case (*Federal Republic of Germany v. Iceland*), Jurisdiction, Judgment, ICJ Rep. 1973, p. 63, para 36; Gabcikovo-Nagymaros Project (Hungary/Slovakia), Judgment, ICJ Rep. 1997, p. 38, para 46. The European Court of Justice holds a similar view on this point. A/CN.4/592, 27 February 2008, p. 4. See also von Heinegg 2014.

5.3 Direct Approach: Interpretative Agreement at an NPT Review Conference

As discussed above, it is hard to interpret Article III.1 of the NPT as legally requiring its non-nuclear-weapon States Parties to conclude an Additional Protocol. However, what has been said thus far does not rule out the possibility that NPT States Parties agree at a Review Conference or elsewhere that the 'safeguards' referred to in Article III.1, include not only those provided by a CSA but also those supplemented by an Additional Protocol to it. If that happens, the above counter-arguments will lose all their validity because States Parties are the masters of their treaty. An effort in this direction may be called a 'direct approach' to the universalization of the Additional Protocol. How can one assess such a possibility in legal terms?

5.3.1 Powers and Functions of NPT Review Conference

First, we have to identify the powers and functions of the NPT Review Conference. According to Article VIII.3 of the NPT, its Review Conferences are convened 'in order to *review the operation* of this Treaty with a view to assuring that the purposes of the Preamble and the provisions of the Treaty are being realised' (emphasis added). While it would not follow from this that the Review Conferences have the power to give an authentic interpretation of the Treaty, it is also true that it is necessary to interpret treaty provisions in order to review its operation. To that extent, the work of the NPT Review Conference could involve interpretation of the Treaty. There are in fact examples in which a review conference of an arms control and disarmament treaty has given a (new) interpretation of its provisions.

For instance, the Fourth Review Conference of the Biological Weapons Convention (BWC) held in 1996 agreed, regarding the interpretation of Article I of the Convention (prohibiting States Parties from developing, producing, stockpiling or otherwise acquiring or retaining microbial or other biological agents or toxins), as follows: 'the *use* by the States Parties, in any way and under any circumstances, of microbial or other biological agents or toxins … is effectively a violation of Article I of the Convention'[28] (emphasis added). This agreement was recorded in the Final Declaration of the Conference. It may be said that this interpretation is a corollary to the prohibitions in Article I because it is impossible to 'use' the

[28] 'Final Declaration of the Fourth Review Conference of the Parties to the Convention on the Prohibition of the Development, Production and Stockpiling of Bacteriological (Biological) and Toxin Weapons and on Their Destruction', *United Nations Disarmament Yearbook,* Vol. 21 (1996), p. 217, Article I, para 3.

prohibited agents without first 'acquiring' them. Still, it is noteworthy that the BWC Review Conference agreed, by way of interpretation, that the 'use' of said agents is also prohibited under Article I.

At the same time, it is undeniable that the NPT, like other arms control and disarmament treaties, does not *expressly* stipulate that its Review Conferences have the power to give an authentic interpretation of the Treaty. Moreover, States Parties absent from the Review Conference in which a new interpretation of the term 'safeguards' may be agreed upon, may argue that they cannot accept the new interpretation as an authentic interpretation of the Treaty. Although they are expected to attend Review Conferences, their argument would not be unreasonable. If so, a possible agreement on a new interpretation of Article III.1 at a Review Conference would provide, to put it in extreme terms, no more than one of the elements for interpretation, though it may carry weight. How important that element is would depend on the way in which the agreement is phrased, formulated and adopted at the Conference.

According to the Rules of Procedure of the NPT Review Conference, decisions on substantive matters, including the adoption of the Final Document, are, in principle, to be taken by consensus. If consensus is not attainable, the decisions are to be taken by a two-thirds majority of those present and voting, provided that they include at least a majority of the participants.[29] Thus, although so far the NPT Review Conferences have adopted all their decisions by consensus, a Review Conference could adopt its Final Document containing a new interpretation of Article III.1 by a two-thirds majority, if consensus could not be reached on the interpretation. In that case, the new interpretation might lose much of its authority, depending on the concrete vote result. For this reason, and in view of the Review Conference's established practice of consensus decision, the Conference under such circumstances would most likely choose not to adopt the new interpretation or the Final Document containing it. Should the Conference adopt it, the interpretation would not be opposable to those States Parties that opposed to it,[30] simply because the Review Conference does not have the authority to give an authentic interpretation of the Treaty.

One of the most telling stories in this context[31] can be found in a debate regarding the Final Document of the Sixth NPT Review Conference of 2000. A section

[29]Rule 28 of the Rules of Procedure. See, e.g. NPT/CONF.2010/1, 20 May 2010, pp. 37–38; NPT/CONF.2010/50 (Vol. I), New York, 2010, p. 36, para 9.

[30]In addition, the interpretation might not be opposable to those States Parties that were absent from the Conference.

[31]Another telling story may be found with regard to para 12 of the Principles and Objectives decision adopted by consensus at the NPT Review and Extension Conference in 1995 (see Sect. 5.4.1). It provides that the NPT parties should require the recipient to accept the IAEA's full-scope safeguards and legally binding commitments not to acquire nuclear weapons for new supply arrangements for the transfer of nuclear material or equipment to non-nuclear-weapon States. The NSG decision on the India-specific exemption of 6 September 2008 deviating from the above NPT decision was made without following any procedure in the framework of the NPT. For the India-specific exemption decision by the NSG, see below n. 80.

of the Final Document dealing with Article VI of the NPT (on nuclear disarmament) enumerates thirteen specific measures as 'practical steps for the systematic and progressive efforts to implement article VI', including, for example, ratification of the Comprehensive Nuclear-Test-Ban Treaty (CTBT), a moratorium on nuclear test explosions and negotiations on a Fissile Material Cut-Off Treaty (FMCT).[32] These so-called '13 steps' have sometimes been described as 'the common interpretation [by] the NPT community of how Article VI is meant to be fulfilled' (Harald Müller).[33] On the other hand, Christopher Ford, US Special Representative for Nuclear Nonproliferation, in criticizing Müller's contention, argues that '[i]t would be absurd ... to suggest that the [13] steps constituted a legally binding obligation'.[34] This might look as if it is for the sake of criticizing, because in the same sentence Müller himself describes the 13 steps as '*politically* binding' (emphasis added) as opposed to legally binding. In any case, it is important to note that both Müller and Ford agree that the 13 steps are not legally binding, particularly since the Final Document of the 2000 Review Conference containing these steps was adopted by consensus with the participation of 158 States Parties.

5.3.2 Interpretative Agreement as a 'Subsequent Agreement' or 'Subsequent Practice'

Recall that the rule of 'fundamental change of circumstances' is a rule for the termination or suspension of the operation of a treaty or withdrawal therefrom, rather than for the interpretation of a treaty. However, there are some rules of interpretation that take into account what happens after the conclusion of a treaty; these are the rules on 'subsequent agreement' and 'subsequent practice'.[35] Indeed, there are writers who argue that the Final Declarations/Documents of the Review Conferences may constitute a 'subsequent agreement' or 'subsequent practice'.[36]

As regards 'subsequent agreement', the Vienna Convention on the Law of Treaties refers to 'subsequent agreement between the parties regarding the interpretation of the treaty or the application of its provisions' as an element to be taken into account in interpreting a treaty (Article 31, para 3(a)). It is natural to consider that if States Parties agree on an interpretation of a specific provision of a treaty even after they conclude it, the interpretation becomes the authentic

---

[32]See NPT/CONF.2000/28 (Parts I and II), New York, 2000, pp. 14–15.

[33]Müller 2005, p. 13.

[34]Ford 2007, p. 412.

[35]For an ICJ judgment declaring that Article 31, para 3, of the Vienna Convention 'reflects customary law', see *Kasikili/Sedudu Island (Botswana/Namibia)*, Judgment, ICJ Rep. 1999, p. 1075, para 48.

[36]See, e.g. Carnahan 1987, pp. 229–230; Jonas 2006, pp. 634–635; Ahlström 2006, pp. 678–679.

interpretation of it, since the power of interpreting a treaty rests with its States Parties. The Commentary of the UN International Law Commission (ILC) which drafted the Vienna Convention states that: 'an agreement as to the interpretation of a provision reached after the conclusion of the treaty represents an *authentic* interpretation by the parties which must be read into the treaty for purposes of its interpretation'[37] (emphasis added). The question then becomes what kind of agreement could constitute a 'subsequent agreement' here, particularly in terms of participation in the agreement. On this question, it should be concluded that such an agreement ought to be one that includes *all* the States Parties to the treaty[38] in light of a similar requirement for the 'subsequent practice', to be discussed below.[39]

With this requirement, a possible agreement at a Review Conference on a new interpretation of Article III.1 of the NPT would not qualify as a 'subsequent agreement', since it is next to impossible for a Review Conference to be attended by all the parties to the NPT. Even the 1995 Review and Extension Conference of the NPT, which decided on the future life of the Treaty, was not attended by all the States Parties at that time.[40]

Still, if a Review Conference agrees on a new interpretation by consensus, it could count as an agreement of a substantial number of States Parties. Furthermore, the agreement could become an authentic interpretation of the article by acquiescence, that is, if those absent from the Conference do not raise any objection to the agreement. Abstract possibility aside, however, this is not likely to happen with the interpretation of Article III.1, given that there are several States Parties to the NPT that openly objected or expressed reservations about the Additional Protocol[41] and many more States Parties are not in a position to accept the mandatory nature of the Additional Protocol.

Along with 'subsequent agreement', the Vienna Convention refers to 'subsequent practice in the application of the treaty which establishes the agreement of the parties regarding its interpretation' as another element to be taken into account in interpreting a treaty (Article 31, para 3(b)). According to the Commentary of the ILC, the Commission considered that 'subsequent practice establishing the understanding of the parties regarding the interpretation of a treaty should be included in para 3 as an *authentic* means of interpretation alongside interpretative

[37] *Yearbook of the International Law Commission*, 1966, Vol. II, p. 221, Commentary to Article 27, para 14.

[38] The same view is held by Professor Georg Nolte, member of the UN International Law Commission, as far as the requirement itself is concerned. A/CN.4/L.741, 5 August 2008, p. 32, para 24.

[39] See below n. 43 and accompanying text.

[40] Out of the 178 States Parties at that time, 175 participated in the Conference. NPT/CONF.1995/32 (Part I), above n. 20, pp. 3–4, para 13.

[41] Brazil, for instance, is one of such States. Huntington 2005, p. 37.

agreements', and that 'the phrase "the understanding of the parties"[42] necessarily means "the parties *as a whole*"'[43] (emphasis added).

Subsequent 'practice' in our context means the conclusion and bringing into force of an Additional Protocol by NPT parties. In order for such a practice to become 'subsequent practice' in the sense of Article 31, para 3(b), of the Vienna Convention, the practice would have to be such as to establish the agreement of *all* the States Parties to the NPT that the conclusion of an Additional Protocol is an obligation under the NPT. This does not mean that all the States Parties must conclude an Additional Protocol for the practice to constitute 'subsequent practice' under the Vienna Convention. Such a requirement would make almost meaningless the interpretation that Article III of the NPT obliges States Parties to conclude an Additional Protocol; if all the States Parties have already concluded an Additional Protocol, there is no practical need to think of the possibility of making it an obligation, except for those very few which will adhere to the Treaty in the future. It would suffice that all the States Parties either actually conclude an Additional Protocol or accept the conclusion as a practice adopted pursuant to Article III.1 of the NPT. The ILC's Commentary states that it is not necessary for every party to individually have engaged in the practice, and that 'it suffices that [every party] should have accepted the practice'.[44]

However, it would not be easy to establish that all the States Parties that have not concluded an Additional Protocol have accepted such a conclusion as something done pursuant to Article III.1. In practical terms, moreover, it is unlikely that they would accept it as such in light of the attitude of some States Parties toward the Additional Protocol, as mentioned above.

What would, then, be the value of an agreement or practice with less than all the States Parties involved therein in light of the rules of treaty interpretation? Generally speaking, it could be submitted, as the ILC also suggested, that the value of such an agreement or practice 'varies according as it shows the common understanding of the parties as to the meaning of the terms'.[45] Speaking of the rules of treaty interpretation as contained in the Vienna Convention, such an agreement or practice may be considered as one of the 'supplementary means of interpretation' in the sense of Article 32 of the Convention. Article 32 provides that

---

[42]ILC's draft Article 27, para 3(b), read as follows: '(b) Any subsequent practice in the application of the treaty which establishes *the understanding of the parties* regarding its interpretation' (emphasis added).

[43]*Yearbook of the International Law Commission*, 1966, Vol. II, p. 222, Commentary to Article 27, para 15. The Commission also said that: '[t]he text provisionally adopted in 1964 spoke of a practice which "establishes the understanding of all the parties"'; '[b]y omitting the word "all" the Commission did not intend to change the rule'; and that '[i]t omitted the word "all" merely to avoid any possible misconception that every party must individually have engaged in the practice where it suffices that it should have accepted the practice'. Ibid., para 15. See also Aust 2013, p. 215.

[44]*Yearbook of the International Law Commission*, 1966, Vol. II, p. 222, Commentary to Article 27, para 15.

[45]Ibid., para 15. This is what the ILC said regarding subsequent practice.

recourse may be had to 'supplementary means of interpretation, *including* the preparatory work of the treaty and the circumstances of its conclusion' (emphasis added). Thus, such 'supplementary means' may *also include other means*, including an agreement that does not qualify as a 'subsequent agreement' and practice that does not qualify as 'subsequent practice' under Article 31, para 3.[46]

However, it is also noted that, according to Article 32, supplementary means may be resorted to either in order to confirm the meaning resulting from the application of Article 31 or to determine the meaning in cases of ambiguity or absurdity. As such, an agreement or practice that is less than a 'subsequent agreement' or 'subsequent practice' could not carry as much significance as it might appear. It is said that '[a]n interpretation agreed [upon] between some only of the parties to a multilateral treaty may ... not be conclusive, since the interests and intentions of the other parties may have to be taken into consideration'.[47]

With this theoretical background information in mind, let us now examine the present level of agreement or acceptance of the NPT States Parties regarding the conclusion of an Additional Protocol.

5.3.3 Discussions on the Universalization of Additional Protocol at the NPT Review Conference

The 2010 NPT Review Conference did not differ much from the previous Conferences and their Preparatory Committees in that there was a fundamental conflict of views between the five nuclear-weapon and Western non-nuclear-weapon States Parties (hereinafter collectively referred to as 'developed States Parties') on the one hand and NAM States Parties on the other. The developed States Parties argued in three different ways in support of their positions.[48] First,

[46]Yasseen 1976, p. 52; Sinclair 1984, p. 138.

[47]Jennings and Watts 1992, p. 1268.

[48]NPT/CONF.2010/WP.21 (Vienna Group), 29 March 2010, p. 5, paras 11–14; NPT/CONF.2010/WP.5 (Japan), 19 March 2010, p. 1, paras 2, 3, p. 2, paras 6, 7; Statement by Australia, Main Committee II, 10 May 2010, p. 2; Statement by Japan, Main Committee II, 10 May 2010, p. 3; Statement by Ukraine, Main Committee II, 12 May 2010, p. 1; NPT/CONF.2010/WP.31 (EU), 14 April 2010, p. 8, paras 37–39; NPT/CONF.2010/WP.32 (France), 14 April 2010, pp. 2–3; NPT/CONF.2010/WP.38 (Vienna Group), 20 April 2010, p. 1; NPT/CONF.2010/WP.48 (OSCE), 30 April 2010, p. 3; NPT/CONF.2010/WP.56 (EU), 4 May 2010, p. 3; NPT/CONF.2010/WP.64 (China), 6 May 2010, p. 2, para 7; Statement by EU, Main Committee II, 10 May 2010, p. 5, para 15; Statement by New Zealand, Main Committee II, 10 May 2010, p. 2; Statement by the United States, Main Committee II, 10 May 2010, pp. 1–2; Statement by Canada, Main Committee II, 10 May 2010, p. 2; Statement by Norway, Main Committee II, 10 May 2010, p. 2; Statement by Russia, Main Committee II, 12 May 2010, p. 3; 'Statement by the People's Republic of China, France, the Russian Federation, the United Kingdom of Great Britain and Northern Ireland, and the United States of America to the 2010 Non-Proliferation Treaty Review Conference', 5 May 2010, para 11.

they said that the Additional Protocol should be universalized and those States Parties that have not concluded an Additional Protocol should do so as soon as possible. Their second argument was that measures contained in the CSA and the Additional Protocol were now the 'verification (or safeguards) standard' of the NPT. Thirdly, they described the Additional Protocol as an 'integral part of the IAEA safeguards system'.

While they all aim at the same objective of universalizing the Additional Protocol, one may be able to point out certain nuanced differences among them. The first argument is a most straightforward description of the objective. Yet, it does not carry much weight other than just expressing the hope. The second argument can be considered as aiming reservedly at an evolutive interpretation of Article III.1 of the NPT by using the word 'standard'. 'Standard' is something established 'as a model or example' to be followed,[49] but falls short of an obligation. The third argument would enable one to contend that the conclusion of an Additional Protocol is now an obligation under Article III.1. As we discussed earlier (Sect. 5.2.2), if the Additional Protocol becomes an 'integral part of the IAEA safeguards system', its conclusion can be regarded as an obligation for non-nuclear-weapon States Parties to the NPT because the said article obliges them to conclude an agreement with the IAEA in accordance with 'the Agency's safeguards system'.[50]

NAM States Parties, on the other hand, remained of the view that it is fundamental to make a 'distinction between legal obligations and voluntary confidence-building measures', in order to 'ensure that such voluntary undertakings are not turned into safeguards obligations'.[51] Although there were several NAM States Parties, including Singapore, the United Arab Emirates (UAE) and Chile,[52] that expressed concurrence to the first and second arguments of the developed States Parties, the negative voices of the leading NAM States Parties, particularly those of Egypt and Iran, as well as the voice of Brazil (non-NAM), were so strong that they prevailed in the discussions on the Additional Protocol not only among the NAM members but in the wider forum of the Review Conference itself.

[49]See *Merriam-Webster Online Dictionary*.

[50]At the 2005 NPT Review Conference, IAEA Director-General Mohamed ElBaradei already argued in this line by stating that: 'I would welcome an acknowledgement by this Conference that the additional protocol is *an integral part of Agency safeguards* in every country party to the NPT' (emphasis added). IAEA Director-General Dr Mohamed ElBaradei, Statement to the NPT Review Conference, 2 May 2005.

[51]NPT/CONF. 2010/WP.46 (NAM), 28 April 2010, p. 7, Rec. 33; Statement by NAM, Main Committee II, 10 May 2010, para 23. See also Statement by the League of Arab States, General Debate, 6 May 2010, p. 4; NPT/CONF.2010/WP.30 (League of Arab States), 13 April 2010, p. 2; Statement by Egypt, Main Committee II, 10 May 2010, p. 1; Statement by Iran, Main Committee II, 10 May 2010, p. 2; Statement by Lebanon, Main Committee III, 11 May 2010, p. 2; NPT/CONF.2010/WP.51 (Syria), 3 May 2010, p. 3, paras 12–13. Cf. Statement by Brazil (non-NAM), Main Committee II, 10 May 2010, p. 2.

[52]Cf. Potter et al., above n. 19, p. 14. See also NPT/CONF.2010/WP.5/Rev.1, 7 May 2010, p. 1, para 3; Statement by Sri Lanka, General Debate, 6 May 2010, p. 1.

As a result, the relevant paragraphs of the Final Document of the 2010 NPT Review Conference (paras 17 and 18), which the Conference took note of,[53] spelled out the developed States Parties' views in a considerably diluted manner. In addition to 'encourage[ing]' all States Parties that have not yet done so to conclude and bring into force an Additional Protocol, the Conference noted: (a) that '*numerous States* were of the view that those measures [specified in the model additional protocol] have been *introduced* as *an integral part of the IAEA safeguards system*'; (b) that 'it is the *sovereign decision* of any State to conclude an additional protocol, but once in force, the additional protocol is a legal obligation'; (c) that '*many States* recognize that comprehensive safeguards agreements and additional protocols are *among the integral elements of the IAEA safeguards system*'; and (d) that '*in the case of a State party* with a comprehensive safeguards agreement *concluded pursuant to article III, paragraph 1, of the Treaty* and supplemented by an additional protocol in force, measures contained in both instruments represent the enhanced *verification standard for that State*'[54] (emphasis added).

In regard to the first argument of the developed States Parties (i.e. those States Parties that have not concluded an Additional Protocol should do so as soon as possible), the Review Conference only 'encourage[d]', rather than called for (as in Security Council Resolution 1887 (2009) of 24 September 2009 adopted unanimously when the Council met in a summit to discuss nuclear non-proliferation and nuclear disarmament),[55] the conclusion of an Additional Protocol.

On their second argument (i.e. measures contained in the CSA and the Additional Protocol are now the verification standard of the NPT), the Conference in (d) above noted that measures contained in a CSA and an Additional Protocol represent the enhanced 'verification standard'. However, it said that they represent a verification standard only for a State Party with these instruments in force. This is entirely different from stating that measures contained in the CSA and the Additional Protocol represent the verification standard for all States Parties to the NPT. It is also to be noted that (d) referred to Article III.1 of the NPT only in relation to the CSA and not in relation to the Additional Protocol, just like Article 8 of the Treaty of Semipalatinsk mentioned earlier.

With reference to the third argument of the developed States Parties (i.e. the Additional Protocol is an integral part of the IAEA safeguards system), it is true that in (a) above the Conference referred to the measures in the Model Additional Protocol as an 'integral part of the IAEA safeguards system'. Precisely speaking, however, it

[53]The Final Document (Part I) of the 2010 NPT Review Conference consists of two parts: the part of 'Review of the operation of the Treaty' and the part of 'Conclusions and recommendations for follow-on actions'. The former part reflects to the best of the President's (of the Review Conference) knowledge what transpired at the Review Conference with regard to matters under review, which the Conference took note of on its final day, while the Conference adopted the latter part by consensus. NPT/CONF.2010/50 (Vol. I), above n. 29, p. 2, footnote 1, p. 40, para 30. The paragraphs referred to in this section all belong to the former part.

[54]NPT/CONF.2010/50 (Vol. I), above n. 29, p. 4, paras 17, 18.

[55]Security Council Resolution 1887(2009) '[c]all[ed] upon' all States to sign, ratify and implement an Additional Protocol (para 15.b).

only said that they have been 'introduced' as such; it did not say that they in fact 'constitute' an integral part of the IAEA safeguards system. Indeed, the Conference in (c) above described CSAs and Additional Protocols 'among the integral elements' of the IAEA safeguards system, instead of 'an integral part' of it—a nuanced difference over which developed and NAM States Parties disputed at the Conference. More important, in both (a) and (c), it was indicated that there was no consensus on the above views by saying that 'numerous' or 'many'—not all—States held those views.

In addition, the Review Conference explicitly showed that the Additional Protocol is an option and not a legal requirement by stating in (b) above that concluding an Additional Protocol is a 'sovereign decision' of each State. Even the Vienna Group countries,[56] consisting of 11 strongest advocates of the universalization of the Additional Protocol, stated in their working paper presented at the Conference that: 'the Group acknowledges that it is the sovereign right of any State to decide to conclude an additional protocol', while, at the same time, considering that both a CSA and an Additional Protocol are necessary to properly meet the safeguards requirement of the NPT.[57] Thus, at this stage, there is no factual basis upon which we could argue that the States Parties to the NPT are legally obligated to conclude an Additional Protocol and bring it into force.

It should perhaps be added that both the United States and Russia also hold the same view on this point. US Under Secretary of State Robert Joseph said in 2005 as follows: 'non-nuclear weapon states party to the NPT are obliged under the NPT to bring into force a full-scope safeguards agreement [i.e. comprehensive safeguards agreement], effectively covering all nuclear material in the state. The NPT does not, however, require such a party to either sign or bring into force an Additional Protocol, whose provisions strengthen the safeguards agreement beyond what is required by the NPT'.[58] Also, the Russian Federation stated in Main Committee II of the 2010 NPT Review Conference that: 'conclusion of the Additional Protocol remains a purely voluntary act'.[59]

5.4 Indirect Approach: Additional Protocol as a Condition for Nuclear Transfers

As we have seen, it is difficult to establish that States Parties are now of the view that the conclusion and bringing into force of an Additional Protocol is an obligation under Article III.1 of the NPT. Therefore, the only way to achieve the

[56]'The Vienna Group of Ten' consists of the following eleven States: Australia, Austria, Canada, Denmark, Finland, Hungary, Ireland, The Netherlands, New Zealand, Norway and Sweden.

[57]NPT/CONF.2010/WP.21, above n. 48, p. 5, para 12.

[58]Questions for the Record Submitted to Under Secretary Robert Joseph by Chairman Richard G. Lugar (#12), Senate Foreign Relations Committee: Safeguards Verification and Compliance, 2 November 2005.

[59]Statement by Russia, Main Committee II, above n. 48, p. 3.

objective of universalization of the Additional Protocol is to take steps involving incentives to conclude it—an indirect approach. One such step is to require the conclusion of an Additional Protocol as a condition for nuclear transfers. A proposal to that effect was put forward by US President George W. Bush in 2004. In his National Defense University address of 11 February 2004, President Bush proposed that 'only states that have signed the Additional Protocol be allowed to import equipment for their civilian nuclear programs'.[60] Although he said 'sign' the Additional Protocol, he may well have meant that the Protocol should be brought into force,[61] because he added that nations that are serious about fighting proliferation will 'approve and implement' the Additional Protocol.

5.4.1 Conditionality for Nuclear Transfers

Nuclear and nuclear-related exports have mainly been governed by the guidelines of the Nuclear Suppliers Group (NSG), an informal (i.e. not treaty-based) group established in 1975 in response to the Indian nuclear explosions in the previous year.[62] Today, its two sets of guidelines provide a policy to be followed by the Group's Participating Governments in supplying items especially designed or prepared for nuclear use (nuclear transfer) and nuclear-related dual-use items (nuclear-related transfer).

In 1992, spurred on by the revelations of Iraq's illegal nuclear weapons development, the former guidelines for nuclear transfer were amended to include the entry into force of a CSA as a precondition for nuclear supply.[63] This revision was supported by the NPT Parties in 1995 when they adopted a decision on the 'Principles and Objectives for Nuclear Non-Proliferation and Disarmament' (hereinafter referred to as the 'Principles and Objectives') at the NPT Review and Extension Conference. Paragraph 12 of the Principles and Objectives stipulates that:

---

[60]White House, President Announces New Measures to Counter the Threat of WMD: Remarks by the President on Weapons of Mass Destruction Proliferation, National Defense University, Washington, D.C., 11 February 2004.

[61]The expression 'sign (up to a treaty)' is often used by a government minister to mean being bound legally. Aust 2013, p. 105.

[62]For a history of the NSG, see INFCIRC/539/Rev.4, 5 November 2009.

[63]'Guidelines for Nuclear Transfers', INFCIRC/254/Rev.1/Part 1/Mod.1, July 1993, Annex, p. 1, para 4(a). For the current version of NGS Guidelines Part 1 on nuclear transfer, which also control the transfer of 'related technology' in addition to the 'trigger list items', see 'Guidelines for Nuclear Transfers', INFCIRC/254/Rev.12/Part 1, 13 November 2013, para 4(a). This sub-paragraph partly provides that: '[s]uppliers should transfer trigger list items or related technology to a non-nuclear weapon State only when the receiving State has brought into force an agreement with the IAEA requiring the application of safeguards on all source and special fissionable material in its current and future peaceful activities'.

> New supply arrangements for the transfer of source or special fissionable material or equipment or material especially designed or prepared for the processing, use or production of special fissionable material to non-nuclear-weapon States should require, as a necessary precondition, acceptance of the [International Atomic Energy] Agency's full-scope safeguards and internationally legally binding commitments not to acquire nuclear weapons or other nuclear explosive devices.[64]

In 2000, the NPT parties 'reaffirm[ed]' the above new rule in the Final Document of the Sixth Review Conference of the NPT.[65]

The proposal put forward by President Bush in 2004 was designed to go one step further by making the signing of an *Additional Protocol* a precondition for nuclear transfer. In the NSG plenary of that year the Participating Governments expressed different views on the proposal. For instance, Argentina and Brazil argued that this criterion should be voluntary; Russia and other States argued that such a restriction should be limited to enrichment and reprocessing transfers as the most sensitive part of the nuclear fuel cycle.[66] To date, the NSG has not been able to agree on this particular proposal by President Bush.

However, since there still is a possibility of the NSG guidelines making the conclusion of an Additional Protocol a condition for nuclear transfers, such conditionality merits legal evaluation in light of the NPT provisions, particularly those related to the States Parties' obligation of export control (Article III.2) as well as their right to the peaceful uses of nuclear energy (Article IV).

5.4.2 *Rights and Obligations of the States Parties Under Articles III and IV of the NPT*

The NPT in Article III.2, provides as follows:

> Each State Party to the Treaty undertakes not to provide: (a) source or special fissionable material, or (b) equipment or material especially designed or prepared for the processing, use or production of special fissionable material, to any non-nuclear-weapon State for peaceful purposes, unless the source or special fissionable material shall be subject to the safeguards required by this Article.

This is an obligation of nuclear suppliers party to the NPT to require the recipient State to apply safeguards to 'the source or special fissionable material' (nuclear material) *relevant to the particular nuclear transfers* (covering both transfers of nuclear material and equipment) (hereinafter referred to as 'item-specific

---

[64]NPT/CONF.1995/32 (Part I), above n. 20, Annex, Decision 2, para 12.

[65]NPT/CONF.2000/28 (Parts I and II), above n. 32, p. 6, para 36.

[66]Boese 2004, p. 19. Enrichment of uranium is a necessary step in making uranium-type nuclear weapons, and reprocessing is a method to extract plutonium from spent fuel of nuclear reactors for plutonium-type nuclear weapons.

safeguards' as opposed to 'comprehensive safeguards').[67] The proposal to require more than item-specific safeguards for nuclear transfers should be looked at from two different standpoints: from the supplier's and from the recipient's, in the context of their respective rights and obligations under the NPT.

From the *supplier*'s standpoint, it would not be counter to its obligations under the NPT for the supplier State Party to do more than what the Treaty obliges it to do by requiring the recipient State to apply a CSA or even an Additional Protocol, rather than simply requiring the application of item-specific safeguards as prescribed by Article III.2 of the NPT. On the contrary, such a step would be in conformity with and even promote the nuclear non-proliferation objectives of the NPT.

From the *recipient*'s point of view, on the other hand, legal questions may arise if the recipient is a party to the NPT, particularly with regard to its rights under Article IV of the Treaty. Article IV.2, of the NPT provides:

> All the Parties to the Treaty undertake to facilitate, and have the right to participate in, the fullest possible exchange of equipment, materials and scientific and technological information for the peaceful uses of nuclear energy. Parties to the Treaty in a position to do so shall also co-operate in contributing alone or together with other States or international organizations to the further development of the applications of nuclear energy for peaceful purposes, especially in the territories of non-nuclear-weapon States Party to the Treaty ...

Thus, the recipients party to the NPT are guaranteed their 'right' to participate in the 'fullest possible exchange' of nuclear equipment, etc., as long as they comply with their (basic) obligations under the Treaty.[68] In the case of non-nuclear-weapon States Parties to the NPT, their main obligations include: not to receive or acquire nuclear weapons or other nuclear explosive devices (Article II) and to accept comprehensive safeguards and conclude an agreement with the IAEA for that purpose (Article III). Requiring what is not required under the NPT, and categorically rejecting nuclear cooperation with States Parties not meeting the new requirement, could raise a legal problem.

---

[67]There is another way of interpreting Article III.2, according to which 'safeguards' in that paragraph refer to comprehensive safeguards. Michel 2007, p. 25. But this interpretation is not widely supported. The Zangger Committee, an informal group to reach a common understanding on the obligations of Article III.2 of the NPT, has considered the safeguards under that paragraph to be item specific. INFCIRC/209, 3 September 1974, Memorandum A, para 3.b; INFCIRC/209/Rev.2, 9 March 2000, Memorandum A, para 3(b).

[68]Compliance with the (basic) obligations is not explicitly mentioned in Article IV of the NPT as a condition for the exercise of the right provided therein. But according to the Vienna Convention on the Law of Treaties, a 'material breach' of a multilateral treaty by one of the parties may lead to a suspension of the operation of the treaty in whole or in part or to the termination of it (Article 60, para 2); and a 'material breach' is defined by the Convention as including 'violation of a provision essential to the accomplishment of the object or purpose of the treaty' (Article 60, para 3(b)). For the meaning of the latter phrase, see, e.g. Simma and Tams 2011, pp. 1358–1360. A working paper submitted to the 2010 NPT Review Conference by 23 States Parties, including both nuclear-weapon and non-nuclear-weapon and both developed and NAM States Parties states that: '[they] recognize that nuclear cooperation should take place only among States that are in full compliance with their IAEA safeguards obligations'. NPT/CONF.2010/WP.71, 12 May 2010, p. 2, para 7.

Based on these general considerations, we should distinguish between requiring the acceptance of comprehensive safeguards as in the NSG guidelines as amended in 1992 or in the NPT Principles and Objectives of 1995 on the one hand, and requiring the conclusion of an Additional Protocol as in the Bush proposal of 2004 on the other. In the former case, the right of the non-nuclear-weapon recipient party to the NPT would not be undermined by the new requirement, because they are already obliged to accept comprehensive safeguards as parties to the Treaty (Article III.1). It would be difficult for a non-nuclear-weapon State Party to the NPT to complain about restricted nuclear cooperation without fulfilling its obligations under Article III. However, requiring the conclusion of an Additional Protocol, which exceeds what the non-nuclear-weapon States Parties are obliged to do under the NPT, as a condition for nuclear cooperation that is guaranteed to them under Article IV of the Treaty, could pose a legal problem of infringement of their right.

That said, it should be pointed out that the 'right' that may be considered infringed upon here is relatively moderate in nature. The obligation of the suppliers party to the NPT corresponding to that right is just to 'facilitate' the fullest possible exchange of nuclear equipment, materials and information as well as merely to 'co-operate in contributing' to the further development of the applications of nuclear energy for peaceful purposes (Article IV.2).

The moderate nature of the rights and obligations under Article IV.2, of the NPT can be confirmed by its drafting history.[69] Although the finally agreed upon provisions of Article IV.2, do not dramatically differ from the original draft of the article, there were several proposals to clarify the content of the provisions during the negotiations of the Treaty, including one by Mexico. Mexico proposed that Article IV.2, use the following language: 'Those Parties that are in a position to do so, have the *duty to contribute* ... to the further development of the production, industries, and other applications of nuclear energy for peaceful purposes, especially in the territories of non-nuclear-weapon States,[70] (emphasis added). However, other States such as Canada and the UK argued that the term 'duty' was too broad and could be interpreted to mean that a nuclear-weapon State would be forced to respond to *any* request by any non-nuclear-weapon State.[71] The United States also stated that, while it shares the objectives sought to be advanced by the Mexican suggestion, '[concerns have] been pointed out by some delegations that the precise terms of the Mexican formulation may in some respects create too sweeping and too general an obligation'.[72] Consequently, the Mexican proposal was not adopted.

[69]See Ford 2010, pp. 308–309; Zhang 2006, pp. 660–661; Shaker 1980, pp. 328–331.

[70]ENDC/196, 19 September 1967, reproduced in US Arms Control and Disarmament Agency, *Documents on Disarmament 1967* (US Government Printing Office, 1968), p. 395.

[71]Firmage 1969, p. 728.

[72]ENDC/PV.338, 12 October 1967, p. 8, para 16.

From all this, we could conclude that, strictly speaking, NPT parties are not really obligated under the Treaty to actually supply any nuclear equipment, materials or information to any demander party to the NPT. In other words, it could be said that requiring the conclusion of an Additional Protocol as a condition for nuclear transfer is not necessarily barred by Article IV of the NPT[73] and, as such, is worth pursuing.

Nevertheless, what is legally possible and what the parties wish to do are two separate matters. In order to further clarify the latter question in a wider forum, we will see the discussions on it at the 2010 NPT Review Conference.

5.4.3 Discussions on the Conditionality for Nuclear Transfers at the NPT Review Conference

At the 2010 NPT Review Conference, the idea of making the conclusion of an Additional Protocol a condition for nuclear transfers caused much discussion, and opinions were expressed in three different ways. First, the Vienna Group States and the EU Member States specifically promoted such an idea of conditionality.[74] For instance, a working paper presented by the Vienna Group stated that: 'this verification standard [i.e. a CSA together with an additional protocol] should be a *condition* for new supply arrangements to non-nuclear-weapon States (emphasis added). There are States, such as Australia, which have already made adherence to an Additional Protocol a condition for nuclear transfers (in the case of Australia, the supply of Australian uranium).[75] Secondly, certain NAM countries argue that supplier States should *consider* whether recipient States have concluded an Additional Protocol in making nuclear export decisions.[76] This is also what the Security Council '[e]ncourage[d]' in its Resolution 1887(2009) of 24 September 2009.[77]

---

[73]For a different view, see Goldschmidt 1977, p. 80. Goldschmidt argues that 'restrictions on transmission of sensitive [nuclear] technologies can be construed as a breach of the promise given in Article IV of the NPT'.

[74]NPT/CONF.2010/WP.17 (Vienna Group), 29 March 2010, p. 5, para 13; NPT/CONF. 2010/WP.31, above n. 48, p. 8, para 46; Statement by EU, Main Committee II, above n. 48, p. 6, para 19. See also Statement by New Zealand, Main Committee II, above n. 48, p. 2.

[75]Statement by Australia, General Debate, 3 May 2010, p. 5; Statement by Australia, Main Committee II, above n. 48, p. 3.

[76]For instance, the United Arab Emirates stated that given the importance of the Additional Protocol, export of nuclear technology should give a priority for countries that have the Additional Protocol in force. Statement by the UAE, General Debate, 4 May 2010, p. 2.

[77]S/RES/1887(2009), 24 September 2009, para 19, which '[e]ncourage[d] States to consider whether a recipient State has signed and ratified an additional protocol based on the model additional protocol in making nuclear export decisions'.

On the other hand, the NAM States Parties as a group underscored the 'inalienable right' of the NPT parties to the peaceful uses of nuclear technology, and pointed out that they did not see any room for reinterpretation or setting of conditions for such uses.[78] More specifically, the League of Arab States stressed the optional nature of the Additional Protocol and said that they did 'not agree to rendering it a mandatory instrument that becomes the standard upon which NPT parties receive nuclear technology for peaceful purposes'.[79]

Moreover, some of the NAM States Parties even took up this question in the context of the US–Indian nuclear cooperation, which allows the United States to give full civil nuclear energy cooperation to India.[80] They criticized that the United States and some other nuclear supplier States have applied a double standard by promising on the one hand to provide nuclear cooperation to India, a country that is neither a party to the NPT nor has concluded a CSA, while on the other hand requiring non-nuclear-weapon States Parties to the NPT to conclude not only CSAs but also Additional Protocols before receiving nuclear cooperation. NAM countries further argued that the US–Indian deal and the NSG decision endorsing the deal were a violation of above-quoted para 12[81] of the 1995 Principles and Objectives providing for the requirement of CSA as a precondition for any new nuclear supply arrangement, and also contended that it should be prohibited to provide nuclear cooperation to non-party to the NPT.[82]

Reflecting these sharp confrontations, the compromise language in the Final Document of the 2010 NPT Review Conference included a phrase which is

[78]Statement by NAM, General Debate, 3 May 2010, p. 4.

[79]Statement by the League of Arab States, General Debate, above n. 51, p. 4. See also NPT/CONF.2010/WP.59 (Iraq), 5 May 2010, p. 2.

[80]Under the US–India Joint Statement issued on 18 July 2005, India committed itself, among others, to separation of its nuclear facilities between civilian and military, placing its civilian nuclear facilities under IAEA safeguards, and to signing and adhering to an Additional Protocol with respect to civilian facilities (but not to the adherence to the NPT nor the conclusion of a CSA). On the other hand, the United States promised to work to achieve full civil nuclear energy cooperation with India by seeking agreement from Congress and friends and allies to adjust US laws and international regimes to enable such cooperation. White House, 'Joint Statement between President George W. Bush and Prime Minister Manmohan Singh', 18 July 2005.
On 6 September 2008, the NSG endorsed this arrangement by adopting a policy under which, notwithstanding certain provisions of the NSG guidelines (including the conditionality of CSA), the Participating Governments may transfer to India trigger list (nuclear) items and/or related technology for peaceful purposes. Although this policy also refers to an exemption from rules contained in the NSG guidelines Part 2 for transfers of nuclear-related dual-use items, Part 2 itself does not necessarily prohibit transfers of such items to States not having a CSA in place, but it only refers to such a factor (not having a CSA in place) as one of the factors to be taken into account in authorizing a transfer of those items. 'Statement on Civil Nuclear Cooperation with India', INFCIRC/734 (Corr.), 19 September 2008; INFCIRC/254/Rev.9/Part 1, November 2007, paras 4(a), 4(b), 4(c); INFCIRC/254/Rev.7/Part 2, February 2006, paras 4(a), 4(b). See generally Ntoubandi 2008, pp. 273–287.

[81]See Sect. 5.4.1.

[82]Statement by Iran, Main Committee III, 11 May 2010, p. 2; NPT/CONF.2010/WP.61 (Iran), 6 May 2010, p. 2, para 5, p. 3, para 9; Statement by Algeria, General Debate, 4 May 2010, p. 4.

difficult to understand without tracing its drafting history. In the initial draft proposed by the President of the Review Conference (Ambassador Libran Cabactulan of the Philippines), it was provided that: 'The Conference encourages States parties to consider whether a recipient State has brought into force *an additional protocol* ... in making nuclear export decisions'[83] (emphasis added). This was virtually the same language as is found in Security Council Resolution 1887(2009) adopted by the Council summit meeting in the previous year, and also reflected what certain NAM countries advanced at the Review Conference.[84]

However, the President's revised text, which was finally adopted by the Conference, read as follows: 'The Conference encourages States parties to consider whether a recipient State has brought into force *IAEA safeguards obligations* in making nuclear export decisions'[85] (Action 37, emphasis added). It is not easy to figure out what is meant by 'IAEA safeguards obligations', but it seems most natural to read it as meaning comprehensive safeguards, because the Additional Protocol is not part of safeguards 'obligations' to be brought into force.[86] If so, the language of the Final Document represented an apparent retreat from that of the corresponding provision of Resolution 1887(2009), though the two provisions adopted in two different forums cannot simply be compared.

With regard to the US–Indian deal, the initial draft of the President of the Review Conference reaffirmed that '[... *existing or new* supply arrangements for the transfer ... shall require, as a necessary precondition, acceptance of IAEA full scope safeguards and internationally legally binding commitments not to acquire nuclear weapons or other nuclear explosive devices]'[87] (emphasis added, square brackets original). This was an almost faithful reproduction of para 12 of the 1995

[83]NPT/CONF.2010/CRP.2/Rev.1, 25 May 2010, p. 26, para 17.

[84]See above n. 76, 77.

[85]NPT/CONF.2010/L.2, 27 May 2010, p. 23, Action 37; NPT/CONF.2010/50 (Vol. I), above n. 29, p. 26, Action 37. Action 37 belongs to the 'Conclusions and recommendations' part of the Final Document, which the Conference adopted by consensus. For the different status of the two parts of the Final Document of the 2010 NPT Review Conference, see above n. 53.

[86]It might also be interpreted to mean the conclusion of an item-specific safeguards agreement (INFCIRC/66) in cases where the recipient State is a non-party to the NPT. But such an interpretation would be inconsistent with other paragraphs of the Final Document, including its para 12, which recalled para 12 of the 1995 Principles and Objectives decision. The said paragraph of the 1995 decision requires NPT parties to make the acceptance of the IAEA's *full-scope safeguards* one of the conditions for new supply arrangements for the transfer of nuclear material or equipment to *non-nuclear-weapon States*.

[87]NPT/CONF.2010/CRP.2/Rev.1, above n. 83, p. 18, para 125.

Principles and Objectives decision, with the exception, *inter alia*, that it not only referred to 'new' supply arrangements but also 'existing' supply arrangements.[88] This latter phrase was clearly intended to point to the US–Indian arrangement for nuclear cooperation, and the language of the initial draft, if adopted as it was, would have had the effect of negating the US–Indian nuclear agreement at least politically. With this potential effect in mind, the United States strongly opposed the provision and stuck to the deletion of the reference to 'existing' supply arrangements. As a result, the revised and final version of the President's draft Final Document deleted the word 'existing' and read that 'new supply arrangements for the transfer ... should require, as a necessary precondition, acceptance of IAEA full scope safeguards and internationally legally binding commitments not to acquire nuclear weapons or other nuclear explosive devices'[89] (para 117).

Thus, while the acceptance of full-scope safeguards (or comprehensive safeguards) as a condition for nuclear transfer was reaffirmed repeatedly in one way or another in the Final Document of the 2010 NPT Review Conference,[90] it failed to agree on the conditionality of the conclusion and bringing into force of an Additional Protocol for such transfer. It must be admitted, however, that as far as the 2010 Review Conference goes, the advocates for the conditionality of Additional Protocol for nuclear transfer still remained a minority. At the same time, it is also to be noted that few States Parties discussed that making the conclusion of an Additional Protocol a condition for nuclear transfers would infringe on the States Parties' rights under the NPT.[91] This coincides with the conclusion of our legal analysis in Sect. 5.4.2. If so, it is not ruled out for individual States or groups of States to require the conclusion of an Additional Protocol as a prerequisite for nuclear supply in a bilateral nuclear cooperation agreement or in a multilateral agreement or arrangement among like-minded countries.

---

[88]There is another deviation. While para 12 of the 1995 Principles and Objectives decision refers to new supply arrangements for nuclear transfers 'to non-nuclear-weapon States', the relevant paragraph of the 2010 Final Document, as well as its earlier draft, does not refer to the above quoted words. If one reads it literally, it may be read to mean that because of this omission the requirements of IAEA full-scope safeguards and abandonment of nuclear weapons option would also apply to *nuclear-weapon States,* and that these States could not make a new supply arrangement with an NPT party unless they fulfil these requirements, which is, however, virtually impossible. The above paragraph of the Final Document should not be read that way. Instead, attention should be paid to the fact that this paragraph is located in a section dealing with the universality of the NPT. By doing so, it is understood that the paragraph is designed to regulate the transfer of nuclear material and equipment to *non-NPT States Parties*. As nuclear-weapon States are all NPT parties, the paragraph should not be read to be intended to apply to nuclear-weapon States.

[89]NPT/CONF.2010/L.2, above n. 85, p. 15, para 118; NPT/CONF.2010/50 (Vol. I), above n. 29, p. 18, para 117. This paragraph belongs to the 'Review' part of the Final Document, which the Conference simply took note of. For the different status of the two parts of the Final Document of the 2010 NPT Review Conference, see above n. 53.

[90]See NPT/CONF.2010/50 (Vol. I), above n. 29, p. 4, para 12, p. 18, para 117 (and p. 26, Action 37).

[91]Perhaps the only exception was Iran, who argued without elaboration that such conditionality would be in contravention of the provisions of Article IV of the NPT.

5.4.4 *Bilateral and Multilateral Agreements or Arrangements Including Conditionality of Additional Protocol*

5.4.4.1 Multilateral Endeavours

As discussed earlier, the NSG has so far failed to agree on the measures proposed by US President Bush in 2004, requiring the recipient State to sign an Additional Protocol before being allowed to import civilian nuclear equipment. However, there have been some related developments in the context of another proposal by President Bush that was made on the same occasion concerning a ban on the transfer of enrichment and reprocessing facilities, equipment and technology[92] (hereinafter collectively referred to as 'sensitive nuclear transfer').

At the L'Aquila summit meeting held in July 2009, the Group of Eight (G8) countries agreed in their L'Aquila Statement on Non-Proliferation to 'implement [the NSG's 'clean text' of 20 November 2008] on a national basis in the next year'[93] (para 8). The NSG's 'clean text' of 20 November 2008—a draft for the revision of the NSG guidelines eventually to be agreed upon in June 2011—was designed to regulate the transfer of enrichment and reprocessing facilities, equipment and technology, and to make the bringing into force of an Additional Protocol one of the many conditions ('criteria') for the recipient State to meet before receiving the transfer of these sensitive items and technology. However, the bringing into force of an Additional Protocol itself was not an absolute condition as, in an effort to accommodate Brazil, the rules allowed the Additional Protocol requirement to be met alternatively by having regional arrangements in place if they could offer similar levels of non-proliferation confidence.[94]

The L'Aquila summit statement had the effect of making such (somewhat relaxed) conditionality applicable among the G8 members in their supply activities, although it was only effective with regard to *sensitive* nuclear transfers, only among G8 members (which nevertheless include major nuclear suppliers), only for 1 year and was only politically binding. While the NSG again failed to agree on the 'clean text' (or its variant) in June 2010,[95] the G8 members did agree, in their June 2010 summit meeting in Muskoka, to extend the measures they had agreed upon in

---

[92]The original Bush proposal in this regard was for the NSG to agree on a total ban on the sensitive nuclear transfers to 'any state that does not already possess full-scale, functioning enrichment or reprocessing plants'. White House, above n. 60.

[93]'L'Aquila Statement on Non-Proliferation' (8 July 2009), para 8.

[94]Pomper 2008, p. 52. One of the criteria for sensitive nuclear transfers under the 'clean text' was that the recipient 'has in force an Additional Protocol *or* has signed, ratified and is implementing a regional arrangement approved by the IAEA which operates to achieve the same objective by providing confidence in the peaceful nature of civilian nuclear programs' (emphasis added). 'Revised Paragraphs 6 and 7 of INFCIRC/Part 1', 20 November 2008, para 6(a)(ii).

[95]Horner 2010, p. 45.

2009 (i.e. the same conditionality) for one more year by stating that '[they] reiterate [their] commitment as found in paragraph 8 of the L'Aquila Statement on Non-Proliferation'.[96] An almost identical provision was also included in the G8 Declaration adopted at its Deauville summit meeting in May 2011,[97] the last G8 summit meeting before the NSG agreed on a revision of its guidelines.

The NSG finally agreed on a revision of its nuclear transfer guidelines in June 2011 concerning the sensitive nuclear transfers and involving an element of Additional Protocol. The newly introduced para 6 of the revised guidelines provides as follows: the suppliers should authorize the transfer of enrichment or reprocessing facilities, equipment or technology, 'only when the recipient has brought into force a Comprehensive Safeguards Agreement, and an Additional Protocol… *or*, pending this, is implementing appropriate safeguards agreements in cooperation with the IAEA, including a regional accounting and control arrangement for nuclear materials, as approved by the IAEA Board of Governors'[98] (emphasis added). The conditionality of Additional Protocol is still not absolute in nature and looks further relaxed than the 'clean text', since the finally agreed text allows the recipient to implement an 'appropriate safeguards' agreement in place of Additional Protocol in the final analysis. Nonetheless, compared with the guidelines having no Additional Protocol criterion at all, the revised guidelines can be assessed positively from the perspective of promoting the universality of Additional Protocol, as they treat the possible exemption from the Additional Protocol requirement as something provisional by referring to 'pending this'.

Although not so many members are major nuclear suppliers, the States Parties to the newest nuclear-weapon-free zone treaty for Central Asia are not only obligated to conclude an Additional Protocol themselves,[99] but also obliged not to transfer nuclear material and equipment to any non-nuclear-weapon State that have not concluded a CSA and an Additional Protocol. The Treaty of Semipalatinsk in Article 8 stipulates as follows:

> Each Party undertakes: … (c) [n]ot to provide: (i) source or special fissionable material or (ii) equipment or material especially designed or prepared for the processing, use or production of special fissionable material, to any non-nuclear-weapon State, unless that State has concluded with the IAEA a comprehensive safeguards agreement and its Additional Protocol …

This is perhaps the only multilateral (plurilateral) treaty to date which provides for the conditionality of Additional Protocol for the transfer of nuclear material and equipment. It is true that the membership of the Semipalatinsk Treaty cannot

---

[96]'G8 Muskoka Declaration: Recovery and New Beginnings', Muskoka, Canada, 25–26 June 2010, para 29.

[97]'G8 Declaration: Renewed Commitment for Freedom and Democracy', Deauville, France, 26–27 May 2011, para 79.

[98]INFCIRC/254/Rev.10/Part 1, 26 July 2011, p. 3, para 6(c).

[99]Article 8, para (b). All five States Parties to the Treaty of Semipalatinsk have concluded and brought into force an Additional Protocol.

be compared with that of the NSG in terms of nuclear supply capabilities, but it includes Kazakhstan, which is now the number one producer of natural uranium in the world. Kazakhstan may be seen as another Australia in making the Additional Protocol a condition for its uranium supply. In fact, it is doing much more. Kazakhstan is legally obliged, not as a policy as in the case of Australia, to require the conclusion of an Additional Protocol before supplying its uranium to any other non-nuclear-weapon State. Such conditionality now also apply to the supply of other nuclear material and equipment in addition to uranium.

5.4.4.2 Bilateral Endeavours

There is also a bilateral endeavour to accomplish a similar objective. In May 2009, the United States concluded with the United Arab Emirates (UAE) an Agreement for Cooperation Concerning Peaceful Uses of Nuclear Energy[100] (hereinafter referred to as the 'US-UAE Agreement'). This is an ordinary bilateral nuclear cooperation agreement, which enables the parties to exchange information, material, equipment and components for the peaceful uses of nuclear energy. In the Agreed Minute attached to the Agreement as an integral part thereof, it is provided that:

> Prior to the licensing by the Government of the United States of America of exports of nuclear material, equipment, components, or technology pursuant to this Agreement, the Government of the United Arab Emirates shall … bring into force the Additional Protocol approved by the IAEA Board of Governors on March 3, 2009 …[101]

This can be seen as a realization of the Bush proposal regarding the conditionality of Additional Protocol on a bilateral basis, as it required the UAE to bring an Additional Protocol into force as a condition for actual nuclear transfers *in general*. As such, the conditionality in the US-UAE Agreement is, just like in the Treaty of Semipalatinsk, wider in scope than that of the G8 arrangements during 2009–2011 and of the NSG's revised guidelines, which are only for sensitive nuclear transfers. The UAE signed an Additional Protocol on 8 April 2009 and brought it into force on 20 December 2010.

It should be noted that although both the Treaty of Semipalatinsk and the US-UAE Agreement serve the common objective of promoting the universality of Additional Protocol, their respective roles are somewhat different. While the former Treaty obligates its States Parties to require the *recipient of their nuclear material or equipment* to conclude an Additional Protocol, the latter Agreement

[100]For the whole text of the Agreement, see Agreement for Cooperation between the Government of the United States and the Government of the United Arab Emirates: Message from the President of the United States (hereinafter cited as 'US-UAE Agreement: Message from the President') (US Government Printing Office 2009).

[101]Agreed Minute of the US-UAE Agreement, in ibid., p. 17.

obliges *the other State Party itself* to have an Additional Protocol in force. Thus, the Treaty of Semipalatinsk functions in such a way as to require its States Parties to *ensure* the conclusion of an Additional Protocol by the recipients of their nuclear material and equipment, by concluding a US-UAE type of bilateral nuclear cooperation agreement or by requiring the other party to a bilateral nuclear cooperation agreement to have an Additional Protocol in force beforehand, i.e. before concluding such bilateral agreement.

How much importance the United States has placed on this Agreement with the UAE can be found in Secretary of State Hillary Clinton and Secretary of Energy Steven Chu's statement in their Memorandum for the President provided to him in relation to the Agreement. It stated that it is the intention of the United States to use this Agreement 'as a model for other countries in the region that wish to pursue responsible nuclear energy development'.[102] Indeed, it has been said that the US–UAE Agreement, including the UAE's renunciation of enrichment and reprocessing as well as the conditionality of Additional Protocol, created a 'gold standard' for the future US peaceful nuclear cooperation agreements.[103] However, whether it could actually serve as a model or gold standard depends on the will of the regional countries concerned, which might complain about such a special rule for the region as 'biased' or 'unfair'.[104]

Moreover, the US–UAE Agreement itself appears to contain some weak points. In the Agreed Minute attached to the Agreement, it is further provided that: 'the fields of cooperation, terms and conditions' accorded by the United States to the UAE shall be 'no less favorable in scope and effect than those which may be accorded, from time to time, to any other non-nuclear weapon State in the Middle

[102]Secretaries Clinton and Chu, after referring to Article 7 (on the UAE abandonment of possession of sensitive nuclear facilities) and Article 13 (on the cessation of further cooperation, return of materials and equipment, and the termination of the Agreement, in cases of material violation of Article 7 and certain other provisions) of the Agreement, said that: 'In view of these and *other* nonproliferation features, we believe the Agreement can serve as a model for other countries in the region that wish to pursue responsible nuclear energy development' (emphasis added). Ibid., p. 25.

[103]See, e.g. E.M. Grossman, U.S. Nonproliferation Legislation Could Gain Steam in GOP-led House, Global Security Newswire, 3 November 2010, http://www.globalsecuritynewswire.org/gsn/archive.php?Date=11/03/2010. For criticism of such an argument particularly with regard to the requirement of abandoning possession of sensitive nuclear facilities, see F. McGoldrick, The U.S.-UAE Peaceful Nuclear Cooperation Agreement: A Gold Standard or Fool's Gold?, CSIS Policy Perspectives, 30 November 2010.

[104]It is said that several Middle Eastern States, including Turkey, Egypt, Saudi Arabia and Jordan, have refused US requests to adopt the UAE standard. H. Sokolski, Nuclear Cooperation and the Atomic Energy Act: Ten Worries, Five Remedies, Testimony submitted to the House Committee on Foreign Affairs: Nuclear Cooperation after Khan and Iran: Time for a New Paradigm, 22 September 2010, p. 3.

East in a peaceful nuclear cooperation agreement'.[105] As a provision similar to the so-called 'most-favored-nation (MFN) clause', it may be viewed as having the potential of changing the conditions of US–UAE nuclear cooperation, including the requirement of an Additional Protocol, upon signing of a new nuclear cooperation agreement with the United States by another regional State.

However, the above Agreed Minute provision of the US-UAE Agreement does not operate in such an automatic way as an MFN clause does. According to the same Agreed Minute, it is necessary to 'amend' the Agreement[106] in order to change the conditions of cooperation.[107] Thus, the conditionality is not as fragile as it may look. Moreover, it is hard to imagine, if not impossible, that the UAE would denounce its Additional Protocol simply because another regional State without having an Additional Protocol in force concluded a nuclear cooperation agreement with the United States with similar content.

At any rate, this is really a small step, covering only one small country in the region. Whether it could become a standard norm for nuclear cooperation with countries in the region and beyond, will depend on the future efforts of not only the United States but also other supplier States.[108]

[105]US-UAE Agreement: Message from the President, above n. 100, p. 21. This is a provision whose origin can be found in the Agreed Minute of the Agreement for Cooperation between the Government of the United States of America and the Government of the Arab Republic of Egypt Concerning Peaceful Uses of Nuclear Energy (hereinafter referred to as the 'US-Egyptian Agreement'), signed at Washington on 29 June 1981. The US-Egyptian Agreement provides that '[t]he Government of the United States confirms that fields of cooperation, terms and conditions accorded by the United States to the Arab Republic of Egypt for cooperation in the peaceful uses of nuclear energy shall be no less favourable in scope and effect than those which may be accorded by the United States to any other non-nuclear weapon state in the Middle East in a peaceful nuclear cooperation agreement'.

[106]Note that the Agreed Minute containing this conditionality forms an 'integral part of the Agreement'.

[107]The Agreed Minute provides that 'the Government of the United States of America … if requested by the Government of the United Arab Emirates, will consult with the Government of the United Arab Emirates regarding the possibility of *amending* this Agreement' (emphasis added) in order to restore the position that the cooperation accorded to the UAE shall be no less favourable than those accorded to other non-nuclear-weapon States in the region. US-UAE Agreement: Message from the President, above n. 100, pp. 21–22. The above-quoted part cannot be found in the corresponding Agreed Minute of the US-Egyptian Agreement of 1981.

[108]It is regrettable to note that the situation does not look very favourable in this respect. Henry Sokolski of the Nonproliferation Policy Education Center points out that: '[n]early all of the world's key suppliers—i.e. Russia, France, Japan, South Korea, Canada, and China—are undercutting U.S. efforts to establish the UAE deal as an international standard'. Sokolski, above n. 104, p. 3. In addition, the IAEA did not include the requirement of Additional Protocol in the eligibility criteria for nuclear fuel supply to a Member State under the IAEA Low Enriched Uranium (LEU) Bank scheme approved by the IAEA Board of Governors in December 2010. GOV/2010/67, 26 November 2010, p. 5, para 19.

5.5 Conclusions

On 28 May 2010, the States Parties to the NPT took note of the 'Review' part of the Final Document of the 2010 NPT Review Conference and adopted by consensus its 'Conclusions and recommendations' part. The NPT Review Conference adopted its Final Document for the first time since it had done so 10 years ago, and the 2010 Conference has largely been recognized as 'incremental success'.[109] However, if one looks closely at its content, the evaluation may become different, depending on the part and the criteria. As far as the universalization of the Additional Protocol is concerned, the Final Document does not seem to deserve high appreciation.[110] On the contrary, the language in the Final Document represents a general retreat from that in Security Council Resolution 1887(2009) adopted 8 months before, in respect of both direct and indirect approaches to the universalization of the Protocol.

With regard to the direct approach—i.e. calling directly for the conclusion of an Additional Protocol—Security Council Resolution 1887(2009) '[c]all[ed] upon' all States to sign, ratify and implement an Additional Protocol, and described the Protocol as 'constitut[ing] essential elements' of the IAEA safeguards system (para 15.b). However, the Final Document of the 2010 NPT Review Conference somewhat toned down by only '[e]ncourag[ing]' all States Parties to conclude and bring into force an Additional Protocol (para 18). It also somewhat qualified the description of the Protocol by stating that '*many*' [i.e. not all] States recognize that CSAs and Additional Protocols are '*among* the integral elements' (emphasis added) of the IAEA safeguards system (para 18).

The situation is much worse with reference to the indirect approach—i.e. taking measures to promote the conclusion of an Additional Protocol. In Resolution 1887(2009), it was encouraged that States consider whether a recipient State has 'signed and ratified an additional protocol' in making nuclear export decisions (para 19). However, in the 2010 Final Document, it was encouraged that States Parties to the NPT to consider whether a recipient State has brought into force 'IAEA safeguards obligations' in making nuclear export decisions (Action 37). It is a common understanding among NPT Parties that whatever 'IAEA safeguards obligations' means, they do not include the conclusion of an Additional Protocol.

It would, however, be wrong if one concludes from these facts that the international community retreated in its endeavour to universalize the Additional Protocol in less than 1 year. The Security Council, which adopted Resolution 1887(2009), consists only of 15 members, and its five permanent members exercise overwhelming power in the Council both politically and procedurally, including veto

[109]See, e.g. G. Perkovich, Nuclear Conference's "Incremental Success", Council on Foreign Relations Interview, 31 May 2010; Choubey 2010, p. 25.

[110]For a similar assessment, see D. Albright and A. Sticker, After the 2010 NPT Review Conference: Advancing the Non-Proliferation Pillar, ISIS (Institute for Science and International Security) Report, 15 July 2010, p. 1.

power. It is natural that the views of the permanent members of the Council, who are all advocates of the universalization of the Additional Protocol, were reflected in the resolution to the maximum. In other words, it may be that Security Council Resolution 1887(2009) did not necessarily reflect the general views of the international community as a whole.

By contrast, the Review Conference of the NPT functions by consensus as a rule, and the 116 NAM members party to the Treaty, the most influential of whom have taken a negative position toward the Additional Protocol, always have a powerful voice. If one attaches great importance to the 'adoption' *per se* of a Final Document under such circumstances, the part dealing with non-proliferation, including the universalization of the Additional Protocol, over which the NAM States Parties are not enthusiastic, may inevitably become slim in substance. This should not be called a 'retreat'.

Rather, the 2010 NPT Review Conference should be noted with its new trends in which some NAM States Parties talked about the Additional Protocol in a similar tone as those of the nuclear-weapon and western non-nuclear-weapon States Parties. This is a result of more and more NAM States Parties joining the Additional Protocol club. This trend will never reverse. Thus, the future of the project to universalize the Additional Protocol seems brighter, despite the gloomy paragraphs on it contained in the Final Document of the 2010 NPT Review Conference. In addition, as more and more States, including NAM members, conclude an Additional Protocol, a sense of norm will naturally be created that measures contained in the CSA and the Additional Protocol constitute the verification standard of the NPT. There is no doubt that the world is progressing in this direction.

Having said all this, however, from a nuclear non-proliferation perspective, the real problem lies in the fact that those States that have been suspected of developing nuclear weapons or of having interest in it have not concluded an Additional Protocol.[111] It is hard to imagine that they will do so simply because a sense of norm regarding the NPT verification standard has been generated among many States. There must be some incentives for them to go ahead with the Additional Protocol. For instance, it seems effective to introduce a mechanism in which States will suffer disadvantages in receiving nuclear material, equipment and technology if they are outside the Additional Protocol circle. In this respect, one of the most regrettable facts is that the NSG is very slow in agreeing on a strict conditionality involving the Additional Protocol in its export control policies. Given such reality,

[111] According to Mark Hibbs, '[t]oday, six states with significant nuclear activities—Argentina, Brazil, Egypt, North Korea, Syria, and Venezuel—have no Additional Protocol. Iran has signed an Additional Protocol but is not implementing it. Fifteen countries, which in recent years have announced that they are interested in deploying nuclear power reactors in the future, also do not have a protocol in force'. M. Hibbs, Nuclear Suppliers Group and the IAEA Additional Protocol, Nuclear Energy Brief, Carnegie Endowment for International Peace, 18 August 2010.

all we can hope for the moment is that unilateral (such as Australia[112]), bilateral (such as US-UAE) and multilateral (such as Treaty of Semipalatinsk) initiatives that have already been instituted to promote the universality of the Additional Protocol in their own ways will be continued, renewed and followed by others, despite their hitherto limited effect.[113]

References

Ahlström C (2006) Legal aspects of the Indian-US civil nuclear cooperation initiative. SIPRI yearbook, pp 669–685

Asada M (2004) Arms control law in crisis?: a study of the North Korean nuclear issue. J Conflict Secur Law 9:331–355

Aust A (2013) Modern treaty law and practice, 3rd edn. Cambridge University Press, Cambridge

Boese W (2004) U.S. nuclear trade restriction initiatives still on hold. Arms Control Today 34:19

Brownlie I (2008) Principles of public international law, 7th edn. Oxford University Press, Oxford

Carnahan BM (1987) Treaty review conferences. AJIL 81:226–230

Choubey D (2010) Future prospects for the NPT. Arms Control Today 40:25–29

Crail P (2009) IAEA approves India additional protocol. Arms Control Today 39:39–40

Doherty B (2013) Australia and India to Start Uranium Sale Talks, Sydney Morning Herald, 7 March 2013

Firmage EB (1969) The treaty on the non-proliferation of nuclear weapons. AJIL 63:711–746

Fischer D (1997) History of the International Atomic Energy Agency: the first forty years. IAEA, Vienna

Ford CA (2007) Interpreting article vi of the treaty on the non-proliferation of nuclear weapons. Nonproliferation Rev 14:401–428

Ford CA (2010) Nuclear technology rights and wrongs: the nuclear nonproliferation treaty, article iv, and nonproliferation. In: Sokolski H (ed) Reviewing the nuclear nonproliferation treaty (NPT). Strategic Studies Institute, Carlisle, pp 237–383

---

[112]Australia has urged (encouraged) all other uranium (nuclear) suppliers to do likewise (adopt a similar approach). Statement by Australia, General Debate, 30 April 2007, p. 2; Statement by Australia, General Debate, above n. 75, p. 5; Statement by Australia, Main Committee II, above n. 48, p. 3. Note that Australia recently revised its long-standing policy of not exporting its uranium to non-NPT States, including India, and started negotiations with India for its uranium sale. Doherty 2013; 'Australian Uranium Shipments Planned for 2015 as India Ramps Up Nuclear Power', *Sydney Morning Herald*, 18 November 2014. With respect to Australia's conditionality of Additional Protocol, India signed an Additional Protocol with the IAEA on 15 May 2009, and brought it into force on 25 July 2014. However, its content is less than satisfactory as it does not contain anything related to the expanded declaration or complementary access. Crail 2009, p. 40.

[113]The Australian measure is limited to Australia and to the supply of its uranium. Moreover, it is only a policy and not a legal obligation, and, as such, may change anytime. In contrast, the conditionality of Additional Protocol in a bilateral agreement requiring the other party to have an Additional Protocol in force, such as the US-UAE Agreement, may cover all areas of nuclear cooperation and is legally binding. However, such conditionality is applicable only between the two States concerned. The Treaty of Semipalatinsk provides for a mandatory conditionality of Additional Protocol for all possible nuclear transfers by its States Parties, and its States Parties include such uranium producing countries as Kazakhstan and Uzbekistan.

Goldschmidt B (1977) A historical survey of nonproliferation policies. Int Secur 2:69–87
von Heinegg WH (2014) Treaties, fundamental change of circumstances, Max Planck encyclopedia of public international law. http://www.mpepil.com
Hirsch T (2004) The IAEA additional protocol: what it is and why it matters. Nonproliferation Rev 11:140–166
Horner D (2010) NSG makes little headway at meeting. Arms Control Today 40:45
Huntington W (2005) Brazilian regulator denies uranium claims. Arms Control Today 35:37
Jennings R, Watts A (eds) (1992) Oppenheim's international law, vol I, 9th edn. Longman, Harlow
Jonas DS (2006) The new U.S. approach to the fissile material cutoff treaty: will deletion of a verification regime provide a way out of the wilderness? Florida J Int Law 18:597–677
Michel Q (2007) Critical reflections on the treaty on the non-proliferation of nuclear weapons. Nucl Law Bull 80:21–28
Müller H (2005) Farewell to arms: what's blocking nuclear disarmament? IAEA Bull 46:12–15
Ntoubandi FZ (2008) Reflections on the USA-India atomic energy cooperation. J Conflict Secur Law 13:273–287
Pomper MA (2008) Nuclear suppliers make progress on new rules. Arms Control Today 38:52–53
Shaker MI (1980) The nuclear non-proliferation treaty: origin and implementation 1959–1979, vol I. Oceana Publications, London
Simma B, Tams CJ (2011) Article 60: termination or suspension of the operation of a treaty as a consequence of its breach. In: Corten O, Klein P (eds), The Vienna Conventions on the law of treaties: a commentary, vol. II. Oxford University Press, Oxford, pp 1351–1378
Sinclair I (1984) The Vienna Convention on the law of treaties, 2nd edn. Manchester University Press, Manchester
Yasseen MK (1976) L'interprétation des traités d'après la Convention de Vienne sur le droit des traités. Recueil des Cours 151:1–114
Zhang X (2006) The Riddle of "inalienable right" in article iv of the treaty on the non-proliferation of nuclear weapons: intentional ambiguity. Chin J Int Law 5:647–662

Chapter 6
The Comprehensive Nuclear-Test-Ban Treaty Organization (CTBTO): Current and Future Role in the Verification Regime of the Nuclear-Test-Ban Treaty

Sabine Bauer and Cormac O'Reilly

Abstract Almost 20 years ago, on 10 September 1996, the United Nations General Assembly adopted the Comprehensive Nuclear-Test-Ban Treaty (CTBT). This Treaty, which seeks to prohibit any nuclear test explosion in any environment, including underground, was part of a carefully balanced diplomatic deal struck in 1995 that made an indefinite extension of the Non-Proliferation Treaty (NPT) possible. As the time span for entry into force of the Treaty was envisaged to last only a few years, States signatories of the Treaty simultaneously established a Preparatory Commission, which is under international law considered a separate international organization from the Comprehensive Nuclear-Test-Ban Treaty Organization (CTBTO) proper. Since 1997 the Commission has worked tirelessly to prepare for the Treaty's entry into force, in particular by building up an elaborately designed universal verification regime. This verification regime is now largely complete and of proven effectiveness and robustness, despite the

---

Sabine Bauer is a Special Assistant to the Executive Secretary of the Preparatory Commission for the Comprehensive Nuclear Test ban Treaty organization, with a background in international law and the laws of international organizations and 18 years of practical legal experience in international organizations, She is admitted to practice law at the New York State Bar.
Cormac O'Reilly is an External Relations Officer at the Provisional Technical Secretariat. He has worked for 14 years in multilateral affairs and disarmament issues, including in the Ministry of Foreign Affairs of Ireland, and is a barrister-at-law and member of the Inn of Court of Northern Ireland.
The views of the authors are personal and may not be attributed in any way to reflect the views of the Commission and its State signatories.

S. Bauer (✉) · C. O'Reilly (✉)
Vienna International Centre, 1200, 1400 Vienna, Austria
e-mail: Sabine.Bauer@ctbto.org
URL: http://www.ctbto.org

C. O'Reilly
e-mail: Cormac.OREILLY@ctbto.org

J.L. Black-Branch and D. Fleck (eds.), *Nuclear Non-Proliferation in International Law - Volume II*, DOI 10.1007/978-94-6265-075-6_6

unforeseen fact that, close to 20 years after its opening for signature, the Treaty has yet to reach full legal standing. This chapter will elucidate in more detail the present legal status of the CTBT, the functioning of its verification regime as it exists to date, as well as the means for completing the verification regime as foreseen in the Treaty.

Keywords Comprehensive Nuclear Test-Ban Treaty (CTBT) · CTBT verification regime · Nuclear testing · Preparatory commission · Treaty on Non-Proliferation of Nuclear Weapons (NPT)

Contents

6.1 Introduction

Adopted through the United Nations General Assembly Resolution 50/245 in September 1996, the Comprehensive Nuclear-Test-Ban Treaty (the Treaty, CTBT) prohibits all nuclear explosions whether for military or for peaceful purposes by anyone and everywhere—on the Earth's surface, in the atmosphere, underwater and underground. In order to fulfil these ambitious objectives, the Treaty provides in its Article II for the establishment of the Comprehensive Nuclear-Test-Ban Treaty Organization (CTBTO), which would carry out the necessary measures to implement the Treaty though a global verification regime while also providing a forum for consultation and international cooperation. However, the CTBT is facing a seemingly challenging situation: although to date 183 States have signed and 164 have ratified the CTBT, the Treaty is still pending entry into force. This is due to the complexity of Article XIV, which determines that 44 States possessing nuclear capabilities must ratify the Treaty before it enters into force. Only 8 States among these 44 have not completed the ratification process to date.[1] Of these, China, Egypt, Iran, Israel and the United States are signatories; while the Democratic People's Republic of Korea (DPRK), India and Pakistan are non-signatories.

As a result, the CTBTO as an international organization does not yet exist *de jure* and the question of its legal existence and impact on current activities linked to the Treaty has received academic attention. However, a Preparatory Commission for the Comprehensive Nuclear-Test-Ban Treaty Organization (the Commission) consisting of all State signatories was established by resolution of the States signatories[2] in the same year of the Treaty's adoption with the ambitious mandate of preparing the Treaty's entry into force as well as setting up and financing the global verification regime that would underpin the Treaty upon entry into force. The standing of the Commission as an international organization in its own right is therefore clearly established in law. It has its own regulatory framework, a permanent structure with technical and administrative divisions and enjoys privileges and immunities applicable to the United Nations organizations.

Almost 20 years later the Treaty's global verification regime is well advanced. It consists largely of an International Monitoring System comprising 337 facilities (321 monitoring stations and 16 radionuclide laboratories), which is now almost 90 % complete. Information from these stations is transmitted continuously via a Global Communications Infrastructure, established by the Commission, to the International Data Centre in Vienna, which collects, analyses and disseminates data and data products to the States signatories. In addition, on-site inspection capabilities have been developed and have demonstrated a high degree of readiness ahead of entry into force. While an international, independent and effective verification tool for the Treaty has now been established, with the Commission able to reliably detect nuclear test explosions, the question arises whether entry into force of the Treaty is indeed critical to the continuation of an emerging norm against nuclear testing.

This chapter will elucidate in detail the present legal status of the CTBT, the functioning of its verification regime as it exists to date, as well as the means for completing the verification regime as foreseen in the Treaty. The authors will demonstrate that the legal status of a norm against nuclear testing remains precarious, and that achieving the ultimate purpose of the CTBT necessitates ratification by the remaining eight States referred to above.

---

[1]An analysis of why these eight States are yet to ratify is beyond the scope of this chapter. For a discussion of some of the possible domestic political and geopolitical reasons, see Dahlman et al. 2009, Chap. 11.

[2]CTBT/MSS/RES/1.

6.2 The Present Legal Status of the CTBT

6.2.1 Origin and Obligations Arising Under the Treaty

The opening for signature of the CTBT in September 1996 marked a significant waypoint on what had to date been a drawn-out process. Whether one traces the genesis of the CTBT to the first proposals by Prime Minister Jawaharlal Nehru of India in 1954 for a 'stillstand agreement' on nuclear testing[3] or even to the more recent post-Cold War thaw that saw considerable forward movement on a range of non-proliferation and disarmament issues,[4] the importance of the moment was not lost as United States President Clinton lauded the international community for having in its grasp 'the longest-sought, hardest-fought prize in the history of arms control'.[5]

In his address to the United Nations General Assembly, Clinton was further able to point to the leadership shown by the United States in becoming the first State to sign the CTBT, and set out his country's understanding of the effect that the Treaty would have: '[i]t will help to prevent the nuclear powers from developing more advanced and more dangerous weapons. It will limit the possibilities for other States to acquire such devices […]'.[6] Moreover, with the length of the process thus far in mind, he called for entry into force 'as soon as possible'.[7]

The negotiation of the CTBT in the Conference on Disarmament (CD) from 1994 onwards was given considerable impetus by the consensus decision of contracting parties to the Treaty on the Non-Proliferation of Nuclear Weapons (NPT) during its 1995 Review and Extension Conference of the Parties to indefinitely extend the NPT. The Conference's Final Document specifically adopted as a goal '[t]he completion by the Conference on Disarmament of the negotiations on a universal and internationally and effectively verifiable Comprehensive Nuclear-Test-Ban Treaty no later than 1996'.[8] Achieving a test ban had, from the earliest days of the NPT, been regarded by a number of States not in possession of nuclear weapons as a key indication of the commitment of nuclear-weapon States (NWS)[9] to the disarmament provisions in Article VI of the NPT.[10]

---

[3]See Johnson 2009.

[4]See generally Moxley 2000, Chap. 1.

[5]Address to the 52nd Session of the United Nations General Assembly, 22 September 1996.

[6]Ibid.

[7]Ibid.

[8]NPT/CONF.1995/32 (Part I), para 4(a).

[9]In the sense of nuclear-weapon States Parties to the NPT, in essence the five Permanent Members of the United Nations Security Council.

[10]The NPT, which entered into force in 1970, was originally conceived with a limited duration of 25 years. Its preamble recalls the determination of States Parties to the Partial Test-Ban Treaty of 1963 to 'seek to achieve the discontinuance of all test explosions of nuclear weapons for all time and to continue negotiations to this end'.

Before considering the current legal status of the Treaty, it is useful to recall the basic obligations arising under its provisions. Following a preamble that outlines the significance of the Treaty as an important nuclear non-proliferation and disarmament measure, Article I stipulates the basic obligations of States Parties. In language that almost mirrors that of the Partial-Test-Ban Treaty of 1963, each State Party undertakes 'not to carry out any nuclear weapon test explosion or any other nuclear explosion, and to prohibit and prevent any such nuclear explosion at any place under its jurisdiction or control',[11] while further undertaking 'to refrain from causing, encouraging, or in any way participating in the carrying out of any nuclear weapon test explosion or any other nuclear explosion'.[12] This formula followed much discussion, even pre-dating the negotiations, on whether a total prohibition on nuclear testing was verifiable or even desirable, or if an allowance for low-yield nuclear explosions should be given.[13] This total ban on nuclear explosions,[14] which applies to all States Parties equally, is supported by a verification regime described in Article IV and comprising (a) an International Monitoring System (IMS); (b) a means for consultation and clarification; (c) a mechanism for on-site inspections; and (d) a provision for confidence-building measures. The current status of this verification regime is explored in Sect. 6.3. In order to maintain the regime and support the responsibilities and needs of States Parties, a Comprehensive Nuclear-Test-Ban Treaty Organization is provided for in Article II. This article goes into detail on the structure and functions of the Organization, which comprise a Conference of States Parties as its principal organ; an elected 51-member Executive Council to which a number of decision-making powers are reserved; and a Technical Secretariat charged with the quotidian maintenance of the verification regime.

6.2.2 Article XIV and Entry into Force of the Treaty

Almost 20 years on, many ironies and paradoxes face the practitioner of international relations or international law when it comes to the CTBT. As of writing, 183 States have signed and 163 have ratified the Treaty, making it one of the most

---

[11]CTBT Article I.1.

[12]CTBT Article I.2.

[13]See Ramaker et al. 2003; Hansen 2006; Johnson 2009. Arguments for the desirability of allowing low-yield nuclear tests were posited, *inter alia*, on the basis of the potential use of so-called 'Peaceful Nuclear Explosions' for civil purposes such as mining or harbor-building; concerns among some NWS about the stewardship of nuclear weapons stockpiles in the absence of testing; and doubts about the credibility of a verification regime targeting a zero-yield threshold.

[14]As opposed to sub-critical, hydro-dynamic or computer simulation experiments, which are not referred to in the Treaty and which quickly became the basis of stockpile stewardship for Nuclear Weapons States. See, for example, http://www.state.gov/1997-2001NOPDFS/global/arms/factsheets/wmd/nuclear/ctbt/fs_991008_stockpile.html.

universally adhered-to arms control instruments ever in existence. Nevertheless, the Treaty is not yet in force. This curious State of affairs results from a somewhat burdensome entry into force provision contained in Article XIV, which requires ratification by each of 44 countries listed in Annex 2 of the Treaty. Annex 2, arrived at through identifying inclusions in two IAEA lists of countries with nuclear research or power reactors, and cross-checking these against members of the Conference on Disarmament (CD) who had participated in the CTBT negotiations in June 1996, was one of a number of attempts to devise a formula[15] that would require ratification by all nuclear-weapon States as well as any States suspected of holding nuclear weapons outside the NPT regime, in addition to so-called 'nuclear threshold' States, i.e. those States that have chosen to exercise complete restraint in the militarization of existing nuclear capabilities.[16]

Although regarded by some analysts as 'bad policy and bad lawyering'[17] or, even more provocatively, as 'the worst entry-into-force provision ever negotiated',[18] it appears that most negotiators did not imagine a delay of more than a few years at most before entry into force was achieved.[19] The interim period could be put to good use by readying the Treaty's extensive verification regime under the auspices of a Preparatory Commission for the CTBTO established by resolution of the States signatories,[20] itself a legally binding international agreement.[21]

Where prospects for entry into force are concerned, the fortunes of the CTBT have waxed and waned in the intervening years. Hopes for hastening ratifications among all Annex 2 States were dealt a significant blow by the failure of the United States Senate to give its advice and consent on the Treaty in 1999, as well as by the policy position against the CTBT taken by the administration of President G.W. Bush from 2001 onwards.[22] While the succeeding Obama administration reinstated executive support for the Treaty, it has not yet been taken up again by

[15]For a description of many of these attempts from the vantage point of the Chair of negotiations in the CD, see Ramaker et al. 2003, pp. 235–244.

[16]For a discussion on latter-day threshold States, see Rublee 2010.

[17]Lenefsky 1999, p. 255.

[18]Krepon 2012, p. 28.

[19]See, for example, the comments of Weston 2012, p. 9: 'It was my assumption, and I think the assumption of most other people in the CD at the time, that all the NWS would ratify… and that they would join with other ratifiers to encourage others…'.

[20]Resolution establishing the Preparatory Commission for the Comprehensive Nuclear-Test-Ban Treaty Organization, CTBT/MSS/RES/1, 17 October 1996. For detailed information on the verification regime, see below, Sect. 6.3. The CTBT itself also refers in several places to 'the Preparatory Commission', assuming its existence as a matter of fact. See Article II, paras 10, 26(h) and 49.

[21]See below, Sect. 6.3.2, on how the legal obligations contained therein pertain to the build-up of the verification regime.

[22]A number of non-NWS Annex 2 States did ratify the Treaty over the following decade. Although the Russian Federation ratified the Treaty shortly after the Senate vote, on 30 June 2000, no NWS has done so since.

the Senate for consideration. A number of other States listed in Annex 2 are still to ratify, due to several national, regional and geopolitical factors.

Currently, eight Annex 2 States are yet to complete their respective ratification processes: China, the Democratic People's Republic of Korea (DPRK), Egypt, India, Iran, Israel, Pakistan and the United States. Of these, India, Pakistan and the DPRK remain non-signatories. Efforts to secure these ratifications continue apace, including through a series of biennial conferences held according to Article XIV[23] with the aim of reaching early entry into force. Although some commentators[24] have queried the effectiveness of these conferences, they have served as an important means of keeping the legal status of the Treaty on the diplomatic agenda and integrate well with the work of the Commission in promoting the CTBT.[25]

6.2.3 The Status of the CTBT as a Unique Politico-Legal Construction

Rather than spelling the end of the Treaty and its verification regime, the fact that the Article XIV requirements have not yet been met have led to the growth of a curious politico-legal construction unprecedented in the international system.

Since the opening for signature of the Treaty, all but three States—India, Pakistan and the DPRK—have refrained from the testing of nuclear weapons. Moreover, since the dawn of the current century, only the DPRK has conducted nuclear tests. This almost universal observance of a nuclear test ban is a result, strictly speaking, of continued adherence by certain States to declared moratoria on testing,[26] coupled with the continued abidance of States signatories to the object and purpose of the Treaty. The latter is in keeping with customary international law as codified in Article 18 of the Vienna Convention on the Law of Treaties (VC), which provides that a State is obliged to refrain from acts which would defeat the object and purpose of a treaty it has signed.

---

[23]Article XIV(2) provides that, if the Treaty has not entered into force 3 years after the date of the anniversary of its opening for signature, 'the Depositary shall convene a Conference of the States that have already deposited their instruments of ratification upon the request of a majority of those States. That Conference shall… consider and decide by consensus what measures consistent with international law may be undertaken to accelerate the ratification process in order to facilitate the early entry into force of [the] Treaty.'

[24]Such as Venturini 2014, p. 147.

[25]*Inter alia* through the establishment in 2013 by the Commission's Executive Secretary, Lassina Zerbo, of a Group of Eminent Persons (GEM) to support and complement efforts to promote the Treaty's entry into force. See more on GEM below Sect. 6.3.

[26]For example, in 1992 the United States adopted legislation confirming a moratorium, while both India and Pakistan declared voluntary moratoria following tests conducted in 1998. The latter was reaffirmed by both parties in 2004 (see Ministry of External Affairs of India, Joint Statement, India-Pakistan Expert-Level Talks on Nuclear CBMs [Confidence-Building Measures], June 20, 2004.

In tandem with this, the United Nations Security Council (UNSC) has taken a strong position against incidences of nuclear testing, adopting resolutions[27] in response to the DPRK's tests in 2006, 2009 and 2013, each of which described the tests as contrary to international efforts aimed at strengthening the global nuclear non-proliferation regime. Not only did the resolutions condemn the respective nuclear tests, but they also explicitly held that the DPRK shall not conduct any further nuclear tests.[28]

At the same time, the Commission worked to put in place the verification regime detailed in Article IV of the Treaty, *inter alia* by setting up the global network of the International Monitoring System (IMS), connected to an International Data Centre (IDC) in Vienna, Austria, and by preparing the means for on-site inspections (OSI).[29] While this is discussed in further detail below (Sect. 6.3), it is important to note for the purpose of discussion on the legal status of the Treaty that the IMS is at an advanced State of completion and that data received and processed by the IDC accurately provided States signatories with information on each DPRK nuclear test within the timeframe laid down by the draft operational manual for the IDC, as elaborated by the Commission.[30]

All of the above together have given rise to a situation in which testing by States considered to possess a credible nuclear weapon capability has ceased entirely, in which the sole new tester is consistently regarded by the international community as acting outside the bounds of expected global practice, and in which reliable data on suspected nuclear tests can be made available rapidly by an existing multilateral organization in the shape of the Commission, itself often referred to in shorthand by the fully fledged acronym, CTBTO. In that light, even before entry into force, there is not only a globally emerging norm against nuclear testing,[31] but also a verification architecture in place that already surpasses those of many legally binding instruments in international arms control. This unusual

[27]SC Res 1695 (2006); 1718 (2006); 1874 (2009); and 2094 (2013).

[28]See for example SC Res 2094 (2013), para 1.

[29]While the Treaty stipulates in Article IV(D) that on-site inspections can only be invoked once it has entered into force, the Preparatory Commission and its Provisional Technical Secretariat are obliged by resolution CTBT/MSS/RES/1 to prepare all aspects of the verification regime in advance. Where OSI is concerned, this has meant constant revision of the draft operational manual and the conducting of major simulation exercises (see above Sect. 6.3.4).

[30]Part I of the Protocol to the CTBT provides in F. 17 that '[t]he procedures and standard event screening criteria to be used by the International Data Centre in carrying out its agreed functions, in particular for the production of standard reporting products and for the performance of standard range of services for States Parties, shall be elaborated in the Operational Manual for the International Data Centre and shall be progressively developed. The procedures and criteria developed initially by the Preparatory Commission shall be approved by the Conference at its initial session.'

[31]The Commission's Executive Secretary, Lassina Zerbo has asserted that the norm exists *de facto* (see, e.g. Address by the Executive Secretary to the 58th Regular Session of the General Conference of the IAEA, September 2014 at www.ctbto.org/fileadmin/user_upload/public_information/2014/14-09-24_IAEA_GC_Statement.pdf).

development has been of interest to international lawyers in examining whether, through an amalgam of customary international law—perhaps reinforced or added to by the CTBT—provisions of other treaties in force that ban nuclear weapons testing in various circumstances and regions,[32] and SC resolutions of a quasi-legislative nature, a *de jure* global ban against nuclear testing can be said to exist.[33] While the academic discourse remains unsettled on that question,[34] and further detailed analysis is not within the scope of the present chapter, it is beyond dispute that in the absence of entry into force and universalization of the CTBT there is no single, irrefutable, legal instrument that binds all States to such a norm. Moreover, within the space in which international law and practice on arms control coexist, the putative existence of such an obligation on the basis of customary international law is no comfortable substitute for the clarity that flows from a treaty, the most important source of obligation in international law.[35] Finally, key elements of a non-discriminatory, multilateral verification regime—consultation and clarification, confidence-building measures, and, above all, on-site inspections—will not be in place prior to entry into force, and nor will the CTBTO, *stricto sensu*, be established with a full range of powers that exceed those of the Commission.

6.2.4 Future Risks and Opportunities for a Legally Binding CTBT

Given that the twentieth anniversary of the Treaty's opening for signature is fast approaching, it is not surprising that thoughts have turned to how to best secure the full range of its benefits, including the elements of the verification regime currently inaccessible to States signatories. Some of the literature in international law and international relations has tended to seek out alternative futures for the CTBT, be it through provisional application[36] under a construction deriving from Article 25 of

[32]Such as the Antarctic Treaty of 1959, the Partial Test Ban Treaty of 1963, the Outer Space Treaty of 1967, the Treaty of Tlatelolco of 1968, the Sea-Bed Treaty of 1971, the Moon Treaty of 1979, the Treaty of Rarotonga of 1985, the Treaty of Bangkok of 1995, the Treaty of Pelindaba of 1996, and the Treaty of Semipalatinsk of 2006.

[33]See Tabassi 2009; Venturini 2014.

[34]Indeed, further potential anchors of a test-ban in specific areas of international law such as environmental law, health law, and humanitarian law continue to be explored. For the latter, see a range of papers and presentations delivered during the course of a series of conferences on the humanitarian impact of nuclear weapons, the most recent of which was held in Vienna, Austria, in December 2014: http://www.bmeia.gv.at/en/european-foreign-policy/disarmament/weapons-of-mass-destruction/nuclear-weapons-and-nuclear-terrorism/vienna-conference-on-the-humanitarian-impact-of-nuclear-weapons/.

[35]On which see generally McNair 1961; Klabbers 1996.

[36]See Michie 2009; Johnson 2009, pp. 227–230.

the Vienna Convention on the Law of Treaties (VCLT)[37] or even through dismantling the current institutional structure and placing control of the IMS under an organization such as the International Atomic Energy Agency (IAEA).[38] The possibility of seeking to further expand the role of the Commission could also be explored. The suggestion that the IMS could be re-assigned to the IAEA is in stark contrast to the decision of negotiators of the CTBT to establish an independent international organization to implement the Treaty and, bearing in mind the archival evidence that separate identity from the IAEA was a *sine qua non* for a number of members of the CD, it is an unlikely and undesirable prospect on political, legal and practical levels.[39]

The argument for provisional application is also problematic. From the legal perspective, it is not clear how negotiating States might satisfy Article 25 VCLT,[40] while in terms of policy it could act as a disincentive for the remaining Annex 2 States to complete their ratification procedures. In addition, it would run the risk of lessening support for the Treaty among some of those who have already ratified, given that they would be subject to strict legal provisions against nuclear testing while countries potentially more like to test would not.[41] It is in fact arguable that such an approach would *decrease* the universality of the CTBT, thereby undermining the entirety of the disarmament and non-proliferation regime.

Attempts to further bolster the role of the Commission are also not straightforward. While the Commission's Provisional Technical Secretariat has been able to act in some ways beyond its strict mandate, for example in the use of IMS data for civil and scientific applications, it is unlikely that the majority of States signatories would support a significant expansion of its functions in order to make them comparable with those of the Organization established under the Treaty.[42]

Entry into force of the Treaty remains the most appropriate way of securing its benefits. Both adherence to the *status quo* or pursuit of the alternative means outlined above carry profound risks which could result in a return to unfettered nuclear testing by NWS. While the present situation of an emerging norm supported by a real, existing verification regime is of great practical use, and while alternative legal futures for the CTBT are of academic interest, it is imperative that

[37]Article 25 provides that '[a] treaty or part of a treaty is applied provisionally pending its entry into force is (a) the treaty so provides, or (b) if the negotiating States have in some other manner so agreed.' As the CTBT does not provide for provisional application, another mechanism for so agreeing—such as through a specially convened conference—would need to be pursued.

[38]Venturini 2014, p. 155.

[39]While the IAEA was created to promote the peaceful use of nuclear energy and to inhibit the latter's diversion towards military means, it does not have a mandate or expertise in monitoring, detecting and inspecting for nuclear explosions. See Hansen 2006, pp. 29–32 on the range of political, legal and practical impediments to including the IMS in the IAEA.

[40]Both in terms of the proper forum and in the inclusion of all 'negotiating States under Article 25.

[41]Potentially leading some States to invoke the 'supreme interest'clause in Article X, allowing them to withdraw from the Treaty.

[42]From the strictly legal perspective, this could be achieved through a resolution of States Signatories.

the political processes towards entry into force run their course. This will require greater policy coordination in support of entry into force from States signatories, and especially from ratifying States. That support should seek to make increasingly visible the role of the verification regime as a central part, not only of the Treaty, but of the intricately linked disarmament and non-proliferation architecture. Current efforts in this regard are examined in Sect. 6.3.4.

6.3 Functioning of the Verification Regime

6.3.1 Definition of Verification

In order to explain the CTBT verification regime in more detail, it is useful to reiterate what constitutes an adequate legal definition of verification. Commonly, the most important elements of verification used in arms control and disarmament agreements were based on the 16 Principles of Verification developed by the United Nations Disarmament Commission and endorsed by consensus by the General Assembly in 1988.[43] Of note specifically is Principle 13 stating

> [V]erification of compliance with the obligations imposed by an arms limitation and disarmament agreement is an activity conducted by the parties to an arms limitation agreement or an organization at the request and the specific consents of the parties and is an expression of the sovereign right of States to enter into such arrangements.

Hence, verification can be described as an activity or process, which establishes whether a State Party is complying with its obligation under the agreement. The verification activity or process involves data collection, monitoring, examining and analysing information for the purposes of assessing compliance with the treaty concerned.[44] However, some authors expanded the definition of three additional elements: the establishment of facts, a legal assessment of a conduct vis-à-vis a norm and a political reaction as a result of a determination of a violation of a norm.[45] In order for verification to be adequate and effective, respective arrangements must be capable of providing, in a timely fashion, clear and convincing evidence of compliance or non-compliance. Continued confirmation of compliance is considered an important element to build confidence and trust among the parties.[46]

In course of the development of various multilateral disarmament and non-proliferation treaties and arrangements the following principles for effective and adequate

[43]Official Record of the General Assembly (1998), 15th Special Session, Supplement No. 3 (A/S-15/3), para 60 (para 6 Section I).

[44]Pawlak 1991, pp. 129–130.

[45]Ibid.

[46]UN Department of Disarmament Affairs, The United Nations Disarmament Yearbook, Volume 29 (2004); Chapter V Related Issues and Approaches 'Arms limitation and disarmament agreements, including verification of compliance', p. 187.

verification gained importance: non-discrimination, universality, transparency, impartiality and objectivity. The CTBT's verification regime, in contrast to many other non-proliferation and disarmament arrangements of bilateral or multilateral nature, will fulfil any of these criteria upon entry into force of the Treaty. Yet, even prior to this, the operation of an elaborate verification regime on a provisional basis serves as a core element and confidence building measure in the nuclear disarmament and non-proliferation discourse. Therefore, in order to progress on the nuclear disarmament front, the lessons learned and procedures developed under the Commission's auspices are crucial elements for nuclear disarmament; it arguably impedes both vertical (the quality of weapons) and horizontal (the quantity of possessors) proliferation of nuclear weapons.[47] 'Without the CTBT, all the nuclear-armed states would still be conducting nuclear tests, and new proliferators would have one less hurdle to overcome.'[48]

6.3.2 Legal Requirements of Operability of the CTBT Verification Regime Before Its Entry into Force

The Partial Test-Ban Treaty 1963 (PTBT), which prohibited nuclear explosions under water and in the atmosphere, did not foresee any independent, multilateral and objective verification entity or measures, as national technical means (NTMs) were considered sufficiently reliable unilateral means of monitoring compliance with the PTBT. However, although it entered into force in the same year, the PTBT did not address underground testing, a method increasingly preferred. Nor did it bring about universalization or effectively end nuclear testing by the major nuclear powers as neither China nor France were Parties. This was not achieved until the CTBT was opened for signature in September 1996.

As outlined in Sect. 6.2, the CTBT did not only create an independent body for monitoring the implementation of the Treaty but also provided for two important verification measures, namely the International Monitoring System, and on-site inspections in addition to a mandatory consultation and clarification process and confidence building measures.[49] It is widely recognized that the most notable feature of the Treaty is the verification regime to monitor compliance with the Treaty obligations.[50] Yet, the question arises as to how a verification regime can become fully operational as long as a treaty has not entered into force.

The legal effect of the operability of the verification regime where State Signatories are concerned[51] pending entry into force can be derived from the

[47]Collina and Kimball 2010; Assada 2002, pp. 88–89.

[48]R. Johnson, Option to facilitate the CTBT's entry into force: embedding the CTBT in norms, law and practice, www.nonproliferation.eu/documents/kickoff2/johnson.pdf, p. 2.

[49]Asada 2002; Venturini 2014, p. 145.

[50]Tavernier 1996, pp. 131–133; Asada 2002, pp. 90–91; Johnson 2009, pp. 145–174; Venturini 2014, pp. 145–147.

[51]In keeping with Article 18 VCLT, as discussed in Sect. 6.2.3.

Treaty text itself, namely its Article IV(A) 1 which stipulates that '*[a]t entry into force of this Treaty*, the verification regime *shall be capable* of meeting the verification requirements of this Treaty' [emphasis added].[52] This Article when interpreted in connection with para 14 of the Annex adopted by States signatories in the 1996 Resolution[53] presupposes the will of States signatories that the verification regime must exist prior to entry into force in order to meet the Treaty's verification standards the time of entry into force. One commentator therefore concluded that Article IVA(1) as a norm *sui generis* should be taken as having an interim legally binding effect on State signatories prior to the entry into force of the Treaty.[54] This is further evidenced in the Annex adopted by State Signatories in the 1996 Resolution,[55] which created a separate international organization (see above Sect. 6.2), namely a Preparatory Commission, with the mandate to carry out the necessary preparations for the effective implementation of the CTBT. Paragraph 13 of the Annex specifically stipulates in relations to Article IV of the Treaty:

> [The Commission shall] undertake all necessary preparations to ensure the operationalization of the Treaty's verification regime at entry into force, pursuant to Article IV, paragraph 1, and shall develop appropriate procedures for its operation [...].

This resolution can be considered a legally binding international agreement among its State signatories, as it creates rights and obligations among its mandatory membership of States. Hence, the readiness of the system to verify a comprehensive nuclear test ban at the time of entry into force is neither facultative nor discretionary.[56] As a result, States signatories indeed undertook a legal obligation to make the verification regime of the CTBT fully operable and functional prior to its entry into force.

6.3.3 The CTBT Verification Regime to Date

According to the Treaty, the verification regime consists of 321 monitoring stations and 16 laboratories in about 90 States worldwide, which can be divided into

[52]General Assembly Resolution 50/245 of 10 September 1996 Asada 2002, pp. 104–105.

[53]Paragraph 14 of CTBT/MSS/RES/1 stipulates that "the Commission shall supervise and coordinate in *fullfiling the requirements of the Treaty and its Protocol*, the development of [...] and pending their formal commissioning, [...] the provisional operation as necessary of the International Monitoring System [emphasis added].

[54]Asada 2002, pp. 113, 121–122.

[55]CTBT/MSS/RES/1.

[56]*United Nations Juridical Year Boo*, 2012, Chapter VI, Legal Opinions of the Secretariats of Intergovernmental Organizations related to the United Nations; Legal Opinion on the status of the resolution establishing the Preparatory Commission for the Comprehensive Nuclear Test Ban Treaty Organization, pp. 507–523.

four major technologies: seismic, infrasound, hydroacoustic and radionuclide. The global seismic network (consisting of 50 primary and 120 auxiliary stations), which some authors describe as the core[57] or heart of the verification regime, is set out in Annex 1 to the Protocol to the Treaty. The stations, which are located in 79 countries, detect and monitor shockwaves underground. Primary stations continuously send data in real time to the International Data Centre (IDC) in Vienna. Auxiliary stations send data only upon request.[58] Due to the unique signature of the seismic waves, regular earthquakes can be distinguished from nuclear explosions.[59]

According to the Treaty obligations (Article IV para 19) the primary seismic network is funded by the Organization, while the installation costs for auxiliary stations are to be borne by the host country, except where the provision and authentication of data and some technical upgrades are concerned. The obligation to provisionally fund and operate this system is as set out in the Resolution establishing the Commission (para 14 CTBT/MSS/RES/1), specifically the Appendix which provides for an indicative list of verification tasks, and which requires the Commission to *inter alia* 'develop procedures and a *formal basis* for the provisional operation and *funding* of the provisional IMS' [emphasis added].[60] As recently as early 2014, China began to send continuous data from its stations to the IDC in Vienna. This is considered a major achievement and a sign of the confidence that also non-ratifying States (China is a signatory to the CTBT) increasingly have in the technological advances and capabilities of the verification regime.

In addition, the verification regime consists of eleven hydroacoustic stations (six of which are under water), which monitor for any explosion that occurs in the sea and underground in marine environments. Hydroacoustic technology is used to measure changes in the water pressure caused by sound waves which travel long distances. These stations are complex and costly to set up and maintain as they are located in extremely inhospitable environments and are subject to freezing temperatures, high pressure and saline corrosion.[61] In Spring 2014, the hydroacoustic station Juan Fernandez Island, off the coast of Chile, which had been destroyed by a tsunami four years before, was reinstalled and commissioned successfully again and has since then transmitted data uninterruptedly. Another hydroacoustic station, on France's Crozet Island south of the Indian Ocean, suffered a similar fate as the Juan Fernadez station, and is currently under reconstruction. These are multi-year, multi-million dollar projects, which serve as a strong demonstration of State signatories' 'commitment to complete the verification regime prior to entry into force of

[57]Johnson 2009, p. 151.

[58]www.ctbto.org/verificationregime/monitoring-technologies-how-they-work.

[59]Johnson 2009.

[60]Appendix to CTBT/MSS/RES/1.

[61]www.ctbto.org/verificationregime/monitoring-technologies-how-they-work.

the Treaty. As with all the verification technologies, hydroacoustic stations sent data via a global communications infrastructure (GCI) consisting of five satellites, to the IDC on a constant basis.

Sixty infrasound stations in thirty-five countries monitor nuclear explosions in the atmosphere by picking up acoustic waves that are inaudible to the human ear. Similar to other technologies, these stations transmit non-stop data to the IDC. Infrasound science has been revitalized since the adoption of the CTBT and has proven useful for the civil and scientific application of the verification regime, in particular for disaster warning and mitigation.[62] Eighty radionuclide stations (forty of which are equipped with noble gas monitoring equipment) and sixteen radionuclide laboratories are widely considered the means of detecting the 'smoking gun' or 'forensic' proof to allow States to determine conclusively whether or not an explosion detected by the other three technologies is indicative of a nuclear explosion. These stations measure the radioactive particles and noble gases in the air emitted during a nuclear explosion, even in miniscule portions.[63] Use of this technology has allowed the Commission to provide clear information on the nature of the DPRK nuclear tests in 2006 and 2013.

The verification regime is almost 90 % complete.[64] At the end of 2014, 300 out of 337 facilities were installed worldwide. This is an impressive undertaking and goes to demonstrate that the verification regime is reliable and trustworthy in the eyes of the Treaty's 183 State signatories. As United States Secretary of State, John Kerry, on the occasion of the 7th Ministerial Meeting promoting the early entry into force of the CTBT in September 2014 in New York, stated

> [The CTBT] verification regime is one of the great accomplishments of the modern world. The international monitoring system is nearly complete; it is robust, it is effective, and it has contributed critical scientific data on everything from tsunami warnings to tracking radioactivity and nuclear reactor accidents.

As outlined by Secretary Kerry, the technical benefits of the verification regime go over and beyond the mere monitoring of the Treaty obligations by State signatories. The use of CTBT data to track the dispersion of radioactivity in the wake of the 2011 nuclear power plant accident in Fukushima, Japan, has for example demonstrated how the regime can assist in disaster risk reduction.

Despite this remarkable technological achievement, delayed entry into force of the Treaty, coupled with persistent financial constraints worldwide, risk endangering the verification regime. Hence, it is not surprising that, in the past, some States openly expressed doubts about the build-up and provisional operation of such an elaborate and technically advanced regime while entry into force still seemed elusive. It is, therefore, increasingly the case that civil and scientific applications,

---

[62]Ibid.

[63]Ibid.

[64]2015 IMS Stations Overiew www.ctbto.org/tiles/pdf/CTBTO-Map-IMS-2015-01-23-All_Stations-Overview.pdf.

while not the main objective of the CTBT, have become an important factor for many States in politically supporting the consensus for the provisional operation of the regime by providing tangible benefits, constituting a return on the substantial financial investment made. For example, the data collected, analysed and disseminated to States signatories are used for tsunami warning and mitigation, and can also be used in areas as diverse as the monitoring of the ash clouds that emanate from volcanic eruptions, of interest to civil aviation; the recording of whale sounds in order to gain insight into migration patterns; and in learning about climate change and weather patterns. These activities constitute recognized and worthwhile spin off effects of the data collection, analysis and products of the verification regime.[65] Indeed, in 2012 the Commission has also become a member of the Inter-Agency Committee on Radiological and Nuclear Emergencies, which the IAEA serves as Secretariat.

In order to keep abreast of technology advances, and to build strong ties with the broader scientific community, the Commission has since 2006 organized bi-annual Science and Technology Conferences. The last Science and Technology Conference in 2013 brought together over 750 participants, and featured 80 oral presentations and over 250 poster presentations.[66] For the fifth time, the Science and Technology Conference was organized in June 2015 and for the first time also included a new theme on 'performance optimization'.[67] Hence, from all of the above, it can be concluded that the verification regime as it currently stands is almost fully functional, robust and reliable and that its positive non-verification activities alone make it a worthwhile and sound investment for members of the Commission, which is also evidenced by the collection rate on annual assessed contribution from those States amounting to well over 90 %.[68]

6.3.4 *Impediments to Completion of the Verification Regime*

The key impediment in the way of completion and effective implementation of the verification regime is its lack of full legal standing prior to entry into force. Despite an operational IMS and the availability of usable data from the IDC, formal verification measures cannot be invoked at this stage. This is best illustrated by the provision in the Treaty for on-site inspections.[69] Although regarded as the

[65]CTBTO website: www.ctbto.org/verification-regime/spin-offs-disaster-warning-and-science.

[66]Science and Technology Conference 2013: www.ctbto.org/press-centre/highlights/2013/the-science-and-technology-conference-2013/.

[67]Science and Technology Conference 2015: www.ctbto.org/specials/snt2015.

[68]2014 Member States Payments of Assessed contributions, www.ctbto.org/fileadmin/user_upload/treasury/52_24_Dec_2014_Member_States__Payments.pdf.

[69]Further examples might be the mandatory consultation and clarification process and confidence building measures, as there is no Executive Council yet in place to authorize their implementation.

ultimate verification measure, this significant part of the verification regime has only so far been tested through simulation exercises. On-site inspections are the ultimate means under the CTBT to prove incontrovertibly whether a country has conducted a nuclear test explosion, and their main purpose is to deter possible violators from conducting such explosions. Under the Treaty Article IV D, any State has the right to request an on-site inspection in another State or a territory controlled by another State, irrespective of whether the source of a possible event came from the data collected by the IMS, on the basis of technical information obtained by national technical means as long as these comply with the principles of international law, or a combination thereof. Although not specifically labelled as such, only such 'challenge inspections', where there is a specific request by a State, are foreseen by the Treaty and the State Party subject to the request cannot refuse.[70] Yet the Treaty links the conduct of on-site inspections to entry into force as any on-site inspection request has to be submitted to the Organization's Executive Council for decision-making within 96 h upon receipt of the request.[71] In addition, the relevant operational manual and the list of inspection equipment must be approved by the Conference of States Parties at its initial session, to be held 30 days after entry into force.[72]

Irrespective of this linkage to entry into force, Commission members also tasked themselves to prepare all on-site mechanisms and procedures that must be in advance of this. The procedures and processes are regularly tested in tabletop exercises and field experiments, complemented by workshops and trainings.[73] Most recently, in November 2014, the largest ever on-site inspection integrated field exercise took place in Jordan (IFE14). This was based on a technically realistic but fictional scenario. During the five-week long exercise, the inspection team searched an inspection area of nearly 1,000 km^2 using 15 of the 17 techniques permissible under the Treaty. Due the complex operational nature of an on-site inspection which has to be conducted in a very narrow time span, IFE14 took 4 years of preparation, used 150 tonnes of specialized equipment that was shipped largely in air-freight containers and saw over 200 international experts participate in the exercise over 5 weeks. In the course of 2015, the Commission and IFE14 participants drew their conclusions on the on-site inspection techniques, identifying areas for improvement and refining the on-site inspection procedures and methods further.[74]

[70] See http://www.ctbto.org/verification-regime/on-site-inspection/the-final-verification-measure.

[71] CTBT Article IV para 46.

[72] CTBT Article II para 26 h, Part II paras 13 and 36 of the Protocol of the Treaty.

[73] www.ctbto.org/verification-regime/on-site-inspection/the-final-verification-measure/.

[74] 2014 Largest Ever CTBT On-Site Inspection Exercise Concludes Successfully: www.ctbto.org/press-centre/press-releases/2014/largest-ever-ctbt-on-site-inspection-exercise-concludes-successfully/.

Therefore, irrespective of the fact that on-site inspections cannot yet be invoked, this important aspect of the regime has not been neglected by States; signatories and is largely ready for operationalization and at the disposal for the international community. As one commentator recently stated, 'the CTBT procedures for on-site inspection decisions deserve close attention as we think about nuclear disarmament process'.[75] One finds it hard to imagine that State signatories would continue to invest the time, money and effort in the verification regime as a whole and in the development of on-site inspections methods and procedures in particular, if there was not an overall conviction that entry into force, while not yet achieved, was nevertheless within reach.

6.3.5 How to Achieve Full Completion of the Verification Regime

Although there are several possibilities, both legal and political, to attempt to overcome the challenges to completion of the verification regime without entry into force (see Sect. 6.2), the authors are of the opinion that the only viable solution is the continuous pursuit of the path of entry into force while at the same time continuing to complete the verification regime and advancing its various technologies. Otherwise, a significant risk remains that the NWS could resume testing, while other States with potential nuclear weapon capability could follow.[76]

How to achieve this? It is important to build up the confidence of the remaining Annex 2 States that the verification regime is not only capable of detecting significantly small yield nuclear explosions but also that entry into force would lend an additional benefit to the ratifying States Parties, namely the power to request an on-site inspection in case of a suspicious event.[77] Moreover, further efforts could be made to continue to involve both the scientific as well as political leadership of the remaining hold-out States and to demonstrate to them the added benefits for their national security by joining the CTBT verification regime through signing (for example in the cases of India and Pakistan). This could be achieved by involving politicians and scientists in training and other scientific conferences. As a case in point, in 2013 the newly elected Executive Secretary of the Commission, Lassina Zerbo, established a Group of Eminent Persons (GEM), comprised of prominent policymakers and international experts from several countries. Through its collective expertise, experience and political standing, the GEM supports and complements efforts to promote the Treaty. In April 2014, during a meeting hosted

---

[75]Nikolai Sokov, Senior Fellow Presentation at a seminar on multilateral verification, VCDNP, December 5, 2013.

[76]See above n. 34, p. 5.

[77]See above n. 34, p. 12.

by the Swedish Ministry of Foreign Affairs in Stockholm, the GEM discussed a range of strategic approaches and modes of action to assist the Executive Secretary in securing the CTBT's entry into force. At the conclusion of the meeting, the GEM issued a joint statement where it stipulated that the entry into force of the CTBT is 'within reach' and it would support

> entry into force and universalization of the CTBT through multilayered engagement at the national, regional and global levels, including direct engagement with policymakers; active participation in significant public events at which the CTBT can be raised; promotion of the Treaty through media outreach; and utilization of networks and force multipliers, including political, civil society, and academic links, to broaden and diversify support for the Treaty.[78]

Several of its members have since then conducted visits, engaged with media, and included the importance of the CTBT in their high-level discussions with policy makers in different Annex 2 States.[79] This initiative has already met with political recognition by States, signatories, as evidenced in the joint statement delivered at the 7th Ministerial Meeting promoting the early entry into force of the CTBT in September 2014 in New York.[80] Only such a persistent international political focus to bring about the entry into force of the CTBT will ensure that the substantial advancement of the disarmament and non-proliferation agenda is not undermined.

6.4 Conclusions

Entry into force of the Treaty remains the most appropriate way of securing its benefits. Both adherence to the *status quo* or pursuit of the alternative means outlined above carry profound risks which could result in a return to unfettered nuclear testing by NWS. While the present situation of an emerging global norm supported by a real, existing verification regime is of great practical use, and while alternative legal futures for the CTBT are of academic interest, it is imperative that the political processes that lead to entry into force run their course. Otherwise, the risk remains that some State actors could cease to fully appreciate the benefits of the Treaty and revert to nuclear testing as a means to further enhance or even build for the first time their own nuclear weapon arsenal. As a result the effects of the Commission's significant achievement in building up an effective, robust and

[78] 2014 Statement of GEM Stockholm, www.ctbto.org/fileadmin/user_upload/public_information/2014/Statement_of_GEM_Stockholm_FINAL.pdf.

[79] 2014 Interview with GEM Member Wolfgang Hoffmann, www.ctbto.org/press-centre/highlights/2014/interview-with-gem-member-wolfgang-hoffmann-on-his-recent-visit-to-pakistan-and-india.

[80] 2014 Ministerial Statement, www.ctbto.org/fileadmin/user_upload/statements/2014_minsterial_meeting/2014_joint_ministerial_statement_final.pdf.

tested Treaty verification regime could be reversed to the detriment of humankind, the environment and generations to come. Only a convergence of both the political will of the international community and the legal procedure necessary will make the Treaty fully effective and implementable.

References

Asada M (2002) CTBT: legal questions arising from its non-entry into force. J Confl Secur Law 7(1):85–122

Collina TZ, Kimball DG (2010) Now more than ever. The case for the comprehensive nuclear test ban-treaty. Arms Control Association. www.armscontrol.org/system/files/ACA_CTB_Briefing_Book.pdf

Dahlman O, Haak HW, Mykkeltveit S (2009) Nuclear test ban: converting political visions to reality. Springer

Hansen KA (2006) The comprehensive nuclear test ban treaty: an insider's perspective. Stanford University Press

Johnson R (2009) Unfinished business: the negotiation of the CTBT and the end of nuclear testing. United Nations

Klabbers J (1996) The concept of treaty in international law. Nijhoff

Krepon M (2012) The CTBTO and the CTBT: securing their valuable global services, in CTBT at 15: status and prospects. Arms Control Association

Lenefsky D (1999) The entry-into-force provision of the comprehensive test ban treaty: an example of bad international lawyering. NYL Sch J Int Comp L 19:255

McNair AD (1961) The law of treaties. Oxford University Press

Michie A (2009) Provisional application of non-proliferation treaties. In: Joyner DH, Roscini M (eds) Non-proliferation law as a special regime, Chapter 2. Cambridge University Press, pp 55–86

Moxley CJ (2000) Nuclear weapons and international law in the post cold war world. Austin & Winfield

Pawlak S (1991) The legal aspects of verification. The international law of arms control and disarmament. United Nations, New York, pp 127–144

Ramaker J, Mackby J, Marshall PD, Geil R (2003) The final test: a history of the comprehensive nuclear-test-ban treaty negotiations. CTBTO, Vienna

Rublee MR (2010) The nuclear threshold states: challenges and opportunities posed by Brazil and Japan. Nonproliferation Rev 17(1):49–70

Tabassi L (2009) The nuclear test ban: *lex lata* or *de lege ferenda*? J Confl Secur Law 14(2):309–352

Tavernier P (1996) L'adoption du traité d'interdiction complète des essais nucléaires. Annuaire français de droit Int 42:118–136

Venturini G (2014) Test-bans and the Comprehensive Test Ban Treaty Organization. In: Black-Branch JL, Fleck D (eds) Nuclear non-proliferation in international law, vol I. Springer.TMC Asser Press, The Hague, pp 133–158

Weston M (2012) The CTBT's role in curbing vertical and horizontal proliferation. In CTBT at 15: status and prospects. Arms Control Association, pp 8–9

Chapter 7
The Nuclear Safeguards Regime of EURATOM: A Regional Cornerstone of the Verification of Non-Proliferation Obligations in the European Union

Wolfgang Kilb

Abstract The European Atomic Energy Community exists next to the European Union as separate legal entity: EURATOM. Regardless of whether the 28 Member States have opted for nuclear power, the European Commission as the main executive body ensures that civil nuclear material is not diverted from its intended and declared use. The EURATOM safeguards system is a regional cornerstone of the verification of non-proliferation obligations in the European Union. Europe's regional "soft" power is backed by "hard" legal competences. Decisions by the Court of Justice of the European Union have clarified and confirmed the extraordinary competences of the European Commission. Given the complexity of the revision process of the EU Treaties, for which unanimity amongst all Member States is required, it seems unlikely that the EURATOM legal framework for nuclear safeguards will change in the nearer future. It is its concrete application in the field that matters. The EURATOM safeguards system, in its 56 years of existence, has been recognized an important contributor to the global task of non-proliferation and a guarantee for European citizens that nuclear power is used for peaceful purposes. The good track record of the European regional system should allow the IAEA to make increased use of EURATOM safeguards.

Keywords European Atomic Energy Community (EURATOM) · European union case law · Safeguards · Sanctions · State-level concept

---

Wolfgang Kilb is a principal lawyer in the European Commission's Directorate-General for Energy, Directorate Nuclear Safeguards. The views expressed are purely those of the author and may not under any circumstances be regarded as stating an official position of the European Commission.

W. Kilb (✉)
Commission Européenne, Direction H Energie Nucléaire, Maison de L'Europe,
2920 Luxembourg, Luxembourg
e-mail: Wolfgang.KILB@ec.europa.eu

J.L. Black-Branch and D. Fleck (eds.), *Nuclear Non-Proliferation in International Law - Volume II*, DOI 10.1007/978-94-6265-075-6_7

Contents

7.1 Introduction

Based on the Treaty on European Union (TEU)[1] for the overall 'constitutional' framework and the Treaty on the Functioning of the European Union (TFEU)[2] for procedures and policies, European law has, in the more than five decades of its existence, developed into a plethora of legislation and jurisprudence. At first sight, primary (=Treaty) law in the field of energy consists of only one provision: Article 194 TFEU.

Post-war European integration started with the Treaty establishing the European Coal and Steel Community (ECSC) of 1951 ('Paris Treaty').[3] The Treaty establishing the European Atomic Energy Community (EAEC or 'EURATOM')[4] was signed together with the Treaty establishing the European Economic Community (EEC)[5] in 1957 ('Treaties of Rome'). Hence, two of the three initial European Communities—that are now commonly referred to as the European Union (EU)—deal with energy questions in great detail. While the ECSC expired in 2002, the EAEC still exists as a separate primary law Treaty.[6]

---

[1]Treaty on European Union (TEU), OJ C 326 of 26 October 2012, 13 et seq. (consolidated version).

[2]Treaty on the Functioning of the European Union (TFEU), OJ C 326 of 26 October 2012, 47 et seq. (consolidated version).

[3]Treaty establishing the European Coal and Steel Community (ECSC) of 1951 ('Paris Treaty'), http://eur-lex.europa.eu/legal-content/EN/TXT/?uri=CELEX:11951K/TXT.

[4]Treaty establishing the European Atomic Energy Community, OJ C 327 of 26 October 2012, 1 et seq. (consolidated version).

[5]Treaty establishing the European Economic Community, http://eur-lex.europa.eu/legal-content/EN/TXT/?uri=CELEX:11957E/TXT.

[6]Overview on the Treaty cf. W. Kilb, The European Atomic Energy Community and its primary and secondary law. In: International nuclear law: history, evolution and outlook, 10th anniversary of the International School of Nuclear Law, Organisation for Economic Cooperation and Development (OECD). Nuclear Energy Agency (NEA), 2010, http://www.oecd-nea.org/law/isnl/10th/isnl-10th-anniversary.pdf, pp. 43–90.

The long negotiations on the European constitution, its rejection and the renegotiation of the TEU and TFEU ('Lisbon Treaty'),[7] which entered into force on 1 December 2009 left the EURATOM Treaty largely unchanged. Although a new title (XXI with its sole Article 194 TFEU) on Energy was introduced by the Lisbon Treaty, agreement could not be reached on an incorporation of nuclear energy issues into the main Treaties. Hence, the EURATOM Treaty was adapted only to reflect the general (mostly institutional) changes. It was the Fukushima nuclear accident of March 2011 that revived public interest in its provisions with a focus on nuclear safety[8] and security. By contrast, nuclear safeguards are an area of European law which remains largely *terra incognita* and which has been left 'legally untouched' by the Fukushima accident.[9]

As fissile nuclear materials can be used both for peaceful and military purposes, EURATOM nuclear safeguards were established as an international requirement and guarantee for the citizens to ensure that nuclear materials are only used for their declared and intended (peaceful) purposes. It was also a condition for overseas support in developing a nuclear industry in Europe in the 1950s and 1960s.

In other words, nuclear safeguards is one of the major guarantees, in addition to nuclear safety and nuclear security that nuclear energy is used in the safest and most secure way in the EU. Independent of the wish of individual Member States to opt for nuclear power or not, a choice guaranteed under Article 194 TFEU, it is the task of the European Commission to ensure that nuclear material is not diverted.

EURATOM safeguards have four distinguishable legal dimensions: First, the 'supranational' relation with the Member States, which gives extraordinary legal powers to the Commission, unrivalled in other fields of European law. Second, the classic 'international' relation with third countries outside the Community, based on bilateral EURATOM agreements with third countries, often suppliers of nuclear material. Third, the 'cooperation' relation with the International Atomic Energy Agency (IAEA) that rests on multilateral agreements between EURATOM, the International Atomic Energy Agency and Member States. Referring to Article III of the Non-Proliferation Treaty, these agreements contain principles of cooperation between the two international organizations in Europe. Fourth, the direct 'supervision' relation with nuclear operators: The Commission carries out verification of nuclear material in the European Union, where it has enforcement rights not only vis-à-vis Member States but also directly against nuclear operators: The Commission can issue directives against Member States and impose sanctions on nuclear operators, in the form of decisions. The Community is also legal owner of special fissile materials.

---

[7]OJ C 306 of 17 December 2007, 1 et seq.

[8]See the 2014 amendment of the 2009 Nuclear Safety Directive: Council Directive 2014/87/EURATOM of 8 July 2014 amending Directive 2009/71/Euratom establishing a Community framework for the nuclear safety of nuclear installations, OJ L 219 of 25 July 2014, p. 42 et seq.

[9]Overview of pre-Fukushima developments in Grunwald 2010, pp. 407–449 (pp. 437–439).

All four dimensions will be dealt with along the lines of the relevant legal instruments, starting with primary and secondary European law, followed by bi- and multilateral international agreements, then individual decisions and finally (scarce) case law.

7.2 Primary and Secondary European Law

Unlike the TEU and the TFEU, the 'sectorial' EURATOM Treaty,[10] dealing only with the peaceful use of nuclear energy, goes into much greater detail on a variety of issues like research, dissemination of information, health and safety, investment, supplies, etc. This chapter on nuclear safeguards is very concrete with regard to rights and obligations of the European Commission, Member States and nuclear operators. Technical details are spelled out in a Commission Regulation, which in turn is interpreted by two Commission recommendations, while other legislative acts regulate more technical details.

7.2.1 Primary Law

Chapter 7 of the EURATOM Treaty is entitled 'Safeguards'. It defines in Article 77 the duty of the European Commission to 'satisfy itself that (…) ores, source materials and special fissile materials are not diverted from their intended uses…' and that 'safeguarding obligations (…) under an agreement concluded with a third State or an international organization are complied with'. The first obligation relates to the overall duty to ensure non-proliferation of nuclear materials to non-civil use by controlling nuclear operators, while the second refers to the international obligations of the Community vis-à-vis third States and international organizations such as the IAEA.

The chapter defines the duties of nuclear operators, which have to declare to the Commission the basic technical characteristics (BTC) of their nuclear installations (Article 78) and are obliged to keep operating records to permit accounting for nuclear materials (Article 79).[11]

7.2.1.1 Extraordinary Rights of the European Commission

The Commission may send inspectors into the territories of Member States. They have direct rights vis-à-vis nuclear operators as 'inspectors shall at all times have

[10]All articles quoted without further specification are those of the EURATOM Treaty.

[11]Overview in Schärf 2008, Chap. 16, J Überwachung (control).

access to all places and data and to all persons … to the extent necessary in order to apply … safeguards to ores, source materials and special fissile materials'.

In case of opposition to an inspection, an urgency procedure is foreseen which requires the President of the Court of Justice of the European Union either to decide within 3 days (!) on an 'order to ensure that the inspection be carried out compulsorily'. The right to directly inspect (private) parties—and not only to instruct the Member State to execute a European decision—and the (very short) delays for the Court to decide on these inspections, constitute extraordinary powers for the Commission. By contrast, the IAEA can only call upon the Member State, in which a nuclear installation is situated, to take corrective action in case of non-compliance of a nuclear operator.[12]

Article 81 limits the right of the Commission to send inspectors to the EU Member States' only by two conditions: First, 'before sending an inspector on his first assignment … the Commission shall consult the State concerned; such consultation shall suffice to cover all future assignments of this inspector'. This does neither mean that the Member State has to *approve* the nomination of an inspector at the beginning of his career in the Commission nor that such consultation takes place before *every* inspection. Second, inspectors act 'on presentation of a document establishing their authority', i.e. by showing at least their inspector's card to the nuclear operator.

As there are no legal precedents, the test of how the President of the Court of Justice of the European Union would decide on a dispute within three days is still to be made.

7.2.1.2 Infringement Procedures Against Member States: Penalty Payments

In case of an infringement, the Commission has equally strong rights vis-à-vis the Member States (MS): It may issue a 'directive' (in fact: a decision) 'calling upon the Member State (…) to bring such [an] infringement to an end …' Again, due to the potential danger of infringements related to nuclear material, if the Member State does not comply by the time limit set, 'the Commission or any Member State concerned may … refer the matter to the Court of Justice of the European Union direct' (Article 82). Hence, the procedure is significantly streamlined when compared to the standard and time-consuming infringement procedure of Articles 258 and 259 TFEU.

Article 106a of the Euratom Treaty refers to a number of key provisions in the TEU and TFEU, including Article 260 TFEU.[13] Under this Article, the Court of Justice of the European Union can, if a Member State is found to have failed to

---

[12]See Article XII of the Statute of the International Atomic Energy Agency (IAEA) on Nuclear Safeguards at https://www.iaea.org/sites/default/files/statute.pdf.

[13]On Article 106a, see Papenkort 2008, pp. 84–107.

fulfil an obligation under the Treaties, require this Member State 'to take the necessary measures required to comply with the judgement of the Court'.

In a second step, the European Commission can bring the same Member State before the Court again if it considers that the Member State has not taken the necessary measures to comply with the judgment of the Court. The Court can then, if it finds that the Member State has in fact not complied with its judgment, impose either a lump sum or penalty payment on it. Such lump sum depends on the seriousness of the infringement, its duration and the need to ensure that the penalty itself is a deterrent to further infringements.

In determining the amount of the lump sum or the penalty, the gross national product (GDP) of the Member State is taken into account, meaning that Germany (being the EU's biggest Member State) would pay a multiple of Malta (the EU's smallest Member State).

7.2.1.3 Infringement Procedures Against Nuclear Operators: Sanctions

In the event of an infringement on the part of the nuclear operator 'the Commission may impose sanctions', i.e. in order of severity: a warning, the withdrawal of special benefits, the placing under administration or the 'total or partial withdrawal of source materials of special fissile materials' (Article 83). Once more, the right to directly sanction a (private) party—without the detour via the Member State in which the party is domiciled—constitutes an extraordinary power attributed to the Commission and has its equivalent only in very few other EU policy areas, e.g. competition law under Article 101 et seq. TFEU.

7.2.1.4 Ownership of Special Fissile Materials

Finally, special fissile materials in the sense of Article 197, i.e. plutonium-239, uranium-233 and uranium enriched in uranium-235 or uranium-233, are subject to a special owner-user relationship[14]:

Article 86 foresees that these materials 'shall be the property of the Community', regardless of whether they are produced in or imported by a Member State. Member States or nuclear operators 'shall have the unlimited right of use and consumption' under the conditions that (1) such materials have properly come into their possession and (2) the obligations imposed on them by the Treaty have been fulfilled, 'in particular those relating to safeguards'.

The right of ownership is potentially a powerful tool for the EURATOM Supply Agency (ESA) to ensure 'by means of a common supply policy on the principle of equal access to sources of supply' (Article 52).

[14]Grunwald 2003, pp. 265–266.

7.2.2 Secondary Law

7.2.2.1 Commission Regulation No. 302/2005 and Particular Safeguard Provisions

The obligations of nuclear operators under Chapter 7 are set out in more detail in Commission Regulation (EURATOM) No. 302/2005 of 8 February 2005 on the application of EURATOM safeguards.[15] This Regulation, based on Article 79, specifies the information to be declared by nuclear operators to the European Commission, and how and when these declarations must be produced. It also specifies the records that nuclear operators are obliged to produce, in order to allow the European Commission to fulfil its duties imposed by Article 77.

Finally, secondary law comes in the form of Particular Safeguard Provisions (PSP). Having their legal foundation in Article 6 of Commission Regulation 302/2005, these Commission decisions contain details of safeguards for individual nuclear installations. They are decisions directly addressed to a specific nuclear operator and therefore are not published in the Official Journal (OJ).

7.2.2.2 Recommendations of 2005 and 2009

On the one hand, Commission Recommendation of 15 December 2005 on guidelines for the application of Regulation (EURATOM) No. 302/2005 on the application of EURATOM safeguards (2006/40/Euratom)[16] provides guidance to the nuclear operators on the information to be provided to the European Commission. Being a recommendation, it is of a legally non-binding nature (cf. Article 288 TFEU) while in practice it is widely recognized as 'soft law'.

On the other hand, Commission Recommendation of 11 February 2009 on the implementation of a nuclear material accountancy and control system by operators of nuclear installations (2009/120/Euratom)[17] provides guidance to nuclear operators on how to implement a high quality Nuclear Material Accountancy and Control (NMAC) system, fulfilling the requirements of Regulation 302/2005. Again, this 'soft law' act is not legally binding.

7.3 International Agreements

Article 77(b) stipulates that 'the Commission shall satisfy itself that (…) any particular safeguarding obligations assumed by the Community under an agreement concluded with a third State or with an international organization are complied with'.

[15] OJ L 54 of 28 February 2005, 1 et seq.

[16] OJ L 28 of 1 February 2006, 1 et seq.

[17] OJ L 41 of 12 February 2009, 17 et seq.

Next to the classic international dimension of the first alternative of Article 77(b), which finds its expression in bilateral EURATOM agreements between the Community and third countries, the cooperation dimension with the other main players in the field of nuclear safeguards is important: The second alternative of Article 77(b) relates to multilateral agreements between EURATOM, the IAEA and the non-nuclear-weapon States (NNWS) of the Community as well as to trilateral agreements with the nuclear-weapon States (NWS) United Kingdom and France.

7.3.1 Bilateral Agreements with Third Countries

The European Atomic Energy Community (EAEC) has concluded a number of bilateral international agreements under Article 101 EURATOM Treaty. Provisions in various areas related to the civil use of nuclear energy are complemented by commitments on non-proliferation, safeguards, physical protection and export controls for nuclear materials. They were concluded with the USA (1958, replaced in 1995),[18] Canada (1959, replacement expected in 2015),[19] Australia (1982, replaced in 2012),[20] Argentina (1997),[21] Uzbekistan (2004),[22] Japan (2006),[23] Ukraine (2006),[24] Kazakhstan (2008)[25] and South Africa (2013, not yet in force).[26] More bilateral agreements are currently being negotiated (e.g. the revised agreement with Canada) and there is a proposal of a negotiating mandate for such negotiations with South Korea.

These agreements vary widely in scope while key elements are nuclear safeguards clauses. For example, the Euratom Agreement with the Government of Australia (2012) expressly stipulates in its Article VII that 'Nuclear material … shall be subject to … the EURATOM safeguards pursuant to the Euratom Treaty and to the IAEA safeguards pursuant to … safeguards agreements…'. Again, in case of an infringement of a safeguards obligation, the Member State is potentially subject to an accelerated infringement procedure (Article 82) and the nuclear operator may face sanctions (Article 83).

---

[18]OJ L 120 of 20 May 1996, 1 et seq.

[19]OJ 60 of 24 November 1959, 1165 et seq.

[20]OJ L 29 of 1 February 2012, 4 et seq.

[21]OJ L 296 of 30 October 1997, 32 et seq.

[22]OJ L 269 of 21 October 2003, 9 et seq.

[23]OJ L 32 of 6 February 2007, 65 et seq.

[24]OJ L 261 of 22 September 2006, 27 et seq.

[25]OJ L 10 of 15 January 2009, 16 et seq.

[26]OJ L 204 of 31 July 2013, 3 et seq.

7.3.2 *Multilateral Agreements Between EURATOM, EU Member States and the IAEA*

Amongst the 28 EU Member States, a distinction has to be made between the vast majority of the 26 non-nuclear-weapon States (NNWS) and the two nuclear-weapon States with a permanent seat in the United Nations (UN) Security Council, i.e. the United Kingdom and France.

7.3.2.1 Non-Nuclear-Weapon States (NNWS)

The Agreement between the non-nuclear-weapon States (NNWS), the European Atomic Energy Community and the International Atomic Energy Agency[27] in implementation of Article III(1) and (4) of the Treaty on the Non-Proliferation of Nuclear Weapons (NPT) was signed in 1973 and came into force in 1978.[28] Recognizing the existence of a Community-wide system of EURATOM safeguards, it contains the general principles of cooperation and details for nuclear safeguards arrangements. It also comprises a Protocol amplifying certain provisions, especially the means to avoid unnecessary duplication of the Community's safeguards activities. Article 23 of the Agreement provides for the accession to the Agreement of all non-nuclear weapon States that become Member States of the EU and EURATOM, e.g. Croatia in 2013.

An Additional Protocol (AP) to the Safeguards Agreement was signed in 1998 and came into force in 2004.[29] It contains provisions to further enhance non-proliferation by strengthening effectiveness and efficiency of the IAEA's safeguards system. Both the IAEA and the Community have an interest in deepening their cooperation in order to free resources on the side of the IAEA for its activities outside the EU. Hence, the AP foresees increased cooperation and provides the IAEA with the means to enhance its capabilities to detect undeclared activities.

Both organizations cooperate on the basis of a partnership approach agreed in 1992.[30] Such cooperation relates, for example, to common development of instruments and techniques, common training, or common inspection approaches and procedures. However, it also comprises the possibility of performing certain inspection activities by only one party (European Commission or the IAEA) and the full use of the results of these activities by the other. This is based on the general principle that each party can fulfil its objectives and draw its conclusions independently.

---

[27]Cf detailed overview on the IAEA's safeguards system in: DeFrancia 2011, pp. 37–39.

[28]OJ L 51 of 22 February 1978, 1 et seq. (also published by the IAEA as Information Circular INFCIRC/193).

[29]OJ L 67 of 13 March 1999, 1 et seq. (also published by the IAEA as INFCIRC/193/Add8).

[30]IAEA GOV/INF/654 of 13 May 1992, http://www.iaea.org/About/Policy/GC/GC37/GC37Documents/English/gc37-1073_en.pdf (Nos. 19–22).

7.3.2.2 The State-Level Concept of the IAEA and Its Impact in Europe

The EURATOM system was the first full-scope nuclear safeguards system, preceding the one of the IAEA, and has a very good track record.[31] The European Commission and the IAEA are continuously discussing further enhancement of this cooperation. In 2013, the IAEA issued a report on 'The Conceptualization and Development of Safeguards Implementation at the State Level',[32] to which in 2014 a Supplementary Document[33] provided clarifications and additional information.

In short, the State-level concept (SLC) refers to the general notion of implementing safeguards in a manner that considers a State's nuclear and nuclear-related activities and capabilities as a whole within the existing legal framework, e.g. the scope of the State's safeguards agreement. It should replace a mechanistic or standardized 'one size fits all' approach. It is supported by the EU Members States and the European Commission with the following qualifications:

In Europe, the described EURATOM nuclear safeguards regime contains a range of unique legal features (ownership of special fissile materials, robust infringement procedures against Member States and effective sanctions against nuclear operators). Lessons learned from its application in Europe in more than half a century include the need for independence of the inspectorate and the robustness of its legal and practical powers. By ensuring that infringements by Member States' duties in handling nuclear materials are followed up and, if needed, operators sanctioned, EURATOM has contributed to making the EU a safer place.

EURATOM as a regional system recognized by the IAEA, with which it shares common duties and interests, could enhance its role in an ever-closer co-operation with the IAEA so that the latter can focus on other areas of the world. To this end, the IAEA's State-Level Concept approach could ultimately be widened it to a 'Regional Level Concept' (RLC).

7.3.2.3 Nuclear-Weapon States (NWS)

Both the United Kingdom (UK) and France as nuclear-weapon States are legitimate holders of nuclear weapons in terms of the NPT. As Permanent Members of the Security Council of the United Nations both enjoy a privileged status, while NNWS such as Germany can only become Non-Permanent Members for a period of 2 years.[34] Moreover, the Euratom Treaty in general does not apply to military

[31]See Kobia 2008, pp. 31–53 (42–44).

[32]GOV/2013/38 of 12 August 2013.

[33]GOV/2014/41 of 13 August 2014 and Corrigenda GOV/2014/41/Corr. 1 of 10 September 2014.

[34]See Article 23 of the Charter of the United Nations at http://www.un.org/en/documents/charter/chapter5.shtml.

use of nuclear energy, a principle which for nuclear safeguards is expressly stipulated in Article 84(3).

However, both the UK[35] and France[36] have voluntarily concluded separate trilateral Agreements with the European Atomic Energy Community and the IAEA in 1976 and 1978. Both legally binding Agreements contain, as above, a main text and a Protocol, amplifying certain provisions of the Agreements. The respective Additional Protocol (AP) to both Agreements was signed in 1998.[37, 38]

Whereas EURATOM safeguards activities relate to all nuclear material in peaceful use in the UK and in France, IAEA safeguards is only applied in a relatively small number of civil nuclear installations in these two Member States.

7.4 Individual Decisions and Case Law

Compared to the standard infringement procedures against Member States only (Articles 258, 260 TFEU), the EURATOM Treaty gives the European Commission extraordinary powers: Both the Article 82 directives against Member States and the Article 83 decisions against nuclear operators take into account the potential danger and hence the need for urgency action in case of non-compliance.

7.4.1 Article 82: Directives Against Member States

The infringement procedure of Article 82(3) is directed against a Member State failing to fulfil its safeguards obligations. This can be the case if a Member State itself acts as a nuclear operator or, in any other way, infringes safeguards obligations.

To date, only one case of infringement came close to an Article 82 but was not referred to the Court of Justice: the Sellafield (BNFL) pond B30 case. Following a Commission Directive, the obligation to submit a comprehensive plan to bring several infringements to an end was imposed on the United Kingdom.[39]

In this context, the general duty of cooperation enshrined in Article 192 obliges the Member States to 'take all appropriate measures … to ensure fulfilment of the obligations arising out of this Treaty or resulting from action taken by the institutions of the Community. They shall facilitate the achievement of the Community's

[35]INFCIRC/263.

[36]INFCIRC/290.

[37]INFCIRC/263/Add 1.

[38]INFCIRC/290/Add 1.

[39]Kilb 2014, p. 107.

task. They shall abstain from any measure which could jeopardize the attainment of the objectives of this Treaty'.

7.4.2 Article 83: Sanctions Against Nuclear Operators

Article 83(1) foresees that 'in the event of an infringement on the part of persons or undertakings of the obligations imposed on them…, the Commission may impose sanctions…. These sanctions shall be in order of severity: (a) a warning, (b) the withdrawal of special benefits, (c) the placing … under … administration and (d) total or partial withdrawal of source materials or special fissile materials'.

Whereas sanctions as the withdrawal of special benefits or of nuclear materials have, so far, never been imposed, a number of nuclear operators were subject to warnings for various breaches of safeguards obligations.[40] In one case, *Advanced Nuclear Fuels v. Commission*,[41] a nuclear operator was even placed under administration.

Sanctions, even in the mildest form of warnings, have proven to be efficient: Operators fear the negative repercussions on their image and their shares, leading them to contest even a simple warning, especially its publication in the Official Journal.[42]

7.4.3 Court of Justice of the European Union Case Law

Only few cases in the field of the EURATOM Treaty have reached the Court of Justice of the European Union.[43] Those that did (around 30) mostly concerned other areas. However, two decisions are worth mentioning because they are of specific interest to nuclear safeguards:

---

[40]UKAEA Dounreay (UK), Commission decision of 4 March 1992 (92/194/Euratom), OJ L 88 of 3 April 1992, pp. 54 et seq.; Escuela Técnica Superior de Ingenieros Industriales de la Universidad Politécnica de Madrid (ES), Commission decision of 21 December 1994 (94/955/Euratom), OJ L 371 of 31 December 1994, pp. 16 et seq.; Enusa Juzbado (ES), Commission decision of 12 December 1997 (97/873/Euratom), OJ L 354 of 30 December 1997, pp. 30 et seq.; Sellafield (UK), THORP Fuel Reprocessing Plant, Commission decision C(2006)412 of 15 February 2006, repealed by Commission decision C(2009)6055 of 3 August 2009, OJ C 16 of 22 January 2010, 17 et seq.

[41]See below Sect. 7.4.3.2 and n. 44.

[42]See action brought on 25 April 2006—*British Nuclear Group Sellafield Ltd. v. Commission* (Case T-121/06), in: OJ C 154 of 1 July 2006, 19–20.

[43]Overview in W. Sebastian, Euratom before the Court: A Political Theory of Legal Non-Integration, European Integration online Papers (EIoP), vol. 15, Article 10, http://eiop.or.at/eiop/texte/2011-010a.htm.

7.4.3.1 Case C-61/03 (*Commission v. United Kingdom*—'Jason Reactor'), 2005

In this action against the United Kingdom, the Commission tried to extend the scope of EURATOM law to security and defence policy. The Commission argued that EURATOM secondary law applies to the decommissioning of a military nuclear reactor and to the safety risks arising from a damaged nuclear-powered submarine. Although only a few provisions of the Euratom Treaty deal explicitly with security and defence policy (e.g. Articles 24–28), the Court ruled that EURATOM law generally does not apply to military installations and activities: 'It is necessary ... to emphasise the fact that the Treaty in not applicable to uses of nuclear energy for military purposes...'.[44]

This confirms the literal interpretation of Article 84(3) that 'The safeguards may not extend to materials intended to meet defence requirements ...'.

7.4.3.2 Case C-308/90 (*Advanced Nuclear Fuels GmbH v. Commission*—'ANF Lingen'), 1993

In this action against the Commission, the nuclear company *Advanced Nuclear Fuels GmbH* (ANF) unsuccessfully challenged the sanction imposed by the Commission under Article 83.[45] The facts of the case merit to be presented as they are an example of the (human) risks involved in nuclear operations and the necessity of a robust nuclear safeguards regime:

A pallet with two containers was moved from the storage area at the nuclear site of the applicant to the material entry lock at the plant for the purpose of removing a box containing uranium pellets. Once completed, the pallet was mistakenly placed outside, close to the storage area for empty containers, and forgotten about. The pallet was loaded by mistake onto a lorry belonging to a normal goods transport company.

The employee in charge believed the containers (standing in the area for empty containers) to be empty and removed the labels indicating the presence of nuclear materials, replacing them with ones indicating that the containers were empty. The lorry was unloaded at Luxembourg airport and the containers transported to the USA. The recipient in the USA, after carrying out a routine dosimetric check had established the presence of nuclear materials in the containers that were supposed to be empty. An examination of the seals revealed that no material could have been removed from the boxes. The nuclear operator notified the European Commission's Safeguards Directorate and the EURATOM Supply Agency (ESA) of this occurrence.

---

[44]Judgment of 12 April 2005, ECR I-2477, Section 44.

[45]ANF Lingen (DE), Commission decision of 1 August 1990 (90/413/Euratom), OJ L 209 of 8 August 1990, 27 et seq. and OJ L 241 of 4 September 1990, 14.

In its sanctioning decision, the Commission placed the operator under administration for a period of 4 months. Whereas from a subjective point of view there was no intention behind the actions and that these should not be seen as a form of diversion, the objective facts breached essential elements of safeguards rules, especially with regard to the control of export of nuclear materials outside the EU. Moreover, the seriousness of the case was reinforced by the fact that it involved a significant quantity of material.

Although the operator himself notified EURATOM authorities of his errors, the Court held that neither a continuation of the infringement (which had ended) was necessary to uphold the Commission's sanctioning decision nor that the sanction itself was disproportionate. The application of ANF was therefore dismissed in its entirety.[46]

7.5 Conclusion and Outlook

Before the International Atomic Energy Agency established its own safeguards system and before the Non-Proliferation Treaty was signed in 1968, the EURATOM Treaty had already established a regional system to guarantee the intended and declared peaceful use of nuclear material at the end of the 1950s. While not all cases of non-conformity could be prevented (e.g. at Sellafield), it contributes to the global safeguards and thus non-proliferation system.[47]

The European Union is often described as a 'soft power'. In the field of nuclear safeguards, however, the European Atomic Energy Community (EURATOM) has been given rights and obligations that amount to 'hard' legal competences: Not only is the Community the legal owner of special fissile materials (Article 86), it also has wide-ranging powers to pursue Member States in infringement procedures (Article 82) that can result in financial penalties (Articles 106a and 260 TFEU). Finally, use has been made of the explicit power to impose sanctions on nuclear operators breaching their safeguards obligations (Article 83).

The European Commission as main executive body of the EU/EURATOM, in its role as 'Guardian of the Treaties' (Article 17 TEU), is therefore a key regional player in the 28 Member States. It is in charge of ensuring the proper use of nuclear material in a region with the world's most developed nuclear infrastructure and over 500 million citizens.

This role of the Commission should allow the IAEA to fully implement the cooperation agreements with EURATOM and its Member States, i.e. to make increased use of EURATOM safeguards and focus on more dangerous countries

---

[46]Judgment of 21 January 1993, ECR-I-349.

[47]Cf. also Nuclear Safeguards Conclusions, Report on the Implementation of Euratom Safeguards in 2013, pp. 2–3, http://ec.europa.eu/energy/nuclear/safeguards/doc/201405_euratom_safeguards_2013_report.pdf.

outside the EU. Hence, the IAEA's State-level concept could be supplemented by a European Regional-level concept.

De lege lata, and in the context of a supranational organization, the European Commission's competences in the field of nuclear safeguards are already very far-reaching. *De lege ferenda*, the experience of the failed attempt to adopt a genuine European Constitution and the ensuing revision process of the European Treaties (Lisbon Treaty 2009) do not give reason to be overly optimistic for a Treaty revision. Under Article 48 TEU, unanimity amongst all Member States is required so that it seems unlikely that the EURATOM legal framework for nuclear safeguards will change in the nearer future. It is its concrete application in the field that matters.

References

DeFrancia C (2011) The continuing role of item-specific agreements in the IAEA safeguards system. Nucl Law Bull (NLB) 88:37–59, http://www.oecd-nea.org/law/nlb/nlb88.pdf#page=39

Grunwald J (2003) Europäisches Energierecht (European Energy Law). De Gruyter, Berlin

Grunwald J (2010) Neuere Entwicklungen des Euratom-Rechts (Latest developments of Euratom law). Z europarechtliche Studien 13:407–449

Kilb W (2014) The nuclear safeguards system of the European Atomic Energy Community (Euratom). In: Raetzke C (ed) Nuclear law in the EU and beyond [Atomrecht in Deutschland, der EU und weltweit]. Proceedings of the AIDN/INLA Regional Conference 2013 in Leipzig. Nomos, Baden-Baden, pp 97–111

Kobia R (2008) The EU and non-proliferation: need for a quantum leap? Nucl Law Bull (NLB) 81:31–53

Papenkort K (2008) Der Euratom-Vertrag im Lichte des Vertrags über eine Verfassung für Europa [The Euratom treaty in the light of a treaty on a constitution for Europe]. Schriftenreihe zum deutschen und internationalen Wirtschaftsrecht. Nomos, Baden-Baden

Schärf W-G (2008) Europäisches Nuklearrecht (European Nuclear Law). De Gruyter, Berlin

Chapter 8
Technical Limits of Verification and Their Implications for Treaty Design

Gerald Kirchner and Stefan Oeter

Abstract Verification regimes to support nuclear non-proliferation are largely based on cooperative schemes. By becoming a member of a treaty (such as the NPT), members accept both substantial non-proliferation obligations and intrusive (cooperative) verification including on-site inspections. But such on-site inspections at short notice have of necessity to be based on additional cooperative action, and in the NPT case acceptance of an additional legal Protocol. As a result, the verification regime of the NPT is open to weakness when genuine cooperation is missing. This chapter will start by looking at the technical limits of verification if a Member State engages in non-cooperative behaviour. This requires an on-site inspection at short notice, since routine inspections may be subject to manipulative tactics to hide nuclear weapons activities. In an optimal treaty design, verification regimes need to combine routine cooperative verification activities with a safety net of unilateral technical verification options such as short-notice on-site inspections. This raises the practical issues of the degree to which unilateral verification measures are technically and politically feasible in circumstances where the State concerned refuses to cooperate, and what information should be sought through on-site inspections at

Gerald Kirchner—Director of the Carl-Friedrich von Weizsäcker Center for Science and Peace Research, University of Hamburg. Formerly Member of the German Radiation Protection Commission and of the United Nations Scientific Committee on the Effects of Atomic Radiation.

Stefan Oeter—Professor of Public International Law and Director of the Institute of International Affairs, University of Hamburg; President of the Historical Commission of the International Society for Military Law and the Laws of War; Member of the German Commission for International Humanitarian Law.

G. Kirchner (✉)
Universität Hamburg, ZNF, Beim Schlump 83, D-20144 Hamburg, Germany
e-mail: gerald.kirchner@uni-hamburg.de

S. Oeter (✉)
Universität Hamburg, IIA, Fakultät Für Rechtswissenschaft, Rothenbaumchaussee 33, D-20148 Hamburg, Germany
e-mail: stefan.oeter@jura.uni-hamburg.de

J.L. Black-Branch and D. Fleck (eds.), *Nuclear Non-Proliferation in International Law - Volume II*, DOI 10.1007/978-94-6265-075-6_8

short notice. The chapter will therefore provide an overview of the technical options for both routine and unilateral verification activities. This will be followed by an examination of the impact upon treaty design of a broad range of verification measures, and whether it is possible to include non-cooperative means of technical verification in the design of a treaty-based verification regime. Also, given the limited possibilities to amend the wording of a multilateral treaty like the NPT, could the existing cooperative verification regime be strengthened by 'bolting-on' some additional means of external and non-cooperative technical verification? The wording of the NPT does not explicitly exclude this. Indeed one option may be to insert such an amendment into the existing IAEA-NPT safeguarding arrangements.

Keywords Distance from emitter · International Atomic Energy Agency (IAEA) Safeguards · On-site inspections · Radionuclides · Technical limits · Treaty on Non-proliferation of Nuclear Weapons (NPT) · Verification

Contents

8.1 Introduction

Article III of the Treaty on the Non-Proliferation of Nuclear Weapons (NPT)[1] establishes the safeguards system which has to be accepted by any non-nuclear-weapon State Party to this treaty. The exclusive purpose of this safeguards system is the '… verification of the fulfilment of its obligations assumed under this Treaty with a view to preventing diversion of nuclear energy from peaceful uses to nuclear weapons …'

[1]Treaty on the Non-Proliferation of Nuclear Weapons (1 July 1968), 729 UNTS 161.

(Article III.1). Its implementation focuses on individual comprehensive safeguards agreements between the International Atomic Energy Agency (IAEA) and non-nuclear-weapon States. These are based on a generic agreement known as INFCIRC/153 (Corr.).[2] This document unambiguously defines the objectives of these safeguards as '… the timely detection of diversion of significant quantities of nuclear material from peaceful nuclear activities to the manufacture of nuclear weapons …, and deterrence of such diversion by the risk of early detection'.[3]

A variety of technologies[4] have been adopted or specifically developed to be able to apply IAEA safeguards effectively at all facilities subject to them, such as nuclear research and power reactors. These include the use of identification codes (e.g. of nuclear fuel elements), of tags (e.g. for canisters in storage rooms), optical surveillance of areas by camera and video, motion and radiation detectors. Also, measuring techniques for bulk nuclear materials contained within a material balance area, and highly sophisticated analytical procedures for detecting trace concentrations of material potentially on swipe and environmental samples are available.

The purpose of comprehensive safeguards agreements is to assure others that a States declaration of nuclear material stocks is both correct and complete. However, the discovery of Iraq's clandestine nuclear weapon programme in 1991 demonstrated that the existing tools available to the IAEA through its comprehensive safeguards agreements were often inadequate to verify the completeness of a States factual declaration. As a consequence, the Model Additional Protocol[5] was developed and approved by the Board of Governors of the IAEA in 1997 and is now in force for 119 States.[6] Signatory States accepted a variety of additional safeguarding procedures including *inter alia* access to sites and locations within them at 24 hours notice; environmental sampling on sites not included in existing comprehensive safeguards agreements; and the use of information provided by sources external to the IAEA and the State involved (e.g. scientific literature, commercial satellite imagery, intelligence information from third parties). The Additional Protocol also gives the IAEA access for wide-area environmental sampling to detect particles of relevant nuclear-related materials, though its use requires approval by the Board of Governors and consultation with the State concerned.

In what follows the conditions under which valuable information can be obtained from environmental sampling and its analysis is discussed, and some conclusions derived from this concerning the existing legal IAEA safeguards framework.

---

[2]International Atomic Energy Agency: The Structure and Content of Agreements Between the Agency and States Required in Connection with the Treaty on the Non-Proliferation of Nuclear Weapons. (International Atomic Energy Agency Information Circular) INFCIRC/153 (Corr.), 1972.

[3]Ibid., para 28.

[4]International Atomic Energy Agency: Safeguards Techniques and Equipment: 2011 Edition. International Nuclear Verification Series No. 1 (Rev. 2), 2011.

[5]International Atomic Energy Agency: Model Protocol Additional to the Agreement(s) Between State(s) and the International Atomic Energy Agency for the Application of Safeguards. INCIRC/540 (Corr.), 1998.

[6]See http://www.iaea.org/safeguards/what.html.

8.2 Limitations of Technical Verification

8.2.1 General Purpose of On-site Inspections

The major purpose of the on-site inspections at short notice contained in the Additional Protocol was to clarify the existence or otherwise of potential nuclear declared or not fully declared activities within a State. This could include the operation of undeclared nuclear facilities capable of irradiating, separating or otherwise processing (e.g. purifying or enriching) nuclear materials. Such a site could be an undeclared facility either at a site where other nuclear activities had been declared to the IAEA or a site with no declared activities.

Almost inevitably, nuclear activities involve the production or emission of radionuclides which leave traces of their existence both in-plants (e.g. on filters and pipelines) and/or in the environment. Detection of such radionuclides may provide evidence of both nuclear activities in general and the operation of specific facilities. Radionuclides may be released though emissions into the atmosphere from chimneys, pipes, stacks, etc., but also by liquid discharges into a river or coastal marine waters. However, radionuclide concentrations from both types of emission will be highly diluted and difficult to detect.

It is reasonable to assume that any State operating an undeclared facility will make every effort to shut down and clean the plant after an announcement of an on-site inspection. This may pose an additional challenge for an on-site inspection team, since the radionuclide signal becomes transient and thus weaker after active emissions have ceased through either radioactive decay or dilution through transport in the environment.

8.2.2 Limitation (1): Distance from Emitter

Radionuclides emitted into the atmosphere will be transported by wind. They are highly diluted by atmospheric turbulences. Since most of the radionuclides are aerosols,[7] a small fraction is deposited at the ground due to gravity and washout during rainfall events. This results in a gradual accumulation of those radionuclides in the vicinity of an operating nuclear plant, and in the case of long-lived isotopes, some nuclear residues after a plant has been shutdown after the announcement of an on-site inspection. Thus, analysis of soil and surface vegetation sampled on-site close to a suspected non-declared nuclear facility appears initially to be a highly attractive process. In practice, however, dilution of the radionuclides during atmospheric transport and deposition may restrict the usefulness of this technique. This is illustrated in Table 8.1; it gives estimates of radionuclide emissions which are necessary for causing a deposition of 1 Bq/m^2. This is a

[7]Exceptions are tritium, carbon-14 (as carbon dioxide) and noble gases.

Table 8.1 Atmospheric emissions required for a deposition of 1 Bq/m^2 at various distances from the emitter

Distance from emitter [km]	Needed activity [10^6 Bq]
0.5	700
1	1250
2	2650
5	9400

Calculated using a dry deposition velocity of 1.5 mm/s and the generic atmospheric dispersion model given in United Nations Scientific Committee on the Effects of Ionizing Radiation: Sources and Effects of Ionizing Radiation. UNSCEAR 2000 Report to the General Assembly, Vol. 1: Sources. United Nations, New York, 2000

low contamination, but can still be detected. As Table 8.1 shows, with increasing distance the emission required for creating a detectable contamination increases drastically and even at moderate distances exceeds the values that can be expected for routine operations of nuclear facilities. Although these estimates may vary considerably depending on stack height, local atmospheric dispersion conditions and precipitation, they clearly document a major limitation of environmental sampling. Already at moderate distances from a potential emitter, radionuclide counting may no longer provide evidence of atmospheric emissions caused by suspected nuclear activities. This means that the huge dilution that produces the absence of detectable contamination prevents any conclusion being drawn using this technique.

For liquid emissions, dilution in the sea or rivers can be expected to be lower than in the atmosphere, since most radionuclides[8] will be absorbed by sediments within short distances from the source. Thus, analysis of sediment samples may be promising—in particular if these are not mixed (physically or by biological activity). Indeed the resultant sediment layers may provide a long-lasting historical archive of liquid emissions of long-lived radionuclides.

8.2.3 Limitation (2): Background Levels

Various radionuclides of interest already exist in the environment surrounding a potential non-declared nuclear facility. They arise from three sources: natural radioactive decay chains (thorium, uranium); historic nuclear weapons testing fallout (plutonium, cesium-137, strontium-90); and emissions of long-lived radionuclides from declared nuclear installations. Typical background inventories in surface soils (0–10 cm) and sediments are[9, 10]:

---

[8]This does not apply for tritium and only to a limited extent for iodine and technetium isotopes.

[9]Based on data compiled by the United Nations Scientific Committee on the Effects of Atomic Radiation (UNSCEAR) (ibid.) and on own measurements.

[10]Weapons fallout inventories refer to the mid-latitudes of the Northern hemisphere and are corrected for radioactive decay.

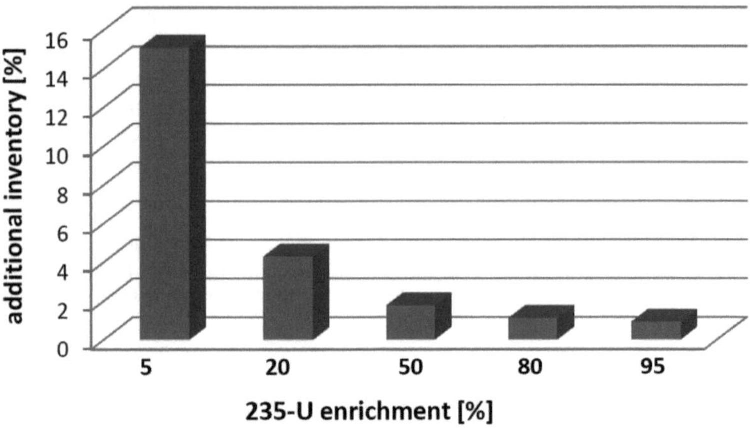

Fig. 8.1 Inventory additional to background of natural U required for detecting emissions of enriched uranium

Uranium	52,500 Bq/m^2	Natural
Plutonium	100 Bq/m^2	Weapons fallout
Caesium-137	2,000 Bq/m^2	Weapons fallout
Strontium-90	1,000 Bq/m^2	Weapons fallout

This ubiquitous radiocaesium and strontium background is further enhanced in regions that had been affected by fallout from nuclear accidents (Chernobyl, Fukushima). Obviously, such background levels drastically reduce the sensitivity of environmental sampling and analysis, since depositions by an undeclared facility must be high enough for discriminating them from the existing background and its common spatial variability.

For nuclear facilities which enrich uranium or process such material, discrimination of uranium emissions from natural background is made possible by the differing uranium isotope ratios of both sources. This method is illustrated in Fig. 8.1. For various enrichment levels, it shows the additional inventory (in percent of background) required for a statistically significant[11] detection of the presence of various levels of the enrichment of uranium-235. Obviously, this fraction becomes low at high enrichments due to the isotopic changes taking place from baseline natural uranium, but even then emissions required for detection will be unrealistically high, at least for atmospheric releases.

8.2.4 *Limitation (3): Time After Announcement of an On-site Inspection*

It is reasonable to assume that after announcement of an on-site inspection any non-declared nuclear activity will be stopped immediately. Thus radionuclide

[11]With 95 % confidence assuming measurement uncertainties of 5 % (uranium-235) and 1 % (uranium-238), respectively.

emissions will cease. However, radionuclides emitted previously may be present for a considerable time in the atmosphere, but at a decreasing level as distance from the source increased. Having access to a wide area around a suspected emitter may allow detecting those radionuclides. Because their concentration decreases with distance, a 'catch-the-plume' approach has been suggested. Based on simulations of the atmospheric transport and dilution of radioactive emissions, samples could be taken in the centre of this plume where concentrations are likely to be highest. The potential of this approach has been systematically explored[12] for emissions of krypton-85 (12.76 years half-life) from nuclear fuel reprocessing plants, which would indicate the existence of a non-declared plant for the separation of plutonium. Simulations assumed atmospheric releases would last 6 h at various hypothetical locations and took into account the variability of regional atmospheric winds and dispersion conditions. Results showed that a 'catch-the-plume' strategy would provide a high probability of detecting the krypon-85 within the first 24 h after its emission, but that after 6 days the detection probability is reduced to about 50 % for a release caused by the separation of about one significant quantity[13] of weapons-grade plutonium.

This result implies that wide-area environmental sampling will have to be conducted within a few days after announcement of an on-site inspection if it is to be of value to the investigators. It should be noted that various organizational issues will have to be resolved within the same short period of time including the availability of aircraft capable of undertaking a 'catch-the-plume' sampling campaign.

8.2.5 Implications

The limitations which should be taken into account in planning environmental sampling in case of an on-site inspection can be summarized as follows. After being emitted radionuclides will always be subject to huge dilutions of their concentrations. This effect increases with distance from the emitter. In general, this effect is less pronounced for those liquid emissions which become adsorbed in sediments. For atmospheric releases, however, concentrations may become too low to allow any inference of the existence of non-declared nuclear activities. In environmental samples, background concentrations of the radionuclide(s) of interest may mask any new signals. This is to be expected for natural radionuclides (uranium) and for long-lived nuclear weapons testing radionuclides, but may also include artificial radionuclides at sites where there are various nuclear facilities.

[12] Ross et al. 2009.

[13] The significant quantity specifies the mass of a fissile material sufficient for building a nuclear weapon. For safeguards, IAEA has set this value to 8 kg for plutonium.

Wide-area sampling may require fast access and may need logistic support. When incorporating tools of wide-area sampling into the additional safeguards, one could profit from the relevant experiences of the OPCW in dealing with chemical warfare agents, as the OPCW is the body most familiar at a working level with these issues, especially in the period in the later 1990s when it was being created.

Such requirements to supplement the existing safeguards with additional tools of verification, deriving from the inherent physical limitations of technical means of verification, pose a significant challenge to the design of treaties in the field of nuclear non-proliferation. To implement a sensible scheme of technical verification, this message must be repeated, fast access to the area around a nuclear facility is needed, as well as the availability of the necessary technical equipment and the logistical support required for its use.

8.3 Implications for Treaty Design, in Particular Safeguards Regimes

8.3.1 The Significance of Safeguards for the Regime Architecture of the NPT

The technical and organizational requirements for effective verification of suspected violations of the NPT's non-proliferation obligations are thus quite challenging. The kind of detection technology described above needs careful preparation in order to function efficiently in the timeframe set by the physical nature of nuclear material released into the relevant environment. The physical limitations of detection of nuclear activities—and detection is the purpose of various forms of on-site inspection and environmental sampling—have obvious repercussions on treaty design, in particular as far as its safeguarding regimes are concerned.[14] The NPT is seen by many to be based on a 'grand bargain' which attempts to integrate concerns to prevent the further proliferation of nuclear weapons with assistance for all States involved in civilian uses of nuclear energy as well as obligations placed on existing NPT nuclear-weapon States to disarm.[15] The credibility of the non-proliferation policies contained in Article II of the NPT depends heavily on the effectiveness of the externally-based IAEA-NPT safeguards specified in Article III of the NPT.[16] The commitments of the 190 Parties to the treaty have made this non-proliferation undertaking credible. But there exist amongst them a limited number of member States who others claim to possess a

[14]See in general on the IAEA safeguards regime Rockwood 2013, pp. 11 et seq., 17 et seq., 21 et seq.

[15]See, for instance, Black-Branch and Fleck 2014, p. 5 et seq.; Denza 2005, p. 290.

[16]See, for instance, Gilligan 2014, p. 96 et seq.

hidden nuclear weapons programme and to have been undeterred from circumventing their non-proliferation obligations by IAEA safeguards. Nominally, the current safeguards regime was created to prevent such covert activities, but as a result of the fundamental political principle of the sovereign equality of States, it was unable to focus on problematic member States alone.[17] Yet without a reliable safeguards regime, nuclear weapon States will never enter into serious efforts of nuclear disarmament to achieve the objective of 'global zero'. At the same time, potential suppliers of nuclear technology and technical equipment needed for the peaceful uses of nuclear energy are discouraged from delivering technology and technical equipment to States they suspect of pursuing a clandestine programme of nuclear armament. A reliable and efficient safeguards regime is thus of utmost importance for the future functioning of the overall regime of the NPT.[18]

8.3.2 The Construction of Safeguards

NPT safeguards are a product of individual safeguards agreements between an NPT non-nuclear-weapon State and the IAEA, which acts as the technical guardian of the NPT regime.[19] These agreements are implemented through regular on-site visits by IAEA inspectors, known as 'routine inspections', supplemented by a limited possibility of 'special inspections'.[20] The inspectors visit nuclear facilities in Member States and monitor the movement of fissionable materials, together with the technical operations taking place within a nuclear site. Their objective is to assess whether the installation might be involved in a nuclear weapons programme by removing nuclear material from the regular cycle of peaceful use and redirected for military purposes. For the purpose of remote monitoring of the ordinary operation of the installation among others, the inspectors may install technical equipment in the installation, such as video cameras, monitors or certain types of sensors.[21]

These routine inspections give the inspection team a relatively clear picture of the technical installations, their technical procedures for processing fissile materials and the technical capabilities of each installation. In most cases an experienced inspector can easily deduce from its technical capabilities that a given installation

[17] See Gilligan 2014, pp. 97–99.

[18] See also Gilligan 2014, pp. 93–96.

[19] On the IAEA safeguards regime see, for instance, Rockwood 2012, pp. 304 et seq.; see also Meier, 2014 pp. 10 et seq.; Szasz 1996, p. 239 et seq.; ElBaradei 1995, pp. 347 et seq.; Scheinman 1995, pp. 133 et seq.

[20] See Rockwood 2013, pp. 22–23.

[21] See, for instance, Rockwood 2012, pp. 310–312.

is not being used in a nuclear weapons programme. Assessing with certainty whether minor quantities of fissile material is being diverted from civil to military use is more difficult. A tight control of fissile material may limit the volume of diverted materials and larger quantities of missing material are difficult to hide. The security thus gained is only relative, but sufficient to deter most would-be proliferators.

Those not deterred from diversion include States that invest significant resources in a military programme physically independent from any civil activities and doing everything possible to hide this from the IAEA's routine inspections. These are not designed to cover up a deliberate attempt at cheating by pursuing such a hidden programme.[22] For a State deciding to follow such a path there will exist a number of possibilities to circumvent inspection schemes and outmanoeuvre the inspection teams. The easiest way of doing so is the one noted earlier of constructing secret research and development sites geographically separate from declared nuclear facilities. Another is to build additional facilities masked as harmless technical annexes linked to existing facilities.[23] In the existing patterns of routine inspections it seems extremely difficult to uncover and adequately inspect such secret and hidden military programmes.[24]

The story of the secret nuclear weapons programme of Iraq under Saddam Hussein in the 1980s and early 1990s is a striking demonstration of the limitations of the routine inspection scheme.[25] The Saddam Hussein regime developed an impressive determination to develop (and potentially use) weapons of mass destruction, including a nuclear weapons programme, and invested a huge amount of resources in them. It was only after the liberation of Kuwait in 1991 and the intrusive sanctions regime imposed upon Iran by the UN that their inspectors revealed the size and intensity of its (hidden) nuclear weapons programme.[26] The ordinary safeguards regime of the IAEA, to which Iraq had subjected itself many years before, had proven incapable of detecting these massive endeavours to develop military nuclear technology. The precedent of these experiences of the limitations of IAEA safeguards diminished t trust in the reliability of the NPT's compliance control mechanisms, and made all States aware that the existing safeguards mechanism was not sufficient to counter deliberate attempts at proliferation.[27]

The usual routine inspections under the Comprehensive Safeguards Agreements created to check the quantities of nuclear fission materials in declared nuclear

---

[22]See, however, the decision of the IAEA Board of Governors that the scope of safeguards agreements includes verifying the absence of undeclared nuclear material and activities in the State ('correctness and completeness')—Rockwood 2013, p. 19.

[23]As a paradigmatic example for such situation see the Iran case—Meier 2014, p. 10 et seq.

[24]See Petritz 2012, pp. 134–139.

[25]See, for instance, Negm 2009, p. 160 et seq.; Simpson 1992, p. 249 et seq.

[26]See Negm 2009, p. 170 et seq.; Zedalis 2006, p. 115 et seq.; Findlay 2004, pp. 65–83.

[27]See Reed and Sullivan 2009, p. 145.

facilities were clearly not robust enough to prevent the development of covert military nuclear programmes based on installations and facilities divorced from civil activities. It also opened to doubt whether diversion of fissile materials from IAEA-monitored civilian facilities could be prevented under the existing inspection regime. It seemed that grey zones existed in the IAEA counting procedures which could allow limited diversions from civil facilities. This was not a new insight but their limitations were obvious at an early point to scientists and lawyers dealing with NPT safeguards. As a result, the IAEA developed additional, complementary but voluntary controls including on-site inspections through what became known as Additional Protocols.

8.3.3 The On-site Inspections Under the Additional Protocols

The Additional Protocols reinforce routine inspections in declared civil facilities but cannot guarantee the detection of covert programmes of research and development of nuclear weapons.[28] The tool now needed to counter hidden military nuclear programmes is to give IAEA inspectors the power to visit and inspect undeclared (and thus not monitored) installations. As was the case in the Iran dispute, internal opposition groups might forward information on covert nuclear programmes and hidden installations to the IAEA and other NPT States parties.[29] The same might result from the intelligence operations of third States that sometimes detect indications for a covert military nuclear programme. Both sources might even be able to pinpoint where these facilities are situated. When such information reaches the IAEA, it could open the way for urgent action, in the form of an on-site visit at very short notice.[30] However, this action will only be possible if significant legal issues confronting the IAEA can be overcome. Foreign inspectors may only be allowed to undertake such an inspection with the cooperation of the government concerned. Also, if a government wants to conceal a covert military programme from an ad hoc inspection, it would have many legal options to prevent such a move. These include failing to provide IAEA inspectors with visas[31]; claims that the installations are military sites where the presence of foreigners is not allowed; and preventing inspectors importing and using the range of technical means necessary to analyse the character and nature of the activities being

[28]See, for instance, Denza 2005, p. 291; but also Rockwood 2013, p. 13; Meier 2014, pp. 12–14; Asada 2011, pp. 3–11; Rockwood 2002, pp. 127–136.

[29]On the background of the Iran nuclear issue see, for instance, Ronen 2010, pp. 16 et seq.; Khan 2010, pp. 63 et seq., 89 et seq.; Meier 2014, pp. 10–16.

[30]See, for instance, Petritz 2012, p. 125 et seq.

[31]See Rockwood 2013, p. 23.

inspected by denying them entry. And entry into the State concerned has to be made very quickly, otherwise (as discussed above) the physical indicators will disappear or become too weak for safe conclusions to be drawn. Indeed for such a system of short notice inspections on suspicion to work, all legal and practical details must be fixed in advance—a path taken by the IAEA, but with limited success, as not all IAEA Member States have signed and ratified an Additional Protocol.[32]

A tendency to automatically deny access to suspect sites is to be expected if it involves authoritarian regimes, who are likely to view IAEA inspectors as spies of enemy powers. In these circumstances, asking this type of government for an unfettered right in advance to inspect all its relevant installations is unlikely to be granted. As a result, concluding Additional Protocols with those States where suspicions exist that they are engaged in covert nuclear programmes of a military nature is virtually impossible.[33] Moreover, on-site inspection at very short notice is inherently very challenging for the IAEA and its team of inspectors. Its safeguards branch must be able to mobilize a team of inspectors with the right skills and mix of expertise and access to adequate technical equipment on rather short notice, especially given the limitations on the financial resources available to the Agency.

8.3.4 Fast Atmospheric Sampling as an Alternative Option

If one wants to avoid the intricacies of on-site inspections at short notice through all States agreeing to implement an Additional Protocol, the only alternative technical option appears to be to use fast atmospheric sampling.[34] This would not require direct access to installations, and thus is less prone to legal and other obstruction by governments that want to hide covert activities. If undertaken quickly enough after a claim about the existence of covert nuclear activities, such atmospheric samplings might enable third-party observers to detect and verify the existence of irregular activities in an efficient manner. It also seems at first sight to involve fewer political issues than on-site inspections, since it appears less intrusive in terms of a States sovereignty.

In practice, however, this option does involve both legal and political challenges in technical preparation and obtaining cooperation from the State concerned. Atmospheric sampling needs access to suitable aircraft to undertake this task; they have to be based in an area close to relevant airspace; some cooperation from the State involved may be necessary; and all this be available at very short

[32]See http://www.iaea.org/safeguards/documents/AP_status_list.pdf; Petritz 2012, pp. 125–127.

[33]See, for instance, Meier 2014, above n. 19, p. 30.

[34]See, as a general introduction to the advantages (and inherent problems) of airborne measurements, Wendisch and Brenquier 2013.

notice. The aircraft cannot be easily leased on the spot: what will be needed is a specific type of aircraft equipped with the technical devices needed for atmospheric sampling. All of these requirements are not easy to meet without prior preparations. An aircraft cannot simply fly at random in the airspace of a suspect State. It must ask for the permit to enter the airspace and must obey the orders of the States air surveillance authorities[35]—a requirement which again is open to tactics of obstruction. Thus, for this technique to be used effectively it requires the existence of a previous legal arrangement between the State concerned and the IAEA (or the organization involved in collecting the sampling) in order to secure the necessary flight rights for atmospheric sampling (and to counter potential obstruction strategies).

8.3.5 The Legal Path Towards a More Efficient Safeguards System

The results of the above reflections on the technical as well as the legal conditions of an efficient safeguards regime are quite disillusioning. Introducing such new mechanisms is not easy. Intrusive on-site inspections on short notice at unknown places are challenging from both a technical and organizational perspective; even more challenging is the need for a strengthened framework that sets the legal conditions for such inspections. This also applies to atmospheric sampling; although seemingly less intrusive and less dependent on government cooperation, it involves significant technical, organizational and legal challenges if the obstructive tactics of a suspect State concerned are to be overcome.

If the safeguards regime is to become efficient, it will have to take care not only of '... the timely detection of diversion of significant quantities of nuclear material from peaceful nuclear activities to the manufacture of nuclear weapons',[36] but also contribute to the goal of 'deterrence of such diversion by the risk of early detection'. In addition, if States are to be deterred from unlawful activities in the research and development of nuclear weapons (as defined by Article II of the NPT), the whole IAEA safeguards regime must be strengthened. One such strengthening would consist in a hardened mechanism of on-site inspections on short notice. Such a development requires the creation of a relatively far-reaching and watertight legal arrangement, where State parties give consent in advance to intrusive technical inspections at research facilities and military installations usually closed to foreigners. This requires changes to the arrangements for IAEA

[35]See in general on the requirement of prior permit for overflight Wouters and Demeyere 2008, paras 13–22.

[36]International Atomic Energy Agency: The Structure and Content of Agreements Between the Agency and States Required in Connection with the Treaty on the Non-Proliferation of Nuclear Weapons. INFCIRC/153 (Corr.), 1972, para 28.

inspectors to enter the territory of any suspect State; simplifying the customs requirement for importing relevant technical equipment; and guaranteeing access to relevant installations without lengthy prior notice. The cooperation of the State agents on site must be secured, including access to all areas and the right to installation of relevant technical equipment. The legal implications of such changes are not insignificant.

Opening up possibilities for atmospheric sampling also requires quite significant preparations. In this case the need for prior consent concerns less the access to installations and facilities, than the prior consent to entering the airspace of the State concerned.

Such consents cannot be read into the existing Comprehensive Safeguards Agreements and Additional Protocols. They would require a new type of Additional Protocol[37] far more intrusive than the existing one. This is likely to produce resistance from a number of States against such a far-reaching development of safeguards. They can easily hide behind arguments of preservation of sovereignty and equal rights under international law. Also, the inequality of the five NPT nuclear weapon States being exempt from similar intrusive monitoring mechanisms offers a pretence to obstruct moves in such a direction.

8.3.6 The Legal Consequences of a New Type of Safeguards

It is thus not realistic to introduce a new type of (deeply intrusive) legally based safeguards system on a broad scale, since a number of important members of the non-proliferation regime would openly object to any new arrangement involving differential treatment of States similar to that found in the NPT's original legal architecture. This system of different obligations for Nuclear-Weapon States—Articles I and VI—and of Non-Nuclear-Weapon States—mainly Articles II and III—distinguishes in a fundamental way between *beati possidentes* of the nuclear world order and the nuclear have-nots.[38] The obligations placed on non-nuclear-weapon States under Articles II and III of the NPT are in principle the same for all the NNWS concerned. However, the system of individual Safeguard Agreements concluded between the IAEA and individual States differentiates to some extent between their individual obligations under Article III NPT,[39] although the existence of the model Comprehensive Safeguards Agreement guarantees some consistence between them. The introduction of Additional Protocols again has introduced a new element of a differentiation of obligations among the NPT's Member States, since not all NPT/IAEA members have ratified Additional

[37]See also Cooley 2003, pp. 29–44.

[38]See, for instance, Nye 1985, p. 123 et seq.

[39]See also Cooley 2003, pp. 36–39.

Protocols.[40] The introduction of a new type of an even more intrusive Additional Protocol would further expand this trend towards differential treatment. As an alternative to such further fragmentation of the NPT's set of obligations, one theoretical option would be for States to make an individual voluntary commitment (similar to that involved in accepting the Additional Protocol) to allow greater access by the IAEA if claims of non-compliance were to be made against them. Indeed an individual commitment in a very specific form of special safeguards arrangement may well be the outcome of the ongoing negotiations between the P5 + 1 and Iran.[41] Such an individual commitment would create a new kind of flexibility in the treaty architecture of the NPT, though its justification would have to be that it is a reaction to the specific problems that have been encountered in the past practice of operating safeguards,[42] which have demonstrated that such additional commitments might be useful. This could, however, result in a set of ad hoc arrangements, where individual commitments of this type are only be negotiated after problems have occurred.

The flexibility in treaty design that such an initiative requires would mean a deliberate departure from the rule of equal treatment of treaty parties. Additional safeguards with intrusive inspections and atmospheric sampling would not be needed in the majority of cases where routine inspections would suffice. They are needed, however, where a State raises suspicion of the existence of covert nuclear programmes of a military nature, cooperation in clearing up claims of proliferation proves to be limited, and there are signs of obstruction. It would only be in these cases that a more thorough and intrusive system of monitoring and verification would be needed.[43] But do States accept there is a potential need for such intrusive means of monitoring and verification, or are they only willing to contemplate such schemes in individual cases, even though this would be a departure from the basic principle of equal treatment of Contracting Parties? It would break with that fundamental principle of equal treatment.[44]

It may be that States are *de facto* not always treated equal under international law, as also the NPT demonstrates; but at least in principle States have a right to be treated in the same way as any other State. In practice this may be counterfactual, but from a normative perspective one should not easily dispense with the fundamental structural principle of sovereign equality, closely linked to the core values of self-determination of peoples.[45] Of course there exist differences in terms of power and resources between different peoples (and States) of the world;

---

[40]See, for instance, Meier 2014, above n. 20, p. 30; see also, with a strategy how to universalize the system of Additional Protocols, Asada 2011, at pp. 20–34; see also Chap. 5 in this volume.

[41]See in this regard also Meier 2014, pp. 14–16, 28–32.

[42]See on this point also Cooley 2003, pp. 30–33.

[43]The same objective is pursued by the program of 'integrated safeguards', see Cooley 2003, pp. 31–39.

[44]See Kokott 2011, paras 43–49.

[45]See, for instance, Oeter 2012, in particular para 37.

but this does not mean that one people, simply as a result of its size and resources, has a different normative value than the other. The principle of sovereign equality protects the community of States against any attempt to force peoples (and States) into a normatively consolidated hierarchy, thus dispossessing them of their chance to decide their own way of social and political organization. Why is the likelihood of Iran possessing nuclear weapons a threat to the security of Israel, the United States and others, whereas the assumed possession of nuclear weapons by Israel is not? The normative difference between the two cases is difficult to argue on the basis of principles—unless one relies on context-specific arguments that always tend towards differential treatment.[46]

But are States of the global South willing to accept such differential treatment? They know from the beginning that the departure from the principle of sovereign equality will not work in their favour. Differential treatment will give the powerful more rights, the powerless fewer rights—and that might be perceived as a danger in a world order that is characterized by strong tendencies of 'exceptionalism' by the great powers.[47] Powers like the United States and Russia know that the other States cannot force them to account for their violations of public international law in the existing institutional framework of the United Nations, and they accordingly tend to behave as if they were above the law.[48] But should we institutionalize such inequality in formal legal arrangements of differentiated treatment? The answer by most of the peoples of the world probably would be: 'No!' If we cannot avoid the phenomena of 'exceptionalism' and differential rights in a (limited) number of treaty regimes, we should keep as limited as possible these exceptions to the basic paradigm of sovereign equality. We thus cannot expect third-world States to accept constructions of differential responsibilities which they believe penalize them.

8.4 Conclusion: The Linkage Between Efficiency of Safeguards and the Disarmament Obligation of Nuclear-Weapon States

The NPT with its differential construction of different sets of obligations for nuclear-weapon States and non-nuclear-weapon States has always been a fragile construction in terms of legitimacy.[49] The concentration on non-proliferation and

[46]See as radical examples of such a differential, context-related treatment Pollack 2013, p. 158 et seq., 224 et seq.; Glennon 2013, pp. 124–127.

[47]See, for instance, Gunn 2002, p. 137 et seq.; Koh 2003, p. 1479 et seq.; Nolte and Aust 2013, p. 407 et seq.

[48]See, for instance Krisch 2003, p. 135 et seq.

[49]See, for instance, Garvey 2013, pp. 29–33.

the hardening of the efficiency of safeguards that dominates the agenda of a superpower like the United States overstretches the tolerance of most of the member States of the NPT. Far-reaching non-proliferation obligations have been acceptable as long as the cooperation and assistance of the nuclear powers in developing civilian uses of nuclear energy offered them advantages.[50] As long as nuclear energy was perceived as the energy of the future, the *quid pro quo* of non-proliferation obligations and access to civilian uses of nuclear energy seemed a fair deal. But the euphoric belief in nuclear energy as the miraculous solution of all future energy problems has faded away. The dangers (and societal costs) of nuclear energy have become obvious, and a growing number of States have decided to abstain from any civilian use of nuclear energy. In these circumstances, what is left of the original perceived deal over the NPT?

The third pillar of the NPT comes into play again. The 'grand bargain' of the Treaty from its beginnings rested on three pillars, not two.[51] Non-proliferation obligations and the access to civilian uses of nuclear energy were complemented by the disarmament obligations of the nuclear powers laid down in Article VII NPT.[52] Renunciation of any recourse to nuclear armament would demonstrate the existence of the reciprocal set of obligations falling upon nuclear-weapon States. The first is the renunciation of any use of nuclear weapons against a non-nuclear-weapon State. If nuclear powers would be allowed to intimidate non-nuclear-weapon States with the threat of using nuclear weapons against them, there would be no incentive for them to renounce the development, production and stockpiling of nuclear weapons. On the contrary, any sensible State would desperately try to acquire these weapons in order to deter others from nuclear attacks. The same logic might even work in the event of conventional threats. If Ukraine would have known that Russia would attack it in a foreseeable future, it would never have relinquished its arsenal of nuclear weaponry to the advantage of Russia's position as the sole nuclear-weapon State in the succession to the Soviet Union. A more or less comparable reasoning seems to be identifiable behind the Israeli and North Korean nuclear weapons programme and the Iranian attempts to at least obtain an option of the future development of nuclear weaponry.[53]

The underlying feature of the NPT is a clear linkage between the non-proliferation obligations of non-nuclear-weapon States and the *pactum de contrahendo* that binds the traditional nuclear powers to negotiate and agree on substantial disarmament/reductions in their nuclear weapons,[54] with the final objective of 'global

---

[50]See in detail Joyner 2011, pp. 47–74, 78–94.

[51]See, for instance, Gilligan 2014, pp. 93–95.

[52]See in detail on Article VI NPT, Rietiker 2014, pp. 47 et seq.; Joyner 2011, pp. 95–108.

[53]See, for instance, Roehrig 2012, pp. 81 et seq.; Jones and Holmes 2012, pp. 201 et seq.; Sagan et al. 2012, pp. 175 et seq.; Said 2011, pp. 39 et seq.

[54]See in detail Rietiker 2014, p. 53.

zero'.[55] Safeguards Agreements and the issue of efficiency of safeguards are a sub-set of obligations resulting from non-proliferation. But what remains of the NPT *quid pro quo* after nearly five decades without any significant agreement on a general move towards nuclear disarmament? Non-nuclear-weapon States show signs of a loss of patience. Why should non-nuclear-weapon States subject themselves to ever more intrusive schemes of monitoring and verification of non-proliferation obligations whilst the nuclear-weapon States handle their basic obligations of nuclear disarmament with evident negligence? Non-nuclear-weapon States have an interest in avoiding further proliferation of nuclear weapons, since that might set into motion a process of escalation forcing them to enter the club of nuclear aspirants, if not nuclear powers. But reminders from nuclear-weapon States that the have-nots should invest more efforts in the fulfilment of their obligations, whereas they themselves neglect their own obligations,[56] are unlikely to fall onto fertile ground given the normative intuitions of non-nuclear weapon States.

The resulting insight might be perceived as heretic in traditional circles of security specialists, but it should be nevertheless formulated bluntly. Further changes in the safeguards regime including more intrusive safeguards and introducing additional means of monitoring and verification of suspected violations of non-proliferation obligations, will only be politically possible if the nuclear powers show a serious commitment to make significant progress in nuclear disarmament (as specified in Article VI of the NPT). Only if its basic reciprocity of the rights and duties accepted by both nuclear-weapon and non-nuclear-weapon States is taken seriously will here will be a realistic chance of further strengthening of the Treaty. This will involve creating a comprehensive system of safeguards that effectively deters States from circumventing the non-proliferation obligations. Whether it is realistic to expect the nuclear powers to follow that insight might be open to doubts, but they bear a fundamental responsibility for the future of the NPT.

The very survival of mankind depends on sustaining the commitments contained in the Non-Proliferation Treaty, while banning the use of nuclear weapons.[57] Only when the nuclear-weapon States take seriously their obligations to engage in measurable disarmament will the NPT have a fair chance to solve the problem of nuclear weapons.[58] At its core, the NPT is a treaty regime based on a fundamental *do ut des*, with a basic feature of reciprocity between rights and duties of the different groups of contracting States—notwithstanding the normative architecture of differential obligations imposed upon nuclear-weapon States and non-nuclear-weapon States. To forget about this would not only hinder further progressive development of the Treaty, but would in the long run endanger its entire existence.

[55]See Falk and Krieger 2012, p. 191 et seq.

[56]See Holloway 2011, pp. 151 et seq.; Joyner 2011, pp. 95–108.

[57]See, for instance, Falk and Krieger 2008, pp. 29 et seq., 39 et seq., 209 et seq.

[58]In this sense see also Rietiker 2014, p. 81; Garvey 2013, pp. 22–28.

References

Asada M (2011) The treaty on the non-proliferation of nuclear weapons and the universalization of the additional protocol. J Confl Secur L 16:3–34

Black-Branch JL, Fleck D (2014) Nuclear weapons, non-proliferation and disarmament: a comprehensive audit of relevant legal issues and international concerns. In: Black-Branch JL, Fleck D (eds) Nuclear non-proliferation in international law. TMC Asser Press, The Hague, pp 1–21

Cooley JN (2003) Integrated nuclear safeguards: genesis and evolution. Verification Yearbook 2003:29–44

Denza E (2005) Non-proliferation of nuclear weapons: the European Union and Iran. Eur Foreign Aff Rev 10:289–311

ElBaradei M (1995) Verifying non-proliferation pledges. The evolution and future direction of the IAEA safeguards system. Leiden J Int Law 8:347–359

Falk RA, Krieger D (2008) At the nuclear precipice: catastrophe or transformation? Palgrave Macmillan, New York

Falk RA, Krieger D (2012) The path to zero: dialogues on nuclear dangers. Paradigm Publishers, Boulder, London

Findlay T (2004) The lessons of UNSCOM and UNMOVIC. Verification Yearbook 2004:65–86

Garvey JI (2013) Nuclear weapons counterproliferation: a new grand bargain. Oxford University Press, Oxford

Gilligan K (2014) The non-proliferation regime and the NPT. In: Black-Branch JL, Fleck D (eds) Nuclear non-proliferation in international law. TMC Asser Press, The Hague, pp 85–104

Glennon MJ (2013) Pre-empting proliferation: international law, morality, and nuclear weapons. Eur J Int Law 24:109–127

Gunn TJ (2002) American exceptionalism and globalist double standards. Columbia J Transnational Law 41:137–152

Holloway D (2011) The United States and the NPT 'double bargain'. In: Njølstad O (ed), Nuclear proliferation and international order. Nobel symposium 142. Routledge, London, pp 151–166

Jones SA, Holmes JR (2012) Regime type, nuclear reversals, and nuclear strategy: the ambiguous case of Iran. In: Yoshihara T, Holmes JR (eds) Strategy in the second nuclear age: power, ambition, and the ultimate weapon. Georgetown University Press, Washington, DC, pp 201–224

Joyner DH (2011) Interpreting the nuclear non-proliferation treaty. Oxford University Press, Oxford

Khan S (2010) Iran and nuclear weapons: protracted conflict and proliferation. Routledge, London

Koh HH (2003) On American exceptionalism. Stanford Law Rev 55:1479–1527

Kokott J (2011) Sovereign equality. In: Wolfrum R (ed), Max Planck encyclopedia of public international law: MPEPIL. Oxford University Press, Oxford (online edn)

Krisch N (2003) More equal than the rest? Hierarchy, equality, and US predominance in international law. In: Byers M, Nolte G (eds) United States hegemony and the foundations of international law. Cambridge University Press, Cambridge, pp 135–175

Meier O (2014) In der Krise liegt die Chance. Der Atomkonflikt mit Iran und seine Auswirkungen auf das nukleare Nichtverbreitungsregime. SWP-Studie S 17/Okt. 2014, http://www.swp-berlin.org/fileadmin/contents/products/studien/2014_S17_mro.pdf

Negm N (2009) Transfer of nuclear technology under international law: case study of Iraq, Iran and Israel. Nijhoff, Leiden

Nolte G, Aust HP (2013) European exceptionalism? Global Constitutionalism 2:407–436

Nye JS (1985) NPT: the logic of inequality. Foreign Policy 59:123–131

Oeter S (2012) Self-determination. In: Simma B et al (eds) The charter of the United Nations: a commentary, vol I, 3rd edn. Oxford University Press, Oxford, pp 313–334
Petritz W (2012) Vor dem Aus? Der Vertrag über die Nichtweiterverbreitung von Kernwaffen: Funktion und Relevanz anhand zweier Beispiele. Peter Lang, Frankfurt am Main
Pollack KM (2013) Unthinkable: Iran, the bomb, and American strategy. Simon & Schuster, New York
Reed TC, Sullivan DB (2009) The nuclear express. Zenith Press, Minneapolis
Rietiker D (2014) The meaning of article VI of the Treaty on the Non-Proliferation of Nuclear Weapons: analysis under the rules of treaty interpretation. In: Black-Branch JL, Fleck D (eds) Nuclear non-proliferation in international law. TMC Asser Press, The Hague, pp 47–84
Rockwood L (2002) The IAEA's strengthened safeguards system. J Confl Secur L 7:123–136
Rockwood L (2012) Ensuring compliance with standards on the peaceful use of nuclear energy. In: Cassese A (ed) Realizing utopia. The future of international law. Oxford University Press, Oxford, pp 304–317
Rockwood L (2013) Legal framework for IAEA safeguards. IAEA, Vienna
Roehrig T (2012) North Korea's nuclear weapons program: motivations, strategy, and doctrine. In: Yoshihara T, Holmes JR (eds), Strategy in the second nuclear age: power, ambition, and the ultimate weapon. Georgetown University Press, pp 81–98
Ronen Y (2010) The Iran nuclear issue. Hart, Oxford
Ross O et al. (2009) Simulation of Atmospheric Noble Gas Concentrations to Assess Sampling Procedures for the Detection of Clandestine Reprocessing. Joint Programme on the Technical Development and Further Improvement of IAEA Safeguards Between the Government of the Federal Republic of Germany and the IAEA, JOPAG/01.09-PRG-373. Hamburg
Sagan SD, Waltz KM, Rapp-Hooper M (2012) Iraq, North Korea, and Iran. In: Sagan SD, Waltz KM (eds) The spread of nuclear weapons: an enduring debate. W.W. Norton, New York, pp 175–214
Said MK (2011) Israel's nuclear capability: implications on Middle East security. In: Njølstad O (ed), Nuclear proliferation and international order. Nobel symposium 142. Routledge, London, pp 39–61
Scheinman L (1995) Nuclear safeguards and non-proliferation in a changing world order. In: Evan WM (ed) Nuclear proliferation and the legality of nuclear weapons. University Press of America, Lanham, pp 133–149
Simpson J (1992) The Iraqi nuclear programme and the future of the IAEA safeguards system. Verification report. Yearbook Arms control Environ Agreements 12:249–253
Szasz PC (1996) IAEA safeguards for NPT. Rev Eur Community Int Environ Law 5:239–245
Wendisch M, Brenquier J-L (2013) Airborne measurements for environmental research. Wiley, Weinheim
Wouters J, Demeyere B (2008) Overflight. In: Wolfrum R (ed) Max Planck encyclopedia of public international law: MPEPIL. Oxford University Press, Oxford (online edn)
Zedalis RJ (2006) Weapons of mass destruction in Iraq. Int Peacekeeping 10:115–161

Chapter 9
Next Generation Nuclear Technologies: New Challenges to the Legal Framework of the IAEA from Intense Neutron Sources

Matthias Englert and Anne Harrington

Abstract In this chapter, we take intense neutron sources (INS) as a somewhat futuristic case to unveil another dimension in disputes over the application of safeguards to nuclear technologies. The current IAEA safeguards regime is built on a distinction between facilities and materials. The assumption underlying such a distinction is that facilities are not a concern in the absence of nuclear materials. Historically, such a distinction made sense because there was no reason to operate nuclear fuel cycle facilities in the absence of nuclear materials. However, INS facilities do not require nuclear materials under normal operating procedures, yet they hold out the potential for producing weapons-grade plutonium in a shorter period of time and with less source material than existing facilities. As a result, they present a new challenge to the IAEA safeguards regime. We present a comparison of the timeline to produce weapons-grade plutonium with reactors, spallation neutron sources and fusion plants and discuss possible advantages and disadvantages of the respective technologies. One focus will be the possibility of fusion plants and spallation sources producing significant quantities of plutonium

Matthias Englert, Öko-Institut e.V., Darmstadt, Germany. Dr. rer. nat in Physics. Formerly Researcher and Coordinator at the Interdisciplinary Research Group in Science Technology and Security (IANUS) at Darmstadt University of Technology (2011–2012), Science Fellow at the Center for International Security and Cooperation, Stanford University (2009–2011).

Anne. I. Harrington, Ph.D. in Political Science (University of Chicago, Researcher, Center for Security Studies, ETH Zurich; formerly Postdoctoral Research Fellow, James Martin Center for Non-proliferation Studies, Monterey Institute of International Studies (2011–2013); Stanton Nuclear Security Postdoctoral Fellow, Center for International Security and Cooperation, Stanford University (2010–2011).

M. Englert (✉)
Öko-Institut e.V., Rheinstr. 95, 64295 Darmstadt, Germany
e-mail: matthias.englert@dialectics.de

A. Harrington
Center for Security Studies, ETH Zurich, Haldeneggsteig 4, IFW, 8092 Zurich, Switzerland
e-mail: anne.harrington@sipo.gess.ethz.ch

J.L. Black-Branch and D. Fleck (eds.), *Nuclear Non-Proliferation in International Law - Volume II*, DOI 10.1007/978-94-6265-075-6_9

with less source material than 'one effective kilogram' of uranium. Furthermore, the question will be raised if the corresponding technologies are adequately covered by current IAEA terms like 'facility' and 'reactor'.

Keywords Fission reactors · Fusion power plants · Intense neutron sources (INS) · International Atomic Energy Agency (IAEA) · Isotope separation plant · Plutonium production · Reprocessing plant · Spallation neutron sources

Contents

9.1 Introduction

The legal framework of the International Atomic Energy Agency (IAEA) was established to verify compliance with the Nuclear Non-proliferation Treaty (NPT)[1] by upholding a comprehensive regime of technical safeguards. These technical measures are designed to ensure that no fissile material is diverted from a civilian energy program for military purposes.

Implicit in the design of the comprehensive safeguards regime is the assumption that facilities in and of themselves are not a proliferation threat until nuclear materials[2] are introduced. However, this assumption does not necessarily hold

[1]Treaty on the Non-Proliferation of Nuclear Weapons (1 July 1968), 729 UNTS 161.

[2]'*Nuclear Material* means any source or any special fissionable material as defined in Article XX of the Statute' (International Atomic Energy Agency Information Circular (INFCIRC/153)). 'The term *source material* means uranium containing the mixture of isotopes occurring in nature; uranium depleted in the isotope 235; thorium; any of the foregoing in the form of metal, alloy, chemical compound, or concentrate; any other material containing one or more of the foregoing in such concentration as the Board of Governors shall from time to time determine; and such other material as the Board of Governors shall from time to time determine' (IAEA statute). The term *special fissionable material* means plutonium-239; uranium-233; uranium enriched in the isotopes 235 or 233; any material containing one or more of the foregoing; and such other fissionable material as the Board of Governors shall from time to time determine; but the term *special fissionable material* does not include source material.

true. The safeguards system was designed to verify declarations that specify how much nuclear material is present in a facility and in the nuclear fuel cycle as a whole.[3] The underlying assumption is that if all nuclear material flows in the nuclear fuel cycle are known from cradle to grave and no nuclear materials cross State borders, a facility in and of itself will not pose a risk. However, historically the facilities in question, such as fission reactors, were not of much use without the introduction of nuclear materials. This will not necessarily be the case with new intense neutron sources (INS). Normal operating conditions at an INS facility will not require the presence of nuclear materials, which means that they will not be part of the traditional nuclear fuel cycle.

INS is an umbrella term that the IAEA uses to describe technologies with a higher rate of flow of neutrons per area (neutron flux)[4] than a fission reactor normally produces. INS covers spallation and fusion technologies. Common uses for spallation sources include research into the physical structure of materials and boosting fission reactors (accelerator-driven systems). Like spallation sources, a common use for fusion reactors is research. Additionally, in the future they may become a more attractive nuclear energy source than fission reactors.

In this chapter, we take intense neutron sources as a somewhat futuristic case to raise the question of whether the corresponding technologies are adequately covered by the current IAEA mandate and safeguards practices. We present a comparison of the timeline for producing plutonium with reactors, spallation neutron sources and fusion plants, and the possible advantages and disadvantages of the respective technologies. What this comparison reveals is that INS sources need much less nuclear material to produce 'one effective kilogram'[5] or a 'significant quantity'[6] of plutonium than fission reactors. Fusion reactors, in particular, have an exceptional capability to rapidly produce weapons-grade plutonium. In spite of the fact that INS do not require nuclear materials under normal operating conditions, refining the operational capabilities of these facilities even in the absence of nuclear materials will produce tacit knowledge[7] that could significantly reduce the timeline for a State that wants to breakout of the safeguards regime and produce a

---

[3]Design documents of the facility and their correctness are also important to verify that no fissile material diversion could take place.

[4]The technical term is *neutron flux*: the distance all neutrons travel through a certain volume in a specific time. The higher the flux the higher the reaction rate for a specific reaction of neutrons with the nucleus of other atoms in the material. These processes can be fission, capture, scattering and others. A helpful visualization is the billiard table.

[5]See below n. 37.

[6]'The approximate amount of nuclear material for which the possibility of manufacturing a nuclear explosive device cannot be excluded' (IAEA 2001). A significant quantity (SQ) of direct use nuclear material is 8 kg of plutonium containing less than 80 % plutonium-238, 25 kg of highly enriched uranium with enrichment higher than 20 % in uranium-235. For indirect nuclear use material it is 75 kg uranium-235, the amount that is roughly contained in 10t of natural uranium or 20t of depleted uranium (see also the definition of one effective kilogram below n. 37). Other isotopes are 8 kg of uranium-233 and 20t of thorium.

[7]MacKenzie and Spinardi 1995, p. 45.

nuclear weapon. Therefore, they are covered under the IAEA's verification mandate. However, the distinction between facilities and materials on which the comprehensive safeguards regime is built creates an exploitable gap in the safeguards regime into which INS facilities fall.

There are some who would agree with our conclusion that INS facilities are a proliferation concern, but still argue that there is no exploitable gap because the existence of an Additional Protocol (AP) safeguards agreement is sufficient to cover neutron sources. The AP model explicitly allows for the inspection not only of the correctness of a declaration, but also of a complete accounting of fissile materials. Therefore, facilities in and of themselves would still not be a concern. Others point to an expansive interpretation of the completeness paradigm, the State level approach, under which even standard Comprehensive Safeguards Agreements (CSA's) accommodate completeness. Yet the fact remains that the safeguards regime is built around the presence of fissile materials, not the facilities in which they are processed and it is facilities that will increase the ambivalence inherent to nuclear programs by significantly reducing the timeline to produce fissile materials for a nuclear arsenal.

Another common objection to the significance of the problem that intense neutron facilities present for IAEA safeguards is that the technology is not yet mature enough to warrant concern. The next step to the commercialization of fusion power is the successful operation of the International Thermonuclear Experimental Facility (ITER) in Cardarache France. Although ITER itself does not pose any serious proliferation risk as it is not capable of producing enough neutrons for a significant plutonium production, it will set precedencies for the development of the technology. Preventive measures to increase the proliferation resistance of the facility should be integrated in the design process, e.g. by researching and developing safeguards by design. If ITER is successful, there are plans for nation States or international consortia similar to the ITER consortium to open several Demonstration Power Plants for operation in the 2030s. The demonstration phase is intended to develop commercial plants that will produce energy by 2050.[8]

Given this timeline, the future of the nuclear fusion power industry is not predictable today. It is too early to know whether or not fusion facilities will become commercially available to those States currently alleged to present a proliferation threat.[9] However, that is not a reason to forego the opportunity to start planning for their incorporation into the safeguards system. It is precisely during the current design phase that there is the largest window of opportunity to shape the proliferation resistance of these facilities. Moreover, the problem of INS facilities opens a window onto the larger issue of how States are able to exploit the ambivalence of

[8]EFDA, Fusion Electricity. A Roadmap to the Realisation of Fusion Energy. In: European Fusion Development Agreement (ed), www.efda.org/wpcms/wp-content/uploads/2013/01/JG12.356-web.pdf. Accessed 5 April 2015.

[9]A more detailed argumentation under what political and technological conditions fusion energy could become proliferation relevant with regard to a widespread use in the energy mix of certain countries in the future can be found in Franscheschini et al. 2013.

nuclear technology in order to trade on 'latent' or 'virtual' military capability in the context of negotiations over the status of their peaceful nuclear program.

After having considered the specific case of INS facilities, the chapter presents arguments for and against different options the IAEA may consider when deciding how to integrate INS into the existing safeguards regime. It concludes with a broader discussion of the limits of technical verification in the IAEA safeguards regime and the inherent ambivalence of nuclear technologies.

9.2 Plutonium Producing Technologies

In this section, we compare the advantages and disadvantages of physical processes that breed plutonium in light of the IAEA safeguards regime. We consider dedicated fission reactors alongside fusion reactors and spallation neutron sources to assess the proliferation concerns associated with each type of facility.

In principle, all neutron sources are capable of producing fissile materials. The physical process that drives the reaction to produce plutonium is the capture of a neutron by the nucleus of a uranium atom yielding a plutonium atom after undergoing radioactive decay. Historically, the production of plutonium for weapon purposes took place in dedicated fission reactors. However, there are several other physical processes that will be able to reach neutron fluxes as high as or higher than in a reactor, namely fusion and spallation. Criteria to compare the proliferation characteristics of these different technologies in terms of their underlying physical processes include:

(a) *The plutonium production rate.* This is a measure of how much plutonium can be produced per unit time. The higher the production rate, the less time is required to produce enough plutonium for a nuclear weapon (a significant quantity).
(b) *The minimum amount of uranium required as source material to produce one significant quantity.* The more uranium is needed the more difficult it will be to divert it to a weapons program
(c) *The end concentration of plutonium isotopes in the heavy metal.* The more plutonium is produced per mass of uranium (source material[10]) the less chemical reprocessing is required to separate the plutonium from the uranium, transuranic elements and fission products.
(d) *The isotopic composition of the plutonium.* The higher the percentage of the isotope Pu-239, the more attractive the material is for weapons purposes.

These criteria will vary in these different processes depending on (1) the time under neutron irradiation, (2) the energy distribution of the neutrons in the materials (neutron spectrum) and (3) the neutron flux (rate of flow). We will show that

[10]See above n. 2.

once they are technically mature fusion reactors in particular will have advantages in producing large amounts of weapons-grade plutonium.

The comparison offers two significant findings that should shape IAEA considerations of how to integrate INS facilities into the safeguards regime. First, fusion reactors have an exceptional capability for weapons-grade plutonium production. If they mature to industrial operation, this inherent potential renders them the optimal choice for quick production of large amounts of fuel for nuclear weapons. This latent capability would be relevant for States that want to quickly produce larger amounts of fissile material in the future. Second, fusion reactors have a very low source material requirement to produce a significant quantity of 8 kg weapons-grade plutonium. No material is needed to maintain a fission chain reaction, so only several hundred kilograms of uranium or even depleted uranium would be sufficient. This is much less than the roughly 10 tons of uranium that would be required as source material to fuel the core of a fission reactor large enough for a similar plutonium production. Such an amount of uranium is the threshold in many IAEA protocols and definitions. Not only could less uranium be exempted from safeguards, but also it is no longer only natural uranium that poses a concern; in an INS depleted uranium could be used instead. Depleted uranium is widely available e.g. in conventional ammunition. Detecting the diversion of such low amounts of source material will be very challenging for a verification regime so that safeguards on the facility itself are even more important.

9.2.1 Fission Reactors

In the early fissile material production programs the five recognized Nuclear Weapon States (the United States, the Soviet Union, Great Britain, France and China) commonly used graphite moderated fission reactors like the G1-Reactor at Marcoule in France or the N-Reactor at the Hanford site in the US.[11] Heavy water moderated fission reactors were used in the programs of NPT outliers Israel, India and Pakistan. Both reactor types have advantages for plutonium production compared to the light water moderated fission reactor (LWR), which is predominantly used in commercial energy production today.

Regardless of which fission reactor design is being used, the proper balance has to be struck between the quantity and quality of plutonium produced. The total production of plutonium in a fuel element (quantity) is inversely related to the

[11]Modern light water reactors slow down the neutrons to low energies by using light water as moderator. Neutrons released by atomic fission events are very fast (high energy), but to induce further fissions in other fissile atoms (chain reaction) it is advantageous to slow them down (moderate them) to lower energies. A process that is also called thermalization if the neutrons are slowed down to the ambient temperatures of thermal reactors. In fast reactors the neutrons are not slowed down as much. The use of different moderators (graphite, light water, heavy water) allows to influence the energy distribution (speed distribution) of the neutrons on a reactor core to tailor this distribution to the processes that would gain from it.

attractiveness of the plutonium for weapon purposes (quality). The longer that uranium is exposed to neutrons in the reactor core, the more plutonium is produced. However, longer irradiation times lead to a buildup of heat producing plutonium isotopes (plutonium-238) or isotopes which undergo spontaneous fission reactions and release additional neutrons (plutonium-240, plutonium-242, plutonium-238). Beyond a certain threshold, neutrons from spontaneous fission might start the nuclear chain reaction too early when the bomb is triggered and together with the additional heat production would increase technical sophistication of the weapons design. Although all plutonium isotopes are weapon usable—it is only a matter of technical sophistication and know-how that determines if such plutonium can be used in a nuclear weapon—in order to maximize the quality of plutonium for weapons use, the exposure time has to be kept short.

In commercial operations with LWR, it is not necessary to take into account the tradeoff between quality and quantity. Uranium fuel is used in a reactor as long as it is technically feasible regardless of the plutonium produced. The time is only constrained by safety considerations, e.g. due to material fatigue and by the number of fissile atoms in the fuel that can still contribute to energy production. At 'end of life', uranium fuel contains roughly 1 % plutonium. Of that 1 % more than 40 % is the unwanted plutonium isotopes. In typical military production the uranium fuel contains a concentration of less than 0.1 % plutonium, only one-tenth of the plutonium in commercial spent fuel, but more than 93 % of it is the attractive plutonium-239, perfect for weapon purposes. Due to the low concentrations of plutonium in the irradiated uranium fuel, larger amounts of uranium are necessary to produce a significant quantity of plutonium compared to a commercial operation.

Total production rates for a sample of fission reactors are given in Table 9.1.[12] The table summarizes factors that influence the proliferation characteristics of a system for plutonium production. The total amount of plutonium that can be produced per year (PU rate), the weapons attractiveness of the produced plutonium (Burnup), the amount of uranium needed for the operation (Initial Uranium Loading), the final concentration of plutonium in the uranium (plutonium in fuel) and the size and technical sophistication, i.e. the cost of the system itself (power).

For the low-power reactors, like the French G-1 with about 40 Megawatt (MW) power, production rates of 11 kg plutonium-239 per year can be calculated for an initial uranium loading of roughly 100 tons.[13] For an advanced production reactor like Hanford-N in the US with 4000 MW thermal power, the production rate is significantly higher as the core contains much more fuel and is one hundred times more powerful. A commercial LWR will usually be operated to yield much higher burnups and the final plutonium concentration will be much higher. But high burnups will also increase the content of unwanted plutonium isotopes, so that the

[12]The production rates were calculated using conversion factors for plutonium production and using the nominal thermal power of the reactors. See Albright et al. 1997, Annex A.

[13]Albright et al. 1997, Chap. 3.

Table 9.1 Comparison of different specifications for the production of plutonium with reactors

Reactor	Power [MWth]	Burnup [GWd/t]	Initial uranium loading [t]	Years in reactor core	Plutonium in fuel [kg/tHM]	Conversion ratio [g/MWd]	Pu rate [kg/y]
PWR commercial	3000	30	100	3.4	8.5	0.3	250
PWR weapons	3000	1	100	0.15	~0.5	0.5	330
France G1	~40	0.2	100	1.7	0.2	0.95	11
Calder Hall	180	0.4	112	0.8	0.4	0.9	50
Hanford-N	4000	1.2	380	0.4	0.9	0.5	580
Yong-byon	~25	0.3	48	2.0	0.3	~0.9	7

All reactor production rates calculated according to Albright et al. 1997 and for 80 % capacity factor (60 % for possible military use of an LWR. Data for North Korean reactor Yong-byon see Albright 1994

content of plutonium-239 will be well below 70 %. This in turn will demand a higher technical sophistication for a practical weapon design.

If the operation of a LWR is not optimized for commercial but for military purposes, the fuel elements will have to be exchanged more frequently to prevent the buildup of unwanted plutonium isotopes and get higher quality plutonium for weapon purposes. As constant refuelling is not possible in an LWR,[14] the operating time and therefore the capacity per year would drop as a consequence to an estimated maximum of 60 % or lower.[15]

These calculations give only a rough estimate. The real plutonium production in a LWR might be somewhat higher or lower, but for the purpose of this article we are not interested in the complexity of nuclear archeology[16] and the estimates will be sufficient for comparison with other neutron producing technologies.

9.2.2 Spallation Neutron Sources

In contrast to fission reactors spallation neutron sources (SNS) will be able to produce plutonium during operation once uranium is inserted, but do not require uranium under normal operating conditions and therefore are a challenge to the current safeguards regime. In an SNS, elementary particles like protons pick up speed in an accelerator by electromagnetic force. When they hit a heavy metal target made of liquid lead or mercury, or possibly also uranium, they are travelling near the speed of light. The protons hit the atomic nuclei of the target and spall the nuclei in the process releasing a zoo of elementary particles and fractions of the nucleus together with several neutrons.

A spallation neutron source (SNS) has two primary purposes. It is useful for research purposes (research SNS), or as a driver for a subcritical reactor core in an accelerator-driven system (ADS)—a machine that combines a subcritical reactor with a SNS for energy production. The SNS provides just enough neutrons so that the subcritical reactor multiplies the neutrons to produce energy. In contrast to a pure SNS without the additional reactor core an ADS will contain nuclear material under normal operating procedures and will be subject to IAEA safeguards just like a normal reactor.

[14] To operate such reactors the primary cooling loop has to be closed and the reactor vessel sealed.

[15] For the proliferation concerns associated with light water reactors, cf. Gilinsky et al. 2004.

[16] Fetter 1993; IPFM, Global Fissile Material Report, by the International Panel on Fissile Materials 2009.

A first analysis of the proliferation potential of SNS, and more specifically ADS, can be found in Magill and Peerani 1999 and Riendeau et al. 1998.[17] Such analysis was necessary as in the last decades SNS performance increased significantly.[18] In particular, there is a renewed interest in SNS for research facilities and for industrial application, e.g. accelerator transmutation of waste and ADS. Additionally, dynamics of accelerator development led to more sophisticated, smaller accelerators and there is a growing commercial market for accelerator technology and components.

The power of a SNS directly depends on the proton beam current and energy. The technological developments of the last decades raised available currents from several 100 μA (Mikroampere) to several Milliampere today. Beam currents up to 100 mA for linear accelerators have been proven successfully. For the purpose of this assessment beam currents of 100 μA can be considered a conservative assumption, 1 mA a moderate and 10 mA progressive.

Calculations of research SNS show that possible plutonium production rates scale linearly with the beam current as well as with the beam energy.[19] For SNS powers above 1 MW, the achievable production rates are assessed to be comparable to a small fission reactor. The plutonium produced in a uranium target will be super weapons-grade plutonium with 99 % plutonium-239 even after 1-year irradiation time. This means, in essence, that due to the neutron energy characteristics the quantity (total plutonium production) will have almost no influence on the quality (weapon attractiveness) of the produced plutonium, so that regardless of the irradiation time super-grade weapons plutonium will always be produced.

9.2.3 Fusion Power Plants

Just like research SNS, fusion power plants challenge the existing safeguards regime as they do not require uranium under normal operating conditions for the production of energy. But once uranium is inserted they have a potential to produce a significant quantity of weapons-grade plutonium in a small part of the reactor by diverting neutrons for this purpose in a concealed operation, or they could produce huge amounts of plutonium in a breakout scenario to fuel a quickly growing nuclear arsenal far exceeding production rates in a comparable fission reactor.

In the fusion reaction, deuterium fuses with tritium yielding one Helium atom and a neutron with high energies. This energy is deposited in the structural

[17]Magill and Peerani 1999 also mentions several programs set up since the 1950s which were dedicated to investigate electronuclear fissile material production. See also Riendeau et al. 1998.

[18]See Bauer 2001, Fig. 13, at p. 520.

[19]This applies for energies above ~300 MeV. There are also limits to the total production due to technical constraints of heat removal, accelerator current and accelerator reliability. See Englert et al. 2006; Englert 2009, Englert et al. 2010.

materials of the fusion chamber, heating the chamber walls in the process.[20] Large amounts of tritium will be used for the fusion reactions. Therefore, the plasma chamber walls contain breeding blankets in which tritium is continuously reproduced by lithium atoms that capture neutrons. With this process, the reactor provides its own fuel.

Due to the high neutron flux that deposits heat and breeds tritium, fusion power plants will have a remarkable potential to produce fissile materials during operation. One only has to insert uranium into the blankets to transmute it into plutonium. This is similar to the process that happens in fission reactor fuel, but in a *pure* fusion reactor fertile or fissile material is not used under normal operating conditions. This characteristic distinguishes it not only from fission reactors, but also from fusion–fission hybrid reactor concepts, which would contain fissile or fertile material either to produce even more energy or to produce plutonium to fuel a satellite fleet of fast reactors.[21] The idea of fusion–fission hybrids is discussed since fusion research started. However, currently most conceptual studies of a future power plant only consider a pure fusion facility.[22]

Five technical reasons are decisive for why a fusion power plant would be attractive for a proliferator:

(1) *High plutonium production potential.* We calculated plutonium production rates in fusion power plants using the conceptual design of a magnetic

[20]There are two technical approaches to commercialize fusion, one is magnetic confinement fusion the other inertial confinement fusion. In Magnetic confinement fusion a plasma of deuterium and tritium will be heated to extreme temperatures so that the atoms will hit each other and fuse together. The plasma chamber is formed like a torus (donut) and very strong magnetic fields will keep the plasma from touching the wall. In inertial confinement fusion, large laser beams will compress a small deuterium-tritium pellet in one laser shot, and thereby fuse the atoms. In this article we only consider magnetic confinement fusion. For proliferation concerns of inertial confinement fusion, see Goldston and Glaser 2011.

[21]Bethe 1979; Holdren 1981.

[22]China and India still show interest in fusion–fission hybrid reactor development. Recently there is new interest in such reactor concepts (Freidberg and Kadak 2009; Gerstner 2009). Proliferation risks associated with fusion power plants are discussed in J.P. Holdren, D.H. Berwald, R.J. Budnitz, J.G. Crocker, J.G. Delene and R.D. Endicott, Report of the Senior Committee on Environmental, Safety, and Economic Aspects of Magnetic Fusion Energy, UCRL-53766 (Lawrence Livermore National Laboratory), Raeder 1995; I. Cook, G. Marbach, L. di Pace, C. Girard, Taylor NP, Safety and Environmental Impact of Fusion, EFDA–S–RE-1 (European Fusion Development Agreement, April 2001), Faghihi et al. 2008; Sievert and Johnson 2010; Goldston 2011; Glaser and Goldston 2012; Franceschini et al. 2013, G. Franceschini and M. Englert, Safeguarding fusion reactors, Plädoyer für eine proliferationsresistente Gestaltung der Kernfusion, HSFK Report No. 7/2013, IAEA Report of the consultancy meeting on Non-Proliferation Challenges in Connection with Magnetic Fusion Power Plants, IAEA Headquarters, Vienna, 26–28 June 2013, Reproduced by the IAEA, May 2014.

Table 9.2 Plutonium production in a fusion reactor

Fusion reactor	Mass [t]	Years in blanket	Conc. Bl. [kg/tHM]	Pu Rate [kg/y]
One blanket	0.22	1	21	4
Complete reactor	11.8	1	Var.	1300

confinement fusion power plant (tokamak)[23] published by the European Fusion Development Agency (EFDA) in 2006.[24] We reproduce some results (Table 9.2) without the details of the underlying assumptions. Under normal operation the blankets in the reactor chamber walls are used for tritium production and filled with a liquid Lead-Lithium (Pb-17Li) alloy. To calculate possible plutonium production rates we added one percent of natural uranium to the alloy in our 'monte carlo' computer model.

Table 9.2 shows two exemplary operations of a much broader parametric study. One of the blankets close to the plasma (2 cm) alone filled with 220 kg of uranium would yield 4 kg weapons-grade plutonium per year. That is half of a significant quantity needed for one bomb according to the IAEA and such plutonium production is comparable to a small fission reactor.

Other blankets will be further away from the plasma and produce less plutonium as less neutrons will travel that far. But using more than one blanket would have a cumulative effect and much higher production rates could be achievable. In total, this reactor contains some 189 breeding blankets with different volumes. The blankets are closer or farther away from the plasma. If all were filled with 1 % uranium the whole reactor could produce more than a ton of weapon-grade plutonium per year. Although technically challenging, this potential exceeds anything we know from the world of fission reactors.[25]

(2) *Extremely low source material requirements.* If used for military purposes, another main advantage over fission reactors would be a relatively small requirement of

---

[23]Term is a transliteration from the Russian acronym. In english it would be TOroidal CHAmber with MAgnetic Coils (tochamac).

[24]D. Maisonnier, I. Cook, P. Sardain, R. Andreani, L. di Pace, R. Forrest, L. Giancarli, S. Hermsmeyer, P. Norajitra, N. Taylor and D. Ward, A Conceptual Study of Commercial Fusions Power Plants. EFDA-RP-RE-5.0. Detailed calculations and discussions of results are published in Englert 2009; Englert et al. 2010; Englert et al. 2011; Englert et al. 2014.

[25]As for the case of spallation these calculations are only rough estimates under several simplifying assumption which are described in (Englert 2009; Englert et al. 2010) in greater detail. For restrictions on the amount of uranium in such a plant see the literature referenced above. Also parts of the plant, especially the breeding blankets would have to be converted to accommodate uranium without jeopardizing their other functions. Such changes will give an inspector leverage to detect any unusual uses in a fusion plant.

source material (natural or depleted uranium).[26] Even with masses much lower than 1t natural (or even depleted) uranium, plutonium production rates on the order of kilograms are possible. The minimum amount of natural uranium[27] necessary to operate a small fission reactor is roughly 10t of natural uranium.

(3) *High end concentrations of plutonium.* Additionally, the achievable concentration of plutonium in the uranium can be much higher than in a fission reactor, reducing the requirements for the uranium mass that has to be irradiated with neutrons. Such a high plutonium concentration in the uranium is also advantageous for reprocessing campaigns to extract plutonium from the uranium breeding targets.

(4) *Plutonium is always weapons-grade.* Due to the hard neutron flux in a fusion reactor Pu-239 fractions and hence the weapon usability are typically higher than in fission reactors of comparable power. The isotopic composition will contain more than 90 % plutonium-239 even for extremely high burnup. So the plutonium produced will be always weapons quality.

There is a fifth proliferation concern associated with fission reactors that is not directly related to the four underlying physical properties associated with plutonium production. That is the use of tritium in a fusion reactor. Tritium is under export control in some countries but not part of the safeguards architecture. However, tritium is used in advanced weapon designs to boost the fission reaction with additional neutrons and enhance the efficiency of a weapon. This reduces the mass of fissile material needed to achieve a certain weapon yield. Tritium boosting is considered as one of the important steps in weapon design to minimize the size of a warhead that it is usable on, e.g. a missile. Typically, only several grams of tritium are sufficient for boosting. In a large fusion power plant, several kilograms will be in the inventory and the annual production rate well beyond 100 kg.[28]

9.2.4 Potential Proliferation Concerns

On the basis of all four of the relevant physical criteria listed above, either research SNS or fusion reactors promise to provide advantages over fission reactors for potential proliferators. First, in the case of fusion plants the total

[26]Since fusion reactors and SNS—unlike fission reactors—do not require critical masses of uranium, these uranium insertions can be arbitrarily small.
Natural uranium consists of two different isotopes uranium-235 and uranium-238. Only uranium-238 contributes to the fission chain reaction in a typical light water reactor for power production. Since natural uranium only has a fraction of 0.7 % uranium-235 with the remaining 99.3 % being uranium-238, the fraction of uranium-235 has to be increased by enrichment to roughly 3–5 % for use in light water reactors. As a waste stream the enrichment process also produces depleted uranium with a uranium-235 content below the natural enrichment.

[27]Or the natural uranium equivalent in case such a reactor operates with enriched fuel.

[28]More on the proliferation impact of tritium can be found in (Kalinowski and Colschen 1995; Kalinowski 2004).

plutonium production rate could exceed that of a fission reactor. (This does not apply to research SNS.) Second, both fusion and research SNS require a relatively low initial mass of natural or even depleted uranium to produce a significant quantity of plutonium (in a research SNS or a fusion reactor there is no need to keep up criticality like in the early production reactors), a fact that poses a problem for safeguards if the minimum threshold for verification of INS as a 'facility' under comprehensive safeguards agreements is one effective kilogram. Third, the possibility of achieving high concentrations in the material without reducing the Pu-239 content in the isotopic composition means that research SNS and fusion reactors will require less chemical reprocessing to separate the plutonium from the uranium, transuranic elements, and fission products. Fourth, even for high burnup, the weapon usability is high with much higher plutonium-239 fractions than in fission reactors. The total irradiation time for both INS technologies is only limited by the radiation and thermal stress of the target material.

9.3 Is There an Exploitable Gap?

In the previous section, we compared the main technical advantages of research SNS and a fusion plant to the production of plutonium in a fission reactor. In this section, we argue that the findings from our comparison point towards the need to focus on facilities, rather than merely on nuclear material and how it is flowing through the nuclear fuel cycle. Research SNS and fusion reactors are a different type of proliferation challenge than fission reactors because they carry military potential, yet none of the materials used under normal operating conditions are subject to the provisions of the non-proliferation treaty. Therefore, although INS are covered by the verification mandate of the IAEA, the conditions under which they are subject to specific safeguards requirements remain underspecified.

The IAEA is well aware that INS have the potential for military use and is collecting data on the specifics of accelerators, spallation neutron sources and fusion plants. In 2014, the IAEA convened a consultancy group on Non-Proliferation Challenges in Connection with Magnetic Fusion Power Plants, in which Dr. Englert, one of the authors of this paper, took part. The consultancy group agreed that the IAEA has a mandate to address the issue of INS. That mandate derives its legitimacy from Article IV of the NPT and the IAEA Statute.[29] Furthermore, the

[29]Article II: 'The Agency shall seek to accelerate and enlarge the contribution of atomic energy to peace, health and prosperity throughout the world. It shall ensure, so far as it is able, that assistance provided by it or at its request or under its supervision or control is not used in such a way as to further any military purpose.'
Article III.5: 'The Agency is authorized: [...] To establish and administer safeguards designed to ensure that special fissionable and other materials, services, equipment, facilities, and information made available by the Agency or at its request or under its supervision or control are not used in such a way as to further any military purpose; and to apply safeguards, at the request of

group recommended that a regular verification process would be needed to ensure that fusion reactors are not used for military purposes. However, the group did not specify how INS should be integrated into the IAEA verification regime, only that it would become necessary to do so.[30]

The question of whether or not existing Comprehensive Safeguards Agreements (CSA) with their materials-based approach are sufficient to encompass regular verification procedures at INS facilities is not one of legitimacy, but rather of scope and frequency. The argument for why existing CSAs are sufficient depends upon a broad-scope interpretation of the IAEA's mandate known as the 'State level approach.' This 'holistic' approach to safeguards screens the nuclear program of a State in its entirety. Unlike traditional interpretations of the comprehensive safeguards regime, which construed the task of the IAEA narrowly to be the verification of the correctness of a States declarations, this broad interpretation adds to correctness the demand of completeness, meaning that the IAEA also has the ability to undertake inspections of suspicious activities in order to confirm that a State has declared *all* material flows in compliance with its reporting requirements.[31]

Arguments that the State-level approach provides for regular inspections of INS facilities are particularly effective in cases where a State has agreed to supplement its CSA with an Additional Protocol (AP). The AP makes explicit the fact that IAEA inspectors may visit, not only declared facilities, but also *locations outside of facilities*.[32]

There are, however, differing opinions on whether the State-level approach might be sufficient to provide timely warning of a military use of INS. Regular verification similar to safeguards, including inspections, might be needed, to verify the absence of fissile material and to detect a missing declaration of the use of uranium in such a facility. The consultancy group on fusion recommended to that end that it would be "advantageous to include fusion in existing verification regimes"

Footnote 29 (continued)
the parties, to any bilateral or multilateral arrangement, or at the request of a State, to any of that State's activities in the field of atomic energy.'

It has to be noted that 'atomic energy' does not necessarily include all physical processes that emit neutrons, e.g. in the US 'atomic energy' in the Atomic Energy Act statutory definition limits the definition to energy released in fission and fusion *not* spallation, which would be a non-nuclear activity according to such a logic.

[30]IAEA, Report of the consultancy meeting on Non-Proliferation Challenges in Connection with Magnetic Fusion Power Plants, IAEA Headquarters, Vienna, 26–28 June 2013, Reproduced by the IAEA, May 2014.

[31]For the discussion on completeness and correctness see also Chap. 2 'The General Framework of IAEA Safeguards' (Tariq Rauf); Chap. 3 (Interpretation of Nuclear Safeguards Commitments: the role of subsequent agreements and practice (Pierre-Emmanuel Dupont); Chap. 4 'Verification of Correctness and Completeness in the Implementation of IAEA Safeguards: the law and practice (Laura Rockwood and Larry Johnson)'; Chap. 5 'The NPT and the IAEA Additional Protocol (Masahiko Asada)'; and Chap. 8 'Technical Limits of Verification and Their Implications for Treaty Design (Gerald Kirchner and Stefan Oeter)' in this volume.

[32]*Location outside facilities* means any installation or location, which is not a *facility*, where *nuclear material* is customarily used in amounts of one effective kilogram or less. INFCIRC/540.

and that the IAEA should provide guidance on those issues.[33] Even so, the conclusion of the consultancy group pointed to the difficulty of covering facilities with agreements drafted with material flows in mind:

> [c]urrent verification frameworks are based on the assumption that nuclear materials are used in any facility that requires verification, following the logic of the material flows in the various possible fission systems. The design flow and/or inventory of source or special fissionable material is also used to determine the frequency of inspections.[34]

While it may be possible to accommodate INS facilities under existing agreements in principle, in practice the focus on material flows opens up an exploitable gap in the regulatory framework that States can use to contest legitimate access, and what does and does not constitute non-compliance with CSA and AP requirements.

There are two features of this gap. First, the fact that fusion reactors would require far less uranium than envisioned by the current standard for 'one effective kilogram' and second INS facilities are not covered by the current definition of 'facility'. Neither the materials centric framework of CSAs nor the relative silence of the AP on the frequency or duration of inspections at locations outside facilities, makes explicit the regularity with which access to INS facilities would be required in order to verify that uranium had not been introduced.

9.3.1 Plutonium Production with Less Than One Effective Kilogram

Nearly every State party to the NPT has a comprehensive safeguards agreement with the IAEA.[35] Safeguards are applied without exception when *any* nuclear material

> of a composition and purity suitable for fuel fabrication or for being isotopically enriched leaves the plant or the process stage in which it has been produced, or when such *nuclear material*, or any other *nuclear material* produced at a later stage in the nuclear fuel cycle, is imported into the State [...].[36]

The CSA document also specifies that *all* materials that contain uranium or thorium have to be reported to the IAEA if these materials are exported from or imported in a Non-Nuclear Weapon State, unless the material is imported for

33IAEA (2014) Report of the consultancy meeting on Non-Proliferation Challenges in Connection with Magnetic Fusion Power Plants, IAEA Headquarters, Vienna, 26–28 June 2013, Reproduced by the IAEA, May 2014.

34Idem.

35International Atomic Energy Agency: The Structure and Content of Agreements Between the Agency and States Required in Connection with the Treaty on the Non-Proliferation of Nuclear Weapons. INFCIRC/153 (Corr.), 1972, para 28.

36Ibid.

specifically non-nuclear purposes. For such material it is sufficient to specify the composition and quantity, and the destination in case of an export.

As noted above, amounts far less than one effective kilogram[37] of uranium are sufficient for significant plutonium production in a fusion reactor:

(a) At the request of the Non-Nuclear Weapon State, one effective kilogram can be exempted from safeguards. This includes ten tons in total of natural uranium, ten tons depleted uranium (>0.5 % enrichment) or 20 tons (<0.5 % enrichment) according to the standard definition of one effective kilogram.[38] It is also unclear in the definitions what exactly is termed to be a non-nuclear purpose or 'non-nuclear activity'. Construction and operation of an SNS in the U.S. e.g. is not a nuclear activity since the term 'atomic energy' in the Atomic Energy Act statutory definition limits the definition to energy released in fission and fusion.[39]

(b) Even depleted uranium can be used and is widely available in small quantities such as in ammunition.[40] It would be extremely challenging to account for depleted uranium amounts with such a precision, that a diversion would be detected in a timely manner. The situation is comparable to the challenge of Material Unaccounted For (MUF) in larger fuel cycle facilities such as reprocessing and enrichment plants: the precision to reduce the error bar of MUF increases costs, and a balance between efficiency and effectiveness has to be chosen to fulfill the objective of safeguards (INFCIRC/153, para 28): the credible deterrence of diversion.

(c) Current inspection frequencies are not adequate. In the CSA inspection frequencies are specified according to the amount of effective kilograms used in such a facility,

---

[37]Effective kilogram (ekg): (a) for plutonium , its weight in kilograms (1 kg plutonium is 1 effective kilogram). (b) For uranium with enrichment of 1 % and above, its weight in kilogram is multiplied by the square of its enrichment (e.g. 25 kg 20 % low enriched uranium is 1 effective kilogram). (c) For uranium enriched to 0.5–1 % its weight in kilogram multiplied by 0.0001 (10t uranium is 1 effective kilogram), (c) for depleted uranium with and enrichment of 0.5 % or below, and for thorium, its weight in kilograms multiplied by 0.00005 (20t uranium or thorium is 1 effective kilogram). Paragraph 104 of INFCIRC/153.

[38]The definition of the "Consolidated Trigger List" of the Zangger Committees (INFCIRC/209, Rev. 2) exempts only 50 g plutonium from declaration for import and export.
In the Convention on the Physical Protection of Nuclear Materials (INFCIRC/255 Rev. 3) three categories (I-III) are applied based on masses requiring different protection measures: For unirradiated plutonium: category I: >2 kg, category II: >500 g, category III >15 g. For uranium with >20 % enrichment I: >5 kg, II: >1 kg, III: >15 g. For uranium with 10–20 % enrichment I: –, II: >10 kg, III: 1–10 kg. For uranium with <10 % enrichment I: –, II: –, III: >10 kg. For uranium-233 I: >2 kg, II: >500 g, III: >15 g.

[39]Thanks to David Moses, Oak Ridge National Laboratory, for this and several other arguments in this section.

[40]E.g. a 25 mm uranium projectile contains 200 g depleted uranium. A 120 mm armour-piercing penetrator as it used on Abrams tanks contains 4.5 kg. Depleted uranium ammunition is used by several countries worldwide.

> in the case of *facilities* [...] with a content or annual throughput whichever is greater, of *nuclear material* not exceeding five effective kilograms routine inspections shall not exceed one per year.[41]

This is not sufficient for timely detection in the light of the potential plutonium production rates. Reactors, e.g. have a maximum of 50 days in which one Inspector can be On-Site at one facility (INFCIRC/153, para 80.a).[42]

9.3.2 Definition of a Facility

The IAEA should receive declarations about the 'facilities' in a country. The IAEA defines a 'facility' as:

(a) A reactor, a critical facility, a conversion plant, a fabrication plant, a reprocessing plant, an isotope separation plant or a separate storage installation; or
(b) Any location where nuclear material in amounts greater than one effective kilogram is customarily used.[43]

Neither spallation nor fusion facilities would fall under the term 'facility', as they are neither reactors[44] nor critical facilities nor locations where nuclear material in

[41]International Atomic Energy Agency: The Structure and Content of Agreements Between the Agency and States Required in Connection with the Treaty on the Non-Proliferation of Nuclear Weapons. INFCIRC/153 (Corr.), 1972, para 28.

[42]For facilities containing more than 5 effective kilogram (ekg) those involving enriched uranium (>5 %) and plutonium, it is 30 times the square root of one ekg, (30*Sqrt[ekg]), for all other facilities it is (0.4*ekg).

[43]International Atomic Energy Agency: The Structure and Content of Agreements Between the Agency and States Required in Connection with the Treaty on the Non-Proliferation of Nuclear Weapons. INFCIRC/153 (Corr.), 1972, para 28.

[44]The definition of a reactor is specified in the IAEA glossary according to the definition in the older facility-specific safeguards (INFCIRC/66) and is based on the terms fission and chain reaction. 'Reactor' means any device in which a controlled, self-sustaining fission chain reaction can be maintained (INFCIRC/66). Facility-specific safeguards according to INFCIRC/66 were replaced by the comprehensive safeguards INFCIRC/153 and exist for only few facilities in countries outside the NPT regime. The IAEA glossary contains the following definition. 'Nuclear reactor means an apparatus, other than an atomic weapon, designed or used to sustain nuclear fission in a self-supporting chain reaction' IAEA 2001. References to the term reactor in the Additional Protocol (INFCIRC/540), which is not ratified yet by all Members of the NPT, is also based on this terminology. Article 1.1 of Annex II lists specified equipment for reporting of exports and imports: 'Nuclear reactors capable of operation so as to maintain a controlled self-sustaining fission chain reaction, excluding zero energy reactors, the latter being defined as reactors with a designed maximum rate of production of plutonium not exceeding 100 g per year.' The explanatory note provides: 'A nuclear reactor basically includes the items within or attached directly to the reactor vessel, the equipment which controls the level of power in the core, and the components which normally contain or come in direct contact with or control the primary coolant of the reactor core. It is not intended to exclude reactors which could reasonably be capable of modification to produce significantly more than 100 g of plutonium per year. Reactors designed for sustained operation at significant power levels, regardless of their capacity for plutonium production, are not considered as 'zero energy reactors.'

quantities more than one *effective kilogram* is customarily used. In a pure fusion reactor, *no nuclear material at all* should be present at the site at any time by design.

One could argue through backward reasoning that a fusion plant (or a research SNS) would fall under the IAEA definition of a 'facility' and thus should be considered for inspection as its operation might involve a *potential* production of more than one effective kilogram of plutonium. To verify the absence of *actual* production the IAEA needs to inspect the facility regularly. Such an understanding of the wording of INFCIRC/153 ('customarily used') would interpret 'use' modally (possible, contingent) and not factually and expand the scope of the inspection mandate to a new category of facilities. Such an interpretation would also be along the line of a completeness paradigm that certifies the absence of nuclear material at a site because before absence is an empiric fact it is a possible presence and invokes inspection given some rationally deductible clues for suspision. However the fact remains that INS, are usually not associated with the 'customary use' of more than one effective kilogram of nuclear material.

The current definitions of facilities are inadequate as they do not intergrate the neutron producing capacity of INS. The best way to trigger safeguards would be to not only specify facilities by the presence of nuclear material under normal operation but also directly in terms of fissile material production capacities—in case of INS that would be plutonium production capacity. The old facility-specific safeguards (INFCIRC/66) and the Additional Protocol, e.g. specify an annual production rate of 100 g plutonium per year as a threshold. Quantitative proxies for plutonium production could be also the neutron flux or the thermal power of a system.[45]

9.4 Legal Challenges and the Limits of Technical Verification

There is a relatively straightforward fix to close both of the gaps identified in the previous section. Updating the definition of a 'facility' to include quantified parameters that describe a latent fissile material production capability would close the gap created by a materials-based definition of a facility by specifying a certain threshold that would trigger regular safeguards for a timely detection of such a use. This solution would clarify the right of the IAEA to continuously verify the absence of nuclear material, effectively also closing the gap created by the fact that an INS facility would require less than one effective kilogram of uranium to produce a significant quantity of weapons-grade plutonium.

What this straightforward solution does not resolve is the fact that verifying the absence of nuclear materials does not preclude the military potential of the facility. Nuclear facilities are not simply 'dual-use'. Describing facilities as dual-use

[45]INFCIRC/66 specified a thermal power of 3 MW as an additional threshold for reactors.

falsely ascribes an either/or characteristic to the technology. Such a characterization implies that it is possible to separate the uses and to guarantee that utilizing the facility for one purpose precludes its simultaneous use for the other. Dual-use is not a property of the technology, but rather an ideal that the safeguards regime is designed to achieve.

Pointing out the fiction of dual-use as an either/or choice between civilian and military purposes is not a new observation. Scholars have been talking about the problem of 'threshold States and 'latent nuclear arsenals' since at least the 1970s. In 1976 Thomas Schelling, for instance, argued that:

> Until recently, having or not having nuclear weapons appeared to be, and was treated as, a question of yes or no. From now on it will make more sense to describe a country's nuclear weapon status not with a yes or a no but with a time schedule. The answer will be a chart, giving the number of weapons of certain energy yields and certain physical characteristics that could be available after elapsed hours, days or weeks from the decisions to assemble them.[46]

What Schelling describes in this passage is not a world in which there are nuclear 'haves' and 'have-nots', but rather one in which the ability to manufacture nuclear materials locates non-nuclear weapon States along an ambiguous continuum. These States are what Mohamed ElBaradei and others have described as 'virtual nuclear weapon States'.[47] Virtual nuclear weapons States have the know-how, experts, materials and facilities so that they come close to the civil-military boundary. ElBaradei considered as many as forty States as virtual nuclear weapon States with latent capabilities. These States are in possession of—in our terminology—ambivalent nuclear technology and know-how. The must obvious ones are Japan, Germany, South Korea, Iran but also others less obvious ones like Sweden, Switzerland, South Africa, Argentina, Brazil, etc. have a history of using the ambivalent potentiality of nuclear technologies and politicizing them for other gains.

The timeline to having a nuclear weapon that Schelling envisions is more politically salient than ever today. Yet, the language we use to describe this dynamic remains unrefined. Wolfgang Liebert and Itty Abraham separately have both suggested that a more accurate descriptor for nuclear technology than dual-use is ambivalent,[48] meaning that the uses of nuclear technology are simultaneous and contradictory by nature. The technology always carries both potentialities and they are realized in context at any one moment in time. Negatively, the intrinsic ambivalent characteristics of nuclear technologies undermine the civil-military boundaries and jeopardize the careful work done by State governments, international institutions and nongovernmental organizations to carefully draw a line between the two. Positively, the ambivalence of nuclear technology *makes it possible* for different actors to read contradictory interpretations onto the same materials and facilities. It opens a space for politics.

---

[46]Schelling 1976.

[47]M.E. Baradei, U.N.'s ElBaradei warns of nuclear apocalypse, Reuters, 6 May 2005.

[48]Harrington and Englert 2014; Abraham 2010; Liebert et al. 1994.

Ambivalence plays an important political role in non-proliferation agreements. As is often said, negotiation is the art of "removing the brackets" by which diplomats mean that there is a process by which disagreements about the language of an agreement is slowly resolved by reconciling differences. The fact that nuclear technology is inherently ambivalent allows diplomats to ratchet down the language, making it ever more rigid and specified. At the same time, everyone knows that the technology carries another possibility within it. Ambivalent technology functions like a pressure release valve within the rigid 'have' and 'have not' NPT system.

Arguably, manipulating the ambivalence of nuclear technology in order to circumvent, or at least challenge, the boundaries of the NPT is what Iran has been doing in the negotiations with the five permanent members of the United Nations Security Council (US, Russia, China, France, Great Britain) plus Germany (P5 + 1). The success of the negotiations for the P5 + 1 is measured in terms of their ability to extend the Iranian timeline to having enough enriched uranium or weapons-grade plutonium for a bomb. Although we have cast the exploitable gap created by a materials-based approach as a somewhat futurist case study with INS at its centre, a similar dynamic is at work in the Iranian nuclear strategy today.

Uranium enrichment plants clearly fall under CSAs since they use natural uranium and produce low enriched uranium. But what happens if the gas centrifuges in the uranium enrichment plant are not fed with uranium but stay under vacuum or enrich the isotopes of elements other than uranium? This might be the outcome for the fortified underground uranium enrichment site at Fordow, Iran. As of the writing of this chapter, under a negotiated settlement Fordow would be converted to a nuclear research centre with a maximum of a thousand centrifuges which would not be fed with uranium. (The difference between INS and a nuclear material-free Fordow plant, however, is that Fordow is still a *facility* under CSA as it is an enrichment plant and that it could not produce a significant quantity with less than one effective kilogram of source material.)[49] In order for this solution to work, it will be necessary to identify what kind of research the plant will be useful for achieving.[50] In other words, as it now stands at the end of April 2015 a successful deal between the P5 + 1 and Iran hinges on accentuating the inherent ambivalence of nuclear technology, so much so that there is a need to create ambiguity by repurposing a uranium enrichment facility so that it will not require uranium under normal operating conditions.

---

[49]To produce one significant quantity (25 kg) of highly enriched uranium within a year, roughly 10t of natural uranium (*one effective kilogram*) would be needed, calculated for an optimal production with 93 % enriched HEU and a depletion to 0.48 % with a facility that would have a separative power of 4070 SWU. This is comparable to the enrichment capacity allowed for Natanz under such an agreement with 5000 centrifuges each having roughly 0.8 SWU capacity per centrifuge.

[50]The European Enrichment Consortium URENCO enriches certain stable nonradioactive isotopes like Titanium, Nickel, Molybdenum, Zinc, Cadmium, Silicium, Germanium and others for industrial and medical applications.

Interestingly, enhancing the ambivalence of the Fordow enrichment facility may become one of the cornerstones of the negotiated settlement that would close the gap in the definition of a facility. Iran first began exploiting this gap more than a decade ago by repeatedly constructing, but not immediately disclosing, uranium enrichment facilities. Whether or not Iran has therefore violated its obligations to the IAEA has been a key point of contention throughout the conflict.

According to Code 3.1. in the subsidiary agreement to the CSA between Iran and the IAEA. Such subsidiary agreements

> shall specify in detail, to the extent necessary to permit the Agency to fulfill its responsibilities under the Agreement in an effective and efficient manner, how the procedures laid down in the Agreement are to be applied.[51]

Code 3.1 of the Subsidiary Arrangements General Part as agreed to in 1976 provides for the submission of design information for new facilities 'normally not later than 180 days before the facility is scheduled to receive nuclear material for the first time'.[52]

Before the Iranian program was even disclosed the IAEA wanted to change this policy to allow for more time to verify the design information of such complex facilities as enrichment or reprocessing plants, arguing that, '[t]he modified text agreed to in 2003, […] provides for the submission of such information as soon as the decision to construct, or to authorize construction, of such a facility has been taken, whichever is earlier'.[53] In 2007 Iran, however, informed the IAEA that it wanted to return to the old specification of code 3.1. with the 180 days of advanced notice to the IAEA. Then in 2009 the existence of the Fordow plant was disclosed to the IAEA and caused a dispute if Iran was in compliance with its obligations.

Apart from the legal question of whether or not these subsidiary agreements constitute a treaty and could be changed unilaterally, as Iran claimed, or not as the IAEA legal advisers argue,[54] a position later affirmed by the Security Council Resolution 1929. The fact is that Iran contested the agreed boundaries. Iran did so by pointing at a loophole in the system: when exactly a latent capability needs to be disclosed to the IAEA. Beyond the issue of sufficient time to verify a facility design, the similarity between INS and *facilities* under code 3.1. in subsidiary agreements to the CSA before 2003 is the ambivalent status of when exactly a facility turns into a *facility*.

---

[51]INFCIRC/153.

[52]IAEA (2007), Implementation of the NPT Safeguards Agreement and relevant provisions of Security Council resolutions 1737 (2006) and 1747 (2007) in the Islamic Republic of Iran GOV/2007/58, 15. November 2007.

[53]Ibid.

[54]D.N. Joyner, The Qom Enrichment Facility: Was Iran Legally Bound to Disclose, Comment on jurist.org http://jurist.org/forum/2010/03/qom-enrichment-facility-was-iran.php. Accessed 5 April 2015, IAEA, Statement by the Legal Advisors to the Meeting of the Board of Governors March 2009. Available at http://www.armscontrolwonk.com/file_download/162/Legal_Adviser_Iran.pdf. Accessed 5 April 2015.

The Iranian example illustrates how nuclear technologies can be used to transgress boundaries. Verification is intended to ensure timely detection of such transgressions and deter actors. What verification does not do is reduce ambivalence. Specifying verification rules under agreements with the intent of reducing and quantifying uncertainty is important not only to detect transgressions but also to have the legal means to enforce compliance. However, politically, once a boundary is specified, the boundary itself can offer leverage as a point of resistance.

From this perspective, the term ambivalence captures the tension between the safeguards regime and the technology it is designed to regulate, a tension that the redefinition of the term 'facilities' to integrate INS will not resolve. The larger problem of technical verification is an over reliance on scientific verification techniques in an effort to eliminate ambivalence by replacing it with the certainty of objectivity. INS highlight this as they even allow to exert a clear-cut criterion for safeguard purposes as detecting any nuclear materials or products from fission processes in a 'pure' plant would immediately raise suspicion unless the facility was designed for such a use (fusion-fission hybrid or an uranium target in a research SNS). The technical implementation of instrumentation and measurement devices in a pure INS plant would also be relatively simple compared to the complexity of material flows in other fuel cycle facilities. Paradoxically, closing the current legal gaps to safeguard these facilities is a logical step, but rather than being a solution it only highlights the problem—much like a bandage that temporarily fixes and simultaneously points to the underlying issue—the limit of technical verification.

9.5 Conclusions

As all neutron sources are capable in principal of producing fissile materials like plutonium, in this paper, we compared reactors with intense neutron sources regarding the potential to produce fissile material. Possible advantages and disadvantages of the respective technologies with their completely different underlying physical processes were discussed. In research SNS and fusion facilities high concentrations of plutonium can be bred thus reducing the amount of source material necessary for production. Even with amounts well below one effective kilogram, which can be exempt from safeguards, significant production of weapon-grade plutonium is possible. Fusion reactors have in addition the capacity to produce huge amounts of plutonium.

Today, there is no immediate proliferation concern with regard to SNS and fusion, as both technologies are currently not yet widely used or in the case of fusion, development for commercial application will take another 20–30 years. However, research and implementation of preventive technical mechanisms to enhance the proliferation resistance by developing safeguard procedures and by finding, if applicable, proliferation resistant designs should be integral part of the technological progress as early as possible.

Intense neutron sources are currently not directly covered by the IAEA regulatory practice. However, the physical attributes of those machines to produce fissile material raise a number of questions about the legitimacy and scope of the different IAEA mechanisms to separate military and civil use of nuclear technologies and about the strategies of potential proliferators. Intense neutron sources challenge the regime built around accounting for the presence of fissile materials, as opposed to a broader view of nuclear-capable technologies more generally. Unlike existing nuclear energy reactors, intense neutron sources do not require nuclear materials to produce energy.

We identified possible gaps in the current definitions of the IAEA, e.g. what defines 'one effective kilogram', or in the current IAEA terminology of what constitutes a 'facility'. Some of the issues could be addressed under the broader mandate of the Additional Protocol, e.g. by complementary inspection authority, but regular inspections similar to those under the standard protocol INFCIRC/153 are needed. In any case, the current focus on existing nuclear material and the loophole on production potentials of facilities will need some legal amendment and clarification on the long run. We argued that rather than focusing on the presence of fissile material in a facility alone the definition of a 'facility' should include quantified parameters that describe a latent fissile material production capability ('virtual' fissile materials).

Although military potentiality is a common feature in nuclear technologies like reactors or enrichment and reprocessing plants, INS and especially fusion plants highlight military potentiality due to their operability without nuclear materials. Even if legal fixes and technical measures were applied to close current loopholes by verifying the absence of nuclear material, INS facilities and especially fusion plants will remain attractive for a proliferator due to their exceptional latent characteristics to produce large quantities of weapons-grade plutonium quickly with low source material requirements.

Rather from being a purely abstract point the latent use of nuclear potentialities is at work in the Iranian nuclear strategy today and will become an even bigger issue in the future. Technical verification and its legal implementation in institutional arrangements or treaties like safeguards agreements is and will remain important to reduce uncertainties and refine early detection of military uses. But it will not eradicate the ambivalent nature of nuclear technologies. In consequence 'the emphasis has to shift from physical denial and technological secrecy to the things that determine incentives and motivations and expectation.'[55] The question is not 'how do we prevent cheating?' but rather how do the mechanisms of denial structure incentives for a State that have a desire to resist through proliferation: 'how do safeguards shape motivations?'

---

[55]Schelling 1976.

References

Abraham I (2010) 'Who's next?' Nuclear ambivalence and the contradictions of non-proliferation policy. Econ Polit Wkly 45(43):18–20

Albright D (1994) North Korean plutonium production. Sci Global Secur 5:63–87

Albright D, Berkhout F, Walker W (1997) Plutonium and highly enriched uranium 1996, world inventories, capabilities and policies. SIPRI Yearbook, Oxford University Press

Bauer GS (2001) Nuclear instruments and methods A 463:505–543

Bethe HA, et seq. (1979) The fusion hybrid. Phys Today 44

Englert M (2009) Neutronic simulation calculations to assess the proliferation resistance of nuclear technologies, Neutronenphysikalische Simulationsrechnungen zur Proliferationsresistenz nuklearer Technologien, Dissertation, Department of Physics, Darmstadt University of Technology

Englert M, Liebert W, Pistner C (2006) Neutronics calculations for the assessment of proliferation risks associated with spallation neutron sources. J Nucl Instrum Methods Phys Res A 562:557–560

Englert M, Balloni F, Liebert W (2010) Possible Proliferation Risks of Future Tokamak Fusion Reactors, Proceedings of the 51st INMM Annual Meeting 11–15 July 2010, Baltimore

Englert M, Franceschini G, Liebert W (2011) Strong Neutron Sources—How to Cope with Weapon Material Production Capabilities of Fusion and Spallation Neutron Sources? ESARDA-INMM Meeting, Aix-en-Provence, 2011

Englert M, Franceschini G, Kütt M, Frieß, M (2014) Proliferation Aspects of Future Commercial Fusion Power Plants, Proceedings of the 55th INMM Annual Meeting July 21–14, Atlanta

Faghihi F, Havasi H, Amin-Mozafari M (2008) Plutonium-239 production rate study using a typical fusion reactor. Ann Nucl Energy 35:759–766

Fetter S (1993) Nuclear archeology: verifying declarations of fissile-material production. Sci Global Secur 3:237–259

Franceschini G, Englert M, Liebert W (2013) Nuclear fusion power for weapons purposes. An exercise in nuclear proliferation forecasting. Nonproliferation Rev 20(3):525–544

Freidberg J, Kadak AC (2009) Fusion-fission hybrids revisited. Nat Phys 5:370–372

Gerstner E (2009) The hybrid returns. Nature 460:25–28

Glaser A, Goldston RJ (2012) Proliferation risks of magnetic fusion energy: clandestine production, covert production and breakout. Nucl Fusion 52:1–9

Goldston RJ (2011) Climate change, nuclear power and nuclear proliferation: magnitude matters. Sci Global Secur 19:130–165

Goldston RJ, Glaser A (2011) Inertial confinement fusion energy R&D and nuclear proliferation: the need for direct and transparent review. Bull At Scientists 67(3):50–66

Gilinsky V, Miller M, Hubbard H (2004) A fresh examination of the proliferation dangers of light water reactors. Nonproliferation Policy Education Center

Harrington A, Englert M (2014) How much is enough? The politics of technology and weaponless nuclear deterrence. In: Mayer M, Carpes M, Knoblich R (eds) International relations and the global politics of science and technology, vol II. Springer, pp 287–302

Holdren JP (1981) Fusion-fission hybrids: environmental aspects and their role in hybrid rationale. J Fusion Energy 1(2):197–210

IAEA (2001) Safeguards glossary, 2001 edn. International nuclear verification series no. 3

Kalinowski MB (2004) International control of tritium for nuclear nonproliferation and disarmament. Science and global security monograph series

Kalinowski MB, Colschen MBL (1995) International control of tritium to prevent horizontal proliferation and to foster nuclear disarmament. Sci Global Security 5:131–203

Liebert W, Rilling R, Scheffran J (1994) Die Janusköpfigkeit von Forschung und Technik – Zum Problem der zivil-militärischen Ambivalenz. BdWi, Marburg

Magill J, Peerani P (1999) (Non-)proliferation aspects of accelerator driven systems. J Phys IV Fr 9:167–181

MacKenzie D, Spinardi G (1995) Tacit knowledge, weapons design and the uninvention of knowledge. Am J Sociol 101:44–99
Raeder J (1995) Report on the European safety and environmental assessment of fusion power (SEAFP). Fusion Eng Des 29:121–140
Riendeau CD, Moses DL, Olso AP (1998) Proliferation potential of accelerator-driven systems: feasibility calculations, U.S. Department of Energy, K/NSP-778
Schelling T (1976) Who will have the bomb. Int Secur 1(1):77–91
Sievert F, Johnson D (2010) Creating suns on earth: ITER, LIFE, and the policy and nonproliferation implications of nuclear fusion energy. Nonproliferation Rev 17:323–346

Chapter 10
The Proliferation Security Initiative: A Tentative Assessment

Gabriella Venturini

Abstract The PSI was launched by the United States in 2003 as a programme aimed at interdicting the transfer or transport of WMD, their delivery systems and related materials to and from States and non-State actors of proliferation concern. Being a voluntary activity and not an international organization, its structure is not institutionalized. Although more than 100 countries have endorsed the PSI, some important States are absent especially in the Asian region and in the Arabic peninsula. The PSI activities are based on the Principles of Interdiction, which do not conflict with existing international law, notably the freedom of the high seas and the principle of flag State consent. Accordingly, a number of ship-boarding agreements have been reached and amendments to the SUA Convention have been adopted to legitimize the interdiction of vessels involved in WMD smuggling. Since 2003 PSI cooperation has gradually contributed to the development of participating States' critical capabilities and practices in relation to the interdiction of WMD and related materials, although a proper evaluation of the PSI's effectiveness is difficult to make due to its lack of transparency. In the future, the Initiative would benefit from a greater involvement of civilian law enforcement authorities for the interdiction of dual-use goods, as well as from a geographical expansion of its scope.

Keywords Beijing convention on the suppression of unlawful acts relating to international civil aviation · Delivery systems · Interdiction · Ship-boarding agreements for the suppression of unlawful acts against the safety of maritime navigation (SUA Convention) · Proliferation Security Initiative (PSI) · United Nations Convention on the Law of the Sea (UNCLOS) · Weapons of Mass Destruction (WMD)

Professor of Human Rights in Armed Conflict, Geneva Academy of International Humanitarian Law and Human Rights; former Director of the Department of International Studies, Università degli Studi di Milano, Italy; Member of the ILA Committee on Nuclear Weapons, Non-Proliferation and Contemporary International Law. The author is grateful to Natalino Ronzitti for his helpful comments on an earlier version of this chapter.

G. Venturini (✉)
Via Fratelli Cervi, Milano Due, Residenza Dei Mestieri 222, 20090 Segrate, MI, Italy
e-mail: venturini.gabriella@gmail.com

J.L. Black-Branch and D. Fleck (eds.), *Nuclear Non-Proliferation in International Law - Volume II*, DOI 10.1007/978-94-6265-075-6_10

Contents

10.1 Introduction

After September 2001, the international community focused on counter-proliferation efforts in order to defeat the threat and/or the use of weapons of mass destruction (WMD) by States or non-State actors of proliferation concern.

Counter-proliferation strategies are important tools for ensuring compliance with non-proliferation obligations. They include a broad range of activities such as export and border controls, nuclear security and physical protection, prevention of terrorist financing, intelligence, monitoring and active and passive defence actions. Within this context a variety of programmes are implemented to prevent the transfer of WMD, their delivery system and related materials, technology and expertise to States and non-State actors of proliferation concern.

This chapter focuses on one of these programmes, which was launched and is being driven by the United States: the Proliferation Security Initiative (PSI). Section 10.2 describes the PSI's structure and discusses its legal nature and founding document, i.e. the Statement of Interdiction Principles (SIP). Section 10.3 assesses the lawfulness of the SIP with respect to general international law and the attitude of the UN towards the PSI. Section 10.4 offers an overview of the multilateral counter-terrorism conventions in the fields of maritime navigation and civil aviation, in respect of which the PSI may be viewed as complementary. Section 10.4, within the limits of the available sources, provides a tentative assessment of the PSI's practice and effectiveness. Finally, the last section contains some concluding remarks.

10.2 The PSI

The PSI was announced by former President George W. Bush in Krakow, Poland, on 31 May 2003 as a programme aimed at complementing non-proliferation and disarmament treaties (NPT,[1] CWC[2] and BWC[3]) and frameworks (such as the voluntary export-control regimes[4]).[5] The Obama administration has been strongly supporting the PSI, since in his famous speech on 5 April 2009 in Prague the US President recognized the importance of continuing and enhancing cooperation in counter-proliferation.[6] The 2010 White House's National Security Strategy also mentions the PSI as a means to detect and intercept the illicit trade in nuclear materials and technologies.[7]

10.2.1 Legal Nature

The PSI's legal nature has been described in a variety of ways, such as 'a cooperative multilateral framework'; 'a group of like-minded States'; 'a set of activities'; 'an informal agreement'; 'a loose consortium of nation-States'; 'a political understanding'; 'an informal network of States'.[8] While each of these definitions

[1]Treaty on the Non-Proliferation of Nuclear Weapons (NPT) of 1 July 1968, 729 UNTS 161.

[2]Convention on the Prohibition of the Development, Production, Stockpiling and Use of Chemical Weapons and on Their Destruction (13 January 1993) 1974 UNTS 45.

[3]Convention on the Prohibition of the Development and Stockpiling of Bacteriological (Biological) and Toxin Weapons and on their Destruction (10 April 1972) 1015 UNTS 163.

[4]Zangger Committee, http://fas.org/nuke/control/zangger/; Nuclear Suppliers Group (NSG), http://www.nuclearsuppliersgroup.org/Leng/default.htm; Australia Group fighting the spread of chemical and biological weapons, http://www.australiagroup.net/en/index.html; Wassenaar Arrangement on Export Controls for Conventional Arms and Dual-Use Goods and Technologies, http://www.wassenaar.org/; Missile Technology Control Regime (MTCR), http://www.mtcr.info/english/index.html; Global Initiative to Combat Nuclear Terrorism (GICNT), http://www.state.gov/t/isn/c37079.htm.

[5]http://georgewbush-whitehouse.archives.gov/news/releases/2003/05/20030531-3.html; see S.J. Koch, The Proliferation Security Initiative: Origins and Evolution, Center for the Study of Weapons of Mass Destruction Occasional Paper No. 9, National Defense University Press, Washington, DC, pp. 8–10.

[6]http://www.whitehouse.gov/the_press_office/Remarks-By-President-Barack-Obama-In-Prague-As-Delivered.

[7]Nuclear Security Strategy, May 2010, The White House, http://www.whitehouse.gov/sites/default/files/rss_viewer/national_security_strategy.pdf, p. 24. Accessed 13 January 2015.

[8]See Lehrman 2004, p. 225; Winner 2005, p. 130; Heupel 2007, pp. 57–66, p. 58; Malisch and Prill 2007, p. 232; Holmes and Winner 2009, p. 140; Thomas 2009, p. 661; Durkalec 2010, p. 1.

stresses a specific feature of the Initiative, all express the basic concept that the PSI is not grounded on an international treaty. As the group's core members have declared, the PSI is 'an activity, not an organization' possessing its own international legal personality.[9] It does not have members, but participating (partner) States; it does not enact hard law measures, instead it builds on a network of cooperating countries which endorse its purposes, while deciding freely how to implement strategies to achieve its goals. Thus, the PSI complements those political and administrative frameworks and non-binding guidelines which contribute to ensuring control over export and re-export of proliferation-sensitive materials including the Zangger Committee, the Nuclear Suppliers Group, the Australia Group and the Missile Technology Control Regime.

10.2.2 Participating States

Besides the USA, the original group of PSI participating States[10] was mainly composed of European States, most of them being members of the European Union (EU). Since then the Initiative has progressively expanded to the present number of 102 endorsing States.[11] Efforts were made to secure participation of nuclear States, on the one hand and, on the other hand, of countries having larger maritime fleets. Among the nuclear States, Russia joined the PSI in 2003,[12] while China, India and Pakistan have not so far formally endorsed the Initiative.[13] Israel, which is widely believed to possess nuclear weapons, supports the PSI. As regards the most registered flags, countries representing about 80 per cent of the world's fleet (in deadweight tonnage) are currently participating in the PSI.[14]

---

[9]See Proliferation Security Initiative: Chairman's Conclusions at the Fourth Meeting, London, October 10, 2003. http://www.state.gov/t/isn/115305.htm.

[10]Australia, France, Germany, Italy, Japan, the Netherlands, Poland, Portugal, Spain, the UK and the USA.

[11]For a list of the 102 participating States see *SIPRI Yearbook 2014*, p. 527 and http://www.state.gov/t/isn/c27732.htm.

[12]See A. Kaliadine (2005) Russia in the PSI: The Modalities of Russian Participation in the Proliferation Security Initiative, WMDC Paper No. 29, The Weapons of Mass Destruction Commission, Stockholm, at: http://www.un.org/disarmament/education/wmdcommission/files/No29.pdf, pp. 8–11 reporting the domestic debates about Russian participation in the PSI and discussing Russia's role in the PSI.

[13]These countries' concerns over the PSI are especially related to interception on the high seas, the status of warships or military aircraft and the determination of the States of proliferation concern. See Becker 2005, pp. 165–167; Allen 2007, p. 58; Bocheński 2007, pp. 74–77; Thomas 2009, p. 678; Klein 2012, p. 196. It should be mentioned, however, that China, India and Pakistan are among the partner nations of the Global Initiative to Combat Nuclear Terrorism (GICNT, http://www.gicnt.org/), co-chaired by the USA and Russia, which promotes nuclear security through deterrence, prevention, detection, and response activities.

[14]See above n. 7.

European States count for about half of the PSI participants. While all the EU members have endorsed the Initiative, the EU itself is not a partner.[15] Apparently this depends on the attitude of the USA attaching more importance to the involvement of an increased number of States in the PSI in order to make it more balanced.[16] As a matter of fact, the regional imbalance in PSI participation is a critical element. In view of today's major geopolitical tensions that involve States and entities of proliferation concern, the absence of some key States in the international scenario from the PSI is arguably a factor that may adversely affect the acceptability and effectiveness of the Initiative. In this perspective, participation by States such as Brazil, China, India, Pakistan, Indonesia, Malaysia, Vietnam, Egypt and South Africa would be important in order to continue and to consolidate cooperation within the PSI.[17]

10.2.3 Structure

Being an informal cooperative network of States, the PSI does not rely on a formal institutional framework. In the view of some commentators this is a serious shortcoming of the Initiative.[18] However, an organizational mechanism has been set up to enhance cooperation. Initially, this was based on an informal 'core group' of countries composed of the eleven original participating States together with Canada, Norway, Russia and Singapore. In 2004, the increasing expansion of PSI's training exercises prompted the establishment of an Operational Experts Group (OEG) with the mandate of hosting PSI meetings, workshops and exercises as well as contributing customs, law enforcement, military and other security experts and assets to interdiction exercises. Presently the OEG is composed of 21 countries; it meets annually and forms working groups in specific areas of

[15]However, in 2004, the EU Council issued a statement on 'Non-proliferation: Support of the Proliferation Security Initiative (PSI)', Brussels, 1 June 2004, 10052/04 (Presse 189).

[16]See J. Durkalec, The Proliferation Security Initiative: Evolution and Future Prospects, EU Non-Proliferation Consortium, Non-Proliferation Papers No. 16, at: http://www.nonproliferation.eu/documents/nonproliferationpapers/jacekdurkalec4fcc7fd95cfff.pdf, pp. 10–11.

[17]This issue intermingles with the question of the U.S. ratification of the United Nations Convention on the Law of the Sea (UNCLOS) which, despite efforts displayed both by the Bush and the Obama administration, is still pending. Some US military and government officials argue that PSI would be positively affected by US participation in UNCLOS, while others deem that it would limit the US sovereignty under customary law. See M.B. Nikitin, Proliferation Security Initiative (PSI), CRS Report for Congress RL34327, http://www.fas.org/sgp/crs/nuke/RL34327.pdf, p. 8.

[18]See Becker 2005, p. 228; Garvey 2005, pp. 137–139 and Valencia 2006, p. 128, arguing that the legitimacy and effectiveness of interdiction would require the establishment of an institutional organization, possibly within the UN system.

cooperation.[19] The 'core group' has been replaced by High Level Political Meetings which are open to all PSI endorsing States, but are convened less frequently.[20] Since 2009, the USA has acted as 'focal point' to coordinate cooperation among all PSI participants. As a consequence the present structure, although informal, resembles the institutional framework of an international organization, the High Level Political Meetings corresponding to the assembly of States parties, the OEG to the executive body and the 'focal point' to a secretariat.

10.2.4 Statement of Interdiction Principles

The Statement of Interdiction Principles (SIP) lays down the mandate of the PSI. It was adopted by the original PSI partners on 4 September 2003.[21] This set of principles commit all PSI participating States, either alone or in concert with other States, to adopt a number of measures and procedures 'for interdicting the transfer or transport of WMD, their delivery systems and related materials to and from States and non-State actors of proliferation concern' (Principle 1). To this end the PSI partners exchange information concerning suspected proliferation activity, dedicate appropriate resources and efforts to interdiction operations and capabilities, and maximize coordination among participating States in interdiction efforts (Principle 2). To accomplish these objectives they will strengthen their relevant national legal authorities as well as the 'relevant international law and frameworks' (Principle 3). Actions taken in support of interdiction efforts must be consistent with States' obligations under such 'international law and frameworks' (Principle 4). In support of interdiction efforts, PSI partners refrain from transporting, assisting in, or allowing the transport of cargoes of WMD, their delivery systems or related materials, to or from States or non-State actors

[19]http://www.state.gov/t/isn/c27726.htm. See J. Durkalec, The Proliferation Security Initiative: Evolution and Future Prospects, EU Non-Proliferation Consortium, Non-Proliferation Papers No. 16, at: http://www.nonproliferation.eu/documents/nonproliferationpapers/jacekdurkalec4fcc7fd95cfff.pdf, pp. 6–8 and S.J. Koch, The Proliferation Security Initiative: Origins and Evolution, Center for the Study of Weapons of Mass Destruction Occasional Paper No. 9, National Defense University Press, Washington, DC, p. 21.

[20]The 10th Anniversary High Level Political Meeting of the PSI was held in Warsaw, Poland on 27–29 May 2013, http://www.state.gov/t/isn/c10390.htm.

[21]The SIP is analyzed in detail by PSI commentators, especially Lehrman 2004, pp. 226–227, 231–233; Persbo and Davis 2004, pp. 22–36; Ahlström 2005, pp. 748–755; Winner 2005, pp. 132–134; Song 2007, pp. 105–110; Thomas 2009, pp. 664–667; Durkalec 2010, pp. 3–6; Dunne 2013, pp. 13–18.

of proliferation concern (Principle 4, para a). As for maritime interdiction, action is to be taken to board and search any vessel flying their flag in their internal waters or territorial seas, or areas beyond the territorial seas of any other State that is reasonably suspected of transporting WMD-related cargoes, and to seize such cargoes after identification (Principle 4, para b). PSI partners 'seriously consider providing consent' to the boarding and searching of their own flag vessels by other States, as well as to the seizure of the WMD-related cargoes (Principle 4, para c). They will take action to stop and/or search suspected vessels in their internal waters, territorial seas or contiguous zones and to enforce appropriate conditions (such as boarding, search and seizure of the cargo) on such vessels when entering or leaving their ports, internal waters or territorial seas (Principle 4, para d). As for air interdiction, aircraft that are reasonably suspected of carrying WMD-related cargoes to or from States or non-State actors of proliferation concern will be denied transit rights in the airspace of PSI partners; such aircraft will be required to land for inspection and cargo seized upon identification when transiting in the airspace of a PSI participating State (Principle 4, para e). Finally, vessels, aircraft or other modes of transport reasonably suspected of carrying WMD-related cargoes are to be inspected and seized after identification in ports, airfields or other facilities are used as trans-shipment points in the territory of participants (Principle 4, para f).

10.3 The PSI and International Law

Principle 1 of the SIP entrusts the PSI participating States with the responsibility of establishing which 'States or non-State actors of proliferation concern' should be subject to interdiction activities because they are engaged in proliferation. Criteria for making such a determination include the existence of efforts to develop or acquire chemical, biological or nuclear weapons and associated delivery systems, and/or the participation in transfers (either selling, receiving or facilitating) of WMD, their delivery systems or related materials.[22] The SIP, however, does not provide a definition of 'WMD, their delivery systems or related

[22]At the time of PSI's adoption the term was understood with reference to States such as the Democratic People's Republic of Korea (DPRK), Iran, Libya and Syria. See A. Persbo and I. Davis, Sailing into Uncharted Waters? The Proliferation Security Initiative and the Law of the Sea, Basic Research Report, The British American Information Council, http://www.basicint.org/sites/default/files/basic_psi_report_final_all.pdf, pp. 28–29; Heintschel von Heinegg 2006, p. 56; Allen 2007, p. 50; Bocheński 2007, pp. 78–79; Song 2007, p. 106. The archetype of 'non-State actor of proliferation concern' was the nuclear smuggling network established in the 1980s by the Pakistani scientist Abdul Qadeer Khan. See Kaliadine 2005, p. 1.

materials'. Such a definition may be found in an asterisk to the preamble of Resolution 1540 adopted by the United Nations Security Council (UNSC) on 28 April 2004.[23] Res. 1540 also refers to relevant multilateral treaties and arrangements and national control lists. Thus, a rather broad margin of appreciation is left to PSI partners as regards dual-use items.[24]

Principle 4 mentions consistency of actions taken in furtherance of the PSI objectives with international law. Furthermore, Principle 3 commits the partners to endeavour to strengthen the 'relevant international law and frameworks'. This explains the efforts of PSI participants to adopt binding rules through UNSC resolutions, on the one hand, and to negotiate new agreements in the subject matter, on the other.[25] In a broader sense, Principle 3 could also be read as an encouragement to change international customary law through the participating States' official practice.[26] This interpretation has raised concerns by third States as well as criticism by a number of commentators, which are addressed below.

10.3.1 The PSI and the Law of the Sea

Principle 4, para (b)–(d) of the SIP dealing with maritime interdiction attracted the attention of commentators in the years following the adoption of the PSI because of the possible consequences of their implementation on States' rights and obligations under the law of the sea (LOS). Those who put the accent on the declared compliance of the PSI with international law expressed a positive opinion about its consistency with States' obligations under customary law and treaties,[27] namely

[23]'Means of delivery: missiles, rockets and other unmanned systems capable of delivering nuclear, chemical, or biological weapons, that are specially designed for such use. [...] Related materials: materials, equipment and technology covered by relevant multilateral treaties and arrangements, or included on national control lists, which could be used for the design, development, production or use of nuclear, chemical and biological weapons and their means of delivery.' See A. Persbo and I. Davis,) Sailing into Uncharted Waters? The Proliferation Security Initiative and the Law of the Sea, Basic Research Report, The British American Information Council, http ://www.basicint.org/sites/default/files/basic_psi_report_final_all.pdf, pp. 30–31 assessing alternative definitions of WMD. SC Res. 1540 (2004) is discussed below in Sect. 10.3.3.

[24]See Becker 2005, p. 183; Song 2007, p. 115; Holmes and Winner 2009, p. 151 and Joyner 2009, p. 324 considering problems arising with defining dual-use materials for interdiction purposes.

[25]See below Sects. 10.3.3 and 10.4.

[26]See Klein 2012, p. 198.

[27]Logan 2005, p. 271; Winner 2005, p. 134; J. Durkalec, The Proliferation Security Initiative: Evolution and Future Prospects, EU Non-Proliferation Consortium, Non-Proliferation Papers No. 16, at: http://www.nonproliferation.eu/documents/nonproliferationpapers/jacekdurkalec4fcc7fd95cfff.pdf, p. 19. But see Doolin 2006, p. 50 and Garvey 2013, p. 196 arguing that the PSI may gradually give rise to a new customary exception to the right of free navigation, and Perry 2006, p. 40 contending that it will affect the customary international law of the sea by blurring its jurisdictional boundaries.

the UNCLOS.[28] Indeed any State has the authority to enforce its laws and regulations over a ship registered under its flag.[29] Yet, it is necessary that appropriate legislation be enacted to prohibit the movement of WMD materials. Likewise, the coastal State has the right to inspect foreign ships (except for those enjoying immunity) when in internal waters (ports, bays and water on the landward side of the baseline), over which it has complete sovereignty.

Some questions arise with regard to the interdiction of a foreign vessel in the territorial waters or the contiguous zone of a coastal State. With the exception of innocent passage, coastal States are granted broad jurisdiction in the territorial sea. The transport of WMD is clearly prejudicial to the coastal State when it is bound for its ports, internal waters or territory, without proper authorization. But the shipment of dual-use items may give rise to the problem of assessing the security risk. And the mere passage of a foreign vessel carrying WMD-related materials destined to a third State could hardly be perceived as a danger to the peace, good order and security of the coastal State.[30] Even more so if the foreign flagged ship is transiting in the contiguous zone, where the coastal State may exercise more limited powers of control. Self-defence or State of necessity could be invoked only in the case of an armed attack or of an imminent and grave threat, which would not necessarily be triggered by the fact that a foreign vessel is loaded with WMD-related materials.[31]

The most controversial aspect of the PSI is related to interdiction in the high seas. Indeed, Article 110 UNCLOS does not mention WMD transport as a circumstance allowing warships to board foreign vessels in the high seas. The SIP, however, explicitly addresses that issue in para (c) of Principle 4, recommending that the partner States authorize the boarding and searching of their own flag vessels by other participating States, consistent with the general principle that consent precludes wrongfulness. In addition, the UNCLOS has codified the customary rule that ships without nationality are liable to be boarded by any warship in the high seas.[32] As a consequence, nothing in the SIP may be construed as derogation from the principle of the freedom of the high seas.[33] In the absence of consent, self-defence or a

[28]United Nations Convention on the Law of the Sea, 10 December 1982, 1833 UNTS 397. Although the USA is not a party to the UNCLOS, its provisions applicable to PSI activities are recognized as part of international customary law.

[29]Article 110 para (1*e*) UNCLOS. See Klein 2012, p. 202.

[30]Byers 2004, p. 532; Ronzitti 2008, p. 274.

[31]A. Persbo and I. Davis, Sailing into Uncharted Waters? The Proliferation Security Initiative and the Law of the Sea, Basic Research Report, The British American Information Council, http://www.basicint.org/sites/default/files/basic_psi_report_final_all.pdf, pp. 64–68, Logan 2005, pp. 269–270; Allen 2007, p. 171. But see Heintschel von Heinegg 2006, p. 65 arguing that in case of a terrorist background interception, boarding, search or arrest of a vessel finds its legal basis either in the right of self-defence or in the international law of counter-measures.

[32]Article 110 para (1e) UNCLOS.

[33]See Lehrman 2004, p. 253; Heintschel von Heinegg 2006, p. 70; Malisch and Prill 2007, p. 240; Song 2007, p. 134; Joyner 2009, p. 315.

State of necessity could arguably justify a coercive interdiction, but only under the strict requirements of the law of international responsibility, including the obligation to pay compensation for damages caused by unjustified measures.[34]

10.3.2 Air and Land Interdiction

Although the SIP is mostly focused on maritime areas, para (e) of Principle 4 extends the Initiative to air interdiction. The partner States are committed to deny transit through their airspace to aircraft that are reasonably suspected of carrying WMD-related cargoes, to or from States or non-State actors of proliferation concern; in case such aircraft is transiting in their airspace, it should land and be submitted to inspection and its cargo seized if the case demands. No action on international airspace is envisaged.

The air freedoms rights granted to civil aviation under he 1944 Chicago Convention on International Civil Aviation and the Air Service Agreements do not prejudice the territorial State's power to require landing and State aircraft are not entitled to fly over (or land on) the territory of a foreign State without authorization.[35] Thus para (e) of Principle 4 is consistent with international law. If a suspected aircraft does not comply with the request to land, however, the territorial State must act in accordance with Article 3*bis* of the Chicago Convention prohibiting the use of weapons against civil aircraft in flight in case of interception. This norm is widely deemed to correspond to customary international law. Therefore, legislation allowing the use of weapons against aircraft in flight that have been hijacked by terrorists, as adopted by some States, is inconsistent with international law.[36]

As a rule, international law does not restrict interdiction and seizure of WMD and related materials on land in the territory of a State. Thus identification and inspection of transportation suspected of carrying WMD-related cargoes at customs areas or trans-shipment points (Principle 4, para f) are the least problematic type of interdiction operations.[37] Likewise, if a suspected foreign aircraft has

---

[34]Draft Articles on Responsibility of States for Internationally Wrongful Acts, 'Report of the International Law Commission on the work of its fifty-third session', *ILC Yearbook* (2001, Vol. II, Part One) Articles 24 and 25, 27, 31 Issues of international responsibility for unlawful interdictions and the settlement of related claims are discussed by Becker 2005, pp. 227–228; Ronzitti 2008, pp. 281–283 and Guilfoyle 2009, pp. 324–330.

[35]Convention on Civil Aviation, 7 December 1944, 15 UNTS 295, Articles (3*c*), 3*bis*(*b*), 5, 6.

[36]See Ronzitti 2008, p. 278 referring to the German law of June 2004 and to the Russian law of March 2006. On 15 February 2006 the German Federal Constitutional Court overruled the German law as contrary to constitutional norms. 1 BvR 357/05, http://www.bundesverfassungsgericht.de/entscheidungen/rs20060215_1bvr035705en.html. See Nickel 2010, pp. 625–627.

[37]See Ahlström 2005, p. 749; Joyner 2009, p. 329; J. Durkalec, The Proliferation Security Initiative: Evolution and Future Prospects, EU Non-Proliferation Consortium, Non-Proliferation Papers No. 16, at: http://www.nonproliferation.eu/documents/nonproliferationpapers/jacekdurkalec4fcc7fd95cfff.pdf, p. 4 and A. Dunne (2013) The Proliferation Security Initiative. Legal Considerations and Operational Realities, SIPRI Policy Paper No. 36, pp. 22–23.

landed or is parked in a PSI participating State's airfield the territorial State has the right to inspect it and to seize that cargo which is identified as a prohibited one. Nevertheless, in times of peace, foreign State aircraft (as well as warships and State-owned ships used for sovereign purposes) are immune from search and seizure under customary international law. This is one of the PSI's inherent shortcomings preventing the interdiction of foreign military aircraft and vessels.

10.3.3 The United Nations and the PSI

In 2004 the PSI received endorsement from the High-level Panel on Threats, Challenges and Changes, which praised the Initiative and encouraged all States to join.[38] Subsequently, the UN Secretary-General publicly commended the PSI as an effort to fill gaps in the defence against terrorism.[39]

The Security Council has been more wary of recommending action. Resolution 1540 of 28 April 2004 calls for multilateral cooperation in the wide area of non-proliferation within the framework of the relevant international organizations and treaties, but it does not mention interdiction operations as a means of control for non-proliferation purposes.[40] Thus a number of commentators maintain that the said resolution does not confer new powers to States besides those granted by international law,[41] while others emphasize that it provides an enhanced legal framework for cooperation among States.[42]

In the following years, the Security Council adopted sanctions against the Democratic Republic of Korea (DPRK) for the launches of ballistic missiles and

---

[38]A More Secure World: Our Shared Responsibility, Report of the Secretary General's High-level Panel on Threats, Challenges and Change (2004) para 132, http://www.un.org/en/peacebuilding/pdf/historical/hlp_more_secure_world.pdf.

[39]Secretary-General Offers Global Strategy for Fighting Terrorism, in Address to Madrid Summit, Press Release SG/SM/9757, 10/03/2005, http://www.un.org/News/Press/docs/2005/sgsm9757.doc.htm.

[40]While the USA attempted to incorporate an endorsement of interdiction in the resolution, this was prevented by the opposition of China and Russia. See Valencia 2006, p. 126 and Winner 2005, p. 136.

[41]Byers 2004, pp. 531–532; Logan 2005, p. 270; Allen 2007, p. 59; M. Heupel, The Proliferation Security Initiative: Advancing Commitment and Capacity for WMD Interdictions, Disarmament Forum, Central Asia at the Crossroads at: http://www.unidir.org/pdf/articles/pdf-art2688.pdf, p. 60; Malisch and Prill 2007, p. 236; Joyner 2009, pp. 320–322.

[42]Persbo and Davis 2004, p. 66; Kaliadine 2005, p. 7; Doolin 2006, pp. 45–46; Heintschel von Heinegg 2006, p. 68; Roach 2006, p. 358. See also Guilfoyle 2009, p. 243 arguing that Res. 1540 'leaves a great deal of flexibility to national law in its implementation.'

the conduct of nuclear explosion tests, and against Iran for failing to comply with previous resolutions concerning its nuclear programme.[43] Resolution 1874 of 12 June 2009 calls upon all States to inspect all cargo to and from the DPRK, in their territory, including seaports and airports, if the State concerned has information that provides reasonable grounds to believe the cargo contains embargoed goods. The resolution further calls upon member States, on the basis of similar information, to inspect vessels, with the consent of the flag State, on the high seas; pursuant to the resolution, if the flag State does not consent to inspection on the high seas it must nevertheless direct the vessel to an appropriate port for the required inspection. As a consequence, a flag State cannot totally deny inspection.[44] Moreover, Resolution 2094 of 7 March 2013 commits member States to deny permission to any aircraft to take off from, land in or overfly their territory, if they have reasonable grounds to believe the aircraft contains prohibited items.[45]

Resolution 1929 of 9 June 2010 imposing a ban on sales of heavy weapons to Iran is worded in more general terms. It merely 'notes' that States, consistent with international law and with the consent of the flag State, 'may' request inspections of vessels on the high seas if there is information that provides reasonable grounds to believe the vessel is carrying items the supply, sale, transfer, or export of which is prohibited.[46]

As resulting from the examples above, the Security Council is slowly moving to authorize maritime and air interdiction for counter-proliferation purposes but on a case-by-case basis and not as a general policy.[47]

10.3.4 Bilateral Ship-Boarding Agreements

Article 110 UNCLOS concedes that acts of interference with the navigation on the high seas may derive form powers conferred by treaty. Thus, bilateral agreements can provide authority to contracting States to board ships suspected of carrying shipment of WMD, their delivery system or related materials. Since the inception of the PSI, the USA has been pursuing bilateral ship-boarding agreements with States holding the largest shipping registries. The first agreements were concluded in 2004 with Panama and the Marshall Islands and in 2005 with Belize, Croatia, Cyprus and Liberia; from 2007 to 2010 Malta, Mongolia, the Bahamas, Saint

[43]See J.L. Black-Branch in Chap. 16 in this volume.

[44]SC Res. 1874 (2009), paras 11–13.

[45]SC Res. 2094 (2013), paras 16–17.

[46]SC Res. 1929 (2010), para 15.

[47]According to Garvey 2013, pp. 201–204 the PSI's effectiveness would be enhanced if the Initiative as a whole were covered by a Security Council mandate. This appears unlikely at this stage.

Vincent and the Grenadines and Antigua and Barbuda entered into such agreements.[48]

The PSI ship-boarding agreements (which usually take the form of an exchange of notes) are modelled on similar arrangements in the field of counter-narcotics.[49] They routinely recall the relevant treaties and UN resolutions. If a vessel registered in the USA or in a partner country, or a vessel without nationality, is suspected of carrying WMD-related cargo in international waters, either one of the parties can request the other to confirm the nationality of the ship in question and to authorize the boarding, search and detention of the vessel, cargo and persons on board. The agreements also establish general and specific safeguards to be respected in the conduct of the boarding operations. Actions permissible in case of refusal to comply with the request for boarding may include the use of force to the minimum degree necessary under the circumstances.[50] Jurisdiction over detained vessels rests primarily with the flag State, which may waive its right and consent to the exercise of jurisdiction by the other party.

Ship-boarding agreements are an important, although restricted practice regarding WMD interdictions. The USA is a constant party to these agreements; no other PSI participating State has concluded a similar network of bilateral treaties. This highlights the dominance of the USA within the Initiative, enabling them to visit and search a considerable portion of the world's merchant fleet in the high seas.

10.4 The Role of Multilateral Conventions

The PSI as a counter-proliferation programme is a part of a broader context including voluntary export regimes, implementation of UN resolutions as well as a number of international treaties and agreements. Thus, the participating States' like-mindedness has been an instrument to pursue counter-proliferation efforts through the adoption of new binding legal instruments. This endeavour has found a breeding ground on the existing multilateral treaties for the protection of international sea and air traffic against terrorism. Unlike the PSI, which is focused on interdiction of WMD-related cargoes, those treaties are aimed at prosecuting persons having committed acts of terrorism. During the first decade of the present

[48]For the text of existing PSI ship-boarding agreements see http://www.state.gov/t/isn/c27733.htm. Their role and scope of application are discussed by Spadi 2006, pp. 257–267; Byers 2007, paras 10–15; Guilfoyle 2009, pp. 246–254; Klein 2012, pp. 184–192; Garvey 2013, pp. 192–193 and 200–201.

[49]See Byers 2004, pp. 538–540 and Lehrman 2004, p. 251 reviewing precedents for ship-boarding agreements in the fight against slave trade, the preservation of straddling fish stocks and the interdiction of drug smuggling. See also Byers 2007 arguing that 'the widespread conclusion of such treaties could itself generate a new rule of customary international law in parallel to treaty obligations' (para 21).

[50]See Roach 2006, providing an analytical commentary to the provisions of a standard ship-boarding agreement (at pp. 360–416).

century, new agreements were concluded in this area indirectly strengthening counter-proliferation and—in one case—providing a new legal basis for maritime interdiction under international law.

10.4.1 The 2005 Protocols to the 1988 SUA Treaties

The 1988 SUA treaties[51] are aimed at fostering international cooperation in criminal matters related to acts of terrorism against ships and fixed platforms, such as seizure by force, killings and other acts of violence against persons, and the placing of devices which are likely to destroy or damage a ship or a platform.[52] States parties undertake to make those offences punishable by appropriate penalties, to prosecute or extradite the alleged offenders and to afford one another assistance in connection with criminal proceedings brought in respect of the said offences.[53] The SUA treaties, however, do not envisage the boarding of vessels seized by terrorists or any other coercive measure.

The amendments adopted in 2005 in the form of two new protocols[54] considerably expand the scope of the 1988 SUA treaties. A new Article 3*bis* includes in the offences within the meaning of the SUA Convention a number of acts performed for terrorist purposes. Among these are the unlawful and intentional uses against or on a ship, discharging from a ship or transport of any explosive, radioactive material or BCN (biological, chemical, nuclear) weapon, as well as the transport of any equipment, material or software that significantly contributes to the design, manufacture or delivery of a BCN weapon.[55] State parties of the NPT, however,

[51]Convention for the Suppression of Unlawful Acts Against the Safety of Maritime Navigation, 10 March 1988 (SUA Convention), 1678 UNTS 221 and Protocol for the Suppression of Unlawful Acts Against the Safety of Fixed Platforms Located on the Continental Shelf (SUA Protocol 1988) 1678 UNTS 304. Both treaties entered into force on 1st May 1992. http://www.imo.org/About/Conventions/StatusOfConventions/Pages/Default.aspx.

[52]SUA Convention Article 3, SUA Protocol 1988 Article 2.

[53]See Kieserman 2006, pp. 427–430; Tuerk 2008, pp. 341–353 and Klein 2012, pp. 151–154 describing the background and analyzing the basic provisions of the SUA Convention.

[54]Protocol of 2005 to the Convention for the Suppression of Unlawful Acts against the Safety of Maritime Navigation, 14 October 2005. http://www.refworld.org/docid/49f58c8a2.html. Protocol of 2005 to the Protocol for the Suppression of Unlawful Acts against the Safety of Fixed Platforms Located on the Continental Shelf, 14 October 2005. http://www.refworld.org/docid/49f58cee2.html. Both Protocols entered into force on 28 July 2010.

[55]See Spadi 2006, pp. 269–274; Malisch and Prill 2007, pp. 236–238; Tuerk 2008, pp. 358–365; Guilfoyle 2009, pp. 254–259; Klein 2012, pp. 172–173 and A. Dunne, The Proliferation Security Initiative. Legal Considerations and Operational Realities, SIPRI Policy Paper No. 36, pp. 21–22 analyzing the new provisions included in the SUA Convention by the 2005 Protocol. See also Joyner 2009, p. 318 and J. Durkalec, The Proliferation Security Initiative: Evolution and Future Prospects, EU Non-Proliferation Consortium, Non-Proliferation Papers No. 16, at: http://www.nonproliferation.eu/documents/nonproliferationpapers/jacekdurkalec4fcc7fd95cfff.pdf, p. 14 elaborating upon their limited influence over the PSI so far.

are exempt from the latter provision insofar as the transport is not contrary to their obligations under that treaty.[56]

10.4.2 Regulating Maritime Interdiction

The provision relevant to maritime interdiction is the new Article 8*bis* of the SUA Convention 2005 which establishes procedures to facilitate ship-boarding when a State party has reasonable grounds to suspect that a ship or a person on board a ship flying the flag of another State party is involved in the commission of an offence under the Convention. To this end the authorization and cooperation of the flag State is required.[57] Upon ratification of, or accession to the 2005 Protocol, a State party can declare that it allows authorization to board and search a vessel flying its flag if it does not respond to the request for authorization within four hours.[58] The use of force must be avoided except when necessary to ensure the safety of officials and persons on board, or if the officials are obstructed to the execution of authorized actions; a number of safeguards are established including consistency of boarding and search with applicable international law.[59] The Convention does not apply to the activities of armed forces during an armed conflict or undertaken in the exercise of their official duties, insofar as they are governed by other rules of international law.[60]

Although currently it has only limited participation,[61] the advantage of the SUA Convention as amended by the 2005 Protocol over the PSI framework resides in the binding obligations undertaken by States parties to adapt their domestic legislation accordingly, to prosecute or extradite alleged offenders, and to cooperate in criminal proceedings. If the number of States parties to the amended Convention gradually increases this will promote the inclusion of WMD-related crimes in domestic legislation and facilitate collaborative actions for their prosecution.

---

[56]SUA Convention 2005 Article 3*bis* para 2. See Thomas 2009, p. 678 making reference to India's disagreement with the discriminatory stance of that provision.

[57]SUA Convention 2005 Article 8*bis* paras 4, 5(a)–(c). The 2005 Protocol to the 1988 SUA Protocol does not include provisions on inspection of fixed platforms.

[58]Idem., para 5(d).

[59]Idem., paras 9–10. See Heintschel von Heinegg 2010, pp. 391–393 describing the generally accepted principles and procedures for visit and search.

[60]SUA Convention 2005 Article 2*bis* para 2.

[61]As at 31 March 2013 the SUA Convention as amended in 2005 has 33 States parties totalling about 36 % of the world's merchant fleet tonnage. While more than twenty are PSI participating States, the USA is not among them. http://www.imo.org/About/Conventions/StatusOfConventions/Pages/Default.aspx.

10.4.3 The 2010 Beijing Convention and Protocol

The 2005 Protocols to the SUA treaties served as models for the negotiation of new counter-terrorism instruments in the field of civil aviation, where a number of treaties on aviation security exist since the 1960s.[62] The agreements concluded on 10 September 2010 are the Beijing Convention on the Suppression of Unlawful Acts Relating to International Civil Aviation (which will replace the 1971 Montreal Convention, of the same heading) and the Beijing Protocol Supplementary to the 1970 Hague Convention for the Suppression of Unlawful seizure of Aircraft.[63]

The importance of the 2010 Beijing Convention for counter-proliferation rests on the new offences it covers. Examples include releasing or discharging from a civil aircraft any BCN weapon or explosive, radioactive or similar substances to cause death, serious bodily injury or serious damage to property or environment; using BCN weapons against or on board an aircraft; transporting explosive or radioactive material, a BCN weapon or source or special fissionable material knowing they will be used for terrorist purposes.[64] The Convention, however, does not contain provisions on air or ground interdiction. Moreover, unlike the 2005 SUA Protocols which were adopted by consensus, the 2010 agreements were adopted by majority vote since the Asian and Middle-Eastern countries opposed provisions preserving the rights of the NPT States parties and exempting the armed forces from the scope of the Convention.[65] As a consequence, among the seventy-one States which attended the 2010 Diplomatic Conference only twenty-seven have signed the Convention and twenty-nine the Protocol. Twenty-two ratifications are required to bring each of them into force.[66] Unless a dramatic change of attitude is forthcoming, it is unlikely that these two instruments will significantly contribute to enhance counter-proliferation efforts in the near future.

---

[62]See Huang 2009, pp. 112–155 describing the network of treaties concluded under the auspices of the International Civil Aviation Organization (ICAO) to strengthen aviation safety against unlawful interference.

[63]http://www.icao.int/secretariat/legal/Pages/TreatyCollection.aspx. The two treaties are not yet in force. http://www.icao.int/secretariat/legal/Lists/Current%20lists%20of%20parties/AllItems.aspx.

[64]Beijing Convention 2010 Article 1 para 1(g), (h), (i). See Abeyratne 2011, pp. 136–140 reviewing the offences under the new Convention.

[65]See D. van der Toorn, September 11 Inspired Aviation Counter-terrorism Convention and Protocol Adopted, 15 ASIL Insights (3), http://www.asil.org/files/insight110126pdf.pdf explaining the negotiating positions at the 2010 Diplomatic Conference.

[66]Beijing Convention 2010 Article 22, Beijing Protocol 2010 Article XXIII.

10.5 The PSI in Practice

The PSI's practice is difficult to evaluate due to a lack of official and publicly available information on its operation.[67] As a matter of fact, since the Initiative has neither legal personality nor autonomy in decision-making, it is not so much PSI's practice but rather State practice of interdictions.[68] Although the SIP requires the PSI participating States to exchange the relevant information which they hold in relation to suspected proliferation activities, it also protects the confidential character of information so provided by other participating States (Principle 2). Reporting on implementation is not envisaged.

Interdiction of WMD, their delivery systems and related materials, however, is not the sole activity that characterizes the PSI. Indeed, the development by participating States of significant interdiction capabilities and practices is a necessary prerequisite to achieve the purposes of the Initiative. This has been pursued through a number of practical activities that presently represent the main area of cooperation among the PSI partners.

10.5.1 Joint Training Exercises

Since the adoption of the PSI many widely publicized multinational exercises and interdiction simulations have taken place including maritime manoeuvers, air or ground exercises, or a combination of any.[69] While their primary aim is to strengthen PSI participating States' capabilities and practices for interdiction, they

---

[67]See Bocheński 2007, p. 71, M. Heupel, The Proliferation Security Initiative: Advancing Commitment and Capacity for WMD Interdictions, Disarmament Forum, Central Asia at the Crossroads at: http://www.unidir.org/pdf/articles/pdf-art2688.pdf, p. 62, Holmes and Winner 2009, p. 145, M.B. Nikitin, Proliferation Security Initiative (PSI), CRS Report for Congress RL34327, http://www.fas.org/sgp/crs/nuke/RL34327.pdf, pp. 7–8, Klein 2012, p. 206 and S.J. Koch, The Proliferation Security Initiative: Origins and Evolution, Center for the Study of Weapons of Mass Destruction Occasional Paper No. 9, National Defense University Press, Washington, DC, pp. 24–25 highlighting criticism of the PSI's lack of transparency.

[68]See J. Durkalec, The Proliferation Security Initiative: Evolution and Future Prospects, EU Non-Proliferation Consortium, Non-Proliferation Papers No. 16, at: http://www.nonproliferation.eu/documents/nonproliferationpapers/jacekdurkalec4fcc7fd95cfff.pdf, p. 18 describing PSI interdiction as every interdiction operation involving a PSI participating State or intentionally linked to the Initiative.

[69]Detailed accounts of PSI interdiction training exercises are given by Song 2007, pp. 108–109, J. Durkalec, The Proliferation Security Initiative: Evolution and Future Prospects, EU Non-Proliferation Consortium, Non-Proliferation Papers No. 16, at: http://www.nonproliferation.eu/documents/nonproliferationpapers/jacekdurkalec4fcc7fd95cfff.pdf, pp. 14–15 and S.J. Koch, The Proliferation Security Initiative: Origins and Evolution, Center for the Study of Weapons of Mass Destruction Occasional Paper No 9, National Defense University Press, Washington, DC, pp. 22–23.

serve multiple purposes within that strategy. First, they facilitate cooperation in both the national and international context among the different agencies involved in interdiction issues, including the armed forces, customs, police, intelligence and other administrations. Second, they offer to non-participants the opportunity to observe the PSI's activities and to benefit from its operation. Third, they are meant to have a deterrent effect on potential proliferators.[70]

Civilian law enforcement authorities are deeply involved in PSI activities related to interdiction of dual-use goods. Yet the greater part of PSI exercises maintain a prevailing military nature.[71] Given the relevance of proliferation-sensitive dual-use trade, this aspect cast some doubts on the ability of the PSI to really meet the challenges of proliferation of WMD-related materials.

10.5.2 Interdiction Operations

In view of the paucity of reliable information on PSI interdictions, it is not surprising that the evaluation of their effectiveness is complicated and their consistency with international law even more uncertain. A number of interdictions of maritime shipments occurred during the first years of PSI's operation were reported by the US government, including the most celebrated diversion and seizure in 2003 of the BBC China, a German-owned freighter bound to Libya, which was found to carry parts for gas centrifuges of a kind used to enrich uranium.[72] The 2014 Report of the Panel of Experts which investigated alleged violations of Security Council Resolution 1929 (2010) imposing sanctions against Iran examined, *inter alia*, a significant number of interdictions of dual use items on the basis of intelligence information that they were intended for use in Iran's prohibited activities.[73] The

[70]See Winner 2005, p. 134; Doolin 2006, p. 43; Bocheński 2007, p. 69, M. Heupel (2007) The Proliferation Security Initiative: Advancing Commitment and Capacity for WMD Interdictions, Disarmament Forum, Central Asia at the Crossroads at: http://www.unidir.org/pdf/articles/pdf-art2688.pdf, p. 61 assessing the results of joint training exercises.

[71]J. Durkalec, The Proliferation Security Initiative: Evolution and Future Prospects, EU Non-Proliferation Consortium, Non-Proliferation Papers No. 16, at: http://www.nonproliferation.eu/documents/nonproliferationpapers/jacekdurkalec4fcc7fd95cfff.pdf, p. 16.

[72]Remarks on the Second Anniversary of the Proliferation Security Initiative, Secretary Condoleezza Rice, http://2001-2009.state.gov/secretary/rm/2005/46951.htm. Accessed 16 January 2015. See Winner 2005, p. 137; Byers 2007, paras 8–9; M. Heupel, The Proliferation Security Initiative: Advancing Commitment and Capacity for WMD Interdictions, Disarmament Forum, Central Asia at the Crossroads at: http://www.unidir.org/pdf/articles/pdf-art2688.pdf, p. 58; Malisch and Prill 2007, p. 231. Some other maritime interdiction incidents possibly related with the PSI are reported by Song 2007, p. 119.

[73]Final Report of the UN Panel of Experts Established Pursuant to Resolution 1929 (2010), S/2014/394 of 11 June 2014 paras 19–30.

report does not reveal where the interdictions took place; according to external sources, however, certain cases involved PSI participant States.[74]

Arguably most interdictions have not been made known to the public or perhaps they were carried out either independently or on the basis of non-PSI cooperation.[75] Be it as it may, it is interesting to see that maritime interdictions, which have attracted the greatest attention and have been discussed in depth by many commentators, are rare in practice. Usually interdiction operations take place in ports, on the ground or at customs.[76] This suggests that interdiction in international waters is not the main application of the PSI, which effectively works through ordinary means of enforcement of domestic and international regulations.

10.6 Concluding Remarks

More than ten years after adoption, concerns about legitimacy of the PSI seem to have been largely superseded by the smooth management of its activities. Freedom of the high seas and the principle of flag State consent remain untouched, as bilateral ship-boarding agreements and efforts to strengthen multilateral treaties demonstrate. Put into perspective, a voluntary initiative such as the PSI and the multilateral treaties on sea and air security may be seen as complementary. The former provides practical training on how to execute interdictions, while the latter stipulate binding rules to be followed with respect to prosecution of those responsible of WMD trafficking and to judicial cooperation in criminal matters.

Although a proper evaluation of the PSI's effectiveness is difficult to make due to its lack of transparency, it is reasonable to assume that joint training exercises regularly performed since 2003 have contributed to the development of participating States' critical capabilities and practices in relation to interdiction of WMD and related materials. These routine activities are unlikely to be transformed into an institutional organization or brought into the UN system. The role of the Security Council comes into play but if and when interdiction needs specific authorization. As long as voluntary cooperation keeps within the limits of international and domestic law it serves counter-proliferation egregiously, provided that

[74]This was the case, for instance, of a shipment of 1800 bobbins of carbon fibre that was reportedly seized in Singapore in December 2012 aboard the *Shahraz*, a ship en route from China to Bandar Abbas in Iran. See N. Gillard, Interdicted Carbon Fibre. Proliferation Case Study Series. Project Alpha, Center for Science and Security Studies, King's College London 26 September 2014, 20140926_-_Project_Alpha_-_Carbon_fibre-2.pdf, p. 5.

[75]Joyner 2009, p. 302, M.B. Nikitin, Proliferation Security Initiative (PSI), CRS Report for Congress RL34327, http://www.fas.org/sgp/crs/nuke/RL34327.pdf, pp. 2–3.

[76]See Allen 2007, p. 113; Song 2007, p. 132; J. Durkalec, The Proliferation Security Initiative: Evolution and Future Prospects, EU Non-Proliferation Consortium, Non-Proliferation Papers No. 16, at: http://www.nonproliferation.eu/documents/nonproliferationpapers/jacekdurkalec4fcc7fd95cfff.pdf, p. 17 and A. Dunne, The Proliferation Security Initiative. Legal Considerations and Operational Realities, SIPRI Policy Paper No. 36, pp. 31–33.

civilian law enforcement authorities are increasingly involved in the interdiction of dual-use goods.

Notwithstanding the wide share of PSI participants in the world's fleet, a shortcoming of the Initiative is still the absence of important States, especially in the Asian region and in the Arabic peninsula. A broader participation of key States belonging to different geopolitical areas would be an important condition for securing PSI's effectiveness in counter-proliferation. Ratification of the UNCLOS by the US could also have a positive, albeit indirect effect on further geographical expansion of the Initiative.

References

Abeyratne R (2011) The Beijing Convention of 2010 on the suppression of unlawful acts relating to international civil aviation—an interpretative study. J Trans Secur 4(2):131–143

Ahlström C (2005) The proliferation security initiative: international law aspects of the statement of interdiction principles, SIPRI yearbook (2005) Nonproliferation, arms control, disarmament. Oxford University Press, Oxford-New York, pp 741–767

Allen C (2007) Maritime counter proliferation operations and the rule of law. Praeger Security International, Westport, pp 143–178

Becker MA (2005) The shifting public order of the oceans: freedom of navigation and the interdiction of ships at sea. Harvard Int Law J 46:131–230

Bocheński S (2007) Quart J. Winter 2007:62–81

Byers M (2004) Policing the high seas: the proliferation security initiative. AJIL 98:526–541

Byers M (2007) Proliferation security initiative. In: Wolfrum R (ed), Max Planck encyclopedia of public international law, 10 vols. Oxford University Press. http://opil.ouplaw.com/view/10.1093/law:epil/9780199231690/law-9780199231690-e1209?prd=EPIL. Accessed June 2015

Doolin JA (2006) The proliferation security initiative: cornerstone of a new international norm. Naval War College Rev 59(2):29–57

Dunne A (2013) The Proliferation Security Initiative. Legal Considerations and Operational Realities, SIPRI Policy Paper No. 36, http://books.sipri.org/product_info?c_product_id=459

Durkalec J (2010) The Proliferation Security Initiative: Evolution and Future Prospects, EU Non-Proliferation Consortium, Non-Proliferation Papers No. 16, http://www.sipri.org/research/disarmament/eu-consortium/publications/nonproliferation-paper-16

Garvey JI (2005) The international institutional imperative for countering the spread of weapons of mass destruction: assessing the proliferation security initiative. J Confl Secur Law 10:125–147

Garvey JI (2013) Counter proliferation of nuclear weapons: a new grand bargain. Oxford University Press, Oxford

Guilfoyle D (2009) Shipping interdiction and the law of the sea. Cambridge University Press, Cambridge, pp 232–262

Heintschel von Heinegg W (2006) The proliferation security initiative: security versus freedom of navigation? In: Sparks TMcK, Sulmasy GM (eds), International law challenges: homeland security and combating terrorism. International law studies, vol 81, pp 55–76

Heintschel von Heinegg W (2010) Maritime interception/interdiction operations. In: Gill TD, Fleck D (eds) The handbook of the international law of military operations. Oxford University Press, Oxford, pp 375–393

Heupel M (2007) The Proliferation Security Initiative: Advancing Commitment and Capacity for WMD Interdictions, Disarmament Forum, Central Asia at the Crossroads at: http://www.unidir.org/pdf/articles/pdf-art2688.pdf

Holmes GR, Winner AC (2009) The proliferation security initiative. In: Busch NE, Joyner DH (eds) Combating weapons of mass destruction, the future of international nonproliferation policy. University of Georgia Press, Athens, pp 139–155
Huang J (2009) Aviation safety through the rule of law: ICAO's mechanisms and practices. Kluwer Law International, Alphen aan den Rijn, pp 112–155
Joyner DH (2009) International law and the proliferation of weapons of mass destruction. Oxford University Press, Oxford-New York, pp 301–332
Kaliadine A (2005) Russia in the PSI: The Modalities of Russian Participation in the Proliferation Security Initiative, WMDC Paper No. 29, The Weapons of Mass Destruction Commission, Stockholm, at: http://www.un.org/disarmament/education/wmdcommission/files/ No29.pdf
Kieserman B (2006) Preventing & defeating terrorism at sea: practical considerations for implementation of the draft protocol to the convention for the suppression of unlawful acts against the safety of maritime navigation (SUA). In: Nordquist MH, Moore JN, Fu K-C (eds) Recent developments in the law of the sea and China. Martinus Nijhoff Publishers, Leiden/Boston, pp 425–464
Klein N (2012) Maritime security and the law of the sea. Oxford University Press, Oxford, pp 147–210
Lehrman TD (2004) Enhancing the proliferation security initiative: the case for a decentralized nonproliferation architecture. Virginia J Int Law 45:223–276
Logan SE (2005) The proliferation security initiative: navigating the legal challenge. J Trans Law Policy 14:253–274
Malisch M, Prill F (2007) The proliferation security initiative and the 2005 protocol to the SUA convention. ZaöRV 67:229–240
Nickel R (2010) Data mining and "renegade" aircrafts: the states as agents of a global militant security governance network – the German example. Emory Int Law Rev 24:619–651
Perry TC (2006) Blurring the ocean zones: the effect of the proliferation security initiative on the customary international law of the sea. Ocean Dev Int Law 37:33–53
Persbo A, Davis I (2004) Sailing into Uncharted Waters? The Proliferation Security Initiative and the Law of the Sea, Basic Research Report, The British American Information Council, http://www.basicint.org/sites/default/files/basic_psi_report_final_all.pdf
Roach JA (2006) Proliferation security initiative (PSI)—countering proliferation by sea. In: Nordquist MH, Moore JN, Fu K-c (eds), Recent developments in the law of the sea and China. Martinus Nijhoff Publishers, Leiden/Boston, pp 351–424
Ronzitti N (2008) The proliferation security initiative and international law. In: Fischer-Lescano A, Gasser H-P, Marauhn T, Ronzitti N (eds), Frieden in Freiheit—peace in liberty—paix en liberté. Festschrift für Michael Bothe zum 70. Geburtstag. Nomos Verlagsgesellschaft. Baden-Baden, pp 269–284
Song Y-H (2007) The U.S.-led proliferation security initiative and UNCLOS: legality, implementation and an assessment. Ocean Dev Int Law 38:101–145
Spadi F (2006) Bolstering the proliferation security initiative at sea: a comparative analysis of ship-boarding as a bilateral and multilateral implementing mechanism. Nordic J Int Law 75:249–278
Thomas TV (2009) The proliferation security initiative: towards relegation of navigational freedoms in UNCLOS? An Indian perspective. Chinese J Int Law 8(3):657–680
Tuerk H (2008) Combating terrorism at sea—the suppression of unlawful acts against the safety of maritime navigation. Univ Miami Int Comp Law Rev 15:337–367
Valencia MJ (2006) Is the PSI really the cornerstone of a new international norm? Naval War College Rev 59(2):123–130
Winner A (2005) The proliferation security initiative: the new face of interdiction. The Wash Quart 28:129–143

Chapter 11
Enforcing Nuclear Non-Proliferation—The Role of Verification

Barry Kellman

Abstract Nuclear non-proliferation verification should be framed as a multiple negative in connection with deterring and detecting States' nuclear activities so as to impel States to neither develop nor otherwise acquire disallowed weapons. Accordingly, international authorities must have legal authority to determine whether non-proliferation obligations are satisfied, to resolve doubts about compliance, and in the rare case to coercively enforce such obligations. Ultimately, verification necessarily entails an elevation of legal authority to judge a State's behaviour from self-appointed State political and military elites to technical elites within the United Nations or other international organizations, thereby strengthening global governance in the cause of peace and security. The international community must know what States are doing with and about nuclear and other weapons, and this superior interest must trump the strategic interests of any particular State. This chapter first asserts that the core imperative of verification must be to enable detection of violations of non-proliferation obligations, and it frames the International Atomic Energy Agency's (IAEA) role in verifying compliance with States' mutual commitment to nuclear non-proliferation. It then addresses two controversies associated with nuclear non-proliferation verification, respectively: the scope of States' legal obligation to allow the IAEA to resolve doubts about compliance, and the Security Council's authority to impose sanctions for non-compliance with nuclear non-proliferation obligations pursuant to recent international law decisions. The author concludes that the IAEA is fully mandated to verify not only the correctness but also the completeness of a State's reports, and the Security Council has unreviewable authority to enforce international obligations in the maintenance of peace and security.

Professor and Director, International Weapons Control Center, DePaul University College of Law.

B. Kellman (✉)
International Weapons Control Center, DePaul University College of Law,
Loop Campus, E. Jackson Blvd, 25, Chicago, IL 60604, USA
e-mail: BKELLMAN@depaul.edu

J.L. Black-Branch and D. Fleck (eds.), *Nuclear Non-Proliferation in International Law - Volume II*, DOI 10.1007/978-94-6265-075-6_11

Keywords Completeness · Compliance · Correctness · Enforcement · International Atomic Energy Agency (IAEA) · Nuclear non-proliferation · Sanctions · Verification

Contents

11.1 Introduction

This chapter is about how international law operates with regard to nuclear non-proliferation verification. My contention is that international law should and does add clarity to the operation of verification mechanisms, and this contribution supports humanity's existential interests in stanching the spread of nuclear weapons. This chapter's purpose is to portray nuclear non-proliferation verification as a legal system, notably as a legal system that works reasonably effectively.

This is no straightforward matter. There is no 'International Treaty on Verification' that stipulates what verification is, what obligations are assumed by States, and what authority may be exercised by an international agency. Verification regimes differ by the type of weapon subject to control; some non-proliferation obligations come without any explicit mechanisms of verification. Existing mechanisms vary depending on the stage of the weapons' lifecycle that is subject to verification: verification of research and development obligations is a very different undertaking, both technologically and legally, than verification of weapons dismantlement obligations.

Some pundits may suggest that the term lacks objective legal meaning, that verification is inherently contextual, lacking any criteria or metrics that can be useful trans-contextually. It is as if there is an Alice in Wonderland quality to 'verification'—the term means precisely whatever the speaker says it means, no more, no less, depending on what strategic objectives are sought to be achieved, what levels of distrust apply among principal States, and what are States willing to be transparent (or at least translucent) about.

Following this logic, international lawyers parse verification obligations mechanistically: if the verification system calls for regular filing of reports, then compliance with the verification system is measured by the regularity of filed reports. But if required reports are designed to be uninformative, there may be ready willingness to prepare and submit them; such compliance says little about whether critical behaviour has actually been steered towards international peace and security. Such an approach is void of content, a tautological exercise in which 'international law' is defined to mean whatever self-serving answer might appear useful, as if each advocate could be its own judge. With regard to the nuclear non-proliferation imperative, such a fatuous approach is not only wrong but dangerous.

In sharp contrast, my thesis can be framed as follows: Verification necessarily entails an elevation of legal authority to judge a State's behaviour from self-appointed State political and military elites to technical elites within the United Nations or other international organizations, thereby strengthening global governance in the cause of peace and security. The international community must know what States are doing with and about nuclear and other weapons, and this superior interest must trump the strategic interests of any particular State.

This chapter asserts the importance of enabling international authorities to determine if non-proliferation verification obligations are satisfied, to resolve doubts about compliance, and in the rare case to coercively enforce such obligations. Disregard for the imperative of coercive enforcement of non-proliferation verification obligations, in this writer's view, leads to crisis where political leaders face a binary dilemma of either resorting to armed force or ignoring proliferation. Affirming this imperative, by contrast, opens alternative policy options for peaceful resolution of disputes.

I advance this thesis in three parts. Section 11.2 is foundational, asserting that the core imperative of verification must be to enable detection of violations of non-proliferation obligations and framing the International Atomic Energy Agency's (IAEA) role in verifying compliance with States' mutual commitment to nuclear non-proliferation. Sections 11.3 and 11.4 address two controversies associated with nuclear non-proliferation verification, respectively: the scope of States' legal obligation to allow the IAEA to resolve doubts about compliance, and the Security Council's authority to impose sanctions for non-compliance with nuclear non-proliferation obligations pursuant to recent international law decisions.

Looking forward, the imminent challenges of nuclear weapons control—e.g. control of fissile materials; nuclear weapons stockpile containment and reduction; expansion and enforcement of nuclear-weapon-free zones; and eventual genuine and complete disarmament—should, in this writer's opinion, be based on a legal predicate of verification that enables coercive enforcement. The same may be said with regard to a host of other (not nuclear) weapons such as directed energy and space-based weapons. Understanding how verification contributes to enforcing nuclear non-proliferation obligations can inform progress in meeting these challenges.[1]

11.2 On Verification of Nuclear Non-Proliferation Obligations

'Verification' refers to a process to systemize obligations in the pursuit of peaceful resolution of disputes, and, by that systemization, avoidance of disputes. Without verification, suspicious behaviour or breach of even a minor obligation may trigger an over-reaction, even a use of force, regardless of whether a significant weapons capability has been obtained.

By replacing innuendo and distrust with objectively quantifiable evidence that States are meeting their commitments, verification helps assure States, regardless of their condition of mutual distrust, to gain mutual confidence that others are not pursuing prohibited weapons. Reinforcing States' confidence in the non-proliferation regime encourages all States to reduce their capacity and eventual interest in strategic breakout that would upend their balance of power. Ultimately, non-proliferation verification serves the fundamental purpose to coerce State compliance with humanity's prime imperative of controlling nuclear weapons.

Non-proliferation verification should therefore be framed as a multiple negative in connection with deterring, detecting and ultimately taking enforcement measures so as to impel States to neither develop nor otherwise acquire disallowed weapons. Accordingly, the level and variety of verification mechanisms should strive to be proportional to risks of evasive wrongful conduct. If the mechanisms of verification are insufficiently rigorous, then finding no evidence of non-compliance with stipulated requirements may be merely suggestive of institutional failure to see through the façade of technical evasion, undermining confidence in the entire regime.

Verification requirements should be sufficiently rigorous to detect violations of non-proliferation obligations, to reach objective and insightful conclusions about those violations, and, if necessary, to justify a collective security response that reinforces non-proliferation policy goals. Key here is the timeliness of detection. Only by providing timely warning before a weapons program has proceeded beyond the point where intervention can be effective can a verification system actually contribute to security by enabling the international community to take preventative action.[2]

---

[1]For a useful introduction on how understanding non-proliferation verification can offer useful insights for controlling other weapons, see M. Dreicer and G. Stein, Applicability of Non-Proliferation Tools and Concepts to Future Arms Control, Lawrence Livermore National Laboratory, LLNL-CONG-636652 (May 2013) and C.R. Wuest, The Challenge for Arms Control Verification in the Post-New START World, Lawrence Livermore National Laboratory, LLNL-TR-564612.

[2]See generally, Avenhaus and Kyriakopoulos 2006.

Of course, among States of good will for whom pursuit of a prohibited weapons program is not a goal, verification requirements can and should operate with a maximum degree of cooperation, rewarding positive indicators of continued peaceful intentions and providing capacities for States to address any confusion or mistake of fact so as to demonstrate compliance with commitments. The aspiration of cooperation is no doubt to be applauded. Yet, it is obvious that if all States were so inclined, verification would be of incidental note. In a world run by flower children, verification of non-proliferation obligations would be both easy and unnecessary, but this is a patently ridiculous characterization of our world.

In this world where acquisition of prohibited weapons holds allure for some State and non-State actors, a legal assessment of verification is more aptly correlated, not with compliance, but with non-compliance and enforcement. Again, the logic of multiple negatives is manifest: mechanisms for gathering information (declarations, inspections, remote monitoring, etc.) are valuable primarily to the extent that they identify no evidence of non-compliance and thereby mutually assure participating States of their non-hostile intentions.

Yet, there will always be a limit to detecting violations, and to think that verification must eradicate all doubt is unrealistic. Verification mechanisms specified in treaties are based on compromises balancing the need to collect data for verifying compliance with the need to protect classified and proprietary information. An additional important factor is cost; if too high, States would be unwilling to bear it. There may also be technological limitations on how to verify, whether of detection capability or of assessment capacity.

Implementation of verification mechanisms in several States should be based on the proliferation risks associated with each State—assessment of such risks should be according to consistent and non-discriminatory analytical criteria. Yet, it is also appropriate to customize risk assessment to reflect subjective factors that experience shows to be potential indicators of proliferation risk: What is the history of deception, ambiguity, hedging behavior, non-cooperation, suspect rhetoric and pursuit of unnecessary dual-use technologies? How responsive is a State to diplomatic engagement? What are the purposes and patterns of its military establishment? How likely is a State's deviation from the rules indicative of wrongful intentions? What are the risks of undetected violations?[3] Thus, any set of verification requirements must be appreciated in the strategic context from which those requirements emerged.

[3]See Verification in All Its Aspects: Study on the Role of the United Nations in the Field of Verification, UN Doc. A/45/372 (1990).

11.2.1 Emergence of Nuclear Verification

The entire concept of verification emerged amid the most unique geostrategic environment humanity has ever faced. Over 80 million people had been violently killed from 1914 to 1945, and the sole basis of trust between the U.S. and U.S.S.R. was the hope that the adversary would not deliberately pursue its self-annihilation. Nuclear weapons came to signify, simultaneously, the means by which WW III would be fought *and* the means by which WW III would be avoided. A remarkably delicate chess game began, but a game with no agreement as to the rules, nor did players have, at least not initially, vast options about how to play. In many respects, 'nuclear arms control' was about doing what could be done with unprecedented technology in unprecedented strategic circumstances—at best, it was the art of the possible.

To gain confidence that the adversary would not suddenly break out of an agreement's proscriptions, verification emerged as sets of bilateral obligations whereby each State was required to reveal critical items of information in return for access to comparable items of information from the adversary. By no means were mechanisms of verification designed to be failsafe; indeed, they were designed to be incremental, both providing some assurance of each side's compliance and supporting mutual confidence upon which more rigorous mechanisms could be built. In the bilateral context, verification focused less on how to detect non-compliance than on enabling participants to gain confidence about each other's intentions. These arrangements were not viewed as needing to be coercive; 'enforcement' was the very thing that all participants deeply sought to avoid.[4]

The major elements comprising verification emerged from the context of the superpower security confrontation:

- *Surveillance* using whatever tools might be available (national technical means, including satellite reconnaissance and national intelligence). Surveillance may or may not be consensual; consensual surveillance is often called *monitoring.* Consensual surveillance has been widely viewed as preferable; on-site monitors tend to be more precise than remote and covert observation technologies.
- *Declarations* (sworn statements of relevant facts by each participant intended for review by other participants and international agents). The contents of such declarations can be stipulated and their submission can be dictated. In various contexts, however, declarations can be more or less voluntary; such voluntary declarations are often referred to as *confidence building measures.*
- *On-site inspections* of critical sites. As an aside, while legal attention has tended to focus on issues associated with inspections because of the perceived potential for misuse (e.g. to gain access to confidential technological information), in the superpower nuclear arms control context, inspections have been the least significant pillar of the verification triad.

---

[4]See generally, Schelling 1966.

11.2.2 The Nuclear Non-Proliferation Commitment

The global commitment to prevent proliferation of nuclear weapons is essential to and complementary of the nuclear arms control and disarmament commitment because the potential spread of nuclear weapons inherently contradicts pursuit of a world free of nuclear weapons. The nuclear non-proliferation commitment asserts as a prime imperative of humanity that the problem of nuclear weapons must be contained. This commitment does not so much advocate changing the prevailing strategic relationships that affect humanity's nuclear future as ensuring that the problems associated with nuclear weapons do not become more intractable and more vulnerable to violent use.

Verification of the nuclear non-proliferation commitment drew on the same triad of elements of verifying superpower nuclear arms control, albeit with somewhat less emphasis on remote surveillance than on declarations and inspections. The tight correlation between these complementary commitments is manifest in the Trilateral Initiative between the United States, Russia and the IAEA, launched in 1996, to examine the technical, legal and financial issues associated with IAEA verification of weapon origin and other fissile material released from defense programs in those two countries.[5] Yet, despite conjoined history and shared ultimate mission, the nuclear non-proliferation commitment is distinguishable from the superpowers' pursuit of nuclear weapons control: the nuclear non-proliferation commitment is not, fundamentally, a trans-national but an international undertaking. From the perspective of international law, this distinction is fundamental.

Trans-national arrangements (whether or not embodied in a treaty) may readily be conceived as horizontal or contractual agreements among legally equal parties that expresses the parties' mutual obligations without engaging the international community, at least not institutionally. An *international regime*, by contrast, is inherently a three-dimensional arrangement whereby the interests of the international community are legally predominant.[6] In an international regime, fundamental obligations are owed by States *erga omnes*. The underlying spirit of an international regime and the *erga omnes* obligation is the mutuality of commitment in light of which many other States adjust their behaviour for the common good. States owe obligations principally to the international community, and one State's non-compliance with its commitments is an offense to each and to all.

The nuclear non-proliferation regime is perhaps law's most deeply rooted and nuanced international regime, premised on the shared commitment to reduce the gravest known danger to humanity. The alternative is too dire to accept.

[5]At the recent Nuclear Security Summit, 2014, 35 nations agreed to implement nuclear security recommendations from the IAEA. See generally Partnership for Global Security, Nuclear Security Summit Paves Way for Future Regime, (7 April 2014), http://partnershipforglobalsecurity.org/2014/04/07/2014-nuclear-security-summit-paves-way-for-future-regime/.

[6]See generally, Kellman 1994.

At the heart of this regime is the Nuclear Non-proliferation Treaty which embodies a fundamental policy keystone that more States having nuclear weapons threatens peace and security. The NPT ensconces the strategic reality that in the late 1960s, five States already had nuclear weapons as the core of their national security strategy and were not about to give them up. These five nuclear-weapon States (NWS) accepted the Article VI obligation to negotiate general and complete nuclear disarmament, but there is certainly substantial debate about whether they have upheld their end of the bargain—a question of utmost significance that may soon be judicially addressed.[7]

Regardless of one's view regarding compliance with Article VI, it is certainly true that the NPT is an important manifestation but not an encapsulation of the larger nuclear non-proliferation commitment; there are many other manifestations of that commitment. It inheres in prohibitions on emplacement of nuclear weapons in outer space, in Antarctica, and on the oceans' deep seabed. Regional nuclear weapons free zones are also a significant component of nuclear non-proliferation. These constraints serve to fix boundaries into which nuclear weapons may not pass, thereby enabling resolution of disputes about these areas to be resolved without the existential specter of nuclear weapons and, into the future, enabling eventual nuclear disarmament to be more easily pursued. Restraints on the trans-national movement of nuclear materials and technology through mechanisms of technology export control arrangements are also extremely important. Not yet an agreed-upon part of the non-proliferation commitment but conceptually very relevant are controls on fissile material production.[8]

11.2.3 The IAEA's Role in the Nuclear Non-Proliferation Commitment

Although an institutional focus on nuclear non-proliferation verification necessarily concentrates on the IAEA, non-proliferation verification is not exclusively a matter for the IAEA. More accurate would be to acknowledge the intricate network of institutions that oversee global nuclear energy, including regional organizations, national regulatory officials, trans-national epistemic communities and others. The IAEA sits atop this structure, and non-proliferation verification is among the most important regulatory functions it undertakes, but by no means is

[7]See ICJ Press Release, http://www.icj-cij.org/presscom/files/0/18300.pdf; see also http://www.icj-cij.org/docket/files/160/18332.pdf; International Association of Lawyers Against Nuclear Arms, The Marshall Islands Case, Special Newsletter, July 2014, http://www.lcnp.org/RMI/IALANA-Newsletter_14_7.pdf.

[8]See generally, S. Johnson, The Safeguards at Reprocessing Plants under a Fissile Material (Cutoff) Treaty, Research Report No. 6, International Panel on Fissile Materials.

non-proliferation verification the only thing that the IAEA does, nor is the IAEA the sole party engaged in non-proliferation verification.[9]

According to the United Nations' Statement of principles issued in the NPT drafting process, the Treaty 'should be void of any loop-holes which might permit nuclear or non-nuclear powers to proliferate, directly or indirectly, nuclear weapons in any form.'[10] Accomplishment of that objective was delegated to the IAEA. Critically, the IAEA is the only international organization having central responsibilities for weapons non-proliferation that was not created by the international agreement that defines those responsibilities.

Indeed, the IAEA predates the NPT by more than a decade. In 1953, President Eisenhower proposed creation of an international atomic energy agency because he believed that the United States was not the credible guardian for world nuclear materials. At the time, no international organization had ever existed to oversee how national governments put to use any technology, least of all a technology with such significant weapons capabilities.[11] The IAEA emerged as a cooperative initiative of the U.S. and the U.S.S.R. (and other States), established by an international treaty.[12]

The point here is that the IAEA is not an institution created by the NPT to carry out treaty (NPT)-related functions. More accurately, the NPT assigned the IAEA independent authority to verify that nations do not use their peaceful nuclear activities to make nuclear weapons. It was the NPT that, as a matter of law, correlated 'safeguards' and 'verification' and this is what States agreed to by becoming parties to the NPT.

This is not the place to offer a report card on the IAEA and on the nuclear non-proliferation regime generally.[13] But it may be confidently offered that the IAEA's role with regard to humanity's use of nuclear energy is substantially different, and greater than, the OPCW's role with regard to humanity's use of chemistry, and nothing comparable exists with regard to biotechnology or any other technological domain. In part, this reflects the sheer uniqueness of the nuclear fuel cycle and physicists' remarkable capacity to measure minute quantities of fissile material.

It may be momentarily pondered: if nuclear weapons had not been invented, would Cold War antagonists have put biological weapons at the heart of strategic deterrence, and, if so, what verification mechanisms would have emerged to cope with the fact that biological agents could not be measured with anywhere near the precision or confidence of measuring fissile materials, which explains, in

[9]See Van de Graaf and Lesage 2009.

[10]G.A. Res. 2028 (XX), p. 2(a), UN Doc. A/6014 (Nov. 19, 1965), cited in DeFrancia 2012.

[11]C. Kessler, Presentation, The International Atomic Energy Agency—The Global Guardian of Non-Proliferation, Brookhaven National Laboratory, BNL-100895-2013-CP.

[12]Statute of the International Atomic Energy Agency.

[13]See, G. Evans and Y. Kawaguchi, Eliminating Nuclear Threats, A Practical Agenda for Global Policymakers, Report of the International Commission on Nuclear Non-Proliferation and Disarmament, recommending regular preparation of a 'Report Card' on the IAEA and the nuclear non-proliferation regime generally.

substantial part, why there exists today no Organization for the Prohibition of Biological Weapons to complement the IAEA and the OPCW.[14] Even if biological weapons had been considered a comparably dire threat, a lower threshold of verification would have had to have been tolerated because of the inherent difficulties of monitoring pathogens and bio-labs.

In any event, it may fairly be said that the IAEA is 'the paramount instrument of global governance in nuclear non-proliferation, nuclear security and nuclear safety'.[15] The IAEA is, first of all, a central repository of technology for measuring nuclear materials and technology.[16] The IAEA also undertakes long-term research and development to enhance, for example, analytical methodologies to detect undeclared nuclear activities including weaponization.[17] Its charge is not only to lead prevention of nuclear weapons proliferation but to promote the peaceful and safe use of nuclear energy. Moreover, the IAEA has primary international responsibility for responding to nuclear accidents.

On a policy level, it is the IAEA which convenes international fora on nuclear matters.[18] The IAEA is the centre of a global network of data centres and is primarily responsible for their collaboration.[19] The growth of nuclear Centers of Excellence (CoEs) and Nuclear Security Support Centers (NSSCs) is a more recent demonstration of this commitment and an acknowledgement of the benefits of sharing international experience and resources for strengthening nuclear security globally.[20]

11.2.4 IAEA Safeguards

The success of the global nuclear non-proliferation regime depends entirely on a functional, globally applicable and effective safeguards system—agreed practices

[14]At the heart of failure of the Biological Weapons Convention Verification Protocol was the virtual impossibility of adapting such finely tuned measurements into the world of biological laboratories. See generally, Kellman 2007.

[15]Wang et al. 2011.

[16]For example, the United States provides support through the State Department International Safeguards Project; Office; National Nuclear Security Administration, NA-22, NA-24.

[17]IAEA Department of Safeguards Long-Term R&D Plan, 2012–2023, available at http://www.iaea.org/safeguards/documents/STR_375_--_IAEA_Department_of_Safeguards_Long-Term_R&D_Plan_2012-2023.pdf.

[18]See, e.g. IAEA Department of Safeguards Long-Term R&D Plan, 2012–2023, available at http://www.iaea.org/safeguards/documents/STR_375_--_IAEA_Department_of_Safeguards_Long-Term_R&D_Plan_2012-2023.pdf. Nuclear Disarmament Safeguards and Physical Protection (S98) Source/Report, February 2012; JAEA-REVIEW--2011-038, http://jolissrch-inter.tokai-sc.jaea.go.jp/pdfdata/JAEA-Review-2011-038.pdf.

[19]See, e.g. Otuka et al. 2014.

[20]See, J.E. Doyle, Towards an INSEN Strategy for Engaging International Centers for Nuclear Security. International Conference on Nuclear Security: Enhancing Global Efforts. Proceedings of the International Conference.

that enable the IAEA to gain a clear picture of a State's nuclear activities. Safeguards constitute both the start point and end point for verification that a State's nuclear energy program is used for peaceful purposes and does not pose risks of nuclear weapons proliferation. 'Balancing rights to peaceful use with the proliferation concerns posed by sensitive activities is, in the end, a question of whether those activities are adequately safeguarded.'[21]

Safeguards are based on the methodology of nuclear material accountancy. States must file reports of safeguarded nuclear material and the features of facilities relevant to safeguarding such material. Material balance areas (MBAs) are identified, and the quantity of material in each MBA is identified. A book inventory of that MBA may be maintained by recording measured flows into and out of the area. The correspondence between the contents of the MBA on paper and these records is the basis to judge whether any material is unaccounted for. Material unaccounted for is then evaluated by refined statistical methods to establish, with reasonable confidence, if significant losses or diversions have occurred.

Further to verify, the IAEA is empowered to examine each safeguarded facility's design to ensure that it will not be used for military purposes. INFCIRC/153 requires States to share design plans of facilities and allow on-site inspections and surveillance.[22] States must permit *ad hoc* and routine inspections (as well as special inspections) to verify the consistency of reported information with records, the location and composition of all safeguarded nuclear material and information on the possible reasons for material unaccounted for or uncertainties in the records. Further details relating to material accountancy, access specifications, reporting of nuclear facility designs and notice periods for new facilities are specified in Subsidiary Arrangements concluded pursuant to the comprehensive safeguards agreements (CSAs).[23]

Measures to prevent proliferation necessarily target information about "proliferation-sensitive" activities, i.e. information 'which is not available to the public and which is important to the design, construction, fabrication, operation or maintenance of a uranium enrichment or nuclear fuel reprocessing facility or a facility for the production of heavy water'.[24] Key indicators of risk guide the IAEA's practice in assessing nuclear activities at the State level. This approach involves 'relevant indicators of the existence or development of processes associated with nuclear-related activities', including weaponization.[25]

The IAEA draws safeguards conclusions of a State's nuclear activities and plans on the basis of wide and integrated assessment of the totality of information

[21]DeFrancia 2012, p. 721.

[22](International Atom Energy Agency Information Circular) INFCIRC/153. The IAEA's statute contemplates the possibility of broad safeguards authorities, including facility design approval authority and anytime/anywhere inspections access.

[23]See generally, Scheinman 1992.

[24]United States Nuclear Non-proliferation Act of 1978, Section 4(a)(6). See generally IAEA Safeguards System, para 12.

[25]DeFrancia 2012, p. 729.

available to the IAEA. In addition to information provided by States or derived from on-site inspections, the IAEA may base its conclusions from other sources including information from internal IAEA collections of scientific and technical literature, news media (including news service data bases), country-specific web-sites and satellite imagery. Such information can shed light on safeguards-related concerns such as research into sensitive technologies, details about source and nuclear material production, location data, imports and exports of dual-use or single-use technologies applicable to the nuclear fuel cycle.[26]

Moreover, the IAEA has developed its own capabilities for in-depth analysis and evaluation of nuclear trade activities on a global scale. These new capabilities involve techniques to enhance the collection and analysis of information about nuclear supply and procurement activities and the investigation of covert nuclear trade networks with a view to assessing whether these networks are supporting undeclared nuclear activities.[27] In this regard, the entire issue of inspectors' access may be growing less salient as alternative technological capacities for gathering and tracking information are emerging.

11.2.5 Summary

Viewed from the perspective of international law, assignment of authority to the IAEA should be understood as the manifestation of an intention, backed by deliberate design and reinforced by decades of practice, to delegate determinations of *verifiability* to an international technical secretariat.[28] The IAEA is not a contracting party but the chief global regulatory institution responsible for a complex system that involves specified processes inputs, outputs and feedback, enhancing achievement of policy imperatives by strengthening coherence and coordination over time. While this institutional framework 'should be inclusive, transparent and effective and it should find common solutions related to global challenges',[29] the IAEA's relationship to States is not horizontal but vertical.

11.3 Resolving Doubts About Compliance with Nuclear Non-Proliferation Obligations

Inevitably, safeguards entail intrusion into domains that participating States might not want revealed, and thus inherent in verification is a conflict between the need of verifiers to access information and the preference of any State to deny access.

[26]Cooley 2006, p. 67.

[27]See Kellman 1996.

[28]Cooley 2006.

[29]UN General Assembly, The future we want, Resolution 66 (2012): 288, para 75.

This has led to ongoing disagreements about the right of non-nuclear-weapon States (NNWS) to undertake proliferation-sensitive activities which, in turn, have provoked defenses of selective targeting of developing States for special treatment.

The thesis of this part is as follows: To resolve such disagreements by construing safeguards agreements as disaggregated bilateral treaties between the IAEA and each NNWS is to ignore the subsidiary relationship that safeguards agreements bear to the NPT itself. More incisively, a verification dispute between the IAEA and an NPT State Party should not be viewed as a stand-alone two-party controversy, but should be resolved so as to strengthen international confidence in compliance with the nuclear non-proliferation commitment.

Section 11.3.1 discusses the NPT's obligation that States accept safeguards on their peaceful nuclear activities. Section 11.3.2 addresses whether refusal to re-negotiate a safeguards agreement in light of the IAEA's Additional Protocol may justify a State's refusal to allow inspectors to resolve disputes about compliance. Section 11.3.3 frames the entire question of inspectors' access under the legal principle of 'right to truth'.

11.3.1 The NPT Article III Obligation to Accept Safeguards

NPT Article III(1) obligates each State Party to accept safeguards to verify fulfillment of its non-proliferation obligations "with a view to preventing diversion of nuclear energy from peaceful uses to nuclear weapons or other nuclear explosive devices." Safeguards "shall be applied on all source or special fissionable material in all peaceful nuclear activities" within the State's territory, jurisdiction or control. This obligation both respects a State's governance of activities inside its territory and constrains how States may exercise that governance.

Article III is framed entirely in obligatory terms: each NNWS must 'conclude agreements with the International Atomic Energy Agency to meet the requirements of this Article'. No language in the Article III obligation to accept safeguards suggests what might be a legal basis for limiting the scope of safeguards and thus inspectors' access. Certainly, the obligation to negotiate safeguards does not, by requiring State consent to such safeguards, authorize a State to refuse to accept safeguards agreements so as to hide wrongful activities from detection. To infer from this positive obligation a double negative permission for States to deny access where no safeguards agreement has explicitly mandated such access—no safeguards agreement exists because the State in question refuses to agree to such an agreement—is to invert the logic of verification. Safeguards agreements are the legal manifestation of consent to comply, not to evade.

As limitations of access must not be negotiated to shield noncompliant behaviour from detection—in legal terms, as the right to withhold consent is not unlimited—limitations of access may be negotiated only for a justifiable reason, and there are not infinite 'justifiable reasons'. Throughout weapons control treaties and other legal arrangements, access may be limited to protect privileged information relating to: (1) confidential or proprietary matters and (2) national security.[30] These justifications deserve a moment's consideration.

Both the nuclear and the chemical non-proliferation verification systems were designed to address concerns that intrusive inspections could jeopardize the security of confidential business or other types of proprietary information. *Managed access* mechanisms have been devised for shielding confidential information while enabling verification inspections. Principles of managed access are both limiting and enabling: they limit inspectors' capacity to purloin market-valuable information while enabling inspectors to gather information relevant to verifying compliance. By reducing the risk of loss of confidential or proprietary information, non-proliferation verification systems corral any legal basis for a State to limit access in order to protect such information and place on the State a significant burden for defending such concerns.[31]

Protection of "national security" interests is a broad but not unlimited justification for denying inspectors' access. Notably, the so-called right of States to limit access on the grounds of national security was developed in the superpower nuclear arms control context which necessarily involved visits to military bases to examine large weapons systems. It is not at all clear whether this justification for denying inspectors' access even applies in the nuclear non-proliferation context where the appearance of items for verification at a military installation would itself be grounds for concern. As it has never been successfully argued to any court to this writer's knowledge that a State may exercise a national security justification to limit verifiers' access, it is difficult to assess what facts might justify claiming a national security justification for limiting verifiers' access.

11.3.2 Safeguards Agreements as Constraints on Verification?

Disputes about access of IAEA inspectors are most acute when the IAEA has already negotiated a safeguards agreement with a State that specifies limitations on access, but, later, the IAEA seeks to expand the scope of that access. A legal question arises whether a negotiated and in-place safeguards agreement serves to legally curtail access only to points identified in the pre-existing safeguards agreement. This has been at the heart of most NPT controversies, including the 'discovery' of Iraq's undeclared nuclear facilities and, more recently, the dispute over Iran's nuclear program. Approaches to addressing this question have most certainly evolved over the decades, and that evolution itself says a great deal about identifying *lex lata* in this domain.

[30]INFCIRC/153, para 5 requires that the IAEA take every precaution to protect commercial and industrial secrets and other confidential information coming to its knowledge in the implementation of the Agreement. See generally Gualtieri and Kellman 1995.

[31]See generally, Kellman et al. 1995.

To put the question more legalistically: does the specification of access in a safeguards agreement create a legal right in the inspected State to deny access to places that it would not necessarily have had a right to deny access when negotiating its safeguards agreement pursuant to its Article III obligation? Does the existence of such agreement establish a contractually enforceable right to deny access to critical places even though no such right inheres in Article III? More concretely, is a negotiated safeguards agreement a legal constraint to deny inspectors access to proliferation-sensitive information that is outside the boundaries of agreement-specified authorization such that inspectors may not legally go? Or is the safeguards agreement merely a mechanism for enabling smooth operation of most inspections; authority for conducting inspections is broader, deriving from the earlier mentioned Article III obligation to enable verification of each State's compliance?

11.3.2.1 Safeguards Under INFCIRC/153 and the Additional Protocol

A brief review of safeguards based on INFCIRC/153's requirements reveals the core problem. Safeguards began at the point where nuclear material is of suitable composition and purity to be enriched in an isotope separation plant or to be fabricated into fuel elements. Materials 'in mining or ore processing activities' were, by INFCIRC/153, specifically exempted from NPT safeguards. Thus, '[n]o matter how thorough and effective the Agency's controls of these materials are, it is in principle possible for a State to have an unregistered domestic source of nuclear material and clandestine production facilities'.[32] Over two decades ago, the IAEA itself appreciated the paradox of being able to verify only the nuclear material under safeguards but not being able to pursue the potential for extraneous nuclear materials or facilities.[33]

Indeed, obtaining information relating to clandestine activities has been one of weapons control's greatest challenges. In both the nuclear weapons and chemical weapons contexts, concerns about non-compliance have focused not only on the risk of diversion of critical materials from within the verification system but also on the risk that critical materials never enter the verification system. During negotiation and implementation of the Chemical Weapons Convention (CWC), this issue concerning the scope of verifier's access was profoundly appreciated. The CWC's detailed verification system was designed, at its core, to explicitly reject the proposition that a State may refuse inspectors access beyond narrow perimeters of sites wherein States' declarations announce that chemicals of concern can be found.[34]

[32] Staasz 1973.

[33] Kellman 2000.

[34] If CWC inspectors request access to areas not covered by the facility agreement in order to clarify an ambiguity, the inspected State must provide information and grant access to the inspection team. CWC Verification Annex, Part VII, Section 25.

To bring nuclear non-proliferation verification into conformity with this understanding, the IAEA developed the Additional Protocol (AP) to give the IAEA more authority than existing safeguards agreements to both information and sites. The AP requires provision of information about, and IAEA inspector access to, all parts of their nuclear fuel cycle as well as to any other location where nuclear material is or may be present. Under the AP's 'complementary access' system, the IAEA has the right to collect environmental samples at locations beyond declared sites if it deems it necessary to do so. In addition, the AP authorizes the IAEA to conduct random short notice inspections at all nuclear and nuclear-related locations and of suspected undeclared nuclear activities.[35]

11.3.2.2 Legal Implications of Non-acceptance of the Additional Protocol

A legal issue has arisen as to a State's right to restrict access if it has not accepted the AP nor negotiated new safeguards agreements based on it. Experts debate whether safeguards agreements negotiated pursuant to INFCIRC/153 authorize inspectors' access to places or activities that do not involve safeguarded material.[36] A related question is whether the AP may be binding on States such that they have no right to refuse to re-negotiate their safeguards agreements pursuant to its terms. May an NPT NNWS, by indicating its non-acceptance of the AP, deny consent to its requirements?

Professor Asada's analysis of whether the AP is an NPT obligation is worth attention here.[37] He notes that the AP, while intended to apply universally, has not been treated as binding on NNWS that have declined to accept it. Reinforcing the conclusion that the AP is not mandatory is the fact that the United Nations Security Council has called on but not required States to ratify the AP, nor has it required adoption of a safeguards agreement based on the AP as a corrective measure to remedy a serious case of non-compliance.[38] Moreover, as Professor Asada points out: "if the conclusion of an additional protocol was an obligation under Article III, it would follow that quite a number of NPT States Parties are in 'violation'" as only 96 out of 185 NNWS have concluded an AP.[39]

---

[35]J. Carlson, IAEA Safeguards Additional Protocol, International Commission on Nuclear Non-Proliferation and Disarmament, 20 January 2009.

[36]See Dupont, Chap. 3 in this volume and Johnson and Rockwood, Chap. 4 in this volume. See also L. Rockwood, The IAEA's State-Level Concept and the Law of Unintended Consequences, Arms Control Today, available at http://www.armscontrol.org/act/2014_09/Features/The-IAEAs-State-Level-Concept-and-the-Law-of-Unintended-Consequences and D. Joyner, A Response to Laura Rockwood, Arms Control Law, http://armscontrollaw.com/page/2/.

[37]Asada 2011.

[38]SC Res 1887 (2009), para 15(b).

[39]Ibid., at p. 7.

Tellingly, Professor Asada notes that Australia and Canada proposed in a Preparatory Committee for the 2005 NPT Review Conference that the Conference decide that the AP is mandatory under Article III because safeguards requirements have evolved over time and must continue to evolve to meet present and future challenges, '...[n]o proliferation tool is perfect'. However, this argument failed in favour of keeping the AP 'a voluntary confidence-building measure', reflecting non-aligned movement (NAM) countries' preference to distinguish 'between legal obligations and voluntary confidence-building measures to ensure that such voluntary undertaking are not turned into legal safeguards obligations'.[40] Asada notes that while the Model AP was adopted by the IAEA's Board of Governors, 'the more teleological argument that the Article III obligation must evolve as the IAEA's safeguards system evolves would not easily be accepted by the States parties who have power to give authentic interpretation of the NPT'.[41]

In this writer's view, Professor Asada's conclusion is the right answer to a somewhat inaptly framed question. All any verification system can do is assure confidence and detect non-compliance. No verification system can force access if a State decides to deny it, for whatever reason. But, under the NPT, it is wholly within the IAEA's authority to conclude that it cannot verify compliance; each NNWS bears the burden to demonstrate compliance, as will be developed below.

11.3.3 Inspectors' Scope of Access Pursuant to the Right to Truth

The right to truth is a developing concept in international law, increasingly recognized by international tribunals.[42] Conceived and initially applied in connection with gross human rights violations, this right's core principles obligate States to enable understanding of their behaviour in relation to preeminent global commitments. The right to truth is inherently entwined with principles of accountability; it signifies a negation of claims of impunity, whether purported as claims of executive secrecy or official interruptions of investigations.[43] This section asserts that the right to truth is a legal obligation that is akin to verification, and application of the right to truth to nuclear non-proliferation verification informs an understanding of States' purported justification for resisting types of verification mechanisms.

The right to truth belongs to society at large,[44] and comes into play with regard to matters of significance. As States deceive and obfuscate routinely, the right to truth is reserved for matters of substantial international importance lest overuse

[40]Asada 2011; see also Asada, Chap. 5 in this volume.

[41]Ibid.

[42]See generally, Groome 2011.

[43]*Al Nashiri v. Poland*, European Court of Human Rights, para 481 (24 July 2014).

[44]Ibid., para 482.

deprive the concept of its compulsory character. The right to truth implies not only clarification of the circumstances of particular violations but also clarification of the general context, the policies and institutional failures and decisions that enabled their occurrence. Thus, the right is best conceived as a proactive obligation on all States to have ways to ascertain the truth. Accordingly, States must have in place and not impede processes for undertaking inquiry when serious allegations arise as to non-compliance with their legal obligations.

In such circumstances, the right to truth calls on the State to undertake an effective investigation and specifies: (1) the investigation must be prompt and thorough; (2) all reasonably available steps must be taken to secure evidence; and (3) the investigation should be independent of the executive. Most important, the concept signifies that negative inferences may be drawn from the absence of such capacities or their ineffectiveness in any particular case. That is, the right to truth posits that a State's failure to inquire as to serious allegations of breach of significant obligations, or its interference with such inquiries, raises, in and of itself, inferences of non-compliance.[45] Finally, even if there is a strong State interest in maintaining the secrecy of information that might justify less than full transparency, 'the difficulties that this causes should be counterbalanced' in a way that allows legal interests to be effectively defended.[46]

The right to truth does not specifically prescribe the exact scope of any specific mode of inquiry but only that the product of such inquiry satisfy international standards of truth in order to enable accountability. The right to truth, therefore, does not give IAEA inspectors access to places that safeguards might deny, but it posits that negative inferences may be drawn from constraints on investigations, especially if constraints are not accompanied by alternative modes of inquiry. This is, of course, precisely consistent with an IAEA determination that it is unable to confirm a State's compliance with its non-proliferation obligations.

11.3.4 Summary

If the IAEA Board of Governors determines that significant questions of compliance remain unaddressed, it can report such questions to the Security Council. The question of State non-compliance here is not a trial, and the burden is not on the IAEA to prove non-compliance. More appropriate is to observe that no State has the legal authority to review an IAEA determination that it lacks sufficient information to verify compliance. The relevant legal question, therefore, is whether the IAEA has legal authority to determine that, absent access called for by the AP, a State party may be identified as unable to confirm compliance. So framed, the question scarcely deserves debate.

[45]Ibid., paras 490–491.

[46]Ibid., para 492.

11.4 The Security Council's Authority to Enforce Compliance with Nuclear Non-Proliferation Verification Requirements

The international order must be a coercive order.[47] In our international order, coercion is the province of the United Nations Security Council pursuant to Chapter VII of the Charter. With regard to all weapons of mass destruction (nuclear, biological, chemical), the ultimate success of the non-proliferation commitment depends on how effectively the Security Council compels non-complying States to hew their behaviour to international norms. These judgments are not subject to judicial scrutiny, of course, and the facts identified by verification, and the analyses of those facts, are not evidence in a trial. Verification is, conceptually and in fact, separate from enforcement in the international legal system. Yet, verification can add legitimacy to Security Council actions by establishing the factual foundation for enforcement measures.

It may be readily conceded that questions of *enforceability* plague all of international law, but the question here can be confined specifically to resolving doubts about compliance with nuclear non-proliferation obligations and initiating enforcement measures when those doubts are not adequately resolved. As earlier mentioned, while a verification system can and should be designed to reinforce assurance in the Parties' mutual compliance, such a system can be successful only to the extent that it enables collective security mechanisms to compel compliance of recalcitrant States.

11.4.1 The International Legal Standard of 'Objectively Justifiable'

This discussion begins with the question, recently answered by the International Court of Justice, of how an allegation of non-compliance with an international legal obligation should be judged. In *Australia v. Japan*,[48] the ICJ considered the legality of Japan's permits for whaling, purportedly issued pursuant to the International Whaling Convention's Article VII exception for whale hunting 'for scientific purposes'. The case is important from an international law perspective, raising an issue of breach of a treaty that explicitly imposes obligations on States with regard to prevention of harm to the international commons as distinct from breach of an obligation that States may owe each other *inter se*.

Japan neither denied authorizing whale hunting nor contended that its hunting would be lawful absent the scientific purposes exception. Japan explained that it

---

[47] Kelsen 1944.

[48] *Whaling in the Antarctic* (*Australia v. Japan: New Zealand Intervening*), Judgment (31 March 2014).

initiated permitting of whale hunting because 'the justification for the moratorium was that data on whale stocks was inadequate to manage commercial whaling properly' and it was therefore 'best to start the research program as soon as possible'.[49] Overall, the litigating States disagreed whether Japan's permitting of whaling made a scientific contribution to the conservation and management of whales.

Japan based its defense on the grounds that it, Japan, had sole legal authority to determine if its whale hunting program complied with the treaty's obligations, notably with the exception for hunting for scientific purposes. Japan argued that the criteria for judging its non-compliance should be limited 'to ascertaining whether the determination (issuance of such permits) was "arbitrary or capricious", "manifestly unreasonable" or made in bad faith'. Japan also stressed that matters of scientific policy cannot be properly appraised by the Court. The role of the Court, argued Japan, is 'to secure the integrity of the process by which the decision is made, but not to review the decision itself'.[50]

The ICJ's response to this argument deserves careful consideration. The standard of judging non-compliance, said the Court, was whether a State's actions were objectively justifiable. That is, with regard to whether Japan's issuance of permits complied with the Convention, the Court exercising its international authority, not the State, must make such a determination on the basis of 'objective justifiability'. Not only is the authority to judge non-compliance pursuant to the standard of objective justifiability vested at the international level, but the burden is on the State 'to explain the objective basis for its determination'. As Japan did not, in the Court's view, bear its burden, it was found to be in non-compliance with its obligations. The ICJ enjoined operation of Japan's whaling program, ordering Japan to revoke any authorization to kill, take or treat whales and refrain from granting any further permits.[51]

To return to the topic of nuclear non-proliferation, the Security Council, as already mentioned, is not at all the juridical equivalent of the ICJ, and a complaint of breach brought by a State is not at all the juridical equivalent of an IAEA determination (discussed below) in the face of State-imposed restrictions on access that it cannot verify compliance. Yet, in both contexts, the standard of *objectively justifiable* is essentially identical. It scarcely bears mention that mechanisms of verification in weapons control regimes, especially the nuclear non-proliferation regime, are designed to enable determinations of fact that are objectively justifiable.

This core notion of international law that the State bears the burden of establishing the objective justifiability of its compliance is foundational here. In any dispute, the State must have ample opportunity to explain why, objectively, its behaviour satisfied its obligations, but that explanation is itself subject to objective review. In the context of an international regime's pursuit of a global goal, no

[49]Ibid., para 102.

[50]Ibid., para 65.

[51]Ibid., para 245.

State may be permitted to rationalize its behaviour as if non-compliance with treaty obligations is to be judged at the State level. The ICJ has made clear in this regard, 'objective' means 'international'. Accordingly, non-compliance is the legal condition of a State not being able (or willing) to objectively justify its behaviour as being in satisfaction of its international obligations.

11.4.2 Enforcement, Viewed Comparatively

Problems of non-compliance arise when a State eludes, or is perceived to elude, verification. As mentioned, no verification system can force access for inspectors if a State denies it, for whatever reason. But a verification system can stipulate the predicates of a finding of compliance such that, absent those predicates, the inspecting agency (the IAEA in the NPT context) may rest its conclusion of 'inability to confirm compliance' and thereby initiate enforcement actions.

This section compares the nuclear non-proliferation enforcement scheme with the Chemical Weapons Convention's enforcement scheme. It is very notable that the role of verification in the enforcement of nuclear non-proliferation obligations is slightly different than its role in enforcement of chemical non-proliferation obligations (and altogether incomparable to anything relevant in the biological weapons context).

11.4.2.1 Nuclear Non-Proliferation Enforcement

Under the IAEA's Statute, safeguards inspectors have the responsibility of determining whether a State is in compliance with its safeguards agreement. An assessment of 'completeness' is a condition *sine qua non* of a safeguards conclusion that all of a State's nuclear material has been placed under safeguards and remains in peaceful nuclear activities or has otherwise been accounted for.

If a State refuses to grant access to the IAEA for the purpose of carrying out safeguards, the inspectors must so report to the IAEA's Board of Governors which can 'call upon' the State to take required action (i.e. agree to grant access) without delay.[52] As verification obligations are essential to the nuclear non-proliferation imperative, the IAEA Board has legal authority to not confirm that there has been no diversion due to the State's refusal to consent to inspections without providing IAEA-acceptable alternative proof of compliance. If the State refuses to 'take fully corrective action within a reasonable time, the IAEA Board of Governors may: (1) curtail or suspend assistance being provided by the IAEA or by another State Party and call for the return of material and equipment made available to the State Party

[52] INFCIRC/153, para 18.

in non-compliance, or (2) suspend the non-complying State Party from the exercise of the privileges and rights of membership in the IAEA Statute.[53]

In addition to the findings of declarations and on-site verification activities, the evaluation process should consider information from open and other sources, including information from internal IAEA collections of scientific and technical literature, news media (including news service data bases), country-specific websites and commercial satellite imagery. Such information can shed light on safeguards-related concerns such as research into sensitive technologies, details about source and nuclear material production, location data, imports and exports of dual-use or single-use technologies applicable to the nuclear fuel cycle.[54] Moreover, the IAEA has developed its own capabilities for in-depth analysis and evaluation of nuclear trade activities on a global scale. These capabilities involve techniques to enhance the collection and analysis of information about supply and procurement of critical nuclear items and investigation of covert nuclear trade networks with a view to assessing whether these networks are supporting undeclared nuclear activities.[55]

Ultimately, the IAEA Board shall report a State's non-compliance to the Security Council.[56] The IAEA Statute and comprehensive safeguards agreements set out the circumstances in which a non-compliance finding should be reached and reported to the Security Council.[57] The IAEA must ensure that this is done in a timely way. Thus, the IAEA's members do not explicitly pass judgment on another State's compliance, leaving such questions to the purview of the Security Council.

11.4.2.2 Chemical Weapons Non-Proliferation Enforcement

The CWC enforcement scheme is broadly similar to nuclear non-proliferation enforcement. Like the IAEA, the OPCW is authorized to identify and take into consider information outside or beyond the information generated by declarations and inspections.[58] In some respects, the CWC verification scheme is even more intrusive than its nuclear predecessor. The scope of access question was addressed more clearly in the CWC than in the NPT, and the CWC specifies a system of challenge inspections although it denies authority to the Executive Council to demand a challenge inspection.

---

[53]IAEA Statute, Article XII(c).

[54]Statute of the IAEA, Article XII(c). Whether the IAEA *must* so report to the Security Council or *may* so report has been the subject of active debate.

[55]Idem.

[56]Idem.

[57]The Statute provides that: '... if in connexion with the activities of the Agency there should arise questions that are within the competence of the Security Council, the Agency shall notify the Security Council, as the organ bearing the main responsibility for the maintenance of international peace and security'.

[58]See generally Gualtieri and Kellman 1995.

In cases where the Executive Council has requested that a State Party redress a situation and the State Party has failed to do so within the specified time, the Conference of States Parties (Conference) may restrict or suspend a State Party's rights and privileges under the CWC until it confirms to its obligations. The CWC does not specify possible sanctions for violations of specific obligations, giving flexibility to the Conference to react as it deems appropriate in a specific case.

Where the State Party's action threatens the Convention's object and purpose, collective measures may be recommended, including withholding from the malefactor any relevant exports of chemicals, technical equipment and scientific-technical know-how. A State Party may not be deprived of its membership, however.[59] In the end, the Conference may bring cases of particular gravity to the United Nations, which can respond in any way authorized by the Charter.[60]

Like enforcement of nuclear non-proliferation, the CWC enforcement scheme begins with the possibility of a State Party refusing inspectors' access and ends with the matter being transferred to the Security Council. But, in between, there are differences of note. The CWC does not contemplate a body with comparable powers to the IAEA's Board of Governors, a reflection of the earlier mentioned fact that the IAEA (in contrast to the OPCW) was not established by the NPT but received authority by the NPT's entry into force. In the CWC context, the OPCW Conference has a more substantial role than the IAEA Conference, reflecting the CWC-negotiators' preference for a level of political decision-making short of the United Nations. The fact that, technically, the OPCW is not part of the United Nations system (unlike the IAEA) reinforces the political significance of the OPCW Conference.

11.4.3 The Security Council's Authority to Target Sanctions

The separation between the IAEA's authority to verify compliance from the Security Council's authority to assess non-compliance is a hallmark of the international nuclear weapons non-proliferation regime. Thus, while State compliance with safeguards agreements is a key factor in determining whether a State is satisfying its non-proliferation obligations, determinations of non-compliance with the NPT are not directly the province of the IAEA but belong to the Security Council whose principal role is to address threats to international peace and security. The Security Council's role in addressing a State's non-compliance with non-proliferation obligations underscores the depth of international concern about the issue.

The Security Council has long considered nuclear weapons proliferation to be a threat to international peace and security and the duty to not proliferate nuclear weapons is an obligation owed broadly by States to the international community. Under Article 41 of the Charter, the Security Council is empowered to undertake

[59] See Gualtieri and Kellman 1995, p. 1051.

[60] CWC, Aricles XII, VIII paras 2, 36; Krutzsch and Trapp 1994, pp. 218–228.

coercive measures not involving the use of force as may be necessary to prevent or respond to the spread of nuclear weapons. These measures may involve, *inter alia*, economic sanctions, interruption of communication and a cessation of diplomatic relations.[61] As there can be no judicial review of the Security Council's exercise of its authority,[62] final responsibility for determining the scope of the Security Council's authority is for the Security Council to decide.

The decision of the European Court of Justice in *Kadi and Al Barakaat*[63] deserves careful attention in this context. Two private entities challenged the imposition of restrictive measures against them by the Council of Europe, taken to implement Security Council enforcement measures directed at ensuring that no national or anyone in a State's territory makes available financial resources for the benefit of the Taliban or Al Qaeda. The Security Council instructed the Sanctions Committee to maintain an updated list of sanctioned individuals.

The Court of First Instance (lower court) concluded that Security Council resolutions under Chapter VII are reviewable to assess their lawfulness 'with regard to *jus cogens*'—higher rules of international law binding on all subjects, including the bodies of the United Nations. The Court of First Instance held that the violations of the claimants' rights did not amount to *jus cogens*. The Appellate Panel disagreed as to the reviewability of Security Council resolutions, holding that 'it is not for the Community judicature to review the lawfulness of such a resolution adopted by an international body, even if that review were to be limited to examination of the compatibility of that resolution with jus cogens'.[64]

The Appellate Panel carefully delimited its review to the European Council's implementation of the Security Council's mandate. How members of the United Nations implement that mandate may be reviewed, not the mandate itself.[65] In making such a determination, special importance must be attached

> to the fact that adoption by the Security Council of resolutions under Chapter VII of the Charter constitutes the exercise of the primary responsibility with which that international body is invested for the maintenance of peace and security at the global level, a responsibility which includes the power to determine what and who poses a threat to international peace and security and to take the measures necessary to maintain or restore them.[66]

More specifically, 'the freezing of assets, in and of itself, could not be regarded as inappropriate or disproportionate to the fundamental interest in fighting acts of terrorism'.[67]

---

[61] DiFrancia 2012, p. 710.

[62] See Legal Consequences for States of the Continued Presence of South Africa in Namibia (southwest Africa) notwithstanding Security Council Resolution 276 (1970).

[63] *Kadi and Al Barakaat International Foundation v. Council and Commission,* Case C-402/05 P and C-415/05 [2008] ECR I-6351.

[64] Ibid., para 287.

[65] Ibid., para 298. See Kokott and Sobotta 2012.

[66] Ibid., para 294.

[67] Ibid., para 363.

The problem for the Appellate Panel was the Community's refusal to 'communicate the grounds on which the name of a person or entity is included in its list of restricted measures ... to enable the persons to whom restrictive measures are addressed to defend their rights'.[68] In *Kadi II*, the Court considered the core issue of whether the evidence against the petitioners satisfied minimal standards of effective judicial protection against wrongful confiscation of property. The Court found that the evidence against them was in the sole possession of the Security Council Sanctions Committee or the country which proposed the listing; the summary provided by the Sanctions Committee was adjudged to be insufficiently detailed to sustain the imposition of sanctions as to them.[69] Notably, by the time of *Kadi II*, the Security Council had established the Office of an independent Ombudsperson tasked with processing the requests of individuals or entities to be deleted from the sanctions list. The Ombudsperson had effectively intervened on behalf of a number of subjects of sanctions, including Kadi.[70]

In the context of sanctions to enforce compliance with nuclear non-proliferation obligations, not a word of either *Kadi* decisions would suggest a basis for any tribunal to review the Security Council's authority under Article 41 of the Charter to impose sanctions, and by virtue of Article 48(2) of the Charter, the obligation on all members of the United Nations to carry out such measures. At issue was only the narrower issue of denying basic human rights in connection with implementing sanctions on particular persons or entities. To be more specific, in the *Kadi* case, the issue was most definitely not about the designation of the Taliban and Al Qaeda as terrorist organizations and the targeting of sanctions on these organizations, and no court would seriously entertain the idea that Al Qaeda could challenge the basis for such targeted sanctions. Only at issue was Kadi's right to deny the application of sanctions to him as an alleged supporter of terrorism.

Thus, in the non-proliferation context, the Security Council's imposition of sanctions on a State whose unresolved non-compliance has provoked the Council's attention is not a matter for judicial review on any level, international or national. The decisions in *Kadi* suggests only that an individual or private entity who is alleged to have dealings with the noncompliant sanctioned State should have the opportunity to be confronted by evidence with an opportunity to rebut.

In brief, as nuclear proliferation poses a threat to international peace and security, there should be no question concerning the Security Council's authority to impose enforcement measures to secure non-proliferation commitments. If there is anything *lex lata* in this domain, it should be the Security Council's unreviewable authority to enforce international obligations against States.

---

[68]Ibid., paras 336–337. By not communicating to the appellants the evidence against them, the appellants' rights of defense were not respected, ruled the Appellate Panel. Ibid., para 348.

[69]Ibid., paras 140–142.

[70]Kokott and Sobotta 2012, p. 1020.

11.4.4 Limitations on Enforcement Measures Not Involving the Use of Force

A final question here is whether a State or group of States may legally undertake enforcement measures in excess of what the Security Council may require in a particular case. This is the mirror opposite question of the issue in *Kadi* involving the bindingness of Security Council resolutions. Here the issue is one of implicit preemption: has the Security Council, by undertaking enforcement measures, necessarily occupied this domain such that States would be said to contravene the Security Council by undertaking their own, excessive, enforcement measures? And if the Security Council's measures do not preclude States from undertaking harsher enforcement measures not involving the use of force, does the law of countermeasures prescribe limitations on State enforcement measures?

A distinction deserves to be drawn here between actions outside of the Security Council's Article 41 authority and actions outside its Article 42 authority. With regard to the use of force in a manner not contemplated by a Security Council authorization under Article 42, there may be constraints on what the State(s) may do. But there would seem to be little logic to extend such constraints to measures under Article 41. The ICJ has confirmed that economic measures directed at other States do not violate the customary international principle of non-intervention in the internal or external affairs of a State. Economic measures are not within the ambit of Article 2(4).[71]

More pivotally with regard to sanctions for non-compliance with non-proliferation obligations is the question of whether a State that unilaterally imposes widespread sanctions might violate the international legal prohibition against one State interfering with the foreign relations of another State. The problem was most pronounced two decades ago with a controversy over United States legislation imposing legal consequences on foreign entities doing business with Cuba. The European Union, Canada and others protested that the United States was undertaking a unilateral secondary boycott, using sanctions to interfere with sovereign States' foreign policy and trade policies.[72]

Worth noting here are the contrasts between the dispute over Cuban sanctions and the issue of unilaterally imposed sanctions for nuclear non-proliferation non-compliance in excess of the Security Council's sanctions. First, in the Cuban context, the United States' policy towards Cuba was wholly without support and contrary to the policies of virtually every other State, while in the non-proliferation context the existence of Security Council sanctions against a State manifests a policy

---

[71] *Case Concerning Military and Paramilitary Activities In and Against Nicaragua (Nicaragua v. United States of America); Merits*, International Court of Justice (ICJ), 27 June 1986, *Merits*.

[72] See generally B. Flowe and R. Gold, The Legality of US Sanctions. 2 Global Dialogue, http://www.worlddialogue.org/content.php?id=98; Meyer 2009.

consensus for punishing that State. Second, the controversy over U.S. sanctions on parties doing business with Cuba happened in a strategic environment where imposition of sanctions was a comparatively rare event; in this century, sanctions have been much more widely used to isolate, pressure and punish behaviour deemed to be starkly, and potentially violently, contrary to the interests of international peace and security.

To come to the core point, the international nuclear non-proliferation regime is humanity's most sophisticated manifestation of pursuit of international peace and security through a dual-level collective security apparatus that enables enforcement both under the Security Council's authority and outside of it. This proposition inheres from nearly seven decades of sanctions practice. The long-standing and often repeated nature of such practice stands in sharp contrast to the complete absence of any legal claim ever successfully litigated against any sanction-imposing State. Adding further support to the conclusion that such sanctions do not contravene the Security Council's authority is that the Security Council, when determining and imposing enforcement measures, has not specified that sanctions in excess of what it imposes are disallowed.

Some experts have called for further elaboration of the international law of countermeasures pertaining to collective nonviolent interventions, including sanctions and controlled disruption.[73] Not only is the topic outside the scope of this chapter, the sheer pace of activity may prove a challenge to any scholarly effort to address it. In this writer's view, the question of whether a State may undertake enforcement measures that do not involve the use of force in connection with non-compliance with nuclear non-proliferation obligations but in excess of measures imposed by the Security Council is a question not at all appropriately viewed as governed by the law of countermeasures. The non-compliance concerns that prompt such excessive sanctions are an enforcement challenge for the entire international community, and the Security Council's imposition of sanctions should therefore be seen as a floor, not a ceiling, on what States may do, short of the use of force, to compel compliance.

It may be, perhaps, that particular sanctions contravene trade conventions or some aspect of international regulatory law, in which case, the sanctioning State may be legally bound to constrain its sanctions. It is entirely fair to suggest, therefore, that enforcement measures against nuclear weapons proliferation should be judged pursuant to all relevant international regulations. Yet, absent any such regulatory prohibitions or injunctions, the law of countermeasures, developed long ago and never seriously designed to address threats to international peace and security especially in the nuclear weapons era, is inapposite to the question of sanctions to enforce compliance with non-proliferation obligations.

[73] DiFrancia 2012.

11.5 Conclusion

In the virtually anarchic post-WW II strategic environment threatened by nuclear holocaust, systems of legal obligations, some more or less binding, were put into place to diminish risks of ever again using nuclear weapons and to curtail the vast allocation of blood and treasure attendant to living with nuclear weapons. The set of legal obligations that comprise the nuclear non-proliferation commitment were without precedent or guarantee of efficacy. These obligations emerged in response to conditions of diplomatic distrust, differentiated technological capabilities and to the very real political imperative of doing what, realistically, could be done at particular moments in history.

Verification of non-proliferation and other weapons control obligations is an important pillar of modern international peace and security. In the context of nuclear weapons non-proliferation, verification mechanisms have become the measure of amicable intentions—the substitute for arms escalation and deterrence by mutual terror.

Looking backward, the nuclear non-proliferation commitment is humanity's longest-standing and most deeply cherished legal regime for governing weapons—one of humanity's greatest unfinished accomplishments. Looking forward, important questions loom concerning the authority of the international system to compel all States to comply with their obligations concerning nuclear weapons. At this time, appreciating the legal role of verification in sustaining the strength of the nuclear non-proliferation commitment is imperative.

References

Asada M (2011) The treaty on the non-proliferation of nuclear weapons and the universalization of the additional protocol. J Confl Secur L 16:3

Avenhaus R, Kyriakopoulos N (2006) Conceptual framework. In: Avenhaus R et al. (eds) Verifying treaty compliance. Springer, pp 13–37

Cooley JN (2006) International atomic energy agency safeguards under the treaty on the non-proliferation of nuclear weapons: challenges in implementation. In: Avenhaus R et al. (eds) Verifying treaty compliance. Springer, pp 61–76

DeFrancia C (2012) Enforcing the nuclear non-proliferation regime: the legality of preventive measures. Vand J Trans L 45:705

Groome D (2011) The right to truth in the fight against impunity. Berkeley J Int L 29:175

Gualtieri D, Kellman B (1995) Advancing the law of weapons control—comparative approaches to strengthen nuclear non-proliferation. Mich J Int L 16:1029

Kellman B (1994) Bridling the international trade of catastrophic weaponry. Amer U L R 43:755

Kellman B (1996) Barricading the nuclear window a legal regime to curtail nuclear smuggling. U Ill L Rev 667

Kellman B (2000) Protection of nuclear materials. In: Shelton D (ed), Commitment and compliance: the role of non-binding norms in the international legal system. Oxford University Press, pp 486–505

Kellman B (2007) Bioviolence—preventing biological terror and crime. Cambridge University Press

Kellman B et al (1995) Disarmament and disclosure: how arms control verification can proceed without threatening confidential business information. Harv Int L J 36:71

Kelsen H (1944) Peace through law. Lawbook Exchange Ltd, London

Kokott J, Sobotta C (2012) The Kadi case—constitutional core values and international law—finding the balance? Eur J Int L 23:1015

Krutzsch W, Trapp R (1994) A commentary on the chemical weapons convention. Martinus Nijhoff, Dordrecht

Meyer JA (2009) Second thoughts on secondary sanctions. U Pa J Int L 30:905

Otuka N et al (2014) Towards a more complete and accurate experimental nuclear reaction data library (EXFOR): international collaboration between nuclear reaction data centres (NRDC). Nucl Data Sheets 120:272–276

Scheinman L (1992) Nuclear safeguards and non-proliferation in a changing world order. Security Dialogue 23:39

Schelling TC (1966) Arms and influence. Yale University Press

Staasz PC, et al (1973) International atomic energy safeguards. In: Willrich M (ed) International safeguards and nuclear industry. The Johns Hopkins University Press, p 95

Van de Graaf T, Lesage D (2009) The international energy agency after 35 years: reform needs and institutional adaptability. Rev Int Orgs 4:293–317

Wang Q et al (2011) Remaking the international atomic energy agency. Environ Sci Technol 42:587

Chapter 12
Best Practice Guidelines for Cooperative Compliance with Nuclear Non-Proliferation Obligations

Ilaria Anna Colussi and Maurizio Martellini

Abstract The fundamental role of the law governing nuclear technologies and nuclear weapons is clear and unambiguous. The law seeks to regulate existing nuclear activities, or—at a preliminary stage—to (try to) prevent and govern the risks arising from the misuse of nuclear technologies, or to tackle the problem of nuclear proliferation. However, on many occasions, it appears that the law is inefficient in dealing with these issues. Thus, this paper proposes some 'best practice' legal ways as a guide to help build nuclear compliance and cooperation at a global level. The analysis starts from the focus on the Treaty on Nuclear Non-Proliferation (NPT), highlighting the content of Article VI as judicially interpreted by the International Court of Justice, and examining the gaps and limits within the NPT framework. Then in the context of 'verification, compliance and enforcement', the paper concentrates on some methods and mechanisms that have been established at the international law level, with the aim of ensuring compliance with international rules. As a useful comparison and source of inspiration for the non-proliferation field, links have been drawn with verification and compliance procedures in respect of environmental law and trade law. On the basis of such comparison, a set of guidelines for enhancing cooperative compliance in

Ilaria Anna Colussi—Lawyer, PhD, Post doctoral fellow, Faculty of Law, Political Science and Criminology, Department of Political Science, European Studies Unit, University of Liège (ULg), Belgium.

Maurizio Martellini—Professor of Physics, Insubria Center on International Security (ICIS), Como, Italy.

I.A. Colussi (✉)
Faculty of Law, Political Science and Criminology, Department of Political Science, European Studies Unit, University of Liège (ULg), Quartier Agora, Place des Orateurs n. 3, 4000 Liège, Belgium
e-mail: ilariaanna.colussi@gmail.com

M. Martellini (✉)
Insubria Center on International Security (ICIS), via Natta, n. 14, 22100 Como, Italy
e-mail: maurizio.martellini@uninsubria.it

J.L. Black-Branch and D. Fleck (eds.), *Nuclear Non-Proliferation in International Law - Volume II*, DOI 10.1007/978-94-6265-075-6_12

the nuclear field is proposed. Aspects of particular importance are: (a) to collect and monitor the data; (b) to reinforce the structure and action of the International Atomic Energy Agency (IAEA); (c) to involve other UN bodies, of States and civil society and (d) to follow the principles of (i) the rule of law, (ii) impartiality and non-discrimination, (iii) transparency and (iv) responsibility.

Keywords Civil society · Compliance · Enforcement · International Atomic Energy Agency (IAEA) · Rule of law, impartiality · Non-discrimination, nuclear non-proliferation · Transparency, responsibility · Treaty on Non-Proliferation of Nuclear Weapons (NPT) · Verification

Contents

12.1 Introduction: The Role of the Law in Relation to Nuclear Non-Proliferation

The discovery of the structure of atoms and of their potential in terms of the uses of radiation and production of energy represents one of the most significant developments by mankind.[1] However, nuclear sciences and technologies can have a dual use[2]: on the one hand they can be used for both civilian and military pur-

[1]See the discovery of radioactivity by Henri Becquerel and the studies conducted by Pierre and Marie Curie. For deepening the history of nuclear science and technology, see http://www.world-nuclear.org/info/Current-and-Future-Generation/Outline-History-of-NUclear-Energy/.

[2]See Miller and Sagan 2009, pp. 7–18.

poses, for medical applications (e.g. medical radiography or radiopharmaceuticals) or for industrial and commercial applications or in agriculture for food radiation, whilst on the other, for the production of nuclear weapons.

Nuclear weapons are one of the most destructive weapons of mass destruction, whose use would lead to indiscriminate deaths and, arguably, even the survival of the human race. On the one hand, if nuclear weapons are used by one State against another, they would risk determining a world of 'nuclear armed anarchy'.[3] On the other hand, if they were handled by terrorists, they could subvert the legal and political foundations of liberal democracy. Therefore, nuclear proliferation poses a severe threat to the international community.

The role of the law in respect of nuclear technologies and nuclear weapons is therefore crucial and meaningful. The law is a means to regulate existing nuclear activities, or—at a preliminary stage—to (try to) govern the risks arising from the misuse of nuclear technologies, or prevent the occurrence of negative events linked to nuclear technologies. In respect of nuclear weapons, the law could also tackle the problem of nuclear proliferation.

However, on many occasions, it appears that the law is inefficient to deal with these issues, and the rules do not seem to work. In a provocative way, Michael Waltzer in *Just and Unjust Wars*, affirms that 'the lawyers have constructed a paper world, which fails at crucial points to correspond to the world the rest of us still live in',[4] so that the law is not effective, and it looks like a pure theory, which is useless when faced with reality. This occurs because of the absence of a clear consensus around rules, the lack of trust and lack of compliance.

Thus, the role of law in the relationship with nuclear non-proliferation needs to be restored, as well as a usable analysis about the ways that need to be followed in order to build relevant nuclear compliance and cooperation at a global level. In this regard, the words expressed by Moxley, Burroughs and Granoff should be kept in mind:

> Law is a means of controlling, directing, and constraining potential actions. If law as an institution is to have international relevance, it must apply to critical issues. The survival of humanity depends on how threats posed by nuclear weapons are addressed. Science, in the service of excessive military means of pursuing peace and security, has placed civilization at risk. Law has a duty to control this risk.[5]

12.2 The Treaty on Non-Proliferation of Nuclear Weapons (NPT) and Its Gaps

The notion of 'non-proliferation' refers to: (a) containment of the number of States that possess nuclear weapons or the control of non-State actors, such as terrorists, who can use such weapons (horizontal non-proliferation), and (b) reduction of the

[3] Cooper 2003, p. 63.

[4] Walzer 2006, p. xxi.

[5] Moxley Jr. et al. 2001, p. 596.

number of existing arsenals both qualitatively and quantitatively (disarm or vertical non-proliferation).[6]

At the international law level, no provisions exist regarding vertical non-proliferation, only bilateral or multilateral agreements, which ban weapons of mass destruction in certain areas. These include the Treaty on the prohibition of proofs of nuclear weapons in the atmosphere and submarine territories (Moscow 1963);[7] the Treaty on the use of nuclear weapons in the depth of sea and ocean (Washington, London, Moscow 1971);[8] and the Agreements which establish the zones of atomic exclusion (e.g. 1968 Tlatelolco Treaty,[9] 1985 Raratonga Treaty,[10] 1995 South-Eastern Asia Treaty,[11] and the 1996 Pelindaba Treaty[12]).

With respect to horizontal non-proliferation, instead, the issue has mainly been dealt with by the International Treaty on the Non-Proliferation of Nuclear Weapons (NPT), which was signed in 1968,[13] and entered into force in 1970. The Treaty aims at preventing the spread of nuclear weapons and weapons technology, and promoting cooperation in the peaceful uses of nuclear energy, thereby seeking to achieve complete nuclear disarmament.

12.2.1 The NPT and Its Legal Principles and Rules

The Treaty provides a comprehensive legal structure of rights and duties designed to protect humanity from nuclear aggression.[14] It tries to regulate nuclear energy both from the perspective of its civil uses, and from its potential use in weapons.

---

[6]R. Alcaro, Il regime di non proliferazione nucleare. Obiettivi, struttura e fattori di rischio. In Studi e Ricerche del Servizio Affari Internazionali del Senato della Repubblica Italiana, N. 66, 2007, Roma, p. 5.

[7]The Limited Test Ban Treaty was adopted on 5 August 1963 and entered into force on 10 October 1963.

[8]The Treaty on the Prohibition of the Emplacement of Nuclear Weapons and Other Weapons of Mass Destruction on the Seabed and Ocean Floor and in the Subsoil Thereof (Seabed Treaty) was adopted on 11 February 1971 and entered into force on 18 May 1972.

[9]The Treaty of Tlatelolco is the conventional name given to the Treaty for the Prohibition of Nuclear Weapons in Latin America and the Caribbean. It was adopted on 14 February 1967 and entered into force on 22 April 1968.

[10]The Treaty of Rarotonga is the common name for the South Pacific Nuclear Free Zone Treaty. It was adopted on 6 August 1985.

[11]The Treaty of Bangkok is the common name for the Treaty on the Southeast Asia Nuclear-Weapon-Free Zone. It was adopted on 15 December 1995 and entered into force on 27 March 1997.

[12]The Treaty of Pelindaba is the common name for the African Nuclear-Weapon-Free Zone Treaty. It was adopted on 11 April 1996, but is not entered into force yet.

[13]The Treaty on the Non-Proliferation of Nuclear Weapons (NPT) was opened for signature in 1968, and entered into force in 1970. On 11 May 1995, the Treaty was extended indefinitely.

[14]See Simpson and Ogilvie-White 2003.

Whilst not explicit, the Treaty is widely acknowledged to be based on three pillars, each equally important and equally significant.[15] They are the principles of 'peaceful use, disarmament, and non-proliferation'.

Instead of embracing the idea of combining deterrence and counter proliferation, such as suggested by the present international security environment, the treaty sought to break new ground by seeking universal abolition of nuclear weapons under international supervision, whilst working meanwhile for the strengthening of legal mechanisms for the development of international security.

12.2.2 Article VI and Its Judicial Interpretation

Among the provisions of the Treaty, Article VI places the focus on nuclear disarmament. Its purpose and meaning were shaped by the International Court of Justice in its well-known 1996 Advisory Opinion,[16] released in response to the United Nations General Assembly's question: 'Is the threat or use of nuclear weapons permitted in any circumstance under international law?' The Court affirmed that 'the threat or use of nuclear weapons would generally be contrary to the rules of international law applicable to armed conflict, and in particular the principles and rules of humanitarian law', but could not 'conclude definitely whether the threat or use of nuclear weapons would be lawful or unlawful in an extreme circumstance of self-defense, in which the very survival of a State would be at stake'.[17]

In particular, with reference to Article VI of the NPT, the Court pointed out that the Article entailed both an obligation of conduct and of result upon States: the conduct should consist of pursuing negotiations towards disarmament in good faith, and the result consists of achieving nuclear disarmament in all its aspects. Indeed, the Court unanimously ruled:

> There exists an obligation to pursue in good faith and bring to a conclusion negotiations leading to nuclear disarmament in all its aspects under strict and effective international control.[18]

Thus, the treaty provisions seem literally clear.[19]

---

[15]At this regard, see Joyner 2011.

[16]International Court of Justice (ICJ), Advisory Opinion. Legality of the Threat or Use of Nuclear Weapons, ICJ Rep. 1996, 226–267. July 8 1996, http://www.icj-cij.org/docket/files/95/7495.pdf.

[17]ICJ, Advisory Opinion, here 266. It can be observed that Judge Shahabuddeen of Guyana, Judge Weeramantry of Sri Lanka, and Judge Koroma of Sierra Leone wrote separate opinions, explaining that the reason they were dissenting was their view that there is no exception under any circumstances (including that of ensuring the survival of a State) to the general principle that use of nuclear weapons is illegal. Vice President Schwebel remarked in his dissenting opinion that it could never be accepted that the use of nuclear weapons could be lawful.

[18]ICJ, Advisory Opinion, here 262.

[19]See Rietker 2014, pp. 47–84.

12.2.3 The Gaps and Limits of the NPT

The treaty is widely accepted as an historical compromise between States, reached during the Cold War, when the world was in fear of nuclear weapons. On the one hand the NNWS renounced any intention to develop nuclear weapons, or seek to acquire or develop nuclear technologies for weapons purposes, whilst the NWS agreed to take steps towards disarmament, and not to transfer nuclear weapons to NNWS. NWS also agreed to assist NNWS in the provision of nuclear technology for peaceful purposes. However, the perception of the international community was that NWS made no progress on implementing their side of the agreement, and gave greater emphasis on counter proliferation policies rather than disarmament efforts that would prevent proliferation.

The road towards nuclear disarmament is still a long one, and the fear of proliferation remains real. For this reason it is evident that the implementation of this Treaty and full compliance with its provisions will always be difficult to obtain.

In 1995, the NPT was prolonged indefinitely and, on that occasion, the principles and purposes of non-proliferation were explicitly stated. Moreover, during the Review Conference in 2000,[20] the main practical steps to be followed were also provided. Meanwhile, many worrying elements arose. These included (a) new international actors trying to legitimize their military nuclear status (India and Pakistan); (b) ambiguous actors such as Israel; (c) the detonation of nuclear explosive devices in North Korea and (d) new threats after 09/11.

When parties to the NPT met again in May 2010, they reaffirmed 'the need for all States at all times to comply with applicable international law, including international humanitarian law'.[21] It should be noted that there is still a gap between NNWS and NWS (the United States, Russia, China, France and the United Kingdom). The limits of the NPT have been convincingly highlighted as follows:[22]

- universal membership is missing: not all States are members of the Treaty;
- the International Atomic Energy Agency (IAEA), which is called upon for the supervision and inspection of the compliance of the Treaty, seems not always able to perform its role in an effective way: indeed, the IAEA verifies only the peaceful nature of atomic programs developed by Non-Nuclear States (Article III) through bilateral agreements known as Comprehensive Safeguards that aim at preventing the transformation of civil nuclear activities to military ones. An Additional Protocol (AP) to a State's Safeguards Agreement with the IAEA, allows the IAEA, in those States that have signed one, to conduct challenge inspections, to

---

[20]See at http://www.un.org/disarmament/WMD/Nuclear/2000-NPT/2000NPT.shtml.

[21]2010 Review Conference of the Parties to the Treaty on the Non-Proliferation of Nuclear Weapons, May 3–28, 2010, Final Document, pts. 1, 19, UN Doc. NPT/CONF.2010/50 (Vol. 1) (2010).

[22]R. Alcaro, Il regime di non proliferazione nucleare. Obiettivi, struttura e fattori di rischio. In Studi e Ricerche del Servizio Affari Internazionali del Senato della Repubblica Italiana, N. 66, 2007, Roma, p. 10.

take samples from the sites and enlarge its investigations even to places where the presence of fissile material has not been declared. However, the adherence to such Additional Protocol is not compulsory and left to the States' will.

- the lack of 'action mechanisms' in the case of non-compliance or the withdrawal from NPT. The Treaty simply refers to the Security Council for the management of non-compliance, but the latter is weak in this regard. A specific body for the enforcement of sanctions against violations of the Treaty does not exist, although a certain power is conferred to the UN Security Council;[23]
- the Review Conferences, which are organized every 5 years in order to monitor the State of implementation of the NPT, are not meant to modify the Treaty, but simply to discuss its general obligations;
- there is a right of withdrawal from the Treaty (Article X). There is no control measure from IAEA. Even if the UN Security Council has adopted some resolutions against the withdrawing States,[24] there is no legal provision that orders the restitution of the acquired sensitive technologies. However, in practice, States maintain technologies after an exit from the Treaty (as demonstrated by the North Korean case);
- the Treaty suffers from a legitimacy crisis, as it can be changed only through unanimous decisions, which are clearly difficult to achieve.

In general, in the nuclear arena, there is a stalemate in the process of disarmament; the availability of nuclear technologies and materials is growing; the threats of preemptive use of force in response of proliferation of weapons of mass destruction are always present; and there is a resistance in accepting the International Court of Justice's rulings.

A misbalance can be observed between horizontal and vertical non-proliferation, since the insistence on activities of interdiction, control, sanctions and prohibitions is stronger than the insistence on the development of international rules and systems of compliance with the law.

Nuclear weapons policy among NWS is still based on deterrence[25] and more dramatic is still the key role of nuclear weapons in the military doctrines of the

[23]The Security Council has a central role to "ensure prompt and effective action by the United Nations" (Article 24 of the UN Charter). Furthermore, under Article 39, the Security Council is allowed to enact a determination that a situation or action constitutes a threat to international peace and security, and it is authorized to decide under Chapter VII of the UN Charter on measures, including economic and military sanctions, which are binding.

[24]SC Res. 1695 (2006), 1718 (2006), 1874 (2009), 2050 (2012), 2087 (2013), 2094 (2013) against North Korea.

[25]Deterrence theory is based on raising the cost of an adversary's actions to unacceptably high levels through utilizing the threat of nuclear attack to deter an unwanted action Green 2000. Portions of the text are available at http://www.disarmsecure/publications/books.org. As Granoff stated, the moral position of the nuclear weapon states is essentially that the threat to commit an illegal act—massive destruction of innocent people—is legal because it is so horrible to contemplate that it ensures the peace. Thus the argument is that the threat of committing that which is patently illegal is made legal by its own intrinsic illogic. The reliance on the value of the doctrine of nuclear deterrence impedes progress in moving towards the elimination of nuclear weapons' Granoff 2000, p. 1437.

main nuclear powers, namely the US and the Russian Federation, that together hold 95 % of the world's nuclear weapon stockpiles, and also of all other States having nuclear weapons.

So, the NPT has some gaps in the compliance and enforcement areas.

12.3 Methods and Mechanisms of Verification, Compliance and Enforcement at the International Law Level

In general, the notion of 'verification' refers to 'the process of gathering, analyzing and using information to make a judgment about compliance or non-compliance with an agreement'.[26] The notion of 'compliance' refers to a set of methods and mechanisms in order to make the rules be respected by the addressees, taking action on the basis of verification.[27] The notion of 'enforcement' corresponds to the act of compelling observance or compliance with a law, rule, or obligation.[28]

As affirmed by Patricia Lewis, verification, compliance, and enforcement are

> the Golden or Bermuda Triangle of issues. [...]The three issues are intertwined in a perpetual embrace. Without information provided by verification, the determination of compliance or non-compliance of nuclear disarmament treaties will rest solely in the hands of a few (one? two? three?) national intelligence agencies – and the consequences of that approach are still fresh [...]. Without law, without impartial evidence, there can be no chance of enforcement. And without enforcement, the whole web of verification deterrence against the spectrum of possible infringement would have little meaning and the rule of law would be undermined.[29]

As known, the international community is a system of States competing within an anarchic international environment, where no overarching authority exists and where the goal of every State is to maximize its relative power in order to survive. International law does not have an international police force, and international bodies do not possess ultimate sanction authority to issue and enforce decisions. Notwithstanding the existence of the United Nations system and the International Court of Justice, international law is based on States' voluntary commitments to international rules. Enforcement mechanisms that require strict compliance are still lacking, or where they exist they are still weak.

A general principle of international requires that treaties must be observed. It is the so called *pacta sunt servanda* principle, which has been codified in the 1969 Vienna Convention on the Law of Treaties (Article 26). It entails that every treaty in force is binding upon the parties to it and must be carried out by them in good faith. However, this is not always the case, and things are not so simple. In

[26]T. Findlay, The Verification and Compliance Regime for a Nuclear Weapon-Free World. A Role for the UK, VERTIC Briefing Paper 5:1–8.

[27]See Oxford Dictionaries.

[28]See Oxford Dictionaries.

[29]Lewis 2009, pp. 233–234.

the international arena, the verification of adherence to an agreement can occur through:

- declarations by the Parties of the treaty with regard to the respect of the agreement;
- inspections by competent surveillance bodies;
- controls and monitoring;
- diplomatic meetings;
- court adjudications.

Compliance could be undertaken by:

- administrative bodies;
- expert/scientific bodies;
- judicial bodies and
- political bodies.

The subdivision is, however, not rigid and models of compliance can provide the involvement of all these actors.

In the origins of international law, systems were State-centred. Therefore, the mechanisms were self-help based, and each State decided which rights had been violated and how to comply with them. Nowadays, many obligations are *erga omnes*, and the ways of compliance can rely on supranational institutions and/or supranational tribunals as well.

There are two predominant perspectives in the compliance framework. Some scholars[30] think that what is posed in the legal system is law and is automatically binding and should be complied with ('positivist theory'). That scheme entails 'norm/sanction'. The other position is a 'constructivist' one, and it affirms that norms come from social consent and need a shared agreement and cooperation between the addressees or the social members in order to be respected.[31]

Among the duties that the aforementioned actors could be called upon to perform, there are: investigative duties; collection of data and declarations; monitoring; controlling and reviewing functions and action duties (behaviors, enactment of sanction, drafting of declarations, activities of negotiation and mediation, assistance, judicial intervention, etc.).

As regards enforcement, the mechanisms can be classified into positive and negative:[32]

- the positive ones encourage compliance with an agreement by providing rewards or 'incentives';
- the negative ones encourage compliance by threatening (and using) punishments or 'disincentives'.

---

[30]See Ago 1984, p. 385.

[31]Katzenstein et al. 1998, p. 658.

[32]J. Ouellet, Enforcement Mechanisms http://www.beyondintractability.org/essay/enforcement-mechanisms.

Positive incentives can promise monetary, or political or social rewards. One incentive for compliance is also transparency, which includes the sharing of information and publication of data, so as to create trust and the psychological will to comply with agreements. Dispute Resolution Processes are considered enforcement mechanisms as well, since they create space for mediation and allow discussion and revision of unclear aspects of agreements.

Negative enforcement mechanisms are sanctions, reparations, and withdrawal from the Treaty. The sanctions could be social, political or economic. The reparations impose the author of damage to restore the status quo ante, or pay for the damage occurred. Through agreement withdrawal, the parties adhering an agreement are obliged to exit from it.

From the comparison with other systems of compliance in the international arena, positive suggestions could emerge to be applied in the nuclear non-proliferation field.[33]

In particular, compliance in the environmental field and within the World Trade Organization provides useful precedents. The former model has been chosen for its proximity to the non-proliferation mechanisms. Indeed, many bodies and organisms that have been established in the environmental area are similar to the ones adopted in the non-proliferation field. However, following analysis, it emerges that environmental compliance is more effective than that in the non-proliferation arena, and thus the comparison can offer possible streams for the implementation of the existing mechanisms provided by the NPT. The latter model (WTO), instead, has been chosen for its completely different structure in respect to the NPT mechanisms. Using these opposing systems, each grounded on a sort of judicial framework, can help stimulate thoughts about effective mechanisms for the NPT.

12.4 Compliance in the Environmental Field

In the environmental area,[34] compliance mechanisms have recently been established. Indeed, the recognition of the need to protect the environment and the importance of drafting rules for its respect have only really been taken seriously in the last few decades.[35] The environmental scenario is dominated by multilateral agreements. Widely accepted elements for verifying non-compliance are:

[33]See also Dorn and Scott 2000, pp. 229–247.

[34]See W. Lang, Compliance Control in International Environmental Law: Institutional Necessities, Max-Planck-Institut für ausländisches öffentliches Recht und Völkerrecht, http://www.zaoerv.de.

[35]For deepening the issues of compliance in environmental field, see S.A. Hajost and Q.J. Sea, An Overview of Enforcement And Compliance Mechanisms in International Environmental Agreements, www.inece.org/1stvol1/hajost.htm.

- collecting information about the non-compliant Party, through a clearing house[36] that (a) collects and systematizes data; (b) facilitates the sharing of information and exchange of scientific, technical, environmental and legal information on the environmental theme at stake and (c) provides a dynamic platform where information is registered and can be easily searched and retrieved. Information content and management are provided in a timely manner;
- reporting obligations: the Parties to a multilateral environmental agreement may be required by the terms of the agreement to report information on their implementation of the agreement.[37] This helps to identify specific non-compliance by the individual State. Such reporting obligations increase cooperation among States, as has occurred in the fields of air pollution, and nuclear accidents;
- observation, inspections, monitoring,[38] conducted by multilateral environmental agreement bodies in the case of monitoring, or by designated observers or inspectors in the case of observation or inspection. This is a 'top down' control. The experts are nominated by the States. This option is based on the idea that it is considered more useful to have measures that prevent the occurrence of environmental damage, rather than rules governing State liability once environmental damage has already occurred; and/or
- initiating a non-compliance procedure.

When a case of non-compliance is identified, response measures must be taken. One of the most adopted mechanisms is the call for reparation. In case of violation of a norm, the reparation should, as far as possible, erase the consequences of the violation and re-establish the situation as it was before the violation occurred (i.e. the *status quo ante*). If reparation is not possible, another mechanism is the imposition of monetary compensation, i.e. payment for damage created. It should be noted that this measure is not so effective, since it can be difficult to determine (and subjectively to apply any conditions) on monetary damages, and they do not prevent the occurrence of future pollution events. States can find simpler compensation measures that do not imply an active obligation to reduce an activity or to remove the pollution, etc. Other, contrasting, mechanisms to be adopted between States are the ones based on negotiation, conciliation, arbitration and adjudication. In many treaties a 'compromisory clause' is inserted.

---

[36]See the Biosafety Clearing House, which is an international mechanism set up by Cartagena Protocol on Biosafety 2003, Article 20 para 1, in order to ensure the safe handling, transport and use of living modified organisms (LMOs) and assist the Parties to better comply with and implement their obligations under the Cartagena Protocol on Biosafety.

[37]See the Montreal Protocol on Substances that Deplete the Ozone Layer (1987) for reporting obligations. It also requires that parties notify the Secretariat of any allowed transfer of production between parties and of any addition to calculated production levels allowed by the Protocol. The treaty was opened for signature on 16 September 1987, and entered into force on 1 January 1989, followed by a first meeting in Helsinki, in May 1989.

[38]See the Kyoto Protocol, which assigns an important role to the monitoring and emissions inventory reporting requirements, and to expert reviews of parties' reports. This Protocol extends the 1992 United Nations Framework Convention on Climate Change (UNFCCC). It was adopted on 11 December 1997 and entered into force on 16 February 2005.

Through negotiation, the parties directly communicate and bargain with each other in an attempt to agree on a settlement of the issue. Conciliation can be voluntary or compulsory. A conciliation commission can be established in order to make proposals for the resolution of the dispute, which the Parties concerned must consider in good faith. The decisions are thus non-legally binding. With arbitration, the States agree that in case of dispute they will refer the issue to one tribunal ad hoc.[39] Through adjudication, the parties assign the case to the Court of Justice, or some other standing and permanent judicial body, for a binding decision.

Most of the multilateral environmental agreements have dispute settlement provisions. Generally, these provisions tend to be weak as States are often reluctant to accept a legal obligation to submit their environmental disputes to binding dispute settlement systems. With regards to the bodies involved in the compliance mechanisms, it is meaningful to observe that the Montreal Protocol provides the presence of:

- the Secretariat (bureaucratic body): this is in charge of receiving the relevant data from the Parties and incorporating them into sophisticated documents, and of undertaking *ad hoc* investigation if there is a suspicion that a party has not accomplished to its duties;
- the Implementation Committee, which has the function to review and investigate the issues (also through on-site inspections if accepted by the Party to be inspected), and to recommend to the main political organ, the Meeting of the Parties, what measures are adapt in cases of non-compliance;
- the Meeting of the Parties, namely the political body, which is entitled to take measures such as sanctions, or assistance, or issue recommendations or suspend rights and privileges.
- The non-compliance procedure provided by the Montreal Protocol may be initiated by any party to the Protocol that suspects another party of non-compliance; by the Secretariat, or through self-reporting.

The Kyoto Protocol provides a compliance body,[40] which is aimed at resolving all the compliance questions relating to parties' emission target-related commitments. In case of non-compliance, the consequences are the suspension of eligibility or the deduction of excess emissions.[41]

In conclusion, it appears that in the environmental area, there is a good combination of both institutions or "top down" bodies, and expert groups, NGOs and business groups. They all play a role in the compliance process. Different

[39]See, for instance, the 1969 International Convention Relating to Intervention on the High Seas in Cases of Oil Pollution Casualties (Article VIII) and its 1973 Protocol Relating to Intervention on the High Seas in Cases of Marine Pollution by Substances other than Oil.

[40]The Kyoto Protocol extends the 1992 United Nations Framework Convention on Climate Change (UNFCCC). It was adopted on 11 December 1997 and entered into force on 16 February 2005. Here see II 2.

[41]See Brunnée 2006.

mechanisms of compliance are also adopted, even if dispute resolution mechanisms are largely employed on a State-to-State basis rather than as part of an institutional process.

12.4.1 Comparison Between Environmental Mechanisms of Compliance and the NPT

Trying to delineate a comparison between the NPT system and environmental mechanisms of compliance, it emerges that the environmental system is stronger than the one provided by the NPT. The latter employs trained professionals to conduct on-site inspections of States' nuclear facilities and materials. These inspections are part of what is known as 'safeguards', and they take place under the auspices of the International Atomic Energy Agency (IAEA). The IAEA, thus, works as a central body that collects information given by States or requested, where admitted, at its own initiative, and it also undertakes inspections and safeguards activities (as verification mechanisms), in order to ensure that fissionable materials, services, equipment, facilities and information are not used for military purposes. The IAEA, thus, assist States in their efforts to prevent the further spread of nuclear weapons and to prevent, detect and respond to illicit uses of nuclear material. This system functions not only as a confidence building measure, but also as an early warning mechanism.

It should be noted that Safeguards may also apply to bilateral or multilateral agreements between countries. So, multilateral agreements are promoted in the non-proliferation field in the same way that they are in the environmental arena.

A certain similarity can be noted between the Secretariat and the Meeting of the Parties provided by the Montreal Protocol, on the one hand, and the IAEA's Secretariat and the Board of Governors, on the other. The Secretariats have a 'technical' function to collect and receive data, and undertake investigations, while the Meeting of the Parties or the Board of Governors has a 'political' role, which consists of taking the relevant decisions, on the basis of the collected data. However, notwithstanding the similar bodies, it could be observed that the environmental mechanisms appear stronger than those adopted in the non-proliferation system. Political bodies in the environmental area have more 'intrusive' powers; they can opt for compensation, sanctions and suspension of rights. Moreover, the Dispute settlement bodies are entitled to release binding decisions in cases of non-compliance with environmental duties. These mechanisms are still lacking for compliance with the NPT. Indeed, attempts to strengthen the IAEA through the enactment of Additional Protocols—that, as we are going to show later on in more detail, require States parties to report on all aspects of its nuclear fuel cycle. While an Additional Protocol allows for short-notice inspections to all facilities on a nuclear site and access to other nuclear-related sites, signature of an AP is still voluntary and not universal.

12.5 The WTO Compliance System

The World Trade Organization (WTO) is the heir to the General Agreement on Tariffs and Trade (GATT) agreement, signed in 1947.[42] The WTO agreement was signed in Marrakesh in 1994.[43] Unlike many other international organizations, WTO members are subject to a dispute settlement system (DSS), disciplined by the Understanding on Rules and Procedures Governing the Settlement of Disputes (DSU). The system is generally binding. However, the WTO authorizes countermeasures to be taken by individual States.

The dispute settlement mechanism consists of Panels (they can be interpreted as 'courts' of first instance in the national legal system), and a standing Appellate Body. The Panels issue reports with findings and recommendations on a dispute, which is followed by an appeal process, if this is desired. In order to obtain legal status these reports also have to be adopted by the WTO's Dispute Settlement Body (DSB), a political organ of all members. If violation of the WTO rules is found, the DSB firstly gives a recommendation to the State to 'bring the measure into conformity' with the WTO agreement (DSU Article 19:1).

A WTO dispute follows three steps: consultation; formal litigation; and, if necessary, implementation. The Complainant State raises its objections to the trade measures of another member State (the Appellant). The Appellant and the Complainant must try to negotiate a satisfactory solution within 60 days. If the consultation does not work, a panel proceeding can be requested, and the formal litigation begins.

The Panel releases an 'interim report'. The parties can still look for negotiation. If that is not possible, the Panel releases the definitive report. If the parties do not agree, there is the right to appeal. The Appellate Body intervenes, and it decides. If this verdict favours the defendant, the case typically ends. If this verdict, instead, favours the complainant, the dispute may proceed to the implementation stage. An Appellate Body report shall be adopted by the Dispute Settlement Body. If compliance is not achieved after a reasonable period of time (up to 15 months), the complainant can request a compliance panel to intervene. If no agreement is reached about the reasonable period for compliance, that issue is then the subject of binding arbitration; the arbitrator is appointed by agreement between the parties. If there is a disagreement as to the satisfactory nature of the measures adopted by the respondent State to comply with the report, such disagreement is to be decided by a panel. If possible this is the same panel that heard the original dispute, but apparently without the possibility of appeal from its decision. If all else fails, two more possibilities are set out in the DSU:

- if a member fails within the 'reasonable period' to carry out the recommendations and rulings, it may negotiate with the complaining State for a mutually

[42]The General Agreement on Tariffs and Trade (GATT) was signed on 30 October 1947.

[43]See at http://www.wto.org/english/docs_e/legal_e/04-wto.pdf.

acceptable compensation. Compensation consists of the grant of a concession by the respondent State on a product or service of interest to the complainant State;

- if no agreement on compensation is reached within 20 days of the expiry of the 'reasonable period', the prevailing State may request authorization from the DSB to suspend application to the member concerned of concessions or other obligations under the covered agreements. Any suspension or concession or other obligation is to be temporary. If the respondent State objects to the level of suspension proposed or to the consistency of the proposed suspension with the DSU principles, arbitration is still provided.[44]

12.5.1 Comparison Between the WTO and NPT Mechanisms

The compliance system adopted in the trade system is rather different to that adopted in the non-proliferation area. Indeed, the WTO is based on a sort of judicial framework, where the bodies act as judges with decisions and appeals, and at the same time mechanisms of compensation and suspensions of benefits are adopted in case of non-compliance. Within the IAEA system, there are no such binding reports or decisions. Moreover, the insistence on arbitration, compensation and suspensions of rights is not in the IAEA Statute. However, a good "lesson" to be taken from WTO is that the States are involved in the compliance itself, beyond the institutional mechanism and international bodies.

12.6 Lessons from Other Mechanisms of Compliance Relevant to the Nuclear Disarmament Field

In the area of nuclear non-proliferation, the IAEA has the central verification role in ensuring that the world's nuclear facilities are directed towards peaceful purposes.[45] It is true that, beyond the IAEA, there are other regional safeguards bodies, such as EURATOM and the Brazilian–Argentine Agency for Accounting

[44]See Imdad Ali 2003.

[45]It could be noted that other organizations in the nuclear area exist, but they do not have the mandate of nuclear watchdog, as IAEA own. For instance, the European Atomic Energy Community (EURATOM), even if it was established before the IAEA (in 1957), is an international organization with the purpose of creating a specialist market for nuclear power in Europe, developing nuclear energy and distributing it to its member States while selling the surplus to non-member States. Moreover, the Comprehensive Nuclear-Test-Ban Treaty Organization (CTBTO) is an international organization, whose tasks are not in force yet. It will be tasked with verifying the ban on nuclear tests and will operate therefore a worldwide monitoring system and may conduct on-site inspections.

and Control of Nuclear Materials (ABACC). However, the IAEA is the sole organization having an international mandate to sign safeguards agreement with the NPT State Parties. Therefore, the issue of verification is at the core of IAEA's duties.

Verification is not just an assessment that nuclear weapons arsenals have been destroyed, but it also involves the creation of confidence that the world will remain free of nuclear weapons.[46] In this sense, there is always going to be more that the IAEA safeguards system can do to improve and ensure compliance, but improvement must be achieved in accordance with international law.

As aforementioned, nuclear safeguards constitute the main way of verifying compliance with a State's commitments under the NPT.[47] Each State Party to the NPT is required under the treaty to conclude a 'comprehensive safeguards agreement' with the IAEA to facilitate verification by the Agency of the State's compliance with its treaty obligations. Non-nuclear weapon States declare their nuclear facilities, and update the data every year.

Under Comprehensive Safeguards Agreements (CSAs), the Agency has both the right and the obligation to verify the correctness and completeness of States' declarations, so that there is credible assurance of the non-diversion of nuclear material from declared activities. Traditionally, the IAEA could only inspect facilities that had been declared by States. However, at the end of 1993, the Agency embarked on a broad development programme (Programme 93 + 2) to further strengthen safeguards implementation under CSAs by enhancing the Agency's ability to consider a State as whole, included undeclared activities. This process brought about the adoption by the IAEA Board of Governors of the model Additional Protocol to Safeguards Agreements, to supplement full-scope safeguards (May 1997) and strengthen the IAEA's role.[48]

The efficiency of safeguards has been also increased through Integrated Safeguards adopted in 2002, with the purpose, not least, of easing the verification burden by using remote sensing devices and automated systems for data evaluation. A 'State-level concept (SLC)' was introduced,[49] taking State-specific factors into account and enabling consideration of a State's nuclear and nuclear-related activities and capabilities as a whole to be made, within the scope of the State's

---

[46]A. Schaper and K. Frank, A Nuclear Weapon Free World—Can It Be Verified?, PRIF Reports, Frankfurt.

[47]The IAEA defines nuclear safeguards as 'technical means used to verify that a State's nuclear activities are in conformity with the undertakings that the State has given about the nature and scope of these activities' (IAEA, The Evolution of IAEA Safeguards, International Nuclear Verification Series, No. 2, Vienna, Austria, 1998, p. 32).

[48]See O. Meier, Fulfilling the NPT: strengthened nuclear safeguards. VERTIC Briefing Paper, 2000, 2:1–12.

[49]This model was introduced by the IAEA Board of Governors in the Safeguards Implementation Report (SIR) in 2004.

safeguards agreement.[50] However, integrated safeguards are still slow to be implemented, and they also show some gaps of transparency. In the following section, the aim is therefore to draw some guiding rules for cooperative compliance with nuclear non-proliferation obligations.

12.6.1 Collection of Data and Monitoring

The fundamental requirement of verification with regard to the dismantlement of nuclear arsenals is the collection of the States' declarations about their nuclear materials, location, personnel, etc. The IAEA has an important role in this sense. There is arguably a need to control verification standards through more detailed examination, experimentation and analysis, including procedural analysis. A proper assessment could be undertaken along the lines of the environmental mechanisms noted earlier. States could certainly collaborate with the IAEA to assist the Agency in this regard. For such verification, it would be useful to involve nuclear scientists from both Nuclear States and Non-Nuclear, through a thorough engagement process. There is potential to improve information sharing and improve cooperation in a transparent way.

The end goal is to ensure that nuclear sites and devices can be monitored constantly and at the international level, through constant inspections *on situ* and through suitable devices. The authentication of potential nuclear facilities should be conducted through a constant constructive dialogue with the NNWSs, as well as the traceability of transports. A prompt detection and reporting of nuclear work of concern in any NNWS that is a party to the NPT should be further encouraged.

12.6.2 Guidelines for Action in Case of Non-compliance

The IAEA's structure works in such a way that, first of all, IAEA inspectors are called upon in order to determine whether there is compliance with the CSA between the Agency and the State. The non-compliance matters are reported to the

[50] It should be noted that on 12 August 2013, the IAEA's Director General submitted to the Board of Governors a report entitled "The Conceptualization and Development of Safeguards Implementation at the State Level" (GOV/2013/38). After a consultation process, the "Supplementary Document to the Report on The Conceptualization and Development of Safeguards Implementation at the State Level" of 13 August 2014, GOV/2014/41 has been released. The latter specifies that the safeguards agreement and, where applicable, the Additional Protocol concluded between the Agency and a State govern the safeguards implementation by the Agency for that State. It can be read: "The implementation does not entail the introduction of any additional rights or obligations on the part of either States or the Agency, nor any modification in the interpretation of existing rights and obligations under safeguards agreements and, where applicable, APs" (p. 13).

Director General, who has to transmit to the Board of Governors all non-compliance reports. The IAEA Board of Governors must decide if the safeguards breaches and failures reported by the Secretariat constitute non-compliance under the Statute and, if so, when they must be reported to the UN Security Council (whose role is defined by Chapter VII of the UN Charter[51]).

The notion of 'non-compliance' is, though, not so easy to define. There could be cases of clear diversion from Safeguard Agreements, and others that are more ambiguous to determine. On the one hand, the discovery of undeclared nuclear materials or activities does not necessarily indicate an intention to produce nuclear weapons. On the other hand, any request for proof of the existence of a nuclear weapon program as a result of finding 'non-compliance' is unrealistic, and it places an impossible burden upon the IAEA. Any moves in this direction would discourage the IAEA's mission and credibility at international level. Therefore, it would be meaningful to draw a set of guidelines within the IAEA, in order to determine when there is non-compliance. This would increase confidence and transparency in the IAEA's process, and it would also limit the arbitrary discretion that the IAEA is alleged to use. Indeed,

> reinforcing confidence in, and commitment to, the non-proliferation regime depends not only on proficient verification but also, where necessary, on effective action to uphold treaty compliance. Well-functioning procedures for determining non-compliance are essential to this.[52]

Hence neither a rigid list of non-compliance hypotheses should be adopted, nor should the IAEA be authorized to use unlimited discretionary power. For this reason, a set of guidelines could be important for assisting the IAEA's work.

12.6.3 Involvement of UN Bodies, States and Civil Society

Since the role of the Security Council attracts considerable criticism and it has been accused of being incapable of addressing the current challenges of society, it would be important to involve UN bodies, beyond the IAEA, in the compliance process to nuclear non-proliferation. For instance, the UN General Assembly (UNGA) could be proactively invited to discuss and develop the guidelines and principles for verification and compliance. The same is valid for the UN Office for Disarmament Affairs, whose assistance in verification and compliance of disarmament obligations, through the participation in the meetings of the Non-Proliferation Treaty and of the UNGA Disarmament and Security Committee could be a meaningful one.

---

[51] See the Articles about 'Functions and Powers', namely Article 24, Article 25, and Article 26 of Chapter VII of the Charter of the UN.

[52] Carlson 2009.

Beyond the technical means and the intervention of international agencies/organizations, and national States, it is also important not to neglect the role of civil society, which complements the official verification system. This 'societal verification' involves civil society, including investigative journalists, non-governmental organizations, professional organizations (such as academics, scientists and engineers) and individuals, to monitor the activities of governments and denounce suspected cases.

From the environmental experience, it appears that States should be more involved, for example through a Conference of State Parties or boosting the cooperation through shared mechanisms of data and information.

Beyond verification as such, it can be noted that the path towards better non-proliferation also involves the responsibility of individual States' and civil society. Indeed, treaties should not be the only vehicle to invoke disarmament commitments. Improving the sense of responsibility in the framework of a 'nuclear ethics'code, upon both the governments and the scientists, through binding rules, guidelines and codes of conducts, is a core goal. Experience in environmental law, as shown above, can be inspiring in this regard. Nuclear and non-nuclear weapon States should also promote academic programs for improving verification skills, and build awareness about verification concepts. They are deemed to provide basic knowledge, build capacity in functional areas and promote sustainability.

12.6.4 Best Practice Principles

Among the principles to be followed we in particular suggest the following:

- *The rule of law* which entails the respect of the normative texts and judicial interpretations, such as those coming from the ICJ. In particular, as the experience in trade law system shows, the adherence and respect of the principle of legality and of the judicial rulings (in the form of dispute settlement as well) are significant elements for the nuclear non-proliferation area too. This is not to say that a model like the one adopted within the WTO should be compulsorily followed by the international community for the non-proliferation area, but the principle of the rule of law deriving from both normative and judicial sources of the law should be followed. Therefore, for instance, the decisions of the International Court of Justice in this area should have an impact. As observed before,

  > There is an increasing urgency for the strengthening of legal norms to constrain the possession, threat or use of nuclear weapons, and for the development of legal regimes to control, reduce and eventually eliminate such weapons. The alternative – a world governed by increasing threats to use force, including the use of nuclear weapons – is likely to occur should the rule of force not be replaced by the rule of law.[53]

- *Impartiality and non-discrimination*, by which all Parties must be treated equally before the law: the principle of non-discrimination means that the same

[53]Ware 2003, p. 244.

compliance to duties that are placed on Non-Nuclear States should also be required of Nuclear Weapons States as well. Cases of non-compliance should be labelled in the same way for all the States that adopt the same behaviour. As known, the problem remains the fact that the CSAs are requested only to NNWS, while the NWS are permitted to give voluntary declarations as regards the State of security of their nuclear facilities. Therefore, a high level of discrimination remains, and the NPT itself is a discriminatory Treaty insofar as it created an improper subdivision between States whilst seeking to impede NNWS in becoming NWS. Indeed, while the Biological and Chemical Weapons Conventions State an absolute ban of these weapons, for the nuclear ones a discriminatory regime has been provided (for historical reasons) with the aim to arrive at complete disarmament according to a sort of 'step by step' procedure. This regime has, though, created discrimination between States.

- *Transparency*,[54] which has high importance in the reduction of nuclear arsenals. It can accelerate the disarmament process. The Document of the 2010 Review Conference of the Parties to the NPT underlines that

  > nuclear disarmament and achieving the peace and security of a world without nuclear weapons will require openness and cooperation and enhanced confidence through increased transparency and effective verification.[55]

  Therefore, transparency is an element of compliance and an instrument to cooperation. Indeed, transparency minimizes the possibilities of misunderstanding and it ensures trust from the Nuclear and Non-Nuclear Weapon States. In a world dominated by secrecy in nuclear practices, growing use of intelligence data in the Safeguards verification and monitoring (which is of course without attribution) and discriminatory policies, improved nuclear transparency at each level, and *in primis* by the IAEA, constitutes real progress. Especially, transparency in sharing information, in declaring the number of nuclear arsenals, and in reporting the status of these arsenals would increase accountability in the disarmament and non-proliferation processes.
- *Responsibility*.[56] It entails attention towards safety, security, environment, society, human rights and that of future generations in the undertaking of nuclear technologies. This responsibility, meant as a moral obligation, is a development (and revision) of Hans Jonas's perspective, and it shall govern negotiation, discussion, and the involvement of stakeholders. Indeed, it shall be promoted towards scientists and the scientific community, legislators, governments, and international organizations, and it shall be the basis for a new effort to ban and eliminate nuclear weapons. In particular, this effort could build on: (i) the 1996 Advisory Opinion of the International Court of Justice; (ii) the 'global awareness

---

[54]See Hibbs 2012; P. Podvig. Transparency in Nuclear Disarmament, UNIDIR Resources, Ideas for Peace and Security, http://unidir.org/files/publications/pdfs/transparency-in-nuclear-disarmament-390.pdf.

[55]Final Document of the 2010 Review Conference of the Parties to the Treaty of Non-Proliferation of Nuclear Weapons, document NPT/CONF.2010/50 (Vol. I), 2010.

[56]Jonas 2006.

of the catastrophic consequences of atomic warfare', as promoted by the International Physicians for the Prevention of Nuclear War (which was awarded with the Nobel Peace Prize in 1985); (iii) the development of a 'Nuclear Weapons Convention (NWC)' modelled on the conventions that already prohibit and require the complete elimination of the biological and chemical weapons. It can be noted that a draft of a NWC was introduced by Costa Rica at the UN in 1997 and it was revised in 2007 by the so-called International Campaign to Abolish Nuclear Weapons. It would be very interesting to investigate the evolution of the notions of the trilogy 'verification, compliance and enforcement' within a NWC framework that could be (a) legally binding, (b) universal (including all the States), (c) nondiscriminatory (applying the same rules to all the States), (d) multilateral (so that the States not belonging to the NPT could enter) and (e) able to generate trust and credibility in its mechanisms among the States. This Convention could be, indeed, the proper framework for 'translating' nuclear ethics, founded on responsibility, into a legal dimension.

12.7 Conclusion

In drawing some conclusions, it is difficult to deal with the nuclear conundrum created by the 'have' and the 'have not' reality, and to State fixed and decisive points for increasing compliance with the NPT. What our contribution has tried to suggest is a set of guidelines, rather than a group of binding behaviours and norms to follow.

In our perspective, compliance with nuclear non-proliferation obligations is not a 'technological machine' to be fixed by the imposition of further constraints, massive use of intelligence gathering, automatisms inbuilt in the UNSC, or transformation of 'political assessments' in technical facts, etc. Indeed, the adoption of such formulae would be against the spirit of the 'rule of law' and would not bring more stability to a world with nuclear weapons. Instead, endorsement of the 'nuclear ethics' code by all the relevant stakeholders, through the involvement of all the 'actors on the stage', and the strengthening of responsibility and transparency principles, can allow an endorsement of the 'nuclear norm' against the use of the nuclear weapons. This perspective could create, in our view, the conditions for a future global elimination of nuclear WMD.

References

Ago R (1984) Positivism. In: Bernhardt R (ed) Encyclopedia of public international law, vol 7. North-Holland, Amsterdam, pp 388–392

Brunnée J (2006) Enforcement mechanisms in international law and international environmental law. In: Beyerlin U et al (eds) Ensuring compliance with multilateral environmental agreements: a dialogue between practitioners and academia. Martinus Nijhoff Publishers, Boston, pp 1–24

Carlson J (2009) IAEA Safeguards Additional Protocol, International Commission on Nuclear Non-Proliferation and Disarmament. Accessed 20 January 2009

Cooper R (2003) The breaking of nations: order and chaos in the twenty-first century. Grove/Atlantic Monthly Press

Dorn W, Scott DS (2000) Compliance mechanisms for disarmament treaties. In: Findlay T (ed) Verification yearbook 2000. VERTIC, London, pp 229–247

Granoff J (2000) Nuclear weapons, ethics, morals, and law. Brigham Young Univ Law Rev 2000(4):1413–1442

Green R (2000) The naked nuclear emperor: debunking nuclear deterrence. Disarmament and Security Centre, Christchurch, New Zealand

Hibbs M (2012) The plan for IAEA safeguards. Carnegie Endowment for International Peace, Washington

Imdad Ali A (2003) Non-compliance and ultimate remedies under the wto dispute settlement system. J Public Int Aff 14:1–22

Jonas DS (2006) The new U.S. approach to the fissile material cutoff treaty: will deletion of a verification regime provide a way out of the wilderness? Florida J Int Law 18:597–677

Joyner DH (2011) Interpreting the nuclear non-proliferation treaty. Oxford University Press, Oxford

Katzenstein PJ et al (1998) International organization and the study of world politics. Int Organ 52(4):645–685

Lewis P (2009) Verification, compliance, and enforcement. In: Perkovich G, Acton JM (eds) Abolishing nuclear weapons: a debate. Carnegie Endowment for International Peace, Washington, pp 233–240

Miller SE, Sagan SD (2009) Nuclear power without nuclear proliferation? Daedalus 138(4):7–18

Moxley CJ Jr et al (2001) Nuclear weapons and compliance with international humanitarian law and the nuclear non-proliferation treaty. Fordham Int Law J 34:595–696

Rietker D (2014) The meaning of article vi of the treaty on the non-proliferation of nuclear weapons: analysis under the rules of treaty interpretation. In: Black-Branch J, Fleck D (eds) Nuclear non-proliferation in international law, vol I. TMC Asser Press, The Hague, pp 47–84

Simpson J, Ogilvie-White T (eds) (2003) NPT briefing book, vol. 1: the evolution of the nuclear non-proliferation regime. Mountbatten Centre for International Studies, Southampton

Walzer M (2006) Just and unjust wars: a moral argument with historical illustrations. Basic Books, New York

Ware A (2003) Rule of force or rule of law? legal responses to nuclear threats from terrorism, proliferation, and war. Seattle J Soc Justice 2(1):243–286

Chapter 13
The Legal Nature of Unilateral Security Assurances: Conceptualizing Positive and Negative Security Assurances as Unilateral Juridical Acts

Eva Kassoti

Abstract This contribution explores the juridical nature of unilateral security assurances within the framework of the doctrine of unilateral acts of States. It will be shown that, according to the doctrine, unilateral acts have two essential elements: unilateralism and the intention to be bound. In the first part of the chapter, these two elements are discussed and defined. Furthermore, a set of factors to be taken into account when determining the existence of the element of intention will be identified. In the second part of the chapter, existing unilateral security assurances will be tested against the background of the doctrine of unilateral acts. It is asserted that these security assurances—despite their shortcomings in terms of scope and content—may be validly considered as binding undertakings to the extent that they manifest the intention of their authors to be bound. On this basis, it is concluded that such assurances, when viewed from the perspective of unilateral juridical acts, play an important role in non-proliferation dynamics.

Keywords Intention to be bound · Negative security assurances · Positive security assurances · Security assurances · Unilateral acts

Contents

Dr E. Kassoti, Lecturer in International Law, The Hague University of Applied Sciences, The Netherlands.

E. Kassoti (✉)
The Hague University, Johana Westerdijkplein 75, 2521 EN The Hague, The Netherlands
e-mail: e.kassoti@hhs.nl

J.L. Black-Branch and D. Fleck (eds.), *Nuclear Non-Proliferation in International Law - Volume II*, DOI 10.1007/978-94-6265-075-6_13

13.1 Introduction

The legal nature of unilateral security assurances, namely unilateral guarantees in the form of oral or written declarations given by nuclear-weapon States (NWS)[1] to non-nuclear-weapon States (NNWS), under which the former undertake to assist them in case of a nuclear attack (positive security assurances) or not to use or threaten to use such weapons against them (negative security assurances), has been the subject of fierce debate since the 1970s. While some international lawyers consider them legally binding and on a par with the French guarantees given in the context of the *Nuclear Tests* cases,[2] others perceive them as mere political statements and thus, incapable of producing any legal effects.[3] In the same vein, international jurisprudence is of little avail in clarifying the legal status of these assurances. The International Court of Justice (ICJ), in its *Advisory Opinion on the Legality of the Threat or Use of Nuclear Weapons*, took note of such assurances, but refrained from drawing specific legal consequences from them.[4] At the same time, the need to shed light on the juridical nature of these assurances is as great as ever. Although NNWS have long insisted on the incorporation of such assurances in international agreements,[5] NWS have not yielded much ground over the years.

---

[1]According to the definition of 'nuclear-weapon States' under Article 9 para 3 of the 1968 Treaty on the Non-Proliferation of Nuclear Weapons (NPT), 729 UNTS 161, the NPT nuclear-weapon States are: Russia, France, the UK, the US and China. India and Pakistan are not parties to the NPT but have openly declared that they possess nuclear weapons. See Khan 2008, p. 84. Israel is widely believed to have nuclear weapons, although it maintains a policy of 'nuclear opacity'. See Cohen 1998. North Korea, which withdrew from the NPT in 2003, has also openly declared that it has manufactured nuclear weapons. See http://www.washingtonpost.com/wp-dyn/articles/A12836-2005Feb10.html. My analysis will focus on the security assurances given by the NPT NWS since these have triggered- and remain at the centre of -the relevant debate.

[2]See for example Eckart 2012, p. 165.

[3]See for example B. Fihn, The Conference on Disarmament and Negative Security Assurances, http://www.unidir.org/files/publications/pdfs/the-conference-on-disarmament-and-negative-security-assurances-369.pdf; Goldbat 2009, p. 67.

[4]Legality of the Threat or Use of Nuclear Weapons, Advisory Opinion, ICJ Rep. 1996, p. 226.

[5]See for example the memorandum circulated by Nigeria during the 1990 NPT Conference and the proposed agreement on the prohibition of the use or threat of use of nuclear weapons against non-nuclear-weapon States parties to the NPT contained therein, Doc. NPT/CONF.IV/17,1 June 1990, p. 2 et seq., available at http://www.un.org/disarmament/WMD/Nuclear/pdf/finaldocs/1991%20-%20Geneva%20-%20NPT%20Review%20Conference%20-%20Final%20Document%20Part%20%20II.pdf.

The relevant discussions both within the context of the Conference of Disarmament (CD) and of the Non Proliferation Treaty (NPT) Review Conferences have reached a deadlock and efforts to persuade NWS to provide assurances by means of regional agreements have had limited success.[6]

In this light, this contribution purports to revisit the question of the legal nature of unilateral security assurances and more particularly the question as to whether and under which circumstances these assurances may be considered as binding upon their author States. In order to do so, the chapter will draw upon the so far underdeveloped theory of unilateral juridical acts,[7] the main tenets of which were proclaimed by the ICJ in the *Nuclear Tests* case,[8] verified in subsequent case-law and elaborated by the International Law Commission (ILC).[9]

To this end, the chapter is divided in two parts. In the first part, I will provide a brief account of the doctrine of unilateral juridical acts in international law. Here, I will analyze the two essential elements of the legal nature of these acts (unilateralism and the element of the intention to be bound) with reference both to the relevant jurisprudence of international courts and tribunals and to the work of the ILC on the topic. On this basis, I will argue that, under international law, a unilateral act has binding force to the extent that it expresses *the autonomous and manifest intention of its author to be bound*. This part will conclude by providing a set of interpretative tools for ascertaining the manifest intention to be bound in practice.

Against this background, the second part of the chapter will focus on unilateral security assurances. For reasons of clarity, I will first discuss the positive security assurances given by NWS in 1968 and in 1995 and then I will turn to the negative security assurances offered in 1978–1982 and in 1995. Both types of assurances will be analyzed within the theoretical framework established in the first part of this chapter. I will argue that, while their content and scope leaves much to be desired, unilateral security assurances are internationally binding instruments. The chapter will conclude by stressing the importance of conceptualizing negative and positive security assurances within the framework of unilateral juridical acts for the purpose of enhancing their importance as a non-proliferation tool.

---

[6]A number of regional agreements have been concluded establishing Nuclear Weapon Free Zones (NWFZs). These agreements include protocols on security assurances for the NWS to sign and ratify. For an overview, see Venturini 2011, pp. 359–362. However, only Additional Protocol II to the Treaty of Tlatelolco has been signed and ratified by all five NPT nuclear weapon States. See http://disarmament.un.org/treaties/t/tlateloco_p2.

[7]The term ‘juridical’ or ‘legal’ is employed throughout the text to connote acts that have binding effects on the international plane, as opposed to ‘political’ acts, i.e. acts that lie outside the ambit of law.

[8]*Nuclear Tests* cases, *Australia v. France,* ICJ Rep. 1974, p. 253, *New Zealand v. France,* ICJ Rep. 1974, p. 457. The Court’s judgments in these two cases are almost identical. Hereinafter, all references made to the *Nuclear Tests* case will concern the case between Australia and France.

[9]Analytical guide to the work of the ILC on Unilateral Acts of States http://legal.un.org/ilc/guide/9_9.htm. For the final product of the ILC’s work on the topic, see the Guiding Principles Applicable to Unilateral Declarations of States Capable of Creating Legal Obligations, adopted by the ILC at its 58th session in 2006, *Yrbk of the ILC* 2006, Vol. II, p. 369. Hereinafter referred to as the ‘2006 Guiding Principles’, or ‘Guiding Principles’.

13.2 The Doctrine of Unilateral Juridical Acts in International Law

Here, I will briefly examine the legal nature of unilateral acts of States in order to provide the necessary analytical framework for the discussion of unilateral security assurances in the second part of the chapter. This part will begin with an introduction to the *problématique* surrounding the concept of unilateral acts in international law. It will be shown that, according to the ICJ, two elements are crucial in determining the juridical nature of a unilateral act: its unilateral nature, or unilateralism, and the element of the intention to be bound. I will then proceed to analyze each of these elements in turn. It will be asserted that the biggest hurdle to establishing that a unilateral act is binding is ascertaining the existence of the element of the intention to be bound. In order to tackle this problem, this part will conclude by compiling a list of indicators of the manifest intent to be bound on the basis of relevant international jurisprudence. These include the content of the act; its publicity; the forum in which the act was made and the authority which made the act on behalf of the State.

The question whether a State may be bound by means of a unilateral statement had been the subject of—admittedly mostly academic—debate[10] until the ICJ delivered its judgment in the *Nuclear Tests* case in 1974. In one of its most controversial dicta, the Court asserted that: 'It is well recognised that declarations made by way of unilateral acts … may have the effect of creating legal obligations.'[11] The Court continued by stipulating the elements of the legal nature of these acts:

> When it is the *intention* of the State making the declaration that it should become bound according to its terms, that intention confers on the declaration the character of a legal undertaking … In these circumstances, nothing in the nature of a quid pro quo, nor any subsequent acceptance of the declaration, nor even a reply or reaction from other States, is required for the declaration to take effect, since such a requirement would be inconsistent with the *strictly unilateral nature of the juridical act* by which the pronouncement by the State was made.[12]

Thus, according to the Court, two main elements comprise the legal nature of unilateral juridical acts: unilateralism and the intention to be bound.

The judgment was met with vociferous criticism in the literature. A number of international lawyers, such as A. Rubin[13] and H. Thirlway,[14] accused the Court of conjuring the concept of 'unilateral juridical acts' out of thin air in order to avoid ruling on the politically sensitive question of the legality of nuclear tests. Notwithstanding this, the Court has in its subsequent jurisprudence (including the

[10]For early works on the topic, see Suy 1962; Garner 1933.

[11]*Nuclear Tests* case, above n. 8, para 43.

[12]Ibid. (emphasis added).

[13]Rubin 1977, p. 24; Franck 1975.

[14]Thirlway 2014, p. 112.

Nicaragua case,[15] the *Frontier Dispute* case,[16] the *Armed Activities* case[17] and more recently the case concerning Questions Relating to the Seizure and Detention of certain Documents and Data[18]) upheld the principle enunciated in the *Nuclear Tests* case, namely that acts of purely unilateral origin are binding on their author States to the extent that they manifest an intention to be bound according to their terms. However, aside from confirming the validity of the *Nuclear Tests* judgment, the Court has not elaborated on the elements of unilateralism or intention in its later case-law. Thus, the Court's 1974 judgment still stands as the only major judicial pronouncement in the field.

In this light and taking into account the fact that unilateral declarations have become a standard tool of modern State interaction, the ILC decided to codify the legal regime applicable to them in 1996. However, it soon became clear that the project was plagued with difficulties: due to irreconcilable differences amongst its members,[19] the Commission abandoned its efforts of codification in 2006 and adopted instead a set of ten Guiding Principles applicable to unilateral declarations of States.[20] The final product of the Commission's 10-year struggle with the topic leaves a lot to be desired. The 2006 Guiding Principles have three main weaknesses. First, they fail to define the element of unilateralism. Protracted disagreement over the question of the unilateral nature of unilateral acts[21] resulted in the omission of any reference to unilateralism in the final text. Second, they fail to establish clear boundaries between estoppel and unilateral acts. Already from the preamble it is noted that 'in practice, it is often difficult to establish whether the legal effects stemming from the unilateral behaviour of a State are the consequence of the intent that it has expressed or depend on the expectations that its conduct has raised among other subjects of international law.'[22] Moreover, Guiding Principle 1 oscillates between the intention of the author State and the reliance placed upon the act by other States as the decisive factor in attributing legal effects to unilateral acts: 'Declarations publicly made and manifesting the will to be bound may have the effect of creating legal obligations… *States*

[15] *Case concerning Military and Paramilitary Activities in and against Nicaragua,* ICJ Rep. 1986, p. 14.

[16] *Case concerning the Frontier Dispute*, ICJ Rep. 1986, p. 554.

[17] *Case concerning Armed Activities on the Territory of the Congo (New Application: 2002),* ICJ Reports 2006, p. 1.

[18] *Case concerning Questions Relating to the Seizure and Detention of Certain Documents and Data*, 3 March 2014, Order for Provisional Measures, available at http://www.icj-cij.org/docket/files/156/18078.pdf.

[19] See generally Tomuschat 2008.

[20] Guiding Principles, above n. 9.

[21] Compare for example the statements made by Pellet, Candioti, Addo to the ones made by Rosenstock, Lukashuk and Economides, Summary record of the 2603th meeting, *Yrbk of the ILC* 1999, Vol. I, pp. 261–264, paras 12–35.

[22] Guiding Principles, above n. 9.

concerned may then take them into consideration and rely on them; such States are entitled to require that such obligations be respected.'[23] Finally, the Guiding Principles fail to provide a clear distinction between unilateral juridical and unilateral political acts. While both the text of the 2006 Principles and the accompanying commentary[24] emphasize the importance of the intention of the author State in the context of unilateral acts, they offer no concrete interpretative tools for establishing this very element. Thus, it seems that the ILC's decade-long efforts failed to provide much-needed clarity on the topic and that 40 years after the *Nuclear Tests* judgment, the legal regime applicable to unilateral acts is still opaque. For this reason, I will next turn to the elements of the legal nature of these acts—as these were identified by the Court—in order to establish: (a) their definition and (b) a set of tools for ascertaining their existence in practice.

13.2.1 The Unilateral Nature of Unilateral Juridical Acts: Unilateralism

In general, the idea that binding effects may arise from a unilateral act without more has not sat comfortably with a number of international lawyers- especially those with a common law background. For them, the binding force of an act of seemingly unilateral origin does not stem from the act *per se*, but from the reciprocal relationship of which the act forms part. In this vein, opponents of the theory of unilateral juridical acts have largely treated these acts as instances of estoppel, thereby justifying their binding effects on the basis of the reliance placed thereon by their addressees.[25] Furthermore, much of the consternation amongst members of the ILC was caused by the blurry lines between unilateral acts and estoppel. While representatives of the civil law tradition within the Commission tended to view such acts as a phenomenon distinct to estoppel, representatives of the common law tradition conceptualized them as instances of estoppel.[26]

[23]Guiding Principle 1, ibid. (emphasis added).

[24]Commentary to Guiding Principle 1, ibid., p. 370. According to the Commentary: 'The wording of Guiding Principle 1, which seeks both to define unilateral acts in the strict sense and to indicate what they are based on, is very directly inspired by the dicta in the judgments handed down by the International court of Justice on 20 December 1974 in the *Nuclear Tests* case. In the case concerning the *Frontier Dispute*, the Court was careful to point out that "it all depends on the intention of the State in question.' Above n. 16, para 49.

[25]See for example, Giganti 1962, p. 351.

[26]This point was highlighted by Crawford during the 1999 session: '[t]he civil law legal systems had a substantial tradition of treating unilateral promises as binding … The common law legal systems generally did not treat such statements as binding and there was therefore no autonomous category of unilateral legal acts in the common law legal system, but it had tried to fill that gap and to deal with the problem of good faith arising from the non-binding character of unilateral statements by reason of the doctrine of estoppel.' Statement by Crawford, Summary record of the 2596th meeting, *Yrbk of the ILC* 1999, Vol I, p. 210.

In view of the doubts surrounding unilateralism, I will examine this element by proving first that estoppel and unilateral acts are two different legal phenomena. I will do so by demonstrating that the binding force of the French statements made in the context of the *Nuclear Tests* case may not be explained on the basis of estoppel. Next, I will focus on the definition of unilateralism provided by the Court in the above case. By analyzing the relevant dictum in the context within which it was made, I will prove that unilateralism refers to the *autonomy of the intention of the author State to produce legal effects irrespective of any kind of acceptance or reliance on behalf of the addressee.*

Estoppel originates from the general principle of good faith and it is the equivalent at the international level of the simple principle "that a man is not allowed to blow hot and cold- to affirm at one time and deny at another."[27] As far as judicial practice is concerned, both the Permanent Court and the International Court of Justice have on various occasions applied the principle of estoppel.[28] On all these occasions, estoppel was neither interpreted nor applied broadly. On the contrary, throughout the case-law, some essential conditions for the application of the principle have arisen. Bowett, in his article on estoppel,[29] has enumerated them: (a) The meaning of the statement must be clear and unambiguous; (b) The statement or representation must be voluntary, unconditional and authorized and (c) Reliance in good faith upon the representation of one party by the other party to his detriment (or to the advantage of the party making the representation. The latter is of particular significance for present purposes.

In the *Nuclear Tests* case, the element of detrimental reliance—or, for that matter, any kind of reliance—was patently absent. Far from relying on the French statements, both New Zealand and Australia expressly declared them to have fallen short of the firm and unequivocal assurances they hoped to receive. In the course of the oral proceedings, the Attorney-General of Australia stated that: 'The recent French Presidential statement cannot be read as a firm, explicit and binding undertaking to refrain from further atmospheric tests. It follows that the Government of France is still reserving to itself the right to carry out atmospheric nuclear tests.'[30] In the same vein, New Zealand stated that: 'New Zealand has not been given anything in the nature of an unqualified assurance that 1974 will see the end of atmospheric nuclear testing in the South Pacific.'[31] Thus, the legal effects attributed to the French statements may not be explained on the basis of estoppel.

Speaking more broadly, there is an additional element that differentiates estoppel from unilateral legal acts. This element relates to the time that obligations arise

---

[27]*Cave v. Mills*, 7 *Hurlstone & Norman* 913 (1862), p. 927, as cited in Cheng 2006, p. 141.

[28]See the case-law mentioned in Sinclair 1996, p. 105 et seq.

[29]Bowett 1957, pp. 188–194.

[30]*Nuclear Tests* case *(Australia v. France)*, above n. 8, p. 261, paras 27–28, and p. 268, para 47.

[31]*Nuclear Tests* case *(New Zealand v. France)*, ibid., p. 465, para 27.

under the two legal concepts. In unilateral legal acts, the emphasis is on the intention of the declarant State; thus, the unilateral act becomes binding upon the declarant State immediately upon its expression. The autonomy of the unilateral legal act in producing binding effects the moment that it is formulated was stressed by the ICJ in the *Nuclear Tests* case.[32] On the contrary, in estoppel the emphasis is on the reliance given by the addressee to the declaration, rather than on the intentions of its maker.[33] Logic dictates that reliance involves an element of duration; a period of time, short as it may be, must run for the addressee of the declaration to act or adopt a conduct to its own detriment upon which the element of reliance will be established. Thus, in the case of estoppel, the binding effects of the statement do not arise automatically, i.e. at the moment that the presentation is made. For all of these reasons, the argument that estoppel may serve as the legal basis of unilateral legal acts is, in the opinion of the author, unfounded.

Turning to the definition of unilateralism in the *Nuclear Tests* judgment, the relevant dictum reads:

> An undertaking of this kind, if given publicly, and with an intent to be bound, even though not made within the context of international negotiations, is binding. In these circumstances, nothing in the nature of a *quid pro quo* nor any subsequent acceptance of the declaration, nor even any reply or reaction from other States, is required for the declaration to take effect, since such a requirement would be inconsistent with the strictly unilateral nature of the juridical act by which the pronouncement by the State was made.[34]

Thus, according to the Court, the concept of unilateralism is akin to a concept of autonomy of the act to produce legal effects irrespective of any kind of acceptance, reliance, or even reaction on the part of the addressee. However, what does it really mean that a juridical act must be autonomous in the production of legal effects in order to satisfy the criterion of unilateralism? Is autonomy to be understood as a factual statement merely signifying that the act emanates from a single entity, or is it a legal concept qualifying the relation borne out of an act of unilateral character?

In order to understand the Court's position attention must be paid not only to the wording of the relevant dictum, but also to the context within which it was uttered. The Court referred to unilateralism in the part of the judgment in which the question of the binding force of unilateral acts was addressed. In upholding the binding force of unilateral acts in the form of declarations, the ICJ put primary emphasis on the *intention* of the author State to create legal effects on the international plane. In the text of the judgment directly preceding the dictum on unilateralism the Court stated: 'When it is *the intention* of the State making the declaration that it should become bound according to its terms, *that intention confers on the declaration the character of a legal undertaking*, the State being

[32]Ibid., para 43.

[33]Thirlway 1989, p. 11.

[34]*Nuclear Tests* case, above n. 8, para 43 (emphasis added).

thenceforth legally required to follow a course of conduct consistent with the declaration.'[35]

Thus, it was in the context of stressing the significance of intention in relation to the binding force of unilateral acts that the Court's reference to unilateralism was made. It is worth recalling that the passage on unilateralism begun with the phrase 'in these circumstances.'[36] The use of this phrase indicates that the reference to unilateralism was not made in a vacuum; rather, it was directly linked to the previous discussion regarding the element of intention. Therefore, when the Court alluded to the concept of unilateralism being akin to a concept of autonomy, it essentially referred to the *autonomy of the intention* of the author State to produce legal effects irrespective of any kind of reciprocity/reliance on behalf of the addressee.[37]

13.2.2 The Juridical Nature of Unilateral Juridical Acts: The Intention to Be Bound

The question whether binding effects may arise from unilateral acts has acquired almost Kafkaesque dimensions in literature and it was a point of great friction amongst members of the ILC. The terse exchanges during the ILC's 54th session are characteristic of the diametrically opposed opinions on the subject. In 2003—7 years after the commencement of the Commission's study—Koskenniemi proposed the abandonment of the project since, in his view, unilateral acts do not constitute a legal institution. He argued that these acts are

> a catch-all term to describe ways in which States sometimes were bound other than through the effects of particular institutions, or in which States acted in special ways so as to create legal effects. It was the source of some of the difficulties; the Commission was trying to codify something which did not exist as a legal institution and was at a loss as to how to define it so as to make it a legal institution.[38]

He was rebuked by Pambou-Tchivounda who stated that 'it was impossible not to be shocked by Mr. Koskenniemi's questioning of the existence of unilateral acts of States as a legal category … Unilateral acts of States had both a theoretical and

[35]Ibid. (emphasis added).

[36]'In these circumstances, nothing in the nature of a *quid pro quo* nor any subsequent acceptance of the declaration, nor even any reply or reaction from other States, is required for the declaration to take effect… .' Ibid.

[37]The same view, namely that unilateralism refers to the autonomy of the act to produce legal effects irrespective of acceptance or reliance on behalf of the addressee was also adopted by the Special Rapporteur of the ILC on Unilateral Acts of States. See the Second Report on Unilateral Acts of States, UN Doc. A/CN.4/500, 14/04/1999, p. 11, paras 62–63, available at http://untreaty.un.org/ilc/documentation/english/a_cn4_500.pdf.

[38]See the comments by Koskenniemi, Summary record of the 2772nd meeting, 2003, *Yrbk of the ILC* 2003, Vol. I, para 42.

practical existence, as was evidenced by the numerous references to State practice appearing in the Special Rapporteur's sixth report'.[39]

In this light, this part will explore the question of the juridical nature of unilateral acts. I will argue here that, in a similar vein to international agreements, *the objective or manifest intention—as opposed to the subjective or real intention—of a State to be bound* is the criterion for attributing legal effects to a unilateral act. I will also show that—again, in the same way as with international agreements—international courts and tribunals have established through their practice a list of indicators that facilitate the task of determining whether a particular act expresses the manifest intent of its author to be bound thereby.

The element of the intention to be bound played a central role to the determination of the binding effects of the French statements in the *Nuclear Tests* judgment as the above-cited dictum demonstrates. The passage in question has been repeated almost verbatim in all subsequent judgments pertaining to the topic.[40] Furthermore, intention features heavily both in the reports prepared by the Special Rapporteur[41] and in the 2006 Guiding Principles adopted by the ILC.[42] As far as the debate within the ILC is concerned, there was consensus amongst the members—who accepted unilateral acts as a legal institution in international law—that intention was the main condition for attributing legal effects to unilateral declarations.[43] This mirrors the position taken in relation to juridical acts of a bi/multilateral origin. In the context of international agreements, the intention to be bound is also considered the determinant factor in ascertaining the binding effects of a treaty instrument.[44]

[39]Statement by Pambou-Tchivounda, ibid., para 5.

[40]See for example the *Frontier Dispute* case, above n. 16, para 39. The relevant dictum has been also cited in judgments originating from other international courts and tribunals. See for example *Case Concerning Sections 301–310 of the Trade Act of 1974*, WT/DS152/R, Report of the Panel (Dec. 22, 1999), available at http://www.wto.org/english/tratop_e/dispu_e/cases_e/ds152_e.htm and *Dispute concerning Access to Information under Article 9 of the OSPAR Convention* (OSPAR Arbitration), Final Award, 02/07/2003, available at http://www.pca-cpa.org/showpage.asp?pag_id=1158.

[41]See for example the First Report on Unilateral Acts, UN Doc. A/CN.4/486, 05/03/1998, available at http://untreaty.un.org/ilc/guide/9_9.htm.

[42]According to Guiding Principle 1, 'Declarations publicly made and manifesting the will to be bound may have the effect of creating legal obligations.', above n. 9.

[43]See for example the statements made by Brownlie, Pambou-Tchivoudva, Chee and Addo, Summary record of the 2772nd meeting, *Yrbk of the ILC* 2003, Vol. I, pp. 144–145.

[44]See for example the Separate Opinion of Judge Read in the *International Status of South West Africa Advisory Opinion*, ICJ Rep. 1950, p. 128 at p. 170. As Pellet pointed out during the 2002 session: 'International law was not based entirely on the expression of the will of the States but it was plain that, insofar as they were bound by treaty obligations and by unilateral acts, it was by their own individual or collective wish… Why were States bound under the treaty mechanism? It was because they wished to be bound and limit their freedom of action. The same was true when States formulated unilateral acts. It was indispensable to orderly relations between States that they should be bound by the expression of their will.' See statement by Pellet, Summary record of the 2722nd meeting, *Yrbk of the ILC* 2002, Vol. I, p. 75, para 54.

However, how are we to construe intention? Is the term to be understood as it is used in common parlance, i.e. as a psychological element referring to the state of mind of an individual at a given time (subjective or real intention), or does it refer to what was manifested to the outside world (objective or manifest intention)?[45] There are good reasons for supporting the latter reading of intention. First, as mentioned previously, the intention to be bound is also the law-determining criterion in the context of the law of treaties and, within that context, it has been consistently upheld to denote the objective or manifest intention of States to be bound.[46] Second, an objective reading of the element of the intention to be bound is supported by the text of the *Nuclear Tests* judgment. Having proclaimed the general rule that a unilateral declaration may be binding if it expresses the intention of its author to be bound,[47] the Court proceeded to state that: 'One of the basic principles governing the creation and performance of legal obligations, whatever their source, is the principle of good faith. Trust and confidence are inherent in international relations … Thus interested States may take cognizance of unilateral declarations and place confidence in them, and are entitled to require that the obligation thus created be respected.'[48] By appealing to the principle of good faith and to the trust, confidence and reliance that other States may place in what was manifested to them by a unilateral act, the Court clearly supported an objective understanding of the requisite element of intention. Had the Court adopted the contrary view, i.e. that what matters is only what the author had in mind at the time of formulating the act, there would be no reason to refer to good faith and to other States' reliance. The same opinion, namely that intention in the context of unilateral acts refers to the objective intention of the author State to be bound, also finds widespread support in theory.[49]

However, having established that the element of the manifest intent to be bound is what bestows binding force on unilateral acts is not enough. How are we to determine that an instrument of unilateral origin expresses the manifest intent of its author to be bound? The Court provided limited guidance in this respect: 'Intention is to be ascertained by interpretation of the act… It is from the actual substance of these statements and from the circumstances attending their making, that the legal implications for the unilateral act must be deduced.'[50] Thus,

[45]For the distinction between 'real or subjective intention' and 'objective or manifest intention', see Klabbers 1996, p. 65 and Hollis 2012, pp. 25–28.

[46]See for example the *Maritime Delimitation and Territorial Questions between Qatar and Bahrain Case*, ICJ Rep. 1994, p. 112 and the *Aegean Continental Shelf Case*, ICJ Rep. 1978, p. 3 and the relevant discussion in Klabbers 1996, pp. 65 and Fitzmaurice 2002, pp. 165–168.

[47]*Nuclear Tests* case, above n. 8, para 46.

[48]Ibid., para 48.

[49]Orakhelashvili 2008, p. 466; Eckart 2012, pp. 208–211.

[50]*Nuclear Tests* case, above n. 8, paras 47 and 53.

according to the Court the element of manifest intention is to be established on the basis of the content of the act and of the context surrounding the making thereof.[51]

As far as the content of the act is concerned, the use of clear and specific wording is one of the most reliable indicators of manifest intent. As the Court underlined in the *Armed Activities* case: 'A statement of this kind can create legal obligations only if it is made in clear and specific terms.'[52] The same principle has also been enshrined in the 2006 Guiding Principles. According to Guiding Principle 7, 'a unilateral declaration entails obligations for the formulating State only if it stated in clear and specific terms.'[53]

With respect to the context within which the act is made, a perusal of the relevant international jurisprudence shows that the publicity of the act, the forum in which the act was made and the authority of the person formulating the act on behalf of the State are taken into account when determining the existence of the element of manifest intent. The evidentiary value of publicity was noted both in the *Nuclear Tests* judgment[54] and in the discussions within the ILC.[55] Publicity also features in the 2006 Guiding Principles. According to Guiding Principle 1: 'Declarations publicly made and manifesting the will to be bound may have the effect of creating legal obligations.'[56] The commentary to Guiding Principle 1 explicitly states that the public nature of declarations represents an important indication of their authors' intention to commit themselves.[57] Furthermore, in a string of judgments spanning from 1925 to 2014, international courts and tribunals have confirmed that the fact that declarations are made before an international forum, such as a UN[58] or an international dispute settlement body,[59] evidences the manifest intent of their author/s to

[51]Again, this approach, i.e. the analysis of both the content of the act and of the circumstances surrounding its making, mirrors the way in which intention is identified within the framework of the law of treaties. See Klabbers 1996, pp. 65 et seq. and Fitzmaurice 2002, pp. 165–168.

[52]*Armed Activities* case, above n. 17, para 50.

[53]Guiding Principle 7, above n. 9.

[54]*Nuclear Tests* case, above n. 8, para 46. The relevant passage reads: 'The unilateral statements of the French authorities were made outside the Court, publicly and *erga omnes*... In announcing that the 1974 series of atmospheric tests would be the last, the French Government conveyed to the world at large, including the Applicant, its intention effectively to terminate these tests. It was bound to assume that other States might take note of these statements and rely on their being effective.'

[55]During the 1998 session, Brownlie noted that 'the criterion of publicity... was certainly relevant in terms of evidence.' Statement by Brownlie, Summary record of the 2527th meeting, Yrbk of the ILC 1998. Vol. I, p. 59, para 15.

[56]Guiding Principle 1, above n. 9, p. 370 (emphasis added).

[57]Commentary to Guiding Principle 1, ibid.

[58]See for example the *Armed Activities* case, above n. 17, para 48.

[59]See for example the *Mavrommatis Jerusalem Concessions* case, *PCIJ Reports*, Series A 1924, No. 2, p. 6 at pp. 36–37; *Case concerning Questions Relating to the Obligation to Prosecute or Extradite*, Order of 28 May 2009, paras 72–3, ICJ Rep. 2009, p. 139; *Case Concerning Sections 301–310 of the Trade Act of 1974*, above n. 40, fn. 692; *Case concerning Questions Relating to the Seizure and Detention of Certain Documents and Data*, above n. 18, para 44.

be bound. Finally, the authority making the act on behalf of the State is also relevant in ascertaining the element of manifest intent. Statements emanating from Heads of State, Heads of Government, Ministers for Foreign Affairs, as well as from other official representatives of a State in specific fields carry significant evidentiary weight according both to the ICJ[60] and to the ILC's Guiding Principles.[61]

This section established the standard of interpretation to be applied in determining the *existence of an obligation* created by means of a unilateral act. A final note should be made in relation to the standard of interpretation to be applied in determining the *scope of the obligation* created by means of these acts. According to the ICJ, the latter should be construed in a restrictive manner: 'Of course, not all unilateral acts imply obligation; but a State may choose to take up a certain position in relation to a particular matter with the intention of being bound... When States make statements by which their freedom of action is to be limited, a restrictive interpretation is called for.'[62] Adopting a more rigid standard of interpretation in the context of unilateral acts is understandable; the Court was anxious to ensure that obligations going beyond those intended by the declarant would not be opposable against it, thereby echoing a well-established principle of international law to the effect that States may not be bound against their will.[63] The same

---

[60]In the *Nuclear Tests* judgment, the Court noted that "of the statements made by the French Government now before the Court, the most essential are clearly those made by the President of the Republic." *Nuclear Tests* case, above n. 8, para 51. In the Order of 28 May 2009 given in the context of the *Case concerning Questions relating to the Obligation to Prosecute or Extradite*, the Court clarified that the statements made by the representatives of Senegal before it unequivocally expressed Senegal's intention to be bound thereby. *Case concerning Questions Relating to the Obligation to Prosecute or Extradite*, Order of 28 May 2009, above n. 59, para 70. In the *Armed Activities* case, the Court stressed that: 'It is a well-established rule of international law that the Head of State, the Head of Government and the Minister for Foreign Affairs are deemed to represent the State merely by virtue of exercising their functions, including for the performance, on behalf of the said State, of unilateral acts having the force of international commitments... The Court notes, however, that with increasing frequency in international relations other persons representing a State in specific fields may be authorised by that State to bind it by their statements in respect of matters falling within their purview. This may be true, for example, of holders of technical ministerial portfolios exercising powers in their field of competence in the area of foreign relations, and even of certain officials.' *Armed Activities* case, above n. 17, paras 46–47.

[61]Guiding Principle 4 repeats almost verbatim the above mentioned dictum in the *Armed Activities* case. See Guiding principle 4, above n. 9.

[62]Ibid., para 47.

[63]In the *Lotus* case, the Permanent Court of International Justice stated that: 'International law governs relations between independent States. The rules of law binding upon States therefore emanate from their own free will as expressed in conventions or by usages generally accepted as expressing principles of law and established in order to regulate the relations between these co-existing independent communities or with a view to the achievement of common aims. *Restrictions upon the independence of States cannot therefore be presumed*' (emphasis added). *The Case of the SS Lotus, PCIJ Series* A, No. 10 (1927), p. 4, at p. 18. The restrictive standard of interpretation to be applied to unilateral acts is also mentioned in the 2006 Guiding Principles. According to Guiding Principle 7: 'A unilateral declaration entails obligations for the formulating State only if it is stated in clear and specific terms. *In the case of doubt as to the scope of the obligations resulting from such a declaration*, such obligations must be interpreted *in a restrictive manner*' (emphasis added). See the 2006 Guiding Principles, above n. 9.

restrictive standard of interpretation was also adopted by the WTO Panel in the *Case concerning Sections 301–310 of the Trade Act of 1974*:

> Attributing legal significance to unilateral statements made by a State should not be done lightly and should be subject to strict conditions… A sovereign State should normally not find itself legally affected on the international plane by the casual statement of any of the numerous representatives speaking on its behalf in today's highly interactive and interdependent world … nor by a representation made in the heat of legal argument on a State's behalf.[64]

13.3 Conceptualizing Unilateral Security Assurances as Unilateral Juridical Acts

Having provided a brief overview of the doctrine of unilateral acts, this section turns to the question of whether and to what extent security assurances made by way of unilateral declarations may be conceptualized as unilateral juridical acts. The long and complex history of unilateral security assurances has been set out in detail elsewhere.[65] It suffices to mention here that the debate in literature largely revolves around three sets of assurances, namely the ones given by the US, the UK and the USSR in 1968, the ones given by all five NPT NWS in the period between 1978 and 1982 and the ones given in 1995. Thus, the main focus of this section will be on these three sets of assurances—with occasional references to later declarations strengthening the already existing ones, such as the ones made by the US and the UK in 2010. For reasons of methodological clarity, this part is divided in two sections: the first section will analyze the juridical character of positive security assurances, whereas the second will deal with the same question in the context of negative security assurances.

13.3.1 Positive Security Assurances: 1968–1995

As mentioned earlier, the term 'positive security assurances' is used in nuclear diplomacy jargon to connote promises of assistance made by NWS to NNWS in case of nuclear attacks. Such promises go as far back as the 1960s. Against the backdrop of China's first nuclear tests, US President Johnson stated in 1964 that 'nations that do not seek nuclear weapons can be sure that if they need our strong support against some threat or nuclear blackmail, then they will have it.'[66] This broadly construed and vaguely worded statement gave little by way of reassurance

[64] *Case Concerning Sections 301–310 of the Trade Act of 1974*, above n. 40, para 7.118.

[65] See generally Bernauer 1991.

[66] Simpson 2012, p. 60.

to NNWS but paved the way for the 1968 statements by the US, the UK and the USSR. The latter were made just a few days before the NPT opened for signature.[67] More particularly, they were provided as an incentive for NNWS to join the NPT—despite the fact that such assurances were not part of the treaty. As France expressed its intention not to join the treaty at the time and China was not as yet a member of the UN, the three remaining NWS chose not to incorporate such assurances into the text of the treaty itself.[68] At the same time they were very well aware of the fact that NNWS would not be amenable to forgoing nuclear weaponry without anything in return. In order to solve this conundrum, the UK, the US and the USSR made oral declarations before the Security Council providing positive security assurances to NNWS that would join the NPT.

Ambassador Goldberg made the following declaration on behalf of the US:

> The Government of the United States notes with appreciation the desire expressed by a large number of States to subscribe to the treaty on the non-proliferation of nuclear weapons, ... The United States also notes the concern of certain of these States that, in conjunction with their adherence to the treaty on the non-proliferation of nuclear weapons, appropriate measures be undertaken to safeguard their security... The United States affirms its intention, as a permanent member of the United Nations Security Council, to seek immediate Security Council action to provide assistance, in accordance with the Charter, to any non-nuclear-weapon State party to the treaty on the non-proliferation of nuclear weapons that is a victim of an act of aggression or an object of a threat of aggression in which nuclear weapons are used.[69]

Identical declarations were made by the USSR and the UK.[70] These declarations were then embodied in UN Security Council resolution 255/1968.[71] According to Res. 255/1968, the Security Council '*welcomes* the intention expressed by certain States that they will provide or support immediate assistance, in accordance with the Charter, to any non-nuclear-weapon State party to the Treaty on the Non-Proliferation of Nuclear Weapons that is a victim of an act or an object of a threat of aggression in which nuclear weapons are used.'[72]

First, it needs to be observed that viewing these declarations as anything else than unilateral in origin would amount to stretching the limits of interpretation to a breaking point. Although they were related to the NPT treaty, they were not made within a context of negotiations, nor were they phrased as an offer the acceptance of which would render them effective. On the contrary, they were made as a 'stand-alone' commitment to NNWS States party to the NPT after the failure of

---

[67]Bunn and Timmerbaev 1996, p. 1.

[68]Simpson 2012, pp. 61–62.

[69]US Arms Control and Disarmament Agency, Documents on Disarmament (1968), pp. 439–440, available at http://www.un.org/disarmament/publications/documents_on_disarmament/1968/DoD_1968.pdf.

[70]Ibid., p. 439.

[71]S/RES/255 (1968) available at http://www.un.org/en/ga/search/view_doc.asp?symbol=S/RES/255%281968%29. France along with India, Pakistan, Algeria and Brazil abstained from voting. Ibid.

[72]Ibid., para 2.

the latter to convince them to include a clause on assurances in the treaty itself.[73] Thus, the language of the declarations and the historical context within which they were made verify their unilateral character.

Turning to the question of the binding effects of the 1968 declarations, it seems that both their content and the context within which they were made indicate an intention to become bound, as this element was defined above. The clear and specific language employed; the forum within which the declarations were made, i.e. the Security Council; the fact that these were later incorporated in a UN Security Council resolution; and the fact that they were made by official representatives of the countries in question corroborate the view that, indeed, these statements expressed the manifest intention of their authors to become bound thereby. Thus, from an instrument perspective, the unilateral form of the assurances does not affect their binding force.

What is, however, problematic is the *scope* of obligations undertaken thereunder: the 1968 security assurances merely reaffirm already existing obligations of the relevant States under the UN Charter. This point was also stressed by the French representative before the Security Council in justifying France's voting abstention: 'It is not the French delegation's intention that that abstention should constitute an obstacle to the adoption of a draft *that in no way changes the provisions of Chapter VII of the Charter*, as is clear from the very contents of the draft, from the declared intentions of its sponsors…'.[74] The failure to go beyond already existing obligations also features in literature as one of the main shortcomings of the 1968 assurances.[75] Other oft-cited shortcomings include: the fact that the resolution seems to have given NWS the freedom to take collective military action without consulting the target State[76]; the fact that the resolution did not clearly

---

[73]Nustyen and Graff Hugo 2014, p. 384.

[74]US Arms Control and Disarmament Agency, Documents on Disarmament (1968), above n. 69, p. 442 (emphasis added).

[75]See for example Elaraby 1995, p. 19; Simpson 2012, p. 62; Tertrais 2012, p. 249; Bernauer 1991, p. 4.

[76]See for example the statements by Austria and Switzerland during the 1980 NPT Review Conference. According to Austria: '… a country like Austria, which had committed itself to a status of permanent neutrality, could not agree to confer upon an outside Power the responsibility for the maintenance of its own security. Austria had therefore expressed strict reservations concerning so-called positive security assurances. It must be stated clearly that it was for the Country which was the victim of an act of aggression, or of the threat of such act, to decide by itself whether, and to what extent, any assistance offered in that regard would be accepted.' NPT/CONF.II/C.I/SR.6, at p. 196. Similarly, Switzerland declared that 'only so-called negative security assurances were acceptable to Switzerland as a neutral State. Positive assurances of assistance to a State attacked or threatened by nuclear weapons would not be compatible with Switzerland's status of neutrality.' Ibid., p. 189, both available at http://www.un.org/disarmament/WMD/Nuclear/pdf/finaldocs/1980%20-%20Geneva%20-%20NPT%20Review%20Conference%20-%20Final%20Document%20Part%20II.pdf. Elaraby 1995, p. 19; D. Fleck, Second Report on Legal Aspects of Nuclear Disarmament, International Law Association Committee on Nuclear Weapons, Non Proliferation and Contemporary International Law, Washington Conference Report, available at http://www.ila-hq.org/en/committees/index.cfm/cid/1025, para 16.

specify what kind of assistance would be provided to the target State;[77] and the fact that, in reality, any act triggering the obligation to assist a target State under the resolution could only emanate from a NWS and thus, the same State could veto any response to such act in its capacity as a permanent member of the UN Security Council.[78] The picture that emerges is that the widely acknowledged problems associated with the 1968 positive security assurances concern the substance and scope of the obligations undertaken thereunder, rather that the legal status of the instrument by means of which they arose.

The same observations can be made regarding the 1995 positive assurances given by NWS on the path to the extension of the NPT Treaty. Just a few days prior to the crucial 1995 NPT Review Conference, where the question of extending the treaty indefinitely would be decided, each of the official NWS made declarations containing both positive and negative security assurances. These were largely identical and were communicated as official UN documents.[79] For example, the UK stated that:

> In 1968 the United Kingdom declared that aggression with nuclear weapons, or the threat of such aggression, against a non-nuclear-weapon State would create a qualitatively new situation in which the nuclear-weapon States which are Permanent Members of the United Nations Security Council would have to act immediately through the Security Council to take the measures necessary to counter such aggression or to remove the threat of aggression in accordance with the United Nations Charter, which calls for taking 'effective collective measures for the prevention and removal of threats to the peace, and for the suppression of acts of aggression or other breaches of the peace'. Therefore, any State which commits aggression accompanied by the use of nuclear weapons or which threatens such aggression must be aware that its actions are to be countered effectively by measures to be taken in accordance with the United Nations Charter to suppress the aggression or remove the threat of aggression. I, therefore, recall and reaffirm the intention of the United Kingdom, as a Permanent Member of the United Nations Security Council, to seek immediate Security Council action to provide assistance, in accordance with the Charter, to any non-nuclear-weapon State, party to the Treaty on the Non-Proliferation of Nuclear Weapons, that is a victim of an act of aggression or an object of a threat of aggression in which nuclear weapons are used.[80]

The Security Council adopted resolution 984/1995 repeating almost verbatim the relevant part of the corresponding 1968 resolution and, once again, welcomed 'the intention expressed by certain States that they will provide or support immediate assistance, in accordance with the Charter, to any non-nuclear-weapon State Party to the Treaty on the Non-Proliferation of Nuclear Weapons that is a victim of an act of, or an object of a threat of, aggression in which nuclear weapons are used.'[81] Again, the same conclusions drawn in relation to the 1968 declarations may be

[77] Elaraby 1995, p. 19.

[78] Tertrais 2012, p. 249.

[79] See S/1995/261 for the Russian declaration; S/1995/262 for the British declaration; S/1995/263 for the US declaration; S/1995/264 for the French declaration and S/1995/265 for the Chinese declaration, all available at http://www.securitycouncilreport.org/.

[80] See S/1995/262, ibid.

[81] S/RES/984 (1995), available at http://www.un.org/docs/scres/1995/scres95.htm.

repeated here. While the language and the context within which the 1995 declarations were made lend support to the view that they evidence the manifest intention of their authors to be bound, the content and scope of obligations undertaken thereunder do not add anything to pre-existing obligations under the Charter.

13.3.2 Negative Security Assurances

13.3.2.1 The 1978–1982 Negative Security Assurances

The 1968 positive assurances fell short of NNWS expectations and the topic resurfaced during the 1975 NPT Review Conference. The statement made by the representative of Nigeria, Mr. Clark, is characteristic of the mood prevailing amongst NNWS at the time: 'The so-called guarantees of the three nuclear weapon States Parties to the Treaty supposed to be embodied in Security Council resolution 255 (1968) seemed to deceive no one. That resolution was now significant only for its historical and sentimental value.'[82] In the light of the reluctance of NWS to commit themselves to providing assistance beyond the Charter's prescriptions, it was felt that another type of assurances, namely negative ones, would prove more effective. The Finnish representative stated in this respect:

> From the beginning, a number of non-nuclear-weapon States had expressed misgivings about the effectiveness of the security assurances given in Security Council Resolution 255 (1968). Some of these States had expressed a preference for 'negative assurances', whereby nuclear-weapon States would commit themselves never to use nuclear weapons against non-nuclear-weapon States.[83]

In the face of mounting pressure, the US, the UK, China and the USSR gave a first set of negative security assurances during the First Special Session of the UN General Assembly (GA) devoted to Disarmament in 1978. These were neither uniform, nor—with the exception of the Chinese declaration—unqualified. It is worth quoting the relevant passages in full. The Soviet Union declared that 'it will never use nuclear weapons against those States which renounce the production and acquisition of such weapons and do not have them on their territories.'[84] The British and the American assurances were similar in content. More particularly, the British representative made a pledge to

---

[82]Statement by the representative of Nigeria, Mr. Clark, during the 1975 NPT Review Conference, Doc. NPT/CONF/SR.8, p. 84, available at http://www.un.org/disarmament/WMD/Nuclear/pdf/finaldocs/1975%20-%20Geneva%20-%20NPT%20Review%20Conference%20-%20Final%20document%20Part%20III.pdf.

[83]Statement by the Finnish representative, Mr. Hyväriven, during the 1975 NPT Review Conference, ibid., p. 168. For similar statements see for example the statement by the Syrian representative, Mr. El-Fattal, ibid., p. 98 and the statement by the representative of New Zealand, Mr. Roberts, ibid., p. 108.

[84]Statement by the USSR, May 1978, as quoted in Bernauer 1991, p. 8.

> non-nuclear weapon States that are parties to the Treaty on the Non-Proliferation of Nuclear Weapons and to other internationally binding commitments not to manufacture or acquire nuclear explosive devices: Britain undertakes not to use nuclear weapons against such States except in the case of an attack on the United Kingdom, its dependent territories, its armed forces or its allies by such a State in association or alliance with a nuclear-weapon State.[85]

In a similar fashion, the US stated that they

> will not use nuclear weapons against any non-nuclear-weapon State party to the non-proliferation Treaty or any comparable internationally binding commitment not to acquire nuclear explosive devices, except in the case of an attack on the United States, its territories or armed forces, or its allies, by such a State allied to a nuclear-weapon State or associated with a nuclear-weapon State in carrying out or sustaining the attack.[86]

China was the only State to offer an unconditional assurance. It undertook that "at no time and in no circumstances will it be the first to use nuclear weapons."[87] France, at the time, did not follow the lead of the rest of the NWS and simply indicated its willingness to give such assurances in the future 'in accordance with arrangements to be negotiated, to States which constitute non-nuclear zones.'[88] However, in 1982, France gave an assurance that resembled the 1978 Anglo-American formulation: 'For its part, [France] States that it will not use nuclear arms against a State that does not have them and that has pledged not to seek them, except if an act of aggression is carried out in association or in alliance with a nuclear-weapon State against France or against a State with which France has a security commitment.'[89] The final document of the 1978 G.A. Session made a reference to the negative security assurances given by the NWS. Paragraph 59 of that document reads:

> In the same context, the nuclear-weapon States are called upon to take steps to assure the non-nuclear-weapon States against the use or threat of use of nuclear weapons. The General Assembly notes the declarations made by the nuclear-weapon States and urges them to pursue efforts to conclude, as appropriate, effective arrangements to assure non-nuclear-weapon States against the use or threat of use of nuclear weapons.[90]

What is the legal status of the 1978 assurances? Were these assurances binding upon their authors, or were they mere political statements? The language of the G.A.'s final document is quite circumspect. The fact that NWS were urged to

---

[85]As quoted in NPT/CONF. 1995/6, p. 8, available at http://www.un.org/disarmament/WMD/Nuclear/1995-NPT/1995NPT_OfficialDocs.shtml.

[86]Ibid.

[87]Ibid. In April 1982 China added the following to its 1978 declaration: '[China] undertakes unconditionally not to use or threaten to use nuclear weapons against non-nuclear countries and nuclear-free zones.' As quoted in Bernauer 1991, p. 7.

[88]Bernauer 1991, p. 7.

[89]Bernauer 1991, p. 8.

[90]S-10/2 Final Document of the Tenth Special Session of the General Assembly, June 1978, para 59 available at http://www.un.org/disarmament/HomePage/SSOD/A-S-10-4.pdf.

conclude 'effective arrangements' seems to suggest that their recipients did not consider the 1978 assurances 'effective' enough. However, ineffective does not necessarily mean non-binding. Thus, no definite conclusions about the legal status of the assurances can be drawn from the actual text of the 1978 final document.

George Bunn, in his commentary on the 1978 assurances, concludes that they are binding and ascribes their binding force to estoppel.[91] This position does not seem to be convincing. As mentioned earlier, estoppel in international law requires not simply reliance, but *detrimental* reliance on behalf of the addressee. According to Crawford: 'The essence of estoppel is the element of conduct which causes the other party, in reliance on such conduct, detrimentally to change its position or to suffer some prejudice.'[92] Here, there is little evidence to suggest that NNWS relied upon the 1978 assurances—or, for that matter, that any such reliance was to their detriment. The cautious language of the General Assembly's final document, whereby NWS were 'urged' to conclude effective arrangements to reassure NNWS, is an indication that NNWS were far from satisfied with the negative assurances provided. Furthermore, subsequent debates within the context of the NPT Review Conferences clearly demonstrate that the majority of NNWS did not consider the 1978 assurances as binding undertakings.[93]

There are also *de lege ferenda* reasons for disassociating the binding force of negative security assurances from any type of reliance or acceptance on the part of NNWS. As it is evident from their text and as it will be explained below, the 1978 negative security assurances contained a wide spectrum of qualifications. If the only way to view them as binding would be through the operation of estoppel, this would affect the negotiating power of NNWS: if such assurances are only binding

---

[91]Bunn 1997, p. 9.

[92]Crawford 2012, p. 420.

[93]See for example the statements made by Nigeria, New Zealand and Kenya during the 1980 NPT Review Conference, NPT/CONF.II/SR.8; NPT/CONF.II/SR.9; NPT/CONF.II/SR.11, all available at http://www.un.org/disarmament/WMD/Nuclear/NPT_Review_Conferences.shtml. The Nigerian representative (Mr. Adeniji) stated: 'Effective security assurances against the use or threat of use of nuclear weapons would encourage more African States to become Parties to the Treaty … [T]he parties to the Treaty that had renounced the acquisition of nuclear weapons were entitled to receive *credible and binding assurances* from the nuclear-weapon States parties. Inasmuch as the unilateral declarations they had made at the tenth special session of the General Assembly *were inadequate in that respect*, it was essential to conclude the addition Protocol proposed at the first Review Conference.' (Emphasis added) NPT/CONF.II/SR.8, p. 91, para 40. Similarly, Mr. Roberts (New Zealand) stated: 'The nub of the question of security assurances had been the reluctance of the nuclear-weapon States to enhance the status of the *unilateral policy statements* made at the United Nations special session on disarmament.' (Emphasis added) NPT/CONF.II/SR.9, p. 96, para 7. Mr. Mania (Kenya) stated: 'The question of the security assurances to be extended to non-nuclear-weapon States remained unresolved. The nuclear-weapon States had been reluctant to make *firm commitments* that they would never use or threaten to use nuclear weapons against non-nuclear-weapon States. During the tenth Special Session of the General Assembly, its special session on disarmament, the three nuclear-weapon States party to the Treaty had made *official policy statements* regarding the use of nuclear weapons and the matter had become the subject of negotiations in the Committee on Disarmament' (emphasis added) NPT/CONF.II/SR.11, p. 113, para 31.

to the extent that they have been relied upon, NNWS would have to show some element of reliance in order to be able to claim their binding effect later on. This would, however, mean in practice that NNWS would have to settle for a lot less than what they wanted—or even deserved, if one takes into account the obligations undertaken by these States under the NPT.

Turning back to the question of the legal status of the 1978 assurances, a perusal of relevant literature reveals that the debate has been obfuscated by the conflation of two distinct questions, namely the question of the content and scope of these assurances and that of their legal character.[94] However, this approach is not methodologically sound. Ascertaining the existence of an obligation and ascertaining the content of that obligation are two separate operations. As far as the content of the 1978–1982 declarations is concerned, this certainly leaves a lot to be desired. First, these declarations were not uniform in scope and, thus, not all NNWS could benefit from all of them simultaneously. Only the Chinese declaration was addressed to all NNWS. The Anglo-American declarations were addressed to NNWS parties to the NPT; the French one to NNWS that did not seek to acquire nuclear weapons; and the Soviet one to NNWS that did not seek to produce or acquire such weapons and did not have them on their territory.

A further weakness of the 1978–1982 assurances lies in the broad scope of the qualifications contained therein. More particularly, the permissibility of the use or the threat of use of nuclear weapons in case of an attack by a NNWS 'in association or in alliance' with a NWS raises a number of problems. The term "attack" is not clearly defined and it could be construed very broadly to include even conventional attacks.[95] Similarly, the words 'in association' or 'in alliance' with a NWS raise questions regarding the precise degree of involvement needed to allow nuclear retaliation. On the face of it, it seems that this formulation would allow nuclear retaliation in case of an attack by a NNWS allied to a NWS—even in the absence of knowledge of the attack by the NWS ally of the attacking State.[96] While the Soviet declaration did not contain a 'non-attack' condition, it did contain a 'non-stationing' condition that is equally problematic. The difficulties raised by the Soviet condition were highlighted by the UK in a working paper submitted to the CD in 1981.[97] First, the Soviet declaration gave no indication as to how it would be possible to verify in practice the absence of nuclear weapons from the territory of a given State.[98] Second, a number of NPT NNWS, most notably Germany, would not be able to benefit from the Soviet assurance since they had nuclear weapons stationed on their territories on the basis of security arrangements with NATO.[99]

[94]For an account of the different variables to be taken into consideration in addressing the question of negative security assurances, see Rosas 1982, p. 204.

[95]Rosas 1982, p. 207; Bernauer 1991, p. 10.

[96]Eckart 2012, p. 162; Rosas 1982, p. 207; Bernauer 1991, p. 18.

[97]CD/177 (United Kingdom), 10/04/1981 as quoted in Bernauer 1991, pp. 72–75.

[98]Bernauer 1991, p. 74.

[99]Bernauer 1991, p. 74.

All in all, it seems that dissatisfaction with the content and scope of the 1978–1982 assurances is justified. With the exception of China, the assurances given by the remaining NWS were shaped by their respective nuclear military doctrines and allowed them a lot of room for manoeuvre. However, does this mean that the assurances in question, unsatisfactory as they may be, are not binding upon their authors? An examination of the wording and context within which they were made shows that this is not the case. First, the language of the declarations is the language commonly employed in the creation of legal obligations. The Chinese assurance expressly States that 'China undertakes unconditionally not to use or threaten to use nuclear weapons.'[100] Similarly, the British, American, Soviet and French assurances explicitly articulate a commitment not to use nuclear weapons except in certain scenarios envisaged thereunder.[101] Furthermore, the assurances were given before a UN body. This has significant evidentiary weight in establishing the element of the intention to be bound according to the Court's judgment in the *Armed Activities* case. It also needs to be noted that the persons who offered the assurances on behalf of the NWS in question were all official representatives of their States to the UN and that the 1982 French assurance emanated from the Minister for Foreign Affairs of France.[102]

More importantly, two NWS, the US and the UK, have drawn attention to the fact that the formal status of their assurances would not be enhanced through the conclusion of an international agreement- thereby confirming the binding character of their unilateral declarations.[103] During the 1980 NPT Review Conference, the US representative stated that he

> could not agree with the view expressed by a number of delegations in the general debate that negative security assurances required further strengthening, in particular, through the negotiation of a common formula which could be embodied in a binding international convention. *So far as the United States declaration was concerned, no further steps were necessary to make it a credible and effective assurance. The declaration had been issued by the president of the United States after careful consideration of all its implications, and could and should be regarded as a firm and reliable statement* ... The desire for greater uniformity in the assurances available to non-nuclear weapon States was understandable but the prospects for working out a common formula had to be gauged realistically.[104]

The US has repeatedly stressed the binding character of its 1978 assurance. In 1994, the US delegation at the DC stated that 'the United States of America

[100]See above n. 79.

[101]Ibid. Venturini also notes that—because of their very nature as 'obligations to refrain from certain action'—no-first use commitments are clear and precise. Venturini 2015, p. 9.

[102]Bernauer 1991, p. 8.

[103]Rosas 1982, p. 208. This stands in stark contrast to the position taken by the US and Russia in relation to their pledges to reduce nuclear-armed sea-launched cruise missiles (SLCMs). Both countries have expressly stated that their joint statements on SLCMs are only politically binding. See Venturini 2015, p. 10.

[104]Statement by the US representative, NPT/CONF.II/C.7/SR.6, p. 191, available at http://www.un.org/disarmament/WMD/Nuclear/pdf/finaldocs/1980%20-%20Geneva%20-%20NPT%20Review%20Conference%20-%20Final%20Document%20Part%20II.pdf (emphasis added).

recalled its solemn and binding security assurances of 1978, a position that had been reiterated by every subsequent Administration.'[105] Similarly, the UK, in its 1981 working paper on negative security assurances discussed within the context of the CD, stressed that:

> Much of the discussion about security assurances has been concerned with the possibility of making them 'legally binding'. The United Kingdom has always made it clear that its assurance was solemnly and formally given... *The United Kingdom doubts the need for any ... enhancement of its own assurance since it already regards it as a solemn undertaking*. As has been constantly stressed, the assurance took effect immediately [at the moment] it was given. There is no requirement for Non-Nuclear-Weapon States, in order to benefit from the assurance, to conclude a bilateral agreement, to adhere to a yet-to-be-concluded convention, or for there to be some other form of joint action by the Nuclear-Weapon States.[106]

Again, in 1994, the UK stressed "the continued validity of their unilateral security assurances which were solemn and formal undertakings.[107]

Russia, France and China have also expressly declared that they consider their unilateral assurances binding. In discussions within the context of the CD, France stated that it 'fulfilled its *obligations* since it already granted security assurances to non nuclear-weapon States which had undertaken to retain that status'[108] and China 'reiterated its *commitment* that in no time, and under no circumstances, would it be the first to use nuclear weapons, and that it would not use nuclear weapons against non-nuclear-weapon States and nuclear weapon-free zones.'[109] In the same context, Russia 'reiterated the *legally-binding character* of the unilateral Russian declaration on NSA.'[110]

The proposition put forward here, namely that, while the 1978 assurances left a lot to be desired content-wise, they did evidence the manifest intention of their authors to be bound is also shared by some NPT NNWS. Switzerland, Austria and Italy explicitly referred to the doctrine of unilateral juridical acts in explaining why, in their opinion, the 1978 assurances had binding force on the international plane. During the 1980 NPT Review Conference, Switzerland stated that

> the nuclear Powers have, through unilateral declarations, renounced the use or threat of use of nuclear weapons against non-nuclear weapon States. *These declarations are legal undertakings which are binding upon their authors.* The form of the unilateral

---

[105] 1994 Report of the Ad Hoc Committee on Effective International Arrangements to Assure Non-Nuclear-Weapon States against the Use or Threat of use of Nuclear Weapons, CD/1275, para 25, available at http://daccess-dds-ny.un.org/doc/UNDOC/GEN/G94/641/01/IMG/G9464101.pdf?OpenElement.

[106] CD/177 (United Kingdom), above n. 97, pp. 74–75 (emphasis added).

[107] 1994 Report of the Ad Hoc Committee on Effective International Arrangements to Assure Non-Nuclear-Weapon States against the Use or Threat of use of Nuclear Weapons, above n. 105, para 24.

[108] Ibid., para 23 (emphasis added).

[109] Ibid., para 26.

[110] Ibid., para 28.

> undertaking is well-known in international law, as was confirmed by the International court of Justice in the case of nuclear explosions in the Pacific. It is desirable that these undertakings should be further strengthened and some of the texts concerned rendered more precise.[111]

In a similar fashion, the Austrian delegation took 'note with satisfaction of the respective unilateral declarations issued by the Governments of nuclear weapon States … and joined Switzerland in regarding those declarations binding upon the respective Powers under international law.'[112] In the framework of discussions within the CD on the legal value of the 1978 assurances, the Italian delegation quoted the judgment of the Court in the *Nuclear Tests* case and stated that 'under international law, unilateral declarations might contain a binding obligation insofar as a clear commitment can be drawn by their wording.'[113] Furthermore, this position has also found support in literature: Rosas,[114] Bernauer[115] and Eckart,[116] in their commentaries on the 1978–1982 assurances, have concluded that the main weaknesses of those assurances do not lie in their (lack of) binding force, but in their content and scope.

Finally, it is interesting to note that even negative security assurances contained in instruments of undoubtedly binding character, i.e. protocols attached to international agreements, raise problems in practice. A good example here is Additional Protocol II to the Treaty of Tlatelolco which has been signed and ratified by all five NPT NWS. Under Article 3 of the Additional Protocol, the five NWS have undertaken not to use or threaten to use nuclear weapons against the contracting parties to the treaty.[117] However, upon signing and ratifying the Additional Protocol, all NWS—with the exception of China—made certain interpretative statements that closely resemble the qualifications entered in their 1978–1982 unilateral assurances.[118] For example, in ratifying Additional Protocol II, the UK Stated in 1969 that it would 'in the event of any act of aggression by a Contracting Party to the Treaty in which that Party was supported by a nuclear-weapon State, be free to reconsider the extent to which they could be regarded as committed by the

---

[111]Statement by Switzerland, NPT/CONF.II/C.I/5, available at http://www.un.org/disarmament/WMD/Nuclear/pdf/finaldocs/1980%20-%20Geneva%20-%20NPT%20Review%20Conference%20-%20Final%20Document%20Part%20I.pdf (emphasis added).

[112]Statement by Austria, NPT/CONF.II/C.I/SR.6, p. 195 available at http://www.un.org/disarmament/WMD/Nuclear/pdf/finaldocs/1980%20-%20Geneva%20-%20NPT%20Review%20Conference%20-%20Final%20Document%20Part%20II.pdf.

[113]1993 Report of the Ad Hoc Committee on Effective International Arrangements to Assure Non-Nuclear-Weapon States against the Use or Threat of use of Nuclear Weapons, CD/1219, para 24, available at http://daccess-dds-ny.un.org/doc/UNDOC/GEN/G93/622/54/IMG/G9362254.pdf?OpenElement.

[114]Rosas 1982, p. 208.

[115]Bernauer 1991, p. 9.

[116]Eckart 2012, p. 163.

[117]Article 3 of Additional protocol II to the Treaty of Tlatelolco, above n. 6.

[118]For the text of the interpretative statements in question, see Bernauer 1991, pp. 8–9.

provisions of Additional Protocol II.'[119] However, these statements seriously modify the scope of obligations undertaken under Article 3 and thus, are more akin to reservations, rather than mere interpretative statements.[120] This, in turn, raises its own set of problems to the extent that Article 4 of Additional Protocol II prohibits reservations. This brief excursus to negative security assurances contained in treaties verifies the conclusions drawn above, namely that the problems pertaining to security assurances are essentially problems of content and not problems of form.

13.3.2.2 The 1995 Negative Security Assurances

In the aftermath of the UN G.A.'s First Special Session on Disarmament, the topic of negative security assurances lost some of its salience. The relevant debate was transferred to the CD and an ad hoc committee on negative security assurances was established. However, the ad hoc committee failed to make progress and it soon reached a stalemate.[121] The topic regained momentum on the eve of the NPT Review and Extension Conference. As mentioned above, in 1995 the nuclear powers circulated renewed positive and negative security assurances. The French, British, American and Russian assurances were practically identical, thereby alleviating some of the problems associated with the 1978 declarations. For example, the US assurance reads:

> The United States reaffirms that it will not use nuclear weapons against non-nuclear-weapon States Parties to the Treaty on the Non-Proliferation of Nuclear Weapons except in the case of an invasion or any other attack on the United States, its territories, its armed forces or other troops, its allies, or on a State towards which it has a security commitment, carried out or sustained by such a non-nuclear-weapon State in association or alliance with a nuclear-weapon State.[122]

China reaffirmed its no-first-use commitment[123] and added that it 'undertakes not to use or threaten to use nuclear weapons against non-nuclear-weapon States or nuclear-weapon-free zones at any time or under any circumstances.'[124] Security Council resolution 984/1995 took note with appreciation of the declarations.[125]

---

[119]Bernauer 1991, p. 9.

[120]Rosas 1982, p. 213.

[121]See for example the conclusions of the 1993 Report of the Ad Hoc Committee on Effective International Arrangements to Assure Non-Nuclear-Weapon States against the Use or Threat of use of Nuclear Weapons where it is stated that "the complex nature of the issues involved, as well as, inter alia, differing perceptions of security interests continued to impede the work on the substance of the effective arrangements and the search for a common formula." Above n. 113, para 26.

[122]S/1995/263, above n. 79. For the text of the French, British and Russian negative assurances see ibid.

[123]S/1995/265, ibid.

[124]Ibid. China clarified that its "commitment naturally applies to non-nuclear-weapon States parties to the Treaty on the Non-Proliferation of Nuclear Weapons or non-nuclear-weapon States that have entered into any comparable internationally-binding commitment not to manufacture or acquire nuclear explosive devices."

[125]S/RES/984 (1995), above n. 81.

The 1995 declarations improved on existing assurances in so far as their contents were harmonized and the conditions contained therein clarified. More particularly, the 'non-attack' condition was narrowed down to attacks 'carried out' or 'sustained' in association with a NWS ally. This clarification ended the long-standing controversy over the degree of involvement needed to trigger nuclear retaliation. According to the 1995 formulation, the attack itself needs to be carried out by a NNWS in association with its NWS ally. Thus, mere knowledge of the attack by a NWS ally is not enough to precipitate nuclear reprisals. Furthermore, as a result of the harmonization of the contents of the assurances, the 'non-stationing' condition was omitted from the text of the Russian declaration. However, the French, Russian, American and British assurances still left a lot to be desired. By way of contrast to the Chinese declaration, the rest of the assurances were neither unconditional, nor did they include a no-first-use commitment. As such, they failed to assuage the misgivings of NNWS.[126] The NNWS' discontent was reflected in the second decision adopted by the 1995 Conference. Decision 2 para 8 reads:

> Noting United Nations Security Council resolution 984 (1995) which was adopted unanimously on 11 April 1995, as well as the declarations of the nuclear-weapon States concerning both negative and positive security assurances, further steps should be considered to assure non-nuclear-weapon States party to the Treaty against the use or threat of use of nuclear weapons. *These steps could take the form of an internationally legally binding instrument.*[127]

The text of Decision 2 leaves no doubt that the recipients of the 1995 assurances were not convinced of their binding force. On this basis, Cedeño, the Special Rapporteur of the ILC on unilateral acts, concluded that 'the attitude of the authors and the positions of most States appear to reflect the political nature of these statements.'[128] However, to what extent are the reactions of the addresses of a unilateral

[126]See for example the working paper on negative security assurances to non-nuclear-weapon States submitted by Egypt at the 1995 NPT Conference: 'However, resolution 984 (1995) and the unilateral declarations issued by the permanent members of the Security Council, with the exception of the declaration issued by the People's Republic of China, continue to fall short of the general expectations of non-nuclear-weapon States and leave much to be desired to bestow credibility on the assurances they offer.' NPT/CONF.1995/MC.I/WP.4, p. 290, available at http://www.un.org/disarmament/WMD/Nuclear/pdf/finaldocs/1995%20-%20NY%20-%20NPT%20Review%20Conference%20-%20Final%20Document%20Part%20II.pdf. See also the statement made by Indonesia during the Conference: 'The recent declarations issued by the nuclear Powers had failed to assuage the apprehensions of non-nuclear-weapon States, which had long demanded legally binding commitments… States which had renounced the manufacture or acquisition of nuclear weapons had the inherent right to receive unconditional and legally binding assurances.' NPT/CONF.1995/32 (Part III), pp. 34–35, available at http://www.un.org/disarmament/WMD/Nuclear/pdf/finaldocs/1995%20-%20NY%20-%20NPT%20Review%20Conference%20-%20Final%20Document%20Part%20III.pdf.

[127]Decision 2, Principles and Objectives for Nuclear Non-Proliferation and Disarmament, para 8, available at http://www.un.org/disarmament/WMD/Nuclear/1995-NPT/pdf/1995-NY-NPTReviewConference-FinalDocumentDecision_2.pdf (emphasis added).

[128]See the Eight Report on Unilateral Acts of States, UN Doc. A/CN.4/557, 26/05/2005, para 115, available at http://legal.un.org/ilc/documentation/english/a_cn4_557.pdf.

act relevant in establishing whether the act has legal effects? Would the attitude of the beneficiaries of the 1995 assurances preclude an international adjudicative body from concluding that the assurances have binding force? At this point it is worth recalling that in the *Nuclear Tests* case the Court made it abundantly clear that unilateral acts do not need to be accepted by their addressees in order to have legal effects on the international plane.[129] Rather, as it was shown above, the determinant factor in attributing legal effects to unilateral acts is whether these acts manifest the intention of their authors to be bound according to their terms.

As far as the element of the intention to be bound is concerned, the remarks made in relation to the 1978 assurances are also pertinent here. The clear and specific wording of the 1995 assurances as well as the formal context within which they were made indicate that they are legal undertakings, rather than mere political statements.[130] The Court's *Advisory Opinion on the Legality of the Threat or Use of Nuclear Weapons* substantiates this proposition. Although the Court did not expressly pronounce upon the legal status of the 1995 assurances, it analyzed them alongside relevant international agreements.[131] This approach shows that the Court considered the assurances on a par with applicable treaties.[132] The following unanimous finding also corroborates this view:

> A threat or use of nuclear weapons should also be compatible with the requirements of the international law applicable in armed conflict, particularly those of the principles and rules of international humanitarian law, *as well as with specific obligations under treaties and other undertakings which expressly deal with nuclear weapons.*[133]

Despite the fact that the Court placed unilateral assurances on the same footing as applicable international agreements, NNWS remain dissatisfied with the 1995 assurances. However, the problem lying at the heart of the debate on unilateral assurances appears to be the political, rather than the legal dimension of unilateralism. First, NNWS feel that they received very little in return for voluntarily renouncing their nuclear option. Second, the fact that these assurances were issued in the form of unilateral declarations has deprived NNWS from the opportunity of sitting at the negotiating table and shaping their contents alongside NWS. Repeated references to multilateralism in connection to negative security assurances reinforce this conclusion. For example, during the 1998 session of the CD, the governments of Brazil, Egypt, Ireland, Mexico, New Zealand, Slovenia, South Africa and Sweden issued a joint declaration stressing that 'the maintenance of a world free of nuclear weapons will require the underpinnings of a universal and

[129] *Nuclear Tests* case, above n. 8.

[130] The same view is also shared by Eckart 2012, p. 166. See *contra* Venturini who argues that these assurances are not legal undertakings per se, but rather means of implementation of the obligations arising under Art VI of the NPT. Venturini 2015, p. 11.

[131] *Legality of the Threat or Use of Nuclear Weapons*, above n. 4, paras 62–63.

[132] Eckart 2012, p. 166.

[133] *Legality of the Threat or Use of Nuclear Weapons*, above n. 4, para 105(2)(D).

multilaterally negotiated legally binding instrument or a framework encompassing a mutually reinforcing set of instruments.'[134] Similarly, in the 2012 working paper on negative security assurances submitted by Syria on behalf of member States of G-21, multilateralism was reaffirmed as the 'core principle in resolving disarmament and non-proliferation concerns.'[135]

However, it would be erroneous, in my opinion at least, to assume that assurances in the form of unilateral declarations are of minor importance in disarmament diplomacy. In hindsight, it seems that such instruments offered some level of reassurance at a time when the rigid nuclear postures of NWS precluded much else. Simultaneously, they have provided a starting point for further discussion and debate. This allowed NNWS to exercise political pressure and, indirectly, to shape future assurances, as the harmonized contents of the 1995 assurances evidence. This proposition is also verified by the latest British and American nuclear posture reviews, in which the 'non-attack' condition seems to have been dropped. According to the 2010 US Nuclear Posture Review: 'the United States is now prepared to strengthen its long-standing "negative security assurance" by declaring that the United States will not use or threaten to use nuclear weapons against non-nuclear weapon States that are party to the NPT and in compliance with their nuclear non-proliferation obligations.'[136] In a similar vein, the British government stated in its 2010 Strategic Defence and Security Review that 'we are now able to give an assurance that the UK will not use or threaten to use nuclear weapons against non-nuclear weapon States parties to the NPT. In giving this assurance, we emphasise the need for universal adherence to and compliance with the NPT, and note that this assurance would not apply to any State in material breach of those non-proliferation obligations.'[137] Finally, if one takes into account the problems pertaining to treaty-based security assurances as these were exemplified above, it is fair to say that, despite their shortcomings, unilateral assurances have proven to be a flexible and useful tool of non-proliferation policy.

[134] Joint Declaration by the Ministers for Foreign Affairs of Brazil, Egypt, Ireland, Mexico, New Zealand, Slovenia, South Africa and Sweden, CD/1542, p. 2, available at http://daccess-dds-ny.un.org/doc/UNDOC/GEN/G98/624/76/IMG/G9862476.pdf?OpenElement.

[135] Working Paper by Syrian Arab Republic on behalf of Member States of G-21, CD/1940, para 7, available at http://daccess-dds-ny.un.org/doc/UNDOC/GEN/G12/623/39/PDF/G1262339.pdf?OpenElement.

[136] US Department of Defense, Nuclear Posture Review Report, April 2010, p. viii, available at http://www.defense.gov/npr/.

[137] UK Government, Securing Britain in an Age of Uncertainty: The Strategic Defense and Security Review, October 2010, p. 37, available at https://www.gov.uk/government/publications/the-strategic-defence-and-security-review-securing-britain-in-an-age-of-uncertainty.

13.4 Conclusions

This contribution explored the question as to whether and to what extent unilateral security assurances can be viewed as unilateral juridical acts. It was shown that, unilateral juridical acts have two essential elements: unilateralism and the intention to be bound. These two elements were discussed and defined against the backdrop of relevant judicial practice. It was shown that: (a) unilateralism refers to the autonomy of an act to produce legal effects irrespective of any kind of acceptance or reliance on behalf of the addressee; and (b) that the intention to be bound refers to the manifest intention of the author to create legal effects by means of a unilateral act. On the basis of relevant case-law, the chapter established a set of factors that facilitate the task of determining the existence of the element of intention. These include the content of the act, its publicity, the authority that formulated the act on behalf of the State and the forum within which the act was made. The chapter continued by testing existing unilateral security assurances against the background of the doctrine of unilateral juridical acts. It was shown that existing unilateral security assurances leave much to be desired in terms of content and scope. At the same time, it was argued that these assurances—despite their shortcomings—are binding undertakings to the extent that (a) they are autonomous and (b) they manifest the intention of their authors to be bound. It was concluded that viewing such assurances from the perspective of unilateral juridical acts would further enhance their role as a flexible, yet reliable tool, of non-proliferation diplomacy.

References

Bernauer T (1991) Nuclear issues on the agenda of the conference on disarmament. United Nations Institute for Disarmament Research Centre, Geneva

Bowett DW (1957) Estoppel before international tribunals and its relation to acquiescence. BYIL 33:176–202

Bunn D (1997) The legal status of US negative security assurances to non-nuclear weapon States. Non-Prolif Rev 4:1–17

Bunn G, Timmerbaev R (1996) Security assurances to non-nuclear weapon States: possible options for change. PPNN Issue Rev 7:1–12

Cheng B (2006) General principles of law as applied by international courts and tribunals. Cambridge University Press, Cambridge

Cohen A (1998) Israel and the bomb. Columbia University Press, New York

Crawford J (2012) Brownlie's principles of public international law, 8th edn. Oxford University Press, Oxford

Eckart C (2012) Promises of States under international law. Hart Publishing, Oxford

Elaraby N (1995) Some reflections on disarmament. In: Tomuschat C (ed) The United Nations at fifty: a legal perspective. Kluwer Law International, The Hague, pp 19–24

Fitzmaurice M (2002) The identification and character of treaties and treaty obligations between states in international law. BYIL 73:141–185

Franck T (1975) Word made law: the decision of the ICJ in the nuclear tests case. AJIL 69:612–620

Garner J (1933) The international binding force of unilateral oral declarations. AJIL 27:493–497
Giganti A (1962) The effect of unilateral state acts in international law. NYUJ Int'l L Pol 2:333–362
Goldbat J (2009) Negative security assurances. In: Nikitin A (ed) Lessons to be learned from non-proliferation failures and successes. IOS Press, Amsterdam, pp 64–69
Hollis D (2012) Defining treaties. In: Hollis D (ed) The Oxford guide to treaties. Oxford University Press, Oxford, pp 11–45
Khan S (2008) Nuclear weapons and conflict transformation: the case of India-Pakistan. Routledge, New York
Klabbers J (1996) The concept of treaty in international law. Kluwer Law International, The Hague
Nustyen G, Graff Hugo H (2014) The nuclear non-proliferation treaty. In: Nystuen G et al (eds) Nuclear weapons under international law. Cambridge University Press, Cambridge, pp 374–397
Orakhelashvili A (2008) The interpretation of acts and rules in international law. Oxford University Press, Oxford
Rosas A (1982) Negative security assurances and non-use of nuclear weapons German Yrbk Int'l L 25:199–218
Rubin A (1977) The international legal effects of unilateral declarations. AJIL 71:1–30
Sinclair I (1996) Estoppel and acquiescence. In: Lowe V, Fitzmaurice M (eds) Fifty years of the International Court of Justice: essays in honor of sir R. Cambridge University Press, Cambridge, Jennings, pp 104–120
Simpson J (2012) The role of security assurances in the nuclear nonproliferation regime. In: Knopf J (ed) Security assurances and nuclear nonproliferation. Stanford University Press, Stanford, pp 57–88
Suy E (1962) Les actes juridiques unilateraux en droit international public. P. Richon, Paris
Tertrais B (2012) Security assurances and the future of proliferation. In: Wirtz J, Lavoy P (eds) Over the horizon proliferation threats. Stanford University Press, Stanford, pp 240–265
Thirlway H (1989) The law and procedure of the international court of justice. BYIL 60:1–157
Thirlway H (2014) The sources of international law. In: Evans M (ed) international law, 4th edn. Oxford University Press, Oxford, pp 91–117
Tomuschat C (2008) Unilateral acts under international law. In: Meziou K et al (eds) Droits et culture mélanges en l'honneur du doyen Yadh Ben Achour. Centre de Publication Universitaire, Tunis, pp 1487–1507
Venturini G (2011) Control and verification of multilateral treaties on disarmament and non-proliferation of weapons of mass destruction. UC Davis J Int'l L Pol'y 17:345–383
Venturini G (2015) Nuclear non-proliferation and self-restraint commitments: the role of unilateral declarations. In: Black-Branch J, Fleck D (eds) Nuclear non-proliferation in international law, vol II. TMC Asser Press, The Hague

Chapter 14
Nuclear Non-Proliferation and Self-restraint Commitments: The Role of Unilateral Declarations

Gabriella Venturini

Abstract International practice in the field of nuclear non-proliferation abounds with unilateral declarations made by nuclear-weapon States to give security assurances to non-nuclear-weapon States, to announce reductions in the nuclear weapon stockpiles and in military fissile material stocks, or to introduce moratoriums on fissile material production or nuclear weapons testing. In some cases, declarations are made in parallel and simultaneously. A number of theories have been put forward to try to demonstrate that unilateral declarations can entail legally binding commitments for the declarant State. According to the jurisprudence of the International Court of Justice and to the *Guiding Principles applicable to unilateral declarations of States capable of creating legal obligations*, adopted by the International Law Commission in 2006, unilateral legal acts may have binding force provided that they are public, generally known, and that they clearly reflect an intention to be bound. While the first two conditions are generally met by unilateral declarations in the field of non-proliferation, the last one seems to be lacking. Similarly, the absence of willingness to be bound prevents parallel undertakings from being regarded as executive agreements. Nevertheless, unilateral declarations may give rise to legitimate expectations of third States, especially if they are seen in conjunction with the obligations laid down by NPT Article VI. Several questions are being raised regarding the effective implementation and expediency of unilateral initiatives in nuclear non-proliferation. Especially, the absence of obligatory verification measures is considered as a serious shortcoming. To address this concern it is essential that NWS adopting unilateral commitments secure transparency as a voluntary confidence building measure based on

---

Professor of Human Rights in Armed Conflict, Geneva Academy of International Humanitarian Law and Human Rights, former Director of the Department of International Studies, Università degli Studi di Milano, Italy; Member of the ILA Committee on Nuclear Weapons, Non-Proliferation and Contemporary International Law.

G. Venturini (✉)
Via Fratelli Cervi, Milano Due, Residenza dei Mestieri 222, I-20090 Segrate, MI, Italy
e-mail: venturini.gabriella@gmail.com

J.L. Black-Branch and D. Fleck (eds.), *Nuclear Non-Proliferation in International Law - Volume II*, DOI 10.1007/978-94-6265-075-6_14

disclosure, accessibility and reliability of information. Founded on the principle of good faith, transparency offers a reliable pattern for ensuring implementation of unilateral non-proliferation commitments and it has a central role in the context of nuclear non-proliferation.

Keywords Confidence-building measures · Moratorium · Political commitment · Security assurances · Transparency · Unilateral declarations

Contents

14.1 Introduction

While treaties are undoubtedly the main instrument through which nuclear-weapon States (hereinafter: NWS)[1] accept obligations in the field of non-proliferation, significant commitments may also be undertaken unilaterally or by means of parallel declarations or statements, which may be issued independently or within the framework of previous arms control agreements. Unilateral (sometimes parallel) moratoriums have also been resorted to in the lengthy process of prohibiting

[1]Pursuant to Article IX para 3 of the Treaty on the Non-Proliferation of Nuclear Weapons (NPT) of 1 July 1968, 729 UNTS 161, a nuclear-weapon State is one which has manufactured and exploded a nuclear weapon or other nuclear explosive device prior to 1 January 1967. According to the meaning of the NPT the five NWS are China, France, Russia, the United Kingdom and the United States. Since 1967, India and Pakistan have openly developed nuclear weapons; Israel is widely considered to possess nuclear weapons, although it declines to confirm; the Democratic People's Republic of Korea (DPRK) developed a nuclear explosive capability and has tested nuclear explosive devices and announced them. These four States are not parties to the NPT.

nuclear weapons testing. This practice raises a number of questions that need to be addressed. Which are the advantages and disadvantages of unilateral/parallel declarations compared with the conclusion of a treaty? May unilateral declarations in the field of nuclear non-proliferation have binding legal effects for the declarant States? Are unilateral commitments somehow related to the obligation established by Article VI of the Non-Proliferation Treaty 'to pursue negotiations in good faith on effective measures relating to cessation of the nuclear arms race at an early date and to nuclear disarmament'? Do effective means of verification of such commitments exist and, if they do, how are they actually used?

The purpose of this contribution is to discuss whether and to what extent unilateral declarations such as reduction commitments and nuclear test moratoriums may have binding legal effects, or give rise of legitimate expectations by the addressee or by other States. To this end, the relevant declarations will be analyzed in closer detail and in the light of the general principles of international law governing the formation and execution of legal obligations. Then the existing and prospective confidence-building measures will be examined with a view to determining whether they are suited to ensure transparency and to foster compliance with unilateral commitments.

14.2 Unilateral Declarations in the Field of Nuclear Non-Proliferation: The Practice

International practice shows several types of unilateral declarations in the field of nuclear non-proliferation. The first category is that of security assurances provided by the NWS, including negative security assurances, positive security assurances and no-first-use declarations. A second group consists of pledges by the NWS to reduce the size of their arsenals, occasionally taking the form of parallel undertakings. A third group relates to statements concerning military fissile material. A fourth group involves nuclear test moratoriums, i.e. announcements to cease or suspend nuclear test explosions. With the exception of positive security assurances, unilateral declarations entail self-restraint, thus restricting the freedom of action of NWS.

The purpose of the present contribution is not the drafting of a catalogue of unilateral declarations in the field of nuclear non-proliferation. Instead, it will consider those that might create legal or political commitments, as well as their means of implementation.

14.2.1 Nuclear Security Assurances and No-First-Use Declarations

In the field of nuclear non-proliferation security assurances have been sought by non-NWS in exchange for their renunciation of the right to manufacture, acquire and possess nuclear weapons. Security assurances have been given by NWS in three forms: unilateral declarations undertaking not to use, or threaten to use, their nuclear weapons against non-NWS (negative security assurances); pledges to come to the aid of a non-NWS against which nuclear weapons have been used, or which is threatened by nuclear weapons (positive security assurances) and no-first-use commitments where a NWS undertakes never to be the first to use nuclear weapons (no-first-use declarations). Unlike security assurances, that are addressed to non-NWS, no-first-use declarations are directed to both non-NWS and to other NWS as well, so encompassing both a negative security assurance to non-NWS and a no-attack commitment to other NWS.[2] While NWS practice concerning security assurances is dealt with elsewhere in this volume,[3] it is worthwhile to mention no-first-use commitments which have been given through unilateral declarations. To date, China is the only NWS clearly maintaining a no-first-use commitment.[4] India and the Democratic People's Republic of Korea (DPRK), which possess nuclear weapons but are not parties to the NPT, also made no-first-use pledges, however their policy is more ambiguous with this regard.[5] The Soviet Union undertook a no-first-use commitment in 1982, but the Russian government withdrew it in 1993.[6] The remaining NWS have consistently refused to adopt a no-first-use policy.

14.2.2 Nuclear Weapons Reduction Commitments

Reductions in the nuclear weapon stockpiles are ordinarily carried out unilaterally and independently by NWS depending on their assessment of the forces needed to assure national security. Occasionally, they are made the subject of formal, public declarations. During the last decade of the twentieth century and at the very beginning of the new millennium, three unilateral and parallel schemes of nuclear reductions were undertaken by the US and the USSR and its successor State Russia, which together have the vast majority of nuclear stockpiles: the 1991 Presidential Nuclear Initiatives; the 1997 Russia-United States Joint Statement on Parameters on Future Reduction in Nuclear Forces; and the Russia-United States Strategic Stability Cooperation Initiative in 2000. The two States

[2]See Simpson 1994, pp. 24–26 pointing out the complex nature of no-first-use declarations.

[3]See Chap. 13 in this volume, Kassoti, The Legal Nature of Unilateral Security Assurances: Conceptualizing Positive and Negative Security Assurances as Unilateral Juridical Acts.

[4]China's no-first-use commitment is included in its 1995 statement on negative security assurances (UN Doc. A/50/155 and S/1995/265). See 20 *United Nations Disarmament Yearbook* (1995) p. 10.

[5]The DPRK's no-first-use policy is reported by Yu and Guangqian 2009, p. 81. Sagan 2009, p. 176 raises concerns about India's movement away from a strict no-first-use policy.

[6]See Feiveson and Hogendoorn 2003, p. 3, discussing the USSR's original pledge not to resort to the first use of nuclear weapons.

also issued a number of joint statements, notably within the framework of the 1991 START Treaty.[7]

14.2.2.1 The Presidential Nuclear Initiatives (1991)

The set of commitments collectively known as the 'Presidential Nuclear Initiatives' (PNIs) were launched by the US President George H.W. Bush on 27 September 1991, near the Cold War's end. Through its President, the US pledged to unilaterally and unconditionally withdraw to the United States all ground-launched short-range weapons deployed overseas and destroy them along with existing US stockpiles of the same weapons, and to cease deployment of tactical nuclear weapons on surface ships, attack submarines, and land-based naval aircraft during 'normal circumstances.' A week later, on 5 October, the USSR President Mikhail Gorbachev (who reportedly had been informed just hours before the PNI became public) announced in his turn a number of measures consisting of the elimination of all nuclear artillery munitions, nuclear warheads for tactical missiles and nuclear mines; the removal of all tactical nuclear weapons from surface ships and multipurpose submarines; and the separation of nuclear warheads from air defence missiles and their partial destruction.[8] In December 1991, just before the Soviet Union's breakup, the Soviet Republics of Belarus, Kazakhstan and Ukraine pledged to return all Soviet tactical nuclear weapons on their territories to Russia by 1 July 1992. On 29 January 1992, the Russian President Boris Yeltsin reaffirmed Gorbachev's commitments and expanded on them in response to a second round of unilateral US nuclear weapons reductions. It appears that on that occasion Yeltsin was given more advance notice of the US proposals.[9]

14.2.2.2 Russia–United States Joint Statements on Reductions in Nuclear Forces

On 21 March 1997, President Clinton and President Yeltsin reached a further understanding on nuclear reductions. The international situation seemed favourable since the NPT had been indefinitely extended in 1995 and the Comprehensive

[7]These statements were related to nuclear-armed sea-launched cruise missiles (SLCMs) that were not counted within the Treaty limits. The two governments accepted that the number of deployed nuclear SLCMs would not exceed 880 per year and they undertook to exchange annual declarations specifying the maximum number of deployed nuclear SLCMs planned every 5 years. See A.F. Woolf, Next Steps in Nuclear Arms Control with Russia: Issues for Congress, Congressional Research Service 7-5700, January 6, 201, http://fas.org/sgp/crs/nuke/R43037.pdf, p. 7.

[8]The text of the Presidential Nuclear Initiative announcements is reproduced in Koch 2012, pp. 23–39.

[9]See Arms Control Association, U.S.-Russian Strategic Stability Cooperation Initiative, September 6, 2000. https://www.armscontrol.org/act/2000_10/dococt00.

Nuclear Test Ban Treaty (CTBT) had been signed by both the US and Russia in 1996.[10] The 1997 Joint Statement committed the two States to immediately begin negotiations on a START III after the START II Treaty of 3 January 1993 would enter into force, with a view to promoting the irreversibility of reductions and the prevention of a rapid increase in the number of warheads; to making the START treaties unlimited in duration; and to deactivating the status of all strategic nuclear delivery vehicles to be eliminated under START II by removing their nuclear warheads or taking other jointly agreed steps.[11] Despite these good intentions, the Presidents also reached an agreement to postpone the deadline for the elimination of strategic nuclear delivery vehicles. As a consequence, on 26 September 1997, the Russian Foreign Minister and the US Secretary of State signed a protocol extending the deadline for completing reductions from December 31, 2001 to December 31, 2007.

Additional initiatives were taken by President Clinton and President Vladimir Putin in 2000. The Joint Statement on Principles of Strategic Stability (adopted in Moscow on 4 June 2000) and the Joint Statement on Cooperation on Strategic Stability (adopted in Okinawa on 21 July 2000) resulted in the Strategic Stability Cooperation Initiative adopted at the United Nations Millennium Summit in New York on 6 September 2000.[12] Said declarations, however, were conditional on preserving the Anti-Ballistic Missile (ABM) Treaty and on the entry into force of the START II Treaty and its 1997 Protocol. The US withdrawal from the ABM Treaty in 2002 and the complex events that marked the process of ratification of START II eventually prevented it from coming into effect. As a consequence, the assumption underlying both the 1997 and the 2000 declarations has been lacking.

14.2.2.3 Initiatives to Reduce Military Fissile Material Stocks

Unilateral initiatives relating to fissile material include announcements by the NWS that the production of highly enriched uranium (HEU) or plutonium for use in nuclear weapons has been terminated and declarations that military fissile material has been removed from defense stockpiles and transferred to civil use. Four of the five NWS: the US, Russia, the UK and France have openly declared that they have ended their production of HEU and plutonium for weapon purposes; recently,

---

[10]Comprehensive Nuclear-Test-Ban Treaty, opened for signature at New York on 24 September 1996 (not yet in force).

[11]Russia-United States Joint Statement on Parameters on Future Reduction in Nuclear Forces and Russia-United States Joint Statement Concerning the Anti-Ballistic Missile Treaty, March 21, 1997, Public Papers of the Presidents of the United States, William J. Clinton, 1997, Book 1: January 1 to June 30, 1997 Government Printing Office, 1999, pp. 340–341. http://www.gpo.gov/fdsys/pkg/PPP-1997-book1/pdf/PPP-1997-book1-doc-pg340.pdf.

[12]Strategic Stability Cooperation Initiative Between the United States of America and Russian Federation, Text of the Joint Statement and Implementation Plan, see http://www.state.gov/1997-2001-NOPDFS/global/arms/factsheets/missdef/000906_fswh_tmd.html.

however, Russia announced it would restart limited HEU production for civil uses. China, which did not make a public declaration, is also deemed to have halted its production *de facto*.[13] Pakistan and possibly India are believed to be producing HEU for weapons, while it is uncertain whether the DPRK has been producing HEU. Israel, India, and Pakistan continue to produce plutonium and the DPRK is also believed to have resumed production.[14]

In addition to ending production of fissile material for weapons, the US, Russia and the UK have declared large amounts of existing HEU and plutonium as excess to the requirements of their nuclear force and national security, after dismantlement of tens of thousands warheads. Military fissile material that has been declared excess is to be disposed of or destined for other uses, mostly for civil purposes.[15]

14.2.3 Unilateral Moratoriums on Nuclear Test Explosions

The history of unilateral commitment to halt nuclear test explosions started in 1958, when the USSR first announced a unilateral suspension. Following some initial uncertainty, the moratorium was then accepted by the US and the UK.[16] This boosted political negotiations on an agreement to ban nuclear test explosions in the atmosphere, which eventually resulted in the Partial Test Ban Treaty (PTBT) of 5 August 1963.[17] While the UK, the US and the USSR immediately ratified the treaty, China and France never became parties.

In June 1973, after having been taken before the International Court of Justice (ICJ) by Australia and New Zealand, French authorities publicly and repeatedly declared that after completion of the round then in progress, no further atmospheric nuclear tests would be carried out in the South Pacific.[18] In its judgement

[13]See Feiveson et al. 2014, pp. 43–54 providing an overview of the declarations.

[14]See IPFM, International Panel on Fissile Materials. Global Fissile Material Report. Increasing Transparency of Nuclear Warhead and Fissile Material Stocks as a Step toward Disarmament. http://fissilematerials.org/library/gfmr13.pdf, pp. 3–9.

[15]See IPFM (2013) International Panel on Fissile Materials. Global Fissile Material Report. Increasing Transparency of Nuclear Warhead and Fissile Material Stocks as a Step toward Disarmament. http://fissilematerials.org/library/gfmr13.pdf, pp. 59–70 and Feiveson et al. 2014, pp. 159–177 describing NWS's reduction programs.

[16]See Divine 1986, p. 24 retracing the history of early nuclear test moratoriums.

[17]Treaty Banning Nuclear Weapon Tests in the Atmosphere, in Outer Space and Under Water, opened for signature at London, Moscow and Washington on 8 August 1963, entered into force on 10 October 1963. http://disarmament.un.org/treaties/t/test_ban.

[18]International Court of Justice, *Nuclear Tests* cases, Judgements of 20 December 1974, *Australia v. France*, ICJ Rep. 1974, paras 34–41; *New Zealand v. France*, ICJ Rep. 1974, paras 35–44.

(without fully explaining its reasons), the Court found that the French statements constituted an undertaking possessing legal effect.[19]

Between 1991 and 1992, both Russia and the US adopted domestic legislation declaring national moratoriums on nuclear test explosions. After conducting its 45th test in July 1996, China began in its turn a unilateral moratorium.[20] As a matter of fact, since 1996 none of the five NWS parties to the NPT has conducted any nuclear test explosions.

In 1999, India and Pakistan concluded the Lahore Memorandum of Understanding, a bilateral agreement aimed at the resolution of a number of controversial issues.[21] The Memorandum includes a commitment to 'continue to abide by their respective unilateral moratorium on conducting further nuclear test explosions unless either side, in exercise of its national sovereignty decides that extraordinary events have jeopardised its supreme interests.'[22] The moratoriums are still in effect.

In February 2012, also the North Korean government announced a suspension of nuclear and missile testing as well as uranium enrichment.[23] The moratorium, however, was breached after 1 year by a new underground NTE carried out by the DPRK on 12 February 2013.

14.3 Legal Effects of Unilateral Declarations in the Field of Nuclear Non-Proliferation

A unilateral manifestation by which a State undertakes a legally binding commitment to do or refrain from doing something in the future is commonly referred to as a promise, or a unilateral act *stricto sensu*.[24] It is generally recognized that this kind of commitment may have the effect of creating legal obligations giving the

[19]ICJ *Nuclear Tests* cases, above n. 18, *Australia v. France*, paras 50–52; *New Zealand v. France*, paras 52–55. See Singh and McWhinney 1989, pp. 294–297; Klabbers 1996, pp. 196–199; Kolb 2000, pp. 331–332; Eckart 2012, pp. 116–137, analyzing in critical terms the reasoning of the Court. See also Kassoti, Chap. 13 in this volume.

[20]A comprehensive review of national positions on nuclear testing is given by J. Medalia, Comprehensive Nuclear-Test-Ban Treaty: Background and Current Developments, September 29, 2014, Congressional Research Service, Report for Congress RL33548. http://fas.org/sgp/crs/nuke/RL33548.pdf, pp. 2–12.

[21]Lahore Memorandum of Understanding, 21 February 1999. http://cns.miis.edu/inventory/pdfs/aptlahore.pdf.

[22]Ibid., para 4.

[23]See Chronology of U.S.-North Korean Nuclear and Missile Diplomacy. http://www.armscontrol.org/factsheets/dprkchron.

[24]A systematic discussion of promises within the general framework of unilateral acts of States is given by Eckart 2012, pp. 28–29 and Rodriguez Cedeño and Torres Cazorla 2013, para 1.

addressee, or addressees, the right to request compliance.[25] However, neither unilateral declarations nor promises are mentioned in Article 38 of the ICJ Statute reflecting the sources of international law. As a consequence, their legal weight is to be assessed according to international practice and jurisprudence.

For the purposes of this contribution, the main sources of reference are the ICJ judgements of 20 December 1974 in the *Nuclear Tests* cases and the *Guiding Principles applicable to unilateral declarations of States capable of creating legal obligations* adopted by the International Law Commission (ILC) in 2006.[26] What emerges from these sources is that unilateral declarations must meet a number of conditions to become legally binding. First, the fundamental factor is the intention of the State making the declaration that it should become bound according to its terms.[27] Second, the content of the declaration must be sufficiently clear and specific.[28] Third, the undertaking must be given publicly by an authority vested with the power to express the State's will.[29] Fourth, the obligations resulting from a binding unilateral declaration must be interpreted in a restrictive manner, based on the text of the declaration and taking into account the context as well as the circumstances in which it was formulated.[30]

Both the ICJ judgements and the ILC Principles emphasize that the binding character of an international obligation assumed by unilateral declaration is based on good faith. 'Thus interested States may take cognizance of unilateral declarations and place confidence in them, and are entitled to require that the obligation thus created be respected.'[31]

14.3.1 Statements Made Publicly by Competent Organs

Given the importance of nuclear policy it is hardly surprising that unilateral commitments in the field of non-proliferation are made publicly by heads of State, heads of government, ministers for foreign affairs or other authorities vested with

---

[25]See Kassoti, Chap. 13 in this volume.

[26]International Law Commission, Guiding Principles applicable to unilateral declarations of States capable of creating legal obligations, with commentaries thereto, *Yearbook of the International Law Commission*, 2006, vol. II, Part Two, 369–381. See Pronto and Wood 2010, pp. 547–561; Eckart 2012, pp. 185–194; Rodriguez Cedeño and Torres Cazorla 2013, paras 10–14.

[27]ICJ *Nuclear Tests* cases, above n. 18, Australia v. France, para 43; New Zealand v. France, para 46; ILC *Guiding Principles*, Principle 1.

[28]ICJ *Nuclear Tests* cases, above n. 18; ILC *Guiding Principles*, Principle 7.

[29]ICJ *Nuclear Tests* cases, above n. 18; ILC *Guiding Principles*, Principle 4.

[30]ICJ *Nuclear Tests* cases, above n. 18, *Australia v. France*, para 44; *New Zealand v. France*, para 47; ILC *Guiding Principles*, Principle 7.

[31]ICJ *Nuclear Tests* cases, above n. 20, *Australia v. France*, para 46; *New Zealand v. France*, ICJ Rep. 1974, para 49. The reference to good faith is reiterated by Principle 1 of the ILC *Guiding Principles*.

the power to express the will of the State. For example, the 1995 declarations on nuclear security assurances (including China's no-first-use commitment) were made by the highest authorities of the NWS;[32] the Security Council formally took note 'with appreciation' of the statements made.[33] The 1991 PNIs, as well as the parallel US and Russia declarations on nuclear reduction commitments in 1997 and 2002, were publicly made by presidents George H.W. Bush, Mikhail Gorbachev, William Jefferson Clinton, Boris Yeltsin and Vladimir Putin. End of production and reductions in the stockpiles of military fissile material were also announced by the highest representatives of the State or by competent regulatory authorities. Unilateral moratoriums on nuclear testing adopted by means of national laws were approved by parliamentary organs, however the executive had an initiating and complementary role in decision-making, as well as the power to extend or to terminate the halting. Parliamentary debates were widely available and the resulting legislation was officially communicated to other States in the appropriate international fora.[34] Thus, looking at the unilateral declarations in the field of nuclear non-proliferation in the light of the criteria laid down by the ICJ in the *Nuclear Tests* cases and by the ILC in the *Guiding Principles*, it appears that the requirement of the capacity of State authorities to represent and commit the State internationally is largely met.

14.3.2 Clarity and Precision of Content

Principle 7 of the ILC *Guiding Principles* establishes that a unilateral declaration entails obligations for the declarant State only if it is expressed in clear and specific terms. As a matter of fact, it is hardly possible to say that unilateral declarations in the field of non-proliferation were always clear and specific. Leaving aside the case of nuclear security assurances, which are apparently worded in precise terms but include exceptions that may give rise to dubious interpretations,[35] it can

[32]See UN Doc. A/50/151 and S/1995/261 for the Russian declaration; A/50/1512 and S/1995/262 for the British declaration; A/50/153 and S/1995/263 for the US declaration; A/50/154 and S/1995/264 for the French declaration; A/50/151 and S/1995/265 for the Chinese declaration.

[33]S/RES/984 (1995) para 1.

[34]See W. Burr and H.L. Montford (eds), The Making of the Limited Test Ban Treaty, 1958–1963. http://www2.gwu.edu/~nsarchiv/NSAEBB/NSAEBB94/, presenting a selection of US government documents (especially documents 1 to 8). See also Nuclear Threat Initiative, China Nuclear Chronology. http://www.nti.org/media/pdfs/china_nuclear_3.pdf?_=1364257156, especially pp. 53 and 78.

[35]This is the case of the verb 'sustained' which appears in the US, UK, French and Russian declarations where these States declare that they will not use nuclear weapons against non-NWS parties to the NPT except in the case of an invasion or any other attack 'carried out or sustained' by a non-NWS in association or alliance with a NWS. See Docs. A/50/151–S/1995/261 (Russia), A/50/152–S/1995/262 (United Kingdom), A/50/153–S/1995/263 (United States), A/50/154–S/1995/264 (France), A/50/155–S/1995/265 (China); A/50/151-155. The clearest and most precise wording is that of the Chinese declaration: see Eckart 2012, p. 164.

be noted that while some of the PNIs undertakings were clear and specific, others were indeterminate.[36] The 1997 Joint Statement on Parameters on Future Reduction in Nuclear Forces simply set out the subject of forthcoming negotiations (that eventually did not take place), while the Strategic Stability Cooperation Initiative of 2000 merely reaffirmed in broad terms the two countries' support for a number of existing arms control agreements and objectives. Conversely, declarations relating to reductions in stockpiles of military fissile material provide detailed figures on the amounts and types of materials covered.

No-first-use declarations and unilateral moratoriums (either on production of military fissile material or on nuclear test explosions) being commitments 'not to do', i.e. to refrain from a certain action, are inherently clear and specific. However, in the case of testing moratoriums, the precise meaning of the term 'explosion' may be subject to different interpretations. In sum, the requirement of clear and specific wording is not always satisfied.

14.3.3 Legal or Political Commitments?

As in the case for treaties, a fundamental aspect of unilateral commitments is the declarant State's intent. This may either express an unconditional decision to legally oblige itself or a mere political, not legally binding pledge. Both the ICJ judgements on the *Nuclear Tests* cases and the ILC *Guiding Principles* attach paramount importance to State intent in order to ascertain the legal effects of unilateral declarations. Intent is to be inferred from the text of the declaration and the circumstances in which it was made, on the basis of a restrictive interpretation.[37]

While there are good arguments in favour of considering negative security assurances as legally binding according to the intention of NWS, non-NWS have repeatedly called on NWS to conclude an international legally binding treaty, thus demonstrating that they do not perceive the 1995 statements as legally binding undertakings.[38] This probably means that rules other than non-proliferation obli-

[36]One of the key pledges was to remove the tactical nuclear weapons from surface ships and attack submarines and to place them in central storage, along with nuclear weapons on land-based naval aircraft. President Bush pledged to destroy 'many', President Gorbachev to eliminate 'a portion.' See S.J. Koch, The Presidential Nuclear Initiatives of 1991–1992, Center for the Study of Weapons of Mass Destruction, National Defense University. http://ndupress.ndu.edu/Portals/68/Documents/casestudies/CSWMD_CaseStudy-5.pdf, p. 40.

[37]ICJ *Nuclear Tests* cases, above n. 20, *Australia v. France*, paras 43–44, 49; *New Zealand v. France*, paras 46–47, 51; Principle 7 of the ILC *Guiding Principles*.

[38]See Eckart 2012, pp. 165–166. The UN Secretary-General's remarks delivered at the opening session of the Nuclear Security Summit in The Hague on 24 March 2014 supports the second view since he calls on States parties at the upcoming 2015 NPT Review Conference to 'address the legitimate interest of non-nuclear States in receiving unequivocal and legally-binding security assurances from nuclear-weapon States.' See Press Release SG/SM/15725-DC/3483. http://www.un.org/press/en/2014/sgsm15725.doc.htm.

gations, such as treaties establishing nuclear-weapon-free zones, are a more appropriate legal framework to deal with these aspects.[39]

As regards no-first-use commitments it must be borne in mind that under *ius ad bellum* any first use of nuclear weapons would be clearly contrary to the prohibition of the use of force established by Article 2 para 4 of the UN Charter, which corresponds to customary international law. Thus the obligation not to be the first to make use of nuclear weapons is the result of the existing law and not of a unilateral commitment. Nevertheless, under *ius in bello*, or the law of armed conflict, the legality of the use of nuclear weapons is still the subject of some disagreement. In its *Nuclear Weapons Opinion*, the ICJ held that

> the threat or use of nuclear weapons would generally be contrary to the rules of international law applicable in armed conflict, and in particular the principles and rules of humanitarian law; however, in view of the current State of international law, and of the elements of fact at its disposal, the Court cannot conclude definitively whether the threat or use of nuclear weapons would be lawful or unlawful in an extreme circumstance of self-defence, in which the very survival of a State would be at stake.[40]

A clear and unconditional no-first-use-commitment precludes the declarant State from using first nuclear weapons in any circumstances, even when its very survival would be in danger. In such an extreme situation, however, it seems very difficult that a State could give up its ultimate means of defence.

The Russia-United States joint statements on SLCMs expressly stated that the declarations were only *politically* binding[41] and it is generally recognized that the PNIs commitments were also *politically*, not legally, binding.[42] As a matter of fact

[39]Protocols to nuclear-weapon-free zones (NWFZ) make negative security assurances by NWS obligatory with respect to the parties to the NWFZ. See Additional Protocol II to the Treaty of Tlatelolco Article 3; Protocol II to the Treaty of Rarotonga Article 1; Protocol I to the Pelindaba Treaty Article 1; Protocol to the Bangkok Treaty Article 2; Protocol to the Treaty on a Nuclear-Weapon-Free Zone in Central Asia (CANWFZ) Article 1. This confirms that agreement is the most appropriate instrument for the purpose of giving negative security assurances. It should be noted, however, that only Additional protocol II to the Treaty of Tlatelolco has been ratified by the five NWS; the treaties of Rarotonga and Pelindaba have been ratified by China, France, Russia and the United Kingdom; the CANWFZ has been ratified by France and the United Kingdom, while no NWS has ratified the Protocol to the Bangkok Treaty thus far. http://disarmament.un.org/treaties/. Accessed 18 March 2015.

[40]*Legality of the Threat or Use of Nuclear Weapons*, Advisory Opinion of 8 July 1996, ICJ Rep. 1996, para 105(2) E.

[41]'Politically binding' agreements are generally defined a contrario as 'non legally binding' instruments. Their goals tend to be broad and loosely defined, and the means to achieve them are at the discretion of participants. The fundamental factor in determining whether an international agreement is 'legally binding' depends on the parties' intent to be legally bound. See Klabbers 1996, pp. 216–217.

[42]This topic is discussed by Corin 2004, p. 5; Handler 2002, pp. 107–132, at 107.

these commitments, as well as subsequent Russia-US joint declaration and statements, were motivated primarily by the desire to avoid burdensome and lengthy negotiations as well as the unpredictability of national ratification processes. In other words, the intent to be bound could have been present, but the existing political circumstances prevented it to emerge.[43] Moreover, the two States took advantage of flexibility allowing them to reduce or increase their nuclear forces in response to their changing security needs.[44] It is therefore not possible to consider them as binding unilateral commitments. The same reasoning prevents us from considering parallel unilateral declarations as executive agreements. Despite the apparent consistency of the statements, the marked absence of the will to be bound puts them outside the scope of application of the law of treaties.

In the same vein, unilateral initiatives by NWS on fissile material could hardly be interpreted as legally binding promises. The US, for example, clearly considers that its moratorium on the production of military fissile material would only become legally binding if established through a multilateral treaty.[45] But despite support given by the majority of States, NPT Review Conferences and UNGA's recommendations, negotiations on a Fissile Materials Cutoff Treaty are not yet open within the Conference on Disarmament.

As regards reductions in military fissile material stockpiles, their purpose seems merely aimed at providing information about national policies and not at committing governments to a specified course of action. As a matter of fact, when the intent to be bound is present, declarations are channelled into the framework of bilateral agreements.[46] Nevertheless, decisions by NWS to make available information about their fissile material stocks and related policies certainly increase transparency and, to some extent, they allow the adoption of verification measures.[47]

The legal effects of unilateral moratoriums on nuclear test explosions should be appraised in a wider context. The UN Security Council repeatedly condemned nuclear testing, expressing 'grave concern' at their 'negative effect' on peace and

[43]Klabbers 1996 describes a comparable situation with reference to the 1941 Atlantic Charter, p. 71.

[44]This is still a meaningful option, see Kristensen 2013.

[45]See for example the address by President Clinton to the UN General Assembly on 26 September 1994 and the remarks by President Obama in Prague on 5 April 2009. http://www.state.gov/p/io/potusunga/207377.htm; https://www.whitehouse.gov/the_press_office/Remarks-By-President-Barack-Obama-In-Prague-As-Delivered/. Accessed 23 March 2014.

[46]Such as the agreement between Russia and the US concerning the disposition of Highly-Enriched Uranium (so called 'Megaton to Megawatts program') of 1993 or the Plutonium Management and Disposition Agreement (PMDA) of 2000. http://fissilematerials.org/library/heu93.pdf; http://fissilematerials.org/library/PMDA2010.pdf. Accessed 23 March 2015. See Hafemaister 2013, pp. 98–105 describing Russian-US programmes and agreements on reduction and disposition of fissile material.

[47]Below Sect. 14.4.

stability and referring to Chapter VII of the UN Charter.[48] Among the NWS, France, Russia and the United Kingdom have ratified the CTBT and they are consequently bound not to defeat the object and purpose of the treaty prior to its entry into force. The 'parallel unilateral' moratoriums currently implemented by India and Pakistan are covered by a binding commitment—the Lahore declaration—that in the opinion of the present author does constitute an executive agreement between the two governments. This overall situation reflects recognition on the part of the international community of the emergence of a new rule of customary international law prohibiting all kind of nuclear test explosions.[49]

14.3.4 The Role of Article VI NPT

It follows from the above that unilateral declarations in the field of non-proliferation may hardly give rise to legal obligations on the declarant State; as a consequence they do not *per se* generate rights in favour of addressees and even less of other States. Account must be taken, however, of the NPT and in particular of its Article VI, which commits the Contracting Parties 'to pursue negotiations in good faith on effective measures relating to cessation of the nuclear arms race at an early date and to nuclear disarmament, and on a treaty on general and complete disarmament under strict and effective international control.' Certainly security assurances, no-first-use declarations, reduction commitments and moratoriums do constitute 'effective measures relating to cessation of the nuclear arms race'.[50] As a consequence, non-NWS parties to the NPT may logically place confidence in NWS's unilateral commitments that are in accordance with the aim of Article VI and legitimately rely on their implementation. In this perspective, the abovementioned declarations have no binding legal effects *per se*, but are rather means of implementation of the obligations arising from a multilateral treaty.

---

[48]S/RES/1172 (1998), 6 June 1998, paras 3 and 9 (on the nuclear tests conducted by India and Pakistan); S/RES/1718 (2006) paras 1–2 and S/RES/2094 (2013) paras 1–2 (on the nuclear tests conducted by the DPRK).

[49]A customary prohibition of nuclear test explosions in the atmosphere, underwater, in outer space and on celestial bodies already is closely related to environmental protection. As regards State practice on underground testing see Venturini 2014, pp. 156–157.

[50]Both Russia and the US assert that reductions in nuclear weapons and fissile material stockpiles are a demonstration of their commitment to the obligations under Article VI NPT. See for example the joint Note Verbale from Russia and the US at the 2010 Review Conference of the Parties to the NPT (NPT/CONF.2010/WP.75 of 17 May 2010) or the US NPT Information Paper, (2010) United States Information Pertaining to the Treaty on the Non-Proliferation of Nuclear Weapons. http://www.state.gov/documents/organization/141928.pdf, pp. 31–36. http://www.state.gov/documents/organization/141928.pdf. Accessed 18 March 2015. See also J.E. Doyle, U.S.-Russia Nuclear Arms Reductions. The Next Round, Public Interest Report, Spring 2011. http://fas.org/pubs/pir/2011spring/New-START.pdf, p. 32.

14.4 Verification of Unilateral Reductions and Moratoriums

As a rule, neither unilateral reduction commitments nor moratoriums provide for verification measures, an aspect which has been seen as a major weakness. This, however, does not mean that they can in no circumstances be monitored. On the contrary, the comprehensive toolbox of transparency and confidence-building measures (TCBMs) currently being used to control the application of non-proliferation treaties and agreements are also available to ensure implementation of unilateral commitments.

TCBNs have long been recognized as a key factor in the implementation of arms control and non-proliferation commitments. They are broadly defined as provisions aimed at reducing tensions between States in confrontational situations and making the conduct of countries more predictable.[51] Transparency involves the disclosure, accessibility and reliability of information that was previously kept secret, thus enhancing communication and understanding among States.[52] Transparency measures include the declassification and release of information on nuclear-related data and the voluntary observation of the declared information, for example through observers, on-site inspections or remote monitoring. Confidence-building measures may also impose military constraints on parties such as relocation and/or de-alerting of weapons, limitations of troop movements and restrictions on the number and scope of major military exercises.[53]

As essentially voluntary and unilateral undertakings, TCBMs are based on the fundamental prerequisite of good faith. Although difficult to define in clear-cut terms, good faith forms part of the general principles of law that underpin international legal rules, both customary and conventional. In general terms, it reconciles the exercise of States' rights and freedoms with the rights and interests of other States, in order to allow fair international relations to be maintained; at the same time, it safeguards trust and reliance on international law.[54] As previously mentioned, the ICJ has found that good faith is the basis of unilateral obligations of States in international law.[55] It is all the more important in the implementation of voluntary activities performed by governments in the exercise of sovereign powers.

[51]For an overview of the subject see Goldblat 2003, p. 11; Finger and Meier 2013, p. 9; Kubiak 2014, p. 4.

[52]See Zarimpas 2013, pp. 7–8 discussing definitions and characteristics of transparency.

[53]See the examples listed by UNODA Confidence Building, http://www.un.org/disarmament/convarms/infoCBM/. Accessed 18 March 2015.

[54]According to Kolb good faith as a general principle of law has the function of protecting legitimate expectations and collective interests. See Kolb 2000, pp. 143–153.

[55]Above para 14.3 and n. 33.

14.4.1 Implementing the PNIs

The PNIs were welcomed when they were announced at the end of the Cold War, and certainly at that time both the United States and the USSR, then Russia, considered their unilateral declarations to be strong political commitments. Some commentators, however, expressed concerns about the lack of any monitoring mechanism.[56] Yet the two States could, to a certain degree, monitor the activities of each other making use of their own national technical means of verification (satellites and sensors), and of the existing compliance mechanisms established by the START I Treaty. Initially, they also made unilateral declarations and exchanged implementation reports related to tactical nuclear weapons, but information by Russian authorities decreased over time and eventually the report exchanges ended.[57] On the Western side it is a generally held opinion that the United States completed the implementation of its undertakings under the PNIs,[58] while serious doubts are raised concerning the fulfilment of Russia's unilateral initiatives. Reportedly, in recent years, Russian authorities have claimed that they are not required to comply with PNIs commitments. As a matter of fact, the US Department of State has publicly and repeatedly questioned Russia's PNI record.[59] In sum, the PNI's status of implementation is still controversial, however the absence of binding verification mechanism did not preclude the two States from alertly monitoring each other's behaviour.

14.4.2 Reducing Military Fissile Material Stocks

In 2010, the NPT Review Conference Action Plan 2010 called on NWS to place fissile material designated as excess to military purposes under safeguards to ensure that it remains permanently outside military programmes.[60] The NWS have

---

[56]See Finger and Meier 2013.

[57]Implementation of the PNIs is reviewed by Handler 2002, p. 116; Corin 2004, p. 2; Kubiak 2014, p. 7; A.F. Woolf, Next Steps in Nuclear Arms Control with Russia: Issues for Congress, Congressional Research Service 7-5700, January 6, 2014, http://fas.org/sgp/crs/nuke/R43037.pdf, p. 26.

[58]The US, inter alia, withdrew all of its nuclear-armed SLCMs from deployment. Nevertheless, the US and Russia continued to exchange annual declarations regarding the number of deployed nuclear SLCMs while the START treaty remained in force. See A.F. Woolf, Next Steps in Nuclear Arms Control with Russia: Issues for Congress, Congressional Research Service 7-5700, January 6, 2014. http://fas.org/sgp/crs/nuke/R43037.pdf, p. 7.

[59]See Arms Control Association 2012 and S.J. Koch, The Presidential Nuclear Initiatives of 1991–1992, Center for the Study of Weapons of Mass Destruction, National Defense University. http://ndupress.ndu.edu/Portals/68/Documents/casestudies/CSWMD_CaseStudy-5.pdf, p. 21.

[60]2010 Review Conference of the Parties to the Treaty on the Non-Proliferation of Nuclear Weapons, Final Document, Action 16, p. 23. http://cns.miis.edu/treaty_npt/pdfs/2010_FD_Part_I.pdf. Accessed 23 March 2015.

implemented this recommendation in different ways. Portions of fissile material declared excess to military uses have been made available for Euratom or IAEA safeguards, and the UK and the US include plutonium declared excess to military requirements in their annual statements according to the IAEA *Guidelines for the Management of Plutonium*.[61] Nevertheless, the Agency was not involved in the Russia-US bilateral verification of the 'Megaton to Megawatts' Agreement[62] while verification measures under he PMDA are yet to be agreed.[63]

14.4.3 Monitoring Nuclear Test Moratoriums

Although the CTBT is not yet in force, the largest part of the verification system envisaged by the Treaty is already effective. Since 1996, the Preparatory Commission for the Comprehensive nuclear test-ban treaty organization has been working as an independent international organization tasked with building up the CTBT's verification regime. This is based on an International Monitoring System including more than 300 facilities and laboratories operating in approximately ninety countries around the world. Local institutions manage those facilities and laboratories under contracts with the CTBTO. A Global Communications Infrastructure transmits the data recorded at the IMS stations to an International Data Centre through a network of satellites. At the IDC data is to be processed, analyzed and eventually submitted to member States for evaluation. Today, the CTBTO verification system is almost fully functioning. For example, when the DPRK conducted its nuclear test explosions in April 2013, States received information about the location, magnitude, time and depth of the tests within a few hours and before the actual testing was announced by the North Korean government.[64] This international monitoring mechanism is not a substitute for the comprehensive verification system that will be in place once the CTBT enters into force;[65] nevertheless it allows the international community to check actions taken by a State in spite of the existing moratoriums and to react accordingly.

---

[61]See INFCIRC/549 of 16 March 1998. Annual declarations provide listings of civil plutonium stocks by the five NPS, plus Belgium, Germany, Japan, and Switzerland.

[62]Above n. 46.

[63]See Schaper 2013, pp. 213–226 and Feiveson et al. 2014, pp. 161–164 assessing the feasibility and effectiveness of verification of unilateral commitments and bilateral agreements on reductions of military fissile material stockpiles.

[64]See J. Medalia, Comprehensive Nuclear-Test-Ban Treaty: Background and Current Developments, September 29, 2014, Congressional Research Service, Report for Congress RL33548. http://fas.org/sgp/crs/nuke/RL33548.pdf, pp. 17–18. See also http://www.ctbto.org/the-treaty/developments-after-1996/2013-dprk-announced-nuclear-test/.

[65]The CTBT verification system is established by art IV of the treaty and further detailed by the protocol to the treaty and its annexes. The regime consists of the International Monitoring System, consultation and clarification procedures, on-site inspections and confidence-building measures.

14.5 Concluding Remarks

Given the high political sensitivity of nuclear policy, unilateral declarations play an important role in the context of decisions that are taken by NWS or by non-NPT nuclear weapons possessors in the field of nuclear non-proliferation. This kind of unilateral acts avoid the necessity for laborious negotiations, bypass the complex process of ratification of international treaties and allow governments flexibility in their implementation, to the extent that they do not provide for binding verification measures. This is clearly demonstrated by reduction commitments. As a matter of fact, during the last decades, most reductions of nuclear warheads and military fissile materials made by NWS have been unilateral. Although these commitments cannot, *per se*, establish obligations binding on the declarant States, if they are seen in conjunction with Article VI of the NPT, which aims at the cessation of the nuclear arms race, they may give rise to legitimate expectations on their implementation by non-NWS parties to the Treaty. Indeed, nuclear reductions represent important steps towards achieving this goal. The US, Russia and the UK, which together have the vast majority of nuclear stockpiles, bear a special responsibility in that respect; in turn, non-NWS must continue to put pressure on NWS to adopt further and permanent reductions of their nuclear arsenals.[66]

Transparency is the key to monitor the implementation of commitments taken through unilateral declarations, in a way similar to verification of nuclear non-proliferation and disarmament agreements. Crucial in achieving this result is the initial good faith of States that engage in international agreements, as well as in politically binding commitments. Enhancing the recourse to unilateral commitments in the field of nuclear non-proliferation requires greater openness on the part of the States involved, which should comprise all NWS as well as non-NPT nuclear weapons possessors.

With respect to nuclear tests moratoriums, the fully operational character of the international verification system depends on the entry into force of the CTBT. For this to happen, a joint international effort is needed to urge the non-signatories and non-ratifiers to sign and ratify the treaty. As things stand, since the US and China are the two NWS that have not yet ratified the CTBT, a dialogue between these two States would be the first crucial step towards breaking the deadlock. The

[66]On 25 April 2014 the Republic of the Marshall Islands, referring to declarations accepting the compulsory jurisdiction of the Court, lodged an application before the ICJ against the UK, India and Pakistan accusing them of not fulfilling their obligations with respect to the cessation of the nuclear arms race at an early date and to nuclear disarmament. In relation to the UK the Marshall Islands invokes breaches of Article VI of the NPT, while in relation to India and Pakistan it asserts that the obligations enshrined in Article VI of the NPT apply to all States as a matter of customary international law. The Marshall Island also invited the remaining NWS and non-NPT nuclear weapons possessors (China, the DPRK, France, Israel, Russia and the US) to accept the Court's jurisdiction pursuant to Article 38.5 of the Rules of Court, asserting similar claims.

responsibility to bring pressure on them to join the CTBT weighs especially heavily on those NWS—France, the UK and Russia—which have already ratified the treaty thus demonstrating their willingness to uphold the authority of the international nuclear non-proliferation regime.

References

Corin E (2004) Presidential Nuclear Initiatives: An Alternative Paradigm for Arms Control. http://www.nti.org/analysis/articles/presidential-nuclear-initiatives/

Divine RA (1986) Early record on test moratoriums. Bull At Scientists 42(5):24–26

Eckart C (2012) Promises of states under international law. Hart, Oxford and Portland

Feiveson HA, Hogendoorn EJ (2003) No first use of nuclear weapons. Nonproliferation Rev Summer 2003:1–9

Feiveson HA, Glaser A, Mian Z, von Hippel FN (2014) Unmaking the bomb. a fissile material approach to nuclear disarmament and nonproliferation. The MIT Press, Cambridge

Finger A, Meier O (2013) Confidence-building on tactical nuclear weapons: what's on the table? Hamburger Beiträge zur Friedensforschung und Sicherheitspolitik, Heft 160, Mai 2013, http://d-nb.info/104313851X/34

Goldblat J (2003): Arms control. The new guide to negotiations and agreements, 2nd edn. Sage, London

Hafemeister D (2013) US nuclear security cooperation with Russia and transparency. In: Zarimpas N (ed) Transparency in nuclear warheads and materials: the political and technical dimensions. Oxford University Press, Oxford, pp 80–111

Handler J (2002) The September 1991 presidential nuclear initiatives and the elimination, storing and security aspects of TNWs. In: T. Susiluoto (ed), Tactical Nuclear Weapons: Time for Control, United Nations Institute for Disarmament Research, UNIDIR/2002/11

Klabbers J (1996) The concept of treaty in international law. Kluwer Law International, The Hague

Kolb R (2000) La bonne foi en droit international public. Contribution à l'étude des principes généraux du droit, P.U.F – I.U.H.E.I., Paris; Genève

Kristensen H (2013) Unilateral Versus Bilateral Nuclear Reductions. Prepared remarks, Center for Strategic and International Studies, 27 February 2013 http://www.fas.org/programs/ssp/nukes/publications1/2013_CSISdebate022713.pdf.

Kubiak K (2014) NATO and Russia experiences with nuclear transparency and confidence-building measures, Background paper for the workshop Non-Strategic Nuclear Weapons in Europe: Transparency and Confidence-Building Measures in Practice, SWP, Berlin, 27–28 March 2014 http://www.swpberlin.org/fileadmin/contents/products/arbeitspapiere/wp_kubiak_April2014.pdf.

Rodriguez Cedeño V, Torres Cazorla MI (2013) Unilateral acts of states in international law. Max Planck Encyclopaedia of Public International Law (MPEPIL), http://opil.ouplaw.com/home/EPIL

Sagan S (2009) The case for no first use. Survival 51(3):151–162

Schaper D (2013) Monitoring and verifying the storage and disposition of fissile 206 materials and the closure of nuclear facilities. In: Zarimpas N (ed) Transparency in nuclear warheads and materials: the political and technical dimensions. Oxford University Press, Oxford, pp 206–228

Simpson J (I994) Nuclear non-proliferation in the post-cold war era. Int Aff 70:17–39

Singh N, McWhinney E (1989) Nuclear weapons and contemporary international law, 2nd edn. Martinus Nijhoff Publishers, Dordrecht

Venturini G (2014) Test-bans and the comprehensive test ban treaty organisation. In: Black-Branch JL, Fleck D (eds) Nuclear non-proliferation in international law, vol 1. TMC Asser Press/Springer, The Hague, pp 133–158

Yu R, Guangqian P (2009) Nuclear no-first-use revisited. Chin Secur 5(1):81–90

Zarimpas N (2013) Introduction. In: Zarimpas N (ed) Transparency in nuclear warheads and materials: the political and technical dimensions. Oxford University Press, Oxford, pp 1–12

Chapter 15
Jus ad Bellum: Nuclear Weapons and the Inherent Right of Self-Defence

Francis Grimal

Abstract The lawfulness of a State's recourse to the 'nuclear option' as a means of self-defence is still a discussion which sits uncomfortably amongst most scholars, partly, because the seminal advisory opinion on the *Legality of the Threat or Use of Nuclear Weapons* delivered by the International Court of Justice in 1996 remains shrouded in legal uncertainty and, perhaps more importantly, because the threshold needed to lawfully invoke the doctrine of self-defence is set so high, and rightly so. Only under exceptional circumstances would a State meet the cardinal requirements of 'necessity' and 'proportionality'. The use of a nuclear weapon as a means of self-defence lies at the very edge of the spectrum. That is not to say that recourse to conventional weapons automatically fulfils the necessity and proportionality requirements.

Keywords Necessity · Proportionality · Conventional weapons · Nuclear weapons · Self-defence

Contents

LLB (Hons) (Nottingham), LLM (Reading), PhD (Reading), Senior Lecturer in Public International Law, University of Buckingham, UK; Member of the ILA Committee on Nuclear Weapons, Non-Proliferation and Contemporary International Law.

F. Grimal (✉)
School of Law, University of Buckingham, Hunter Street, Buckingham MK18 1EG, UK
e-mail: francis.grimal@buckingham.ac.uk

J.L. Black-Branch and D. Fleck (eds.), *Nuclear Non-Proliferation in International Law - Volume II*, DOI 10.1007/978-94-6265-075-6_15

15.1 Introduction

The purpose of this chapter is to examine at what point, and under what circumstances, a State is lawfully permitted to defend itself with nuclear weapons. Broadly speaking, there is no paucity of literature on the more general discussion of 'at what point'[1] but the more specific question of 'under what circumstances' has been neglected. Consequently, the chapter will address the specifics and also assess the issue of a State using a threat of force as a means of self-defence—deterrence *par excellence*. Section 15.2 will consider the right of self-defence under international law and the parameters that govern it. Section 15.3 will specifically address how the 'nuclear option' fits within the overarching framework of self-defence. Section 15.4 will consider the practice of deterrence—one State threatening another State with a nuclear attack as a means of self-defence. The lawfulness of such action will be assessed.

15.2 The Law Governing Self-Defence

A State's right of self-defence under international law is an area that continues to attract regular scholarly scrutiny.[2] Moreover, the perennial question concerning whether or not the present UN Charter regime (embodied under Article 51) overrides previous customary law is as present in the literature today as it ever has been.[3] Given that this area is a 'subject in itself', the discussion in *this* chapter will remain confined to examining the main parameters required to calibrate a lawful response of self-defence.

Article 2(4) of the UN Charter contains an absolute prohibition against the threat or use of force by one State against another. Academic opinion is divided, however, with regards to the status of Article 2(4). As submitted by those who deem that the prohibition has peremptory status, a violation of Article 2(4) equates to a violation of a *jus cogens* norm.[4] Others, however, disagree that this conclusion

---

[1]This chapter will confine itself to solely discussing the *jus ad bellum* and not the *jus in bello*. See below nn. 21–25 and accompanying text.

[2]See more recently, Green 2015; Sadoff 2009; Green 2009a; Green 2006; Murphy 2005; Rockefeller 2004; Pierson 2004; Martinez 2003; Byers 2003.

[3]See generally, Gray 2008.

[4]Orakhelashvili 2006.

should be adopted without question.[5] Nevertheless, the effect of the prohibition contained in Article 2(4) is tempered alongside the 'positive duty' contained in Article 2(3)—that States settle their disputes via peaceful means.

Undoubtedly, there exist two well-known exceptions: the use of force in self-defence and an authorization of force by the United Nations Security Council under its chapter VII powers.[6] For the purpose of this chapter and indeed this overall discussion the focus is entirely on the first exception—self-defence.

15.2.1 Self-Defence as It Stands Today

Today's 'regime' governing the lawful invocation of self-defence lies partly in pre-existing customary international law (pre-Charter) and primarily of course in the text of Article 51 of the UN Charter.[7] Compliance with Article 51 means that a State can only invoke its right of self-defence if it has suffered an 'armed attack'—or as a minimum, be faced with a sufficiently serious and imminent threat of suffering an armed attack.[8] Regrettably, Article 51 provides no further guidance as to what form an armed attack may take. However, the ICJ in the *Nicaragua* case[9] and commentators both concur that an 'armed attack' constitutes 'the most grave form of the use of force'—a qualitatively grave use of force—beyond a use of force simpliciter.[10]

15.2.2 Necessity, Proportionality and the Cessation of Force

The cardinal parameters of necessity and proportionality regulate the lawfulness of a State's subsequent response. Necessity and proportionality are grounded within customary international law as espoused in the well-trodden correspondence between the then US Secretary of State Daniel Webster, and his British counterpart Lord Ashburton with regards to and forming part of the *Caroline* incident.[11]

[5]Green 2010.

[6]On this, we can note Green 2015 who refers to the International Law Commission, Text of the Draft Articles on Responsibility of States for Internationally Wrongful Acts, included in the Report of the International Law Commission, 53rd session, UN Doc. A/56/10, 2001, Chapter IV, www.un.org/documents/ga/docs/56/a5610.pdf, Commentary to Articles 22, 177 ('the existence of a general principle admitting self-defence as an exception to the prohibition against the use of force in international relations is *undisputed*', emphasis added).

[7]Green and Grimal 2011, p. 299.

[8]Greig 1991, pp. 366–402.

[9]*Military and Paramilitary Activities in and Against Nicaragua (Nicaragua v. U.S.)*, 1986 ICJ 14, para 191.

[10]Green and Grimal 2011, p. 300, see also Constantinou 2000.

[11]Letter from Daniel Webster to Henry S. Fox (April 24, 1841), in 29 *British and Foreign State Papers* (1841–1842), pp. 1129–1139 (1857).

Daniel Webster's formulation required that the following must be satisfied in order for a State to lawfully invoke self-defence:

> [S]how a necessity of self-defense, instant, overwhelming, leaving no choice of means, and no moment for deliberation. It will be for it to show, also, that… [it] did nothing unreasonable or excessive; since the act, justified by the necessity of self-defense, must be limited by that necessity, and kept clearly within it.

Inherent within this Statement are the inextricably linked principles of necessity and proportionality.[12] The current interpretation of necessity is two-fold: (1) the State must demonstrate that it exhausted all non-forcible measures[13] and (2) it would be wholly unreasonable to expect the responding State to attempt a non-forcible response.[14] In essence, necessity is a concept of last resort. Compliance with the principle of proportionality requires that the 'force employed must not be excessive with regard to the goal of abating or repelling the attack'.[15] As Green and Grimal note, a State's response need not 'mirror' the initial attack numerically speaking. For example, if State A fires ten missiles at State B, State B is not constrained or confined to respond in kind—providing the force is not excessive in abating or repelling the attack.[16]

At this point, it is perhaps useful to draw a distinction between the lawfulness of a defending State's action taken during an on-going armed attack—the so called 'cumulative effect', as coined by Garwood-Gowers,[17] and instances whereby force is used once the armed attack has ceased. In the context of the former, the position, according to Green, is that the responding State is placed under a temporal restriction—there must be a reasonable temporal proximity between the victim State's response and the armed attack itself.[18] Green is the first to concede that the 'reasonableness' parameter is somewhat nebulous, and is certainly open to interpretation along the lines of 'a context-specific appraisal of the various factors that may delay a self-defence action: intelligence gathering, initial resort to negotiation, geographical disparity, and so on'.[19] Broadly speaking, an 'overly tardy' response in Green's view, would negate the necessity requirement and thus may render the action unlawful.[20]

In the context of the latter (when force is used once the armed attack has occurred), it would be incorrect to set out so categorically that a 'defending State' must 'cease and desist'—a forceful response against a non-attacker would no

[12]Green and Grimal 2011, p. 300 and see generally Green 2009b.

[13]Green and Grimal 2011.

[14]Ibid., p. 301.

[15]Constantinou 2000, pp. 159–161, Badr 1980, pp. 25–26, Kretzmer 2005, pp. 187–188.

[16]Green and Grimal 2011, p. 301 and also Judge Higgins's Dissenting Opinion, para 5, p. 583 in Legality of the Threat or Use of Nuclear Weapons, Advisory Opinion, 1996 ICJ 226 (July 8).

[17]See generally Garwood-Gowers 2004.

[18]See Green 2015 in his conclusion.

[19]Ibid.

[20]Ibid.

longer fall within the realm of necessity and would push the State's behaviour into the unlawful territory or reprisals. Rather, there is certainly the notion that to a limited degree, states can extend 'their response in self-defence beyond the moment where the attack being responded to terminated'.[21] Moreover, as Green and Garwood-Gowers independently suggest, there is sense that there exists a 'dual' or 'cumulative affect' argument whereby a State not only needs to respond to the previous attack but be guarded against a future attack.[22]

Before considering the lawfulness of a nuclear response in the section below, it is worth briefly considering the position as to whether it would be lawful to target nuclear facilities in self-defence. The argument 'in favour' of such action would presumably be grounded on the basis that such an attack is less 'destructive' and is a more realistic military option for a NNWS.[23] Arman Sarvarian has covered this very question in some considerable detail in a recent article; so instead, the broad conclusions of the question will be outlined.[24] State practice, endorsed by Sarvarian in his analysis undeniably rejects the possibility that self-defence can ever be employed to justify such an attack.[25] Sarvarian draws our attention to two specific instances: the Cuban Missile Crisis (where nuclear warheads were deployed) and the Osirak attack (an attack against civilian nuclear facilities) and subsequent State practice is used to underpin his analysis of a hypothetical attack by Israel against Iran.[26]

For the purposes of this chapter, the Iranian question so to speak will be avoided. Sarvarian himself concludes that action by Israel against Iran would be unlawful—primarily on the grounds that mere possession of nuclear weapons alone does not constitute an unlawful threat of force in violation of Article 2(4) and much less, that of 'armed attack'. Sarvarian's overall conclusion is that the rather hazardous nature of an attack against either deployed warheads or a civilian nuclear facility in terms of potential fallout, has led States to adopt 'an especially cautious and restrictive interpretation of the temporal scope of self-defence'.[27] Nevertheless, that does not necessarily and categorically, rule out the lawfulness in each and *every* instance. If, a State's possession of nuclear weapons is combined with bellicose rhetoric that goes beyond mere sabre rattling, it's behaviour may well fall within the remit of Article 2(4) and constitute an unlawful threat of force in turn potentially giving rise to anticipatory action.[28]

---

[21]Ibid. And, as helpfully signposted by the anonymous reviewer, this would cover 'Crimea-type' scenarios whereby the 'defending state' has since been occupied.

[22]Ibid. and Garwood-Gowers 2004.

[23]I am grateful to the anonymous reviewer for this observation/question.

[24]Sarvarian 2014, pp. 247–273.

[25]Ibid., p. 271.

[26]Ibid.

[27]Ibid.

[28]See generally Grimal 2012, Chap. 5.

15.3 A Nuclear Response?

When it comes to assessing the lawfulness of self-defence via the 'red button' the difficulty lies in the inherent nature of the nuclear weapons themselves. The destructive nature of the payload invariably shifts the perspective both in terms of when such a response would be deemed necessary and, under what circumstances it would be deemed proportionate. Moreover, if State A attacks State B with 10 MOABs (GBU-43/B Massive Ordnance Air Burst—one of the most powerful 'conventional' ordnances) would State B lawfully be entitled to respond with a compact, low yield nuclear option which, has exactly the same destructive capacity?

Such a discussion is little aided or abetted by the ICJ's seminal *Advisory Opinion* and the subsequent scholarly discussion centred on the 'known unknowns'—the Court allowing a nuclear response under 'exceptional circumstances' without defining precisely what that entails.[29] Paragraph 105(2) of the Advisory Opinion left open the possibility of self-defence under extreme/exceptional circumstances but neither the Court nor the literature addressed the 'devil in the detail'.[30] Indeed, as President Bedjaoui famously professed, 'the *Advisory Opinion* does no more than place on record the existence of legal uncertainty'.[31] In the words of Sheldon, the Court was forthright it its avoidance of providing specific examples of when a State's use of nuclear weapons would comply with the threshold parameters contained in Article 51.[32] Indeed, as Greenwood notes and the Court pronounced, 'the right of self-defence under Article 51 of the Charter was subject to the limitations of proportionality and necessity'—the proportionality element in particular is crucial to such a discussion.[33] Gardam adopts a similar view of the Court's pronouncement and notes the rather unhelpful discussion of proportionality—States must consider the unique nature of nuclear weapons when determining if a response is necessary and proportionate.[34] The overwhelming consensus therefore within the literature is that for a nuclear response to have the slightest chance of being deemed lawfully, it must cross the well-trodden thresholds of necessity and proportionality.[35] In effect, academic consensus goes much further—not only are those threshold parameters very difficult to lawfully 'trigger' the right of self-defence,[36] but really it is only under exceptional circumstances that such action (a nuclear response) could ever be lawfully envisaged.[37]

---

[29]Legality of the Threat or Use of Nuclear Weapons, Advisory Opinion, 1996 ICJ 226 (July 8).

[30]Bodansky 1999, p. 153.

[31]See the declaration of President Bedjaoui in Legality of the Threat or Use of Nuclear Weapons, Advisory Opinion, 1996 ICJ 226 (July 8) whose view was supported by Judges Schwebel and Higgins in their dissenting opinions.

[32]Sheldon 1996, p. 184.

[33]Greenwood 1999, pp. 258–263.

[34]Gardam 1999, p. 286.

[35]See also Mullerson 1999, pp. 267–270; Spierman 1999, p. 148.

[36]See generally Alexandrov 1996; Bowett 1958; Ruys 2010; Green 2009b.

[37]See generally Gardam 2004; Green and Grimal 2011.

The purpose of this section is to address the practical lacunae by reference to two practical if somewhat far-fetched hypothetical examples. This allows a more forensic approach to establish in concrete terms the precise nature of the 'exceptional circumstances' the Court hinted at in para 105(2).[38] As noted in Sect. 15.2, necessity is the exhaustion of all non-forceful measures and for a response to be proportionate, it must not be excessive in abating or repelling the attack (while noting that a mirrored/identical numerical response is not a pre-requisite and is linked to defensive necessity).[39]

15.3.1 Analysis

In terms of the necessity element, if a State waits until it has actually suffered a nuclear 'armed attack', chances are, it will no longer be in a position to defend itself. Therefore, a reasonable interpretation of necessity would be along the *Caroline Incident* lines.[40] In practical terms, once the missiles are either in the 'free flight phase' or ideally at the 'boost phase' (although it is difficult to determine exact trajectory in this phase) any response would fall within the realm of necessity. In other words, a State is acting anticipatorily—something that the Court in *Nicaragua* did not dismiss outright in para 35 and, of course, if one accepts a more general right of anticipated self-defence under international law.[41] A response under those set of circumstances against a nuclear launch (boost phase or free flight) would arguably fall within the necessity requirement.

Such a discussion is of course incomplete without interacting with the issue of what is understood by 'imminence' and clearly to note that it means different things to different commentators.[42] And indeed, and as noted by Green few commentators if any, have actually provided definitive guidance.[43] Nevertheless, both Lubell and Green seemingly agree that in order for imminence to be triggered, there must be 'a *specific* and *identifiable* threat, which is *highly likely* to occur' and there must be 'an objectively verifiable, concretely imminent attack'.[44] In other words, it must effectively fall somewhere 'between (1) absolute certainty of a future attack (which is impossible); and (2) a threat that is not specific, objectively verifiable and already being prepared (which would thus not be sufficiently "imminent")'.[45]

---

[38]Legality of the Threat or Use of Nuclear Weapons, Advisory Opinion, 1996 ICJ 226 (July 8).

[39]See Sect. 15.2.

[40]See Sect. 15.2.

[41]See for example, Antonopoulos 2008.

[42]Dinstein 2012, at pp. 203–204, Dinstein refers to 'interceptive self-defence'.

[43]See generally Green 2015, who refers back to Lubell 2015, p. 702.

[44]Ibid., at pp. 702–705.

[45]Green 2015 and Lubell 2015.

The greatest difficulty lies instead with satisfying the proportionality element. The use of a nuclear response must not be excessive in abating or repelling the attack—a State may be able to defend itself and repel a future attack without necessarily 'wiping the other State off the map'. This is something that this section will consider in more detail by way of two practical and highly hypothetical scenarios.

Scenario 1 The United Kingdom launches an unprovoked nuclear attack (using the Trident option) against State B, noting, that the UK's 'nuclear option' is solely vested in its Vanguard Trident-Class submarines.[46] Leaving all obvious criticisms aside, a perverse interpretation of proportionality would dictate that following such an attack, State B would be constrained into repelling a future attack, i.e. defending itself, simply by nullifying the submarines (admittedly of which, there are not many). Therefore, one could conceivably argue that only an attack against the UK submarines would be a proportionate response. This last comment needs further clarification. Clearly, this would be under a perverse, overly restrictive and inaccurate interpretation of proportionality whereby, the 'response' would be limited to neutralizing the submarines—something that would be both undesirable and impractical.

If we take this rather unlikely scenario a stage further, the key issue vis-à-vis proportionality is *really* to consider the abatement of a subsequent attack—once the initial attack is underway, a responsive attack will not stop it. However, if the UK's nuclear strike has inflicted mass destruction on State B, then inflicting similar destruction on the UK may be the *only* way to convince the UK in refraining from another launch. Moreover, one would have to take a pragmatic view that one of the submarines may 'escape' and therefore the risk of a second attack against State B remains present. Under this analysis, a direct territorial attack may not be deemed excessive.

Scenario 2 The UK's entire land-based conventional capabilities are crippled by a 'conventional' armed attack, which, has taken out all defensive capabilities—a territorial attack. The UK's only means of defending itself, i.e. repelling or abating a further attack is to have recourse to the four Vanguard-Class submarines capable to exercise the 'Trident option'. The necessity elements are seemingly satisfied: this is a last resort option and there are no alternatives. However, given the intertwined nature of necessity and proportionality (proportionate to the defensive necessity is also there), it would certainly repel/abate any future attack but on the other hand, wiping that State off the face of the map might be deemed 'excessive'. The question then becomes does the defensive necessity negate the slightly 'disproportionate' element?

The natural inclination is to conclude that wiping a State off the face of the map is more than likely to be disproportionate. Moreover, the ICJ's *Advisory Opinion* again offers little concrete guidance and patently acknowledges that it 'cannot reach a definitive conclusion as to the legality or illegality of the use of nuclear weapons

[46]See https://www.gov.uk/government/policies/maintaining-an-effective-independent-nuclear-deterrent.

by a State in an extreme circumstance of self-defence, in which its very survival would be at stake'.[47] However, it is possible to distinguish between such an extreme use (obliterating an entire State) which is clearly disproportional, and one, which is more localized in terms of its effect. For example, the dropping of the two atomic bombs over Hiroshima and Nagasaki in World War Two were undoubtedly massively destructive but Japan was not obliterated (in the 'complete' sense).[48] This is of course very much open to criticism and not without it's detractors.[49] Gazzini in particular argues that the necessity element of self-defence had not been fulfilled—Japan's defeat was imminent and there were still other means available.[50] Nonetheless, Singh in his article leaves the door ajar for the use of a nuclear weapon in self-defence when conventional weapons are ineffective.[51] If one accepts the rather controversial view as espoused by Truman[52]—that is to say that Japan's defeat was not *fait accompli* and that conventional weapons were unlikely to yield surrender, then Singh's position would seemingly allow this more 'localized' use of nuclear weapons. One must also stress that it may well be undesirable to discuss the lawfulness of the attacks on Hiroshima and Nagasaki in the sense that hostilities had already started which, would render this discussion within the realms of international humanitarian law/*jus in bello* as espoused in the *Shimoda* case.[53]

15.3.2 Application

Returning to the question posed at the outset of this section: if State A attacks State B with ten MOABs (GBU-43/B Massive Ordnance Air Burst—one of the most powerful 'conventional' ordnances) would State B be lawfully entitled to respond with one compact, low yield nuclear option which, has exactly the same destructive capacity? In other words, would a more limited (albeit still massively destructive) use be able to meet the proportionality threshold?

---

[47]Legality of the Threat or Use of Nuclear Weapons, Advisory Opinion, 1996 ICJ 226 (July 8), paras 90–97.

[48]The author is grateful for a helpful discussion with James A. Green on this point.

[49]For a full discussion on the lawfulness of action in Hiroshima and Nagasaki, please see Gazzini 2005, p. 219; Falk 1997, p. 69; Falk 1965, p. 759. On the point concerning the devastating nature of the use of atomic weapons, see Roberts 1994, pp. 131–132. The above literature is quick to note that Japan was not far off from being defeated, and that the use of atomic weapons was 'unnecessary' in the strict sense.

[50]Gazzini 2005, p. 219.

[51]Singh 1956, pp. 32–34.

[52]See Kennedy and Andreopolous 1994, pp. 217–218. Again, I am grateful to the anonymous reviewer for this helpful observation.

[53]*Shimoda* case (Compensation claim against Japan brought by the residents of Hiroshmina and Nagasaki), Tokyo District Court, 7 December 1963. Again, I am grateful to the anonymous reviewer for this helpful observation.

Clearly if State B has no other military capabilities aside from the nuclear weapon (highly unlikely and most likely moot) then a nuclear response might be both necessary and proportionate. The objection within the literature to such a scenario is firmly on the application of proportionality.[54] For example, Gazzini views that 'the so called mini-nuclear weapons' can hardly satisfy the proportionality requirement.[55] Here one could plausibly take the view that Gazzini is also erring on the side of the IHL consideration of proportionality, which, makes a quantum type assessment between the military gain and the potential damage caused rather than the 'abate and repel' of the *jus ad bellum*. However, if we take Singh's argument to its natural conclusion—that is to say that the use of nuclear weapons is *permissible* when conventional weapons are ineffective, then if a State has no other military capabilities in the first place (other than the nuclear option), the use of a nuclear weapon would indeed be lawful.[56]

15.4 A Threatened Nuclear Response?

Extending this discussion into the realm of State A threatening another State with a nuclear response as a means of self-defence takes the analysis to its natural conclusion. The concept of threatened self-defence has recently surfaced within the literature.[57] Its basic premise is that a State could conceivably threaten another State with force as a means of defending itself rather than having recourse to force itself. State B warns State A that should State A choose to launch an armed attack, State B will defend itself. The reason for including such a discussion within the context of this chapter lies with the very nature of nuclear weapons. One of the inherent purposes of possessing such a weapon is existential deterrence.[58] Strategically, the mere possession of a nuclear weapon may deter another State from attacking it.[59] Unfortunately, the Court chose not to entertain such a discussion.[60] Judge Shi's remarks echoed the overall view taken by the Court that deterrence was a political doctrine rather than a legal one—a perhaps all too convenient policy view.[61]

---

[54]Gazzini 2005, p. 219.

[55]Ibid.

[56]Singh 1956, pp. 32–34.

[57]See, for example, Grimal 2012.

[58]See Legality of the Threat or Use of Nuclear Weapons, Advisory Opinion, 1996 ICJ 226, para 47.

[59]Grimal 2012, p. 61 and Legality of the Threat or Use of Nuclear Weapons, Advisory Opinion, 1996 ICJ 226, para 47.

[60]Legality of the Threat or Use of Nuclear Weapons, Advisory Opinion, 1996 ICJ 226, para 47.

[61]Judge Shi's dissenting opinion in Legality of the Threat or Use of Nuclear Weapons, Advisory Opinion, 1996 ICJ 226.

In March 2013 North Korea threatened to defend itself with nuclear weapons if attacked.[62] This final section of this chapter will therefore examine this type of threat and assess whether the parameters discussed in Sect. 15.3 would remain the same if a State chose to threaten another State with a nuclear response as means of self-defence. In order to undertake such a discussion it is necessary to briefly set out and define what is meant by a threat of force. However, such analysis will be relatively brief as this issue has been covered elsewhere in the literature. Rather the focus will be on the analytical section in terms of assessing under what circumstances a threatened nuclear strike as a means of self-defence would be deemed lawful.

15.4.1 Threats of Force

Threats of force are strictly prohibited by Article 2(4) of the United Nations Charter, but the precise definition of a threat is one remains very much undefined. Commentators broadly accept that a threat is not confined to classical verbal ultimate—actions can also 'speak louder than words'... The author of this chapter maintains both here and elsewhere, that a full assessment of a threat of force cannot be conducted without reference to strategic considerations.[63] Strategic considerations help explain the practical distinction between an empty threat—made by a State which does not possess the means of carrying it out (which out may well violate Article 2(4) but is 'tolerated') and, a threat which is all too 'real'.[64] The threatening State is militarily capable of carrying out its threat and the threat itself is both unlawful under Article 2(4) and intolerable in the eyes of the international community.[65]

15.4.2 Legal Analysis

The current test for determining the lawfulness of a threat of force was articulated by the ICJ in the *Nuclear Weapons* Advisory Opinion[66] and poses a retroactive test to the following hypothetical question. *If* the threat of force were carried out (in other words actual force and not threatened force were to be used) would that be lawful? If yes, that would legitimize the prior threat. If not, (actual force would be deemed unlawful) then so would the threat that precedes it.

---

[62]http://www.reuters.com/article/2013/03/07/us-korea-north-attack-idUSBRE9260BR20130307. Accessed 28 January 2015.

[63]Grimal 2012, p. 61.

[64]Ibid.

[65]Ibid.

[66]Legality of the Threat or Use of Nuclear Weapons, Advisory Opinion, 1996 ICJ 226, para 47; Brownlie 1963, p. 63; see Grimal 2012, Introduction and Chaps. 2 and 4.

The other issue to contend with is whether one can simply transpose the tapestry of necessity and proportionality from 'traditional self-defence and apply them to an instance of threatened self-defence (or in this case, threatened nuclear self-defence). Opinion remains divided on this precise issue. While Green and Grimal both maintain that because a threat of self-defence has a different practical consequence (there is no *actual* force), it should therefore be treated differently, Roscini takes an opposing view.[67] For the purposes of reconciliation—at least in this chapter, one could view that a threat of self-defence would have to be made in response to either an armed attack or a threatened armed attack which is *imminent* in nature.[68]

With regards to necessity and proportionality the necessity requirement is the most difficult to satisfy as it creates a paradox—'it may well be necessary to threaten force when it is not necessary to use it'.[69] Equally, the necessity to use force is only available if there are no other non-forcible measures available (such as a threat of force…).[70] The solution? To interpret necessity along the lines of reasonableness or last resort.[71] Proportionality is less problematic. For a threat to be proportionate, it must pose an effective deterrent—to stop or repel a future attack).[72]

15.4.3 Application

The North Korean example cited above is a useful example as it deals specifically with the declared concept of a nuclear attack. However, in order to make the analysis more plausible, it is preferable to use a neutral example. State A could threaten State B with a nuclear attack as a means of self-defence if State B had launched a prior conventional armed attack providing that a nuclear threat was the only reasonable means of deterring State B from continuing that attack.[73] If it was reasonable, it would satisfy the necessity threshold and even if such a threat would not be commensurate, it would nonetheless fall within the parameter of proportionality.[74]

---

[67]Green and Grimal 2011; Roscini 2007, p. 245.

[68]Green and Grimal 2011, p. 321.

[69]Ibid., at p. 322.

[70]Ibid.

[71]Ibid.

[72]Ibid., at p. 324.

[73]Ibid.

[74]Ibid.

15.5 Conclusion

This chapter has sought to re-dress an arguable deficiency within the literature—namely, the exact point at which a State can lawfully respond with recourse to nuclear weapons with reference to practical examples. In conclusion, under certain limited circumstances, as set out in Sect. 15.3, a nuclear response as a means of self-defence may indeed be possible under current international law. Furthermore, Sect. 15.4 has extended the discussion to include the very real possibility of a threatened nuclear attack as a means of self-defence. Despite the brinkmanship of the Cold War, and in more recent times, posturing by States (albeit in terms of a 'latent' threat since they do not possess weapons capability) such a discussion on the lawfulness of a 'nuclear response' remains thankfully 'hypothetical'.

References

Alexandrov SA (1996) Self-defense against the use of force in international law. Kluwer Law International, The Hague

Antonopoulos C (2008) Force by armed groups as armed attack and the broadening of self-defence. Neth Int'l L Rev 55:159–180

Badr GM (1980) The exculpatory effect of self-defense in state responsibility. Ga J Int'l Comp L 10:1–28

Bodansky D (1999) Non-liquet and the incompleteness of international law. In: Boisson de Chazournes L, Sands P (eds) International law, the International Court of Justice and nuclear weapons. Cambridge University Press, Cambridge, pp 153–170

Bowett D (1958) Self-defence in international law. Manchester University Press, Manchester

Brownlie I (1963) International law and the use of force by states. Oxford University Press, Oxford

Byers M (2003) Preemptive self-defense: hegemony, equality and strategies of legal change. J Polit Philisophy 11:171–190

Constantinou A (2000) The right of self-defence under customary international law and article 51 of the United Nations charter. Ant. N. Sakkoulas, Bruylant, Athènes Bruxelles

Dinstein Y (2012) War aggression and self-defence. Cambridge University Press, Cambridge

Falk R (1965) The Shimoda case: a legal appraisal of the atomic attacks upon Hiroshima and Nagaasaki. AJIL 59:759–793

Falk R (1997) Nuclear weapons, international law and the world court: a historic encounter. AJIL 91:64–75

Gardam J (1999) Proportionality and necessity in the nuclear weapons case. In: Boisson de Chazournes L, Sands P (eds) International law, the International Court of Justice and Nuclear Weapons. Cambridge University Press, Cambridge, pp 275–292

Gardam J (2004) Necessity, proportionality and the use of force by states. Cambridge University Press, Cambridge

Garwood-Gowers A (2004) Self-defence against terrorism in the post-9/11 world QUTLJJ, vol. 4, Issue 2

Gazzini T (2005) The changing rules on the use of force in international law. Manchester University Press, Manchester

Gray C (2008) International law and the use of force. Oxford University Press, Oxford

Green JA (2006) Docking the Caroline: understanding the relevance of the formula in contemporary customary international law concerning self-defense. Cardozo J Int'l Comp L 14:429–480

Green JA (2009a) Fluctuating evidentiary standards for self-defence in the international court of justice. Int Comp Law Q 58:163–178
Green JA (2009b) The international court of justice and self-defence in international law. Hart Publishing, Oxford
Green JA (2010) Questioning the peremptory status of the prohibition of the use of force. Mich J Int'l L 32:215–257
Green JA (2015) The *ratione temporis* elements of self-defence. J Use Force Int Law 2(1) (forthcoming)
Green JA, Grimal F (2011) The threat of force as an action in self-defense under International Law. Vand J Transnat'l L 44:285–329
Greenwood C (1999) Jus ad bellum and jus in bello in the nuclear weapons advisory opinion. In: Boisson de Chazournes L, Sands P (eds), International law, the International Court of Justice and Nuclear Weapons. Cambridge University Press, Cambridge, pp 247–266
Greig D (1991) Self-defence and the Security Council: what does article 51 require? Int Comp Law Q 40:366–402
Grimal F (2012) Threats of force: international law and strategy. Routledge, Abingdon
Kennedy P, Andreopolous GJ (1994) The laws of war: some concluding reflections. In: Howard M, Andreopoulos G, Shulman MR (eds), The laws of war. Yale University Press, New Haven, pp 414–227
Kretzmer D (2005) Killing of suspected terrorists: extra judicial executions or legitimate means of defence? Eur J Int'l L 16:171–212
Lubell N (2015) The problem of imminence in an uncertain world. In: Weller M (ed) The Oxford handbook of the use of force in international law. Oxford University Press, Oxford, pp 697–720
Martinez L (2003) September 11th, Iraq and the doctrine of anticipatory self-defense. UMKC LRev 72:123–182
Mullerson R (1999) On the relationship between jus ad bellum and jus in bello in the General Assembly advisory opinion. In: Boisson de Chazournes L, Sands P (eds), International law, the International Court of Justice and Nuclear Weapons. Cambridge University Press, Cambridge, pp 267–274
Murphy S (2005) Doctrine of preemptive self-defense, the symposium: brave new world: U.S. responses to the rise in International Crime. Vill L Rev 50:699–748
Orakhelashvili A (2006) Peremptory norms in international law. Oxford University Press, Oxford
Pierson C (2004) Preemptive self-defense in an age of weapons of mass destruction: operation Iraqi freedom. Denv J Int'l L Pol'y 33:150–178
Roberts A (1994) Land warfare from Hague to Nuremberg. In: Howard M, Andreopoulos G, Shulman MR (eds) The laws of war. Yale University Press, New Haven, pp 116–139
Rockefeller M (2004) Imminent threat requirement for the use of preemptive military force: is it time for a non-temporal standard, the 2004 Sutton colloquium: 2003–2004 Leonard V.B. Sutton Award. Denv J Int'l L Pol'y 33:131–149
Roscini M (2007) Threats of armed force and contemporary international law. Neth Int'l L Rev 45:229–274
Ruys T (2010) 'Armed attack' and article 51 of the UN charter: evolutions in customary law and practice. Cambridge University Press, Cambridge
Sadoff D (2009) Striking a sensible balance on the legality of defensive first strikes. Vand J Transnat'l L 42:441–500
Sarvarian A (2014) The lawfulness of a use of force upon nuclear facilities in self-defence. J Use Force Int Law 1(2):1–26
Sheldon JM (1996) Nuclear weapons and the laws of war: does customary international law prohibit the use of nuclear weapons in all circumstances? Fordham Int Law J 20:181–261
Singh N (1956) The right of self-defence in relation to the use of nuclear weapons. Indian Yearb Int Aff 5:3–37
Spierman O (1999) Lotus and the double structure of international legal argument. Boisson de Chazournes L, Sands P (eds), International law, the International Court of Justice and Nuclear Weapons. Cambridge University Press, Cambridge, pp 131–152

Chapter 16
Countermeasures to Ensure Compliance with Nuclear Non-Proliferation Obligations

Jonathan L. Black-Branch

Abstract Countermeasures against non-compliance with the Nuclear Non-Proliferation Treaty and other pertinent obligations remain an open option for States and international organizations, even if implementing activities by the International Atomic Energy Agency and nation States are regulated in rather specific form and United Nations Security Council sanctions may come into place. The purpose of this chapter is to explore the role of countermeasures in the case of non-compliance with nuclear non-proliferation obligations relating to their legal requirements, effectiveness and consequences. Gaps in legal regulation are explored to identify the need for legal developments and to promote international cooperation to ensure compliance with existing nuclear obligations. The chapter explores the use of individual, or collective, countermeasures, which may not at first seem like an obvious choice, but employing them to achieve compliance with the Nuclear Non-Proliferation Treaty and other relevant obligations may prove to be a useful and effective device. The author concludes that not only are countermeasures permissible under the 2001 Articles on Responsibility of States for Internationally Wrongful Acts and the 2011 Draft Articles on Responsibility of International Organizations, but they may be necessary to ensure compliance with *erga omnes* obligations and may prove to be a successful option for enforcing requirements under the Nuclear Non-Proliferation Treaty as well as other relevant obligations.

Keywords Countermeasures · Erga omnes obligations · Nuclear non-proliferation · Responsibility of international organizations · Sanctions · Responsibility of States

Professor of International Law, Royal Holloway University of London; a member of Wolfson College, Oxford; Chairman of the International Law Association (ILA) Committee on Nuclear Weapons, Non-Proliferation and Contemporary International Law.

J.L. Black-Branch (✉)
Perseverance Cottage 74 Old High Street, Old Headington, Oxford OX3 9HW, UK
e-mail: blackbranch@binternet.com

J.L. Black-Branch and D. Fleck (eds.), *Nuclear Non-Proliferation in International Law - Volume II*, DOI 10.1007/978-94-6265-075-6_16

Contents

16.1 Introduction

Under the Nuclear Non-Proliferation Treaty (NPT)[1] nuclear-weapon States[2] are under an obligation not to transfer nuclear weapons or other nuclear explosive devices, or control over such weapons or devices, to any recipient whatsoever. Non-nuclear-weapon States are not to receive the transfer of nuclear weapons or other nuclear explosive devices, or have control over such weapons, and not to manufacture or otherwise acquire nuclear weapons or other nuclear devices.[3] Whilst the US and Russia hold an estimated 95 per cent of the world's nuclear arms, three non-nuclear Powers—Israel, India and Pakistan—possess, or are believed to possess, nuclear capacity. The Democratic People's Republic of Korea has withdrawn from the NPT and the Security Council has requested it to retract its withdrawal and abandon all nuclear weapons and existing nuclear programmes in a complete, verifiable and irreversible manner.[4]

Despite various attempts by the Security Council, their Resolutions have often been challenged by a policy of non-compliance. States can exercise their own options to introduce countermeasures particularly if they are dissatisfied with non-compliance at the UN level. A state may exercise the possibility of employing

[1]Treaty on the Non-Proliferation of Nuclear Weapons—NPT—(1 July 1968), 729 UNTS 161 (Article I).

[2]China, France, the Russian Federation, the United Kingdom, and the United States (as defined in Article IX(3) NPT).

[3]Specifically, Article II NPT states that it is the obligation of non-nuclear-weapon States, 'not to receive the transfer from any transferor whatsoever of nuclear weapons or other nuclear devices or of control over such weapons or explosive devices directly, or indirectly' and 'not to manufacture or otherwise acquire nuclear weapons or other nuclear devices'.

[4]The Security Council established a Committee pursuant to resolution 1718 (2006) on 14 October 2006 to oversee the relevant sanctions measures and to undertake various tasks set out in para 12 of that same resolution. Additional functions were entrusted by the Council to the Committee in Resolutions 1874 (2009), 2087 (2013) and 2094 (2013). By its Resolutions 1718 (2006), 1874 (2009), 2087 (2013) and 2094 (2013), the Council imposes certain measures relating to the DPRK.

countermeasures on an individual basis. Since measures taken by the Security Council under Chapter VII of the UN Charter have often proven less than effective to ensure compliance with arms control and disarmament goals, it may be for States to seek viable solutions in exploratory talks and negotiations, to pursue long-term settlements that should endure daily pressures, and to cooperate in dispute settlement as required under the Charter.[5]

The NPT calls on the International Atomic Energy Agency (IAEA) to assist with verification practice,[6] which extends to States not party to the NPT.[7] There is no doubt that the IAEA has succeeded in ensuring credible safeguards even in the absence of explicit obligations under the NPT. That said, its best efforts have been challenged by recalcitrant States, including Iran and North Korea,[8] highlighting inadequacies in the current international enforcement regime and gaps in legal regulation regarding compliance with existing nuclear obligations.

Given the challenges raised by delinquent States, and the difficulties facing such prominent international bodies as the Security Council and the IAEA, a possible way forward may be for individual States themselves, as well as international organizations, to implement individual countermeasures.

Countermeasures by States and international organizations must be used in conformity with existing legal standards as described in Articles 22, and 49 to 54 of the 2001 Articles on Responsibility of States for Internationally Wrongful Acts (ARSIWA)[9] and Articles 22, and 51 to 57 of the 2011 Draft Articles on the Responsibility of International Organizations (DARIO), respectively.[10] In order to meet existing legal limits and to avoid damaging confidence-building exercises, such countermeasures must be employed with care. Furthermore, States may use export limitations, traffic controls, travel restrictions and criminal prosecution to

---

[5]On pacific settlement of nuclear disputes see Chap. 17 in this volume by Dieter Fleck.

[6]Article III.1 NPT: 'Each Non-nuclear-weapon State Party to the Treaty undertakes to accept safeguards, as set forth in an agreement to be negotiated and concluded with the International Atomic Energy Agency in accordance with the Statute of the International Atomic Energy Agency and the Agency's safeguards system, for the exclusive purpose of verification of the fulfilment of its obligations assumed under this Treaty with a view to preventing diversion of nuclear energy from peaceful uses to nuclear weapons or other nuclear explosive devices. …'. Article III.4 NPT: 'Non-nuclear-weapon States Party to the Treaty shall conclude agreements with the International Atomic Energy Agency to meet the requirements of this Article either individually or together with other States in accordance with the Statute of the International Atomic Energy Agency. …'

[7]See Rockwood 2013; Status List of safeguards agreements, additional protocols and small quantities protocols as of 31 December 2014, https://www.iaea.org/safeguards/documents/sir_table.pdf.

[8]See Black-Branch 2015.

[9]Articles on Responsibility of States for Internationally Wrongful Acts—ARSIWA—(2001) UN Doc. A/56/10, Yearbook of the International Law Commission, 2001, vol. II, Part Two, http://legal.un.org/ilc/texts/instruments/english/commentaries/9_6_2001.pdf.

[10]Draft Articles on the Responsibility of International Organizations (DARIO), UN Doc. A/66/10, para 87, Yearbook of the International Law Commission, 2011, vol. II, Part Two, http://legal.un.org/ilc/texts/instruments/english/commentaries/9_11_2011.pdf.

ensure compliance with non-proliferation obligations. Such measures would not fall under the restrictions set up in ARSIWA, as unlike countermeasures they are generally speaking in conformity with international obligations towards the other State, although questions of extra-territorial effects and of the legal limitations to such effects will have to be considered.[11]

In this light, the purpose of this discussion is to explore countermeasures and sanctions in the case of non-compliance with nuclear non-proliferation obligations relating to their legal requirements, effectiveness and consequences for future legal developments and diplomatic cooperation regarding nuclear compliance and weaponization. It first explores the role of countermeasures as part of existing sanctions regimes (Sect. 16.2). As a second step it examines the question of whether countermeasures have a legitimate role when it comes to issues of nuclear disarmament, nuclear arms control and non-proliferation (Sect. 16.3). The third step will be devoted to the notion of injured States (Sect. 16.4): do States, beyond the scope of existing Security Council sanctions, have legal standing under international law to take unilateral countermeasures against other States? The purpose of countermeasures against nuclear proliferation and existing legal limitations is given detailed consideration (Sect. 16.5); and, finally, some conclusions are presented along with recommendations for future development (Sect. 16.6).

16.2 The Role of Countermeasures Complementing Existing Sanctions Regimes

Countermeasures have become a widely accepted means of forcing States to comply with international law. Different from retorsions, countermeasures are defined by their intrinsic unlawfulness which is, however, justified by a wrongful act committed by the State or international organization against which they are directed. Countermeasures are part of regulatory efforts by the ILC (Articles 22, 49–54 ARSIWA and Articles 22, 51–57 DARIO), but this regulation does not extend to the use of sanctions adopted by the Security Council, which do not derive from general international law but from the UN Charter itself and are not characterized by an intrinsic unlawfulness, but by the SC's authority to maintain or restore international peace and security.[12] Even if SC sanctions could be seen as falling under the wider term of countermeasures, DARIO would not apply, as such sanctions would be excluded under the *lex specialis* rule (Article 64 DARIO).

Article 41 of the United Nations Charter makes it clear that the Security Council can take enforcement measures to maintain or restore international peace and

[11] See Chap. 17 in this volume by Dieter Fleck, footnotes 97–99 and accompanying text.

[12] Alland 2010, p. 1135.

security.[13] The term sanctions is commonly used, but the Charter itself does not make use of this term, *per se*; it refers to 'measures' in Article 41. Such measures may range from economic activities and/or other sanctions, economic, diplomatic or otherwise, not involving the use of armed force or international military action.[14]

The primary purpose of sanctions is to apply pressure on a State or entity involved to comply with specific objectives set by the Security Council to bring about a peaceful resolution to a matter of international concern without resorting to the use of force. To that effect, in principle this mechanism offers the Security Council an important facility to enforce its decisions. In practice, however, this mechanism is often viewed as a blunt instrument offering very little, if any, tangible value towards achieving its intentions. On the one hand, the universal character of the United Nations, and, in particular, the role of the Security Council as an organ with law-enforcement powers makes it an especially powerful body to establish and monitor such measures. On the other hand, its utility is often criticized as being less than effective in achieving meaningful change as they are often slow to take effect, whereas countermeasures would invariably apply additional pressure on States not fulfilling their obligations. Countermeasures may be a more direct form, and effective method, of achieving compliance as they can be implemented relatively swiftly by a Nation State with precise aims and objectives directly targeting the non-compliant State. Nevertheless, the Security Council has issued sanctions as an enforcement instrument when the peace has been threatened and other efforts to bring about compliance have failed. The range of sanctions has included comprehensive economic and trade sanctions as well as more targeted measures such as arms embargoes, travel bans, financial or diplomatic restrictions.

One vital difference between measures taken by the Security Council and by and States is that the SC has the advantage of a veiled threat of force as per its powers under Chapter VII looming, whereas nation States could not use or threaten to use force under any circumstance (Article 50). Articles 41 and 42 of the UN Charter, avoiding the term 'sanctions', have endowed the Security Council with specific rights to take coercive action, yet not for the purpose of restoring legality in general, but to give effect to its decisions to maintain or restore international peace and security. A separate issue that is not explored in this discussion but is worth evaluation is legal constraints and limitations that must be observed by the SC in relation to human rights norms in limiting the type of enforcement measures that the Security Council takes in maintaining or restoring international peace and security.[15]

---

[13]Article 41 UN Charter: 'The Security Council may decide what measures not involving the use of armed force are to be employed to give effect to its decisions, and it may call upon the Members of the United Nations to apply such measures. These may include complete or partial interruption of economic relations and of rail, sea, air, postal, telegraphic, radio, and other means of communication, and the severance of diplomatic relations.'

[14]Note that Article 42 allows for the use of force stating: 'Should the Security Council consider that measures provided for in Article 41 would be inadequate or have proved to be inadequate, it may take such action by air, sea, or land forces as may be necessary to maintain or restore international peace and security. Such action may include demonstrations, blockade, and other operations by air, sea, or land forces of Members of the United Nations.'

[15]See de Wet 2004.

Legal regulation of this far-reaching matter is less than comprehensive and practice shows that many sanctions taken by the Council were less than effective. Looking at recent disputes with the Democratic People's Republic of Korea,[16] Iran,[17] India and Pakistan,[18] sanctions have, indeed, not proven to be the most effective means of dispute settlement. As discussed in this volume[19] none of the cases reported to the Security Council have been resolved successfully by Council measures under Chapter VI or VII of the Charter. Even coercive measures of the Council have been disregarded in critical situations and the affected States have insisted on maintaining their own political positions. In extreme situations, disobedience of UN sanctions may even be seen as an exercise of lawful countermeasures, a last resort against what is considered a wrongful act, taken by the Council.[20] Fresh thinking about, and new approaches to, Security Council accountability has convincingly influenced debates in the recent years, yet there is still 'a marked discrepancy between the very idea of sanctions … and the traditional international legal system … characterized by its fundamental decentralization and the absence of any authority over the juxtaposed sovereign States'.[21]

Countermeasures taken by States or regional organizations are not precluded by the Charter and ideally they might support Security Council sanctions. Essential aspects of such countermeasures are now accurately described in ARSIWA and the DARIO.[22] Neither are countermeasures to be suspended in any event, when the Security Council is deciding on sanctions, unless they are incompatible with the measures decided on by the Council.[23]

The European Union has developed significant activities in promoting a stable international and regional environment for securing nuclear non-proliferation. Its basic principles on the Use of Restrictive Measures (Sanctions),[24] specified by Guidelines on Implementation and Evaluation of Restrictive Measures (Sanctions) in the Framework of the EU Common Foreign and Security Policy,[25] are designed to ensure full, effective and timely implementation by the European Union of measures agreed by the UN Security Council in support of efforts to fight terrorism and the proliferation of weapons of mass destruction.[26] A critical characteriza-

---

[16]SC Res. 1874 (2009), 1928 (2010), 1985 (2011), 2050 (2012), 2087 (2013), 2094 (2013).

[17]SC Res. 1696 (2006) and 1737 (2006).

[18]SC Res. 1172 (1998).

[19]See Chap. 17 in this volume by Dieter Fleck.

[20]See Tzanakopoulos 2011, p. 202.

[21]See Pellet and Miron 2012, para 61.

[22]See above n. 9 and 10.

[23]Sicilianos 1990, p. 1142.

[24]EU Doc. 10198/1/04 REV 1 (7 June 2004).

[25]EU Doc. 15114/05 (2 December 2005).

[26]See Hertwig 2014, p. 234.

tion of such autonomous European measures as eventually distorting established rules and principles of international law[27] may remain disputable as long as such measures are not incompatible with Security Council decisions. In fact, European policies including the European WMD Strategy,[28] which accompanies the European Security Strategy[29] of 12 December 2003 and has been implemented *inter alia* in the new Export Control Regime,[30] are designed to strengthen, not obscure, UN Charter principles and rules. They also have the advantage of being fully subject to judicial control. It would be a healthy development, and by no means limiting the effectiveness of acts to ensure non-proliferation of WMD, if judicial control could be made available on acts committed by other international organizations, including the UN thereby adding an additional layer of accountability.

The IAEA may also use sanctions in certain circumstances: in severe cases of non-compliance the Board of Governors is authorized under Article XII(7)(C) of the IAEA Statute to

> direct curtailment or suspension of assistance being provided by the Agency or by a member, and call for the return of materials and equipment made available to the recipient member or group of members. The Agency may also, in accordance with article XIX, suspend any non-complying member from the exercise of the privileges and rights of membership.

The first step, however, is to report the non-compliance to all members as well as to the Security Council and General Assembly of the United Nations. Sanctions do not exclude a resort to countermeasures by States or international organizations when cooperative forms of dispute settlement may not suffice and sanctions may be unsuccessful. It is in such cases that the conformity with existing legal standards as described in Articles 22, and 49 to 54 ARSIWA and Articles 22, and 51 to 57 DARIO becomes relevant. Recent developments by the European Union and the United States regarding Iran demonstrate how an individual State and a Union of States can be used effectively to force negotiations aimed at achieving a workable solution to Iran's non-compliance with its international obligations. Note again that countermeasures taken by States (US sanctions) or the EU are not fully subject to SC mandates, but must observe the rules referred to above.

The main purpose of the 2001 Articles on Responsibility of States for Internationally Wrongful Acts (ARSIWA) is to codify the basic rules of international law concerning the responsibility of States for their internationally wrongful

[27] Dupont 2012, pp. 301–336.

[28] EU Strategy Against Proliferation of Weapons of Mass Destruction, http://europa.eu/legislation_summaries/foreign_and_security_policy/cfsp_and_esdp_implementation/l33234_en.htm.

[29] A secure Europe in a better world—European security strategy, EU Doc. 15895/03, http://www.consilium.europa.eu/uedocs/cmsUpload/78367.pdf.

[30] Council Regulation (EC) No. 428/2009, http://ec.europa.eu/trade/import-and-export-rules/export-from-eu/dual-use-controls/.

acts.[31] It is essential to note that the emphasis is on the secondary rules of State responsibility. The articles do not attempt to define the content of the international obligations, the breach of which gives rise to responsibility. A State is compelled to comply with obligations created under primary rules that established an obligation under international law with which that State must comply under international obligations. Note that an international obligation is distinct from internal state obligation.

A starting point is whether a State may be bound by a treaty, as in the case of North Korea and the NPT. It is a matter for the law of treaties to determine whether a State is a party to a valid treaty, whether the treaty is in force for that State and with respect to which provisions, and how the treaty is to be interpreted. In the case of the NPT, North Korea has expressed its withdrawal. There are varying views as to whether it has technically complied fully with withdrawal procedures. Note that it is the right of an injured State to terminate or suspend a treaty for material breach, as reflected in Article 60 of the 1969 Vienna Convention.[32]

The articles under discussion here deal only with the responsibility for conduct which is internationally wrongful. Thus for the purposes of these articles, international responsibility results exclusively from a wrongful act contrary to international law. This is reflected in the title of the articles. The articles are divided into four main parts; Part Three is of particular relevance to this discussion as it specifies that in certain circumstances, a State or States may take countermeasures as a reaction to internationally wrongful acts in order to ensure cessation of the wrongful act and reparation for its consequences.

Part One of the 2001 ARSIWA defines the general conditions necessary under which State responsibility will arise. Specifically, it lays down three basic principles for responsibility from which the articles as a whole proceed (Chapter I). It defines the conditions under which conduct is attributable to the State (Chapter II);

[31]The issue of individual State countermeasures under State responsibility has had a long history. The Charter of the United Nations provides that the General Assembly 'shall initiate studies and make recommendations for the purpose of … encouraging the progressive development of international law and its codification' (Article 13, para 1(a)). With the establishment of the UN in 1948 the General Assembly set up the International Law Commission (ILC) as a subsidiary organ of the UN, with a mission of seeking to promote the progressive development and codification of primarily public international law. The issue of State Responsibility had been a long-standing area for consideration in the international community extending back to the League of Nations, and indeed it was one of the main subjects reviewed at its conference in The Hague in 1930, albeit unsuccessfully. With the establishment of the ILC, State responsibility was selected as one of the 14 original topics for review and development (for a more complete discussion see J. Crawford, Articles on Responsibility of States for Internationally Wrongful Acts 2001, Historical background and development of codification, UN Audiovisual Library of International Law, http://legal.un.org/avl/ha/rsiwa/rsiwa.html. Over the years several reports were submitted under the work of the various Special Rapporteurs and from 1998 to 2001 Professor James Crawford undertook a comprehensive review of the entire text with the adoption of a new draft, consisting of 59 draft articles, which was subsequently adopted by the General Assembly during its fifty-third session, in 2001.

[32]See Joyner and Roscini 2012; Fleck 2012.

and it lists in general terms the conditions under which such conduct amounts to a breach of an international obligation of the State concerned (Chapter III). Chapter IV deals with certain exceptional cases where one State may be responsible for the conduct of another State not in conformity with an international obligation of the latter. Chapter V defines the circumstances precluding the wrongfulness for conduct not in conformity with the international obligations of a State.[33]

Article 1 highlights the principal responsibility of a State regarding its internationally wrongful acts, stating that, ‘Every internationally wrongful act of a State entails the international responsibility of that State’.[34] The starting point is that there must be a ‘wrongful’ act or omission on the part of a State owing the obligation and it must be ‘international’ in character. This may be seen as enlarging the scope of international legal obligations as it provides a requirement to not act in a wrongful manner at an international level; effectively the rules identify the effects of international wrongful acts. It could be argued that this places a positive obligation on the State involved separate from their contractual obligations described in the treaty in question.

16.3 The Applicability of the Law of Countermeasures as a Means to Ensure Nuclear Non-Proliferation

While the successive and, indeed, progressive acceptance of countermeasures relating to State responsibility and individual State[35] enforcement of international law should not be disputed, as a starting point it is only fitting to examine whether countermeasures actually have a legitimate role when it comes to issues of nuclear disarmament, nuclear arms control and non-proliferation. It could be argued that these areas remain ring-fenced, falling outside the law of countermeasures, as they have not been discussed in the ILC, when ARSIWA were developed.

A peripheral glance at a related topic may be appropriate here: When the law of armed conflict was reaffirmed and further developed by the 1977 Additional Protocols to the Geneva Conventions of 1949, a number of States formally expressed their view, which was and remains substantially supported by their Allies and uncontested by any other Party, that the ‘new rules introduced by Additional Protocol I’ were intended to apply to conventional weapons, irrespective of other rules of international law applicable to other types of weapons, with the result that these rules do not ‘influence, regulate, or prohibit the use of nuclear

[33]See articles on Responsibility of States for Internationally Wrongful Acts, with commentaries 2001, in the Yearbook of the International Law Commission, 2001, vol. II, Part Two.

[34]Chapter I: General Principles.

[35]Including collective.

weapons'.[36] The question is whether the approach taken at that time, which is still of certain relevance today, could be seen as being comparable to the present question. If so, would it be logical to conclude from the absence of any similar statement during the ILC's work and in particular in the commentary to ARSIWA that the new rules on countermeasures are fully applicable in the present case? This author would suggest that the nuclear-weapon States have moved to a certain degree in accepting legal obligations on the regulation of nuclear weapons with the NPT. But they also showed that limits have been reached with their 'nuclear declaration' on Additional Protocol I. To automatically apply ARSIWA (a set of rules that has not even been subjected to formal ratification and thus excludes possibilities of making reservations) in respect to countermeasures against nuclear proliferation may be argued goes too far. It would not be logical to conclude from the absence of any similar statement in the development or commentary to ARSIWA that the new rules on countermeasures are fully applicable in the present case, without more specifically considering the restraints in the articles themselves. This author argues that the NPT treaty are obligations *erga omnes*, elevating this sphere of law as a special domain requiring a unique approach recognizing individual State responsibility as well as collective. What follows is a discussion of restraints to be exercised when implementing countermeasures highlighting that they are fully applicable to countermeasures by nuclear-weapon States against nuclear proliferation by other States and non-State actors.

Article 3 ARSIWA stipulates that the characterization of an act of a State as internationally wrongful is governed by international law (e.g. NPT), not by internal law.[37] Therefore internal law can never be used to justify a breach of an international obligation. This is consistent with Article 27 of the 1969 Vienna Convention on the Law of Treaties, which stipulates that a party may not invoke the provisions of its internal law as justification for its failure to perform a treaty.[38] So domestic legislation enacted to circumvent an obligation under the NPT, for example, either by design or inadvertently could not be relied upon to enable such a breach. This would include a non-nuclear-weapon State introducing a legal framework to develop nuclear weapons or a head of State authorizing the testing

[36]See the statements made on ratification of API by Belgium, Canada, Germany, Italy, The Netherlands, Spain, UK, France,—on its accession on 11 April 2001, and—on signature—by the US, printed in Roberts and Guelff 2000, pp. 499–512, and referred to in UK Ministry of Defence 2004, para 617, p. 117.

[37]Article 3. Characterization of an act of a State as internationally wrongful: 'The characterization of an act of a State as internationally wrongful is governed by international law. Such characterization is not affected by the characterization of the same act as lawful by internal law.'

[38]This rule is without prejudice to Article 46 which states: 1. A State may not invoke the fact that its consent to be bound by a treaty has been expressed in violation of a provision of its internal law regarding competence to conclude treaties as invalidating its consent unless that violation was manifest and concerned a rule of its internal law of fundamental importance. 2. A violation is manifest if it would be objectively evident to any State conducting itself in the matter in accordance with normal practice and in good faith.

of nuclear devices. In addition, even States that are no longer party to the NPT are still bound by continuing obligations under IAEA safeguards. Therefore, North Korean President's authorization of the testing of a nuclear device is contrary to international law.[39]

North American Aerospace Defense Command officials at Peterson Air Force Base, Colorado, reported that U.S. missile warning systems detected and tracked the launch of a North Korean missile.[40] The missile was tracked on a southerly azimuth [angle]. Initial indications are that the first stage fell into the Yellow Sea. The second stage was assessed to fall into the Philippine Sea. Initial indications are that the missile deployed an object that appeared to achieve orbit.[41]

UN Secretary General Ban Ki-moon condemned this action as a 'clear violation' of UN resolutions. That aside, for the purposes of this discussion it could be argued that the North Korean testing also caused an internationally wrongful act that was in clear breach of its obligations rendering itself subject to countermeasures, regardless of whether the action was permissible under domestic Korean law and the President was acting within his authority under that law. Moreover, individual States could take countermeasures as long as they complied with ARSIWA and were in keeping with SC resolutions.

In terms of countermeasures, it should be noted that Article 21 ARSIWA makes it clear that, the wrongfulness of an act of a State is precluded if the act constitutes a lawful measure of self-defence taken in conformity with the Charter of the United Nations. Effectively, self-defence is an exception to the general prohibition against the use of force in international relations. Article 51 of the Charter of the United Nations expressly preserves a State's 'inherent right' of self-defence in the face of an armed attack. This is to be balanced with the general obligation to refrain from the threat or use of force laid down in Article 2, para 4 of the UN Charter in relation to 'territorial independence'.

In the case of North Korea in its testing, the North American Aerospace Defense Command officials at Peterson Air Force Base, Colorado, noted in relation to the North Korean missile: 'At no time was the missile or the resultant debris a threat to North America'.[42] Had the US, or other States, felt it was under attack, it would have been free to exercise its right to self-defence under

[39]The North Korean Central News Agency (KCNA) reported the successful launch of the second version of the DPRK's Kwangmyongsong-3 [Una-3] satellite from the Sohae Space Centre and that the satellite had entered the orbit as planned, http://www.bbc.co.uk/news/world-asia-20690338. 12 December 2012.

[40]http://www.norad.mil/Newsroom/tabid/3170/Article/1666/norad-acknowledges-missile-launch.aspx.

[41]http://www.norad.mil/Newsroom/tabid/3170/Article/1666/norad-acknowledges-missile-launch.aspx.

[42]http://www.norad.mil/Newsroom/tabid/3170/Article/1666/norad-acknowledges-missile-launch.aspx.

Article 51,[43] noting the restraints under Article 51, particularly 'until the Security Council has taken measures necessary to maintain international peace and security'. Also, the general acceptance of self-defence does not allow the breach of principles and rules of well-established and accepted international humanitarian law and human rights obligations. In relation to international humanitarian law the ICJ in the advisory opinion on the Legality of the Threat or Use of Nuclear Weapons, they constitute intransgressible principles of international customary law,[44] highlighting that internal law cannot be used to violate these principles.

Among the most debated issues relating to the responsibility of States for internationally wrongful acts is the issue of countermeasures, regulated under Chapter II of Part Three of the Draft Articles.

Article 22[45] ARSIWA clearly sets out that a State can issue 'countermeasures' in respect of an internationally wrongful act. A State can take countermeasures, if subjected to an internationally wrongful act. Judicial decisions, State practice and doctrine confirm that countermeasures must meet certain substantive and procedural conditions. Whilst historically the terminology was 'legitimate reprisals' or, more generally, measures of 'self-protection' or 'self-help', contemporary literature regarding countermeasures makes specific reference to proportional reactions to internationally wrongful acts. This appears to modernize what was hitherto known as legitimate reprisals or measures of self-protection or self-help regarding wrongful acts. Article 22 must be read in conjunction with the requirements under Part Three, Chapter II which stipulates various conditions of countermeasures, including the temporary or reversible character of countermeasures and the requirement of proportionality.

Article 49[46] establishes the permissible object of countermeasures and places certain limits on their scope, i.e. a State may take measures against another State

[43]Article 51 UN Charter: 'Nothing in the present Charter shall impair the inherent right of individual or collective self-defence if an armed attack occurs against a Member of the United Nations, until the Security Council has taken measures necessary to maintain international peace and security. Measures taken by Members in the exercise of this right of self-defence shall be immediately reported to the Security Council and shall not in any way affect the authority and responsibility of the Security Council under the present Charter to take at any time such action as it deems necessary in order to maintain or restore international peace and security.'

[44]ICJ, Legality of the Threat or Use of Nuclear Weapons, Advisory Opinion, 8 July 1996, ICJ Rep. 1996, 226, at p. 257, para 79.

[45]Article 22 ARSIWA: 'The wrongfulness of an act of a State not in conformity with an international obligation towards another State is precluded if and to the extent that the act constitutes a countermeasure taken against the latter State in accordance with Chapter II of part three.'

[46]Specifically, Article 49 sets out the object and limits of countermeasures stating that, '1. An injured State may only take countermeasures against a State which is responsible for an internationally wrongful act in order to induce that State to comply with its obligations under Part Two. 2. Countermeasures are limited to the non-performance for the time being of international obligations of the State taking the measures towards the responsible State. 3. Countermeasures shall, as far as possible, be taken in such a way as to permit the resumption of performance of the obligations in question.'

for non-compliance with specific nuclear obligations, e.g. the case of North Korea as mentioned above.

Article 50 lists specific obligations which cannot be affected by countermeasures relating to fundamental human rights, prohibiting reprisals and peremptory norms of general international law.[47] In other words, the starting point is that countermeasures taken by States are permissible although subject to specific qualifications. In essence, Article 50 reinforces these obligations under international law, in order to uphold a basic set of core values. Article 50 does not confer any rights, *per se*, it merely reminds States of their existing obligations. In doing so it highlights these existing obligations, which complement the development of nuclear capacity for peaceful purposes only, arms reduction (not proliferation) and nuclear disarmament. It could be said that Article 50 seeks to protect international values and principles that have emerged under customary practice. A more detailed discussion of these obligations is presented in greater depth in Part 4 of this discussion in relation to nuclear obligations.

Furthermore, Article 51[48] establishes the requirement of proportionality stating that countermeasures must be commensurate with the injury suffered, that is to say they must be proportionate to the level and degree of the injury suffered. The State imposing countermeasures must also apply to two further criteria; 'taking into account' the gravity of the internationally wrongful act, and the rights in question.

Needless to say, this may be open to interpretation perhaps requiring both a 'quantitative' and a 'qualitative' element. A major restriction that must be placed on countermeasures is that they cannot be disproportionate or perhaps a better way of framing it would be that they cannot be grotesquely incongruent with the injury caused. Essentially, there is a sliding scale corresponding exacting the countermeasure taken to the injury suffered. Again, in reaching such conclusions one must take into account both the gravity of the internationally wrongful act, and the rights in question. Direct reference to 'the rights in question' leaves this wide open, particularly as it relates to the concept of *erga omnes*. After all, what is proportionate from a quantitative and qualitative perspective when 'all States … have a legal interest'[49] in the outcome? Better still, what is disproportionate? For example, the testing of a nuclear device. How to measure a proportionate respond would depend on a number of factors. Although the starting point is that such

[47]Namely obligations to refrain from the threat or use of force as embodied in the Charter of the United Nations (50(1)(a)); obligations for the protection of fundamental human rights (50(1)(b)); obligations of a humanitarian character prohibiting reprisals (50(1)(c)); as well as other obligations under peremptory norms of general international law (50(1)(d)) including *jus cogens*. Article 50 specifies that a State, in taking countermeasures, is 'not relieved from fulfilling its obligations' (50(2)), particularly those under any dispute settlement procedure applicable between it and the responsible State (50(2)(a)); as well as to respect the inviolability of diplomatic or consular agents, premises, archives and documents (50(2)(b)).

[48]Article 51 states: 'Countermeasures must be commensurate with the injury suffered, taking into account the gravity of the internationally wrongful act and the rights in question.'

[49]Ibid.

testing is a breach of the Non-Proliferation Treaty, the type of countermeasure taken by individual States would depend on factors, including the type of device tested; the strength of the device; where it was deployed; under what conditions was it tested; what communications were made between the State testing the device and the UN, the IAEA and other nation States. Again, using a sliding scale approach, what is proportionate in one set of circumstances may be different in another. North Korea's testing of a nuclear device in one of the most densely populated regions in the world, and arguably one of the most delicate in terms of international diplomacy, secretly without any open communication might be viewed differently from a countermeasures perspective from a lesser devise tested under strict conditions with open communications. Again stressing that both sets of tests are inappropriate, what justifies a proportionate countermeasure might differ from one set of circumstances to the next on a sliding scale model.

What might constitute a clearly disproportionate measure in one case may be view differently as it relates to the issue of nuclear military capacity, particularly as it is in the interests of a State to feel safe and secure. The psychological element involved in a qualitative assessment leaves this element very objective. Proportionality does require that a countermeasure must be commensurate with the injury suffered. How does one quantify injury in cases of this nature? What is proportionate to ensuring compliance with nuclear non-proliferation issues, particularly when it could be argued that non-compliance may be deemed a threat to the peace. Again, what about when 'all States … have a legal interest'?[50]

What distinguishes the nuclear issue is the nature and the strength of the device in question. A widespread attack of any nature is impermissible but that of a nuclear dimension may have lingering effects with various humanitarian implications. After all, it was, in part, the lingering 'indiscriminate' humanitarian concerns that led to the 1997 Ottawa Convention and the 2008 Dublin Convention on Cluster Munitions. Indeed, the enormity of the threat and consequent insecurity relating to nuclear war that leaves wide open the qualitative and quantitative questions regarding appropriate countermeasures regarding a proportionate and commensurate response on a sliding scale model.

Aside from the above limitations, Article 52[51] specifies other conditions relating to a State's resorting to countermeasures. Specifically, Article 52 sets out procedural conditions relating to the application of countermeasures by an injured

---

[50]Ibid., 33.

[51]Article 52 states: '1. Before taking countermeasures, an injured State shall: (a) call upon the responsible State, in accordance with article 43, to fulfil its obligations under part two; (b) notify the responsible State of any decision to take countermeasures and offer to negotiate with that State. 2. Notwithstanding paragraph 1(b), the injured State may take such urgent countermeasures as are necessary to preserve its rights. 3. Countermeasures may not be taken, and if already taken must be suspended without undue delay if: (a) the internationally wrongful act has ceased; and (b) the dispute is pending before a court or tribunal which has the authority to make decisions binding on the parties. 4. Paragraph 3 does not apply if the responsible State fails to implement the dispute settlement procedures in good faith.'

State. In particular, before taking countermeasures an injured State is required to call on the responsible State (in accordance with Article 43) to comply with its obligations under Part Two. Also, the injured State is required to notify the responsible State that it intends to take countermeasures and to offer to negotiate with that State regarding the injury. Notwithstanding this requirement, the injured State may take certain urgent countermeasures to preserve its rights. Note that if the responsible State has ceased the internationally wrongful act and the dispute is before a court or tribunal that has competence over such matters, then countermeasures may not be taken and if they have already been taken, such measures must be suspended. However, this requirement would not apply if the responsible State is failing to implement dispute settlement procedures in good faith.

Countermeasures are a form of taking action in response to the position of the injured State in an international system that presently lacks the impartial settlement of disputes through an independent process of law. The above procedural requirements impose a mechanism for States potentially employing countermeasures to achieve compliance with nuclear non-proliferation obligations. First, the injured State must call on the responsible State to fulfil its obligations under the treaty in question, e.g. the NPT, before resorting to countermeasures (Article 52(1)(a)). This provides the State under scrutiny the opportunity to respond to the injured State, potentially opening dialogue that may move the issue forward. Again, the purpose of the procedure is to bring about compliance and is not to be used as a form of punishment or retribution; any discussions that lead to the cessation of the negative behaviour with the view to full compliance would be deemed valuable. So the offer to negotiate (Article 52(1)(b)) over a disputed point is essential before countermeasures are implemented. Indeed the injured State may already have notified the responsible State about its claim in accordance with Article 43, and if so, it will not have to do it again in order to comply with Article 52(1)(a).

Notwithstanding this, the injured State may take 'such urgent countermeasures as are necessary to preserve its rights' even before any notification of the intention to do so. Reference must be made to the word 'urgent' countermeasures which are necessary to preserve the rights of the injured State, such as temporary stay orders, the temporary freezing of assets and other measures could fall within para 2, depending on the circumstances. Paragraph 3 deals with the case in which the wrongful act has ceased and the dispute is submitted to a court or tribunal which has the authority to decide it with binding effect for the parties. In such a case, and for so long as the dispute settlement procedure is being implemented in good faith, unilateral action by way of countermeasures is not justified. So a case submitted to the ICJ, for example, such as the *Marshall Islands* case, would preclude the Applicant from taking appropriate countermeasures against the six countries privy to the action whilst the action is proceeding. That said, it is essential to note that a resort to countermeasures is not excluded by the obligation to resolve a dispute by peaceful means.

Any countermeasure imposed must cease upon compliance with its obligations by the responsible State (Article 53).[52] Again, this must be read in line with the fact that the action of a countermeasure can neither be permanent in nature, nor generate an internationally wrongful in and of itself.

Article 54[53] refers to measures taken by States other than an injured State. Specifically, the right of an injured State is to take countermeasures against a responsible State in order to induce that State to comply with its obligations of cessation and reparation. However, 'injured' States, as defined in Article 42, are not the only States entitled to invoke the responsibility of a State for an internationally wrongful act under Chapter I of this Part. Article 48 allows such invocation by any State, in the case of the breach of an obligation to the international community as a whole, or by any member of a group of States, in the case of other obligations established for the protection of the collective interest of the group.

Needless to say, this again strengthens an *erga omnes* argument as proposed in this discussion regarding the fulfilment of NPT obligations as it is to the benefit of 'all States' that 'have a legal interest'.[54] By virtue of Article 48, para 2, such States may also demand cessation and performance in the interests of the beneficiaries of the obligation breached. Thus, with respect to the obligations referred to in Article 48, such States are recognized as having a legal interest in compliance. The question is to what extent these States may legitimately assert a right to react against unremedied breaches.[55] Note that under the *lex specialis* rule of Article 55

> [t]hese articles do not apply where and to the extent that the conditions for the existence of an internationally wrongful act or the content or implementation of the international responsibility of a State are governed by special rules of international law.

The States or States in question would have to take into consideration derogation clauses or other treaty provisions.

The developing nature of international law is accounted for under Article 56[56] relating to questions of State responsibility not regulated by these articles. This is of particular relevance to the area of international nuclear legal obligations, which is under continuous treaty development, but more particularly from a customary international law perspective.

---

[52]'Countermeasures shall be terminated as soon as the responsible State has complied with its obligations under Part Two in relation to the internationally wrongful act.'

[53]Article 54 states: 'This chapter does not prejudice the right of any State, entitled under Article 48, paragraph 1, to invoke the responsibility of another State, to take lawful measures against that State to ensure cessation of the breach and reparation in the interest of the injured State or of the beneficiaries of the obligation breached.'

[54]*Barcelona Traction, Light and Power Co. Ltd. (Belg. v. Spain)*, 1970 ICJ 3, 32 (Feb. 5). p. 32, para 33.

[55]See, e.g. Sicilianos 2010; Akehurst 1970; Charney 1989; Simma 1994; and Frowein 1994.

[56]The applicable rules of international law continue to govern questions concerning the responsibility of Article 56 states: for an internationally wrongful act to the extent that they are not regulated by these articles.

The above discussion focused on the nature, scope and limits of individual States using countermeasures to enforce nuclear obligations. It appears that these articles provide a valuable framework regarding individual State non-coercive intervention. In that light, the conventional view that the SC is the only legitimate body for issuing and enforcing sanctions or countermeasures, especially in relation to nuclear issues, often based on information provided by the IAEA, may be challenged. Article 25 of the UN Charter stipulates that, the Members of the United Nations 'agree to accept and carry out the decisions of the Security Council' in accordance with the present Charter. Article 103 states that,

> In the event of a conflict between the obligations of the Members of the United Nations under the present Charter and their obligations under any other international agreement, their obligations under the present Charter shall prevail.

Taking into consideration this traditional deference given to the SC, in relation to its legal authority under the UN system for collective security, a critic may question the rights of States to take countermeasures as a means of enforcing the law of State responsibility. They could argue that it would lead to a patch-work quilt of policies that serve to complicate the enforcement of nuclear obligations rather than simplifying it. Yet, applying the rubric of ARSIWA may assist to enforce nuclear obligations at the State level whilst not affecting the SC's exclusivity over security issues as it relates to coercive means as per Chapter VII. Indeed, as explored above, it could enhance it.

The question remains whether a breach of a multilateral agreement such as the NPT or indeed other pertinent obligations could justify States Parties or international organizations to take their own countermeasure against a responsible State regarding an international wrongful act.

On the one hand, we need confidence building in the international community. Encouraging States parties to make use of bilateral and multilaterally negotiated and agreed guidelines and understandings in developing this sensitive area requires delicate negotiations. If we are aiming for transparency and confidence building, then perhaps acting unilaterally will foster insecurity rather than inspire confidence. On the other hand, continued non-compliance on the part of a collection or recalcitrant States does little to inspire confidence and calls for concerted efforts to force compliance; it seems that States may be better able to achieve this by non-coercive means. Eva Kassoti and Gabriella Venturini in their chapters in this volume looked, *inter alia*, at the effectiveness of unilateralism in implementing safeguards.[57] Turning to the question of whether individual State action might undermine attempts to resolve issues on the international stage, it is to be considered that principle is not effective in every case. Hence, individual and joint countermeasures by States following the rubric of the articles may assist. The articles were codified and developed with the view to clarifying international law and restating practice based on judicial and arbitral rulings, and existing State practice. The inclusion of countermeasures was controversial at the time, but nevertheless,

---

[57]See Chaps. 13 and 14 in this volume.

they were included and not subjected to further restrictions in relation to the law on nuclear non-proliferation.

Whilst these articles are meant to provide a general overview in relation to overall areas of State responsibility, questions remain relating to the NPT and more particularly its three pillars, disarmament, non-proliferation and the development and use of nuclear energy for peaceful purposes.

The starting point under Article 1 ARSIWA is that, '[e]very internationally wrongful act of a State entails the international responsibility of that State'. Jansen Calamita states:

> In general, non-compliance with existing international legal obligations is an internationally wrongful act and provides grounds for other states to invoke the non-complying state's international responsibility.[58]

Calamita highlights the difficult question that arises in the case of non-compliance with multilateral obligations, specifically: whether, and under what circumstances, the response to non-compliance may include the use of unilateral countermeasures. He examines in great depth whether breaches of the NPT can give rise to a right in the other Parties to that treaty to consider themselves as 'injured States' such that they may clearly resort to countermeasures in order to encourage compliance, or whether breaches of the NPT cause a more generalized injury, such that countermeasures are not expressly sanctioned by the articles. In doing so he provides a comprehensive examination of Articles 42 and 48 of the Articles on State Responsibility and the character of the NPT, concluding that

> [b]ecause the NPT agreement is underpinned by a collective belief among the Parties that cooperative action is more valuable than 'the individualistic pursuit of security', it is essential that each State possess not only the right to demand performance from all other States party but also the right to take measures to 'ensure compliance' with the Treaty's provisions.[59]

In examining various restraints it would seem that, *prima facie*, they are fully applicable to countermeasures by nuclear-weapon States against nuclear proliferation by other States and non-State actors.

The Draft Articles on the Responsibility of International Organizations (DARIO), specifically, Articles 22, and 51 to 57, set out similar obligations in respect to international organizations. There are similar obligations in regard to 'the wrongfulness of an act of an international organization not in conformity with an international obligation towards a State or another international organization'.[60]

---

[58]See Calamita 2009, p. 1421.

[59]See Calamita, p. 1428.

[60]Article 22 DARIO: '1. Subject to paragraphs 2 and 3, the wrongfulness of an act of an international organization not in conformity with an international obligation towards a State or another international organization is precluded if and to the extent that the act constitutes a countermeasure taken in accordance with the substantive and procedural conditions required by international law, including those set forth in Chapter II of Part Four for countermeasures taken against another international organization. 2. Subject to paragraph 3, an international organization may not take countermeasures against a responsible member State or international organization unless: (a) the conditions

Also, the conditions for taking countermeasures by members of an international organization,[61] There are those regarding the object and limits of countermeasures,[62] and the 'conditions for taking countermeasures by members of an international organization'[63] and 'obligations not affected by countermeasures'.[64] Similarly, 'countermeasures must be commensurate with the injury suffered, taking into account the gravity of the internationally wrongful act and the rights in question'[65] and must 'be terminated as soon as the responsible international organization has complied with its obligations under Part Three in relation to the internationally wrongful act'.[66]

Footnote 60 (continued)
referred to in paragraph 1 are met; (b) the countermeasures are not inconsistent with the rules of the organization; and (c) no appropriate means are available for otherwise inducing compliance with the obligations of the responsible State or international organization concerning cessation of the breach and reparation. 3. Countermeasures may not be taken by an international organization against a member State or international organization in response to a breach of an international obligation under the rules of the organization unless such countermeasures are provided for by those rules.'

[61]Article 52 DARIO: '1. Subject to paragraph 2, an injured State or international organization which is a member of a responsible international organization may not take countermeasures against that organization unless: (a) the conditions referred to in Article 51 are met; (b) the countermeasures are not inconsistent with the rules of the organization; and (c) no appropriate means are available for otherwise inducing compliance with the obligations of the responsible international organization concerning cessation of the breach and reparation. 2. Countermeasures may not be taken by an injured State or international organization which is a member of a responsible international organization against that organization in response to a breach of an international obligation under the rules of the organization, unless such countermeasures are provided for by those rules.'

[62]Article 50 DARIO: 'This Chapter is without prejudice to the entitlement that a person or entity other than a State or an international organization may have to invoke the international responsibility of an international organization.'

[63]Article 51 DARIO: '1. An injured State or an injured international organization may only take countermeasures against an international organization which is responsible for an internationally wrongful act in order to induce that organization to comply with its obligations under Part Three. 2. Countermeasures are limited to the non-performance for the time being of international obligations of the State or international organization taking the measures towards the responsible international organization. 3. Countermeasures shall, as far as possible, be taken in such a way as to permit the resumption of performance of the obligations in question. 4. Countermeasures shall, as far as possible, be taken in such a way as to limit their effects on the exercise by the responsible international organization of its functions.'

[64]Article 53 DARIO: '1. Countermeasures shall not affect: (a) the obligation to refrain from the threat or use of force as embodied in the Charter of the United Nations; (b) obligations for the protection of human rights; (c) obligations of a humanitarian character prohibiting reprisals; (d) other obligations under peremptory norms of general international law. 2. An injured State or international organization taking countermeasures is not relieved from fulfilling its obligations: (a) under any dispute settlement procedure applicable between it and the responsible international organization; (b) to respect any inviolability of organs or agents of the responsible international organization and of the premises, archives and documents of that organization.'

[65]Article 54 DARIO.

[66]Article 56 DARIO.

16.4 Injured States or Regional Organizations

Article 12 ARSIWA, regarding the existence of a breach of an international obligation specifies that,

> There is a breach of an international obligation by a State when an act of that State is not in conformity with what is required of it by that obligation, regardless of its origin or character.

As discussed above, there is little doubt that countermeasures remain an option for States to enforce nuclear obligations. Yet the question remaining is that of standing: May States or international organizations, other than the SC, take unilateral countermeasures against countries for noncompliance with NPT requirements and other nuclear obligations? Do they have standing, under the law of State responsibility to respond to alleged breaches of the collective non-proliferation obligations contained in the NPT or other nuclear obligations? And if so, upon which particular legal grounding, except responding to a wrongful act involving a breach of their own rights?

A convincing answer to these questions may be found in Article 42[67] ARSIWA, which sets out the conditions regarding the invocation of responsibility by an injured State. There is no surprise that the meaning of this particular article has sparked debate, particularly as it pertains to the NPT and relevant nuclear obligations. Some may argue that an interpretation of its strict construction serves to preclude NPT arguments, thereby eliminating the option for levelling countermeasures. That said, this author feels that these conclusions warrant a fresh analysis.

First, Article 42 recognizes an injured State's entitlement. As discussed in the commentary regarding Responsibility of States for Internationally Wrongful Acts, in order to invoke Article 42, a State would have to claim injury, caused by an internationally wrong act in breach of an obligation as per Article 22. An 'injured State' is defined in a relatively narrow manner and draws a distinction between injury to an individual State or possibly a small number of States and the legal interests of several or all States in certain obligations established in the collective interest.[68] In particular, this chapter of the articles deals with the invocation by a State of the responsibility of another State. It is intended for measures of a formal nature and not simply an act of criticism or protest regarding a breach. The commentary notes that a protest is not considered an invocation of responsibility, *per se*.

---

[67]Article 42 ARSIWA: 'A State is entitled as an injured State to invoke the responsibility of another State if the obligation breached is owed to: (a) That State individually; or (b) A group of States including that State, or the international community as a whole, and the breach of the obligation: (i) Specifically affects that State; or (ii) Is of such a character as radically to change the position of all the other States to which the obligation is owed with respect to the further performance of the obligation.'

[68]Materials on the Responsibility of States for Internationally Wrongful Acts, United Nations Legislative Series, ST/LEG/SER B/25 (2012) at p. 274.

There normally would be a formal claim, such as in the case of the NPT employing countermeasures for the breach against the State in question.

For the purposes of the articles, in order to invoke responsibility, a State must be considered an injured State. In that regard, an injured State as per Article 42 is entitled to resort to all means of redress contemplated in the articles, including countermeasures as stipulated in Article 49 and in accordance with the rules laid down in the articles. The commentary highlights an important distinction between Article 42 ARSIWA and Article 60 of the 1969 Vienna Convention on the Law of Treaties. It notes that although the definition in Article 42 is closely modelled on Article 60, the scope and purpose of the two provisions are somewhat different. Specifically,

> Article 42 is concerned with any breach of an international obligation of whatever character, whereas article 60 is concerned with breach of treaties. Moreover, article 60 is concerned exclusively with the right of a State party to a treaty to invoke a material breach of that treaty by another party as grounds for its suspension or termination. It is not concerned with the question of responsibility for breach of the treaty. ... This is why article 60 is restricted to 'material' breaches of treaties. Only a material breach justifies termination or suspension of the treaty, whereas in the context of State responsibility any breach of a treaty gives rise to responsibility irrespective of its gravity.[69]

The term 'irrespective of its gravity' may be of significance in relation to the current discussion. It could stand that any breach may render a State eligible to invoke countermeasures.

The commentary identifies three possible cases regarding the responsibility of another State as an injured State. First, 'a State must have an individual right to the performance of an obligation, in the way that a State party to a bilateral treaty has vis-à-vis the other State party (subparagraph (a))'.[70] Article 42(a), states that a State is 'injured' if the obligation breached was owed to it individually, such as under a bilateral treaty or in some instances unilateral commitments. The commentary also notes that, subparagraph (a) 'is intended to cover cases where the performance of an obligation under a multilateral treaty or customary international law is owed to one particular State'.[71] Further, the commentary acknowledges that:

> The scope of subparagraph (a) in this respect is different from that of article 60, paragraph 1, of the 1969 Vienna Convention, which relies on the formal criterion of bilateral as compared with multilateral treaties. But although a multilateral treaty will characteristically establish a framework of rules applicable to all the States parties, in certain cases its performance in a given situation involves a relationship of a bilateral character between two parties. Multilateral treaties of this kind have often been referred to as giving rise to 'bundles' of bilateral relations.[72]

Needless to say, the obligations owed pursuant to the NPT are collective in nature, but could it not be argued that under some circumstances there are individual

---

[69]Idem, at p. 275.

[70]Idem, at p. 275.

[71]Idem, at p. 276.

[72]Idem, at p. 276.

obligations implied in this treaty? That is, although the NPT is a multilateral treaty with an established framework of rules applicable to all the States parties, in certain cases its performance in a given situation involves a relationship of a bilateral character between two parties. In the case of a State, for example South Korea, affected by radiation caused by a nuclear test, such as employed by North Korea, could it not be argued that these circumstances involve a relationship similar to that of a bilateral character between the two parties? The injury sustained has denied that States have the duty to uphold their obligations and have been remiss in their actions. Or, in the case of India and Pakistan, could it not be argued that the threat one poses to the other gives rise to a relationship of a bilateral character between two parties, that is, the obligation owed under the NPT is both collective as well as individual. This is especially relevant because although they owe multilateral commitments, their positions appear to be aimed, literally, at one another and not necessarily intended against the international community as a whole. Could it not be argued that these, as well as other situations to be determined on an individual case-by-case basis, give rise to invoking subparagraph (a) of Article 42 allowing them the individual entitlement to invoke countermeasures against the delinquent State Party.

Article 42(b) allows a State to invoke responsibility owed to a 'group of States including that State' or 'the international community as a whole'. Note that this general requirement denotes two separate types of responsibility owed: an individual State affected as part of a group; or as part of the international community as a whole, thus potentially covering both treaty obligations and customary practices. Under these scenarios there are two situations regarding the breach of obligation: (i) the breach specifically affects that State; or (ii) 'the breach is of such a character as radically to change the position of all the other States to which the obligation is owed with respect to the further performance of the obligation'.

In relation to Article 42(b)(i) it could be argued that NPT obligations are owed to a group of States and indeed one individual State has been affected by a breach. Again, South Korea may be affected by radiation fallout caused by a nuclear test by North Korea. As a result a State has been injured by another State owing a responsibility, even though other States were not directly affected. If the State argued they were not Party to the NPT, as in the current case of North Korea, it could be argued that the responsibility is on the international community as a whole and they are bound regardless, thus owing the responsibility to the individually injured State.

As noted in the general commentary, the articles do not define the 'nature or extent of the special impact that a State must have sustained' in order to be considered 'injured'. The commentary notes that such would be assessed on a case-by-case basis, 'having regard to the object and purpose of the primary obligation breached and the facts of each case'.[73] 'For a State to be considered injured, it

[73] Idem, at p. 277.

must be affected by the breach in a way which distinguishes it from the generality of other States to which the obligation is owed'.[74]

In relation to the NPT, most debate focuses on Article 42(b)(ii).[75] As regards this clause, the commentaries emphasize that it may be the case that performance of the obligation by the responsible State is a 'necessary condition of its performance by all the other States (subparagraph (b)(ii)); this is the so-called "integral" or "interdependent" obligation'.

Sahib Singh makes the following observation regarding Article 42(b)(ii):

> There are two ways to read Article 42(b)(ii), namely: (1) it provides standing to the aforementioned states because it is premised on the broad understanding of interdependent obligations in the law treaties – and such an understanding of the concept should be read into the Article. [Or,] (2) it must pertain solely to the situation where it is concerned with the modification of the future performance of the *same specific obligation* that has been breached; this is the only conceptually coherent reading available if one it to maintain the methodology of the ILC Articles on State Responsibility.[76]

By accepting the second argument, a breach of nuclear obligations would trigger Article 42(b)(ii), thereby enabling standing for a State to take countermeasures. Singh notes the following:

> loosely classified the NPT as an interdependent treaty and therefore a breach of the safeguards provisions or substantive provisions would permit recourse to countermeasures through Article 42(b)(ii)…. This approach collapses the distinction between treaties and obligations, as well as, the law of treaties with the law of state responsibility. One must be concerned with classifying *obligations* as interdependent or not; the classification of the treaty is irrelevant.

The commentary highlights that a State is 'injured', if the obligation breached was owed to it individually, whereby the expression 'individually' indicates that in the circumstances, performance of the obligation was owed to that particular State. This author would contend that any individual State may be affected by a breach of the NTP or other relevant nuclear non-proliferation obligations, thus invoking a

---

[74]Idem, at p. 277–278.

[75]See S. Singh, Iran, the Nuclear Issue and Countermeasures, on the Blog of the European Journal of International Law (January 10, 2012), http://www.ejiltalk.org/iran-the-nuclear-issue-countermeasures/. Note that in this instance Singh takes the latter view stating: 'I personally fall into the latter camp, because Article 42(b)(ii) must be conceived of as articulating a rather novel legal position based on conceptualizations with significant intellectual baggage—the relevance of this baggage to the particularities of the law of state responsibility is perhaps to be doubted.' See also Calamita 2009, p. 1421.

[76]See S. Singh, Iran, the Nuclear Issue and Countermeasures, on the Blog of the European Journal of International Law (January 10, 2012), http://www.ejiltalk.org/iran-the-nuclear-issue-countermeasures/. Note that in this instance Singh takes the latter view stating: 'I personally fall into the latter camp, because Article 42(b)(ii) must be conceived of as articulating a rather novel legal position based on conceptualizations with significant intellectual baggage—the relevance of this baggage to the particularities of the law of state responsibility is perhaps to be doubted.' See also Calamita, p. 1421.

right to take countermeasures on an individual basis. Moreover, the international community, as-a-whole, may be injured by wrongful actions and the breach of the obligation, under Article 42 ARSIWA, could be invoked either individually or collectively. The use in Article 42 (b)(ii) of the phrase 'radically to change the position of all the other States to which the obligation is owed with respect to the further performance of the obligation' includes the possibility that *erga omnes* obligations may be invoked, as will be discussed below.

One should note that the articles do not convey rights, *per se*, they merely articulate the entitlement to issue countermeasures in the event of an internationally wrongful action. By virtue of its very nature, it is safe to say that the NPT holds a unique status amongst other treaties by its very design, subject matter and significance to international peace and human security, arguably making it the most important treaty ever negotiated and reviewed; requiring full implementation. A record 190 States[77] are Party to the NPT 'making it the most universal of all disarmament and arms control agreements'.[78] By design, the Non-Proliferation Treaty was negotiated and agreed under an asymmetrical process, whereby States were differently placed in the negotiating process based on their nuclear weapons status at the time, invariably calling into question the principle of 'sovereign equality' on which the United Nations was founded. Equality arguments aside, the Treaty as it stands today recognizes two distinct classes of States, nuclear-weapon States (Article I) and non-nuclear-weapon States (Article II). This asymmetrical design renders the treaty special status as a peculiar arrangement, partially based on compromise to allow certain States differential treatment and partially based on pragmatism highlighting the need to reach agreement before other States acquired nuclear weapons capacity.

The material form and substance make it one of the most unusual and indeed peculiar treaties ever agreed, under what is commonly referred to as the 'grand bargain'.[79] In essence it froze into place a select group of states that perpetually retain a unique status in the international community of supposed 'sovereign equals'. Arguably, this elevates the Nuclear Weapons States to having élite status as regards nuclear weapons ownership and notably precludes other States from achieving the same position. It recognizes and legally enforces two classes of States. Given this anomaly, could it not be argued that this renders the treaty a unique position, one which owes both individual and collective obligations?

Moreover, given the significance of the issues at stake, i.e. nuclear warfare, non-proliferation and disarmament, render the NPT status as a very special treaty amongst others and mounting an argument that it deserves primacy status taking precedent over other matters concerning nation states, regional organizations

[77]Note that India, Israel, and Pakistan are not party to the Treaty. North Korea has stated its withdrawal from it.

[78]Zanders 2010, p. 5.

[79]Moelling 2010.

and the international community as a whole. Again, this author argues that the concerns raised by the treaty are obligations *erga omnes*; a special domain of law requiring a unique approach requiring both individual State and collective responsibility.

It is increasingly recognized that some wrongful acts engage the responsibility of the State concerned towards several or many States or even towards the international community as a whole. The ICJ made a significant step in this direction in the *Barcelona Traction* case when it noted that:

> an essential distinction should be drawn between the obligations of a State towards the international community as a whole, and those arising vis-à-vis another State in the field of diplomatic protection. By their very nature the former are the concern of all States. In view of the importance of the rights involved, all States can be held to have a legal interest in their protection; they are obligations *erga omnes*.[80]

Article 2 ARSIWA[81] specifies the conditions required to establish the existence of an internationally wrongful act. First, the conduct in question must be attributable to the State under international law. Second, the conduct must constitute a breach of an international legal obligation in force for that State at that time. Both these elements are required without exception. The element of attribution has been described as 'subjective' and the element of breach as 'objective' although the articles themselves avoid using such terminology, *per se*. Whether there has been a breach of a rule could well depend on the intention or knowledge of State organs or agents in question and in that sense may be 'subjective'. In other cases, the standard for breach of an obligation may be 'objective', in the sense that the behaviour of relevant State organs or agents may be irrelevant. In determining whether the test of responsibility is 'objective' or 'subjective' this would be confined to the circumstances, based on the facts of the case and the specific primary obligation in question. It goes without saying that the conduct in question must both be characterized as an internationally wrongful act, as well as be attributable to the State in question. Moreover, the act in question should constitute a breach of an international obligation of that State, either treaty or non-treaty.

International law maintains that a breach of an international obligation refers to conduct, contrary to the rights of others. In summary, the two necessary conditions for an internationally wrongful act must be met, conduct attributable to the State under international law, and the breach by that conduct of an international

[80] *Barcelona Traction, Light and Power Co. Ltd. (Belg. v. Spain)*, 1970 ICJ 3, 32 (Feb. 5), p. 32, para 33.

[81] Article 2 ARSIWA. Elements of an internationally wrongful act of a State: 'There is an internationally wrongful act of a State when conduct consisting of an action or omission: (a) is attributable to the State under international law; and (b) constitutes a breach of an international obligation of the State.'

obligation of the State. Of course, what remains is the question of harm. Questions arise as to whether, as an extension of the above requirements a further condition exists, namely, damage, loss, harm or injury to another State. The starting point of this analysis is whether such conditions are required under the primary obligation. In that regard there is no general rule on this matter.

As discussed above, Article 3 stipulates that the internationally wrongfulness of the act in question is governed by international law. Again, in the case of North Korea, it may not invoke internal laws, or constitutional privileges accorded to the President, to justify the testing of a nuclear device.

Article 22 raises questions as to whether countermeasures may be taken by third-party States which are not themselves individually injured by the internationally wrongful act in question, although they are owed the obligation which has been breached. Might it also be said that the degree to which NPT Member States allow other States Parties to breach the NPT they are complicit in the breach of positive obligations under *erga omnes* obligations? Allowing others to breach may constitute a breach in and of itself in a modern world where complicit acts are increasingly deemed negative acts, *per se*. Do States not have positive obligations to ensure compliance with international obligations such as the NPT? There are two points requiring exploration. First, does the breach affect all States to the obligation or simply one State? If it affects only one State then Article 22 would allow third-party intervention.

That said, it depends on how one defines harm. In the case of the North Korean nuclear test, had one state been physically affected by the test, say for example it experienced direct nuclear radiation effects, then the State affected would have had an international wrong committed against it by a State. That said, one could argue that even a State tens of thousands of kilometres away that did not experience any direct physical affects, may also have been injured as there is insecurity, a psychological fear factor, raised by such tests. The fact that they are removed physically from the direct effects does not necessarily mean that they are not affected by the test. Indeed, a large State that has received physical damage may not feel the same level of insecurity or fear as a smaller State seemingly more removed. The recent military matters between Russia and Ukraine may cause direct insecurity for Ukraine, but this is not to say that other smaller States in the region, such as the Baltic States or Moldova, are not as affected in terms of psychological fear of attack. Certain behaviours and actions may well create a level of insecurity amongst a wide collection of seemingly unaffected States. Objectively speaking, it depends on the State's position including its vulnerability and ability to defend itself. In some instances, nuclear testing may well affect a collection of seemingly uninvolved States more psychologically than the State that has been directly and physical affected. In addition, arguably, a State may be injured on an *erga omnes* basis without physical harm, *per se*.

An obligation may be owed to the international community as a whole and in that regard, the ICJ has affirmed that all States have a legal interest in compliance.

In the Barcelona Traction case,[82] the ICJ recognized that there is 'an essential distinction' between 'the obligations of a State towards the international community as a whole. ... [b]y their very nature the former are the concern of all States,' taking into consideration 'the importance of the rights involved'. That is to say that, 'all States can be held to have a legal interest in their protection' under *erga omnes*. Thus, the first criterion of an obligation rising to the level of *erga omnes* is, in the words of the ICJ, 'the obligations of a state towards the international Community as a whole'.[83] While the ICJ goes on to give examples of such obligations in Barcelona Traction, it does not define precisely what meaning it attaches to the phrase 'obligations of a state towards the international community as a whole'. The ICJ also elaborated that,

> Such obligations derive, for example, in contemporary international law, from the outlawing of acts of aggression, and of genocide, as also from the principles and rules concerning the basic rights of the human person, including protection from slavery and racial discrimination.

The concept of obligations *erga omnes* had been used to describe third-party effects of treaties or judgments. In the Barcelona Case it was use to decide whether international law recognized the *jus standi* of Belgium in its claim to protect Belgian shareholding interests in respect of injury caused by a state to a foreign company, as opposed to a claim to protect actual Belgian natural or juristic persons permitted by the principle of diplomatic protection. Needless to say, the ICJ's dictum regarding obligations *erga omnes* has raised debate over the past decades. Whilst some commentators have criticized it, dismissing it as irrelevant, others argue a wider application.[84] That debate aside, the concept has intrigued scholars and practitioners alike over the past forty years. Whilst the ICJ has not taken it upon itself to hear a case in the area outright, it remains a focal point of academic discussion acquiring legitimacy, thus meriting exploration in the case at hand. A question within this context relates to enforcing nuclear non-proliferation obligations.[85]

While countermeasures may only be taken by injured States or an injured international organization, the *erga omnes* nature of non-proliferation obligations could justify more widespread activities in this respect. It is clear that safeguards agreements with the IAEA, both under INFCIRC/153 and an Additional Protocol that could be the object of breaches, are bilateral agreements between a State and the

---

[82]In the *Barcelona Traction* case, the ICJ identified *erga omnes* (*obiter dictum*). *Barcelona Traction, Light and Power Co. Ltd. (Belg. v. Spain)*, 1970 ICJ 3, 32 (Feb. 5).

[83]*Barcelona Traction, Light and Power Co. Ltd. (Belg. v. Spain)*, 1970 ICJ 3, 32 (Feb. 5).

[84]See Tams 2010; and Tzanakopoulos 2011; *Barcelona Traction* at 40: The ICJ as an agent of legal development. Leiden Journal of International Law 23(4):781–800. ISSN 0922-1565.

[85]A detailed treatment can be found, for example, in the following works: Bassiouni 1996; de Hoogh 1996; Tams 2010; Villalpando 2005; Sicilianos 1990; Picone 2006; as well as in the contributions to Tomuschat and Thouvenin 2006. The clearest summary is Frowein 2012. Ragazzi 2010 offers much information on specific examples of obligations *erga omnes*, but curiously neglects the concept's enforcement aspect.

Agency to which no third State is a Party in the formal sense. But the obligations included therein are fully congruent with obligations of third States, as the latter have similar safeguards agreements with the Agency based on the same standards, to protect interests which are shared globally. Hence the right in question is more than a corresponding right, but the same right, stemming from an interdependent obligation,[86] so that in case of breaches third States may, indeed, claim to be injured as well. To avoid escalating effects and limit damage to confidence-building processes, these countermeasures need to be subjected to self-restraint and should be regulated as much as possible.

Again, Article 50 ARSIWA[87] lists the various obligations that are not affected by countermeasures, stipulating specific obligations which may not be impaired by countermeasures under any circumstances, including obligations relating to the protection of fundamental human rights; those of a humanitarian character prohibiting reprisals; and obligations under peremptory norms of general international law may not be affected. In other words, the starting point is that countermeasures taken by States are permissible although subject to these qualifications.

This author contends that Article 50 forms the heart and soul of State Responsibility. It seeks to protect central international values; a core set of principles and norms which no State should violate under any circumstances. It entrenches exiting norms and procedures as to how a State reacts to a wrongful act; additionally, it reinforces that these actions in and of themselves are wrongful acts. This core set of norms and principles have emerged over time under customary law and are recognized throughout the international community under various treaties and doctrines such as the duty to protect as well as peremptory norms such as *jus cogens* and the concept of *erga omnes*.[88] This obligation is owed by States to the international community as a whole, and is intended to protect and promote the basic values and common interests of all humanity[89] and 'all States can be held to have a legal interest in their protection'.[90]

It may be argued that one such 'protection' in which 'all States can be held to have a legal interest' is that of protection from nuclear disaster. The deployment of these weapons is assured to have devastating effects on mass populations, the

[86]See Huesa Vinaixa 2010, p. 951.

[87]Article 50 ARSIWA: '1. Countermeasures shall not affect: (a) the obligation to refrain from the threat or use of force as embodied in the Charter of the United Nations; (b) obligations for the protection of fundamental human rights; (c) obligations of a humanitarian character prohibiting reprisals; (d) other obligations under peremptory norms of general international law. 2. A State taking countermeasures is not relieved from fulfilling its obligations: (a) under any dispute settlement procedure applicable between it and the responsible State; (b) to respect the inviolability of diplomatic or consular agents, premises, archives and documents.'

[88]As referenced in *Barcelona Traction, Light and Power Co. Ltd. (Belg. v. Spain)*, 1970 ICJ 3, 32 (Feb. 5), p. 32, para 33.

[89]For a full discussion see Ragazzi 2010.

[90]*Barcelona Traction, Light and Power Co. Ltd. (Belg. v. Spain)*, 1970 ICJ 3, 32 (Feb. 5). p. 32, para 33.

majority of which is civilians caught in the cross-fire, most likely resulting in the mass movement of people seeking asylum; not to mention the untold environmental effects whereby survivors would need to escape depleted lands for safety as well as economic opportunity post-devastation. Aside from the humanitarian implications likely caused by nuclear disaster is the existing day-to-day insecurity caused by this lingering threat of nuclear war as a result of persistent violations of NPT and other relevant nuclear security obligations.

Indeed, it could be said that Article 50 strengthens the *erga omnes* argument. The purpose of Article 50 could be seen as two-fold for the purposes of this discussion. First, to recognize the limits of the scope of measures a State may place on another to achieve compliance. Second, the spirit of the limitations is to preserve specific principles, norms and values within the domain of international law, specifically the non-threat or use of force, protecting basic human rights, and upholding humanitarian obligations. One could argue that the primary purpose of introducing countermeasures against another State for the enforcement of nuclear obligations is to achieve these exact aims. In other words, one could argue that imposing countermeasures to enforce nuclear obligations is symbiotic to achieving the limitations set out in Article 50. The two are mutually compatible and seek similar ends. Indeed, the purpose of including the various limitations set out in Article 50 was to recognize and reinforce the importance of maintaining certain principles of public international law and international humanitarian law as well as existing peremptory norms of general international law. Is it not these same principles that a State is seeking to achieve when applying countermeasures for non-compliance of nuclear obligations.[91] Specifically, many of the very principles expressed in Article 50 would be those advanced by countermeasures for nuclear compliance, *per se*.

The purpose of Article 50 is to protect these obligations under international law, namely obligations to refrain from the threat or use of force as embodied in the Charter of the United Nations (50(1)(a)); obligations for the protection of fundamental human rights (50(1)(b)); obligations of a humanitarian character prohibiting reprisals (50(1)(c)); as well as other obligations under peremptory norms of general international law (50(1)(d)) including *jus cogens*. Article 50 specifies that a State, in taking countermeasures, is 'not relieved from fulfilling its obligations' (50(2)), particularly those under any dispute settlement procedure applicable between it and the responsible State (50(2)(a)); as well as to respect the inviolability of diplomatic or consular agents, premises, archives and documents (50(2)(b)). In other words, the purpose of Article 50 is to limit countermeasures in order to protect these core values. Article 50 does not confer any rights, *per se*, it merely reminds States of their existing obligations. In doing so, it highlights existing obligations which complement the development of nuclear capacity for peaceful purposes only, arms reduction, not proliferation, and nuclear disarmament. Is it not so that a State applying countermeasures for compliance with the NPT as well as

[91]Note that not each non-compliance act may necessarily in itself endanger peremptory norms.

other relevant nuclear obligations is seeking to actually reinforce these same core values; again, in a symbiotic fashion, one acting to mutually benefit the other as it relates to nuclear requirements, and indeed human security.

So, in relation to countermeasures taken to achieve compliance with non-proliferation and disarmament obligations, not only could one argue that taking appropriate countermeasures would not violate these core obligations but indeed the central purpose of imposing these countermeasures is to preserve them. It might be said that allowing for the use of countermeasures could not have been designed for a more fruitful purpose than railing against non-compliance with international obligations relating to nuclear non-proliferation and disarmament. Whether or not the articles were intended for these purposes is not the point, but upon reflection it could be deemed perfectly designed to achieve the very obligations they were serving to protect in Article 50.

That is, to uphold the highest level of compliance relating to potential threats or uses of force (50(1)(a)). After all, the main purpose of employing countermeasures would be, in part, to bring about full compliance with non-proliferation and disarmament obligations. In seeking to achieve such objectives one would be endeavouring to reduce and/or, to eliminate arms that could potentially threaten peace or be used forcefully against another State or States. Such motives are in keeping with contemporary standards.

In the Declaration on Principles of International Law concerning Friendly Relations and Cooperation among States in accordance with the Charter of the United Nations[92] the General Assembly established two principles on similar lines; that States shall refrain from the threat or use of force against the territorial integrity or political independence of any State or act in any other manner inconsistent with the purposes of the United Nations. Furthermore, States shall settle their international disputes by peaceful means and not endanger international peace and security and justice. Indeed, the preamble listed in the UN Charter itself attests it is 'determined' to save succeeding generations from the scourge of war.

Again, enacting countermeasures aimed at preventing arms proliferation may well be at the heart of Article 50. Indeed, it could be said that the purpose of ARSIWA and DARIO is to both strengthen State and organizational obligations and to provide a legal framework for seeking remedy and redress for internationally wrongful acts. That is, to provide a mechanism for challenging and addressing inappropriate behaviours in the international community. Arguably, defiance of UNSC resolutions and IAEA requirements, or treaty obligations relating to nuclear security owed to nation States, are not just against those States or bodies, respectively, but are against humanity as a whole.

As for obligations for the protection of fundamental human rights (50(1)(b)), again, the purpose of countermeasures of this nature would aim to preserving human rights as enumerated under the Universal Declaration of Human Rights

[92] General Assembly Resolution 2625 (XXV), adopted on a Report from the Sixth Committee (A/8082) on 24 October 1970.

1948; the Convention on the Prevention and Punishment of the Crime of Genocide;[93] the International Covenant on Civil and Political Rights 1966; and, the International Covenant on Economic, Social and Cultural Rights 1966. Article 1(2) of the UN setting out that one of 'the Purposes of the United Nations' is to develop friendly relations among nations based on respect for the principle of equal rights and self-determination of peoples, and to take other appropriate measures to strengthen universal peace. Beyond that the countermeasures would also aim to promote basic rights and fundamental freedoms enlisted in various regional human rights regimes and embraced in States' constitutions, including the European Convention for the Protection of Human Rights and Fundamental Freedoms, 1950;[94] the American Convention on Human Rights;[95] and the African [Banjul] Charter on Human and Peoples' Rights.[96] It should also be noted that they may be deemed imperatives that enforcing compliance is meant to achieve.

Surely, these instruments pursue real goals and are not merely lofty ideals. This author would argue that shortly after the birth of the United Nations much of the international legal agenda was politically hijacked by Cold War politics. Recent decades have seen strenuous attempts to regain a legal agenda whereby treaties and customary laws are enforced legally and not politically negotiated. In that vein, it is fitting to return to the legal requirements of the Charter and human rights instruments and not to pick and choose which articles are more politically palatable based on the regime in place at the time. Applying individual countermeasures provides a means for individual States to assist with an agenda of enforcing basic rights and fundamental freedoms through enforcing nuclear obligations.

Article 50 stipulates that countermeasures cannot affect obligations of a humanitarian character prohibiting reprisals (50(1)(c)). Suffice it to say that countermeasures addressing nuclear proliferation and compliance with disarmament obligations would be consistent with preserving these requirements with specific emphasis on the Geneva Conventions, 1949. Furthermore, countermeasures imposed in accordance with the limitations set out in both ARSIWA and DARIO would actually reinforce the principles that the Geneva Conventions are seeking to protect. Essentially, they are seeking to deter, or even eliminate, situations that give rise to activating the protections accorded under these various Conventions.

[93]Adopted by Resolution 260 (III) A of the United Nations General Assembly on 9 December 1948.

[94]Signed in Rome on 4 November 1950 by 12 member states of the Council of Europe and entered into force on 3 September 1953.

[95]Adopted at the Inter-American Specialized Conference on Human Rights, San José, Costa Rica, 22 November 1969.

[96]The African Charter on Human and Peoples Rights (also known as the Banjul Charter) is an international human rights instrument that is intended to promote and protect human rights and basic freedoms in the African continent. Oversight and interpretation of the Charter is the task of the African Commission on Human and Peoples Rights, which was set up in 1987 and is now headquartered in Banjul, Gambia. A protocol to the Charter was subsequently adopted in 1998 whereby an African Court on Human and Peoples Rights was to be created. The protocol came into effect on 25 January 2005. http://www.achpr.org/instruments/achpr/.

Specifically, these Conventions are activated during armed conflict. Employing countermeasures to achieve compliance with NPT and other nuclear obligations seeks to prevent or to eliminate situations under which the Geneva Conventions 1949 would apply, therefore enforcing their intensions in a proactive fashion.

Countermeasures would not interfere with other obligations under peremptory norms of general international law (50(1)(d)). Indeed, the point would be to preserve such norms, namely *erga omnes*. Again, it seems that Article 50 strengthens this argument.

It must be noted that, countermeasures do not relieve a State from fulfilling its obligations under any dispute settlement procedure applicable between it and the responsible State (50(2)(a)) and to respect the inviolability of diplomatic or consular agents, premises, archives and documents (50(2)(b)). The intention of the countermeasures under review would be to assist the process of peaceful settlement and indeed to utilize diplomatic channels to assist the resolution of non-compliance at the earliest opportunity.

It is argued that the harm levelled by existing insecurity over nuclear proliferation coupled with the need to protect and promote the core international values articulated in Article 50 render the employment of countermeasures, individually or collectively, not simply permissible but indeed desirable for the development of human security under obligations *erga omnes*.

16.5 The Purpose of Countermeasures against Nuclear Proliferation and Existing Legal Limitations

Article 54 ARSIWA leaves open the question whether any State may take measures to ensure compliance with certain international obligations in the general interest as distinct from its own individual interest as an injured State. While Article 22 does not cover measures taken in such a case to the extent that these do not qualify as countermeasures, neither does it exclude that possibility. The starting point is that countermeasures are strictly limited to the requirements of the situation, based on the circumstances in question. Moreover, they require adequate safeguards against abuse as per Article 49. As it pertains to nuclear obligations such as under the NPT, this leaves it open for a State to institute measures to ensure compliance. Indeed, it could be argued that not taking measures to ensure compliance may be deemed to render the State complicit in the breach, imposing a positive obligation on the State to enforce its horizontal obligations under the NPT, as long as the measures taken are limited to the requirement and adequate safeguards are taken.

Again, Article 49 regarding the object and limits of countermeasures describes the permissible object of countermeasures that may be taken by an injured State against the responsible State and places certain limits on their scope. Countermeasures may only be taken by an injured State to induce the responsible State to comply with its obligations under Part Two, namely to cease the internationally wrongful conduct, and to provide reparation. Note that under no circumstances are countermeasures to be used as punishment or for punitive measures. It is to be used for compliance purposes only. In that regard, in taking countermeasures the injured State may withhold performance of one or more international obligations (para 2 of Article 49) or the performance of several obligations simultaneously; para 2 refers to 'obligations' in the plural. So a State may take measures against another State for non-compliance with specific nuclear obligations. For example, it may elect to freeze the assets of a State involved in one or several breaches of NPT obligations. It may place travel bans or revoke visas of specific individuals traveling for diplomatic purposes. The phrase 'for the time being' in para 2 indicates the temporary or provisional character of countermeasures. So again, the object of countermeasures must be limited to the wrongful act in question and be lifted as soon as compliance is achieved. The principal aim of such countermeasures is the restoration of a condition of legality, i.e. legal compliance with the obligation, and not to create new situations or wrongful acts of their own which cannot be rectified or revoked. Actions of a permanent nature are prohibited.

As discussed above, Article 50 stipulates specific *obligations* which *may not be impaired* by countermeasures under any circumstances. In particular, obligations relating to the protection of fundamental human rights; those of a humanitarian character prohibiting reprisals; and, obligations under peremptory norms of general international law may not be affected. In other words, the starting point is that countermeasures taken by States are permissible although subject to qualifications. Indeed, as discussed above, it could be said that Article 50 actually strengthens the *erga omnes* argument. The purpose of Article 50 is to recognize the limits of the scope of measures a State may place on another to achieve compliance as well as the limitations to preserve specific principles within the domain of international law, specifically the non-threat or use of force, protecting basic human rights, and upholding humanitarian obligations. One could argue that the primary purpose of introducing countermeasures against another State for the enforcement of nuclear non-proliferation obligations is to achieve these exact aims. In other words, one could argue that imposing countermeasures to enforce nuclear obligations is symbiotic to achieving the limitations set out in Article 50. The two are mutually compatible and seek similar ends. Indeed, the purpose of including the various limitations set out in Article 50 was to reinforce the importance of maintaining certain principles of public international law and international humanitarian law. Is it not these same principles that a State applying countermeasures for non-compliance of nuclear obligations is trying to achieve? Specifically, many of the very principles that are protected in Article 50 would be those advanced by the countermeasures. Article 50 does not confer any rights, *per se*, it merely reminds States of their existing obligations. In doing so it highlights existing obligations which complement the development of nuclear capacity for peaceful purposes only, arms reduction and nuclear disarmament.

In taking countermeasures to achieve compliance with non-proliferation obligations, again, Article 51 specifies that countermeasures must be commensurate with the injury suffered that is proportionate to the injury suffered, whereby the State imposing countermeasures must 'taking into account' the gravity of the internationally wrongful act, and the rights in question, and open to interpretation requiring both a 'quantitative' and 'qualitative' element. The main restriction would be that such countermeasures cannot be *disproportionate* to the injury caused, taking into account the gravity of the internationally wrongful act and the rights in question. Again, taking into account the *erga omnes* obligation leaves 'the rights in question' wide open: How does one quantify injury in cases of nuclear non-compliance?

Procedural requirements set under Article 52 relating to the application of countermeasures by an injured State (in accordance with Article 43) means that, the injured State must notify the responsible State of its intent to take countermeasures and offer to negotiate with that State regarding the injury. As far as compliance with nuclear non-proliferation obligations, these procedural requirements provide a useful framework for States intending to impose countermeasures to achieve compliance. The injured State calls on the responsible State to fulfil its obligations (Article 52(1)(a)) providing an opportunity to respond to the injured State, along with the offer to negotiate (Article 52(1)(b)) over a disputed point opening potentially fruitful dialogue. The procedure is aimed at achieving compliance with the obligation in question and is not meant for punitive purposes. That said, the injured State may take 'such urgent countermeasures as are necessary to preserve its rights' to preserve its rights including, temporary stay orders, or the temporary freezing of assets. Again, countermeasures must temporary in nature and terminated as soon as compliance is achieved (Article 53) by the responsible State. Under the proviso of the *lex specialis* provision in Article 55, the State or States in question would have to take into consideration derogation clauses or other treaty provisions, reflecting the maxim *lex specialis derogat legi generali*.

16.6 Conclusions

The Articles on Responsibility of States for Internationally Wrongful Acts (ARSIWA) and the Draft Articles on the Responsibility of International Organizations (DARIO) were codified and developed with the view of clarifying international law and restating practice based on judicial and arbitral rulings, and existing State practice. The inclusion of countermeasures was controversial at the time, but nevertheless they were included and not subjected to further development or restrictions in relation to international nuclear law. Whilst these articles are meant to provide a general overview in relation to overall areas of state responsibility, questions remain relating to the NPT and, more particularly, its three pillars: disarmament, non-proliferation and the development and use of nuclear energy for peaceful purposes. This chapter highlights the option of invoking countermeasures against non-compliance with the Nuclear Non-Proliferation Treaty and other pertinent obligations for States and international organizations, even if implementing activities by the International Atomic Energy Agency and nation States are regulated in rather specific form and United Nations Security Council sanctions may come into place. Given the often ineffectiveness of Security Council sanctions, it seems that countermeasures in the case of non-compliance with nuclear non-proliferation obligations relating to international wrongful acts is legally sound if done so in accordance with the stated legal requirements and limitations. Gaps in legal regulation highlight the need for legal developments in this special domain of law in order to promote international cooperation to ensure compliance with existing nuclear obligations.

It seems that employing individual, or collective, countermeasures to achieve compliance with relevant obligations may prove to be a useful and effective device. Indeed, not only are countermeasures permissible under the 2001 Articles on Responsibility of States for Internationally Wrongful Acts and the 2011 Draft Articles on Responsibility of International Organizations, they may be necessary from a positive horizontal perspective to ensure compliance with *erga omnes* obligations and may prove to be a successful option for enforcing requirements under the Nuclear Non-Proliferation Treaty as well as other relevant obligations.

16.6.1 Recommendations

(1) States must acknowledge that they do have standing under Articles on Responsibility of States for Internationally Wrongful Acts, beyond the scope of existing Security Council mandated sanctions, to take unilateral countermeasures against countries for non-compliance with Nuclear Non-Proliferation Treaty as well as other relevant obligations.
(2) International organizations must acknowledge that they do have standing under the 2011 Draft Articles on Responsibility of International Organizations, beyond the scope of existing Security Council mandated sanctions, to take unilateral countermeasures against countries for non-compliance with Nuclear Non-Proliferation Treaty as well as other relevant obligations.
(3) Formal recognition is needed that there are fundamental obligations under the NPT of an *erga omnes* character, all States should cooperate in ensuring compliance with these obligations.
(4) States and international organizations should acknowledge the legal limits of countermeasures and especially that countermeasures are a last resort after trying peaceful dialogue. They should recognize that countermeasures are not meant to punish States, they are aimed at bringing about compliance with international obligations and should acknowledge that countermeasures should be temporary in nature and are to be withdrawn when the act in question ceases.

(5) States and international organizations should consider the relationship between countermeasures and the peaceful settlement of disputes.
(6) States and international organizations should consider countermeasures, including use export limitations, traffic controls and travel restrictions to ensure compliance with non-proliferation obligations.
(7) States should legislate and pursue criminal prosecution to ensure compliance with non-proliferation obligations.

References

Akehurst M (1970) Reprisals by third states. Br Yearb Int Law 44:1

Alland D (2010) The definition of countermeasures. In: Crawford J, Pellet A, Olleson S (eds) The law of international responsibility. Oxford University Press, Oxford, pp 1127–1136

Bassiouni MC (1996) International crimes: jus cogens and obligatio erga omnes. Law Contemp Probl 59(4):63–74

Black-Branch J (2015) (Dis)armament and (non)proliferation in international law: the effectiveness of UN sanctions in the case of North Korea. Eleven International Publishing, The Hague

Calamita NJ (2009) Sanctions, countermeasures, and the Iranian nuclear issue. Vanderbilt J Trans Law 42(5):1393

Charney JI (1989) Third state remedies in international law. Mich J Int Law 10(1):57

Dupont P-E (2012) Countermeasures and collective security: the case of the EU sanctions against Iran. J Conflict Secur Law 17(3):301–336

Fleck D (2012) State responsibility consequences of termination of or withdrawal from non-proliferation treaties. In: Joyner DH, Roscini M (eds), Non-proliferation law as a special regime. a contribution to fragmentation theory in international law. Cambridge University Press, Cambridge, pp 250–269

Frowein JA (1994) Reactions by not directly affected States to breaches of public international law, RdC 1994–IV, vol 248. Martinus Nijhoff, Dordrecht, p 345

Frowein JA (2012) Obligations erga omnes. In: Wolfrum R (ed) Max-Planck encyclopedia of public international law (MPEPIL), vol 10. Oxford University Press, Oxford www.mpepil.com

Herik L vd (2014) Peripheral hegemony in the quest to ensure security council accountability for its individualized UN sanctions regimes. J Conflict Secur Law 19(3):27–449. http://jcsl.oxfordjournals.org/content/current

Hertwig J (2014) European Union initiatives: strategies against proliferation of weapons of mass destruction. In: Black-Branch JL, Fleck D (eds) Nuclear non-proliferation and international law, vol I. Asser Press, The Hague, pp 225–256

de Hoogh A (1996) Obligations erga omnes and international crimes. Nijhoff

Huesa Vinaixa R (2010) Plurality of injured states. In: Crawford J, Pellet A, Olleson S (eds) The law of international responsibility. Oxford University Press, Oxford, pp 949–955

Joyner DH, Roscini M (2012) Withdrawal from non-proliferation treaties. In: Roscini M (ed) Joyner DH. Non-proliferation law as a special regime. A contribution to fragmentation theory in international law. Cambridge University Press, Cambridge, pp 151–171

Moelling C (2010), The grand bargain in the NPT: challenges for the EU beyond 2010. In: Zanders JP (ed), Nuclear weapons after the 2010 NPT review conference. Chaillot papers. European Union Institute for Security Studies

Pellet A, Miron A (2012) Sanctions. In: Wolfrum R (ed) Max-Planck encyclopedia of public international law (MPEPIL), vol 10 Oxford University Press, Oxford. www.mpepil.com, para 61

Picione P (2006) Comunità internazionale e obblighi 'erga omnes'. Jovene, Napoli
Ragazzi M (2010) The concept of international obligations erga omnes. Oxford Scholarship Online
Roberts A, Guelff R (2000) Documents on the laws of war, 3rd edn. Oxford University Press, Oxford
Rockwood L (2013) Legal framework for IAEA safeguards. IAEA
Sicilianos L-A (1990) Les reactions décentralisées á l'illicité: des contre-mesures á la légitime défense. Librairie general de droit et de jurisprudence, Paris
Sicilianos L-A (2010) Countermeasures in Response to grave violations of obligations owed to the international community. In: Crawford J, Pellet A, Olleson S (eds) The law of international responsibility. Oxford University Press, Oxford, pp 1137–1148
Simma B (1994) From bilateralism to community interest in international law. RdC 1994–VI, vol. 250. Martinus Nijhoff, The Hague, p 217
Tams CJ (2010) Enforcing obligations erga omnes in international law, rev edn. Cambridge studies in international and comparative law (44). Cambridge University Press, Cambridge
Tomuschat C (1994) Are counter-measures subject to prior recourse to dispute settlement procedures? EJIL 5:77–88
Tomuschat C (2012a) Article 2(3). In: Simma B et al. (eds), The charter of the United Nations. A commentary, 3rd edn. Oxford University Press, Oxford
Tomuschat C (2012b) Article 33. In: Simma B et al. (eds), The charter of the United Nations. A commentary, 3rd edn. Oxford University Press, Oxford
Tomuschat C, Thouvenin JM (2006) (eds), The fundamental rules of the international legal order—jus cogens and obligations erga omnes. Nijhoff
Tzanakopoulos A (2011) Disobeying the Security Council. Countermeasures against wrongful sanctions. Oxford University Press, Oxford
UK Ministry of Defence (2004) The manual of the law of armed conflict. Oxford University Press, Oxford
Villalpando S (2005) L'emergence de la communauté internationale dans la responsabilité des États. Graduate Institute Publications, Genève:
de Wet E (2004) The Chapter VII Powers of the United Nations Security Council. Hart, Oxford
Zanders JP (2010) Introduction in nuclear weapons after the 2010 NPT review conference. In: Zanders JP (ed), Chaillot papers. European Union Institute for Security Studies

Chapter 17
Disputes on Nuclear Proliferation: Means and Methods for Their Settlement

Dieter Fleck

The present system offers an array of measures ranging from dialogue to sanctions to enforcement actions. But judging by our record in recent years, these measures—rather than being applied in a systematic manner to deal effectively with proliferation issues—are employed haphazardly, and too often with political overtones.
Dialogue is withheld as a reward for good behavior, rather than as a means to change behavior and reconcile differences. Public rhetoric substitutes for effective diplomacy. The lesson should be obvious by now: we cannot bomb our way to security. Rather, we should focus on addressing the underlying causes of insecurity.

Mohamed ElBaradei 2008, p. 211

Abstract Disputes arising from an alleged lack of compliance with the Nuclear Non-Proliferation Treaty (NPT) or initiated by shortcomings of the Treaty text have impeded international cooperation and even led to threats to international peace and security. Means and measures of their effective settlement deserve and require reconsideration. After evaluating some shortcomings and bringing them into context with reported cases of non-compliance, the author examines possible solutions by the Security Council, States and international organizations. In this context various measures of and procedures for dispute settlement are discussed, and the effectiveness of Security Council sanctions under Chapter VII of the UN Charter is critically reviewed in light of the fact that none of the cases reported to the Security Council

Former Director International Agreements & Policy, Federal Ministry of Defence, Germany; Member of the Advisory Board of the Amsterdam Center for International Law (ACIL); Honorary President, International Society for Military Law and the Law of War; Rapporteur of the ILA Committee on Nuclear Weapons, Non-Proliferation and Contemporary International Law.

D. Fleck (✉)
Richard-Wagner-Str. 30, 50999 Cologne, Germany
e-mail: DieterFleck@t-online.de

J.L. Black-Branch and D. Fleck (eds.), *Nuclear Non-Proliferation in International Law - Volume II*, DOI 10.1007/978-94-6265-075-6_17

have been successfully solved by such Council measures. Consequences for States, international organizations, and non-State actors are considered and further studies are suggested on these issues. The author concludes that the obligations under the NPT are clear in principle, requiring no amendment of its text; but the UN Charter rules on pacific dispute settlement, as set out in Article 2(3) and Chapter VI, need to be better implemented and further developed in multilateral cooperation. The General Assembly (Article 11), the Security Council (Article 26), the Secretary-General (Article 99) and States have active roles to fulfil in this regard.

Keywords Brazilian-Argentine Agency for Accounting and Control of Nuclear Materials (ABACC) · International Atomic Energy Agency (IAEA) · Dispute settlement · European Atomic Energy Community (EURATOM) · Incentives for compliance · Nuclear disputes · Preparatory Commission for the Comprehensive Nuclear-Test-Ban Treaty Organization (CTBTO) · Retorsions · Sanctions

Contents

17.1 Introduction

The Nuclear Non-Proliferation Treaty (NPT)[1] calls for horizontal restrictions (in the cooperation between States) and for vertical measures (aiming at the prevention of expansion of existing weapons capabilities and the denial of access to non-State actors) to ensure compliance with its goals and provisions.

Activities for implementation are manifold. While States are required to take effective action for meeting their obligations under the Treaty, they do have considerable discretion in making appropriate choices. Such choices may depend on political principles rather than exact technological requirements. There may be several viable possibilities for taking appropriate action, either unilaterally or as part of international cooperation, to ensure an effective protection of weapons-relevant material and its non-delivery to States or non-State actors. Many pertinent activities, performed by the executive or outsourced to private companies, are not necessarily subject to national legal regulation. It is only for few acts of government,

[1]Treaty on the Non-Proliferation of Nuclear Weapons (1 July 1968), 729 UNTS 161.

such as the penal prosecution of offences,[2] that national legislation will be required, to secure compliance with international non-proliferation obligations.

Issues concerning nuclear non-proliferation obligations may arise when there is uncertainty about compliance or even suspicion of non-compliance. While attempts should be made to remove doubts and clarify any allegations in a cooperative manner, the possibility of a dispute between the International Atomic Energy Agency (IAEA) and a Member State or between States exists.[3] Such disputes may have various reasons. They may be rooted in shortcomings of the treaty text, shortcomings that would have existed since its adoption and may have got new importance. They may result from diverging interests that have developed over time. They may also arise from gaps of legal regulation that were intentionally left open during the negotiations, but have gained greater relevance thereafter, as is the case with compliance by non-State actors with existing obligations.

These different origins of disputes may require different measures and procedures for their pacific settlement. Disputes on nuclear non-proliferation have severely impeded international cooperation and even led to threats to international peace and security. It is important to explore these issues and develop means and methods for strengthening international dispute settlement. As famously stated by Ian Brownlie, 'there is no obligation in general international law to *settle* disputes, and procedures for settlement by formal and legal procedures are consensual in character'.[4] But the strong impact every nuclear dispute has on international security underlines the essential need for peaceful settlement in these cases. Settlement by political means, which is widely informed by international legal principles and rules even where principles of equity have a more dominating impact, cannot be set aside here. Concentrating on legal principles and rules, this chapter will investigate shortcomings of existing treaty law, assess the development of customary principles and rules, and identify gaps of regulation.

After evaluating certain shortcomings of the NPT (Sect. 17.2) and bringing them into context with reported cases of non-compliance (Sect. 17.3), this chapter will discuss possible solutions for ensuring compliance with existing nuclear

[2]See e.g. Convention on the Physical Protection of Nuclear Material—CPPNM—(30 March 1980), 1456 UNTS 125, entered into force on 8 February 1987, amended on 8 July 2005 (International Atomic Energy Agency Information Circular) INFCIRC/274/Rev 1, http://www.iaea.org/Publications/Documents/Conventions/cppnm.html (amendment not yet in force); Convention for the Suppression of Unlawful Acts against the Safety of Maritime Navigation—SUA Convention—(10 March 1988), amended by Protocol of 2005 to the Convention for the Suppression of Unlawful Acts of Violence against the Safety of Maritime Navigation (14 October 2005); Protocol for the Suppression of Unlawful Acts Against the Safety of Fixed Platforms located on the Continental Shelf (10 March 1988), amended on 14 October 2005, www.imo.org/About/Conventions/Pages/Home.aspx; http://www.imo.org/About/Conventions/StatusOfConventions/Documents/Status%20-%202014.docx.pdf; http://www.state.gov/t/isn/trty/81728.htm.

[3]See Bothe 1994, pp. 181–182.

[4]Crawford 2012, p. 718.

non-proliferation obligations and providing pacific dispute settlement (Sect. 17.4).[5] As stated in the UN Charter,[6] any such settlement comprises a variety of efforts, which must be considered as part of a resolution following international principles and rules. A focus on 'legal resolution' in a narrower sense, as comprising third-party settlement by international adjudication and arbitration, but excluding diplomatic activities for settlement,[7] appears to be too limited. Other means of international dispute settlement are likewise influenced by legal principles and rules[8] and judicial settlement is only one option, but not a dominating part of dispute settlement under the Charter.[9] Settlement by negotiation, strongly influenced by auto-interpretation of the relevant treaties and auto-adjudication of the required standards of performance is a typical phenomenon of arms control.[10] While possibilities of making more use of third-party adjudication, arbitration and mediation to solve international disputes should be appreciated, the containment and settlement of nuclear non-proliferation disputes will predominantly remain a task for States and competent international organizations.

It is difficult to develop and confirm general principles for dispute settlement in this field and a need for pragmatic solutions and common sense rather than generic legal regulation must be particularly recognized. Nevertheless, some general conclusions may be drawn from this analysis, to contribute to improving international cooperation and developing proposals for the way ahead (Sect. 17.5).

17.2 Shortcomings of the NPT

The NPT does not regulate all military uses of nuclear material, but only explosive uses. This is to accommodate the interest of a number of States in retaining the right to use nuclear energy for non-explosive military purposes, specifically nuclear naval propulsion. A need for regulation does not necessarily exist insofar as safety is ensured.

---

[5]For countermeasures to ensure compliance with nuclear non-proliferation obligations see Black-Branch, Chap. 16 in this volume.

[6]Far from reducing 'peaceful settlement' to 'judicial settlement', Article 33 UN Charter refers to 'negotiation, enquiry, mediation, conciliation, arbitration, judicial settlement, resort to regional agencies or arrangements, or other peaceful means'. As Article 2(3) UN Charter confirms, such means shall be used 'in such a manner that international peace and security, and justice, are not endangered'.

[7]See Fry 2013, p. 34 and throughout his monograph.

[8]See e.g. R. Higgins, The Place of International Law in the Settlement of Disputes by the Security Council, published in Rosalyn Higgins, Themes and Theories, Oxford University Press, 174–192, Oxford Scholarship Online: March 2012, DOI: 10.1093/acprof:oso/9780198262350.001.0001, especially at pp. 183–185 and 189–192; de Wet 2004, pp. 369–372.

[9]As well put by Shaw 1999, p. 54: 'The Court does not constitute a different or rival system of dispute settlement; it is firmly locked into that integrated and pluralist system established under the Charter'.

[10]See Dahlitz 1984, pp. 212–213.

There are also certain inconsistencies in the Treaty text itself. Some open issues may derive from the lack of definitions of terms such as 'nuclear weapon' or 'manufacture',[11] but it appears that practice has solved these issues in an acceptable manner and allows for a generally effective verification system.

While it was argued decades ago that the Treaty as it stands would be no legal obstacle to a non-nuclear-weapon Party furnishing material assistance to another non-nuclear-weapon State not party to the Treaty for a nuclear weapons programme,[12] such interpretation was successfully rejected by States and may be ruled out today based on widely shared expertise.[13] It would, indeed, hardly match with the obligations of non-nuclear-weapon States 'assumed under this Treaty with a view to preventing diversion of nuclear energy from peaceful uses to nuclear weapons or other nuclear explosive devices' (Article III.1 NPT). It should also be considered that under Article III.2 States' Parties undertake not to provide material or equipment to any non-nuclear-weapon State even for peaceful purposes, unless the source or special fissionable material is subject to safeguards. As will be discussed below,[14] the verification practice of the IAEA has been successful in ensuring credible safeguards even in the absence of explicit obligations under the NPT.

A textual weakness has been seen in the fact that the obligation 'not to transfer to any recipient whatsoever' which is one of nuclear-weapon States under Article I, is not expressly repeated for non-nuclear-weapon States in Article II.[15] This understanding, however, is disputable: Article II fully mirrors the obligation of nuclear-weapons States 'not to transfer to any recipient whatsoever' by establishing an obligation for non-nuclear-weapon States 'not to receive the transfer from any transferor whatsoever'. It should be read in context with Article III under which each non-nuclear-weapon State Party to the NPT clearly has to support the IAEA safeguards system. The latter applies to all kinds of nuclear materials,[16] irrespective of whether relevant facilities are owned or operated by a State or a private enterpriser.

Some loopholes of the NPT are of continuing concern: Only non-nuclear-weapon States are obliged under the Treaty to accept IAEA safeguards (Article III.1), while nuclear-weapon State Parties are not bound in the same manner. There is also no compulsory international control of fissile production. Hence, it is correct to state that an important divide exists under the NPT between nuclear-weapon States and non-nuclear-weapon States. The United States, the Russian

[11]See e.g. Nystuen and Hugo 2014, pp. 387–390; A. Persbo, A Reflection on the Current State of Nuclear Non-Proliferation and Safeguards, EU Non-Proliferation Consortium Non-Proliferation Papers No. 8, http://www.sipri.org/research/disarmament/eu-consortium/publications/publications/non-proliferation-paper-8, pp. 4–5.

[12]Willrich 1968, pp. 1477–1478; Willrich 1969, p. 95.

[13]See the US and Soviet statements, Willrich 1968, p. 1478, n. 73, and the convincing assessment of the negotiations by Shaker 1980, pp. 191–267.

[14]See below, n. 32–36 and accompanying text.

[15]Marauhn 2013, p. 49.

[16]See paras 19–20 INFCIRC/66/Rev.2, The Agency's Safeguards System (16 September 1968), http://www.iaea.org/Publications/Documents/Infcircs/Others/infcirc66r2.pdf.

Federation, China, the United Kingdom and France have a leadership responsibility for taking appropriate action insofar. The extent to which these Powers are meeting this challenge is decisive for the NPT's effectiveness. While the argument has already been made that '[p]erhaps, the NPT legal regime is already legally dead, given the failure of the nuclear weapon States to fulfil their end of the bargain and considering its selective implementation over the years',[17] the challenge for improving compliance continues to exist without acceptable alternative. It extends to all three pillars of the NPT, thus comprising serious steps towards nuclear disarmament, further commitments towards non-proliferation of nuclear weapons and other nuclear explosive devices, and effective measures to ensure safety and security of the use of nuclear energy.

The five Powers have voluntary offered safeguards agreements with the IAEA which cover some or all nuclear material and/or facilities from which the IAEA may select material or facilities for the application of safeguards. They have also signed Additional Protocols that include certain measures provided for in INFCIRC/540[18] and brought them into force.[19] Membership of the IAEA includes certain States not party to the NPT, such as India, Israel and Pakistan, and the IAEA has agreements with these States, specifying the application of safeguards to nuclear material, facilities and other items in accordance with INFCIRC/66/Rev. 2.[20]

During the past decades a considerable number of further international treaties and agreements have been developed for various related purposes: to regulate the use of nuclear energy,[21] to ensure security and safety of peaceful uses of nuclear energy,[22] and to strengthen international responsibility for compliance with these

[17]Falk 2008, p. 47.

[18]IAEA, Model Protocol Additional to the Agreement(s) Between State(s) and the International Atomic Energy Agency for the Application of Safeguards, INFCIRC/540 (Corr.), http://www.iaea.org/Publications/Documents/Infcircs/1997/infcirc540c.pdf.

[19]See e.g. http://www.iaea.org/safeguards/documents/AP_status_list.pdf, and the Additional Protocols concluded with China (INFCIRC/369/Add.1 of 22 April 2002), the United Kingdom (INFCIRC/263/Add.1 of 24 February 2005), France (INFCIRC/290/Add.1 of 24 February 2005), the Russian Federation (INFCIRC/327/Add.1 of 8 January 2008), and the United States (INFCIRC/288/Add.1 of 9 March 2009).

[20]See above n. 18 and the Safeguards Agreements concluded with Israel (INFCIRC/249 of 28 September 1977), India (INFCIRC/754 of 29 May 2009), and Pakistan (INFCIRCs 34, 90, 116, 135, 150, 239, 248, 285, 393, 418, 596, 636, 669, 705, 712, 816, and 832 as listed at http://www.iaea.org/Publications/Documents/Infcircs/Countries/pakistan.shtml).

[21]See e.g. Treaty establishing the European Atomic Energy Community—EURATOM—(25 March 1957), http://eur-lex.europa.eu/en/treaties/dat/12006A/12006A.htm; Paris Convention on Third Party Liability in the Field of Nuclear Energy, last amended on 12 February 2004, http://www.oecd-nea.org/law/Unofficial%20consolidated%20Paris%20Convention.pdf.

[22]See e.g. Convention on Nuclear Safety—CNS—(5 July 1994), INFCIRC/449, http://www.iaea.org/Publications/Documents/Infcircs/Others/inf449.shtml; Agreement between the Republic of Argentina, the Federative Republic of Brazil, the Brazilian-Argentine Agency for Accounting and Control of Nuclear Materials (ABACC) and the International Atomic Energy Agency for the Application of Safeguards (13 December 1991), http://www.iaea.org/Publications/Documents/Infcircs/Others/inf435.shtml.

rules.[23] Yet rather than offering a comprehensive regulatory system, these instruments are characterized by certain differences as well as by overlaps as to their subject matter, participation and implementing mechanisms. This inevitably has led to shortcomings and obvious loopholes in legal regulation, the most significant of which shall briefly be addressed below.

Safety and security of peaceful uses of nuclear energy have proven unsatisfactory. While safety issues include any hazards in the handling of equipment and material, security issues comprise external threats ranging from military assault to individual criminal acts. International legal regulation of nuclear safety, nuclear security and radioactive waste management still require further efforts. The 2012 Nuclear Security Summit addressed existing relations between nuclear safety and security in the context of the Fukushima incident of 11 March 2011, yet a comprehensive international regulation has not been achieved so far.[24] The Nuclear Security Summit, hosted in The Hague on 24 and 25 March 2014,[25] highlighted the importance of the dialogue between governments and industry in promoting nuclear security, in order to enhance information security, and to strengthen sustainability of nuclear security cooperation.[26] While it is technically impossible to guarantee full safety of nuclear energy production, both technical safeguards and liability issues are a matter of concern and they remain subject to continuing challenges. Radioactive waste management, which requires enormous activities to isolate radioactive waste and ensure its containment from the biosphere for hundreds or thousands of years, is far from being settled on a global scale. Shipments of material from nuclear reactors in Japan to the mixed oxide fuel (MOX) plant at Sellafield (UK) and *vice versa* have caused particular controversies in recent

[23]See e.g. IAEA, The Structure and Content of Agreements between the Agency and States Required in Connection with the Treaty on the Non-Proliferation of Nuclear Weapons, INFCIRC/153 (Corr.), http://www.iaea.org/Publications/Documents/Infcircs/Others/infcirc153.pdf.

[24]Nuclear Security Summit 2012, http://armscontrolcenter.org/issues/nuclearterrorism/articles/fact_sheet_2012_seoul_nuclear_security_summit_results/; see Anthony 2013.

[25]Nuclear Security Summit 2014, http://www.denhaag.nl/en/residents/to/Nuclear-Security-Summit-2014-in-The-Hague.htm.

[26]See The Hague Nuclear Security Summit Communiqué, https://www.nss2014.com/sites/default/files/documents/the_hague_nuclear_security_summit_communique_final.pdf, para 25: 'We recognise that nuclear security and safety have the common aim of protecting human health, society and the environment. We reaffirm that nuclear safety measures and nuclear security measures need to be designed and managed in a coherent and coordinated manner in the specific areas where nuclear security and nuclear safety overlap. In these areas, efforts to further improve nuclear security might benefit from experience gained with nuclear safety. We emphasize the need to develop a nuclear security culture, with a particular focus on the coordination of safety and security. Sharing good practices, without detriment to the protection of sensitive information, might also be beneficial. The principle of continuous improvement applies to both safety and security. In this regard we acknowledge the IAEA Nuclear Security Guidance Committee and the IAEA Commission on Safety Standards and their activities aimed at properly addressing safety and security interface issues.'

years. The relevant decisions of the European Court of Justice[27] and the Permanent Court of Arbitration[28] and its consequences for similar cases deserve further exploration. Furthermore, a relationship between nuclear weapons modernization, nuclear disarmament and the safety of peaceful nuclear uses cannot be denied. This aspect calls for more transparency in the dismantlement of nuclear weapons and explosive devices, a matter that still needs to be regulated on an international level.

The challenge of terrorism by actors involving the threat or use of weapons of mass destruction is a serous possibility today.[29] This requires responses, not necessarily to be based on treaty law, but rather on partnerships, arrangements among groups of States, such as the Global Initiative to Combat Nuclear Terrorism (GICNT),[30] the Proliferation Security Initiative (PSI),[31] or the Global Threat Reduction Initiative (GTRI).[32] Measures to be taken in this context are to a large extent voluntary in nature, a fact that does not diminish their importance. As far as legal regulation is concerned, it is widely based on national rules of law enforcement and criminal prosecution, while pertinent principles and rules of international law are still in a developing stage.

It may be considered as a weakness of the IAEA safeguards system that it essentially relies on the voluntary cooperation by States. But the question about realistic alternatives remains open. The Board of Governors of the IAEA has confirmed on numerous occasions since as early as 1992, that the Agency is authorized and required to seek to verify both the non-diversion of nuclear material from declared activities (i.e. correctness) and the absence of undeclared nuclear activities in the State (i.e. completeness).[33] To perform this task effectively, cooperation by States is essential. While there is some controversy on whether the

[27]See ECJ, *Commission of the European Communities v. Ireland* (Case C-459/03), Judgment of 30 May 2006, http://curia.europa.eu/jcms/upload/docs/application/pdf/2009-02/cp060045en.pdf.

[28]See Permanent Court of Arbitration, *Ireland v. United Kingdom* ('*MOX Plant* case', 2001–2008), http://www.pca-cpa.org/showpage.asp?pag_id=1148.

[29]See Wilkinson 2012, pp. 52–61.

[30]See Global Initiative to Combat Nuclear Terrorism (GICNT), http://www.state.gov/t/isn/c37079.htm.

[31]Proliferation Security Initiative (PSI), http://www.state.gov/t/isn/c10390.htm, see Venturini, Chap. 10 in this volume; see US Department of State, 'Proliferation Security Initiative 10th anniversary high-level political meeting outcomes' (28 May 2013), http://www.state.gov/r/pa/prs/ps/2013/05/210010.htm.

[32]See Global Threat Reduction Initiative (GTRI), http://www.cdi.org/program/document.cfm?DocumentID=3650.

[33]See IAEA, *How We Implement Safeguards*, http://www.iaea.org/safeguards/what.html and for example, IAEA Report GOV/2013/6 (21 February 2013), n. 61, http://www.iaea.org/Publications/Documents/Board/2013/gov2013-6.pdf.

IAEA is acting *ultra vires*,[34] a clear distinction between specific reporting obligations of States and the mandate of the Agency remains necessary: Verification cannot be confined to using national reports. Efforts of treaty interpretation should not neglect the purpose of verification, as reflected in the mandate. The importance of verification for ensuring safety and international security must not be ignored. In 1997, the IAEA developed its Model Additional Protocol to strengthen the safeguards regime by improved national reporting, complementary access to locations where nuclear material may be present, and a right for inspections.[35] While many States, including all nuclear-weapons States party to the NPT have committed themselves to the obligations stipulated in the Model Additional Protocol, universal acceptance has so far not been reached.[36] The Agency was able to conclude in its last Annual Report that of the 117 States that had both a Comprehensive Safeguards Agreement under INFCIRC/153 and an Additional Protocol, in 63 States (and Taiwan, China) *all* nuclear material remained in peaceful activities; for the remaining 54 States the necessary evaluation remained ongoing. When an Additional Protocol is not available, the IAEA can only be expected to make such conclusion for *declared* nuclear material.[37] Yet it is free to conduct monitoring activities also beyond verification measures that are regulated in safeguards agreements. For this purpose, e.g. open source information, including satellite imagery and trade information may be used. In accordance with its mandate, the Agency has conceptualized safeguards implementation at the State level. While it seeks support by States for its verification activities, this should not be misunderstood as monitoring States under review only subject to agreement.

States, too, have increased their efforts to ensure non-proliferation and they have developed the effectiveness of measures taken for that purpose. More and more export controls concentrate on end-use rather than considering all specific

[34]See Dupont, Chap. 3 in this volume; Dupont 2014, p. 209; Joyner 2011, pp. 92–93; D.H. Joyner, New IAEA DG report on Iran Still Incorrect on the Legal Mandate of the IAEA (11 March 2013), http://armscontrollaw.com/2013/03/11/new-iaea-dg-report-on-iran-still-incorrect-on-the-legal-mandate-of-the-iaea/; *contra*: Rockwood and Johnson, Chap. 4 in this volume; L. Rockwood, The IAEA's State-Level Concept and the Law of Unintended Consequences, in Arms Control Today (September 2014), https://www.armscontrol.org/act/2014_09/Features/The-IAEAs-State-Level-Concept-and-the-Law-of-Unintended-Consequences; D. Albright, O. Heinonen and O Kittrie, Understanding the IAEA's Mandate in Iran: Avoiding Misinterpretations. http://www.isis-online.org/uploads/isis-reports/documents/Misinterpreting_the_IAEA_27Nov2012.pdf.

[35]See above n. 18.

[36]See http://www.iaea.org/safeguards/documents/AP_status_list.pdf; SC Res. 1887 (2009), para 15b; Asada, Chap. 5 in this volume.

[37]IAEA, Annual Report for 2013, http://www.iaea.org/sites/default/files/anrep2013_full_0.pdf, pp. 8–9. See also ElBaradei 2008, p. 211.

characterizations of items that could contribute to a particular weapons system.[38] This is to avoid unnecessary control steps and ensure that only relevant activities are scrutinized. Similar experience was made with export controls of chemical and biological dual-use items.[39]

Hence, existing shortcomings of treaty regulation notwithstanding, effective cooperation is possible both under and beyond existing treaty provisions, to ensure compliance with international obligations in this field. While such cooperation often appears to be less than straightforward, there is still a considerable potential to dissuade and deny by immediate action, and exercise adequate control and leadership under long-term policies.[40]

17.3 Lack of Implementation

International institutions are deeply involved in the implementation of the NPT, thus supplementing the role of States Parties. The Treaty refers to an existing organization, the IAEA, established in 1956 'to accelerate and enlarge the contribution of atomic energy to peace, health and prosperity throughout the world'.[41] The Agency's safeguards system shall be used to ensure verification of nuclear non-proliferation obligations (Article III NPT).

The practice of the Preparatory Commission for the Comprehensive Nuclear-Test-Ban Organization (CTBTO), founded in 1996, also becomes increasingly relevant for efforts to ensure compliance with existing rules.[42] At regional level the long-standing experience gained by the European Atomic Energy Community (EURATOM)[43] and the Brazilian–Argentine Agency for Accounting and Control of Nuclear Materials (ABACC)[44] provide viable solutions for current legal challenges.

---

[38]See Anthony 2012, pp. 25–44; Zangger Committee, with its Trigger List for the processing, use, or production of special fissionable materials, developed to clarify language in Article III(2) NPT (INFCIRC/209), http://cns.miis.edu/inventory/pdfs/zang.pdf; Nuclear Suppliers Group (NSG) with its Guidelines for Nuclear Transfers (INFCIRC/254, Part 1) and Guidelines for Transfers of Nuclear-Related Dual-Use Equipment, Materials, Software, and Related Technology (INFCIRC/254, Part 2), http://www.nuclearsuppliersgroup.org/Leng/default.htm.

[39]See Australia Group fighting the spread of chemical and biological weapons, http://www.australiagroup.net/en/index.html.

[40]See Franceschini 2008, pp. 173–180.

[41]Article II of the Statute of the International Atomic Energy Agency (26 October 1956, amended 1963, 1973, 1989, and 1999), http://www.nuclearfiles.org/menu/library/treaties/atomic-energy-act/trty_atomic-energy-statute.htm.

[42]See Bauer and O'Reilly, Chap. 6 in this volume; see also Venturini 2014, p. 133.

[43]See Kilb, Chap. 7 in this volume; see also Kilb 2014, p. 97.

[44]Agreement on the Exclusively Peaceful Use of Nuclear Energy (Guadalajara Agreement between Argentina and Brazil, 18 July 1991), http://cns.miis.edu/inventory/pdfs/abacc.pdf; see http://www.abacc.org.br/?page_id=5&lang=en.

The IAEA Board of Governors in its global practice has so far found six of its Member States to be in non-compliance with nuclear non-proliferation obligations: Iraq (1991), Romania (1992), Libya (2004), the Democratic People's Republic of Korea (1987–2002 and 2002–2013), Iran (since 2005) and Syria (2011). Each situation was rather different. Not all cases have been reported to the Security Council and those reported were not solved by Council measures in accordance with Chapters VI or VII of the UN Charter, but had or remain to be solved through international cooperation:

In the decade preceding the 1991 Gulf war, Iraq (a party to the NPT since 1969) had made a number of unsuccessful efforts to produce highly enriched uranium.[45] The IAEA and the United Nations Special Commission (UNSCOM) revealed in 1991 that Iraq had been able to buy unlisted items that were not subject to export control in the exporting State and could make a contribution to an unsafeguarded nuclear fuel cycle, a situation which entailed intense on-site inspections under a Security Council mandate.[46] The IAEA concluded in 1997 that Iraqi weapons of mass destruction (WMD) programmes had been incapacitated.[47] UNSCOM was officially terminated when the Security Council passed Resolution 1284 (1999), which established, again as subsidiary body, the United Nations Monitoring, Verification and Inspection Commission (UNMOVIC), to address unresolved disarmament issues. UNSCOM and UNMOVIC, together with the IAEA, have been involved in the most comprehensive international monitoring system ever established in the sphere of arms control. The final success, however, had not been enabled by Security Council resolutions[48] alone, but it became possible due to continuing multinational pressure supported by all Arab States since the 1989 Paris Conference on Chemical Weapons, demanding that all weapons of mass destruction must be eliminated from the Middle East Region.[49] Iraq had provisionally implemented its Additional Protocol to the Comprehensive Safeguards Agreement with the IAEA since 2010, and ratified it in 2010,[50] so that the Security Council has lifted its Sanctions prohibiting Iraq from pursuing peaceful nuclear technology.[51]

The IAEA was asked in 1992 to verify unreported plutonium separation experiments conducted during the Ceausescu regime in Romania. According to Russian intelligence sources 470 g of plutonium were discovered in a secret laboratory of the Atomic Energy Institute in the city of Pitesti. At the session of the IAEA Board

[45]See Nuclear Threat Initiative, Iraq Country Overview, www.nti.org/e_research/profiles//Iraq/Nuclear/index.html; IAEA Annual Report for 1991.

[46]See SC Res. 681 (1991), para 13; SC Res. 715 (1991), paras 1–8.

[47]IAEA, 'Fourth Consolidated Report of the Director General of the International Atomic Energy Agency under Paragraph 16 of Resolution 1051 (1996)', UN Doc. S/1997/779 (8 October 1997), Iraqwatch.org; Negm 2009, pp. 160–170.

[48]See above n. 45, and SC Res. 687 (1991), 1051 (1996), 1154 (1998), 1284 (1999), 1957 (2010).

[49]See Fleck 2002, p. 108.

[50]See http://www.iaea.org/newscenter/news/2012/iraqap.html.

[51]SC Res. 1957 (2010).

of Governors on 17 June 1992, Bucharest was warned that it had to fully curtail the nuclear military programme and a number of demands were made to ensure monitoring and control. All these conditions were fulfilled by the new Romanian government, as confirmed by an IAEA delegation headed by its Director General Hans Blix in April 1994. Based on these results, Romania was allowed to resume the work of its nuclear centres in reorganized form, acquire nuclear fuel in Canada and the United States for its Cernavoda Nuclear Power Plant, and resume production of heavy water. The IAEA offered a concrete programme of assistance to Romania in the nuclear field worth a total of 1.5 million US dollars; this included a project for ensuring the safe work at Cernavoda, consultations, the delivery of certain types of equipment and instruments, allocation of a number of scholarships for training abroad, and seminars on nuclear problems conducted in Bucharest. The IAEA also made 156 recommendations on conducting activities at the Cernavoda Nuclear Power Plant that the Romanian side implemented in full.[52]

Pakistan, with the help of nuclear scientist A. Q. Khan, distributed sensitive nuclear technology and materials to Libya in 2004 and the Democratic People's Republic of Korea (DPRK) from 1987 to 2002.[53] While Libya agreed to give up its nuclear programme, and its cooperation with the IAEA was confirmed by the Agency,[54] the DPRK continues to openly obstruct IAEA safeguards.[55] It exported non-conventional military technologies in exchange for oil, although it had agreed with the Soviet Union in 1985 to sign the NPT in exchange for a nuclear power plant and extensive economic cooperation.[56] The United States offered the withdrawal of its tactical nuclear weapons from South Korea, suspension of the annual US–Republic of Korea military exercise in 1992 and diplomatic exchange with Pyongyang in January 1992.[57] When the IAEA discovered inconsistencies and demanded special inspections in 1993, Pyongyang declared its withdrawal from the NPT on 12 March 1993, but suspended that declaration on 11 June. As a consequence it achieved another deal with the 1994 Agreed Framework, which included a US commitment not to use nuclear weapons against North Korea, to

[52]See http://fas.org/irp/threat/svr_nuke.htm.

[53]See SC Res. 1695 (2006), 1718 (2006), 1874 (2009), 2050 (2012), 2087 (2013), and 2094 (2013). On the relationship between the DPRK and the IAEA see IAEA Doc. GOV/2013/39-GC(57)/22 (28 August 2013) Application of Safeguards in the Democratic People's Republic of Korea, Report by the Director General, https://www.iaea.org/About/Policy/GC/GC57/GC57Documents/English/gc57-22_en.pdf.

[54]See IAEA Annual Report for 2004, http://www.iaea.org/Publications/Reports/Anrep2004/index.html, p. 9, referring to Libya's past failures to fulfil the requirements of its NPT safeguards agreement, and stating that Libya had taken corrective actions, and decided to sign and implement, pending entry into force, an additional protocol to that agreement. When Libya had submitted its initial declarations under the protocol and showed good cooperation with the Agency, the IAEA Board adopted a resolution on the implementation of safeguards in Libya. See Corea 2006.

[55]See SC Res. 825 (1993).

[56]Solingen 2007, p. 129.

[57]Mazarr 1995, p. 95.

improve diplomatic relations, to provide two light-water nuclear reactors, and shipments of oil in exchange for a freeze on North Korea's weapons programme and unimpeded international inspections.[58] That deal, however, fell apart. In 2003 Pyongyang confirmed its withdrawal from the NPT and eventually conducted nuclear test explosions on 9 October 2006 and 24 May 2009.[59] The Security Council has requested the DPRK to retract its withdrawal and abandon all nuclear weapons and existing nuclear programmes in a complete, verifiable and irreversible manner,[60] but as of to date, none of these requests have been met.

Iran, a State found to be in non-compliance with nuclear non-proliferation obligations over several years,[61] had become a target of unsuccessful Security Council sanctions,[62] before a cooperative solution could be envisaged in negotiations concluded between the E3/EU+3 (China, France, Germany, the Russian Federation, the United Kingdom and the United States, with the High Representative of the European Union for Foreign Affairs and Security Policy) and Iran.[63]

Syria began in 1991 to construct its first research reactor at Al-Kibar (aka Dair Alzour) in northwestern Syria, which was destroyed in September 2007 by the Israeli Air Force, based on US and Israeli intelligence claims that the site was a plutonium production reactor. The Syrian government has denied these allegations, but in 2008 and 2009 IAEA inspectors discovered the presence of undeclared anthropogenic uranium particles on site. Following more than 3 years' investigation, during which Syria did not sufficiently cooperate with the IAEA, the Agency concluded in May 2011 'that it is very likely that the building destroyed at the Dair Alzour site was a nuclear reactor which should have been declared to the Agency.'

---

[58]Agreed Framework of 21 October 1994 Between the United States of America and the Democratic People's Republic of Korea, INFCIRC/457, http://www.iaea.org/Publications/Documents/Infcircs/Others/infcirc457.pdf.

[59]The Democratic People's Republic of Korea had declared its withdrawal from the NPT on 12 March 1993, but suspended that declaration on 11 June 1993. On 10 January 2003 it declared an 'immediate effectuation of its withdrawal from the NPT', see http://www.atomicarchive.com/Docs/Deterrence/DPRKNPTstatement.shtml.

[60]SC Res. 1695 (2006), 1718 (2006), 1874 (2009), 1928 (2010), 2050 (2012), 2087 (2013) and 2094 (2013). See J. Bajora and B. Xu, The Six-Party Talks on North Korea's Nuclear Program', Council on Foreign Relations, http://www.cfr.org/proliferation/six-party-talks-north-koreas-nuclear-program/p13593; Pollack 2011.

[61]See IAEA Report GOV/2013/40 (28 August 2013), http://www.iaea.org/Publications/Documents/Board/2013/gov2013-40.pdf.

[62]SC Res. 1696 (2006), 1737 (2006). 1747 (2007), 1803 (2008), 1835 (2008), 1887 (2009), 1929 (2011), 1984 (2011), 2049 (2012).

[63]See SC Res 2231 (2015); Joint Statement by the IAEA Director General Yukiya Amano and the Vice-President of the Islamic Republic of Iran, President of the Atomic Energy Organization of Iran, Ali Akbar Salehi and Road-map for the clarification of past and present outstanding issues regarding Iran's nuclear program, Vienna 14 July 2015, http://www.iaea.org/newscenter/pressreleases/iaea-director-generals-statement-and-road-map-clarification-past-present-outstanding-issues-regarding-irans-nuclear-program.

On 9 June 2011, the IAEA Board of Governors passed a resolution that found Syria to be in noncompliance with its obligations under its Safeguards Agreement, and reported the case to the Security Council.[64] By the end of that year, however, the Agency reported that Syria cooperated in addressing the Agency's concerns in relation to previously unreported conversion activities at the Miniature Neutron Source Reactor and the origin of anthropogenic natural uranium particles found there; concluding that declared nuclear material remained in peaceful activities.[65]

Alleged nuclear weapon activities by Egypt and the Republic of Korea were also discussed within the IAEA, but no further measures were found necessary:

In 2004, after examining 'open source documents' published by current and former Egyptian Atomic Energy Authority officials, the Agency took note of certain undeclared nuclear activities. It first raised the issue with Egyptian officials and subsequently conducted several inspections of Egypt's nuclear facilities. In November 2004 the Board of Governors was informed. A 14 February 2005 report by IAEA Director-General Mohamed ElBaradei stated that Egypt failed to disclose nuclear facilities, material, and experiments dating back between 15 and 40 years, but there was no indication that Egypt had a nuclear weapons programme, and Cairo had either ceased the nuclear activities in question or placed them under IAEA monitoring.[66]

Following Seoul's disclosure of previously undeclared experiments in which scientists separated and enriched minute amounts of plutonium and uranium, the IAEA launched an investigation in 2004 and stated on 3 June 2008 that its concerns about the peaceful nature of South Korea's nuclear programme had been resolved. The revelations came after Seoul's Additional Protocol to the Comprehensive Safeguards Agreement with the IAEA, which was signed on 21 June 1999, entered into force on 19 February 2004.[67]

Other disputes were brought to the Security Council by States:

After Israel's military attack on the Iraqi nuclear research centre at Osirak the Security Council in its meeting on 19 June 1981 acted at Iraq's request dated 8 June 1981,[68] not without listening to a statement of the IAEA which referred to a Resolution of the IAEA's Board of Governors of 12 June 1981.[69] The Council condemned Israel's attack and called upon Israel to urgently place its nuclear facilities under the safeguards of the IAEA.[70] Israel, a member of the IAEA, but not party to the NPT, did not comply with the Security Council's request. It has concluded a

[64] http://www.nti.org/country-profiles/syria/.

[65] See IAEA Annual Report for 2011, http://www.iaea.org/Publications/Reports/Anrep2011/yearinreview.pdf, p. 11.

[66] See https://www.armscontrol.org/print/1753.

[67] See K. Fishman, IAEA South Korean Concerns Resolved. Arms Control Today, July/August 2008, https://www.armscontrol.org/2008_07-08/SouthKorea.

[68] Letter of the Minister of Foreign Affairs of Iraq dated 8 June 1981, UN Doc. S/14509.

[69] UN Doc. S/14532.

[70] SC Res. 487 (1981).

safeguards agreement with the Agency in 1975 and accepts peer review of the safety of its IRR-1 Reactor, located in the Soreq Nuclear Research Center, as part of the Agency's Integrated Nuclear Safety Assessment of Research Reactors (INSARR),[71] but it deliberately maintains its long-standing policy of nuclear opacity.[72]

Both India and Pakistan were able to produce a nuclear explosive device using items that had been supplied for ostensibly civilian purposes. The nuclear tests conducted by India on 11 and 13 May 1998 and by Pakistan on 28 and 30 May 1998 were even announced beforehand with no settlement procedure in place. The Security Council Resolution condemning these tests made no reference to the IAEA, but welcomed the initiative of the UN Secretary-General to encourage the two States to enter into dialogue.[73] A cooperative solution still remains to be found.[74] While at the time of negotiations of the NPT, Indian and Pakistani support for it might have been reached by stronger disarmament commitments by nuclear-weapon States,[75] such support seems less realistic today, due to changed threat perceptions and a further developing security rivalry between the two States.

This overview of the cases of non-compliance, which had been identified by the IAEA, and other disputes between States shows that shortcomings or loopholes of treaty texts had been of minor importance, whereas changed national interests in a progressively developing security environment were the predominant reasons for disputes. In many cases existing compliance control mechanisms did not suffice to ensure implementation of non-proliferation obligations, so that the characterization of dispute settlement as being only of supplementary value in this field,[76] can no longer be upheld. Without willingness for and the ability to engage in dispute settlement activities control mechanisms will be less than effective.

17.4 Means and Methods of Pacific Dispute Settlement

Due to their consequences for international peace and security, disputes on compliance with nuclear non-proliferation obligations are posing particular challenges for States, the Security Council and international organizations. The present treaty

[71] See http://www.iaea.org/newscenter/news/2013/insarrisrael.html.

[72] Unconfirmed estimates for Israel's nuclear weapons stockpile range around 80 intact nuclear weapons and additional inventories of fissile materials of 0.3 tons highly enriched uranium (HEU) plus 0.84 ± 0.13 tons of separated plutonium. See Schell and Kristensen, p. 333; Glaser and Mian, pp. 326–331; Cohen; Kandel, pp. 173–184. See also reports by the Federation of American Scientists (FAS), http://www.fas.org/nuke/guide/israel/nuke/; Negm 2009, pp. 227–258; Kroenig 2010, pp. 67–110.

[73] SC Res. 1172 (1998).

[74] See Ogden 2012, pp. 149–160; Chakma and Pant 2012, pp. 161–172. On the bilateral U.S.-Indian deal see Handl 2010, pp. 11–15.

[75] See e.g. Shaker, Vol. I, pp. 22, 54 and Vol. II, p. 487.

[76] Marauhn 2007, p. 272.

system should provide sufficient conditions for meeting these challenges. It has already created certain openness and transparency that have supported international cooperation under formal and informal arrangements.[77] There is a wide acceptance for negotiated solutions and the implementation of agreed control procedures. Export controls provide additional means of verification. Cooperative dispute settlement remains, however, necessary and its effectiveness may provide the best incentives for compliance. Opportunities for third-party settlement by the ICJ or international arbitration being relatively small in practice,[78] other means of peaceful settlement must be given continuous attention.

Specific problems for dispute settlement may arise by the existence of inherent limits for any bargaining in this field: there will be no sustainable settlement without convincing assurance that non-proliferation obligations are complied with. This should exclude any weak compromise. Sustainable offsets must be sought through convincing security assurances. At the same time, security challenges are often subject to progressive technological development. Regulatory approaches will have to consider this.

A thorough assessment of existing means of pacific dispute settlement and their limits is essential in this context. While Article 2(3) of the UN Charter underlines the general responsibility of States for the settlement of their disputes by peaceful means 'in such a manner that international peace and security, and justice, are not endangered', Chapter VI addresses the special responsibility of the Security Council for the settlement of any dispute 'the continuance of which is likely to endanger the maintenance of international peace and security'.[79] Pertinent disputes may be of very different nature and quality. Clearly, not all relevant aspects could be discussed in this Chapter. A comparative study in various disputes on nuclear non-proliferation issues, including those mentioned above (Sect. 17.3), may help to develop legal principles and procedures stemming from the relevant Articles 2(3) and 33–38 of the UN Charter and related agreements. Objectives and procedures of verification need to be discussed with a view to improving their effectiveness. This work could add to more transparency, confidence building and regularization in international cooperation in that it might clarify the responsibility and potential of States, the Security Council, international organizations and civil society in this respect.

Beginning with State responsibility, not only those States directly involved in a dispute are to be considered here, as non-compliance with non-proliferation obligations does affect much wider regions even beyond neighbouring States. Third-party dispute settlement is not addressed in the text of the NPT, but it is part of the Treaty's review process. Review conferences are held every 5 years to review the operation of the Treaty with a view to assuring that its purposes and provisions are being realized. IAEA safeguards agreements normally contain arbitration

[77]See Fujita 1994, pp. 92, 101.

[78]See Fry 2013, passim.

[79]Article 33(1) UN Charter.

provisions,[80] but no recourse to arbitration has been made to date in the implementation of safeguards.[81] At a more general level, disputes concerning the interpretation or application of the IAEA Statute may become subject to jurisdiction by the ICJ,[82] but it is very unlikely that the relevant conditions will ever be met in practice. Yet issues of compliance and enforcement have repeatedly been controversial, a situation that underlines the importance of cooperative solutions and responsible action by States, cooperative action that should be regularized and supported by appropriate principles and rules.

The IAEA's Board of Governors shall report disputes on non-compliance that affect international peace and security and cannot be solved in mutual cooperation to the Security Council.[83] As confirmed by Article 33 of the UN Charter, the dispute settlement tasks of the Security Council are primarily ('first of all') those of a non-coercive nature under Chapter VI. As such they have no legally binding character, except for investigations under Article 34.[84] The Council can turn responsibility to the Parties by calling upon them to settle their dispute by peaceful means (Article 33 para 2); it can recommend appropriate procedures or methods of adjustment (Article 36 para 1) or—if it deems that the continuance of the dispute is likely to endanger international peace and security—make suggestions for a substantive settlement (Article 37), before taking measures of a coercive nature under Chapter VII. It is important to note, however, that coercive measures must remain a last resort and that—as shown above—they may not always be successful.

Security Council measures should help to ensure compliance with existing obligations and even create new obligations for maintaining or restoring peace and security. While the Council is generally bound to act in a more or less *ad hoc* manner and its law-making powers are limited to the 'concrete case',[85] it can do so systematically and with great authority. There is also much room for discretion and proportional action to take. In fact, a great variety of non-coercive measures is available to the Security Council before resorting to coercive action under Chapter VII.

Articles III B 4 and XII C of the IAEA Statute also mentions the General Assembly as a recipient of reports on non-compliance in cases that cannot be

[80]INFCIRC/153, para 22, provides for arbitration on disputes arising out of interpretation or implementation of a safeguards agreement, except for disputes on findings of the Board. For an assessment of standard dispute settlement clauses including certain variations in some safeguards agreements with the IAEA see Fry 2013, pp. 268–285.

[81]Rockwood 2013, p. 25.

[82]Article XVII: 'Settlement of disputes. (A) Any question or dispute concerning the interpretation or application of this Statute which is not settled by negotiation shall be referred to the International Court of Justice in conformity with the Statute of the Court, unless the parties concerned agree on another mode of settlement. (B) The General Conference and the Board of Governors are separately empowered, subject to authorization from the General Assembly of the United Nations, to request the International Court of Justice to give an advisory opinion on any legal question arising within the scope of the Agency's activities.'

[83]See Article III B 4 and Article XII (C) IAEA Statute.

[84]See Tomuschat 2012, MN 2.

[85]See Krisch 2012a, MN 34.

solved in cooperation with the State or States concerned. A role of the General Assembly in dispute settlement was envisaged in the Manila Declaration of 1982.[86] Although this role has not been materialized in practice and the primary role of the Security Council in this respect is beyond dispute, the potential of the General Assembly for developing consensus on matters of global importance should not be underestimated.[87] The General Assembly can be invoked to affirm principles of international law and thus contribute to de-escalating existing disputes, while fact-finding, mediation, conciliation, good offices and other peaceful means of dispute settlement will be for the Security Council to initiate.

Beyond the affirmation of existing rules steps towards international law-creation may become relevant in this context. Such steps may be taken by both the General Assembly and the Security Council. The General Assembly may make recommendations with regard to

> the general principles of cooperation in the maintenance of international peace and security, including the principles governing disarmament and the regulation of armaments.[88]

It has in fact passed a great number of resolutions confirming existing principles and rules and making recommendations, interpreting its authority under Article 11 rather broadly.[89] The Security Council in turn is responsible for

> formulating, with the assistance of the Military Staff Committee referred to in Article 47, plans to be submitted to the Members of the United Nations for the establishment of a system for the regulation of armaments.[90]

As practice under this latter provision is still rather scarce, it may be left open in the present context, to what extent the Council is limited here by the requirements to develop such plans as a system constituting a comprehensive and multifactor whole rather than taking action on contentious issues,[91] and to what extent the assistance of the (still dormant) Military Staff Committee would be mandatory for such activities. An increasing density of legal regulation by the Council is, however, available with its practice under Chapter VII: SC Res 1540 (2004) has mandated

[86] Manila Declaration on the Peaceful Settlement of International Disputes, Annex to UNGA Res. 37/10 (15 November 1982).

[87] See also Declaration on the Prevention and Removal of Disputes and Situations Which May Threaten International Peace and Security and on the Role of the United Nations in this Field, UNGA Res. 43/51 (5 December 1988).

[88] Article 11 UN Charter.

[89] Klein and Schmahl 2012, MN 8, 9–17.

[90] Article 26 UN Charter.

[91] Schütz 2012, MN 26. See also Krisch 2012b, MN 16, critically observing with respect to long-term arms restrictions for Iraq, Iran, and North Korea, designed to prevent future aggression, that 'this does not necessarily include a competence to take general measures for the limitation of armaments, or a possibility to regard armament by States in itself as a threat to the peace. In principle, States are free to decide on their armament, and under Article 26 the SC possesses only recommendatory powers for general regulation in this sphere.'

States to criminalize the proliferation of weapons of mass destruction, to adopt strict export controls, and to secure sensitive material. It established a special forum of activities with the 1540 Committee. Concerns with the lack of judicial review and control which had even led the 2005 World Summit to take a rather critical position against the Security Council[92] have lost a great deal of their former relevance due to a self-critical practice of the Security Council.[93] Virtually all UN Member States are supporting Resolution 1540, but the lack of judicial control of acts committed on behalf of the United Nations, which became most evident due to the jurisprudence of the European Court of Justice,[94] remains an issue for further legal development.

The Secretary-General has an active role to fulfil in this context. His right of initiative (Article 99) may become decisive for initiating measures taken by the Security Council and activities by the Secretary-General in implementing such measures will often be essential for securing their effectiveness and strengthening international cooperation.

While coercive measures to ensure compliance include countermeasures by international organizations and by States,[95] below the level of countermeasures States and international organizations may use retorsions, defined in the Commentary to the Articles on State Responsibility, as

> 'unfriendly' conduct which is not inconsistent with any international obligation of the State engaging in it even though it may be a response to an internationally wrongful act.[96]

Such measures may include export or import limitations (unless excluded under treaty law), travel restrictions and enhanced activities of criminal prosecution to ensure compliance with non-proliferation obligations. Generally speaking such measures do not fall under the restrictions described for countermeasures, as long

---

[92]2005 World Summit Outcome UN Doc. A/RES/60/1 (24 October 2005), para 109: 'We … call upon the Security Council … to ensure that fair and clear procedures exist for placing individuals and entities on sanctions and removing them, as well as for granting humanitarian exceptions'.

[93]See Marauhn 2013, pp. 66–68, and also Anthony 2012, p. 37.

[94]*Yassin Abdullah Kadi and Al Barakaat International Foundation v. Council of the European Union* [*Kadi I*] judgment of the Court of Justice (3 September 2008) ECR I-6351; *Yassin Abdullah Kadi v. European Commission,* supported by Council of the European Union, the French Republic and the United Kingdom [Kadi II] judgment of the General Court (Seventh Chamber) of 30 September 2010, http://curia.europa.eu/juris/document/document.jsf;jsessionid=9ea7d0f130d5922fc18d39ee42029102a501ef4d5f41.e34KaxiLc3eQc40LaxqMbN4OahqPe0?text=&docid=83733&pageIndex=0&doclang=EN&mode=lst&dir=&occ=first&part=1&cid=708499; see de Wet 2013.

[95]See Black-Branch, Chap. 16 in this volume.

[96]See Articles on Responsibility of States for Internationally Wrongful Acts—ARSIWA—(2001) UN Doc. A/56/10, Yearbook of the International Law Commission, 2001, Vol. II, Part Two, http://legal.un.org/ilc/texts/instruments/english/commentaries/9_6_2001.pdf, Chapter II, Commentary (before Article 49), para 3, p. 128.

as they are in conformity with international obligations towards the other State[97] and do not disregard legal limitations to certain extra-territorial effects[98] or constitute an abuse of rights, conditions that will, however, hardly become relevant in the present context, given the essential importance of nuclear non-proliferation for the maintenance of peace and security. For international organizations essentially similar rules apply.[99] It is important to note that retorsions are not specifically restricted under the provisions set up in ARSIWA and DARIO, as unlike countermeasures they are generally speaking in conformity with international obligations towards the other State. Hence the legal character of any measures should be made explicit and countermeasures should be avoided when retorsions would suffice for the intended purpose. In the EU practice of 'restrictive measures (sanctions)' such legal clarity is not always present. In particular the EU 'sanctions' against Iran[100] which are mainly focussing on export and import restrictions, restrictions on financing of certain enterprises, traffic and training, do not generally fall under restrictions valid for countermeasures, and are not regulated under DARIO. The fact that they were triggered by Security Council resolutions[101] may give them certain justification, but this does not substitute for effective means of cooperative dispute settlement.

The Security Council so far did not offer any benefits to non-State actors, benefits that may be necessary for gaining their cooperation for exploring and effectively removing root causes of illicit trafficking and offering incentives for compliance. There are no legal instruments available for activities to provide such incentives in the field of nuclear non-proliferation, a fact that marks a big difference between non-proliferation law and other branches of international law, such as for example the law of non-international armed conflict with its special agreements under Article 3(3) common to the Geneva Conventions, Declarations under Article 96(3) of Additional Protocol I or

---

[97]For pertinent principles see Declaration on Principles of International Law concerning Friendly Relations and Co-operation among States in accordance with the Charter of the United Nations, General Assembly Resolution 2625(XXV), adopted on 24 October 1970 (Annex, The principle concerning the duty not to intervene in matters within the domestic jurisdiction of any State, in accordance with the Charter); Charter of Economic Rights and Duties of States, General Assembly Resolution 3281(XXIX), adopted on 12 December 1974 (Article 32); Economic measures as a means of political and economic coercion against developing countries, General Assembly Resolution 44/215, adopted on 22 December 1989; and Unilateral economic measures as a means of political and economic coercion against developing countries, General Assembly Resolution 66/186, adopted on 22 December 2011.

[98]Bothe 2013, para 46.

[99]See Draft Articles on Responsibility of International Organizations (DARIO), UN Doc. A/66/10, para 87, Yearbook of the International Law Commission, 2011, vol. II, Part Two, http://legal.un.org/ilc/texts/instruments/english/commentaries/9_11_2011.pdf.

[100]EU Council Decisions 2010/413 (26 July 2010); 2011/670/CFSP (10 October 2011); and 2012/35/CFSP (23 January 2012).

[101]See EU Council Conclusions on Iran (3142th Foreign Affairs Council meeting, 23 January 2012) Press Release 5592/12, http://www.consilium.europa.eu/uedocs/cms_Data/docs/pressdata/EN/foraff/127480.pdf, para 1: 'Iran's acceleration of enrichment activities is in flagrant violation of six UNSC Resolutions and eleven IAEA Board resolutions and contributes to increasing tensions in the region.'

deeds of commitment deliverable to Geneva Call,[102] which in some cases were quite effective, although not explicitly provided for in treaty law. These examples also show very well that to be successful, incentives for compliance should be developed in cooperation. Furthermore, legal regulation will require legal control. Very small steps have been taken in non-proliferation law with the establishment of the Office of the Ombudsperson under SC Res 1904 (2009), the delisting provisions under SC Res 1988 (2011), and the encouragement of States for making use of exemptions under SC Res 1989 (2011). Indeed, more should be done to really tackle the root causes of international terrorism, integrate various actors, and thus improve nuclear security.

Compliance with nuclear non-proliferation obligations is to be implemented in this complex environment of military and civilian activities, legal and policy commitments, national and international regulation, law enforcement and criminal prosecution, transparency and confidentiality. A number of important issues for the settlement of disputes on nuclear proliferation issues remain to be discussed in greater depth. Should verification efforts on nuclear non-proliferation focus on abilities or quantities? As far as quantities are concerned, should numbers of warheads or general ceilings be focused on? Is the approach to be taken on nuclear non-proliferation different from that on chemical and biological weapons and equipment, as in the latter cases stricter treaty prohibitions apply that would be missing here? Should incentives for compliance and countermeasures in the event of non-compliance be evaluated as to their effectiveness and further regulation be based on such evaluation?

These questions will remain open, as long as the role of States, groups of States, international organizations and civil society in nuclear non-proliferation is less than comprehensive as is the case today and the NPT is not fully used at global scale. Ensuring implementation of existing rules remains a challenge that must be performed between potential competition and shared responsibilities. States and international organizations are called to take appropriate action for this cause. This challenge includes acts committed by non-State actors. Neither listing of individuals nor criminal prosecution of offences is enough to ensure compliance with non-proliferation obligations.

17.5 Conclusions

Shortcomings and loopholes in treaty law, but even more so, gaps in compliance by States with existing non-proliferation obligations in the practice of States and international organizations have highlighted the need to increase incentives for compliance, to further improve verification, and to enforce pertinent rules in an effective manner. A comparative study in various disputes on nuclear non-proliferation issues may reveal legal principles and procedures for peaceful dispute settlement, stemming from the relevant Articles 2(3) and 33-38 of the UN Charter and related agreements. Objectives and procedures of verification need to be discussed

[102] See http://www.genevacall.org/.

with a view to improve their effectiveness. This work could contribute to more transparency and regularization in international cooperation in that it might clarify the responsibility and potential of States, the Security Council, international organizations and civil society in this respect.

For peaceful dispute settlement a great variety of means and procedures is available. States and international organizations including the International Atomic Energy Agency (IAEA), the Preparatory Commission for the Comprehensive Nuclear-Test-Ban Treaty Organization (CTBTO), the European Atomic Energy Community (EURATOM), and the Brazilian-Argentine Agency for Accounting and Control of Nuclear Materials (ABACC) have gained unique experience with control procedures in verification that may best be characterized as cooperative. The roles of the UN Secretary-General (Article 99 UN Charter), the General Assembly (Article 11) and the Security Council (Article 26) may complement each other in reaching non-coercive (cooperative) solutions that may be more effective and longer-lasting than any coercive measure.

While many open issues remain to be explored in this context, the following principles may be suggested as relevant for further cooperation:

(1) More international exchange and deepened cooperation is essential to ensure compliance with non-proliferation obligations.
(2) Not only those States directly involved in a dispute are called to cooperate in this context, as non-compliance with non-proliferation obligations could affect much wider regions even beyond neighbouring States.
(3) Measures by the Security Council may help to ensure nuclear non-proliferation, support strict and effective export controls and provide transparent procedures for pertinent activities.
(4) Recommendations by the General Assembly with regard to principles of cooperation in the maintenance of peace and security and principles governing disarmament and the regulation of armaments may add to transparency in nuclear-non-proliferation.
(5) Reporting activities by the Secretary-General and the exercise of his right of initiative may be essential for nuclear non-proliferation measures taken by the General Assembly, the Security Council and by States.
(6) To ensure compliance with existing rules and best practice, incentives may be more effective and more important than enforcement measures. Incentives should be developed in international cooperation. This might lead to a prioritization of lawful means available and may entail the development of new legal principles and rules.
(7) Procedures and objectives of verification are to be continuously scrutinized. Cooperative action is to be taken to reach nuclear balance at lower levels, ensure non-proliferation of nuclear weapons and nuclear explosive devices, and abolish chemical and biological weapons.
(8) Retorsions, i.e. acts or omissions below the level of countermeasures deserve more attention in current discussions on compliance with arms control obligations.

(9) Incentives for compliance are relevant at all stages of dispute settlement and different forms of cooperation will be required at those different stages.
(10) The lack of judicial control of acts performed on behalf of the United Nations remains an important issue for further legal development in this field.

References

Anthony I (2012) The evolution of dual-use technology controls: a historical perspective. In: Meier O, Daase C (eds) Arms controls in the 21st century: between coercion and cooperation. Routledge

Anthony I (2013) Measures to combat nuclear terrorism. In: SIPRI yearbook 2013. Armaments, disarmaments and international security. Oxford University Press, pp 358–364

Bothe M (1994) Some matters of accommodation—third party input. In: Dahlitz J (ed) Avoidance and settlement of arms control disputes. Vol II arms control and disarmament law. United Nations, pp 181–185

Bothe M (2013) Weapons of mass destruction, counter-proliferation. In: Wolfrum R (ed) Max-Planck encyclopedia of public international law (MPEPIL), vol 10. Oxford University Press

Chakma B, Pant HV (eds) (2012) Handbook of nuclear proliferation. Routledge

Cohen A (1998) Israel and the bomb. Columbia University Press, New York

Corea G (2006) Shipping for bombs. Nuclear proliferation, global insecurity and the rise and fall of the A.Q. network. Oxford University Press

Crawford J (ed) (2012) Brownlie's principles of public international law, 8th edn. Oxford University Press

Dahlitz J (1984) Nuclear arms control with effective international agreements, 2nd edn. Allen and Unwin, London

Dupont P-E (2012) Countermeasures and collective security: the case of the EU sanctions against Iran. J Confl Secur Law 17:301–336

Dupont P-E (2014) Compliance with treaties in the context of nuclear non-proliferation: assessing claims in the case of Iran. J Confl Secur Law 19:161–210

Elbaradei M (2008) Preventing nuclear catastrophe: where do we go from here? In: Falk R, Krieger D (eds) At the nuclear precipice. Catastrophe or transformation? Palgrave Macmillan, New York, pp 209–213

Falk R (2008) Non-proliferation treaty illusion and international lawlessness. In: Falk R, Krieger D (eds) At the nuclear precipice. Catastrophe or transformation? Palgrave Macmillan, New York, pp 39–47

Fleck D (2002) Development of the law of arms control as a result of the Iraq-Kuwait conflict. Eur J Int Law 13(1):105–119

Franceschini G (2008) Assessing the nuclear non-proliferation regime: what are the loopholes? What are the challenges? In: Boutherin G (ed) Europe facing nuclear weapons challenges. Bruylant, Bruxelles, pp 155–180

Fry J D (2013) Legal resolution of nuclear non-proliferation disputes. Cambridge University Press

Fujita H (1994) The role of transparency in the avoidance and settlement of arms control disputes. In: Dahlitz J (ed) Avoidance and settlement of arms control disputes. Vol II arms control and disarmament law. United Nations, pp 87–102

Glaser A, Mian Z (2013) Global stocks and production of fissile materials, 2012. In: SIPRI Yearbook 2013 Oxford University Press, pp 326–331

Handl G (2010) The nuclear non-proliferation regime: legitimacy as a function of process. Tulane J Int Comp Law 19:1–39

Joyner DH (2011) Interpreting the nuclear non-proliferation treaty. Oxford University Press

Kandel A (2012) Israel: origins and implications of nuclear ambiguity. In: Pant HV (ed) Handbook of nuclear proliferation. Routledge, pp 173–184

Kilb W (2014) The nuclear safeguards system of the European atomic energy community (EURATOM). In: Raetzke (ed) Nuclear law in the EU and beyond. Proceedings of the AIDN/INLA Conference 2013 in Leipzig. Nomos, p 97
Klein E, Schmahl S (2012) Art. 11. In: Simma B et al (eds) The charter of the United Nations. A commentary, 3rd edn. Oxford University Press
Krisch N (2012a) Introduction to chapter VII: the general framework. In Simma B et al. (eds) The charter of the United Nations. A commentary, 3rd edn. Oxford University Press
Krisch N (2012b) Art. 39. In Simma B et al. (eds) The charter of the United Nations. A commentary, 3rd edn. Oxford University Press
Kroenig M (2010) Exporting the bomb. Technology transfer and the spread of nuclear weapons. Cornell University Press, Ithaca
Marauhn T (2007) Dispute resolution, compliance control and enforcement of international arms control law. In: Ulfstein G (ed) Making treaties work: human rights, environment and arms control. Cambridge University Press, pp 243–272
Marauhn T (2013) Global governance of dual-use trade. The contribution of international law. In: Meier O (ed) Technology transfers and non–proliferation. Routledge, pp 45–75
Mazarr MJ (1995) Going just a little nuclear: non-proliferation lessons from North Korea. Int Secur 20:92–122
Negm N (2009) Transfer of nuclear technology under international law. Case study of Iraq, Iran and Israel, Nijhoff
Nystuen G, Hugo TG (2014) The nuclear non-proliferation treaty. In: Nystuen G, Casey-Maslen S, Golden Bersagel A (eds) Nuclear weapons under international law. Cambridge University Press, pp 74–396
Ogden C (2012) India: the (accepted) gatecrasher. In Pant HV (ed) Handbook of nuclear proliferation. Routledge, pp 149–160
Pollack JD (2011) No exit. North Korea, nuclear weapons and international security. Routledge/IISS
Rockwood L (2013) Legal framework for IAEA safeguards. IAEA
Schell Ph, Kristensen HM (2014) Israeli nuclear forces. In: SIPRI yearbook 2014. Oxford University Press, pp 333–334
Schütz H-J (2012) Art. 26. In: Simma B et al (eds) The charter of the United Nations. A commentary, 3rd edn. Oxford University Press
Shaker MI (1980) The nuclear nonproliferation treaty: origin and implementation 1959–1979, vol 3. Oceana
Shaw MN (1999) Peaceful resolution of 'political disputes': the desirable parameters of ICJ jurisdiction. In: Hahlitz J (ed) Peaceful resolution of major international disputes. United Nations, New York and Geneva, pp 49–75
Solingen E (2007) Nuclear logics: contrasting paths in east Asia and the Middle East. Princeton University Press
Tomuschat C (2012) Art. 33. In: Simma B et al (eds) The charter of the United Nations. A commentary, 3rd edn. Oxford University Press
Venturini G (2014) Test-bans and the comprehensive Test Ban Treaty Organization. In Black-Branch JL, Fleck D (eds) Nuclear non-proliferation in international law, vol I, Springer/Asser Press, pp 133–158
de Wet E (2004) The chapter vii powers of the United Nations Security Council. Hart, Oxford and Portland Oregon
de Wet E (2013) From Kadi to Nada: judicial techniques favouring human rights over United Nations Security Council sanctions. Chin J Int Law 12(4):787–808. doi:10.1093/chinesejil/jmt034
Wilkinson P (2012) Nuclear weapons and non-state actors. The evolving threat of nuclear terrorism. In Pant HV (ed) Handbook of nuclear proliferation. Routledge, pp 52–61
Willrich M (1968) The treaty on non-proliferation of nuclear weapons: nuclear technology confronts world politics. Yale Law J 77:1447–1519
Willrich M (1969) Non-proliferation treaty: framework for nuclear arms control. The Michie Company, Charlottesville

Index

J.L. Black-Branch and D. Fleck (eds.), *Nuclear Non-Proliferation in International Law - Volume II*, DOI 10.1007/978-94-6265-075-6

MIX
Papier aus verantwortungsvollen Quellen
Paper from responsible sources
FSC® C105338

If you have any concerns about our products,
you can contact us on
ProductSafety@springernature.com

In case Publisher is established outside the EU,
the EU authorized representative is:
Springer Nature Customer Service Center GmbH
Europaplatz 3, 69115 Heidelberg, Germany

Printed by Libri Plureos GmbH
in Hamburg, Germany